'Magnificent ... Mazower traces the rise of some of the most dangerous ideas in history which spread in the wake of the First World War, from virulent nationalism to the increasing importance of race' Alexandra Richie, *Observer*

'Mark Mazower, reconstructing a more honest European history from the skeletons in the 20th-century cupboard ... is anxious to clear away the liberal myth-making and the false history that have served to cloak what actually happened ... *Dark Continent* is an exemplary anti-revisionist tract, written with verve and splendidly argued' Richard Gott, *New Statesman*

'A model of synthesis, sharp, anything but bland, courageous and original' Michael Ignatieff, *Guardian* Books of the Year

'Division and hatred and the reinvention of Europe in this, its most ruinous century are the themes of Mark Mazower's book, the finest essay on Europe of our time' Robert Fox, *European*

'Mark Mazower, one of our brightest young historians, has managed to write about this subject in such a way that you want to turn the pages ... valuable and well written' Norman Stone, *Guardian*

'I was impressed by Mark Mazower's *Dark Continent*. Anyone who still thinks of the history of Europe as the triumph of liberalism and democracy should read this sombre survey of 20th-century Europe as the cradle of barbarity' Eric Hobsbawm, *New Statesman*, Books of the Year

'Mark Mazower has provided a rich mixture in his highly individual and intelligent interpretation of Europe's twentieth-century history' Richard Crampton, *The Times Literary Supplement*

'The central thrust of his argument, expressed with verve and perception, is that the century has seen a fundamental struggle between liberalism, fascism and communism ... Mazower presents a challenging and disturbing thesis' Richard Overy, *Sunday Telegraph*

Mark Mazower is Reader in History at the University of Sussex. He is the author of the prize-winning *Inside Hitler's Greece: The Experience of Occupation, 1941–1944* (co-winner of the Fraenkel Prize and the Longman/*History Today* Book of the Year). He writes and broadcasts regularly on current developments in the Balkans.

MARK MAZOWER

Dark Continent:
Europe's Twentieth Century

PENGUIN BOOKS

PENGUIN BOOKS

Published by the Penguin Group
Penguin Books Ltd, 27 Wrights Lane, London W8 5TZ, England
Penguin Putnam Inc., 375 Hudson Street, New York, New York 10014, USA
Penguin Books Australia Ltd, Ringwood, Victoria, Australia
Penguin Books Canada Ltd, 10 Alcorn Avenue, Toronto, Ontario, Canada M4V 3B2
Penguin Books (NZ) Ltd, Private Bag 102902, NSMC, Auckland, New Zealand

Penguin Books Ltd, Registered Offices: Harmondsworth, Middlesex, England

First published by Allen Lane The Penguin Press 1998
Published in Penguin Books 1999
1 3 5 7 9 10 8 6 4 2

The author and publishers gratefully acknowledge Harcourt Brace & Company
for permission to reprint the map 'The Expulsion of Germans from
Central Europe, 1945–7'

The moral right of the author has been asserted

Printed in England by Clays Ltd, St Ives plc

for Ruthie

and in memory of

Frouma Mazower
Max Mazower
Reg Shaffer

Contents

Preface

Why then do the European states claim for themselves the right
to spread civilization and manners to different continents? Why
not to Europe itself?

– Joseph Roth, 1937[1]*

Europe may seem to be a continent of old states and peoples, yet it is
in many respects very new, inventing and reinventing itself over
this century through often convulsive political transformation. Some
nations – such as Prussia – have been wiped off the map in living
memory; others – like Austria or Macedonia – are less than three
generations old. When my grandmother was born in Warsaw, it was
part of the Tsarist empire, Trieste belonged to the Habsburgs and
Salonika to the Ottomans. The Germans ruled Poles, the English
Ireland, France Algeria. The closest much of Europe came to the
democratic nation-state which has become the norm today were the
monarchies of the Balkans. Nowhere did adults of both sexes have
the vote, and there were few countries where parliaments prevailed
over kings. In short, modern democracy, like the nation-state it is so
closely associated with, is basically the product of the protracted
domestic and international experimentation which followed the collapse of the old European order in 1914.

The First World War mobilized sixty-five million men, killed over
eight million and left another twenty-one million wounded; it swept

* See Notes (page 426 below).

ix

away four of the continent's ancient empires and turned Europe into what Czech politician Thomas Masaryk described as 'a laboratory atop a vast graveyard'. 'The World War', wrote Russian artist El Lissitsky, 'requires us to test all values.' Amid the ruins of the *ancien régime* – with the Kaiser exiled, the Tsar and his family shot – politicians promised the masses, enfranchised and mobilized as never before, a fairer society and a state of their own. The liberal Woodrow Wilson offered a world 'safe for democracy'; Lenin a communal society emancipated from want and free of the exploitative hierarchies of the past. Hitler envisaged a warrior race, purged of alien elements, fulfilling its imperial destiny through the purity of its blood and the unity of its purpose. Each of these three rival ideologies – liberal democracy, communism and fascism – saw itself destined to remake society, the continent and the world in a New Order for mankind. The unremitting struggle between them to define modern Europe lasted most of this century.[2]

In the short run, both Wilson and Lenin failed to build the 'better world' they dreamed of. The communist revolution across Europe did not materialize, and the building of socialism was confined to the Soviet Union; the crisis of liberal democracy followed soon after as one country after another embraced authoritarianism. By the late 1930s the League of Nations had collapsed, the Right was ascendant, and Hitler's New Order looked like Europe's future. Against the liberal defence of individual liberties the Nazis counterposed the racial welfare of the collectivity; against liberalism's doctrine of the formal equality of states it offered Darwinian struggle and rule by racial superiors; against free trade it proposed the coordination of Europe's economies as a single unit under German leadership. Yet how bewilderingly fast fortunes changed in the struggle of ideologies. In the 1940s – the century's watershed – the Nazi utopia reached its zenith, and then as swiftly collapsed. Fascism became the first major ideology to suffer conclusive defeat at the hands of the history it claimed to have mastered.

In the long run, the 1940s were important for another reason too. The exhausting, murderous experience of total war – the culmination of nearly a century of imperial and national struggles inside and outside the continent – led to a growing weariness with ideological politics across the continent. The great tide of mass mobilization began to ebb, and with it the militarism and collectivism of the inter-war years. Believers became cynics at worst, at best apathetic, resigned and domesticated. People rediscovered democracy's quiet virtues – the space it left for privacy, the individual and the family. Thus after 1945, democracy re-emerged in the West, revitalized by the challenge of war against Hitler, newly conscious of its social responsibilities. Only now it faced competition from the Left not the Right, as the Red Army, having crushed Nazi Germany's imperial dreams, brought communism to the new Soviet empire in eastern Europe.

Although the Cold War represented the last stage of the ideological struggle for Europe's future, it differed crucially from earlier phases in its avoidance of real war – at least on the continent itself. To be sure there were crises; but in general, the two superpowers lived in 'peaceful coexistence', aiming at each other's ultimate demise, but accepting each other's right to exist in the present for the sake of continental stability and peace. The two systems armed themselves for a war that could not be fought, and competed to provide welfare for their citizens, and to bring economic growth and material prosperity. Both offered some astonishing initial achievements; but only one proved capable of adapting to the growing pressures of global capitalism. With the collapse of the Soviet empire in 1989, not only the Cold War but the whole era of ideological rivalries which began in 1917 came to an end.

What all ideologies have in common is that they like to present their own utopia as an End to History – whether in the form of universal communism, global democracy or a Thousand Year Reich. They share what Ignazio Silone once described as 'the widespread virtue that identifies History with the winning side'. They read the present back into the past, and assume – for instance – that democracy must be rooted deeply in Europe's soil simply because the Cold War turned out the way it did. Today a different kind of history is needed – less useful as a political instrument but bringing us closer to past realities –

which sees the present as just one possible outcome of our predecessors' struggles and uncertainties. After all, democracy reigned supreme in Europe as the First World War ended, but was virtually moribund two decades later. And if 1989 marked democracy's victory over communism, it was a victory which could not have come about without communism's earlier comprehensive and shattering defeat of National Socialism in the war. It was thus not preordained that democracy should win out over fascism and communism, just as it remains still to be seen what kind of democracy Europe is able and willing to build. In short, what I describe here is a story of narrow squeaks and unexpected twists, not inevitable victories and forward marches.[3]

Ideologies matter, not so much as guides to history, but as vehicles for belief and political action. If the dogmas of the past no longer hold us in their grip, this does not mean they were merely grand deceptions from the start. The end of communism has been described as 'the passing of an illusion', but a funeral oration is not a historical analysis. After 1945, fascism was similarly explained away as a political pathology by which insane dictators led bewitched, hypnotized populations to their doom. Yet the wounds of the continent cannot be dismissed as the work of a few madmen, and its traumas will not be found to lie in the mental condition of Hitler or Stalin. Like it or not, both fascism and communism involved real efforts to tackle the problems of mass politics, of industrialization and social order; liberal democracy did not always have all the answers. 'We can no longer afford to take that which was good in the past and simply call it our heritage,' writes Hannah Arendt, 'to discard the bad and simply think of it as a dead load which by itself time will bury in oblivion.'[4]

National Socialism, in particular, fits into the mainstream not only of German but also of European history far more comfortably than most people like to admit. If Soviet communism involved a truly radical break with the past – an attempt, in Europe's most underdeveloped and war-torn country, to create a new property-less society, to hold together a disintegrating empire and simultaneously to telescope an industrial revolution into a few years – Nazism, by contrast, was less ambitious and far more secure at home, and ultimately far more aggressive abroad. Its revolutionary rhetoric masked greater continuities of ideas and institutions with the past. Its construction of a racial-nationalist welfare system simply pushed to extremes tendencies visible in European thought more generally and it held power against negligible opposition in Europe's most technologically advanced economy. Yet this solidly established regime was committed in a way the Soviet Union never was to overthrowing the Versailles settlement by force. This is why it was the Third Reich which posed the most serious challenge to liberal democracy this century, and why an analysis of the changing content of European democratic thought and practice means acknowledging the very real possibility that emerged in the late 1930s of a continent organized along Nazi lines.

It would of course be possible to take a very different view of the century, focusing less upon fascism than upon communism. Marxist historiography, exemplified recently in Eric Hobsbawm's panoramic *Age of Extremes*, downplays fascism's significance in its concentration upon what it regards as the fundamental struggle between communism and capitalism. If I have chosen not to do that here, it is partly because communism's impact upon *democracy* – important though it was – was in general more indirect and less threatening than the challenge posed by Hitler. But it is also, and more basically, because if this century has shown one thing, it is that politics cannot be reduced to economics: differences in values and ideologies must be taken seriously and not simply regarded as foils for class interest. Fascism, in other words, was more than just another form of capitalism.

Precisely because the Nazi utopia of a dynamic, racially purified German empire required a war for its fulfilment, and because that utopia was also a nightmarish revelation of the destructive potential in European civilization – turning imperialism on its head and treating Europeans as Africans – the experience of fascism's New Order (and its short-lived allure) was forgotten as quickly as possible after 1945. The city council of Bologna melted down its bronze statue of Mussolini on horseback and recast it as a noble pair of partisans; France canonized the memory of a united opposition to Vichy, while Austria shamelessly milked its status as Hitler's first victim and erected memorials to its anti-Nazi 'fighters for Austrian freedom'. These were the foundation myths of a Europe liberated from history; they expunged awkward memories and asserted the inevitability of freedom's triumph.

Keeping intact a sense of European civilizational superiority also involved an endless redrawing of mental boundaries. The so-called 'European Community' implicitly ignored half the continent: post-war Europe became equated with the West. Dismayed East Europeans talked themselves into 'central Europe' to distance themselves from the barbarians. The habit persists today: a leading British historian recently described the war in Bosnia as 'a primitive, tribal conflict only anthropologists can understand', preferring to see Yugoslavia as part of the barbaric Third World than to accept that contemporary Europe itself might be tainted. Not even the murderous record of the twentieth century has yet, it seems, diminished Europeans' capacity for self-delusion.[5]

My own geographical conception of Europe and its limits is basically a pragmatic one. This is a book about events and struggles within Europe rather than about Europe's place in the world. But of course it is not possible to consider Hitler's continental ambitions without seeing them in the context of European imperialism overseas, nor to describe the Cold War without reference to the United States. The Soviet Union – as the great Eurasian power – stands both inside and outside European history at different times. Hence this is a Europe whose boundaries – as in reality – are porous and adaptable. Eastern Europe is no less a part of the story than the West, the Balkans no less than Scandinavia.

As ever, issues of geography disguise arguments about politics, religion and culture, and those who are keen to establish Europe's unity will find my agnosticism deeply unsatisfying. Yet this merely corresponds to the uncertainty which now surrounds the concept of Europe itself. Fascism, after all, was the most Eurocentric of the three major ideologies, far more so than either communism or liberal democracy: a creed which was both anti-American and anti-Bolshevik at least had the virtue of clarity. What Europe means for us today after the end of the Cold War is far vaguer – is it part of the 'West' (itself a notion with an antiquated edge), a western outcrop of 'Eurasia', both or neither? The 'Europe' of the European Union may be a promise or a delusion, but it is not a reality. Taking the divisions and uncertainties of this continent seriously – as I have tried to do here – implies abandoning metaphysics, renouncing the search for some mysterious and essential 'Europe', and exploring instead the constant contest to define what it should mean.

Ultimately it is the question of values which lies at the heart of this history – the values which drove people to act, which shaped and transformed institutions, guided state policy and underpinned communities, families and individuals. 'Every social order is one of the possible solutions to a problem that is not scientific but human, the problem of community life,' wrote the French scholar Raymond Aron in 1954. 'Are Europeans still capable of practising the subtle art required by liberal communities? Have they retained their own system of values?' The 'problem of community life' which Aron raises is perhaps the central theme of this book. Against Aron, however, one must ask: what was Europe's 'own system of values'? Liberalism was but one of them, and there were others. Europe's twentieth century is the story of their conflict.[6]

My primary debt is to the many other scholars upon whose work I have drawn. I owe thanks too to the institutions and individuals who have supported me through hard times for British universities. This book grew out of the uniquely invigorating environment of the University of Sussex, and I would like to thank my students and colleagues in the School of European Studies, and the History and International Relations subject groups, for their help – especially the late Christopher Thorne, Alasdair Smith, Nigel Llewellyn, Rod Kedward, John Röhl and Pat Thane.

Thanks too to Bob Connor, Kent Mullikin and the staff of the National Humanities Center in North Carolina for giving me the opportunity to start this project, and the Annenberg Foundation for making my year there possible. I am very grateful to Dimitri Gondicas and the Program in Hellenic Studies at Princeton University for their continued support, to the staff of the Institut für die Wissenschaften vom Menschen in Vienna, for allowing me to finish the book in such peaceful surroundings, and to Barbara Politi and Walter Lummerding for their truly extraordinary hospitality. Part of this material appeared initially in *Daedalus* and *Diplomacy and Statecraft*, and I thank the editors of these journals for permission to use it here.

Deb Burnstone gave me much confidence in this project from the outset. She, Nikos Alivizatos, Bruce Graham, Dave Mazower, Michael Pinnock, Gyan Prakash, Pat Thane, John Thompson and Johanna Weber offered me encouragement and support, and suggested many improvements. My father's recollections of the 1940s helped me greatly. Peter Mandler gave me all kinds of precious companionship, not least intellectual. Steve Kotkin worked out what I was trying to say before I did, and pushed me to say it. My heartfelt thanks to them all. I dedicate this book to Ruth Shaffer, most remarkable of grandmothers, and to the beloved memory of Grandpa, Frouma and Max. The story of Europe's twentieth century is their story too.

I

The Deserted Temple:
Democracy's Rise and Fall

... a time when one hears talk on all sides of a crisis – and
sometimes even a catastrophe – of democracy.
                                            – Hans Kelsen, 1932[1]

Freedom? Many people smile at the word. Democracy? Parliaments? There are few who do not speak ill of Parliaments . . .
                                            – Francesco Nitti, 1927[2]

At a 'Congress of Dethroned Monarchs' held at Geneva in 192—
Europe's erstwhile crowned heads tried to win back their old supporters. But their stirring proclamation ('Only monarchy is able to
defend European culture from an onslaught of Bolshevik barbarism,
from soulless American mechanization, from the anger of awakening
Asiatic nationalisms ... Europe can choose: annihilation or
monarchy . . .') fell on deaf ears. Bowing to the spirit of the times,
they finally set up their own Republic of Kings on a small island in
the Indian Ocean. There, to their surprise, they were soon forgotten
by their former subjects. The 'twilight of the history of monarchy'
had begun.[3]

That was fiction, as narrated by the Polish writer Alexander Wat
in his 1927 story 'Kings in Exile'. But the real constitutional changes
wrought by the First World War were no less dramatic. In that moment
of 'bourgeois triumph', the *ancien régime* was finally toppled – sultans,
pashas, emperors and dukes reduced to impotence. Before the First
World War there had been just three republics in Europe; by the end

of 1918 there were thirteen. 'In the eyes of a Wilson, a Lloyd George, a Clemenceau, a Masaryk, a Beneš, a Venizelos,' wrote a French commentator, 'the flight of the Kaiser Wilhelm and the departure of the Emperor Charles completed the flight of Louis XVI . . . 1918 was a sort of European 1792.'[4]

Following the wholly unforeseen collapse of the great autocratic empires of Russia, Austria-Hungary, Hohenzollern Germany and Ottoman Turkey, the Paris peace settlement saw parliamentary democracy enthroned across Europe. A belt of democracies – stretching from the Baltic Sea down through Germany and Poland to the Balkans – was equipped with new constitutions drawn up according to the most up-to-date liberal principles. British scholar James Bryce, in his 1921 classic *Modern Democracies*, talked about the 'universal acceptance of democracy as the normal and natural form of government'.[5]

Yet liberalism's triumph proved short-lived. The Russian Revolution and the spectre of communist subversion cast their shadows westwards across the continent. Democratic values disappeared as political polarization brought much of Europe to the verge of civil war. Ruling elites in many countries soon showed themselves to be anti-communists first, democrats second. This became clear as early as 1919 in Hungary with the suppression of the Béla Kun revolutionary government and the installation of Admiral Horthy's regime. In Italy Liberal elites supported the formation of a Fascist government in 1922. Primo de Rivera seized power in Spain; Portugal's republic succumbed to the dictatorship of Professor Salazar. Poland took a sharp turn away from parliamentary rule in 1926, following a period of hyperinflation and political instability. With the onset of the Great Depression in 1929, one government after another moved rightwards. The trend seemed inexorable. 'When one examines the contemporary problem of European dictatorships,' noted an acute Spanish commentator, 'one of the facts which immediately strikes one is the ease with which they have been established and the even greater ease with which they stay in power.'[6]

By the 1930s, parliaments seemed to be going the way of kings. The Left had been vanquished or forced on to the defensive nearly everywhere west of the Soviet Union, and all the key political debates were taking place on the Right. Only on the continent's northern fringes did effective parliamentary rule survive. 'We are living in a period when the most courageous face moments of profound discouragement, when the hopes for social and international appeasement salvaged from the wreckage of the World War, seem sadly illusory,' wrote an analyst of the 'current reaction against democracy' in 1934. As early as 1925 the German legal scholar Moritz Bonn had talked of 'the crisis of European democracy'; Eustace Percy in 1931 saw 'Democracy on Trial' while H. G. Wells looked forward to 'After Democracy'. 'Is this the end of liberty?' asked Salvador de Madariaga in the midst of the Spanish civil war. Professor William Rappard wrote from Geneva that the 'crisis of democracy' had taken 'civilized mankind completely unawares, following the apparent triumph of democracy in the modern world'.[7]

Sitting in Paris in the summer of 1940 as the Germans marched in, the anti-liberal Bertrand de Jouvenel wrote off the 'stream of jurists' who had created 'a mass of parliaments' after the 'bourgeois triumph' of 1918; only gradually, he went on, did people realize that 'the great tide of bourgeois parliamentarism of 1919–1920 had retreated' and that 'in place of that current which had seemed irresistible there appeared another, an authoritarian one'. To de Jouvenel, faced with what seemed to be the definitive collapse of parliamentary democracy in Europe, such institutions as the Presidency of the Republic, the Senate and the Chamber now appeared mere 'fantasies of the Faculty of Law'.[8]

Today, it is hard to see the inter-war experiment with democracy for the novelty it was: yet we should certainly not *assume* that democracy is suited to Europe. Though we may like to think democracy's victory in the Cold War proves its deep roots in Europe's soil, history tells us otherwise. Triumphant in 1918, it was virtually extinct twenty years on. Maybe it was bound to collapse in a time of political crisis and economic turmoil, for its defenders were too utopian, too ambitious, too few. In its focus upon constitutional rights and its neglect of social responsibilities, it often seemed more fitted to the nineteenth than to the twentieth century. By the 1930s the signs were that most Europeans no longer wished to fight for it; there were dynamic non-democratic alternatives to meet the challenges of modernity. Europe found other, authoritarian, forms of political order no more foreign to its traditions, and no less efficient as organizers of society, industry and technology.

MAKING CONSTITUTIONS

'Constitution is such a wonderful thing that he who does not know what it is is a donkey,' exclaimed an inhabitant of Ottoman Salonika in 1908. During the nineteenth century the demand for constitutional government had been a centrepiece of middle-class demands for political reform, and this demand gathered pace in the decade before the outbreak of the First World War, spreading through the empires of Europe and infiltrating St Petersburg, Istanbul and the monarchies of the Balkans.

With the victory of Entente forces and the USA in 1918, the demand for constitutional reform swept central–eastern Europe. Poland and the Baltic states lost no time once Germany was defeated in affirming their liberal ambitions, and drawing up appropriately democratic constitutions. Territories wrested from the former Habsburg empire underwent a similar transformation. In November 1918, a provisional constitution declared Austria to be a 'democratic republic'. The Czech nationalist leaders issued the Declaration of Independence of the Czechoslovak State in October 1918 in Paris. 'We accept and shall adhere to the ideals of modern democracy, as they have been the ideals of our nation for centuries,' they proclaimed. 'We accept the American principles as laid down by President Wilson: the principles of liberated mankind – of the actual equality of nations – and of governments deriving their just power from the consent of the governed.' Early in 1920, the Czech National Assembly adopted the constitution of a democratic republic.[9]

Of course, the key to the future of democracy in Europe – as it would be through the century – was Germany. The Kaiser was forced into exile, and a transitional liberal regime under the constitutionalist

Prince Max of Baden soon made way for a sweeping democratization of the entire political system under the chancellorship of the Social Democratic leader, Friedrich Ebert. In January 1919 a National Constituent Assembly was elected by universal suffrage; six months later it voted for a constitution whose first article affirmed: 'The Reich is a republic. All political authority is derived from the people.' The workers' and soldiers' councils which had been set up at the same time, inspired by the Bolshevik example, were forced to accept the primacy of parliamentary rule.

In this way, amid the chaos and confusion of post-war central Europe, where nationalist paramilitaries, bandits, peasant radicals and pro-Bolsheviks were all seeking to exploit the collapse of the old regime, middle-class lawyers and politicians tried to lay down the bases of a new, democratic, constitutional order. The Russo-French scholar Mirkine-Guetzevitch, in his 1929 survey *Les Constitutions de l'Europe nouvelle*, found no fewer than twenty-two separate cases to discuss, including the constitutions of the Free City of Danzig, of the Vatican, Prussia and Bavaria. In that heady first post-war decade the jurist was king. University professors wielded extraordinary influence and experts like Hugo Preuss in Germany and Hans Kelsen in Austria put their theories into practice in the constitutions of their respective countries.

For inspiration – often taken verbatim – they scoured established liberal polities such as France, the USA, England and Switzerland. But they outdid even these in their zeal to build truly representative and comprehensive democracies. Their handiwork reflected the most modern doctrines of public law and its relationship to politics and society. Their fundamental aim was – in the words of a leading commentator – to subordinate politics to law, to 'rationalize' power and sweep away the inconsistencies and irrational residues of the old feudal order, considering every aspect of social and political life in specific constitutional provisions.[10]

Later, of course, it was the lawyers themselves who would be blamed for the collapse of democratic institutions. They had been naive, unrealistic and too inclined to seek 'juridical perfection' rather than 'political expediency'. Replacing politics with law was a rather quixotic aspiration in the bitterly polarized climate of post-1918 central Europe. Critics charged that such grandiose and ultimately utopian schemes only produced political structures that were unworkable in the real world. These accusations ignored the many other factors that contributed to inter-war political instability – economic crisis, social turmoil, the inequities of the Paris peace settlement. But they did at least recognize the genuine importance and novelty of post-war constitutional arrangements.[11]

Most of the new constitutions began by stressing their democratic, national and republican character. Thus, article 1 of the 1920 Austrian constitution asserted that 'Austria is a democratic republic. Sovereignty is vested in the people.' The Lithuanian constitution opened: 'The state of Lithuania is an independent democratic republic.' Sovereignty was usually stated to reside in 'the people'; in some, however, such as Poland, the Irish Free State (in the 1922 constitution) and Greece, it emanated from the 'nation'. The 1921 constitution of the Kingdom of the Serbs, Croats and Slovenes insisted hopefully that 'there is only one nationality for all the subjects of the Kingdom'; the Czechoslovak wording was almost identical. The Weimar constitution declared similarly its belief in 'the national self-consciousness of a self-organizing people'.

Because so much of bourgeois political life had revolved in the nineteenth century around the struggle with autocratic monarchs and their personalized systems of rule, the new constitutions naturally expressed an overwhelming mistrust of executive authority. Power was heavily concentrated in the legislature. The new constitutions authorized the setting up of parliamentary committees to oversee the workings of the executive and spelled out the circumstances in which a vote of confidence in the government might be called. In some cases, it was stipulated that government ministers were to be nominated by parliament rather than by the prime minister or president. This pre-eminence of parliament was to become, as we shall see, one of the main points of criticism by opponents of the new democratic arrangements.[12]

The same desire for a highly modern, open democracy led often to the adoption of proportional representation in order to produce a legislature which would most closely express the popular will; referendums were also popular for this reason. In order to 'rationalize' the tangled mass of regional legal codes and conventions and create a national body of law, several constitutions tried explicitly to define and restrict the power of local authorities and enhanced the power of the central state. Draft proposals by Polish and Croatian jurists to safeguard the autonomy of local government were rejected. Wilson's legacy, after all, encompassed not just democracy but national self-determination as well, and a strong central authority appealed to Czechs faced with a powerful German minority, to Poles with their Ukrainians, to the Serbs in Yugoslavia. Only in Germany and Austria was the new state constructed on a federal rather than unitary basis, and in those cases not until after a long struggle, nor for very many years. Indeed even before Hitler and Dollfuss centralized power in an unmistakable fashion, the central governments of Germany and Austria had begun to use their special powers in fiscal and welfare legislation.

Where the new constitutions departed sharply and most controversially from nineteenth-century liberal values was in their extension of rights from political and civil liberties to areas of health, welfare, the family and social security. The goals of social policy – new in their ambition and promise – were set out in constitutional provisions, not only in countries like Germany and Austria where the Social Democrats held power at the end of the war, but even in Romania, which talked about the 'social rights of man' and in the Kingdom of Serbs, Croats and Slovenes which mentioned land reform and the need for social and economic legislation. The Spanish constitution declared the country 'a democratic republic of workers of all classes' and laid down that property might be expropriated 'for social uses'.[13]

In these as in other respects, the new constitutions reflected the very diverse political preoccupations of their makers. On the one hand, they were expressions of classic nineteenth-century liberalism; on the other, they attempted to meet popular demands reinforced by the impact of the First World War for a 'genuine social democracy'. This social democratic agenda was clearly a response to events in Russia, and reflected a desire to win the masses away from Bolshevism and over to parliamentarism. 'Either Wilson or Lenin,' wrote Hugo Preuss, who drafted the Weimar constitution and saw it as a bulwark against the Bolshevization of Germany. Thus the new constitutions tried to reconcile old-fashioned parliamentarism with the contemporary pressures of a modern mass society emerging from the devastation of war. A mixture of forward-looking optimism and a new anxiety, they mirrored the ambiguous post-war situation of democracy's defenders – the European bourgeoisie.[14]

EUROPE'S CIVIL WAR

'The soul of the Russian people,' declared Prince Lvov, Prime Minister of the Provisional Government in March 1917, 'turned out by its very nature to be a universal democratic soul. It is prepared not only to merge with the democracy of the whole world, but to stand at the head of it and to lead it along the path of human progress according to the principles of liberty, equality and fraternity.'[15]

For much of 1917 it seemed that Russia would be the site of the first triumph of Europe's democratic revolution. All the parties involved in the overthrow of the old autocracy were committed to preserving their gains from the monarchy's return: liberal democracy was all the rage in early 1917, and if there was an apparent enemy, it lay in the form of the Romanov loyalists not the Bolsheviks. The Left, including Lenin, was pressing for a Constituent Assembly in order to usher in the period of 'bourgeois rule' which according to Marxist theory was now needed. As late as October, when the Bolsheviks seized power, they could not decide whether the revolution they were making was 'bourgeois democratic' or 'proletarian socialist'.

With the Tsarist empire disintegrating, the struggle in 1917–18 with the breakaway Ukrainian and Finnish assemblies helped to push them in favour of the second possibility. Even more important were the results of the Constituent Assembly elections, which represented a vote for the Left but a considerable defeat for the Bolsheviks, who gained under one fourth of the total votes cast, and less than half as many deputies as the Socialist Revolutionaries. In the face of this rejection by the electorate, Lenin adjusted his position: according to his *Theses on the Constituent Assembly* it was true that 'in a bourgeois republic the constituent assembly [is] the highest form of the democratic principle'; however, it now appeared that according to 'revolutionary social-democracy . . . a republic of Soviets [is] a higher form of the democratic principle'. The Assembly became an anachronistic symbol of 'bourgeois counter-revolution'; its members were written off as 'men from another world'. Lenin did not prevent its meeting in January 1918; but one day after it opened, he closed it down by force. This was bad Marxism, according to more moderate Social Democrats, but Lenin hardly cared.[16]

His triumph, like Mussolini's later from the Right, was really the consequence of liberalism's failure. Russia's liberals turned out to be the first, but not the last, to assume mistakenly that a deep-rooted social crisis could be solved by offering 'the people' constitutional liberties. Such liberties were not what 'the people' – and especially Russia's fifteen million peasant conscripts – wanted. They were more interested in peace and land, and the liberals offered them neither, just as they had little to offer the country's urban working class either. In the factories, in the countryside and in the ranks, social order was collapsing, and the middle ground in Russian politics disappeared. Kerensky's Provisional Government had become an empty shell well before Trotsky's Red Guards seized power in Petrograd.

The hopes of Russian constitutionalists lingered on, nevertheless, and in June 1918 they established a short-lived Committee of Members of the Constitutional Assembly in Samara. After the end of the civil war, 'bourgeois counter-revolutionaries' formed a rump Assembly of Members of the Constituent Assembly in Paris – but this bore little relation to the balance of power inside what had by now become the Soviet Union, where the overwhelming desire was not for constitutional liberties but for socio-economic transformation, national consolidation and an end to lawlessness and social anarchy through decisive state action. Thus Russia, liberalism's first wartime triumph, became the scene of its first and most frightening defeat.

In Bolshevik hands, even constitutionalism could be used against the bourgeoisie: why should *their* form of constitution be regarded as the last word? Perhaps it was outmoded and class-ridden, and needed to be replaced by something more modern? 'We'll tell the people that its interests are higher than the interests of democratic institutions,' insisted Lenin in December 1917. Shortly after the dissolution of the Constituent Assembly, he contrasted the 'dead bourgeois parliamentarism' of the assembly, with the 'proletarian, simple, in many ways disorderly and incomplete, but alive and vital Soviet *apparat*'. And it was upon the basis of his Declaration of Rights of the Toiling and Exploited People that the Fifth Congress of Soviets approved its own constitution for the Russian Federated Republic. Through this document the congress sought the creation of socialism by ending exploitation, 'crushing completely' the bourgeoisie and vesting power in the working population as expressed through the Soviets.[17]

Citizenship in this new state was unrestricted – at least in theory – according to sex and place of birth, so that women and some foreigners were enfranchised. It was, however, restricted according to social background in favour of 'the urban and rural proletariat' and 'the poorest peasants': at least seven categories of persons – including rentiers, monks and commercial traders – were denied the vote. Moreover, all rights in law were conditional: they could be withdrawn by the government if their exercise was deemed to prejudice the socialist revolution. When in December 1919, the Menshevik Martov criticized the Revolution's repeated violations of its own constitution, Lenin rejoined that what Martov demanded meant 'back to bourgeois democracy and nothing else', insisting that 'both terror and the Cheka are ... indispensable'. One year later, he was clearer still. 'The scientific term "dictatorship"', he wrote, 'means nothing more or less than authority untrammeled by any laws, absolutely unrestricted by any rules whatever, and based directly on force.' Thus, well before Stalin, the absolutist character of communist rule was made manifest; as in Tsarist times, the regime preserved an administrative conception of law rather than one consistent with the 'bourgeois' separation of powers. It differed, of course, both from Tsarist times and more important, from constitutional innovations elsewhere in Europe, in the priority it gave to socio-economic benefits for the masses – public housing, medical care and schooling, liberalized marriage and divorce laws – over the classical individual freedoms. But it differed too in its conception of revolutionary politics as civil war, wherein state terror had a special role as an instrument of class struggle.[18]

Yet the development of the Soviet system had a less immediate impact on the rest of Europe than seemed likely in 1918. The West's intervention in the Russian Civil War failed to topple the communist regime. But equally across the rest of Europe, the much-feared revolution either failed to materialize, or was easily put down. Despite the wave of soviets, strikes, mutinies and insurrections which swept Europe in 1918–19 from Scotland to the Adriatic, with street fighting in Germany and a violent civil war in Finland, there was only one other country where a Bolshevik regime actually seized power for any length of time, and that was Hungary. As in Russia, civil war was the consequence; the outcome, however, was very different.

In early 1919, the liberal regime of Count Mihály Károlyi was overthrown by a Bolshevik sympathizer called Béla Kun, who immediately proclaimed the establishment of a Soviet republic. But Kun held Budapest for only several months. Backed by the Entente powers, the Romanian army invaded Hungary and the communists fled. In the autumn of 1919, the gentry class returned to power under the regency of Admiral Horthy, established a regime of terror against suspected radicals and quickly won Allied recognition.

At first, Horthy's right-wing regime – anti-communist, anti-democratic – seemed an anomaly in an era of growing democratization, a last gasp of European feudalism. Time would show, however, that it was more than a relic from the past; it was also a vision of the future: the democracies were to be squeezed increasingly tightly between the twin extremes of communism and fascism. These new authoritarian models were soon to challenge the pre-eminence of Versailles liberalism.

BOURGEOIS DOUBTS

At a time when ruling elites feared the prospect of peasants and workers joining hands to seize power, one of the main instruments for building up support for democratic successor states across Europe was land reform – sacrificing the aristocracy to save bourgeois society from the Bolshevik threat to do away with private property completely. Thus throughout eastern and central Europe, large estates were parcelled out to create a new class of peasant smallholders. In general it was hoped that they would prove to be independent, democratic but conservative, immune to the blandishments of communism.

Such a political project could only work, however, where the government was prepared to dispossess the landed classes. Where large estates were in the hands of an ethnic minority, as in the Baltic states, in Czechoslovakia and to some extent in the Balkans, politicians were happier about land reform than in countries like Hungary, where the magnates nipped the reform movement in the bud, or Italy, where landowners were well connected to government. In Weimar Germany, east Elbian Junkers accused the reform-minded Chancellor Brüning of 'Agrarian Bolshevism'. In Spain, of course, fear of agrarian reform was to play a large part in fomenting civil war.

The revolutionary wave of 1918–19 did indeed demonstrate the political conservatism of the landowning peasantry. It was in the cities – Berlin, Munich, Vienna, Budapest – that pro-Bolshevik groups sought power. It was in cities – like Turin in 1920 – that the power of European pro-Bolsheviks expressed itself in strikes, factory occupations and demonstrations. What limited their potential – outside wartime Russia – was their lack of appeal to the rural population. Rarely in Europe did you encounter peasants in as miserable a condition as was to be found in Russia. Most were uninterested in political radicalism – with the partial exception of the Bulgarian Agrarians. Only where you found a landless agricultural workforce as in the Po valley, in the latifundia of Andalusia, or the Great Plain of Hungary, did the Russian Revolution resonate. Whilst Austrian smallholders denounced Red Vienna, Italian *braccianti* were forming powerful socialist leagues. Unwilling to defuse this rural discontent by the only democratic means possible – land reform – political elites in Italy turned to force. Agrarian civil war paved the way for Mussolini.

The rise of Italian Fascism in the early 1920s offers an instructive counter-example to those critics who blamed the new constitutions for democracy's collapse in Europe. After all, when Mussolini became Premier, Charles Albert's *Statuto* of 1848 remained the constitutional foundation of the state. What post-war Italy offered was a picture of liberal uncertainty and weakness, a more or less voluntary renunciation of power to the Right in the face of popular discontent and political instability.

In October 1922, when the King invited Mussolini to form a government, the Fascist movement was still relatively small. What helped it into power was not the impression created by the melodramatic, not to say farcical, March on Rome, but rather the widespread fear of socialism in Italy, generated by the results of the new universal male suffrage in the elections of 1919. It was this fear which explains why such broad strata of the police, the civil service, the Court and parliament looked at the Fascists with sympathy. Mussolini's first government was a coalition with three other political parties. Without their support, especially that of the Liberals, Mussolini would have been unable to form a government. Without their support, and that of the Socialists as well, he would have been unable to push through the electoral reform of 1923 which ensured his government's control of the Chamber of Deputies.

Up to 1925, indeed, many of the Duce's more radical supporters expressed their disappointment at Fascism's compromise with the old system. The conservative Gaetano Serventi, in his book *Ascesa della democrazia europea e prime reazioni storiche* (The Ascent of European Democracy and the First Historical Reactions) not only wrote off post-war democracy as a symptom of 'the rapid and progressive decadence of European values in the world', but, less predictably perhaps, attacked what he called 'parliamentary Fascism' for 'deluding itself that its vitality might exist within a democratic system'. Similarly the Spanish commentator Francisco Cambo warned that Mussolini, by compromising with parliamentarism, had lost his opportunity for a truly revolutionary break with the past. Such criticisms were to be found also within the Fascist movement itself, where calls for revolutionary renewal led to the so-called 'second wave' of 1925–6. Only then were laws passed extending the powers of the prefect in the provinces, depriving the regime's critics of citizenship, suppressing opposition parties and attacking press freedoms and civil liberties. In the fluid political climate of the early 1920s, Fascism no less than democracy was feeling its way.[19]

Over the next four years the outlines of the Fascist state became clearer. Some features from the past were retained: the King remained head of state (although his powers were whittled down), parliament continued its ineffectual debates, while the widespread use of police power in the provinces remained as indispensable as it had done under the Liberals. Thus in some ways Fascism followed on quite smoothly from its Liberal predecessors, and post-war mass democracy looked much like a tiny interlude in a longer history of elite government.

Where Fascism differed sharply from liberalism was in its frank defence of the authoritarian state. 'Discipline must be accepted,' stated Mussolini, who had – after all – chosen the *fasces*, a Roman image of authority, as the symbol of his movement. 'When it is not accepted, it must be imposed.' Individual and collective rights were, of course, harshly curtailed. The virtues of violence and action were extolled, while parliament was denounced for ineffectiveness and useless rhetoric. As the Duce himself put it in his inimitable prose:

Fascism rejects in Democracy the conventional lie of political equality, the spirit of collective irresponsibility and the myth of happiness and indefinite progress . . . One should not exaggerate the importance of Liberalism in the last century and make of it a religion of humanity for all present and future times when in reality it was only one of the many doctrines of that century . . . Now Liberalism is on the point of closing the doors of its deserted temple . . . That is why all the political experiments of the contemporary world are anti-Liberal and the desire to exile them from history is supremely ridiculous: as if history was a hunting preserve for Liberalism and professors, as if Liberalism was the last and incomparable word in civilization . . . The present century is the century of authority, a century of the Right, a Fascist century.[20]

In its attack on liberal individualism, Fascism proposed a social project revolutionary in its implications: the bourgeois division of life into public and private spheres was to be replaced by a 'totalitarian' conception of politics as a complete lived experience: 'One cannot be a Fascist in politics . . . and non-Fascist in school, non-Fascist in the family circle, non-Fascist in the workshop.' Through all the many twists and turns of the Duce's long period in office, these elements at least of Fascism remained constant.[21]

Foreign reaction was largely positive. Outside observers were unimpressed by Italy's experience of parliamentary government, and their approval of Mussolini's achievement often carried undertones of a more general disquiet about the efficacy of parliamentary democracy in the modern world. Condescending English politicians like Churchill or Austen Chamberlain, who doubted whether the parliamentary tradition was for export at all, congratulated the Italians on having liberated themselves from a form of government to which they had clearly been unsuited.

Similar doubts about the universality of the democratic model could be detected more widely. Some questioned whether 'the Latin peoples' with their tradition of absolutism could make of democracy anything more than a 'comedy'. In Portugal, for instance, there had been eight presidents, dozens of governments and innumerable attempted coups in the fifteen years which followed the creation of the republic. Perhaps certain specific historical traditions existed in the Anglo-Saxon world to explain the tenacity of democratic institutions – a long history of successful struggle against monarchy, a deep attachment to the liberties which had been slowly and painfully won during that struggle. The pre-war experience of Greece, Romania, Serbia and indeed Italy itself showed that parliaments were quite compatible with corruption, clientelism and continued backwardness.

At the same time post-war changes in the nature of government and the role of the state had made parliament itself less important as a locus of decision-making than its liberal advocates liked to admit. Now it had to share power with centres of business and union bargaining, and other kinds of interest groups. When one looked more closely at how parliaments actually functioned in the 1920s, the question remained: why bother with them at all?

THE CRITIQUE OF PARLIAMENTARISM

'The reason why "fascisms" come into being', wrote a French critic, 'is the political and social failure of liberal democracy.' The authors of *Fascism for Whom?* (1938) put it more simply: 'Fascism was the product of democratic decay.' This decay was located most obviously in the working of parliament itself. For many Europeans the roots of the post-war 'flourishing of dictatorship' lay 'in the crisis of parliamentary government as practised today'.[22]

Proportional representation – as some critics had warned at the outset – produced fragmented legislatures, with large numbers of parties. The very system designed to reflect the popular will revealed its absence amid a welter of class, ethnic or religious differences. Sixteen parties secured seats in the 1930 Reichstag, for example, nineteen in the 1929 Czech elections, while in Latvia, Estonia and Poland there were sometimes even more. According to Cambo, 'the greatest inefficiency of the Italian parliament coincided with the application of . . . proportional representation' which he described as 'one of the most obvious reasons for the success of the Fascist revolution'.[23]

New electoral laws could discourage this fragmentation. France in 1924 and Greece in 1928 saw systems of proportional representation replaced by majority voting. Critics pointed to the example of Britain in support of their argument that majority voting would increase the stability of democracy. The problem, however, went beyond the electoral system itself. Political parties – highly organized, often with their own educational, cultural, welfare and paramilitary services – were frequently accused of acting as intermediaries for sectional interests rather than standing for the country as a whole. One conservative German theorist talked of the 'egotism' of political parties and regarded their influence as the 'symptom of an illness' and 'a degeneration'. Belgians talked disparagingly of the 'regime of parties' which

held sway. There were Peasant Parties, Communist and Social Democratic Parties for the industrial working class, even a 'Party of the
Middle-Classes, Artisans and Merchants' (in Czechoslovakia). Parties
formed on ethnic lines as well as class. A Party for Spiritual Renewal
made a brief appearance in Weimar. Parliament seemed like a lens,
magnifying rather than resolving the bitter social, national and economic tensions in society at large. To see deputies hurling chairs as
well as insults at each other was not uncommon; in the extreme case,
in the Belgrade Skupština in 1928, a Serbian MP shot dead the Croat
Peasant Party leader at point-blank range, leading King Alexander to
suspend parliamentary business, to revoke the constitution, and, in
an act of extreme hopefulness, to rename the land of the Serbs, Croats
and Slovenes the Kingdom of Yugoslavia. But this did little good and
in 1934 Alexander himself was assassinated by Croat nationalist
extremists.[24]

In his analysis of the Weimar party system, Sigmund Neumann
argued that Germany's political parties were confronting rather than
communicating with one another. Each group of supporters, mobilized
in increasingly militaristic party organizations with their banners and
placards, looked on with hostility at other sections of society. Political
dialogue and coalition government were increasingly intractable, for
'discussion becomes meaningless where one's partner has already
decided on his position before the discussion has begun . . . As a result
the intellectual foundations of liberalism and parliamentarism have
been shaken.' Neumann predicted that 'the breakdown of parliament
will of necessity lead to the rise in importance of other political power
factors, perhaps the Reich president [or] the Reich government'.
Legislative paralysis, according to his colleague Moritz Bonn, 'has
produced the clamor for a dictator who is willing to do the things the
nation wants to be done, but who is not subject to the rule of economic
groups or even of a majority'. Hans Kelsen, one of Europe's most
eminent legal theorists, spoke of 'the crisis of the parliamentary system'
and discussed reinforcing the power of the government vis-à-vis the
Reichstag. Neumann, Bonn and Kelsen were all committed democrats;
but they were all conscious of living in societies split down the
middle in an era of unprecedented economic and political polarization.

Democracy was supposed to have unified the nation; instead it seemed to have divided it.[25]

As a result of the multiplicity of competing party interests, the formation of governments was becoming ever more difficult. There were hardly any countries in Europe after 1918 where the average Cabinet lasted more than a year; in Germany and Austria the average was eight months, in Italy five, in Spain after 1931 under four. In the French Third Republic – the ineffectual model for so many east European constitutions – the average Cabinet lifespan dropped from ten months in 1870–1914, to eight in 1914–32 and a mere four in 1932–40. This reflected the almost universal lack of stable bi-party legislatures, or of parties able to command absolute majorities. 'Restoring the authority of the State in a democracy ... will be ... the first and most essential element of our intended programme,' announced Paul-Boncour in December 1932; his Cabinet fell a month later. Such governments naturally found it difficult to push through the socio-economic reforms which were promised in their constitutions and party programmes.[26]

Impasse in the legislature prompted calls for a strengthening of the executive. In Brussels the Centre d'Études pour la Réforme de l'État pushed hard for the modification of parliamentary procedure; 'Réforme de l'État' became a popular slogan in Belgian politics. The Czech premier Beneš correctly predicted that following the resolution of the European crisis 'there will certainly be a reinforcement and consolidation of the executive power as compared with the last phases of European liberal constitutional democracy'. Neither in Czechoslovakia nor anywhere else would this debate be forgotten after 1945.[27]

In fact, constitutional revisions to strengthen the executive did occur in Poland and Lithuania (1926 and 1935), Austria (1929), and Estonia (1933 and 1937). The 1931 Spanish constitution – the most modern in inter-war Europe – authorized the delegation of substantial legislative power to the executive. Many feared, however, that such moves would turn out – as occurred, for example, under Piłsudski in Poland – to be a step along the road to dictatorship rather than a safeguard for democracy. 'We must defend democracy,' the leading French liberal Victor Basch warned the League of the Rights of Man in May 1934.

'We will not accept Parliament being sent away, nor these decree-laws which may be constitutional but are contrary to the very principles of democracy.'[28]

It is just here that we can discern the clash between, on the one hand, liberal democrats who saw 'in Power an enemy which can never be weakened enough', and, on the other, those more pragmatic constitutionalists who argued that in a crisis the executive should use all available constitutional powers to preserve the substance of democracy. Nowhere did this clash have more profound implications than in Weimar Germany.

By the late 1920s, the right-wing legal theorist Carl Schmitt had already developed his analysis of the 'state of exception' – in which constitutional emergency powers were to be employed to defend the constitution rather than to institute dictatorship. With the Reichstag paralysed, Schmitt promoted the idea of the president as defender of the constitution. Between March 1930 and January 1933, Weimar moved towards a presidential system of government through emergency decrees. In the disastrous elections of September 1930, the Nazis and the Communists emerged as the second and third largest parties, making a majority coalition impossible and giving credence to Schmitt's arguments. Germany now appeared to be in a situation whereby decree-laws issued under article 48 of the constitution were essential if government was not to be turned over into the hands of parties dedicated to the complete overthrow of democracy.[29]

The growing use of article 48, however, made it difficult to determine at what point democracy slid into dictatorship. Between 1925 and 1931 only sixteen emergency decrees were issued; in 1931 there were forty-two as against thirty-five laws passed by the Reichstag; in 1932 there were fifty-nine as against five. On 20 July 1932, Chancellor von Papen used an emergency decree to impose martial law in Prussia and remove the Social Democrat state government. Jurists started talking of the 'dictatorial power of the Reich president'; conservative anti-parliamentarians offered 'democratic dictatorship' as the alternative to parliamentary government. It was scarcely surprising that jurists like Schmitt were widely suspected of laying the groundwork for an authoritarian New State – perhaps under General Schleicher who was known to favour such a solution as a means of keeping out Hitler. One Liberal paper subtitled a 1932 discussion of Schmitt's views 'A Constitutional Guide for Students of Dictatorship'.[30]

The German constitutional debate – paralleled, it must be said, by very similar discussions elsewhere – illuminates the complex relationship between authoritarianism and democracy in the crisis atmosphere of inter-war Europe. Weimar in the 1920s was clearly a democracy; under Chancellor Brüning it was less of one; under von Papen and Schleicher – Hitler's immediate predecessor – it was already very close to being an authoritarian state. Most people felt that the liberal model of parliamentary democracy needed revision; the question was, first, to what extent to transfer powers from legislature to executive, and second, what function parliament should possess once the executive predominated. Parliaments, after all, were rarely abolished entirely or suspended indefinitely; they lingered on in a shadowy half-life in Hitler's Germany, Fascist Italy and in many authoritarian states – a sign that these regimes still craved the kind of popular legitimacy which representative assemblies, however constituted, could offer.

THE CRISIS OF DEMOCRACY

Parliaments were not the only point of controversy; liberal democracy was under attack on a much wider front as well. To put it most simply: how democratically minded was inter-war Europe? Disillusioned jurists argued that the problem lay not in an excess of democratism in the constitutions but rather in a lack of democratic values among the public. Moritz Bonn echoed the views of many when he said that behind the crisis of parliaments lay 'the crisis of European life'.[31]

Anti-liberal and anti-democratic creeds had been gaining ground since the last quarter of the nineteenth century. In the wake of the Great War, they spread fast, through a 'gospel of violence' most visible in the Fascist movement but common to many members of what a later historian was to call the 'generation of 1914'. Reared on war, extremist ideologues preferred violence to reason, action to rhetoric: from Marinetti to Ernst Jünger, many young European males in the 1920s seemed ready to justify and even advocate the politics of confrontation. 'Nothing is ever accomplished without bloodshed,' wrote the young right-wing Frenchman Drieu la Rochelle in *Le Jeune Européen*. 'I look forward to a bloodbath.' Violence obsessed artists from the Expressionists to the Surrealists. Some saw the heritage of the war in the atmosphere of 'internal war' which was polarizing most countries in Europe and which achieved its juridical expression in Lenin's conception of internal civil war and in the Nazi 'state of emergency'.[32]

Among the veterans of the front were thinkers like Jünger and politicians of the Right including Röhm, head of the SA (the Storm Troopers), Oswald Mosley, the Flemish nationalist Joris van Severen, the Hungarian Ferenc Szálasi (founder of the extremist Arrow Cross movement) and, of course, Hitler himself. They assailed democracy for being 'bourgeois': sluggish, materialistic, unexciting and incapable of arousing the sympathy of the masses, reflecting the aspirations of an older generation whose politicians dressed in frock coats and top hats. Bertrand de Jouvenel claimed young people found democracy unappealing; Henri de Montherlant contrasted the 'haggard gaze' of the sedentary bourgeois with the physical vigour of the disciplined young authoritarian, beneficiary of the fascist 'revolution of the body'. Young Romanian intellectuals like Emil Cioran and Mircea Eliade hailed Hitler's assault on 'democratic rationalism', and the energy of messianic and spiritual totalitarianism. Against liberalism's glorification of the selfish individual they proposed the spirit of self-sacrifice, obedience and communal duty.[33]

Nor was it only the confirmed anti-democrats who thought democracy effete and worn out. Robert Musil, author of *The Man without Qualities*, affirmed: 'I do not fight against fascism, but in democracy for her future, thus also against democracy.' H. G. Wells urged Oxford summer-school students to transform themselves into 'Liberal Fascisti' and 'enlightened Nazis' who would compete in their enthusiasm and self-sacrifice with the ardent supporters of dictatorship. Unless democracy was able to mobilize such advocates, he saw little future for it. Liberalism seemed too individualistic to cope with the demands of a more collectivist age.[34]

In 1930 Weimar's Chancellor Hermann Müller warned that 'a democracy without democrats is an internal and external danger'; but the founders of post-war constitutionalism had not given this matter much thought. Kelsen, for instance, had proudly promoted his vision of a 'legal theory purified of all political ideologies'; yet such a theory, by virtue of its detachment from politics, lacked supporters. Kelsen criticized Austria's Christian Socials and Social Democrats for following different legal traditions, contaminated by political Catholicism or Marxism, but they at least had large party memberships and he did not. His position might have been intellectually unassailable; politically he was still living with the comfortable illusions of nineteenth-century bourgeois culture. Democracy in Europe had been shored up briefly after 1918 by an unstable coalition of international and domestic forces which was now breaking down across much of the continent. There were, simply, fewer and fewer committed democrats.

In the first place, democracy's international backers were less supportive as time passed. Woodrow Wilson's legacy of messianic liberalism was undermined by American isolationism, while the European victors – Britain and France – were concerned more about communism than dictatorship; so long as the new states of central–eastern Europe held communism at bay, they cared little for their domestic political arrangements. They made sure that the deposed monarchs and emperors of the Central Powers could not return to power, but were less concerned with other kinds of threat. They failed to realize that if democracy was identified with the peace imposed at Versailles then the abolition of democracy implied an attack on the peace settlement as well. Back from Catalonia, Orwell chafed at the 'deep, deep sleep of England', which by the late 1930s was losing the battle of ideologies by default.

Unambiguous support for democracy was thin on the ground throughout Europe. Guglielmo Ferrero remarked in 1925 that democracy's failure in Italy was chiefly due to the lack of a strong democratic party. But not only in Italy. The core group of old-time liberals were marginal figures in the inter-war years, their battles largely won with the defeat of monarchs and aristocracies. 'The *positive* argument for being a Liberal,' according to John Maynard Keynes in 1925, was 'very weak'. The decline of Britain's Liberals had little impact upon the stability of the political system, but this was not true, for instance, of Weimar's Democratic Party and other classic liberal parties. Mass suffrage threatened them with a marginal political role in the face of the great parties of the Left, of conservatism and nationalism, and of Catholicism. Fear of communism, in particular, drew many liberals towards authoritarian solutions. They were joined there by other kinds of elitists – the social engineers, business managers and techno-crats, who wanted scientific, apolitical solutions to society's ills and were impatient with the instability and incompetence of parliamentary rule.[35]

The European Left was seriously weakened by the split between Social Democrats and Communists, and was never again as strong as in 1918–19. The Communists opposed what they regarded as 'bourgeois formalism' – parliamentary democracy – but could not destroy it, though they tried hard enough, at least before 1934. With the possible exception of 1930s France, they remained on the margins of politics and emerged – in the words of one recent historian – 'on the losing side of all electoral battles of the inter-war years'. 'By any reasoned judgement,' concludes Donald Sassoon, 'the record of pre-war communism in Europe must be described as one of failure.' The Social Democrats did not want to destroy democracy, so long as it could be transformed into socialism. 'Republic, that's not much/ Socialism is the goal' was the ditty which summed up SPD attitudes to Weimar. This was a very provisional kind of backing, based on Marxist premises and reservations, especially once it became clear that many of the social rights set out in the second part of the Weimar constitution would remain a dead letter. At least one percipient critic foresaw the consequences; Hermann Heller warned at the height of the depression that either Weimar would realize its promise to become a *soziale Rechtsstaat* – a state with social and economic justice as foreseen in the constitution – or else it would slide into dictatorship. Only where Social Democrats forged a secure alliance with rural populations – as most notably in Scandinavia – or with conservatives – as in Belgium and Britain – did democracy survive. Elsewhere, constitutional commitments to socio-economic rights and welfare benefits were undermined by the depression and mass unemployment. The healing of the breach on the Left through a Popular Front strategy came too late for Germany and Austria, failed to save the Republic in Spain and ultimately collapsed in its heartland, France, as well.[36]

Many conservatives, for their part, were no happier with inter-war democracy and were keen to see a return to more elitist, aristocratic and occasionally even monarchical modes of government. For them the problem with democracy lay in the power it gave the masses, in the supposed incompatibility of democracy and authority. They were prone to attack democracy on ethical grounds too. It placed too much stress on rights and not enough on duties. It had bred egotism and sectional self-interest and had thus contributed to its own downfall by failing to encourage a civic consciousness or a sense of community, or so many Catholic, Orthodox and nationalist critics of democracy in the 1920s argued. The Spaniard de Madariaga called for liberal democracy to be replaced with 'unanimous organic democracy'; the French social Catholic Emmanuel Mounier greeted the fall of the Third Republic in 1940 by calling for 'a struggle against individualism, a sense of responsibility, restoration of leadership, sense of community . . . [and] a sense of the whole man, flesh and spirit'; his readers were reminded that for years he had been calling for a rejection of the pernicious individualism of 'liberal and popular democracy'.[37]

Such criticisms marked the failure of democracy to live up to its own boast to have embodied and given voice to the nation as a whole. Once it had sounded so confident: 'We, the Czechoslovak Nation, in order to form a more perfect union of the nation . . .' began the preamble to the 1920 Czech constitution, yet it was an open question whether the country's Slovaks, Jews, Hungarians and Germans regarded themselves as included in such a phrase. Hugo Preuss had drawn up his draft of the Weimar constitution noting that 'there is neither a Prussian or Bavarian nation . . . there is only one German nation which is to shape its political organization in the German republic'. And yet facts proved the contrary: Austria was prohibited from joining the new Germany and Bavaria was prevented from seceding; the constitution itself was drafted in an atmosphere of civil war. The confident bourgeois claim that liberal constitutions would both acknowledge and nurture the Nation was belied almost everywhere by ethnic and class cleavages. As a result, those whose highest priority was national unity were increasingly tempted by more integral and authoritarian forms of government; liberal democracy had failed the Nation, and might have to be sacrificed if the Nation was to survive. 'When a constitution proves itself to be useless,' Hitler wrote to Chancellor Brüning in 1931, 'the nation does not die – the constitution is altered.'[38]

It is thus not surprising that by the 1930s many asked why it should ever have been expected that democracy would flower in Europe. This sort of attitude fitted neatly with the British pursuit of appeasement. 'It may be that the system of parliamentary Government which suits Great Britain suits few other countries besides,' sniffed *The Times*, defending non-intervention in Spain: 'Recent Spanish Governments have tried to conform to the parliamentary type of republican democracy, but with scant success.' From this perspective, the crisis of democracy in Europe simply proved Britain's superiority.[39]

But it was not only Little England that took such a view. Karl Loewenstein was just one of many who pointed out how few European countries had any indigenous tradition of democracy. In few states, he argued, had the inhabitants a long tradition of fighting for popular liberties. Did the history of eastern Europe not suggest that democracy had been a last-minute gift – if not an imposition – of the victors at Versailles rather than the result of a popular mobilization? Was it then surprising that people should acquiesce so calmly in the loss of something they had scarcely fought for? Democracy's shallow roots in Europe's political tradition helped explain why anti-liberal regimes were established with such ease and so little protest.[40]

FORMS OF THE RIGHT

Benedetto Croce once described Fascism as a parenthesis in Italian history, implying that liberal democracy was the country's natural condition. Many critics of Fascism liked to see Europe's move to the Right as a burst of collective insanity, a form of mass madness over which reason must eventually prevail. Even today it seems easier for many people to envisage inter-war Europe as a continent led astray by insane dictators than as one which opted to abandon democracy. We lap up books which portray Mussolini as a buffoon, Hitler as a demented and disorganized fanatic, Stalin as a paranoid psychopath. But what, for instance, can Mussolini's life really tell us about Fascism's appeal? It was, Michael Oakeshott noted in 1940, a characteristically liberal failing to see the enemy of liberty as 'the single tyrant, the despot' – first monarchs, then dictators – and to lose sight in the process of where the real challenge to democracy came from.[41]

Oakeshott insists upon the need to take the political doctrines – and practices – of the Right and Left seriously, for 'each of them belongs to some current of tradition . . . in our civilization'. Liberalism had lost 'touch with the contemporary world', unlike fascism, communism, political Catholicism and National Socialism, and could learn from them. 'Democracy should learn, on the basis of the extreme example of Fascism, how to reconcile individual liberty with the regulation and control of social affairs necessitated by the general welfare,' observed a student of Mussolini's Italy. 'With knowledge of the Fascist experiment it may come to realise the futility of applying nineteenth-century standards in the contemporary world.' 'Benevolent despotism', concluded a young American diplomat called George Kennan, 'had greater possibilities for good' than democracy, and he went on to propose that the USA too travel 'along the road which leads through constitutional change to the authoritarian state'.[42]

Given the explicit irrationalism of the Right and its preference for action and intuition over reason and logic, it might seem strange to take theories of the authoritarian state seriously. Right-wing intellectuals such as Carl Schmitt or Martin Heidegger were invariably disappointed in right-wing realities; men such as Mussolini and Hitler took up and dropped their ideas without hesitation. Conversely, the irrationalism of the Right can easily be exaggerated. The Right too had its political theory (or theories) and its own jurisprudence, accepted by millions of people, and continuing earlier traditions no less potent and no less forward-looking than liberalism. 'In the great laboratory of the world today,' declared the Portuguese dictator Salazar in 1934,

when the political systems of the nineteenth century are generally breaking down and the need for adapting institutions to the requirements of new social and economic conditions is being felt more and more urgently, we may be proud . . . because, with our ideas and our achievements, we have made a serious contribution to the understanding of the problems and difficulties which beset all States . . . I am convinced that within twenty years, if there is not some retrograde movement in political evolution, there will be no legislative assemblies left in Europe.[43]

The fact is that in most of Europe by the mid-1930s – outside the northern fringe – liberalism looked tired, the organized Left had been smashed and the sole struggles over ideology and governance were taking place *within* the Right – among authoritarians, traditional conservatives, technocrats and radical right-wing extremists. Only France continued its civil war between Left and Right through the 1930s, until that was ended by Vichy. But civil war had already erupted briefly in Austria (in 1934) and more protractedly in Spain before ending in right-wing triumph. In Italy, central Europe and the Balkans, the Right held sway. Regimes varied from the royal dictatorship of King Carol in Romania, through the military men ruling Spain, Greece and Hungary to the one-party states in Germany and Italy. Not all of these were fascists; indeed, some saw in fascists their most threatening enemies.

The crucial difference was between the regimes of the old Right, who wanted to turn the clock back to a pre-democratic elitist era, and the new Right who seized and sustained power through the instruments of mass politics. The former included General Franco and the Greek dictator Metaxas, men who feared mass politics and allied themselves with bastions of the established order such as the monarchy and the Church. In the Balkans, the Right harked back to the nineteenth century, where a strong, autocratic monarch picked his ministers, supervised political parties and ran closely controlled elections.

The new radical Right, in contrast, rose to power in Italy and Germany through elections and the parliamentary process. Its instrument was the party, which gave it a legitimacy and a power in an era of universal suffrage that allowed it to outflank and weaken old-fashioned conservatives, less used to the new game of mass politics. When Hitler insisted to Chancellor Brüning that 'the fundamental thesis of democracy runs: "All power issues from the People"', he was speaking as the leader of a major vote-winning party. Catch-all movements like the NSDAP (the National Socialist German Workers' Party) were the real successors to the populist impulses of the 1920s, since they recognized the tremendous power embodied in the popular demand for representative government. The very real tension between old and new Right could be detected most obviously in countries like Austria, Hungary and Romania where, in the 1930s, murderous political conflicts erupted between conservatives and radical nationalists.[44]

Of course, this new Right, despite its use of the mass party as its vehicle to power, insisted that it was not continuing the parliamentary game, and proffered alternatives to parliamentarism to satisfy the post-1918 demand for unifying forms of participatory politics. First and most lavishly praised, Mussolini's corporatist state evolved amid much fanfare and international interest in the 1920s. Italian corporatism was publicized as a typically fascist means of organizing the representation of society through associations of producers rather than classes. 'The Corporate State is to Mussolini what the New Deal is to Roosevelt,' declared Fortune magazine in 1934.

In reality, corporatism was a sham, disguising Fascism's taming of the workers and its collaboration with the managerial elite. But its appeal stemmed from the fact that it seemed to point the way to a less divisive and more organic form of political representation. Even its hierarchical character seemed proof to some of its essential modernity. 'Italy shows us', wrote one student of Fascist policy in the 1930s, 'that this central authority can itself be a direct emanation of the existing national syndical structure – a freely chosen elite which, inspired by new ideals of social right and social justice, is ready and able to limit, through its dependent organizations, the freedom of the one in the interests of the many.'[45]

Similar schemes were adopted elsewhere. In 1933, António Salazar introduced a new Portuguese constitution which declared the country a corporative and unitary republic. Individual rights were overridden by the power bestowed upon the government to limit them 'for the common good'. A vestige of parliament survived – as in Nazi Germany – but political parties were banned, and the Prime Minister ruled by decree-law. The Upper House became a Corporative Chamber, and industrial relations were forcibly remodelled along the lines of Catholic organic thought through the National Labour Statute, which outlawed strikes and lockouts, destroyed independent unions and led to the creation of national guilds. In this way, class warfare and capitalist conflict were – at least in theory – replaced by harmony and cooperation. As in Italy, however, the theory turned out to be one-sided – Catholics' fear of communism usually moderated their hostility towards capitalists – and businessmen retained much of their autonomy.[46]

In depression-torn Austria, Hans Kelsen's democratic constitution had been regarded with suspicion by the Austro-Marxists, hostility by the Grossdeutsch Volkspartei (pro-German national liberals), and unenthusiasm by the Christian Socials, who were more interested in their own Catholic corporatism. Chancellor Dollfuss resolved the tension between Marxist Vienna and the Catholic provinces first by suspending parliamentary government (on 4 March 1933, eight days before Hitler followed suit in Germany) and then, the following year, by ordering a military attack upon the great socialist housing estates in the capital. With the destruction of Red Vienna – a further tremendous blow to the Left in Europe – came Dollfuss's creation of a Catholic authoritarian regime, which replaced liberalism and democracy with the doctrine of a 'Christian-German corporate state'.[47]

Austria thus followed Portugal in pioneering the kind of self-consciously Christian nationalism which would later permeate

Slovakia, Spain, Greece, Croatia and Vichy France, as well as right-wing politics in Poland, Hungary and Romania. Violent anti-Semitism was the corollary. When the philosopher Moritz Schlick was murdered by a deranged student inside the hall of the University of Vienna itself, a Catholic-nationalist newspaper responded:

We would like to remind everyone that we are Christians living in a Christian-German state and that it is we who decide which philosophy is good and suitable. The Jews should be allowed their Jewish philosophy in their own Jewish cultural institute! But in the chairs of philosophy in the Viennese university in Christian-German Austria, there belong Christian philosophers! Recently it has been repeatedly explained that a peaceful solution of the Jewish question in Austria is also in the interest of the Jews, for otherwise a violent solution is unavoidable. Hopefully, the terrible murder in the Viennese university will serve to bring about a truly satisfactory solution of the Jewish question![48]

The fact that Schlick was not Jewish himself was evidently less important than that he was associated with 'Jewish' movements in contemporary philosophy! Well before the Nazis marched in, therefore, Austrofascism was pursuing the goal of a *Judenrein* community. The 1938 *Anschluss* might have destroyed Austrian independence, but hardly democracy, since that had already collapsed.

Yet for all the similarities between Austrofascism and National Socialism, there were differences. Austrofascism, under Dollfuss and later Schuschnigg's leadership, aimed at a Catholic authoritarianism. It was no less hostile to democracy and parliaments than was Nazism, but it accepted the Church's leading role in society. As a result a split developed between the regime's supporters and the proponents of racialism – a split which needs to be taken seriously in a climate where, increasingly, the Left's power was on the wane and the major tensions were within the Right itself.

Inter-war Austrian conservative thinkers, who combined German nationalism and Catholicism, always remained ambiguous about whether the doctrine of the corporate state was a universal creed, or designed solely for Catholic Germans. National Socialism was, by contrast, anti-religious and explicitly nationalist. 'National Socialism opposes the dogma of the international universalistic science of liberalism, according to which all human beings are the same, with the knowledge of racial difference,' stated an Austrian philosopher, Ferdinand Weinhandl, in 1940.[49]

Of all the right-wing assaults on parliamentary liberalism, therefore, National Socialism was the most extreme, the most uncompromising: if parliaments were no longer the site of legitimacy, neither was the Church, still less the monarchy. Here was where the difference lay between Dollfuss's Austria, Franco's Spain and Antonescu's Romania, all of which acknowledged and coexisted with traditional bases of authority, and the Third Reich. One kind of Right defended the old order against the forces of mass politics; the other used those forces in a revolutionary attempt to reshape society itself. Even Fascist Italy allowed King and Church to reside alongside the regime. In Nazi Germany, however, legitimacy lay solely in the popular will, as manifested in the decrees of the Führer.[50]

LAW AND THE NATIONAL SOCIALIST STATE

If the liberal European constitutions of the 1920s aimed to subordinate politics to the rule of law, for Hitler, by contrast, law was subordinated to politics. Yet the Third Reich was certainly not a lawless state. On the contrary, the Nazi regime insisted that it was defending law and order against the forces of anarchy, and this claim was vital to its popularity and self-image. Over four thousand statutes, decrees and ordinances were issued in the first three years of the Third Reich in the official law bulletin of the Reich alone. Hitler himself – having murdered his colleague Ernst Röhm in the Night of the Long Knives in 1934 – then issued a retroactive decree which stipulated that 'the measures taken on June 30, July 1 and 2, in order to suppress treasonable attacks, are declared legal'. There was law aplenty in the Third Reich; but it operated in a quite different relation to politics than in the democracies.[51]

The German legal tradition had always been highly conservative. Positivism, the autocratic nature of Wilhelmine administration, and the career structure of the judiciary all led judges to see the law as an instrument for the protection of the state rather than the individual. During Weimar their conservative and nationalist sympathies were revealed in their lenient treatment of the extreme Right. After 1933, they adapted to the new situation, comforting themselves with the view that National Socialism was a legal continuation of the preceding regimes. However it quickly became apparent that behind the veneer of legality, the regime itself harboured revolutionary aspirations.[52]

For a start, Nazis explicitly repudiated the values of liberal jurisprudence, as represented by the Weimar constitution. A Hamburg court stated, for example, that 'the destruction of this constitution has been one of the outstanding goals of National-Socialism for many years' since its 'degenerate form of bourgeois constitutionalism' was repellent to the 'German world view'. Rather than drawing up a new constitution as the Bolsheviks did, Nazi justice was based on the *Führerprinzip* – the view that it must reflect Hitler's will, serving as an instrument of the regime's goal of building up a 'healthy racial community'. The *Führerprinzip* subordinated 'formal legal criteria' to arbitrary measures validated by Hitler's authority. 'Protection of the *Volksgemeinschaft*' meant that the law no longer protected the rights of Jews and gypsies, as well as 'degenerate' classes of Aryans: asocials, homosexuals, the physically and mentally handicapped and others. Police repression and medical violence increased in intensity and replaced the therapeutic schemes of the Weimar welfare state. The notorious Roland Freisler emphasized that 'fundamental rights which create free spheres for individuals untouchable by the state are irreconcilable with the totalitarian principle of the new state'.[53]

For those judges who were conservative nationalists rather than Nazis, the implications of such statements were troubling. They clung to the fiction of a 'National Socialist constitutional order' or argued vainly that the suspension of the Weimar constitution was only temporary. In the first years of the regime, the courts tried to preserve the idea of due process against the depredations of the Gestapo. How, for example, could business operate without some consistency in the application of the law? Max Weber had argued that a rational legal system was necessary for the smooth functioning of a capitalistic economy. In fact the Nazi experience did not disprove his contention: vast areas of private and commercial law were left largely untouched, with the obvious proviso that German Jews were rapidly excluded from their provisions.

But in general radical National Socialism overwhelmed the judges' natural desire for consistency and independence. From the legal point of view, Germany had become a 'dual state', in which an endless stream of arbitrary decrees issued by the political leadership eroded the customary body of law. Restraints on police power were abolished, and the Gestapo often seized people who had been acquitted by the courts and sent them straight to concentration camps. Some judges were outraged at this behaviour, not least because it damaged the dignity of the court; they negotiated a series of arrangements with the Gestapo whom they agreed to notify when acquittals seemed likely. In return, the Gestapo agreed to carry out their arrest of acquitted defendants more discreetly.[54]

Often, lawyers actually anticipated the wishes of the political leadership. For over a year before 'racially mixed' marriages were banned by the Nuremberg 'Law for the Protection of German Blood and German Honour', many judges and other civil servants refused to perform marriage ceremonies in which one of the partners was Jewish. In January 1934 Reich Interior Minister Frick was forced to remind officials of the rules then in existence, ordering them to carry out ceremonies according to the laws then in force even where they 'perhaps appear not to conform fully to National Socialist views'.[55]

The Nazi view, however, was that 'healthy race sentiment' should override 'formal legal criteria'. According to a judge at the Berlin *Landgericht*, 'the view that every single act against Jews must be ordered by the government individually is not correct. If this were the case, it would not be permissible to interpret the law to the disadvantage of the Jews and the Jews would enjoy the protection of the law. It is obvious that this makes no sense.'[56]

The superseding of liberalism in pursuit of a healthy racial community was evident not only in the dominance of ideology over legal precedent, but also in the extension of politics into all areas of life. Nazi law –

even more than that of the Fascist state before it – revealed the new power demanded over every individual by the totalitarian state, with what Hitler himself termed its 'comprehensive claim to power, destroying all liberal forms of autonomy'. The old bourgeois distinction between public and private was challenged by the insistence that 'in the struggle for self-preservation which the German people are waging there are no longer any aspects of life which are non-political'. One Nazi jurist argued that 'the so-called "private sphere" is only relatively private; it is at the same time potentially political'.[57]

On the one hand, members of the *Volksgemeinschaft* reaped the benefits, thanks to an activist state which built public housing, gave advice on child rearing, issued cookbooks and provided free vacations and modern medical care – often continuing the same interventionist welfare policies initiated by Social Democrats in the 1920s, and eliciting the same kind of intense civic idealism. On the other hand, however, the health of the collectivity meant the segregation, sterilization and even killing off of mentally, physically or racially diseased bodies by the state, control of marriage and reproduction, and fierce sanctions against anyone who dissented. The traditional family unit was thereby supported but also subjected to a higher power.

Fear of denunciation and surveillance entered the family, the home and even the subconscious mind. 'It was about nine o'clock in the evening,' started the dream of a forty-five-year-old German doctor in 1934:

My consultations were over, and I was just stretching out on the couch to relax with a book on Matthias Grünewald, when suddenly the walls of my room and then my apartment disappeared. I looked around and discovered to my horror that as far as the eye could see no apartment had walls any longer. Then I heard a loudspeaker boom, 'According to the decree of the 17th of this month on the Abolition of Walls . . .'[58]

Having written down his dream, the doctor then dreamed that he had been accused of writing down dreams. Not even sleep was private any longer.

Since freedom of conscience was not recognized, a Jehovah's Witness who said only 'Heil' rather than 'Heil Hitler' (on the grounds that such a greeting was due only to God) could be legally dismissed from his or her job. Children educated according to values regarded as incompatible with those of the Hitler Youth were said to be 'neglected' by their parents and could be placed in a foster home. In 1938, for instance, one family was broken up because the father had refused to let his children be enrolled in the Hitler Youth. According to the local court, he thereby 'abused his right of custody of his children'.[59]

This abolition of the distinction between private and public spheres of life matters in assessing popular attitudes towards the Nazis. A free citizenry in a democracy chooses whom to support and with what degree of fervour. In the Third Reich, however, anything less than enthusiasm could be seen as potentially subversive and hence punishable. Public opinion did not exist since there was no means to express it; how then do we gauge the popularity of the regime?

Discussing, for example, the question of whether a citizen had a duty to hoist a swastika on festive occasions, one commentator argued that while there was no legal duty, failure to raise the flag might be taken to indicate a want of enthusiasm for National Socialism: the solution, he went on, perhaps lay in a spell in a concentration camp. In another case, a civil servant was prosecuted for refusing to donate money to the Winter Relief Fund. The defendant protested that he gave generously to various other causes, and should be allowed to decide which charity he favoured, especially since donations to the Winter Relief Fund were 'voluntary'. His arguments, however, failed to persuade the court which concluded: 'The defendant's conception of liberty is of an extreme character . . . For him liberty is the right to neglect all of his duties except where they are explicitly required by law.' This had led him to 'a despicable abuse of the liberty which the Leader had granted in full confidence that the German people would not abuse it'.[60]

In this environment, where the individual was no longer permitted the unimpeded exercise of a free judgement, it was no easy matter for observers – whether secret police or underground opposition – to assess the state of popular feeling towards the regime. On specific issues – over food prices, the treatment of the Jews, foreign policy, the Church – people spoke fairly forthrightly; but sweeping judgements about the regime itself rarely surfaced for obvious reasons.

We can, however, point to some general trends. In Nazi Germany, as in the one-party states in Italy and Russia, people routinely drew a distinction between the leader and the party apparatus. Open grumbling and annoyance at the behaviour of local officials were often expressed in the same breath as admiration, reverence and even adoration for the figure of the Leader. The Italian historian Emilio Gentile has talked about the 'sacralization of politics' under Mussolini. Leadership cults – whether of the Duce, Hitler or Stalin – helped to unify and integrate populations and reconcile them to otherwise unpopular regimes.[61] Such a 'sacralization of politics' involved lavish spending on monumental buildings and rallying grounds, propaganda exhibitions and publications. Mass rallies, parades and marches offered ritual and projected a sense of power which underlined the atomization and impotence of the individual. In a world of enemies, the Leader offered inspiration and security. But leadership cults were propagated also through the everyday forms of modern life – the spread of radio, the extension of literacy and increased schooling as well as the militarization of communal life in general.

Nor was this simply a process in which people were hoodwinked by powerful regimes through censorship and manipulation. It is, rather, a story of values shared, and argued over jointly, by leadership and population alike. The fundamental utopian projects – construction of Socialism in One Country, of a German *Volksgemeinschaft* or an imperial Italy – projected positive images of a new, undivided nation and were far from unpopular. Policy issues were now debated not between parties but inside the only one permitted to exist, or across ministries and other public and private institutions. Opposition to aspects of the regime could thus be expressed in many forms besides total rejection of the system: in internal party feuds, or siding with 'normal' people against party fanatics, or with party 'idealists' against those in favour of business as usual.

The high degree of support for the peacetime Reich emerges in other ways as well. Of course, the Nazi regime used the law and the police as a repressive instrument to elicit mass obedience. Before

1939 the courts passed several thousand death sentences; compared with the twenty-nine death sentences passed on political prisoners in Fascist Italy, or the handful passed by Japanese courts, the relative severity of Nazi law stands out. On the other hand, the coercive powers of the state were never nearly as much in evidence in peacetime Nazi Germany as they were in Stalin's Soviet Union: Nazi concentration camps in the 1930s housed some 25,000–50,000 prisoners compared with the millions in the Gulag. Today, those 1950s theories of totalitarianism, which posited a state of affairs in which a small elite kept down an enormous population by sheer terror, look more and more like a comfortable delusion, whose effect is to blind us to the stability of undemocratic regimes in inter-war Europe. The Third Reich was not built on repression alone, nor was that the sole function of its legal system. A majority of the German population failed to vote for Hitler, but also failed to resist him. People accepted the new state of affairs and the regime became part of normal life.[62]

The differences between Europe's two largest one-party states – Nazi Germany and Soviet Russia – outweighed their similarities. Nazism came to power with massive electoral backing, communism through a *coup d'état*. The Third Reich was run by a large party whose leader's power was unquestioned within both party and the country at large. The Soviet Union, with double the population spread over a vast land mass, had a party membership of about the same size, riven by internal and external tensions, beset by an acute succession crisis following Lenin's death, and ultimately run by a leader always nervous of his position as *primus inter pares*. Whereas Hitler valued his fellow 'old fighters' and was acknowledged by them as their *Führer*, Stalin ruthlessly purged the party of his former comrades in order to bolster his personal power. The Night of the Long Knives for all its brutality left the bulk of the Nazi Party untouched; by contrast, the Communist Party of the late 1930s had little in common with the revolutionary force created by Lenin.[63]

These contrasts reflect the fact that the party's ideological purpose was not the same in the two cases. Hitler's Germany was the major industrial power in Europe, with a highly educated labour force; the domestic goal of the NSDAP was the creation of a racial welfare state – the *Volksgemeinschaft* – which built upon and expanded earlier welfare traditions in both its constructive and its coercive aspects. Its key domestic victims were a small minority, unlike the millions of peasants targeted by the Bolsheviks. *Their* goal was far more radical: it involved abolishing private property, developing a new Soviet nationality to hold the Union together, and compressing into a single decade an industrial revolution that had taken much of the latter nineteenth century elsewhere, in the most backward peasant economy in Europe. Hence the extraordinary strains and tensions which the Bolsheviks faced as they tried forcing this project through. It is the difference between these two enterprises which explains the vastly differing levels of domestic violence in the two countries in the 1930s.

But it was precisely because so much of Nazi domestic policy could be fitted smoothly into traditional German life that the genuinely radical proponents of National Socialism, of whom Hitler was the most important, were constantly wary of being buried by business as usual, by the bankers, the middle classes and nationalist conservatives who just wanted order and stability. Normality frightens revolutionaries because it acts as a drag on their utopian dreams, and the German population's easy acceptance of the regime tended to alarm Hitler almost as much as it alarms us. It was one thing to eliminate Röhm and bring his lawless SA under control in 1934 in order to consolidate the Nazi grip on power; another to give in to the bourgeoisie altogether. 'Political lethargy' dismayed the Führer, especially as evidence mounted in 1935–6 of growing public apathy.[64]

Nazi radicals saw the inglorious fate met by the Fascist Party in Italy, which had been ingested after the conquest of power into the state apparatus and had been obliged to abandon thoughts of a radical Fascist revolution. The leaders of the Third Reich had different aspirations. While Mussolini deified the state, Hitler insisted upon the need to control its inertia and passivity through the dynamism of the party. 'Not the state commands us, but we command the state,' he declared at the party congress in 1934. The party's political message must 'penetrate the hearts of the masses for it is our best and strongest belief-carrier'. To what end? The gigantic rearmament programme launched in the 1930s provides the clue. For the Führer – his eyes set upon the millions of Germans living outside the borders of the Reich – there could be only one answer. Only in war could the Nazi project for the racial salvation of the German nation be realized.[65]

2

Empires, Nations, Minorities

By making the State and the nation commensurate with each
other in theory, (nationality) reduces practically to a subject
condition all other nationalities that may be within the boundary
. . . according, therefore, to the degree of humanity and civilization in that dominant body which claims all the rights of the
community, the inferior races are exterminated, or reduced to
servitude, or outlawed, or put in a condition of dependence.

– Lord Acton, 1862[1]

The First World War and the collapse of Europe's old continental
empires signalled the triumph not only of democracy but also – and
far more enduringly – of nationalism. With the extension of the
principle of national self-determination from western to central and
eastern Europe, the Paris peace treaties created a pattern of borders
and territories which has lasted more or less up to the present. Yet
the triumph of nationalism brought bloodshed, war and civil war in
its train, since the spread of the nation-state to the ethnic patchwork
of eastern Europe also meant the rise of the minority as a contemporary
political problem. Where a state derived its sovereignty from the
'people', and the 'people' were defined as a specific nation, the presence
of other ethnic groups inside its borders could not but seem a reproach,
threat or challenge to those who believed in the principle of national
self-determination.

The old nineteenth-century empires had operated very differently.
They had claimed their legitimacy on the basis of dynastic loyalty not

ethnicity, so it was possible for ethnic Germans to rise to high positions in Tsarist administrations, and for diplomats representing the Otto-man Empire in international congresses to be Greek. The war of 1914–18 swept this world away. 'None but members of the nation may be citizens of the state', ran point four of the 1920 Nazi Party programme, speaking, in this respect at least, for much of Europe. Discussing the arguments in favour of changing Turkish and Slavic-sounding place-names into Greek ones, the Greek scholar Kambourog-lou wrote after the war that 'on Greek soil there should remain nothing that is not Greek'.[2]

But the pure nation had to be made, for it was still a dream, not a reality. Neither Greece, nor Germany nor any of the other so-called nation-states of central and eastern Europe were really ethnically homogeneous. Versailles had given sixty million people a state of their own, but it turned another twenty-five million into minorities. They included not only Jews, gypsies, Ukrainians and Macedonians but also former ruling groups such as the Germans, Hungarians and Muslims. Because the latter category in particular regarded themselves as more civilized than the peasant upstarts who now lorded it over them, they did not take easily to the idea that they should assimilate into the new national culture, as liberal political theory proposed. In fact, in inter-war Europe, neither minority nor majority believed in assimilation; the new democracies tended to be exclusionary and antagonistic in their ethnic relations.

The tensions created by the dream of national purification lay at the heart of inter-war European politics. Exterminating minorities – as the Turks tried with the Armenians – was not generally acceptable to international opinion; expelling or swapping minorities, as the Greeks and Turks did in 1922–3, did not seem much of an improve-ment. The victor powers at Versailles tried a different approach – keeping minorities where they were, and giving them protection in international law to make sure they were properly treated so that in time they would acquire a sense of national belonging. But the minority-rights treaties did not work very well, and failed to prevent ill-feeling and discrimination.

It was, in fact, because it was obvious that the principle of national self-determination would create this kind of problem that many people had doubted during the 1914–18 war whether a world of nation-states was such a desirable outcome. Yet for the British and French, whose global empires were now bigger than ever before, such a territorial settlement in central–eastern Europe suited their imperial interests. It created a tier of states which would act as a buffer against both Germany and Russia, allowing them to govern their far-flung colonies while simultaneously dominating the continent.

The imperial ambitions of Germany and Russia, on the other hand, lay in precisely the area occupied by the new nation-states. Their temporary exhaustion in 1918 had allowed the British, French and Americans to impose a new liberal order. But as they regained their power and appetite, they approached the region on a very different basis. The Soviet Union, for example, was basically a federal solution to the ethnic complexities of the old Tsarist domains – or what was left of them, after the losses of the Great War; it centralized power through the Communist Party, while allowing administrative and cultural opportunities to local Ukrainian and Belorussian elites.

Because the Russians effectively gave up dreams of westwards expansion after their defeat in the Russo-Polish war, their Soviet empire was able to coexist with the Versailles system, and indeed actually entered the League of Nations in 1934. But in the 1930s the liberal order of nation-states and minority rights set up by the British and French began to collapse in the face of a more determined challenge. With the rise of Nazi Germany came a new racial nationalism across eastern Europe, a new assault on minorities and, as a result, a fast-growing refugee crisis. At the same time, a new round of empire-building began as the fascist states reasserted themselves against the older imperial powers. Mussolini showed the way with the invasion of Abyssinia; in 1938 Hitler embarked on his quest for empire inside Europe itself.

DISSOLVING THE GREAT EMPIRES

'If you ask me what is my native country,' wrote the playwright Odon von Horvath, author of *Tales from the Vienna Woods*, 'I answer: I was born in Fiume, grew up in Belgrade, Budapest, Pressburg, Vienna and Munich, and I have a Hungarian passport; but I have no fatherland. I am a very typical mix of old Austria-Hungary: at once Magyar, Croatian, German and Czech; my country is Hungary, my mother tongue is German.'

Von Horvath was right: there was nothing unusual about his background. At the turn of the century, the Habsburg city of Czernowitz was home to Hungarians, Ukrainians, Romanians, Poles, Jews and Germans. Further south, the dock workers of Ottoman Selanik (Salonika) routinely spoke six or seven languages: the city included some 70,000 Jews as well as Greeks, Armenians, Turks, Albanians and Bulgarians. This polyglot atmosphere was common in eastern Europe, whose towns and cities were a jumble of diverse religious and ethnic groups. As the doctrine of nationalism gained ground, the problems such places posed provoked discussion among politicians and political theorists alike: how could the constitutional and administrative arrangements of the great multi-ethnic and multi-religious empires be made compatible with the growing swell of national feeling which was moving eastwards across Europe?[3]

During the nineteenth century, nationalism had already begun to corrode the older dynastic or religious sentiments upon which imperial loyalties had once depended. Uprisings in the Ottoman Balkans led to the formation of Greece, Serbia and Bulgaria; the revolutions of 1848 showed the power of German, Italian and Hungarian nationalism in central Europe, while the Polish revolt of 1863 showed the depth of resentment there at Russian rule. The failure of Habsburg neo-absolutism in the 1850s underlined the impossibility of turning the clock back to the eighteenth century.

For the rulers of empire, two strategies presented themselves in the face of nationalism's advance. One was the creation of a new imperial nationalism – Turkification of the Ottoman Empire, Russification of the Tsarist lands, and Magyarization in the Hungarian half of the Habsburg Dual Monarchy. Such policies aimed at the creation of modern, centralized empires. They might try, as the Hungarians did, to win acceptance by offering the possibility of assimilation into the ruling national group, but their intrusion into traditional society, their insistence upon standardization of language and promptly paid taxes often had the undesired effect of creating a backlash and encouraging counter-nationalisms. Hence in the first decade of this century, the Young Turks inadvertently fuelled the rise of Albanian and Macedonian nationalist movements, Hungarian heavy-handedness boosted Romanian and Croatian resistance, while the Russians faced increasing opposition in Finland, the Baltic states and Poland.

The other strategy to cope with nationalism was through a policy of divide and rule. Thus the Ottoman authorities exploited differences between Greeks and Bulgarians by creating a separate Bulgarian Orthodox Church, while the Habsburgs – unable to build up their own imperial nationalism, since there were no Austrians – played off German nationalists against the Czechs. This strategy, of course, opened up possibilities for nationalist groups to gain concessions themselves, and so it is not surprising that in the decade before the First World War, imperial rulers were faced with demands for constitutional reform, a broader suffrage and linguistic and educational rights. The vehicle for such demands was new mass political parties. But these parties almost never envisaged complete national independence. Rather they pressed – with some success – for democratization and greater freedoms within the existing imperial state structures.

It was the Austrian Social Democrats who developed the most interesting discussion of how the empires could be modified to embrace national aspirations. By the turn of the century, Austria-Hungary – that 'historical experiment' (as the constitutionalist Oscar Jaszi once described it) – had fifty-one million inhabitants, two states, ten 'historic nations' and over twenty other ethnic groups. Two things seemed obvious to many Habsburg political thinkers: first, that nationalism was a political force which could not be ignored; and second, that the nation-state was an anachronism in the modern world, since economic progress required states to be organized into much larger units. Modern life therefore required some kind of political structure which did not deny national feelings but did not give in to them completely. British imperial theorists of the 'Commonwealth' idea were thinking on much the same lines.

From the Habsburg perspective before the First World War it seemed possible to pull off this difficult achievement by offering national groups cultural autonomy and an expansion of the franchise within the empire. Many nations, in this view, could live together in a single fatherland. In the words of Yiddish writer I. L. Peretz in 1908: 'Its unique culture rather than its patrolled borders guarantees a nation its independent existence.'[4] Jews like Peretz supported such views because they offered a third way between Zionism (a nationalism which abandoned Europe) and complete assimilation (with its denial of Jewish identity). But similar demands were voiced by the leaders of other national groups; few Czech or South Slav nationalists thought in terms of outright independence until very late in the day. Even in 1918 the Austrian socialist Karl Renner advocated turning the Habsburg empire into a 'state of nationalities' in order 'to present an example for the future national order of mankind'.[5]

If this humane approach failed to materialize in central and eastern Europe, it was less because of pressure from the nationalists themselves than because the empires committed suicide during the 1914–18 war by fomenting nationalism as a form of political warfare against their opponents. John Buchan's best-seller *Greenmantle* reflected British fears that the Turks would lead India's Muslims to revolt. But it was London and Paris who encouraged both Jewish and Arab separatists (with fateful consequences) to rise up against Ottoman rule in the Middle East. Russians and Germans tried the same game, and started a bidding war with the Poles. In August 1914, the Romanov Grand Duke Nikolai pledged autonomy to the Poles in the event of a Russian victory; two years later he was trumped by the Central Powers, who offered independence to a rump Poland wrested back from the Tsarist armies. Two years later still, the Entente reluctantly went one better by pledging an independent Poland with an outlet to the sea. Polish freedom-fighters sensibly moved from one sponsor to the next as the bidding progressed.

In wartime Berlin the Germans helped Ukrainians and Jews for the same short-term ends. They encouraged the formation of a League of Oppressed Nations of Russia to wean support away from the Tsar and to subvert morale inside the multinational Tsarist army: they sponsored Finnish and Ukrainian nationalist groups, supported religious autonomy for Polish Jews, and recognized Yiddish as an official language in Congress Poland. German Zionists formed a Committee for the Liberation of Russian Jews, and proposed an eventual federation of minorities in the Tsarist lands. Had Germany won the First World War the fate of the Jews would have looked very different and we would no doubt be reading monographs on the murderousness of Russian or Polish not German anti-Semitism.

Meanwhile the Entente played exactly the same game against the Central Powers: the anti-Habsburg Congress for Oppressed Nationalities – Czechs, Croats, Slovenes and Poles – convened in Rome. In London the magazine *New Europe* enthusiastically conducted its own campaign for the 'oppressed nationalities' of the Habsburg lands. But not everyone in the British or French governments thought this was such a sensible idea. Lord Robert Cecil, for instance, criticized those who believed 'in nationality as if it were a religion' and warned: 'I do not myself believe that a European peace founded only on nationality, and without any other provisions, is likely to be desirable or even in all respects beneficial.'[6]

Nor did the Central Powers really believe in national self-determination either. The Germans, in particular, had other dreams for solving the ethnographic mess of eastern Europe. One of the most popular of these – in Germany at least – was the idea of an economically coherent *Mitteleuropa*. This was the goal of Chancellor Bethmann-Hollweg's politics, and it was popularized by a wartime bestseller, Friedrich Naumann's *Mitteleuropa*, which outlined the virtues of a German-dominated European heartland. But non-Germans were not so easily convinced of the economic and cultural benefits of enlightened German rule, while the Habsburgs – with whom the Germans were uneasily allied during the war – did not like being made to feel like second-class Germans.

Yet for the more extreme German nationalists the idea of *Mitteleuropa* was far *too* considerate of the sensitivities of other peoples in central–eastern Europe. The generals on the German general staff, men like Hindenburg and Ludendorff, were principally concerned to ensure military and political domination in the East. *Their* vision was an essentially authoritarian one which left little freedom to the Reich's nationalist allies.

For a brief moment near the end of the war, their dreams were realized. In the spring of 1918 – a strange prefiguring of 1941 – they signed the Treaty of Brest-Litovsk with the new Bolshevik Government, which was desperate to make peace and willing to grant the Germans most of what they wanted in the East. This peace treaty offered Berlin influence beyond the wildest dreams of the Pan-German League, and gave it control of a vast area of eastern Europe: client states in the formerly Tsarist lands of Poland, the Ukraine and the Baltic. Austria-Hungary was marginalized and one million tons of wheat were pledged annually in the 'bread peace' from the Ukraine as a condition of its independence. German troops pushed into Finland, the Ukraine and down towards Rostov and the Caucasus. The alliance with Turkey was cemented by the cession of former Russian territory. The war in the east seemed over: Brest-Litovsk had brought a *Pax Germanica* to eastern Europe. If today Brest-Litovsk is almost entirely forgotten, and seems 'a mere bubble', burst by the German collapse a few months later, it did not look that way to the British Foreign Office who feared that Germany would now be able 'to fight the world for ever and be unconquerable'. The combination of Germany and Turkey could threaten India and hold the Eurasian land mass indefinitely: the war might go on for years. Only the Entente victory in the West turned these fears into memories.[7]

After the war the German Right looked back to the Brest-Litovsk interlude as the great might-have-been, the Reich's first grand venture into an east European empire. Few Germans saw that they had been too harsh for their own good and too indifferent to others' national aspirations. For one extreme nationalist, Alfred Rosenberg, writing in 1921, Berlin had in fact been *too* considerate of the rights of the Poles and other national groups. Twenty years later, as Hitler's Minister for the Occupied Eastern Territories in a new war of imperial expansion, he would be well placed to avoid his predecessors' mistake. Right to the end, the authoritarian strand in German nationalism clung instinctively to direct military rule over the Slav 'barbarians' and ignored the advantages which a more cooperative approach might have offered. The Russians, whose own approach to the nationalities problems of eastern Europe was far more sophisticated, reaped the benefits.[8]

One must ask why it was that the Habsburg Empire expired while the Tsarist empire came back to life as the Soviet Union. In part, no doubt, it was because of their differences, most obviously the fact that while Germans and Hungarians never even amounted to one half of the population of the former, Russians alone never comprised less than half the population of the Soviet Union, and together with Ukrainians and Belorussians amounted to around two thirds. An imperial nation predominated there in a way that was not true of the Dual Monarchy, enhancing the tradition of state centralism developed under the Tsars and brought to fruition under Stalin.[9]

But this is only half the answer. It is also true that Russian Marxists learned much from the Habsburg debate about nationality and empire. In some ways, the Soviet Union was the Habsburg Empire's real heir, just as Hitler's New Order was its ultimate rejection. Thanks to the Bund – the Yiddish-speaking Jewish workers' movement – the pre-war Austro-Marxist debate about nationalism had reached Russia and the Bolsheviks. The Bundists had wanted to turn the Russian empire into a federation of peoples, with national-cultural autonomy independent of territory – in line with the Austrian Social Democrat programme for the Habsburg Empire – and attacked the Russian demand for assimilation as a 'nationalism of appropriation'. One leading Bundist presciently attacked Lenin and other Russian Social Democrats in 1902 for their intolerance of Jewish national autonomy, warning that an apparently internationalist workers' movement might become 'nationalistic' if it were 'blinded by the "general-Russian", "general-

Polish" or "general-German" cause which holds the rights of subject nationalities in contempt'.[10]

A decade later Lenin, who had initially been extremely hostile to the Bundist line, became convinced that nationalism could not be wished away. Before the war he had opposed the Bund's federalism as weakening the Russian workers' movement; and he had opposed its nationalism on conventional Marxist grounds, insisting that to oppose assimilation meant 'to turn back the wheel of history', since 'this process of assimilation of nations by capitalism means the greatest historical progress . . . especially in backward countries like Russia'. But during the war, his views began to change. Opposing his comrades' call for 'the liquidation of the national states in Europe', Lenin moved gradually towards a commitment to national self-determination. This commitment, however, was always conditional upon the interests of the proletariat. For Lenin it was necessary to enter into a temporary alliance with nationalist groups for the sake of the revolution. But at what point might this alliance cease to be useful? The difficulty of answering this question helps explain the uncertainty of Bolshevik nationalities policy between 1917 and 1920.[11]

By the end of 1917, as Richard Pipes has put it, Russia 'as a political concept had ceased to exist'. Taking Lenin at his word – or rather, simply reflecting Moscow's lack of power and German dominance – national movements had swept to power in the Baltic states and Finland. Along the southern and eastern rim of the Tsarist dominions, new republics sprang up. Was the doctrine of national self-determination not now simply endangering the revolution? Stalin reached this conclusion well before Lenin, as early as December 1917: the Ukrainian crisis, he argued, showed an independence movement simply masking counter-revolution. With the outbreak of civil war, and Allied intervention from the periphery, such an analysis gained in plausibility.[12]

Thus Bolshevik Russia in the 1920s faced at the outset what the Habsburgs only confronted at their end – 'the management of politically conscious, ambitious nationalities'. To this problem, the Bolsheviks found a solution which was subtle, pioneering and remarkably durable. They created a federal system which was, in effect, a combination of an Austro-Marxist state and a centralized Communist Party. Founded in the 1920s, this system, with all its contradictions, proved more effective in its capacity to manage nationalist politics than anything the Habsburgs or the Germans devised. It was called the Soviet Union.[13]

On the one hand, the Bolsheviks won over the new non-Russian nationalities, offering them real political power through participation in government and administration; economic power by enjoying the benefits of social revolution, in which previously dominant ethnic groups among the urban bourgeoisie and the landowning classes found themselves dispossessed, and peasants took over the cities; and cultural power through new educational rights with the spread of mass literacy and compulsory schooling. In the Ukraine, for instance, 97 per cent of Ukrainian children received instruction in their native language by 1929, something they could only have dreamed of before the revolution; Poland at the same time was busy shutting down its Ukrainian-language schools, whose numbers fell from 3,662 to 144 in the inter-war period.[14]

It is not surprising that Bolshevik nationalities policy, so far from being regarded as oppressive and tyrannical, exerted a powerful attraction over the minorities of central–eastern Europe between the wars. In the 1920s, communist support was high among these groups – Macedonians, Belorussians, Jews and others – who were the chief victims of Versailles's love affair with the nation-state. The Ukrainians themselves could contrast the violent police repression they faced against their culture in Poland with the situation in the Soviet republic, at least until the famine of the early 1930s, and perhaps even after. Only on the basis of this contrast can we understand why so many Ukrainians and Jews celebrated the downfall of the Polish republic and the arrival of the Red Army into the Western Ukraine in the autumn of 1939.[15]

On the other hand, the ostensibly federal structure of the Union of Soviet Socialist Republics, as it emerged in the early 1920s, hid an increasingly centralized reality. Republics may have had greater powers than the so-called autonomous regions, but they were still subject to Moscow, and their constitutional right to secession –

designed to prove the egalitarian nature of the Union – existed only on paper.

In fact the Bolshevik leadership's willingness to consider federalism depended upon real power remaining in the hands of an organization that was not even mentioned in the 1923 USSR constitution – the Communist Party. Lenin might have rebuked Stalin in 1922 for 'Great Russian chauvinism', and stressed the need to avoid 'imperialistic relations towards our oppressed minorities'. But there was no essential disagreement between them over the party's fundamental role in cementing the new empire together. This it carried out successfully enough to make Russia Europe's last imperial power. Communism turned out to be the last, and perhaps the highest, stage of imperialism.[16]

THE LIBERAL VARIANT: TOWARDS MINORITY RIGHTS

Much like the Bolsheviks, the victors at Versailles also had to grope their way towards a policy which could reconcile their pledges of national self-determination with the need for regional stability in Europe. Through the first months of 1918, in fact, many policy-makers in Washington and London still believed the best solution for eastern Europe remained confederation: nation-states would be too small to be viable and too unstable to keep the peace. The Americans planning their version of Europe's future hesitated between recommending independence for Poland and turning it into a federal state in a brand-new Russian democracy; the British Foreign Office only reluctantly abandoned the idea of re-forming the Habsburg Empire.[17]

But the sudden collapse of the old empires made such thinking redundant and as a result brought the minorities issue into the open for the first time, primarily and initially in relation to Poland. Given that, as the Polish nationalist Roman Dmowski put it, 'the aim of this war was to reduce German power to limits which would allow the reestablishment of European equilibrium', Poland played a crucial role in any post-war settlement. But defining Poland was not a straightforward matter in terms of either territory or ethnicity, since the country had not existed as an independent state for over a century, and was home to large communities of Germans, Lithuanians, White Russians, Ukrainians and Jews as well as Poles. Polish nationalists themselves were torn between two visions of past glory: an exclusively Polish nation-state of pristine ethnic purity, or a multi-ethnic Commonwealth under Polish leadership.[18]

Roman Dmowski stood for the first. There was, in his view, 'no place for a small and weak state' if Poland was to serve as a bulwark against Germany. Other ethnic groups would have to be assimilated in a tightly centralized nation-state; federation was a recipe for disintegration. 'I have never been a herald of liberal-humanitarian ideas, and did not belong to any international organisation founded to bring happiness to humanity,' he wrote later, writing off the whole idea of minority protection.[19]

Opposing him, however, was his rival Józef Piłsudski, as well as Ukrainians and Jewish lobby groups in London and Washington. Jewish groups, in particular, played an important role in these early stages of the development of a doctrine of minority rights by alerting British and American policy-makers to the schemes of 'half-crazed nationalists'. The Balkan Wars of 1912–13 – when Ottoman Europe was carved up between Greece, Serbia and Bulgaria – had already revealed to them the dangers nation-states posed to minority groups. Now they pressed for some form of autonomy to be granted minorities in any eventual Polish state. The pogroms carried out by Polish troops in the winter of 1918 only helped their case.[20]

At the Paris Peace Conference, the struggle between these different conceptions of an independent Polish state was eventually to coalesce into a new international policy towards minority rights. The French – pro-Polish, fervently anti-German *and* anti-Bolshevik – were the minorities' stiffest opponents. Their view was that 'the business of the Conference is to create a sovereign state for Poland, not for the Jews.' But the British were less dismissive. Balfour worried that the existence of an independent Poland, 'so far from promoting the cause of European peace, would be a perpetual occasion of European strife'. Lloyd George feared an 'imperialist Poland'. Poland's land-grab in Eastern Galicia and Western Ukraine increased these concerns. By mid-1919, Poland was only two thirds Polish from the ethnic point of view – its population now included four million Ukrainians, three million Jews and one million Germans – and looked very much like the 'reactionary Imperialist, military State', the 'ramshackle Empire', foreseen by the British journalist H. N. Brailsford.[21]

It was already clear to the peacemakers in Paris that the minorities question would not be solved by maps alone: the ethnographic distribution of the population in eastern Europe was so complex that it defied the most expertly drawn of borders. In the British Foreign Office, E. H. Carr suggested offering minorities inducements to migrate to their own nation-state. But what of those who preferred to remain? And what of those, like the Jews, or gypsies, who lacked a national homeland? This was precisely the difficulty raised by the minorities problem in Poland.[22]

Prompted by President Wilson's concern, the newly created New States Committee in Paris decided to tackle the issue. They dismissed Jewish demands for national autonomy for the Jewish minority in Poland; it was undesirable, in their view, to create the danger of a state within a state, or indeed to forestall the process of assimilation which was still believed to be the desirable long-term outcome. On the other hand, the committee insisted that some form of minority rights had to be found if Poland was not, through the Poles' own intolerant nationalism, to create the conditions for an ethnic civil war and consequent instability throughout eastern Europe.[23]

The result – in the teeth of bitter Polish protests – was that the government, as a condition of recognition, signed a treaty guaranteeing certain rights to its minorities. These rights covered citizenship, equality of treatment under the law and religious freedoms as well as minorities protection proper, in other words, rights to certain forms of collective organization such as schooling. The treaty was guaranteed by the League of Nations, which meant that complaints could be brought before the League (though not directly by the minority concerned). In certain circumstances, the League's Council could take action against the Polish government.

During the previous century, the Great Powers had often made recognition of new states dependent upon a commitment to religious freedom and toleration: such had been the case, for example, in Belgium in 1830 and Romania in 1878. But the Polish Minority Rights Treaty took international law into uncharted waters. What was new in 1919 was the concern for 'national' rather than exclusively religious rights, and for collective rights rather than individual liberties, as well as the provision for international deliberation by a supranational body rather than a conclave of Great Powers.

Poland turned out to provide the model for a whole series of minority-rights treaties which the peacemakers in Paris drew up for eastern Europe. Similar obligations were imposed on the other newly created states as well as on former belligerents like Hungary and on older states like Romania and Greece which acquired territory as a result of the war. Thus the League of Nations came to stand for a system which, on the one hand, accepted the nation-state as the norm in international relations and, on the other, made a considered effort to tackle the minority issues which were thereby created. It acknowledged (perhaps thereby sometimes encouraging the creation of) minorities as collective entities.

But the role of the League itself in this system was ambiguous. It was difficult to bring cases to the League's attention, and even more difficult to push them through the Geneva machine and have them taken up by the Council. Although the League had the power to refer cases to the Permanent Court of International Justice in The Hague, it rarely acted on it. On the other hand it jealously guarded this power, and blocked proposals to allow minorities to appeal to the Court more directly. The League secretariat did not see itself as a 'champion of minorities' but more modestly as an interlocutor helping governments carry out their own obligations. The League also had few sanctions against egregious offenders. Thus the notoriously repressive behaviour of Yugoslav gendarmes in Macedonia went unchecked, as did the Polish government's bloody 'pacification campaign' against the Ukrainians in 1930.

Polish or Serbian intolerance did not, however, much bother the French, who were more concerned about the stability of their east European allies than about minorities. Nor, increasingly, did it bother the British, who believed the minorities treaties were hindering the process of assimilation. 'More harm would in the end be done by unnecessary interference than, even at the risk of a little local suffering, to allow these minorities to settle down under their present masters,' wrote a Foreign Office official in London in 1922. 'So long as these people imagine that their grievances can be aired before the League of Nations they will refuse to settle down and the present effervescence will continue indefinitely.'[24]

Facing such indifference from the League's main sponsors, many minority groups and their protectors pushed for a more activist stance. Under the diplomacy of Gustav Stresemann, Weimar Germany entered the League and began to assume the role of 'defender of minorities', with an eye to the millions of ethnic Germans scattered across eastern Europe. German and Jewish groups spearheaded the high-profile lobbying of the European Congress of Nationalities, while Stresemann identified himself closely with the cause of reforming the Geneva machinery by creating a permanent minority rights commission. His efforts had limited results, partly because they were suspected to form part of a more general effort to revise the Versailles settlement. German nationalists at home became convinced that the League would never adequately protect the rights of ethnic Germans abroad. Just as the victors at Versailles had prevented Germans in Austria exercising the right to self-determination through *Anschluss* with Germany in 1918, so in the 1920s they appeared to be turning a blind eye to the grievances of the Germans elsewhere. Tens of thousands in fact migrated to Germany, while the millions who remained were supported through organizations like the two-million-strong Association for Germandom Abroad, and through political movements like the Nazi Party.[25]

At the same time, the minority treaties were bitterly resented as a humiliation by the countries upon whom they had been imposed. They were particularly irritated by the fact that there was no universal minority rights regime, and asked why they had been singled out when no such obligations had been imposed on Germany, and when Fascist Italy persecuted the German-speaking minority in the South Tyrol with impunity. It is true that of the approximately 35 million estimated minority inhabitants in inter-war Europe, only some 8.6 million lived in western Europe (roughly one in twenty of the total population) whereas about 25 million lived in central and eastern Europe (one in four). Thus the minorities question *was* numerically far more important in the East. Even so, the lack of a universal regime was an embarrassment for the Great Powers.[26]

Such an idea had in fact been considered in 1919 in Paris, only to be rejected. As James Headlam-Morley, a leading British policy-maker, noted at the time, fundamental issues of state sovereignty were at stake:

At first there was, so far as I recollect, a proposal that there should be inserted in the League of Nations some general clause giving the League of Nations the right to protect minorities in all countries which were members of the League. This I always most strongly opposed . . . for it would have involved the right to interfere in the internal constitution of every country in the world. As I pointed out, it would give the League of Nations the right to protect the Chinese in Liverpool, the Roman Catholics in France, the French in Canada, quite apart from the more serious problems, such as the Irish. This point of view was, I think, not seriously opposed by any except the unofficial bodies who wished the League of Nations to be a sort of super-state with a general right of guarding democracy and freedom throughout the world . . . My own view was that any right given to the League of Nations must be quite definite and specific, and based on special treaties entered into because of definite exceptional cases, and that such a right could only be recognised in the case of a new or immature state of Eastern Europe or Western Asia. Even if the denial of such a right elsewhere might lead to injustice and oppression, that was better than to allow anything which would mean the negation of the sovereignty of every state in the world.[27]

Thus the Great Powers were happy for the League to interfere in the internal affairs of 'new' states, but not in their own. According to their thinking, 'civilized' states such as those in western Europe had evolved procedures to facilitate the assimilation of minorities which did not yet exist in 'immature states'. That view was, to some extent, true: it was easier for Welsh or Catalan children to make careers in the professions or the civil service than it was, say, for Ukrainians in Poland or Hungarians in Romania where hatreds were more recent. Breton children might suffer at school; they did not have their homes and villages burned down. Thus the minority treaties were a way of educating less civilized nations in international deportment.

But the underlying premise of this thoroughgoing liberalism was that assimilation into the civilized life of the nation was possible and desirable. Mill had argued decades earlier that 'free institutions are next to impossible in a country made up of different nationalities': democracy required assimilation. As a Brazilian delegate put it in Geneva in 1925, the goal of the treaties was not to perpetuate a state of affairs in which certain groups in society saw themselves as 'constantly alien', but rather, to establish the conditions for 'a complete national unity'. From this it was not far to Carl Schmitt's arguments that a modern mass democracy presupposed 'first homogeneity and second – if the need arises – elimination or eradication of heterogeneity'. 'A democracy demonstrates its political power', he went on, 'by knowing how to refuse or keep at bay something foreign and unequal that threatens its homogeneity.'[28]

Liberalism's hypocrisies on this score were obvious, preaching one thing and practising another. After all, how universalist and free of racial assumptions was liberalism itself? In 1919, it was the liberal powers which had rebuffed Japan's suggestion to insert a clause affirming racial equality in the League of Nations covenant. American liberalism coexisted for years with segregation. And the British and French, too, made it very hard for colonial subjects of the wrong skin colour to acquire full citizenship. 'Does the British Empire rest on universal and equal voting rights for all its inhabitants?' Schmitt asked pointedly. 'It could not survive for a week on this foundation; with their terrible majority, the coloureds would dominate the whites. In spite of that the British Empire is a democracy.' Some liberals were concerned at the double standard. 'France cannot in effect show two faces,' wrote Albert Sarraut, a leading colonial commentator, 'that of liberty, turned towards the metropolis, that of tyranny towards its colonies.' Of course it did; the Anglo-French belief in assimilationism only made sense viewed within their national borders.[29]

In the colonies, liberalism was giving way to new doctrines of separate development for different races, segregation and colour bars; full citizenship was a privilege of the state rather than a right. 'Far from a right for natives,' wrote an expert on French colonial law, 'the granting of French citizenship must be considered as a favour accorded by the administration only to those who have shown themselves truly worthy . . . It is permitted to be astonished . . . at the tiny number of naturalizations, or access to French citizenship offered to natives.' The old self-confident sense of a civilizing mission – which led the Portuguese, for instance, to divide the colonial population into unassimilable *indígenas* and assimilated *civilisados* – was waning. In 1919 the French deported tens of thousands of Algerian labourers as 'unassimilable'. In North Africa, they replaced assimilation with the doctrine of associationism, something akin to the British doctrine of indirect rule. Meanwhile, in 1929 the Hilton Young Commission regarded it as an open question whether representative institutions would ever be suitable in Africa. All this undermined the assumption made at Paris in 1919, when the mandate system established the League's control over former German colonies, that natives would and could be educated in a democratic way of life.[30]

Scarcely surprising, then, with such a lead that the nation-states of Europe should also retreat from an assimilationism they had never much believed in. Between the wars, minorities were often seen as fifth columns for neighbours' irredentist ambitions, or for Bolshevism, and were regarded as security risks rather than citizens. Most promises made in the minority treaties were honoured in the breach. Minority-language schools were closed down while ambitious resettlement schemes tried (but usually failed) to alter the demographic balance in sensitive border areas such as Eastern Galicia and Macedonia to the detriment of local minorities. The old empires had handled matters more tolerantly. Before 1914 there had been numerous Czech civil servants in Vienna; after 1918, however, the new Czech state – though undoubtedly the most liberal in central Europe – allowed very few civil servants of German ethnicity, despite the fact that Germans comprised one fifth of the population.

Discrimination against minority rights was not primarily the work of reactionaries and conservatives. On the contrary, in eastern Europe it was above all the work of modernizing liberals who were trying to create a national community through the actions of the state. For them, the state had to show that its power was above 'everyone and everything', and to override its opponents whether these be the Church, brigands, communists or ethnic minorities. Thus it was entirely consistent for the Romanian Liberal Minister of Education, Constantin Angelescu, to criticize not only minorities but also the Church and provincial administrators in his desire to build up a centralized school system, since 'the interests of the State, the interests of the Romanian people, stand above individual interests, be they those of the communities . . . The Romanian State that is ours, all of ours, must be strengthened and . . . this State can only be strengthened by . . . letting the State mold the souls of all its citizens.'[31]

Because democracy was about the creation of *national* communities, it was generally anti-Semitic, or at least more ready to allow anti-Semitism to shape policy – through separate electoral colleges, for example, or entry quotas into the universities and civil-service posts – than old-fashioned royalists had been. In Hungary a 1920 law marked out Jews as a separate race rather than as 'Hungarians of the Mosaic faith'; had the country been more democratic, it would probably have been more anti-Semitic still. 'All citizens in Poland irrespective of creed and nationality must enjoy equal rights,' the Polish Peasant Party announced in 1935, adding the rider that 'the Jews, however, as has been proved, cannot be assimilated and are a consciously alien nation within Poland'. Similar views were evident in Slovakia and Romania. And this was not just an east European problem: such sentiments were on the rise in once ultra-assimilationist France as well, and eventually led to the notorious clause in Vichy's draft constitution describing the Jews as 'a race that conducts itself as a distinct community that resists assimilation'.[32]

It is in this context of widespread, indigenous traditions of anti-Semitism – common to the modernizing, state-building national elites of authoritarian *and* democratic countries alike through much of central and eastern Europe – that Hitler rose to power. Nazi Germany was not an anomaly, nor even a pioneer in such policies of 'cleansing the nation', though it took them to new extremes and sounded the death-knell for the 'assimilation thesis' (as it was dubbed by opponents). And while ethnic nationalism as practised in Warsaw or

Bucharest had limited scope for assimilation, biological racial nationalism of the kind which spread across central and eastern Europe in the 1930s, allowed none. The rise of institutionalized anti-Semitism in Hitler's Germany undermined the whole basis of the League's approach to minorities, since a supposedly 'civilized' state was rejecting the assimilationist idea in the most sweeping possible fashion. In October 1933, Nazi Germany left the League. A year later, the Polish premier, Colonel Beck, drove another nail into the League's coffin when he denounced Poland's minority-rights obligations 'pending the introduction of a general and uniform system for the protection of minorities'. The number of minority petitions received at Geneva fell sharply from 204 in 1930 to 15 in 1936, a drop which can be taken as a barometer of the waning confidence felt by European minorities in the value of the League.[33]

Let us not, though, be too hasty in writing off the League's minority system altogether. In the first place, it did notch up a few successes which offered valuable lessons for the future and showed what was possible with astute and far-sighted government. If these have today been forgotten, it is because they were too peaceful for the history-books. The Åland islands dispute, for instance, between Sweden and Finland was resolved quietly in 1921: the islands remained Finnish, but the Swedish islanders were granted a high degree of administrative autonomy. This compact formed the basis of a solution which removed a major source of tension between the two countries. The Estonian government took the very remarkable step of granting cultural autonomy to its 'national minorities'; the Latvians did not go quite this far, but did offer some concessions in education.

Those who condemn the League's minorities system might also ponder the alternatives. Nation-states were a reality, not merely a creation of wartime Great Power diplomacy. The conversion of the Ottoman Empire into a Turkish national state, for instance, could hardly be attributed to forces outside the country; Mustapha Kemal made the running there, not Lloyd George. And as that example demonstrated, there were several other ways of treating minorities.

'First we kill the Armenians, then the Greeks, then the Kurds,' a Turkish gendarme told a Danish Red Cross nurse in July 1915 as the war accelerated the Turkification of the Ottoman Empire. The attempt to murder the Armenians – chiefly carried out through the so-called Special Organization – was the logical extension of the nationalist programme of the government in Istanbul. Even friendly German observers concluded that beyond the professed concern for military security in border areas the Turks aimed at 'the planned extermination of the Armenian people'. The numbers are disputed, but between 800,000 and 1.3 million may have perished in massacres and death marches. Later this would be termed 'genocide', later still 'ethnic cleansing'. Mass killing, then, was one way of tackling the problem of minorities in a nation-state. Many in the West were filled with horror; few bore in mind that it was the introduction of the Western conception of the nation-state into the multinational societies of the Near East that had led to massacre in the first place.[34]

Just a few years later, the dissolution of the Ottoman Empire provided a second model for dealing with minorities – population exchange. In the aftermath of the Greek defeat in Asia Minor in 1922 – following a decade of fighting between Greeks and Turks – the two governments agreed upon a compulsory version of E. H. Carr's idea of voluntary 'repatriation', which had actually been tried out on a smaller scale between Greece and Bulgaria in 1919. This time, though, the numbers involved were enormous – nearly 1.2 million Greeks, and half a million Turks. Since religion was used as a marker of identity, thousands of Turkish-speaking Orthodox villagers from Asia Minor were expelled to Greece, even though they spoke no Greek, while Greek Muslims, many of whose families had converted to Islam, embarked for Turkey. Such was the logic of European nationalism as it tried to rationalize the end of a multi-confessional empire. People were redefined, nationalities created. The suffering was immense: homes and property abandoned, friends left behind. Only through nationalist blinkers could this look like homecoming.

Yet if not homecoming, then at least the building of a fatherland. Horrible as it was, population 'transfer' was helpful to governments aiming for national homogeneity, and both the Greek and Turkish authorities welcomed it on these grounds: in Greek Macedonia, for example, the flood of refugees Hellenized both the province and its port of Salonika; other ethnic groups – Sephardic Jews, Albanians, Slavic-speaking Macedonians – suddenly found themselves out-numbered.

Given the growing propensity for certain ethnic groups, notably the Germans and the Hungarians, to act as magnets for irredentism, transfer might have seemed an attractive idea to many other states. Still, there were several reasons why the Greco-Turkish population exchange was not more widely followed in inter-war Europe. One was cost: Greece's population increased by a quarter – putting into perspective the recent British refusal to admit three million Hong Kong Chinese – and the strain of resettling so many refugees imposed an awesome social and economic burden on the country. In addition, the two governments wrangled for years over compensation and property valuation; it was doubtful whether bilateral relations were much improved by the exchange. Third, it was obvious that such an arrangement was only feasible where a minority had a 'home' to go to. It was hardly applicable to the Jews, the Macedonians or even the Ukrainians, for example. Finally, of course, the compulsory uprooting of populations offended liberal ideas of individual rights. The forced transfer of 1923 would not find imitators until the collapse of the League and the rise of a Nazi New Order.[35]

The Greco-Turkish exchange of peoples had been reached in part *after* the event, for hundreds of thousands of Greeks had fled Asia Minor to escape the Turkish advance well before the diplomats started talking. They were, in fact, part of the enormous wave of refugees produced by the war, including more than a million Russians fleeing the revolution, Poles, Balts and Germans hounded out of eastern Europe, 350,000 Armenians and many others. Before 1914 they might have found refuge across the Atlantic; after 1921 the doors were closed. Thus Europe's traditional strategy for its displaced populations – transoceanic export – no longer functioned. Meanwhile nation-states drafted citizenship laws which excluded hundreds of thousands of incomers. The result was a vast increase in 'stateless' persons, unable or unwilling to return home, resented in their place of refuge and straining those earlier traditions of asylum which had been so pro-nounced a feature of pre-war liberalism. The 1924 Romanian citizenship law made 100,000 Jews inside Romania stateless; others remained in limbo in Poland. Weimar Germany and France of the Third Republic both locked up thousands in detention camps. Liberals were shocked. 'It is impossible that in the twentieth century, there could be 800,000 men in Europe unprotected by any legal organisation recognised by international law', wrote the president of the International Committee of the Red Cross. As a result of international action, the so-called 'Nansen passport' was created and efforts were made to define a refugee in international law and to provide protection.[36]

The problem did not go away, however; in fact, the economic depression made it worse. Twenty years after the Russian civil war no less than half all Russian émigrés still counted as refugees. The Spanish civil war saw 400,000 republicans flee northwards into France just as the country was expelling hundreds of thousands of foreign workers, chiefly Algerians and Poles. After Hitler's rise to power, hundreds of thousands of Jews fled Germany, Austria and Czechoslo-vakia, and searched for shelter elsewhere. This last wave of refugees in particular illustrated both the value and the limitation of the prevailing minority-rights regime. It brought home in the starkest possible terms the need for minorities to enjoy international protection against the nation-state if Europe was to escape a permanent refugee crisis. To that extent, the minority guarantees system introduced in 1919 was a courageous and imaginative step in the right direction. But that system had never been extended to Germany. What was more, even if it had been, it would have been inoperative, since Germany had pulled out of the League in 1933 and refused to recognize its authority. The minority treaties were part and parcel of the inter-national order established under the League; they stood, and fell, with the authority of the League itself.

IDEALISTS AND REALISTS

What, then, was the League of Nations? A system of alliances, a guarantor of peace, an instrument of arbitration or a proto-federation? For General Smuts in 1918 the answer was simple and radical: 'Europe is being liquidated and the League of Nations must be the heir to this great estate': according to this view (which reflected much older attitudes towards territorial distribution), it was to be a combination of international property manager and nanny, nursing immature societies both inside and outside Europe towards independent statehood. By implication, the great civilized powers were duty-bound to offer guidance.

This quasi-imperial vision of liberal paternalism shaded at one end of the political spectrum into the secret desire of some in Whitehall to see the League as an updated Concert of Great Powers, of the kind which had managed to keep the peace (more or less) for nearly a century after the Congress of Vienna in 1815. At the other, it touched on the Wilsonian dream of a new international order based on equality of nations (or more precisely states) under a strengthened international law. This lofty vision was put to the test early on, when Japanese delegates to the Paris Peace Conference proposed a clause for the League's Covenant enshrining the principle of racial equality. This was too much for the white men – Wilson's adviser Colonel House minuted worriedly: 'It will surely raise the race issue throughout the world' – and the suggestion was unceremoniously rebuffed.[37]

If for idealists the League offered the chance of a new juridical order, for the hard-headed French, on the other hand, the League's chief value lay not in its defence of a new international morality but, far more concretely, in its capacity to defend the Versailles settlement against revision. French interests demanded a League with teeth. They made several attempts to create a supranational military force at the League's disposal, but failed to persuade the British. When Wilson failed to push American membership of the League through Congress, much of the League's deterrent value slipped away.

The British scholar Alfred Zimmern was probably right to see the League in the 1920s as an 'instrument of cooperation'. Even if it disappointed both the idealists and the realists, it was certainly not unimportant: it provided an international forum for discussion, it was a source of influence, and helped tackle the kinds of problems – like the refugee crisis, and other social, economic and legal matters – where a coordinated international response was desirable. Even though it had very limited powers to intervene in the internal affairs of member states, it could help publicize abuses of minority groups, and to that extent expose governments to the pressure of world opinion.

Nevertheless, its influence depended on its members' willingness to work through it. They were not bound to it, and could conduct diplomacy through other channels. And this meant that the rule of international law it embodied ultimately depended upon the political will of its members. The strength of pacifism in Britain and France made public sentiment – which Woodrow Wilson and others had seen as the basis of a strong League – studiously passive in international affairs. As the balance of power in Europe shifted, the League became increasingly marginalized, diplomacy flowed around Geneva rather than through it, and a rival ideological vision of a European order emerged in Berlin.

The defining feature of the European balance of power in 1919 had been the simultaneous exhaustion of Russia and Germany. This was perfectly obvious to observers at the time, though they did not all draw the same lessons from the fact. For the British it was important to recognize that Germany must recover her status as a Great Power, if only to prevent a political understanding between Berlin and Moscow, which would jeopardize the whole settlement. The minorities treaties would help by ensuring the fair treatment of the German minorities outside Germany, as well as by providing a model of tolerant government to the new states more generally.[38]

From France's point of view, on the other hand, Germany had to be kept in her place. The new states of eastern and central Europe would act both as a buffer against Bolshevik revolution and as a check against Germany. The slogan of national self-determination was thus a means to an end, and could be overridden when it clashed with French interests. This explains the French lack of enthusiasm for the minorities treaties – which seemed merely to weaken her new east European allies – and the French refusal in 1918–19 (and again, implicitly, in 1931) to allow Austria and Germany to be united, against the evident wishes of the bulk of the Austrian population.

Despite the creation of the League, then, Great Power politics was far from dead in Europe after 1918. Other, more traditional, diplomatic forums remained influential: the Conference of Ambassadors, for example, a gathering of the Great Powers in the old style, was chosen in preference to the League to settle two major crises in 1923 – over Corfu, between the Greeks and Mussolini's Italy; and Vilna, between the Poles and the Lithuanians. As the French in particular lost faith in the idea of collective security through Geneva, they pursued alternative and more traditional means of guaranteeing their interests.

In 1921, at French prompting, Poland, Czechoslovakia and Romania formed the Little Entente, a bloc directed at Hungary, and indirectly at Germany too. In the next few years, France signed treaties with all these states, as well as with Yugoslavia. France's hold over Germany was manifested much more concretely in her occupation of the Rhineland. When French and Belgian troops invaded the Ruhr in 1923 to force the payment of reparations, it looked like a further expression of French might: the ensuing fiasco, however, and eventual reparations deal was more than a temporary rebuff to Paris. It lost Paris goodwill in London, and demonstrated that the Europeans could not solve their problems without American help.[39]

In the mid-1920s, as French policy became more conciliatory, Germany re-emerged as a major power. At Locarno, in 1925, peace was reaffirmed in western Europe, but the issue of Germany's eastern borders was pointedly left open: the 'spirit of Locarno' pointed more to the revival of Great Power diplomacy than to Geneva. The years 1928–30 saw the last French efforts to achieve stability through Geneva. First there was the meaningless declaration, 'outlawing war', known as the Briand–Kellogg Pact; although many other countries signed up, it was in fact far less than the solid American support France had hoped for. Then came Briand's ill-fated proposal for European unity. Finally, there was the 1932 Disarmament Conference, the largest international gathering since 1919. This met in unpropitious conditions: the Manchurian crisis had exposed the weakness of the League in its first major international challenge; Franco-German relations were at a low, following France's veto of the proposed Austro-German customs union; the economic crisis had plunged the international economy into depression. Again, the French proposed a League of Nations force; again it was rejected. Hitler's election doomed the conference; the German delegation walked out, and Germany left the League in October 1933.

Between 1934 and 1936 the European balance swung inexorably away from Paris and London. The French alliance system was damaged by Poland's decision to sign a non-aggression pact with Germany in January 1934. France then turned towards the Soviet Union, but western and east European anti-communism made it difficult for Moscow to fulfil the role France had once intended for Poland and Czechoslovakia. Even more critical was the Abyssinia crisis of 1935–6, which brought Italy into conflict with the League. The French, in particular, were desperate to keep close links with their Mediterranean neighbour; the sanctions imposed by the League wrecked this hope and pushed Mussolini into Hitler's arms. In 1934 Mussolini had stood up to Hitler and prevented a Nazi takeover of Austria; four years later, he offered no objection and *Anschluss* took place.

The British watched all this happen with some detachment. Suspicious of the French, they were overextended in the Far East and could ill afford further military or naval commitments in Europe. Government policy was affected by pacifism, by a certain liberal sympathy for German ethnographic claims in central Europe, by fiscal conservatism (which opposed rearmament), and by a poor strategic sense which exaggerated Italian power in the Mediterranean and undervalued the significance of eastern Europe.

As for the French, their basic defensiveness was amply illustrated by the construction of the Maginot line: French generals had no offensive plans where Germany was concerned. Defence spending was at low levels, politically the country was deeply divided. From 1937 onwards, these factors produced a growing willingness to come to terms with Germany. At the nadir of French diplomacy, in the winter of 1938, after Munich, there was a Franco-German declaration of friendship, and French politicians indicated a 'fundamental alteration' in France's relations with eastern Europe.

Not surprisingly, these developments doomed the League of Nations. By 1936, with the Disarmament Conference ignominiously wound up and the minorities system more or less moribund, few people looked any longer to Geneva for the answers to Europe's problems. As civil war erupted that summer, Spain was added to Manchuria, Abyssinia and the Rhineland in the roll-call of the League's failures. Not even the ineffectual International Non-Intervention Committee was organized from Geneva. Hardly surprising, then, that the Spanish foreign minister should bitterly reproach the League's Assembly in September 1938 with following 'a strange theory according to which the best method of serving the League was to remove from its purview all questions relating to peace, and the application of the Covenant'. One French supporter of the League, Gaston Riou, saw 1936 bringing to an end a phase of history that had started in 1918: the League had simply been defeated. 'If European democracy binds its living body to the putrefying corpse of the 1919 settlement,' warned E. H. Carr in November 1936, 'then it will merely be committing a particularly unpleasant form of suicide.'[40]

Rather than embodying the nucleus of a new international order, universal in its aspirations, the League was shrinking to something far more modest, a mere coalition of like-minded states which made no claim to monopolize the pattern of international relations. In 1937 a Nazi political scientist pointed out acerbically that there was a kind of 'asserted monopoly of the Geneva system'. In fact, he argued, there was not just one, but several actual or possible systems of collective action. He was right.[41]

In the 1920s there had been fumbling alternative schemes of international cooperation such as the anti-communist White International, sponsored briefly by the Hungarians, or Count Coudenhove-Kalergi's schemes for pan-European union. None of these amounted to very much. Under Hitler's leadership, however, the Third Reich evolved a vision of a European order based on fundamentally different principles from those developed in Geneva. In the ideologically charged climate of inter-war Europe, a shift in the balance of power implied a profound political and moral challenge to the League system. The whole idea of liberal universalism came under attack.

AGAINST THE LIBERAL NEW ORDER

Hitler grew up steeped in the Pan-German nationalism – viciously anti-Slav and anti-Semitic – of the late Habsburg Empire. In 1923 during the Beerhall Putsch, he walked through the streets of Munich alongside the more famous Erich Ludendorff who, together with Hindenburg, had been the architect of Germany's wartime victories in the East. It is, therefore, tempting to interpret National Socialist foreign policy in terms of older German nationalist traditions. Undoubtedly, they were influential both on Hitler personally and on the movement he led. It would, however, be a great error to ignore the substantial differences between him and his predecessors. To imagine that Hitler was merely following in, say, Bismarck's footsteps was profoundly to misunderstand the man and his view of the world. Bismarck thought in terms of great-power politics, Hitler of racial triumph.

Hitler did not object to the League of Nations simply because it defended the Versailles settlement. That would have implied a willingness to participate at Geneva if the settlement could have been revised. Many German nationalists, of course, did take this position, which was also the assumption underlying British appeasement policy. But in *Mein Kampf*, Hitler made it clear that restoring the frontiers of 1914 was certainly not his aim. He was after further *Lebensraum* for the German people. This imperial programme flowed naturally from his broader vision of politics as racial struggle. Such a struggle – seen in Darwinian terms as an existential battle – implied a hierarchical vision of international (or, better, interracial) relations.[42]

The League, after all, was an organization of states. But what was the state? According to Hitler's biological view of politics, it was no less than 'a living organism'. Reflecting the writing of German geopoliticians, he argued that boundaries could not be fixed; they were, rather, 'momentary frontiers in the current political struggle of any period', at the mercy of 'the mighty forces of Nature in a process of continuous growth . . . to be transformed or destroyed tomorrow by greater forces'.[43] Hitler's own vision of global politics – unlike that of many geopoliticians – rested upon race: the state itself was merely the expression of the racial *Volk*. 'Blood is stronger than a passport,' wrote a prominent pan-Germanist in 1937. The German minorities abroad were 'racial comrades' of Reich Germans; the Third Reich had a duty to the whole of the German people, not merely those who happened to live within its current borders.[44]

The fundamental problem, therefore, with the League was not merely that it defended Versailles, but that – in Nazi eyes – it embodied a wholly mistaken philosophy of international affairs. There could be no equality among states, for some 'are not worthy of existence'; there could therefore be no universal morality or law. Even the highly paternalistic liberalism which Geneva embodied reeked of humanitarian weakness to the Nazis. The stronger race must prevail over the weaker; it would thus win the right to impose its own wishes upon the loser. It followed that legal arrangements were purely matters of convenience to be followed or repudiated as the interests of the *Volk* dictated.[45]

It is true that among German political theorists in the 1930s there were endless debates – for or against forms of European federalism, for German-led economic zones, for cooperation with Russia or anti-Bolshevik crusade. Nevertheless, the logic of Hitler's racial obsessions forced the discussion within narrow bounds and gave rise to a National Socialist doctrine of international law that attempted to define Germany's new stance in the world. Equality in international relations was not taken as absolute; it was relative 'to the concrete value of the race represented by the state', in other words 'their natural superiority or inferiority'. Thus was justified the 'hegemony' of some races over others. Not surprisingly, German legal theorists argued that international law had only a very limited role to play in regulating relations between states, and they criticized the League for the way it had led to a 'juridification' of international life. What masqueraded as a liberal philosophy of human rights was really – on this view – nothing other than a fig-leaf for the '1919 Versailles-Diktat', and an expression of 'the Jewish spirit' with its opposition to the life of the *Volk* and hatred of national specificity. Since there existed no 'common rule of law' there was little value in international institutions such as the League or the Permanent Court of International Justice.[46]

That the Nazi challenge to the League went far beyond mere territorial revisionism was clear enough at the time to those who wished to see. For C. A. Macartney, for instance, a leading British expert on central Europe, 'Hitlerism was flatly incompatible with the League system and its philosophy'. One would have 'to succumb to the other'. In a melancholy but fascinating article written in 1938, an émigré lawyer asked whether the collapse of belief in a universal international law did not reflect the 'disintegration of European civilization'. There was no longer a cohesive value-system or an international society in the old sense; social and political divisions in Europe made it a 'fiction' to talk about the 'universal validity of all rules'.[47]

FASCIST EMPIRES

In an era when biological metaphors were widely applied to international relations, when fears of population decline were widespread, and nations themselves (in France, Hungary and Greece just as much as Germany) were seen as bodies – facing extinction, asphyxiation or decline if they could not 'sustain life' within their borders – the need for 'living space' was a common concern across the political spectrum. It was, for instance, not Hitler but Konrad Adenauer, then mayor of Cologne, who in 1928 opened a colonial exhibition entitled *Space without People and People without Space*. Anxious contemporaries saw no inconsistency in arguing simultaneously that their country had too small a population, *and* not enough land.[48]

For both Nazi Germany and Fascist Italy, empire was crucial to their claims to be great powers as well as to their very survival as dynamic nations. Empire was land, and land meant room for settlement, foodstuffs, raw materials and healthy colonists. Never mind the evidence that it was easier to win land than to direct people to it or that in the nineteenth century far more Europeans had preferred to settle in the Americas than in Africa: these were lessons fascist regimes would have to learn the hard way. Fascist empire-building marked the culmination of the process of European imperial expansion that began in the 1870s. Mussolini and Hitler accepted the basic geopolitical tenets of nineteenth-century imperialism, while jettisoning its liberalism.

Fascist empire came first to Ethiopia, following the Italian invasion late in 1935. The fighting itself was conducted with unprecedented brutality by the Italians, who were desperate for a quick victory: gas and chemical warfare, as well as saturation bombing, killed enormous numbers, as did the detention and concentration camps that the Italians brought with them from the pacification campaigns of a few years earlier against the nomadic Senussi. Around 3,000 Italians died compared with tens and perhaps hundreds of thousands of Ethiopians. Neither later nor at the time did this kind of bloodshed occasion much criticism; inside Italy, victory marked the high point of Mussolini's reign, a 'golden age' of 'Fascist empire'.[49]

The peace that followed was equally enlightening. Following an assassination attempt on Viceroy Graziani, notorious for his brutality, Fascist squads went on the rampage in Addis Ababa, killing over a thousand people in cold blood. Others were executed in mass reprisals, including several hundred monks. All this offered a foretaste of what Europe – and Italy – would itself experience a few years later at the hands of the Germans. Meanwhile, Ciano addressed the General Assembly of the League of Nations, and referred to the 'sacred mission of civilization' which Italy was heeding, declaring that his country would 'consider it an honour to inform the League of the progress achieved in its work of civilizing Ethiopia'.[50]

Empire-building was closely connected with racial laws and decrees which were new to Italian Fascism. Considerations of racial 'prestige' led the authorities to try to regulate sexual and other contacts between Italians and Ethiopians, in ways that they had not considered in Libya or on Rhodes. Just as the apartheid of the Nuremberg laws had been prefigured in pre-1914 German colonial policy, so Italian racism in Africa paved the way for the 1938 racial laws inside Italy itself. The infamous Manifesto of Racial Scientists, and the accompanying anti-Semitic laws, were thus not mere mimicry of National Socialism but an expression of Fascism's attempts to create a fitting image for itself as an imperial power.[51]

Fascism's admirers abroad took heart. Sixty-four French academics published a manifesto attacking 'that false juridical universalism that equates superior and inferior, civilized and barbaric'. 'Why continue to lie?' wrote a French journalist. 'There *are* different levels among men; there is a human hierarchy. To deny it is absurd and disregard it a shameful confusion. Leave Ethiopia, two or three Ethiopias if one is not enough ... This is the absolute right of human civilization when the hour comes to impose itself upon barbarism.' Just a few years later, Marshal Pétain would publicly describe Vichy France as 'a social hierarchy ... rejecting the false idea of the natural equality of men'.[52]

Much Italian policy was, of course, reminiscent of Nazi views on race and empire. But between Hitler's and Mussolini's imperial projects there were two key differences. One was that Germans took racial exclusionism (and indeed the law generally) more seriously than Italians: the Nuremberg laws operated more efficiently than the 1938 race laws. The second was that while Fascism – like older imperialisms – saw its civilizing burden lying chiefly outside Europe, National Socialism did not: and just here, no doubt – by turning Europeans back into barbarians and slaves – lay the Nazis' greatest offence against the sensibility of the continent.

Events in 1938–40 showed that the kind of leadership Nazi Germany desired in Europe could be obtained by a combination of conquest and 'hegemony'. Military conquest led to either annexation – as with Austria – or occupation: the invasion of Bohemia-Moravia in the spring of 1939, for example, was interpreted as demonstrating the importance of 'the phenomenon of leadership in the international community'.[53] The second Vienna accord of August 1940 – a deal brokered by Hitler to settle territorial disputes in central Europe – illustrated the possibilities of hegemony: Germany gained rights to Romanian oil exploitation, acted as regional arbiter between Hungary, Slovakia and Romania, and created 'trustee rights' over the German minorities in those countries.

German commentators hailed this last step as a vast improvement on the old League system of minority protection: these 'laws for the protection of the folk-group' gave the 'mother country' the right to intervene in the event of disputes between the minority and the host government; they also turned the entire 'folk-group' into a collective legal entity. But such legislation looked a lot better at the height of German power in the summer of 1940 than it did a mere four years later, for it made ethnic Germans hostage to the fortunes of Hitler's war.[54]

In recent years, a 'little Englander' school of revisionist historians has once again suggested that an Anglo-German war was avoidable. Was there perhaps more to appeasement than subsequent criticism allows, and less, perhaps, to Churchill's insistence on confrontation? What if no British guarantee had been given Poland in 1939? Or if Hitler's peace feelers had not been rebuffed in the summer of 1940? Might Whitehall not have done a deal with Germany which accepted Nazi control of eastern Europe in return for the continued existence of the British Empire? Did it not, perhaps, do something similar with Stalin a few years later?

If Hitler was, as A. J. P. Taylor once famously implied, just another politician, these arguments might have some force. But what weakens Taylor's analysis of the origins of the war is his indifference to the role of ideology. The Second World War did not start because of diplomatic misunderstanding or confusion, nor even because of Hitler's deceit or duplicity. Rather it started because – very late in the day – Hitler's opponents realized they were faced with 'a clash of two worlds'. Berlin and London were not playing the same game, though some on both sides wished they were.[55]

It is true that the British Empire was ruined by the cost of fighting Hitler. What, however, is doubtful is whether it could have been saved by joining him. Germany's own colonial agenda troubled the British, who were reluctant to buy off Nazi demands in Europe with bits of Africa. The ideological gulf between the two powers was evident here too, and Nazi colonial planners harshly criticized the British for their excessively lax racial policies. Any alliance would therefore have involved the British abandoning their liberal imperialist creed (and belief in indirect rule) for hardline racialism. Such an alliance was actually envisaged by Alfred Rosenberg, a leading Nazi ideologue – Britain and Germany together defending the white race by land and sea. It implied, however, an impossible transformation in British values: these were liberal rather than authoritarian, while British racism – which certainly existed – was based more upon culture than biology.[56]

The ideological gulf which existed between British and German society was revealed by the shocked British reaction to news of the Kristallnacht pogrom in November 1938. More than anything else up to that point, this event turned British opinion against appeasement.[57] Over the next few months, the British and French governments were forced to reappraise their entire policy, even though after Munich the omens were poor. 'The first part of Mr Hitler's programme – integration of Germans into the Reich – is completed,' wrote Robert Coulondre, the new French ambassador in Berlin, in December 1938. 'Now the time for *Lebensraum* has arrived.'[58]

Appeasement had been premised on the assumption that Nazi Germany was basically pursuing a revisionist agenda; the invasion of Bohemia-Moravia in March 1939 was the first sign that Hitler's aims went beyond annexing the areas inhabited by ethnic Germans. It also indicated Hitler's contemptuous attitude towards international agreements. In response, Britain and France belatedly sought to resuscitate the eastern security tier which they had created at Versailles by offering security guarantees to Poland and Romania. It was an unconvincing gesture.

Circumstances had changed greatly since 1919. Nazi control of the former Czechoslovakia now made strategic nonsense of an eastern alliance, while assuring Germany of the substantial resources in armaments and gold of the Czech state. There was no serious coordination of military plans between London and Paris, on the one hand, and Warsaw and Bucharest, on the other. Worse still, Russian power was restored, raising the spectre of a German–Soviet carve-up in the East. Blinkered by anti-communism – the same anti-communism which led Lord Halifax to welcome Germany as a 'bastion against Bolshevism' – neither the British nor the French made a serious attempt to reach agreement with Stalin. This failure doomed the new independent states of eastern Europe, and turned the continent itself into an enormous laboratory in Nazi (and later communist) empire-building. The violence, which Europe had found it so easy to ignore when committed abroad in its name, proved harder to stomach at home.

3

Healthy Bodies, Sick Bodies

Ten Commandments for Choosing a Spouse:
1. Remember that you are German.
2. If of sound stock, do not remain unwed.
3. Keep your body pure.
4. Keep spirit and soul pure.
5. As a German, choose someone of German or Nordic blood for your partner.
6. When choosing your spouse, look into their lineage.
7. Health is a precondition of external beauty.
8. Marry only out of love.
9. Seek not a playmate but a partner in marriage.
10. Wish for as many children as possible.

– from the *Hausbuch für die deutsche Familie* (Berlin, n.d.)

These tips for domestic harmony came near the beginning of the *Handbook for the German Family*, which the Nazi authorities routinely issued to every young couple. Its excellent collection of recipes was accompanied by advice on childcare, on looking after the home, diet and racial health. A special section summarized the Nuremberg laws and carried helpful charts to clarify family bloodlines and to investigate genealogies contaminated by marriage with Jews. Domestic health and happiness – readers were reminded – were no longer merely a matter for individual choice and satisfaction. Weimar's self-centred liberalism had been replaced by National Socialism's concern for the community as a whole. Before the recipes came a useful saying of the Führer: 'If one lacks the strength to struggle for one's own health, one loses the right to life in this world of struggle.'

Such a book shows us values which had not only penetrated German life, but were also part of a much broader European discourse about national and family health in the inter-war years. The Third Reich might have taken this discourse to new extremes, and highlighted the role of race in a way unmatched elsewhere. But the idea that family health concerned society more generally, that the nation needed racially sound progeny, that the state should therefore intervene in private life to show people how to live – all this ran right across the political spectrum of inter-war Europe, reflecting the tensions and stresses of an insecure world in which nation-states existed in rivalry with one another, their populations decimated by one war and threatened by the prospect of another.

Fears for national strength were reinforced by the long-term decline in birth rates which had set in before the First World War. 'The attention of many European governments has been called to the decreasing birth rate of the white races during the last decades,' noted an Italian journalist in 1937. 'Most biologists, economists and politicians fully endorse the view that numbers are the strength of the Nation.' After 1918, the state tried to correct this trend by setting up Health Ministries and promoting family values. People were encouraged and exhorted to have more babies, while abortion and contraception were discouraged or criminalized. Living and housing conditions were improved as were municipal amenities for the masses. Physical fitness was promoted through swimming in the new public lidos, rambling in the countryside or cycling during extended paid holidays.

But the development of social policy had a darker side as well: safeguarding the 'quality' as well as the quantity of the nation's human stock – as doctors, scientists and policy-makers recommended – implied reducing the dangers to public health. These were not only slums, poverty and malnutrition; they also encompassed the physically and mentally ill, who were shut away, sterilized or even in the extreme case killed for the greater good of society. Juvenile delinquents or the sexually promiscuous were also seen as jeopardizing family stability and public order. And sometimes the threat to the nation was defined even more broadly in terms of an entire class – as in the so-called 'social problem group', which supposedly existed in inter-war Britain – or in terms of race. The Third Reich combined biological anti-Semitism with a highly efficient state apparatus to produce the most modern form of this kind of racial welfare state in Europe.

As we now know, Sweden, Switzerland and several other European countries continued to employ sterilization and other coercive measures in social policy until relatively recently. Such practices make Hitler's Germany look less exceptional and closer to the mainstream of European thought than once seemed possible. Nevertheless, the similarities should not be exaggerated. The Nazi *Volksgemeinschaft* (or People's Community) was promoted through what one social commentator called the 'life-ensuring state', but of course this 'life-ensuring state' also believed it was necessary to take the life of others, expropriating their goods and redistributing them for the benefit of those inside the nation. Its emergence prompted both imitators (as in Italy) and critics – especially in Britain – who attacked the idea that racism had any basis in science, or more generally that social policy ought to be made on the basis of coercion. The Second World War became a struggle to define the relationship between the community as a whole, the individual citizen and social policy, paving the way for the very different forms of welfare state which would emerge after 1945. Fascist welfare states taught democrats the lesson that granting individual liberties was not enough to secure people's loyalties in an era of mass politics. Hitler's defeat would allow democracy to root itself once more in European life through a new sense of social solidarity and national cohesion.

WAR AND THE DESTRUCTION OF BODIES

Somewhere above eight million men lost their lives in the First World War – over 6,000 deaths each day of the conflict. With the casualties suffered as a result of the Russian Revolution, of flu, typhus and of the other conflicts that continued into the early 1920s, probably as many as thirteen million Europeans died. France lost one in ten of its active male population, Serbia and Romania even more.

Most of the dead were young men, whose absence in post-war Europe had profound and devastating consequences for those who remained. Magnus Hirschfeld, the pioneering researcher into human sexuality, described the war as the 'greatest sexual catastrophe ever suffered by civilised Man'. During the fighting gender roles had already changed dramatically, as women and children fended for themselves without husbands or fathers. After 1918 the traditional family came under even greater strain: by then there were around 500,000 war widows in Germany alone, most of whom would never remarry.[1]

To millions of other women, the men who came home from the war carried the physical and mental scars of their experiences. They were 'destroyed men' (in a contemporary phrase) and 'wounded patriarchs'. Incapable of reintegration into civilian life, haunted by wartime memories, many committed suicide – rates rose fast at the end of the war – drank themselves into oblivion or tried to reassert their authority by beating their wives and children. While governments erected noble monuments to commemorate the dead, mutilated veterans begged at street corners or looked for work. Given this battering inflicted by total war upon Europe's traditional patriarchal family, it is not surprising that there was much talk of 'youth running wild' in a newly 'fatherless community'. The crisis atmosphere of 1918/19 with insurrections, revolution and mutinies, increased the sense of a complete collapse of social order. 'The revolution and its consequences have been particularly harmful for the psyche of many people, particularly of youth,' observed a Prussian civil servant. 'The foundations have been shattered. State institutions have almost completely lost their authority, as has the Church. The educational influence of parents has often been reduced to nil.'[2]

As again after the Second World War, such anxieties provoked the state to act more and more as surrogate parent and fount of moral authority. As divorce rates rose sharply, it reasserted the values of family cohesion – since 'moral order', in Mussolini's words, produces 'public order' – in order to show women and children their proper place. 'A nation is not a collection of individuals placed beside one another; it is a group of interlocking families,' insisted the Radical French politician Édouard Herriot in 1919. 'The organic cell is not the individual but the family.' It was, in other words, not just the Right which felt the vital importance of restoring the family – and if necessary checking individualism – for the sake of the nation's well-being.[3]

All this meant exorcizing a frightening apparition which had emerged during the war – the independent and emancipated young woman with her own place in the labour force and her own income. Tuppence Beresford, for instance – the heroine of Agatha Christie's 1922 thriller *The Secret Adversary* – who had been a wartime nurse, entered the post-war world with new demands for equal work opportunities, sexual independence and an active life. Despite the reality of growing female employment, however, especially in new service industries, role models like Tuppence were increasingly denounced as manifestations of 'sexual Bolshevism', threatening the traditional authority of the male. The *garçonnes* of the 1920s, Bright Young Things with their bobbed hair and slim hips, were accused of displaying a selfish love of pleasure, and a frightening disregard for the nation's future. 'Smoking, wearing short hair, dressed in pyjamas or sportswear . . . women increasingly resemble their companions,' wrote an alarmed Frenchman. How could such androgynes ever be turned into responsible mothers?[4]

To such suspicions there was a nervous political undertone. The Bolsheviks had opened up breathtaking vistas in relations between the sexes, swiftly emancipating Russian women to an extent unparalleled anywhere else in Europe – curbing the power of the Church, sweeping away traditional patriarchal privileges and allowing women to sue for divorce. Some Soviet policy-makers even talked about eventually abolishing marriage altogether and encouraging free unions of men and women; not surprisingly, critics believed that the war-torn Russian family was being encouraged to 'wither away', together with the other institutions of bourgeois life.[5]

All of this – in the anti-Bolshevik climate of the 1920s – hardly helped the cause of female emancipation in the rest of Europe. True, women won the vote under many of the new constitutions, but they still remained without it elsewhere – in France, Italy and Greece, for instance, and only on a very limited basis in the UK before 1930. Moreover, splits opened up within the women's movement: the old suffragist focus on electoral equality was less and less satisfactory to younger activists with more practical concerns. 'For the working woman, the vote . . . does not represent her emancipation,' argued one Greek communist. 'Because in this matter of supreme importance, what concerns her above all is the entire social problem.'[6]

Constitutional provisions for equal opportunities were effectively neutralized by the new cult of the family, and by unchanged male-dominated family-law codes. 'The State recognizes that by her life within the home, woman gives to the State a support without which the common good cannot be achieved,' ran article 41 of the 1937 Irish constitution, making it clear where women were supposed to be working. Conservatives, male-dominated unions and ex-servicemen's organizations blocked many efforts to improve women's employment rights, and often succeeded in forcing them to quit war-time jobs for men, while professional women were often obliged to leave work upon getting married, as was the case for instance inside the British civil service.[7]

In contrast to the selfish hedonism of the single working woman, the wife and mother (for the two were generally equated) encapsulated the 'heroic form of Everyday life'. Or as a Fascist propagandist put it: 'Maternity is the patriotism of women.' Even Stalin came round to a similar view – alarmed by soaring divorce and abortion rates in Russia as peasant women flocked to the cities – and in the mid-1930s the libertarian laws of the early Bolsheviks were replaced by a new Soviet commitment to the traditional family.[8]

This inter-war European ideology of motherhood had deep roots. A long-term fall in national reproduction rates had begun towards the end of the nineteenth century, just as the competition between empires and nations was heating up. The growing importance of conscript armies made the size and health of a country's population an issue of military and national security, especially as Europe's states seemed locked in a Darwinian struggle for mastery. The French worried that Germany's faster population growth meant their own eventual extinction as a great power. The Germans were not so worried about the French but were terrified of the 'teeming Slavic hordes' to the east. Hungarian nationalists believed they faced a 'battle without hope', in the struggle against 'folk-death' at the hands of Slavs, Germans and Romanians. The British, especially after the Boer War, wondered how a 'declining race' could govern a gigantic empire. As Giuseppe Sergi, a leading Italian eugenicist, informed the Italian Society for the Progress of Science in 1916, Europe generally – still in thrall to the idea of empire – was gripped by the fear that its 'superior races' were in decline.[9]

The First World War, of course, made the whole outlook much worse, leading national leaders to peddle the view that 'pregnancy is the woman's active service'. In their effort to encourage births, the French authorities circulated wartime postcards which exhorted soldiers on leave to 'work for repopulation' and asked young women to 'work for France'. British pro-natalists published scary accounts of what awaited their countrymen in books like *The Menace of the Empty Cradle*, or the 1916 *Cradles or Coffins? Our Greatest National Need*. In Germany, the Reichstag passed laws outlawing contraception and restricting abortion. 'The general welfare of the state has to have precedence over women's feelings,' insisted the preamble to the anti-abortion bill.[10]

Nor did the fears of population decline vanish after the war ended. On the contrary, rising divorce rates and a series of gloomy demographic predictions pushed the issue into the headlines. 'Fewer British babies. Sudden birth slump. Population may become stationary in Britain if decline lasts,' warned the *Daily Mail*, after one statistician warned that the population of England and Wales would drop to 31 million by 1975 and to a mere 17.7 million by the century's end. France's leading demographer estimated that his country's population would shrink to 29 million by 1980. Weimar Germany was transfixed by a 1927 pamphlet entitled *Geburtenrückgang* (Birth Decline) (by Richard Korherr, later the head of the SS Statistical Service and as such responsible for estimating the death toll of European Jewry for Himmler during the war), while *Volk ohne Jugend* (People without Youth) was quickly sold out on publication in 1932 and went into three editions. And global anxieties overlapped with national ones. 'The present fall in the European birth rate', warned an Italian commentator on social policy, 'is an evil against which it is necessary to react in the name of Western civilization, the supremacy of which might be threatened by the overflowing masses of the coloured races.'[11]

'Go back home and tell the women I need births, many births,' Mussolini instructed the heads of Fascist women's organizations. But the Duce and Hitler were not the only ones nor even the first to aim in this direction. Many of their propaganda ideas were modelled on the efforts of the French, who issued a medal 'for the French family' to productive mothers – bronze for five children, gold for ten – who did their patriotic duty in the aftermath of the Great War's bloodletting. Lobby groups like Belgium's League of Numerous Families pressed for tax breaks and enjoyed large memberships. Employers promoted family allowances in order to help workers have more children; such measures also made the recipients more loyal to their firm and less likely to strike. In the 1920s, Mother's Day – an invention of florists and stationers – showed in another way how capitalism was able to take advantage of the obsession with motherhood.[12]

Maternalism was drilled into young women from the time they entered school. 'Infant management' and 'domestic science' or 'housecraft' were provided in English schools to teach 'the craft, art and profession of a good mother'. French schoolgirls were trained in 'puericulture', learning how to feed and bathe babies and change their nappies. Later, young mothers were exposed to propaganda health campaigns like National Baby Week, whose Infant Welfare Conference in London in 1923 displayed items for the health-conscious mother, or to the expertise offered in Sir Frederick Truby King's Mothercraft Training Centres. Their German equivalents read magazines like Weimar's *Die Deutsche Hausfrau* (The German Housewife), published by a popular middle-class housewives' organization, or visited one of the many travelling health exhibitions organized by the Dresden Hygiene Museum in order to ensure the 'national fitness and the physical and mental health of future generations'. No fewer than seven million people visited the Ge-So-Lei (*Gesundheit, soziale Fürsorge und*

Leibesübungen/Health, social welfare and exercise) exhibition, with its prominent publicity for the League of Child-Rich Families. For many of these women, the collapse of Weimar marked the culmination of a move 'away from liberalism, towards obligations; away from the career woman, towards the housewife and mother'.[13]

And at the same time as women were being urged to turn into producers of babies, the state was making it harder for them to have abortions. 'Abortion places a heavy burden on the state,' wrote one Soviet doctor, 'because it reduces women's contribution to production.' In 1936 abortion was criminalized in the Soviet Union just as it had been previously in much of the rest of Europe. Far from communism succeeding in spreading its scandalously libertarian ideas through the continent, it had in its turn succumbed to the pro-natalist reassertion of traditional family and gender roles.[14]

Catholic countries had always been sharply opposed to abortion, but their inter-war policies became even more repressive thanks to the intervention of the Vatican, after Pope Pius XI's 1930 encyclical on the sanctity of marriage. Italy introduced heavy penalties for illegal abortion and doctors were obliged to report cases to the authorities. At one stage, the Fascist government even toyed with the idea of registering all pregnancies; its Laws on Public Safety did turn 'impeding the fecundity of the Italian people' into a crime of state, while the 1930 penal code included a chapter headed 'crimes against the integrity and health of the race'. France outlawed abortion in 1920, noting that 'in the aftermath of the war, when almost one and a half million Frenchmen sacrificed their lives so that France could have the right to live in independence and honour, it cannot be tolerated that other French have the right to make a livelihood from the spread of abortion'. But the trend extended beyond the Catholic world: Britain's 1929 Infant (Life Preservation) Act turned abortion into a statutory offence punishable by life imprisonment.[15]

Across Europe, however, the wishes of the state and of women remained far apart. Twentieth-century abortion legislation remained as difficult to police as its Napoleonic equivalent. Prosecutions were few, and failed to have much impact upon a practice which remained widespread among women of all classes. Experts in the 1930s guessed that there were as many as half a million abortions a year in France, 150,000 in Belgium. In Weimar Germany, where there were more prosecutions under anti-abortion laws than in the first years of the Third Reich, anywhere up to 800,000 abortions took place each year. Abortion, in other words, was a regular method of birth control. Laws against it did not have any appreciable impact on birth rates; they simply made the practice more dangerous and furtive for millions of women. Indeed, women may have had greater recourse to abortions than they would have done otherwise because of the state's simultaneous attack on other forms of birth control. France had banned the advertising and sale of contraceptives in 1920, followed by Belgium in 1923 and Italy in 1926. In Franco's Spain, birth control was rejected by the medical profession on religious grounds. 'All restrictions to fertility are dangerous for the health of the woman; all women darken their souls with the black crêpe of mortal sin,' warned one Spanish doctor in 1941.[16]

Outside Catholic Europe the movement for birth control was more powerful, and in the 1920s some highly effective lobby groups were able to counter the pro-natalists and argue in favour of contraception, either as a woman's right or on eugenic grounds as helpful to the nation's health. In Britain, Marie Stopes transfixed the public with her message that birth control was an important element of marital harmony. Her Society for Constructive Birth Control and Racial Progress, alongside other groups, set up birth-control clinics, flooded the country with pamphlets and operated a scheme of missionary Birth Control Caravans.[17]

The German birth control movement was even stronger and more politicized, perhaps because it faced much greater and more determined opposition, amid a far deeper sense of national crisis. For Helene Stöcker – left-wing intellectual, rationalist and leader of the Federation for the Protection of Mothers – the outlawing of contraception implied society surrendering control over nature. In her mind, birth control had a eugenic purpose, for 'as humankind has subjected all other things to its rational insight, so must it become increasingly master over one of the most important matters for humanity: the creation of a new human. One will have to find means of preventing the incurably ill or degenerate from reproducing.' As such statements showed, Left and Right were not so far apart as sometimes appeared. Both dreamed of a eugenic utopia and were confident of their ability to reach it. The Third Reich actually liberalized some Weimar abortion provisions, again on eugenic grounds, but closed down birth-control centres and clamped down on the advertising of contraceptives.[18]

Yet Europe's governments did not find it easy to lever up birth rates, or to force women out of work and into motherhood. Overall, the number of women in the European labour force barely fell, and in some countries actually rose through the inter-war period. There was no dramatic upward trend in birth rates, and the leading authority on inter-war population policies concludes that they largely failed in their purpose. German birth rates did rise through the 1930s, but the reasons probably had little to do with Nazi policy. The regime's demographers argued that National Socialism's 'psychic revolution' had prompted Germans to have more children. That argument, however, was weakened by the fact that SS men, who were expected to lead the way in ideological and sexual fervour, set the rest of the population a poor example: by 1939 61 per cent of the SS were bachelors, and its married men averaged only 1.1 children per family.[19]

Pro-natalism failed between the wars for many reasons. Perhaps the most important was that governments too often made policy on the cheap. Family allowances, tax rebates and housing subsidies were all ways of getting families to have more children, but the desperate financial situation of most governments made them reluctant to set incentives at a high enough level to make much impact. Few resorted to the imaginative Fascist expedient of taxing bachelors. Most relied on cheaper but equally ineffectual methods such as police repression and medals for prolific mothers.

Official propagandists harping away on the family often sent confusing signals. Mothers did not particularly like to see bearing children as a patriotic responsibility, nor to think that their sons would become cannon fodder. The state, by emphasizing the themes of 'duty' and 'responsibility', made parenthood sound like a burden. Worse still, it increasingly *was* a burden from the financial point of view. Job prospects were uncertain, unemployment a constant worry. The very children desired by the state were now prevented by it from paying their way through work, were forced to spend longer at school, and had now to be properly fed and housed. As the manual-labour economy was increasingly replaced by a new demand for a skilled and literate workforce, the economics of the family shifted dramatically. From being essentially a unit of production as had been the case in the traditional farming and working-class world, it was now turning into a unit of consumption.

Perhaps it is reassuring that the inter-war state should have had such little impact on overall population trends, and was unable entirely to control the reproductive decisions of ordinary individuals. What makes people have more or fewer children remains one of the great mysteries – the causes of the long-term decline in European fertility are no more settled today than the reasons for the unexpected baby boom of the 1950s – and this is perhaps why population trends arouse such apocalyptic fears. Nightmarish images of an overcrowded globe, of a Europe – whose own population is dwindling and ageing – being swamped by fast-breeding immigrants from the Third World are the post-war equivalents of those panics of the inter-war years. On the other hand, even if the inter-war state did not achieve what it wanted – faster-growing national populations – it did intervene in larger and larger areas of people's personal lives. In ways that combined encouragement and coercion, the state's desire for an improved bio-logical stock led to a range of new family policies which would endure long after the obsession with population decline had vanished.

THE STATE AS PATERFAMILIAS

Locked away in a Fascist jail, the Italian communist theoretician Antonio Gramsci noted to himself the 'educative and formative role of the state. Its aim is always that of creating new and higher types of civilization . . . of evolving even physically new types of humanity.' The social ambitions of the inter-war state bore him out. Parents were no longer left to bring up their children themselves; the fear of national decline led to the emergence of a vast array of official welfare services alongside older private religious or charitable bodies; with the interventionist public sector came the rise of the professional social worker, the housing manager, the school health visitor and the educational psychologist. The state was meddling in the most intimate matters of private life, offering – it is true – a range of new benefits, but demanding in return adherence to an increasingly explicit model of sexual behaviour.[20]

During, or immediately after, the war, national authorities set up clinics to treat venereal disease and tuberculosis and regulated so far as they could the consumption of that 'racial poison', alcohol. Britain passed laws to bring down infant and maternal mortality, and set up the Ministry of Health in 1919. Its priorities on behalf of child-rearing worried some extreme eugenicists like Sir Robert Hutchinson, President of the Royal College of Physicians, who wondered 'whether the . . . careful saving of infant lives today is really, biologically speaking, as wholesome as the mass production and lavish scrapping of the last century'. But this was very much a minority view: the birth process was increasingly medicalized and professionalized (not always to mothers' benefit), and the proportion of childbirths which took place in hospital rose from 15 per cent in 1927 to 25 per cent ten years later, and 54 per cent by 1946. Outside the UK, the state's role was expanding faster and more decisively. In France, the wartime military health service was turned into a new Ministry of Health in 1920. The Italian National Agency for Maternity and Infancy (set up in 1925) publicized modern methods of infant hygiene and promoted the medicalization of childbirth in a country where 93 per cent of all births still took place at home; running centres for mothers and children in light, new, modernist buildings, seaside sanatoriums for working women, summer camps and medical centres, it was only dissolved in 1975.[21]

The Left – operating usually at the municipal rather than the national level, and strongly influenced by the sweep of Bolshevik ideas in the Soviet Union – developed some of the most comprehensive welfare schemes of the 1920s. Social Democratic town fathers in Germany set up 'family care' offices which aimed to 'grasp the whole family' in their embrace to save it from the disintegrative force of capitalism. In 'Red Vienna' – run between 1919 and 1934 by the most ambitious socialist city council in Europe – Marxist councillors offered a 'social contract' with parents, providing special assistance such as baby clothing for needy couples in return for their commitment to responsible parenting. Where this was lacking, social workers were on hand to remove children to the municipal Child Observation Centres. All this was part of a 'Marriage and Population Policy' designed to guarantee the 'optimal conditions of upbringing' in the family. The Left as much as the Right believed – in the words of the 1937 Irish constitution – that the 'family was the natural, primary and fundamental unit of society', and it was more inclined than old-fashioned conservatives to use public powers to back this up. In turn, its modernizing activism and its ambition to create a 'new human being' provided a model for the interventionist movements of the fascist Right of the 1930s.

Family health was closely connected with living conditions in the built environment. Homes, buildings and the city itself became laboratories for new designs in improved and healthier forms of life. Old nineteenth-century slum dwellings were demolished to make way for family flats on planned estates. Social workers and housing estate managers checked on standards of hygiene and cooking methods. On Red Vienna's great new municipal estates – some 60,000 new family flats built in fifteen years – communal washrooms and bathrooms were provided: 'Instead of densely built house-blocks with narrow courts, only those were erected with large, free inner spaces into which light and air could stream. Each dwelling obtains an ante-room and its own WC inside the dwelling, as well as gas and electric light . . . Basement dwellings were no longer permitted.' Throughout inter-war Europe cities were rationalized with the aid of sweeping town planning laws, while parks were laid out, and lidos and playgrounds gave scope for the new obsession with sunlight and physical fitness. Praising the achievements of the Berlin city authorities in the 1920s, Oberbürgermeister Gustav Boess pointed to 'the new people's parks, athletic fields and playgrounds, the free baths'.[22]

The planning of modern life extended from the city to the interior of the home, systematizing movement in the private as well as the public sphere. Under the influence of the international style, left-wing designers modernized family life by treating household tasks as functions, and the family unit as an element of the Machine Age. 'The layout is designed on the basis of studies of kitchen procedure, actions, movements etc.,' wrote a Czech architect of his new 'production line' kitchen. 'Individual parts of the equipment are placed alongside each other as they come into use. The basic conveyor belt is thus a continuous circle, avoiding criss-crossing and to-and-froing.' With its built-in cupboards and long working surfaces, this kitchen must have seemed highly futuristic to most housewives in the 1920s, a vision of a world in which cooking and indeed daily life were planned and organized along industrial lines. In fact, the mechanization of home life would only really take root in the 1960s with the disappearance of cheap domestic labour; between the wars, middle-class homes in much of Europe still had maid's quarters to house the dishwasher.[23]

The Brave New World of the 1920s combined rationalism with moral high-mindedness. Laws controlled overcrowding in order to ensure 'social hygiene' by eliminating the dangers posed by slum life to morality and health. Members of the Society of Women Housing Estate Managers visited families on properties owned by the Metropolitan Housing Corporation of London and reported that 'the result has been a steady increase in the standards of cleanliness and in the general social health of the majority of their tenants'. The Corporation had set up a 'model flat' which it invited residents to visit, forming an 'ideal towards which many of the tenants are encouraged to work'. The way in which public housing shaped norms of family behaviour was even clearer in Holland, where special blocks were developed for the segregation of 'asocial families'. According to the authorities:

The selected families are placed in these housing compounds on a temporary basis for the purpose of effecting a rehabilitation and making them into clean, dependable and peaceable families. A great deal of attention is given to educating the families in the proper use of their facilities, and in showing them the error of their ways ... When a family has demonstrated that it has become a normal family, it is moved into one of the regular municipal housing estates . . . If it is finally demonstrated that the family is incurable, it is evicted.[24]

'Incurable' families: here was the language of medical science being applied to social norms and morality in a context far removed from that of Nazi Germany. In fact, the Third Reich's obsessions fitted into the broader European debate about social policy. The inter-war state justified its interventions in private life by appealing to notions of professionalism, of scientific expertise and apolitical competence. Middle-class professionals, civil servants and public administrators presented themselves as a modern instrument of social management, doctors working on the body of society and concerned with its health.

American relief officials, for instance, working in Europe after 1918, saw themselves explicitly above the political fray as they distributed food relief to the starving peasants of Poland and the Ukraine, set up children's clinics and free milk in Vienna, or supervised the resettlement of millions of refugees in Greece. The Rockefeller Foundation sponsored campaigns to eradicate tuberculosis by 'applying the art of advertising to the facts of science'. But Europeans, too, liked to see social policy as a non-political matter, a question of 'social hygiene'. In Britain, for instance, members of the British Social Hygiene Council called for the 'institutionalization' of the mentally ill, health and sex education in schools, better housing and sanitation and improvements in child nutrition. In France, the Health Ministry was advised by a Conseil Supérieur d'Hygiène Sociale. Society was seen as an object for social engineering, in which enlightened and impartial policy was made in a spirit of rational detachment from political passions.[25]

Nowhere were the ambiguities of this kind of approach more evident than among the eugenicists – those people, in other words, on both Left and Right who believed that it was indeed possible to produce 'better' human beings through the right kind of social policies. Increasingly accepted by social scientists and administrators before the First World War, the eugenics movement was boosted by the mass killing of the war itself. In his welcome address to the second International Eugenics Congress in 1921, Henry Fairfield Osborn of the American Museum of Natural History observed that 'I doubt that there has ever been a moment in the world's history when an international conference on race character and betterment has been more important than the present. Europe, in patriotic self-sacrifice on both sides of the World War, has lost much of the heritage of centuries of civilization which can never be regained. In certain parts of Europe, the worst elements of society have gained the ascendancy and threaten the destruction of the best.'[26]

Prompted by such fears, societies dedicated to the promotion of eugenics, or to its German cousin 'racial hygiene', spread from western Europe and Scandinavia to Spain and the Soviet Union. Enthusiasts promoted national fitness in Hungary and Czechoslovakia and established ties with patriotic sports associations. The Russian Eugenics Office, founded in 1921, called for 'comparative work on eugenics by scientific and social workers in all specialties' and forged links with the Eugenic Record Office in the USA, the German Society for Race and Social Biology and the British Eugenics Education Society. Thus the movement was not simply the sinister proto-Nazi precursor it looks like today; it was, rather, a broad church with confidence in its own scientific standing. Believers included social democrats and Liberal reformers like Keynes and Beveridge in Britain, as well as conservatives and right-wing authoritarians. Some were anti-Semites, but some leading German 'racial hygienists' were Jews. Some stressed 'negative' measures such as sterilization; others 'positive' policies to improve fitness, nutrition and public health, warding off racial decline through fresh air, regular exercise and sunbathing. What they shared was confidence in the power of the state and public authorities to shape society for the better.

Of course, the nature of the coming 'new man' and the broader social setting were defined rather differently by eugenicists across the political spectrum. Social Democrats focused on the condition of the urban working class, and the city more generally. For many conservatives, on the other hand, the vision of a mechanized industrial world where human beings were reduced to functional components in a labour process was the problem not the answer to the crisis of modern society. Le Corbusier's dreams of 'the contemporary city with three million inhabitants' – 'la Ville radieuse' (1935) – left them cold.

They identified social health not with the city but with the countryside, not with industry and the machine but with the soil and manual labour. For many eugenicists, cities had paradoxical effects upon human fertility: they made the middle classes sterile at the same time as inducing the lower classes to breed with appalling speed. In fact, prompted by eugenic concerns, a deep-rooted ambivalence could be encountered across Europe about the social and biological consequences of urbanization.

Before 1914 Europe's surplus population had been siphoned off across the Atlantic, or settled in far-flung colonies. But after 1918, America closed its doors and transatlantic emigration on the scale of the past became impossible. The imperial powers tried to encourage people to become farmers in Tanganyika, Libya or the East Indies, but few had found this idea attractive in the past, and fewer still were tempted in the 1920s. Peasants looking for work, or refugees from persecution, flocked into the cities, and the number of Europe's conurbations with more than one million inhabitants doubled between the wars. This flight to the cities was on a limited scale compared with what would take place after 1950, yet in the depressed and anxious conditions of the 1920s and 1930s it provoked deep unease.

Alarmed at the growth of the 'Great Cities', the Secretary of the German Society for Housing Reform saw them threatening 'the roots of our whole existence . . . biologically through the enormous decline in birth-rates . . . politically through the negation of the bases of a healthy democracy . . . militarily through the obvious and particularly great vulnerability of big cities in wartime, and morally through the enormous obstacles that the contemporary big city places in the way of the necessary moral regeneration of our nation'. Sir Arthur Keith – an eminent British anthropologist and President of the British Association for the Advancement of Science – contrasted the life led by modern city-dwellers with that of their 'tribal ancestors' and became uneasy about 'the effects of modern civilization on the minds and bodies of those who are subjected to it for many generations'. The biologist Konrad Lorenz, whose writings after 1938 betrayed a sympathy for National Socialism, argued similarly that the 'domestication' of human beings by modern life was leading to racial deterioration and was thus opposed to true evolution. Whereas ancient village life was supposed to have bred a sense of community and encouraged child-rearing, the modern city offered pleasures and temptations which threatened family solidarity and fed individual selfishness and alienation: its bitter fruits were youthful 'asocials' and 'psychopaths' as well as sexual hedonism shaped by the easy availability of casual partners and birth control. Cinema – that post-war apparition – was seen as a poisonous influence, condemned by Church leaders, criticized by conservative politicians and studied by social scientists.[27]

Providing public housing with allotments and private gardens, or shifting the focus of building from city centres to suburban homesteads and new pseudo-villages was one way of trying to cope. In Poland, Scandinavia and Germany, the authorities built as though for urban farmers. In the UK, private builders responded to similar desires among their buyers by offering mock-Tudor and other 'pre-urban' styles.[28] But as the political outlook in Europe darkened, this public love affair with an idealized countryside intensified. Across the continent, the modernist idiom of the 1920s – internationalist, mechanized – gave way in the arts to a more nationalist concern with the organic and with a life close to nature. Rationalism was replaced by an emphasis on the instinctual, individualism by the tribal and communal life, the brain by the body. Weimar's New Realism was succeeded by Hitler's Aryan landscapes of fields and farmers, just as in France the cosmopolitan art scene of Paris was challenged by the avowedly Gallic *paysages* of Dunoyer de Segonzac and Ozenfant. Fascist Italy had started out worshipping the machine, Futurism and the destruction of the past; by the 1930s it had embraced classicism, history and the land.

Yet once again, in practice, the state found it difficult imposing its wishes upon its recalcitrant population. Mussolini tried to prevent country-dwellers settling in towns without work, deporting new unemployed arrivals back to the provinces. This did not work very well. Others tried to make the rural life more attractive by giving loans to new farmers and building new housing estates in country areas. In Eire, the government subsidized remote Gaelic-speaking communities. In Britain – where urbanization had begun earlier than almost anywhere else – access to the countryside was made easier for city-dwellers. It was natural that a prominent eugenicist like Lord Horder, royal physician and President of the Eugenics Society, should have combined an interest in mental health and family planning with a concern for physical fitness, the Boy Scouts and the National Park movement.

But in fact nothing stemmed the movement citywards. Cities remained magnets of employment and cultural freedom. Moreover, the state itself had only a limited interest in following up its own rhetoric: in an era when national power depended upon industrial progress, the country life could never present a convincing alternative to the city. 'It is necessary to correct many legends concerning urbanization and populous cities,' wrote an Italian journalist in 1925. 'The idyllic country, the creator of vigorous loins and the nursery of the long-lived, is a work of poets; in any case, it cannot be in accord with the development of industry.' For nation-states determined to fight for their place in the world, cities might look dangerous to national health and power, but they were indispensable nonetheless.[29]

QUANTITY AND QUALITY

Bodies were on display between the wars as never before, parading in what a previous generation would have regarded as underwear or scandalous near-nudity. Footballers' shorts crept up to around the knee, while the members of the human pyramids photographed by Rodchenko in Russia even went without vests. Open-air public swimming pools were available for recreation and pleasure; new stadia were built – in Wembley, Vienna, Berlin – for grander sporting and political events. Massed together in ranks and rows, these bodies projected collective unity and political might. In 1931, 100,000 socialists marched round Vienna's Ring before watching a show in the new stadium in the Prater in which 4,000 performers enacted the overthrow of capitalism. This was a vast spectacle – with banner parades and mass callisthenics, choruses, chants and oath ceremonies. It represented a deliberate projection of the military might of the workers' movement, inspired in many ways by the Bolshevik Proletkult festivals of the early 1920s. In turn, it looks to us very like the Nuremberg Party rallies of the Nazi Party. Even placid Britain – in a much less charged political atmosphere – offered mass pageants like the 1924 Empire Festival or the Albert Hall spectaculars laid on by the Women's League of Health and Beauty. In most countries, keeping fit was not so much the matter of consumer choice it would become after 1950 as a national or class duty: 'The body culture of the Worker is the Core of Socialist Construction', ran the slogan on a Soviet poster. Right-wing movements from the conservative Boy Scouts to the Romanian fascists in the Iron Guard took a similar view. The more politics was seen in terms of military struggle and national survival, the more important became the physical fitness of the collectivity.

But the state had not merely to promote the healthy body; it had also, in one way or another, to ensure it was not contaminated by the unhealthy. It had, in terms of eugenicist thought, to concern itself with the quality as well as the quantity of the nation's human stock.

Negative eugenics – obsessed by the idea of social degeneration – was especially preoccupied by the threat posed by the mentally ill. Ever since Darwin's cousin, Francis Galton, called for 'stern compulsion' to 'check the birth rate of the unfit', eugenicists had urged state action to stop the breeding of racial inferiors. In Britain, the pre-1914 Liberal government studied the problem of the 'feeble-minded' – a catch-all category which included the deaf and dumb, those 'unable to earn a living' or 'incapable of managing themselves or their affairs with ordinary prudence'. To prime minister Asquith, the young Winston Churchill privately described the high birth rate of the 'mentally deficient' alongside the 'restriction of the progeny among all the thrifty, energetic and superior stocks' as 'a very terrible danger to the race'. In 1913 a law was passed providing for the detention of 'mental defectives' in special institutions in order to prevent them having children.[30]

Poor young women who in one way or another threatened prevailing social norms thereby found themselves at risk of being seized on the flimsiest of pretexts – at the behest of father, husband, doctor or employer – and held for years among those with genuine mental problems. It was, for example, only after his father's death that the Bristol working-class boy called Archie Leach – better known to the world as Cary Grant – found out that the mother he thought had abandoned him and his father was actually living in an institution where his father had placed her in order to be able to live with his mistress.

Yet holding people in asylums – the British solution – was an expensive means of preventing them having children. Sterilization – a cheaper alternative, but one which involved actual physical violence to the body – had been widely discussed in late-nineteenth-century Germany and Scandinavia and actually introduced into several American states. The USA was at the forefront of negative eugenics around this time, and by 1921 2,233 people had been legally sterilized there, mostly in California. But several doctors in Weimar Germany were also carrying out illegal voluntary sterilizations without sanction.[31]

Sterilization was a precise answer to the issue which so worried eugenicists of differential birth rates between 'superior' and 'inferior' population groups. It targeted the fast-breeding inferiors – however defined – and thus supplemented the positive welfare measures which the state could take to encourage more 'valuable' births. The financial crisis of 1929 made sterilization's relative cheapness seem increasingly attractive, and laws providing for voluntary sterilization were passed between 1928 and 1936 in Switzerland, Denmark, Germany, Sweden, Norway, Finland and Estonia. Even in liberal Britain the debate was reopened by the 1929 Wood Report on Mental Deficiency, which found that there had been an alarming growth in mental deficiency over the previous two decades, and warned that there was a 'social problem group' – whose size it estimated at no less than four million, roughly 10 per cent of the total population – which posed an acute threat to national health. Eugenicists proposed sterilization as the answer, after the Eugenics Society's Social Problem Group Investigation Committee found that poor living conditions were caused by mental deficiency. As in our own times, the poor – labelled as 'the socially inadequate' – were being blamed for their own poverty: slum-dwellers were the 'chief architects of slumdom'.[32]

British eugenicists – reflecting the characteristic national obsession with class – ran into a wall of opposition. Church, medical and labour leaders helped block proposed sterilization legislation, and there were legal complications as well. All this reflected the rather mild sense of national crisis which existed there compared with on the Continent. But while eugenics was losing ground in Britain, it was gaining it in Germany, where the desire for national reassertion was as strong as anywhere. The National Socialist seizure of power swiftly ushered in compulsory sterilization laws which targeted first the mentally ill, then 'dangerous habitual criminals', and eventually juvenile offenders as well. By 1937 over 200,000 people had been sterilized, compared with slightly over 3,000 in the USA, among them gypsies, the so-called Rhineland Bastards (children of liaisons between German women and black French soldiers), the 'morally feeble-minded', 'disorderly wanderers', the 'workshy' and 'asocials'.[33]

To this point, Hitler's Germany realized on a massive scale a policy of coercive social engineering which other governments – in Sweden and elsewhere – followed to a more limited extent. But Nazi ambitions ranged further still. In 1939 the regime moved from sterilization to mass murder. Under Hitler's special authorization, between 70,000 and 93,000 inmates of asylums and clinics were gassed before the euthanasia campaign was run down after public opposition from Church leaders. After 1941, the killing of mental patients continued on a smaller scale, mostly by lethal injection, while the euthanasia experts found new employment running the death camps in Poland and operating mobile gassing units.

These measures formed part of a new approach to social policy which promoted the health of the 'national community' at the same time as suppressing its internal biological enemies. On the one hand, it helped newly-weds with marriage loans (granted, naturally, on condition that the woman gave up work, and that both partners were racially sound) and offered child benefits, free vacations and day-care facilities. On the other, it rounded up beggars and assigned them to camps or compulsory labour schemes. 'The construction of a lunatic asylum costs 6 million RM. How many houses at 15,000 RM each could have been built for that amount?' a maths school book asked children. What was striking was not merely the extremism of the regime's philosophy, but the lengths to which the most modern state apparatus in Europe would now go to implement it.

Even before 1933, the German state displayed an ability to organize repressive social policies with unusual efficiency. Special police units targeted the gypsies (helped by the 1926 Bavarian Law for the Combating of Gypsies, Travellers and the Workshy), while unemployed men were labelled as 'workshy antisocials' and dragooned into militarized 'comrade groups' to keep them off the streets. But after 1933, such actions were centralized and intensified, backed by the findings of racial scientists such as Dr Ernst Rüdin, whose 'thirty years of research in psychiatric genealogy' provided the scientific justification for the new sterilization laws. The state financed the country's leading Kaiser Wilhelm Institute for Anthropology, Heredity and Eugenics, to which a young wartime researcher on their staff called Josef Mengele would send eyes and internal human organs back from his laboratory in Auschwitz.

Demographers and statisticians helped organize enormous surveys of criminal and medical records, while doctors, medical researchers and psychologists sat on the Hereditary Health Courts which gave verdicts on cases of sterilization. Criminal biologists conducted investigations into 'criminal types', traced their genealogies and built up data banks. Far from being regarded as unscientific and barbaric, such research was modern enough to interest leading policemen and lawmakers of other countries. Only the outbreak of war in 1939 prevented Sir Norman Kendal, head of Britain's Scotland Yard, from taking up a German invitation to tour the Dachau concentration camp in order to study contemporary policing methods, and to hear Arthur Nebe, head of the Criminal Police, lecturing on new techniques of crime control.

The racial nature of the Nazi welfare state targeted above all the country's Jews. They were gradually but systematically excluded from the 'national community' – first dismissed from public employment, then subjected to economic boycott and deprived of the protection of the law. In 1935, the Nuremberg laws for the first time offered a systematic definition of being Jewish and turned Jews into subjects not citizens: the criminalization of interracial sexual relations and the prohibition of mixed marriages followed swiftly. The systematic Aryanization of Jewish properties – notably in Vienna after the *Anschluss* in 1938 – could also be seen as part of this coercive and exclusionary racial welfare programme: more apartments were obtained by Nazi Aryanization policies in the Austrian capital in three years than had been built by the Social Democrats in the 1920s.

The exclusion, persecution and eventual extermination of the Jews was the culmination of a social philosophy which based itself upon the protection of the *Volksgemeinschaft* – a racially defined national community. '[Weimar governments] failed in the case of community aliens,' wrote a Munich law professor in 1944. 'They did not make knowledge of eugenics and criminal biology the basis of sound welfare and criminal policies. Liberalistic thinking saw only the "rights" of the individual, and was more concerned with the protection of rights vis-à-vis the state than with the well-being of the community. In National Socialism, the individual does not count so far as society is concerned.'[34]

The emergence of the German racial welfare state – which was in so many ways the apotheosis of very widespread trends in European social thought – inevitably provoked an intense debate elsewhere. The exclusion of entire groups from the benefits enjoyed by the 'national community', the definition of that community in terms of racial biology, the recourse to police repression and medical violence highlighted all the ambiguities present in European thinking about race.

In an age of empire and social Darwinism, notions of racial hierarchy were ubiquitous, and few Europeans on Left or Right did not believe in ideas of racial superiority in one form or another, or accept their relevance to colonial policy. So-called 'scientific racism' was taken seriously and influenced public attitudes. Sir Harry Johnston, for instance, a British colonial commentator, had defended the new science of anthropology to the public in 1908 on the grounds that it would help the rulers of empire decide whether races should be preserved, allowed to interbreed, or forced to die out. German anthropologists who shaped SS racial policy in eastern Europe during the Second

World War had begun their careers with scholarly articles on 'race mixing' in pre-1914 colonial Africa and Asia, where their concerns were shared by British and French colleagues.[35]

On the other hand, the application – and in such a radical form – of these ideas inside Europe was another matter entirely. In general, the concept of race had an exceptionally amorphous and indeterminate meaning, and varied widely from one country to another. Hitler's policies made it harder to avoid confronting and working out these ambiguities, especially as they coincided with new discoveries in genetics, serology and the causation of mental illness which cast doubt on earlier assumptions about the scientific foundations of racial thought.

In few countries was biological racism as central to the definition of the nation as it became in inter-war Germany. References to *la stirpe* (race) in Italy, or to 'the health of the race' in Britain were usually vague ways of talking about historical communities, with little impact on policy. Italian eugenicists were, after all, in favour of racial mixing, which they believed led to 'hybrid vigour', while the British were more concerned about differential birth rates between classes. In France, the nation was defined mainly in terms of language and culture, in the Balkans in terms of language and religion. Racial prejudice and anti-Semitism were omnipresent but not necessarily decisive in shaping policy. To be sure, the Third Reich spawned imitators, and hardline racialist movements flourished in Poland and Hungary. In General Metaxas's Greece, Jews were not allowed to enter the regime's youth movement. In Fascist Italy, the 1938 racial laws led to hundreds of dismissals from the universities and the civil service. Yet none of this – not even in Italy – could be compared in extent or intensity with what was happening in Nazi Germany.

In France, bitterly polarized as few other countries were between Left and Right, the 1930s saw a strengthening of both racism and anti-racism. In the 1920s high levels of immigration – from Poland, Algeria and elsewhere – had been welcomed as one way of boosting the birth rate; but in the 1930s anti-immigrant sentiment grew and large crowds – among them the young François Mitterrand – demanded the deportation of the new arrivals. As in the USA and the UK earlier, racial issues were closely tied to calls for immigration controls against 'aliens'. At the same time, tracts like René Martial's 1934 *La Race française* were countered by anti-racist journals like *Races et racisme*. It is, in fact, from this time that the concept of 'racism' itself dates. Ludwig Hirszfeld, who together with his wife Hanna had pioneered research into blood types after the First World War, wrote to dissociate himself 'from those who attach the blood groups to the mystique of race'.[36]

In Britain, the attack on scientific racism was still stronger, though it is not clear whether this was due to better public understanding of the scientific issues, to lower levels of inter-war immigration, a relatively weak and nebulous tradition of thinking about nationalism, or simply greater outright antipathy to trends in Nazi Germany. But leading researchers into the causes of mental illness demolished the myth of the 'social problem group', and with it the mainstay of the hardline eugenicist case in Britain. At the same time, a group of left-wing scientists and intellectuals campaigned against scientific racism.[37]

Typical of the works produced in this spirit in the English-speaking world were Jacques Barzun's *Race: a Study in Modern Superstition* and Ashley Montagu's *Man's Most Dangerous Myth: the Fallacy of Race*. But the sharpest attack of all came in a book called *We Europeans: A Survey of 'Racial' Problems*, which was a best-seller in 1936. Written by the biologist Julian Huxley with the elderly anthropologist A. C. Haddon, *We Europeans* was a ferocious assault on what its authors described as the 'pseudo-science of "racial biology"'. Huxley himself was a confirmed believer in eugenics, who felt Nazi racism had done the movement much harm. He underlined the vagueness of the term 'race' and cast doubt on the existence of such a thing as 'racial group sentiment' (a concept beloved not only by the Nazis but by British racial anthropologists such as Sir Arthur Keith). Huxley observed sarcastically:

Our German neighbours have ascribed to themselves a teutonic type that is fair, long-headed, tall and virile. Let us make a composite picture of a typical Teuton from the most prominent exponents of this view. Let him be as blond as Hitler, as dolichocephalic as Rosenberg, as tall as Goebbels, as slender as Goering and as manly as Streicher. How much would this resemble the German ideal?[38]

In common with other British researchers of the time, Huxley and Haddon insisted that there were no 'pure races' in the biological sense in Europe. Environment, they argued, was more important than heredity in shaping the sense of communal identity, and they recommended using the term 'ethnic group' rather than 'race' as the former lacked the latter's misleading biological associations. But their book ended with a sombre warning:

The violent racialism to be found in Europe today is a symptom of Europe's exaggerated nationalism: it is an attempt to justify nationalism on a non-nationalist basis, to find a firm basis in objective science for ideas and policies which are generated internally by a particular economic and political system, and have real relevance only in reference to that system. The cure for the racial myth, with its accompanying self-exaltation and persecution of others, which now besets Europe, is a re-orientation of the nationalist ideal, and in the practical sphere, an abandonment of claims by nations to absolute sovereign rights. Meanwhile, however, science and the scientific spirit can do something by pointing out the biological realities of the ethnic situation, and by refusing to lend her sanction to the absurdities and horrors perpetrated in her name. Racialism is a myth and a dangerous myth at that.[39]

It was in the Second World War that Sir William Beveridge offered his 'welfare state' as a contrast to the Nazi 'warfare state'. But between the two world wars, welfare and warfare were intimately connected, and social policies to improve population numbers and health reflected the anxieties of nation-states keen to defend or reassert themselves in a world of enemies. The Second World War fostered a new international anti-racist consensus, which was bolstered by new discoveries in genetics, marshalled by politically committed scientists such as Huxley, and reinforced by the knowledge of what Nazi policies had ultimately led to. All of this helped discredit attitudes which had been commonplace in the inter-war era. In Europe, a belief in scientific racism only lingered on among some anthropologists and social scientists in central Europe, who continue to see 'long-skulled' and 'big-boned' racial types around them to this day. But this is a relatively peripheral group with little impact on social policy. In general, it is now hard for us – living in a more individualistic world – to appreciate how far many welfare policies of the post-war decades grew out of a very different set of concerns about the decline, degeneration and reinvigoration of the nation and the race.[40]

4

The Crisis of Capitalism

Father used to joke a lot in those days. But after two years the
picture changed. One day father came home looking downcast.
Mother looked at him and knew what had happened. He had
lost his job . . . Now my father has been unemployed for over
three years. We used to believe he would get a job again one day,
but now even we children have given up all hope.
> – Hanna S. (fourteen years old), December 1932[1]

'This house sees more hope in Moscow than Detroit.'
> – Motion debated at the Cambridge Union, 1932

'It was as if someone had picked up the world and shaken it into utter
confusion,' wrote the novelist Sholem Asch. 'There were no permanent
values. What were paper or diamonds, gold, houses or factories? A
transient illusion, a fleeting gleam, a dissolving fantasy.'[2] After the
Great War, Europe's economic life was in chaos; in Poland, four
currencies were in use simultaneously; 'starving Vienna' had been
turned into a 'giant city' in a dwarf country and its streets were filled
with refugees and hungry former imperial civil servants: by the summer
of 1922 the Austrian crown stood at 83,600 to the dollar. Prices
everywhere were hundreds or thousands of times higher than before
the war. The Greek government pioneered a new approach to taxation
by calling in all banknotes, cutting them in half and returning only
half to their original owners. But matters were not much better in
western Europe, where a brief post-war boom quickly petered out,

leaving more than two million unemployed in Britain alone. In 1923 Weimar Germany was rocked by hyperinflation, the same year that both Hitler and the communists tried to seize power by force: the prospects for reconstructing capitalism in Europe looked bleak.

Four years of total war had completely destroyed the traditional monetary foundations of nineteenth-century bourgeois confidence and economic stability. The war had forced countries to suspend the convertibility of their currencies and to abandon those basic principles of Victorian capitalism: the gold standard and free trade. Governments had accumulated enormous debts to finance the war, and Europe's main creditor powers had ended the conflict in debt to the United States. The war had also boosted the power of organized labour, and made it harder to keep down wages. It had destroyed old trading networks on the Continent itself, and it had encouraged new centres of industrial and agricultural production outside Europe, so that as the war ended Europe's producers faced increased global competition.

At the same time, the success of the Bolshevik Revolution and the emergence of the Soviet Union presented European capitalism with an unprecedented challenge. 'Russia is no Africa, Mexico or Java,' insisted a Russian artist in 1922. 'We and western Europe live in the same times and are no longer distant from one another.' In the aftermath of the 'global social revolution', he continued, it was the Soviet Union which was teaching the rest of the world its future and the possibility of a 'new beginning'. In the early 1920s, in particular, such a prospect made European statesmen shudder, and propelled them to take the task of reconstructing the continent's economy seriously.

In this task, however, there was something of a paradox. Bringing Europe back to the 'normalcy' of the world before 1914, as so many wanted, meant trying to return to free trade, fixed exchange rates and minimal state involvement. This was a world in which the state kept out of economic affairs and left investment decisions to private businessmen and the mass of individual bondholders. The task of fighting a world war had, of course, forced the state to intervene more heavily than before in economic affairs in order to 'organize' economic life; but few in Britain or France, the two countries which would take the lead in Europe's economic reconstruction, wanted to see such wartime state activism continue long into the peace. Thus the first plans drawn up for continental recovery involved statesmen relying heavily on the private sector for backing – with predictably unfruitful results.

Lloyd George and Aristide Briand, the British and French premiers at the start of the 1920s, both activists by temperament, agreed that Europe's problem was common to East and West, and therefore needed an overall approach. As they wrote in a preparatory memorandum:

The markets of Central and Eastern Europe are essential to the well-being of European industry. If those markets cannot be reconstituted, Eastern and South-Eastern Europe will lose millions of their population and reconstruction will become progressively more difficult; and the conditions which produce misery and starvation in the East will doom the industrial population of Western Europe to a long period of under-employment during which they will compete with each other in markets incapable of taking more than a part of the goods they are anxious to produce. In such circumstances, the economic rehabilitation of Europe will be impossible. Inflation will continue, the cost of living will rise, the standard of life will be depressed; and in the West of Europe as in the East, starvation and under-feeding will waste the fibre of the wage-earning and the professional classes . . .[3]

What the British and French proposed was to set up an international investment consortium which would inject private capital into central–eastern Europe. Needless to say, this precursor of the European Bank of Reconstruction and Development (which was entrusted with a similar task in the 1990s) was not a great success: western bankers were not going to lend money until there was some order in eastern Europe; they would follow stability and could not be relied upon to create it. The capitalist equilibrium of the continent had been shattered, but European capitalism itself was capable of only a half-hearted response.

The failure of the Lloyd George–Briand scheme underlined the weakness and hesitancy of post-war market forces and the necessity for some kind of government action if capitalism was to be successfully rebuilt. For this purpose, the British and French turned to their intergovernmental creation, the League of Nations, which did play an important part in the reconstruction effort in the mid-1920s. Not merely a diplomatic forum, the League took an active part in brokering financial deals between impoverished governments and western bond-holders. In Austria, Estonia, Hungary, Greece and elsewhere it raised money for governments on condition they stabilized their budgets, and it insisted upon the foundation of independent central banks. Just as eager Harvard economists rushed into eastern Europe after the fall of communism, so seventy years earlier western bankers and financial experts helped redesign these war-ravaged and impoverished econo-mies on the approved liberal lines. Westerners acted as supervisors of central banks, inspectors of tax revenues and even chaired powerful committees resettling millions of refugees.

Although the League of Nations' key Financial Committee had members drawn from a number of countries, it was the prominent part played by British delegates which attracted comment and sus-picion. Given London's traditional eminence as an international capi-tal market, it was perhaps not surprising that the Bank of England should be accused of financial imperialism and of wishing to bring about 'some sort of dictatorship over the central banks of Europe'. Sir Otto Niemeyer, the most powerful and energetic British delegate, who sat on the Financial Committee from 1922 to 1937, also just happened to be a director of the Bank of England. It was easy to see the League as the cat's-paw of City plutocrats, stretching out over the rich pickings of a defenceless continent.[4]

In fact Montagu Norman, the eccentric Governor of the Bank of England, did have some vague, long-term pipe-dream of a free-trading Europe with central banks linked to sterling. He hoped to preserve London's pre-eminence as a centre of international banking through, for example, the idea of 'an Economic Federation to include half a dozen countries on or near the Danube'. Yet this was very much a *liberal* dream, and was undermined by the British government's reluctance to involve itself in economic affairs. In the long run, in fact, the laissez-faire tradition in British economic diplomacy under-mined all the plans of Niemeyer and Norman, and made Britain a very half-hearted architect of capitalist revival: the market was more sacrosanct in London than perhaps anywhere else. With the exception of Lloyd George, the British government was not convinced that central and eastern Europe really mattered, given the small fraction of British trade and investment the area attracted compared with the USA, western Europe or the empire. The Foreign Office was suspicious of the League of Nations and unimpressed by the work of its Financial Committee. There were thus clear limits to Whitehall's willingness to foster a new economic order in Europe.[5]

Capitalist reconstruction was also weakened by the tensions which surfaced between the Entente powers over the desirability of fostering recovery in Germany, a question discussed largely in relation to the issue of reparations. Britain had little sympathy with what it saw as French anti-Germanism and Paris's efforts to saddle Weimar with a massive reparations bill. The French, in turn, felt let down by London. In early 1923 the tussle across the Rhine reached its climax when, provoked by German non-payments, the French and Belgian governments sent in troops and occupied the Ruhr. In fact, the occupation of the Ruhr was a humiliating fiasco which only served to underline the limits to French power. In Germany itself inflation spiralled out of control, and by December prices were 126 trillion times higher than before the war. The French faced strong pressure from both the British and the Americans to negotiate a way out, just as a budgetary and financial crisis in France itself underlined the country's own fragility. All this helps explain why these events have been seen as 'the end of French predominance in Europe'.

The hard lesson learned from the Ruhr crisis was that the Versailles victors could not win the peace except by joint action. More important, it demonstrated that the capitalist reconstruction of Europe could not be brought about by Europe alone. Among its major economies – France, Britain and Germany – there was simply too much ill-feeling: the USA, turned by the war into the world's greatest creditor power, also had to be involved. Private American loan capital had in fact been flowing into western Europe from the end of the war; American relief organizations had been coping with famine in the Ukraine and refugee resettlement in the Balkans. It was the American *government* that needed to be cajoled out of isolationism. The Ruhr crisis and the resulting diplomatic impasse provided the catalyst, and the Americans were brought back in. For five brief years, an American-brokered deal brought peace on the reparations issue and American capital propped up Europe's recovery.

America's re-entry into Europe's affairs, however, intensified the Old Continent's fears of a transatlantic takeover and reflected all the anxieties and fears that the war had provoked about the decline of European values. For the first time America's economic supremacy challenged its own economic and cultural strength. England's roads, warned J. B. Priestley in his *English Journey* (1934), now 'only differ in a few minor details from a few thousand such roads in the United States, where the same tooth-pastes and soaps and gramophone records are being sold, the very same films are being shown'. Books like André Siegfried's best-seller, *America Comes of Age* (1927), warned of the challenge ahead.[6]

In fact, American multinational expansion abroad may have been faster between 1924 and 1929 than any time in the post-1945 era. Politicians of all hues, unionists and businessmen worried about Europe's inability to compete and drew a now-familiar moral. As British Labour leader Ramsay MacDonald warned: 'The United States has already developed as a super-national power. Unless Europe can do the same, the doom of her economic pretensions is certain. The recognition of these facts is dawning on the Continent . . . The goal is still very far-off . . . But there are signs that a movement towards it has begun, which may prove the decisive issue of the twentieth century.'[7]

Pushed ahead by the French, encouraged by the upswing of the mid-1920s, the proponents of pan-European economic cooperation gathered heart. Signing the 1925 Locarno treaties, which ushered in a new era of Franco-German cooperation, Aristide Briand heralded them as 'the draft of the constitution of a European family within the orbit of the League of Nations . . . the beginning of a magnificent work, the renewal of Europe'. The 1927 International Economic Conference in Geneva, gathered at French initiative, met – according to its chairman – to move towards 'an economic league of Nations whose long-term goal . . . is the creation of a United States of Europe'.

This he envisaged as 'the sole economic formula which can fight effectively against the United States of America'. Leading British industrialists shared this confidence in the inevitability of the emergence of 'an organized European bloc'. But, as the future was to show, the French lacked the strength, the British the will, to realize such a venture. Whitehall was torn between Europe and Empire, and increasingly plumped for the latter. The first time round, the cause of European unity was stillborn; it would require heavy American involvement, a Western-oriented Germany and the Cold War to make it work.[8]

From some points of view, the mid-1920s were a period of prosperity, stabilization and success. One after the other, currencies were brought under control; Britain, Italy, Germany and France all fixed their currencies to gold. Wild fluctuations in exchange rates and hyperinflation were succeeded by a period of gentle inflation which stimulated business and encouraged growth. New central banks started operating, speculation was dampened, investor confidence revived and the main money markets started lending on a large scale throughout Europe. It is an indication of the attractions of this revival of capitalism, and the rewards that apparently lay ahead for those who joined the club, that Yugoslavia returned to the gold standard as late as June 1931.

Yet the recovery was a fragile one and even before the Wall Street crash of late 1929 there were warning signs of what was to come. German and British trade figures remained lower than they had been in 1913. Few countries took advantage of the relatively prosperous mid-1920s to reduce tariffs. They were more concerned to shelter their own producers from the pressure of world markets, where prices for basic commodities were already *falling* from the middle of the decade. 'Today more or less everywhere – in the Far East, India, South America, South Africa – industrial regions are in being, or coming into being,' wrote an alarmed Oswald Spengler, 'which, owing to the low scale of wages, will face us with deadly competition. The unassailable privileges of the white races have been thrown away, squandered, betrayed . . . The exploited world is beginning to take its revenge on its lords.'[9]

In addition to this new global competition with its harshly

deflationary impact, Europe's recovery in the 1920s was also constrained by its own economic policies and theories. The simple fact was that the existing rules of the game were not designed primarily to boost production or to provide work. The overwhelming priority attached to returning to gold required doses of deflation to bring down wage and price levels, and savage welfare cuts. The political consequences could be seen graphically in Britain, where this policy was pursued especially vigorously: it was sterling's return to gold in 1925, driven through by the Chancellor, Winston Churchill, which led directly to the General Strike the following year; and if the crisis of 1929–31 had less impact there than in Germany it was only because unemployment in Britain remained at high levels through the 1920s.

The basic problem across Europe was that the war had bred in the bourgeoisie a desire to return to pre-war stability at the same time that it had led governments to promise working-class and peasant recruits a new, higher standard of living. 'Homes fit for heroes' did not square easily with a return to gold and democracy suffered as a result. Conflicts between labour and capital – loosely patched up during the war – acquired a new intensity which would ease off only with the abandonment of laissez-faire after 1932. Some industrialists and trade unionists called for a very different industrial policy – based on an American model of high wages, high-volume production and high productivity. But fears of inflation ruled this out and it would not be tried until the Americanization of western Europe after 1950.

Most critical of all for the fragile recovery of the 1920s was its dependence upon an inherently unstable international flow of capital. Britain, which had been the world's banker before 1914, was able to lend less than ever before. German reparations to the Allies, and Allied war debt repayments to the USA, were all contingent upon the willingness of Americans to lend to Europe. Because nearly half of the lending to Germany after 1924 was short-term, international financial stability was made dependent upon the decisions of thousands of small investors. After 1945 the Americans learned their lesson, and helped rebuild Europe through government loans, but in the 1920s this would not have fitted with prevailing conceptions of the state's role in international finance, where it was supposed loosely to act as guarantor rather than direct provider of funds. In 1928 investors shifted capital back across the Atlantic to take advantage of a stock exchange boom then developing; the following year, they liquidated what remained of their assets in Europe for the opposite reason. The result was an unparalleled international financial disaster.

The 1929 Wall Street crash led to bank closures, currency depreciations and monetary chaos. In turn, the financial crisis provoked bankruptcies, lower output, shortened working weeks and growing dole queues. International trade was collapsing, helping to provoke an agrarian crisis of immense proportions as sharply falling farm prices drove farmers into debt, leading surpluses of unwanted produce to mount up, reducing the domestic demand for manufactured goods and accelerating the flight of unemployed hands from the country areas into Europe's cities. As food stocks ran to waste or were deliberately destroyed, while hunger and poverty increased, market-driven capitalism seemed less and less rational.

The way governments responded has been a source of controversy ever since. Most followed the conventional wisdom which was to tighten belts, reduce public spending and wait for investor confidence to return. There was no direct policy to tackle unemployment since it was feared that increasing government spending – and therefore debt – in a slump would only drain confidence further in the state's handling of the economy. The position of the British government, a senior civil servant advised Prime Minister Ramsay MacDonald, was like that of 'the captain and officers of a great ship which has run aground on a falling tide; no human endeavour will get the ship afloat until in the course of nature the tide again begins to flow'.[10]

In the meantime, the gold standard remained sacrosanct. 'Industry crucified on a Cross of Gold?' asked one newspaper. When the Bank of England announced an interest rate rise in February 1929, the press saw this as 'the complete and final condemnation of the gospel of deflation, dear money and the exaltation of the paper value of the pound over the practical needs of British industry'. Among policymakers, though, what in Britain was known as 'the Treasury view' was dominant: wages should fall, and unemployment benefits be cut.[11]

A similar official fatalism was evident in Germany. Might the

Brüning government have averted Hitler's rise to power and preserved the Weimar Republic by following a policy of reflation in 1930–32? Some Keynesian economic historians have argued this way. Others point out that the criticism takes no heed of the intellectual climate of the day: interventionists were few in number and defensive about the costs of their schemes. In Germany, as in Poland, Austria and elsewhere, the memory of hyperinflation just a few years earlier made governments very cautious about doing anything that might jeopardize monetary stability. Even so, it is now clear that the deflationary policies pursued by most governments in 1929–31 almost certainly deepened the depression. Governments stumbled across alternatives by accident not design, when forced by the crisis itself to abandon gold.

Because of its multiple nature, the crisis itself cannot be precisely dated. Although world commodity prices started falling around 1926, and export volumes a year or so after, the starting point is usually taken to be 1929. Some countries abandoned gold then, more followed in 1930: by the summer of 1932 only a few countries had not devalued or blocked their exchanges. One of these was France, which was hoarding gold and was not seriously affected by the slump until 1934, by which time most other countries had begun to recover. Its desperate bid to cling to the old order thus weakened its ability to resist the rise of the Third Reich.

The crisis symptoms, too, varied greatly from one country to another. Abandoning fixed exchange rates was more or less universal: countries either moved to a lower rate or allowed their currency to float. Severe drops in trade were also registered across the board, intensified by tariff increases and other forms of protectionism. In Germany, one of the worst-affected countries, the depression was marked by a 46 per cent drop in industrial output, and six million unemployed; in Britain, where unemployment had remained high through the 1920s, the scale of the increase after 1929 was not quite so marked. But industrial output sank between 1929 and 1932 by 28 per cent in France, 33 per cent in Italy and 36 per cent in Czechoslovakia. In the more agrarian economies of central and eastern Europe, the crisis took the form of spiralling farm debt and growing peasant unemployment that was less visible than its industrial counterpart. France cushioned the impact by expelling its foreign labour force, and by sending urban workers back to their smallholdings or villages.

Everywhere, of course, there were hidden costs in terms of deteriorating physical and psychological health. 'Inter-war unemployment bred in the poor the fear that they might be left on the margins,' recalls Dimitri Kazamias, who grew up in the refugee quarters of 1930s Athens. 'You saw the "bum" fear he was losing his worth, and the "scab" his faith in the law and justice.' The slump changed the very rhythms of social and family life. Men out of work walked more slowly than women, who still had housework to do, and stood around aimlessly. 'Nothing is urgent anymore; they have forgotten how to hurry,' noted observers of the unemployed in one German town. 'For the men, the division of the days into hours has long since lost its meaning. Of one hundred men, eighty-eight were not wearing a watch and only thirty-one had a watch at home. Getting up, the midday meal, going to bed, are the only remaining points of reference. In between, time elapses without anyone really knowing what has taken place.'[12]

'Stop This Starvation of Mother and Child!' was a slogan used in Britain by the National Unemployed Workers' Movement. It may not have been greatly exaggerating as there was real hunger in unemployed families. Although British censors cut pictures of NUWM marchers from cinema newsreels, and held up films about workers' suffering like Love on the Dole, the impact of mass unemployment could not be so easily hidden: dragooning unemployed men into labour platoons or forced workfare schemes did not take many off the streets. In Down and Out in Paris and London and The Road to Wigan Pier, George Orwell described the soup kitchens, the hostels and the sheer sense of despair which capitalism's failure had created.[13]

Yet governments responded only slowly and disjointedly and were reluctant to abandon the market wisdoms of the past. Neither the Stresa Conference of 1932 nor the still more ambitious World Monetary and Economic Conference that met in London the following year led to coordinated action: on the contrary, they showed ever more clearly the disarray and growing nationalism which existed among the participants. With the collapse of international cooperation came the end of the gold standard (now confined to France, with her immense gold reserves, and Belgium, the Netherlands, Switzerland, Czechoslovakia and Poland) and the cessation of lending from London and New York. In effect, the drying up of the money markets meant ending the decade-long effort to rebuild Europe's economy through liberal capitalism. France remained on gold, while Britain's attention turned to trade with its empire. Both started to think seriously about colonial development and the economic exploitation of their imperial territories in Africa and Asia. The rest of Europe was left to its own devices.

Thus in the 1930s the financial facts of life forced a new economic nationalism on Europe. This was clearly incompatible with the liberal model of free trade and international capital movements advanced by Britain and France. But it was not incompatible either with Soviet-style communism, or with nationalist capitalism, along the lines developed first in Italy and subsequently in the Third Reich. Both Left and Right thus offered a means of escape from the stranglehold of Anglo-American 'plutocracy'; both placed economic growth above financial rectitude, the nation above the global economy, and production above stable prices and the interests of the rentier class. Above all, both provided *work* and eradicated mass unemployment. Capitalism's great crisis thus carried with it powerful political implications: was there a democratic alternative to fascism and communism that could face up to the economic challenges of the 1930s?

THE COMMUNIST ACHIEVEMENT

Commuters from the suburbs of north-east London who use the London Underground station of Gants Hill may be struck by the huge and magnificent underground concourse with its vaulted roof and chrome-yellow banding. Built in 1937, the station was a British tribute to the Moscow Metro, which had just opened the previous year. Today, after communism's defeat in 1989, the inter-war 'mystique of the Soviet Union' is harder than ever to understand. Yet its traces are scattered widely across Europe. During the 1930s, communism was a success to set against capitalist breakdown, an example of how to tackle the economic difficulties of modern society. It had turned the war-torn Tsarist empire into a major industrial power within a few years: it was a system that worked.

Nowhere had the task of post-war economic reconstruction been more awesome than in Russia, for the wartime collapse there went much further and lasted longer than anywhere else in Europe. The fighting itself only ended in 1921, with a casualty total higher even than that of the First World War. Between 1914 and 1926 an estimated fourteen million civilians died of unnatural causes, with five million victims of the famine of 1921–2 which swept southern Russia at the end of the civil war. Famine on this scale was – as a British relief worker put it – 'a famine of everything', which forced people to eat horses and their harnesses, ground bones, acorns, sawdust and even supposedly the dead. This was human suffering which dwarfed even that produced by the collapse of the other great empires – the Ottoman and Habsburg dynasties – and put western Europe's post-war problems in sobering perspective.[14]

Millions of refugees were on the move: by 1921 20,000 refugees *a day* were pouring through the city of Omsk on the route eastwards. An estimated seven million young orphans wandered through the country. Bandits and other armed groups terrorized the villages and railways. Harvests had plummeted to below pre-war levels, with peasants subjected to conscription and requisitioning from Reds, Whites and Greens alike. Through this chaos the Soviet leadership tried to steer towards socialism. As their efforts to foment revolution in central Europe failed, they were forced to focus upon the lands of the former Tsarist empire. Communism began to emerge as a radical *national* alternative to international capitalism.

The Bolsheviks had at one and the same time to build socialism *and* to create a genuinely unified national economy. This was a country where the spring thaw made roads impassable, where the average speed of a commercial train in 1923 was under ten miles an hour, and where the number of train passengers had fallen to half the 1913 figure. Post offices closed down for lack of snow-cleaners in winter;

telegraph lines in rural areas were often cut. Educational backwardness hindered the state as much as poor transport: illiteracy was widespread. Even a twenty-seven-year-old Red Army veteran and Party cadre who read the press regularly was found not to understand such words as 'class enemy' or the letters 'USSR'![15]

The regime may have adopted Lenin's characteristic tone of dogmatic omniscience towards the outside world, but in fact everything about its colossal new venture remained to be defined, not least in the minds of the leaders. From the outset, it was not clear how quickly and how far capitalism and private property should be abandoned. At first the Bolsheviks adopted a radical approach – with extensive nationalization of the means of production, and an early version of central planning. This helped them win the civil war, but threatened to lose them the peace, as production and distribution dried up, and rural resistance grew. In 1921, in the face of fierce internal opposition, Lenin opted for pragmatism: his New Economic Policy – with its relaxation of central controls – was a retreat from hardline War Communism and an effort to kick-start a ravaged economy. It represented the regime's effort to regain the trust of the peasantry, to regroup politically after the hardships of the previous decade, and perhaps also to try to profit from international trade, business and technology. For a few years, private business was tolerated on a small scale. Agriculture – the mainstay of the Soviet economy – began to recover. The leadership won a breathing space in which to consolidate itself politically and to build up federal institutions.

Yet the NEP was a short-term policy of ambivalence. On the one hand, the private sector though tolerated in theory was often persecuted in practice. On the other, many communist cadres could not see in the NEP the road to socialism for which they had fought; rather they saw the return to power and influence of the old pre-revolutionary technical, administrative and intellectual elites. It was difficult to reconcile the NEP with that utopian zeal to 'build a new world' which was so integral to the communist project. As those with access to markets prospered, the NEP opened up increasing economic inequalities among different groups. Class and regional disparities grew – between richer peasants, wandering tradesmen, and an impoverished and restless urban labour force – and these threatened the always fragile cohesion of the entire economy. The NEP in fact made Soviet growth rates dependent upon the market behaviour of workers and peasants, not the Party or the state. Worst of all, perhaps, for the Moscow elite, it made it harder and harder to control the regions.[16]

After Lenin's death, a fierce debate raged within the Party over the pace and direction of economic policy. Initially Stalin was part of the group which called for continued moderation, against the Left Opposition gathered round Trotsky, who called for heavy investment in industry and harsh measures against the peasantry. But once the Left Opposition had been politically outwitted and Trotsky marginalized, Stalin came closer to their view. The straw which broke the camel's back and led directly to what would become known as Stalinism was the grain crisis of 1927–9. This was the point at which the weakness of the state became manifest. Not surprisingly, given the scarcity of reliable economic information, Stalin was caught completely unawares by what he was soon calling the 'peasants' strike'. Faced with lower grain stocks, rationing in cities, and increasingly expensive food prices, the regime reverted to the methods of War Communism and took emergency measures to collect grain by force.

By 1929, Stalin had won against his critics on both Left *and* Right: communism would be imposed upon the countryside, and farming would be collectivized and mechanized. At the end of the year, Stalin targeted the wealthier peasants, the so-called 'kulaks', and declared himself in favour of the 'liquidation of the kulaks as a class'. According to the instructions issued from Moscow, these were to be divided into three groups: the most dangerous, those in the 'counter-revolutionary kulak *aktiv*', were to be handed over to the OGPU (the state security police); the second group was to be deported to 'far-off' parts of the Soviet Union; the third was to be resettled elsewhere in the region where they lived. The total number of families involved was expected to be around one million in all – or from five to seven million people; in fact, ten million or more may have eventually been deported, and at least thirty thousand were shot out of hand.[17]

Prosecuting the 'truly Bolshevik struggle for grain' involved sending in shock troops of workers, Party cadres and the secret police in what amounted to an internal war – punishing lax local officials and sentencing 'speculators', those peasants, in other words, trying to keep grain for themselves. 'When you are attacking, there is no place for mercy,' said one Party activist. 'Don't think of the kulak's hungry children; in the class struggle philanthropy is evil.' Delivery targets were set which bore little relation to the producers' ability to deliver. Yet local echelons of the state apparatus were under pressure to meet these 'at any price'; their failure could mean punishment for 'rotten liberalism'.

Of course, only a small proportion of peasants had any sort of wealth at all, and only a tiny proportion of farms employed paid workers. 'Why are you constantly yelling about kulaks?' the cadres were asked in one village. 'We have no kulaks here.' Some of the poorer peasants, whom the regime tried to turn against the richer villagers, could see what was coming: 'Now they are confiscating bread from the kulaks; tomorrow they will turn against the middle and poor peasant.' In the spring of 1930 they slaughtered their last cows rather than hand them over; not even the Germans eleven years later would inflict such damage on Soviet cattle stocks.[18]

According to Soviet figures themselves, grain harvests fell in the 1930s, a clear reflection of the disastrous impact collectivization and coercion had had on the countryside; on the other hand, state grain procurements rose steadily from 10.7 million tons in 1928 to 31.9 millions in 1937, or from 14.7 per cent of the total crop to 36.7 per cent. If the figures are unreliable, the general picture is clear enough. The regime had turned its back on those other strategies for industrial development that might have required patience and cooperation with the peasantry, in favour of short-term violence: this brought in the grain it needed but at the cost of long-term damage to Soviet farming, whose consequences for the Union itself would eventually prove fateful.[19]

During the famine of 1932–3 with its millions of victims – a direct consequence of these policies – police kept foreigners out of the afflicted areas, and kept the victims in by reimposing an internal passport system, like the Tsarist model which Lenin had abolished.

But of course many knew what was going on. 'Dniepropetrovsk was overrun with starving peasants,' remembered one Party worker. 'Many of them lay listless, too weak even to beg around the railway stations. Their children were little more than skeletons with swollen bellies.' He was appalled at what was happening, but his superior saw things differently. 'A ruthless struggle is going on between the peasantry and our regime . . . It's a struggle to the death. This year was a test of our strength and their endurance. It took a famine to show them who is master here. It has cost millions of lives, but the collective farm system is here to stay. We've won the war.'[20]

At first many people, inside the Party as well as outside, were bewildered by the scale of the turmoil. There were protests at the deportations, and public expressions of sympathy for the 'kulaks'. Even workers betrayed 'negative attitudes'. 'Were Lenin alive', one remarked, looking at his portrait, 'he would have allowed free trade and eased our lot; afterwards, he would have instituted a shift towards collectivization – not by force, but by consent and persuasion.' But this outrage was overlaid by sheer panic, and growing passivity. 'Earlier an arrested man was led by two militiamen,' it was reported. 'Now one militiaman may lead groups of people, and the latter calmly walk and no one flees.'[21]

The grain procurement drives of the early 1930s became the training ground for a new generation of Party members, who became accustomed to a level of violence and repression which spread to the rest of Soviet society with the Terror a few years later. Their tendency to see a world of conspiracies, with 'wreckers', 'White Russians', terrorists and saboteurs engaged in a war against the Revolution – already visible in the war scare of 1927 – was reinforced. Their strong-arm methods, after all, whipped up the kind of opposition which made such fears seem all too plausible, while official policy created problems, suffering and waste which could not be blamed on their real authors. The deportation of millions of peasants led to the rapid creation of forced-labour colonies, and to the perfection of techniques of population control that Stalin would employ against other class and ethnic minorities – Poles, Chechens, ethnic Germans among them – in the 1930s and 1940s. Last but not least, collectivization opened the way to the headlong industrialization of the first Five-Year Plan.

Forced industrialization was Stalin's policy. He won the argument over the collectivization of agriculture, and now emphasized his desire for fast industrial growth to push Russia into the Machine Age. At stake was the Bolshevik boast to be creating a modern society. And in a hostile world, which had already tried to snuff out the Revolution at birth, the Soviet Union needed rapid industrialization to safeguard socialism. In February 1931 Stalin made a remarkable prophecy. 'Do you want our socialist fatherland to be beaten and to lose its independence?' he asked. 'If you do not want this, you must put an end to its backwardness in the shortest possible time and develop a genuine Bolshevik tempo in building up its socialist economy . . . We are fifty or a hundred years behind the advanced countries. We must catch up this distance in ten years. Either we do it or we go under.' Operation Barbarossa was exactly a decade away.[22]

Stalin's strategy demanded not merely ruthless control of the domestic food supply but high levels of investment in heavy industry, with consequent pressure upon urban living standards. In theory, the means was to be the Plan; but in reality, the Plan functioned chiefly as an unstable source of stimuli and goals, bearing little relation to resources, and frequently supplemented by high publicity 'shock tactics' and 'overfulfilment'. This is what explains the pell-mell rate of industrialization at the very time when the functioning of the state planning agencies was disrupted by deep purges, and when regional Party bosses were competing furiously for investment funds.

The striking thing is to what extent the whole frenzied and disorganized process worked. Real output often fell short of the ludicrous targets proposed in the Plan (which had anyway been wound up one year early), but this is less remarkable than the output gains that did take place. Entire new towns – Magnitogorsk, for example, the world's largest steel plant – were built from nothing; existing metallurgical plants were pushed to their limit. Tractor factories and machine-tool industries developed rapidly to cut down the country's import needs. All this despite the fact that so much investment was channelled into heavy industry that fuel and transport could not keep up, and generated frequent breakdowns and wastage.

In terms of creating work, the regime's policy was an unparalleled and extraordinary success. The urban labour force increased from 11.3 million to 22.8 million between 1927–8 and 1932; by 1939 it had risen to 39 million. At the very time when capitalist Europe was deep in the slump, unemployment had been eliminated, large numbers of women were working, and the country actually suffered from a labour shortage. 'It cannot be regarded as an accident', boasted Stalin in 1934, 'that the country in which Marxism has triumphed is now the only country in the world which knows no crises and no unemployment, whereas in all the other countries including the fascist countries, crisis and unemployment have been reigning for four years now.'[23]

Stalin's policies were creating a new working class, drawn chiefly from the millions of peasants who flocked into the cities in these years, often to escape the new collective farms. Between 1929 and 1933, the number of foremen in industry leapt from 18,700 to 83,800 – the vast majority drawn from the ranks of uneducated workers – the total number of managerial and technical personnel from 82,700 to 312,100. Here was indeed the emergence of a New Civilization, though not perhaps in the sense meant by Sidney and Beatrice Webb. A largely peasant society was being electrified, mechanized and conquered by a modernizing regime, but was also taking it over: peasants were being turned into workers, managers and Party cadres. By the end of the 1930s state, Party and economy were all being run by the beneficiaries of this social revolution.[24]

Of course, the supposed heroes of the Revolution quickly found that they were no freer than anyone else in the all-powerful state and Party machines. When the mostly illiterate and unskilled labourers moved from one job to another, they could be accused of 'petty bourgeois spontaneity'. The imposition of labour discipline emerged as a major preoccupation of the regime, and in the face of growing food shortages, rationing and the scarcity of consumer goods, the labour unions were transformed from protectors of the workers into enforcers of labour discipline in the fight against 'loafing' and 'absenteeism'. The old leadership was dismissed for 'right-wing deviation' and the unions were ordered to 'face production'. This meant, among other things, ignoring the primitive and dangerous conditions at work.

If building socialism sounded exciting to the droves of Western intellectuals who came to watch, it was harsh and injurious in practice. Despite the worship of the Machine, Soviet industrialization was highly labour-intensive and the low level of technical expertise meant that many machines lay idle while work was done by hand: especially in the first few years, lorries and tractors mattered less than horses and wheelbarrows. But labour-intensive is an abstract term: 10 per cent of the 'kulak' forced labourers sent in to construct Magnitogorsk died in the first bitter winter there. Workers building the gigantic hydroelectric power plant at Dneprostroi were little better off: 'Barrack dwellers complained of snow drifting through rooms. Tent dwellers endured temperatures below −13 degrees C in the winter and tornado-strength winds whipped tents away in the summer of 1929.' And these hazards were only made worse by the introduction of 'socialist emulation', or competition spearheaded by 'shock workers' and the hated Stakhanovites.[25]

The entire effort required heavy pressure upon private savings – through the sale of government bonds – and consumer spending. Individual wants were subordinated to the needs of the collectivity – a trend which elicited both grumbling and a feeling of selflessness. Bread rationing was imposed in 1929 and the consumption of meat and dairy products fell. Only in 1935 was there some improvement. The cities were growing all the time – the urban population doubled between 1926 and 1939 – making the perennial housing shortage much worse. Living space norms per person in Moscow fell by one third between 1929 and 1931. The hunger for better housing became just one of the reasons why people entered the Party, before the Party apparatus itself was purged so ruthlessly in the mid-1930s.

But the pressures of Stalinist industrialization were not confined to cramped living quarters: the years of the first Five-Year Plan also witnessed the explosive development of the camp system. Historically, forced labour had been of crucial importance for the economic development of much of the Americas and of the Tsarist empire. Stalin carried this process further than ever before. In 1929 the OGPU's concentration camps were renamed 'labour camps' and were given an explicit economic function. Starting with the mass arrests during collectivization, and fluctuating in intensity throughout the 1930s, the security organs gained control of millions of prisoners in a complex network of prisons, 'corrective labour camps', labour colonies and special settlements: latest estimates put the total number of prisoners as rising from 2.5 million in 1933 to 3.3 million on the eve of the German invasion in 1941.[26]

Forced labour played a significant part in the overall industrialization drive: on the eve of the Second World War, the NKVD (OGPU's successor) was responsible for around 25 per cent of all building work, and dominated construction work in the Urals, Siberia and the far east; a secret-police official publicly praised his organization's camps as 'pioneers in the cultural development of our remote peripheries'. Specific commodities located in these regions – gold and other metals, timber and later, munitions – depended on slave labour. Forced labour also helped construct the White Sea–Baltic canal, one of the regime's propaganda triumphs of the early 1930s. Special settlers were allocated to new industrial sites like Magnitogorsk. By 1939 there were some 107,000 guards working in NKVD camps and colonies alone.[27]

Unlike capitalism, whose view of the world was essentially harmonious and benign, communism saw itself as embattled and beleaguered. Enemies outside had tried to stamp out the Revolution at birth; those within had tried to lead the Party astray through their factionalism and 'deviations'. Coinciding with the height of repression and the onset of the Terror, Soviet industrialization took place in a conspiratorial world of 'saboteurs' and 'counter-revolutionary plots'. From the 1928 trial of foreign engineers onwards, technical experts, managers and Party bosses worked under the threat of arbitrary punishment: failure, personal rivalry, or even a sudden change in the leadership's line might be enough to disgrace them. Tens of thousands of educated professionals were sent to the camps. The need to train a new generation of managers became a priority for the regime, but also an opportunity for social advancement for a younger generation. Stalinism thus meant terror and repression, but also upward mobility and exciting new life chances which compared strikingly with the relatively static and hierarchical structure of Tsarist society: between 1928 and 1933, some 770,000 Party members alone are reckoned to have moved up from the working class into white-collar and administrative jobs.[28]

Today it is natural to castigate Westerners like H. G. Wells, Bernard Shaw or the Webbs for skating over the nastier and more brutal aspects of Stalinism, and for confusing Soviet propaganda and reality. Yet at a time when capitalism appeared to be committing suicide, Stalin's Russia formed a striking contrast to the West – an image of energy, commitment, collective achievement and modernity – the more alluring for being so little understood. The few outspoken and knowledgeable critics, like the former Croat communist Ante Ciliga – whose book *In the Land of the Great Lie* appeared in 1938 – found their exposés largely ignored.[29]

In part this credulity reflected what one historian terms 'the phenomenal will to believe in utopia' which pervaded inter-war Europe. But it also reflected the West's gradual detachment from the realities of Soviet life. Soviet contacts with the rest of Europe in the 1920s had been substantial – in technological, scientific and cultural affairs if not in finance and trade. Teams of American, German and British engineers provided technical advice, while some of Europe's most distinguished architects and town planners including Le Corbusier and Ernst May competed to plan Moscow and other cities. But with the 1930s show trials – whose defendants included Western engineers and businessmen – these contacts dwindled and travel in and out of the country became more difficult. As the Soviet 'economic miracle' forged ahead, Soviet realities disappeared from Europe's view and the country closed in on itself.

It was, above all, the rise of Hitler which made it hard to evaluate Russia objectively. With Nazi Germany emerging as the main threat to democracy in Europe, much of the centre and Left in western Europe combined in a largely pro-Soviet anti-Fascism: 'Support of the Soviet Union at the present juncture is (as the one hope of averting war) of such overwhelming importance', the British publisher Victor Gollancz warned the writer H. N. Brailsford in 1937, 'that anything that could be quoted by the other side should not be said.' For many European intellectuals, the Soviet Union thus became a mirror, reflecting their own obsessions, their hopes and fears of what Nazism held in store.[30]

NATIONAL RECOVERY

Nowhere was the dazzling Soviet achievement watched with more concern than in crisis-torn central and eastern Europe. 'In business and banking circles in Berlin', reported the British ambassador in early 1931, 'the chief topic of conversation has been the menace represented by the progress made by the Soviet Union in carrying out the Five Year Plan, and the necessity of some serious effort being made by the European countries to put their house in order before Soviet economic pressure becomes too strong.'[31]

Britain was unable to provide the necessary leadership. Liberal capitalists talked as though living in an earlier century, and free trade – the British mantra – was an unconvincing and outdated response. Told at Geneva to cut trade barriers and allow in cheap grain from Canada and Argentina, the Yugoslav foreign minister replied bitterly that this was possible 'provided they sacrificed four-fifths of their population'. The only difference, he went on, between the free-trade policy proposed by Britain and Stalin's Five-Year Plan was 'that you do not shoot the population, but starve them'.[32]

Quite fortuitously, though, the collapse of free trade revealed some alternative and unexpected paths out of depression that capitalist countries could follow. Economic nationalism in the 1930s turns out to have been rather more successful than historians have allowed, and many countries did better producing for themselves than they had done struggling to get back on to the gold standard and coping with international competition in the 1920s. Self-sufficiency, to be sure, had its costs. It burdened consumers with expensive home-made goods, but then by the same token it encouraged producers. So did debt standstills which liberated indebted farmers and industrialists alike and boosted domestic demand. The price producers paid for these relatively positive developments was increasing state control.

With the abandonment of laissez-faire, governments suddenly found it necessary to decide where they wanted the exchange rate; they were drawn into trade policy and the allocation of foreign exchange; at home they began to plan output, to foster producers' cartels and intervene in the development and location of new concerns. Thus quite independently of ideology, self-sufficiency altered the relationship between state and private initiative. Capitalist nations took over the idea of planning and state control from the Bolsheviks, and watered it down: the slump prompted the emergence of state-led national capitalism.

In the short term, domestic recovery and industrial growth were impressive. Protected by higher tariffs and non-convertible currencies, prices stopped falling, and employment picked up. Industries aimed at the domestic market such as textiles, chemicals and power generation all grew rapidly, while farming too recovered with the aid of state marketing boards which bought in crops at guaranteed prices. Between 1932 and 1937 industrial output soared by 67 per cent in Sweden and 48 per cent in the UK, while in gold-obsessed Poland, France and Belgium it stagnated. In Nazi Germany – helped by compulsory labour service, rigid control of wages, work creation schemes and a campaign against working women – unemployment fell from 5.6 million to 0.9 million in five years; by 1939 there was full employment.

New domestic sources of financing emerged to replace the capital markets of the West. Defaulting on foreign debt – or 'rescheduling' – was worth a lot to the debtor states of central and eastern Europe – the equivalent of more than 10 per cent of government spending for Greece, Romania and Bulgaria, for example, between 1931 and 1935. What could have been more rational than borrowing heavily in the 1920s and repudiating the debt in the 1930s? British and American bond-holders were resentful but helpless.[33]

Domestically, consumer spending could be squeezed, as could wages, especially in police states where independent unions had been smashed. Inflation, high tax rates, tight control of wages and other forms of forced and 'voluntary' savings kept real wages low and funnelled resources into the state's coffers. The Nazi regime constructed motorways and public buildings, the British council houses;

nearly everyone subsidized farmers and sooner or later invested in rearmament. Thus a third form of development strategy emerged between, on the one hand, relying on foreign borrowing and, on the other, Soviet forced industrialization. It permitted a slower rate of growth than in the Soviet Union, but cost fewer lives and helped stabilize the political class.

On the whole, however, autarky remained a short-term option for European capitalism. True, it encouraged industrial recovery but only in a sheltered and uncompetitive environment. Established firms were shielded from foreign rivals and even from new entrepreneurs at home, through state-sponsored cartel schemes. Lucky businessmen reaped high profits but had little incentive to reinvest these in plant and equipment, especially when this needed to be imported. The main exception was where – as in the Third Reich – the nationalist state made it clear that it expected results for its protection. A Nazi public utility like Volkswagen, or private corporation like Daimler-Benz, laid down plant, equipment and profits in the 1930s (and early 1940s) that would form the basis for post-war growth. But these were the exceptions: most states were either insufficiently nationalist (like the British), or too disorganized (like the French and Italians) to make autarky pay. For all the talk of 'efficiency' and 'coordination', there was overall no leap forward in technology to compare with the 'rationalization' drive of the 1920s, and in some cases actual regression. Not until the 1950s would European industry truly modernize; ironically, the post-war Soviet Union became a case study of what could happen when a country persisted with autarky too long.[34]

In farming the story was similarly mixed, especially in backward eastern Europe. There was some modernization of agriculture – better strains of seed, more intensive use of fertilizers, greater cultivation of cotton and other import substitutes – but too many 'battles for grain' kept the countryside alive yet unable to prosper. Peasants retreated from the market back into a subsistence economy. In the long run, autarky offered no solution to Europe's overcrowded villages: these too would have to wait till the 1950s when communism and international capitalism would between them propel peasants into the towns and create new industrial jobs.

National capitalism in the 1930s had plenty of other drawbacks as well: working-class employment grew but wages were kept low, especially in authoritarian regimes. The Nazi Labour Front organized tourist trips and pressured factory bosses to improve some working conditions, all of which helped dissipate worker dissatisfaction; but none of this helped raise wages substantially. Thus the kind of consumer-led recovery which took place in Britain in the 1930s, based around growing employment in light industry, was essentially incompatible with the kind of recovery pursued in Nazi Germany or Fascist Italy. What, moreover, kept recovery going there was not the consumer but the military state. The Ethiopian war was vital for helping Italy out of recession. Until 1939 German spending on rearmament was roughly double the proportion of GNP that it was in the UK, and ten times what it was in the USA. For Hitler, of course, recovery was not the reason for rearmament; that was, quite simply, the need to prepare for the inevitable 'new conflict' with Soviet Bolshevism. Nevertheless, the consequence was a tremendous stimulus to growth, which generated serious labour shortages and inflationary pressures by the end of the 1930s.

International trade did not come to a complete stop after 1932, but it ran at such reduced levels that it could not stimulate growth in the way it would after 1950. Levels of world trade had plummeted after 1929 and never recovered: even in 1937 world trade was below the 1929 figure, though world production had increased. Europe split into trading blocs with the British building up a zone of Imperial Preference outside the continent, and the French trying unsuccessfully to keep a small gold zone (the Netherlands, Belgium, Switzerland, Poland and Czechoslovakia) in existence. The most determined effort to build a new trading system compatible with autarky was pursued by Germany after 1934 with the New Plan – a network of bilateral clearing accounts with the countries of eastern and south-eastern Europe.

Heralded by some Nazi geopoliticians as the start of a New Order, and attacked by anti-Nazis as a system of fascist exploitation, the New Plan was in reality more modest in its impact. The rather poor and backward economies of eastern Europe were hardly a substitute for Germany's old export markets. The Nazi regime really wanted their goods, not their custom, and they got their way by running large trade deficits with their poorer neighbours. Bulgaria, Yugoslavia and Greece thus helped pay for the German recovery. Yet no one else would take their exports anyway, and governments continued to humour the Germans because it was important to keep their own farmers happy. When the Greek government threatened to stop tobacco sales to the Third Reich because they were not getting much in return, it was the protests of their own tobacco growers that made them think again.

Thus although Germany came to dominate their trade, the Balkan states never became more than minor trading partners for the Reich. Their value lay chiefly in specific commodities – Yugoslav bauxite, Greek tobacco, Romanian oil – vitally needed for the overheated German armaments boom. This was exploitation, perhaps, but not of a kind which could offer a country like Germany anything more than short-term benefits. From 1938, barter trade was overshadowed by more direct forms of economic exploitation: valuable minerals, foreign-exchange reserves and extra steel capacity from the *Anschluss* with Austria; then, with the occupation of Czechoslovakia the following year, more gold and the Škoda works, the most important arms producer in central Europe. Foreign conquest – the primary goal of Nazi economic policy – had begun.[35]

FASCIST CAPITALISM

'We are now burying economic liberalism,' Mussolini proclaimed in 1933. By then, the end of laissez-faire had been accepted by most people. The active state had taken the place of the free market; the liberal's selfish individual had been succeeded by the disciplined collectivity. It was easy to see how such trends might make fascism look like the capitalist economics of the future. But was there a specifically fascist economics? If Liberalism was now dead, did that mean fascism had all the answers?[36]

Fascism certainly brought its own style to the management of the economy – activist, heroic, militaristic: Mussolini's 'Battle of Wheat' was followed by a 'Battle of the Lira', a 'Campaign for the National Product' and later by Hitler's 'Battle for Work'. Fascists also liked to turn 'economic problems' into 'questions of will', which was often another way of saying the leadership had no idea what to do next. In fact, fascist ideology was almost wilfully obscure on economics, partly because the leadership needed to keep both Left and Right wings of the movement happy, but partly too because it was not very interested in the subject, seeing economics as means to an end. Hitler wanted to use 'the production technique of private enterprise in line with the ideas of the common good under state control', a formula which satisfied everyone and no one. Fascism was strongly anti-communist but also anti-plutocratic. It was opposed to international finance – often condemned as 'parasitic' and 'cosmopolitan' – but in favour of national 'production'. Did this make it socialist? Perhaps in a special, airily non-class sense. 'Our socialism is a socialism of heroes, of manliness,' declared Goebbels who came from the left wing of the Party.[37]

A 'socialism of heroes' implied endless hymns to the Worker: every dictator in Europe must have posed at some time as his country's First Peasant or First Worker. But fascism stressed manual labour rather than machinery and technology as in the USSR or the USA. Fascist men wielded scythes, they did not drive tractors. 'I am a socialist', Hitler stated, 'because it appears to me incomprehensible to nurse and handle a machine with care but to allow the most noble representatives of labour, the people, to decay.' Posters emphasized craftsmen and artisans – a look backwards which perhaps helped draw labour away from its contemporary strong class connotations. Even motorway workers – according to Nazi publicity brochures – were pictured above the caption: 'We plough the eternal earth.'[38]

In practice, however, fascism was scarcely the worker's friend. Both Mussolini, the former socialist, and Hitler spoke one way to the workers before they had achieved power, and another way after it. Left-wing Italian Fascists had feared just this, and urged Mussolini not to cave in to the employers; anti-capitalist 'Red Nazis' like the young Goebbels had exactly the same fear. 'All the disgust provoked by parliamentarianism, and the just criticism of socialism and democracy, will end in bitter disappointment and inconclusive rhetoric and – worse still – a fatal reactionary illusion,' a leading pro-labour Fascist warned the Duce, 'if Fascism is not to have a more solid, realistic and human base . . . The Communist utopia might still recover its deleterious influence if the new order were to show itself incapable of ensuring a minimum of economic welfare.' But such warnings not to sell out the workers were disregarded: Fascist and Nazi left-wingers were quietly brought to heel and the principle of private property was never seriously challenged. Left-wing Nazis dreamed of a 'second revolution' against capitalism, but in Germany this prospect ended with the Night of the Long Knives and the murder of Gregor Strasser in 1934; in Italy it had vanished years earlier.[39] In industrial relations, fascist regimes clearly leant towards the bosses. Independent unions were smashed in both Italy and Germany, but employers' associations were permitted to exist, and there was little check to employers' power except through the power of the labour market once full employment returned. Fascism remained a low-wage economy, different in kind from that of post-1945 western Europe.

If the kind of working-class protest which generations of Leftist historians have searched for failed to materialize, this may be partly because of the success of the regime's German Labour Front (DAF) and its subsidiaries in organizing welfare and improving working conditions in the factory; after all, with an income three times that of the Nazi Party itself, and a membership many times larger, the DAF was not completely without influence. In Italy, the Dopolavoro organization also signalled the regime's interest in workers' leisure and welfare. At the same time, the new hierarchical order introduced into workplace relations made collective action harder to achieve.

Perhaps more crucial, though, was the memory of unemployment. As an observer of Germany noted in 1938, 'although [the workers] know there is a labour shortage – they are all scared of losing their jobs. The years of unemployment have not been forgotten.' But the Nazi achievement could also be expressed more positively; in 1938 unemployment stood at just 3 per cent compared with 13 per cent in the UK, 14 per cent in Belgium and 25 per cent in the Netherlands. Much higher levels of unemployment in Italy may explain why Italian workers seemed to stay more alienated from the regime than their German counterparts. Nazi slogans about the 'dignity of work' and the 'honour of German labour' may actually have struck a chord; caught between the threat of 'emergency labour' camps, on the one hand, and organized concerts, films, sports and travel, on the other, the average worker put political struggle behind him.[40]

After all, in both Italy and Germany, private property no longer reigned supreme either. As Hitler put it, one did not require expropriation when one had a strong state. There were now higher values – the Italian 'Nation' and the German *Volk* – in whose name the economy was now to be administered. 'In future the interests of individual gentlemen can no longer play any part in these matters,' Hitler had stated in 1936 as he gave the green light for rearmament. 'There is only one interest, the interest of the nation.' In a wonderfully precise formulation, a senior German civil servant advised businessmen that 'at bottom we do not seek a material but a mental nationalization of the economy'. This was a warning to private enterprise as well as a disclaimer. Likewise, Italian bankers were reminded that 'the Banks are no longer the dominators of the economy of the Nation but only the instrument of the exercise of a particular form of credit'; business had 'the right and the duty to enjoy the use of all the sources of credit which the Nation puts at the disposal of the productive activity of the Italian people'.[41]

Despite the endless appeals to 'efficiency' and 'coordination', though, it is difficult to discern a distinctive fascist approach to the state. The state as modernizer? Hardly. In Italy, the need to rescue failing industrial concerns led to the formation of giant public-sector holding companies. On paper, there was a great increase in state control over the economy. In practice, however, industrial managers continued much as before. The Third Reich developed a panoply of state controls, before the 1936 Four-Year Plan spearheaded the rearmament drive under Goering's leadership: by the late 1930s, his ministry determined around 50 per cent of total industrial investment in Germany. Inspired in part by the Soviet example, the German state undertook a massive scheme of capital investment, building up the most powerful military–industrial complex in Europe. Yet the gargantuan achievements – such as the Brunswick metallurgical works, the world's largest aluminium industry, the high-quality weaponry – belied a chaotic reality, bedevilled by bureaucratic in-fighting and lack of central planning or even mere coordination. Standards of craftsmanship were high, but distracted attention from what was really needed – efficient mass-production. When it was put to the test, the German war economy – despite the attention lavished on it by the Nazi regime – was unable to match its rivals, both capitalist and communist.[42]

REFORMING A DEMOCRATIC CAPITALISM

'It suffices to consider countries as different as the United States of America, Soviet Russia, Italy or Germany,' insisted the leading Belgian socialist Hendrik de Man in October 1933, 'to understand the irresistible force of this push towards a planned national economy.' The question for western Europe in the 1930s was whether democracy could learn from these striking new tendencies in economic life.[43]

The fascist and communist emphasis on will and action impressed west European intellectuals who felt increasingly surrounded by mediocrity and fatalism. After 1933, it was above all younger socialists – stunned by the swift annihilation of German social democracy – who became impatient with their own leaders' caution. Mocking the mood of the French socialist leadership at their 1933 congress, one critic wrote sarcastically that the delegates had been told 'it was necessary to be prudent, it was necessary to be patient, it was necessary to measure the opposing forces accurately. We were not to advance towards power because that would be too dangerous; we would be crushed by the resistance of capitalism itself; we were not to advance toward revolution because we were not ready, because the time was not ripe . . . We are to advance nowhere!'[44]

In Britain, similar feelings attracted Labour MP Oswald Mosley to fascism; he was not alone in feeling exasperated by what a fellow-MP called the Labour leadership's 'passion for evading decisions'. Mosley had proposed a radical plan for economic recovery at the 1930 Labour

Party conference; its rejection by the leadership on grounds of cost prompted him to leave the party and begin the move rightwards which would culminate in the British Union of Fascists.[45]

A generational gulf of outlook and temperament separated young men like Mosley, who had fought in the First World War, from the older socialist leadership. The latter were keen to show the electorate they could play by capitalism's rules; the 'Front Generation' thought the rules themselves irrational and the leadership passive, defeatist and geriatric. 'This age is dynamic, and the pre-war age was static,' argued Mosley. 'The men of the pre-war age are much "nicer" people than we are, just as their age was much more pleasant than the present time. The practical question is whether their ideas for the solution of the problems of the age are better than the ideas of those whom that age has produced.' For many of the 'Front Generation', fascism and communism both represented more 'modern' and more dynamic forms of economic organization than either liberalism or reform socialism.[46]

Their exasperation was understandable. Only occasionally did socialist parties even try rethinking theory and practice in the light of unemployment and the slump. The best example was Sweden, which devalued early and recovered fast, thanks to the reflationary policies of its 1932 Social Democratic government. Here was an administration keen and prepared to use fiscal policy to engineer an upswing. 'There will be no spontaneous recovery,' affirmed the Swedish finance minister in 1933, 'except to the extent that the policy of the state will help to bring it about.' The government gave a massive boost to investment and by 1937–8 unemployment was shrinking fast (from 139,000 in 1933 to under 10,000) and there was a manufacturing boom. Official policy was worked out in advance and carefully planned. It is true that Sweden enjoyed certain economic advantages which protected the country from the worst of the international depression: nevertheless, in its counter-cyclical fiscal policies and the pact between unions and employers which helped regulate industrial relations, it looked ahead to the managed capitalism which the rest of western Europe only adopted after 1945.[47]

Industrial Belgium, clinging to gold and mired in depression, provided the other noteworthy response – capitalist planning. In 1933 Hendrik de Man returned there from Germany to work on his *Plan van der Arbeid*. The novelty of the idea that there might be a socialist effort to plan within a capitalist framework, and within a nationalist one at that, was reflected in the opposition which greeted de Man even within his own Workers' Party:

When I first unfolded the *Plan* before the Executive Bureau of the Workers' Party in October, I met more opposition than I had foreseen. Some said: 'You are really too moderate in that you replace the concept of socialization with that of a directed economy. And in place of loyalty to class struggle you seek an alliance with the middle class and the farmers.' Others: 'What you lay before us is thinly-disguised fascism. You make the state all-powerful and you can only realize your programme through a dictatorship. And above all, you expect everything from the nation and nothing from the International.'[48]

To such objections, de Man replied that the fate of Weimar had revealed what could happen when social democrats refused to cooperate with the middle classes: it was no use proposing schemes for boosting employment which were politically unacceptable to them, nor to talk of doing away with capitalism when the Party lacked the strength or the will for this. Like Mosley, de Man offered cogent insights into the new situation created by the crisis: the need for socialists to come to terms with nationalism, to challenge the gospel of the balanced budget and to offer a decisive alternative to the market. But in practice he was only slightly more successful: as minister of public works in the 1935 Belgian Government of National Renovation, de Man brought down unemployment substantially. But this was chiefly the result of the long-overdue currency devaluation the government imposed at the same time rather than of the *Plan de Man*. His achievement was a real one, but far from the triumph of *planisme* he fought for. Disillusioned, de Man moved slowly to the Right, and he collaborated with the Germans in 1940, declaring that Nazism was 'the German form of socialism'. But his ideas bore fruit after the war: the famous *Plan* was in many ways a model for state planning in much of western Europe after 1945.

In France, the *Plan de Man* was widely discussed, but an equivalent plan was entirely omitted from the Popular Front programme in 1936; worse still, the Blum government tried to satisfy workers' demands at the same time as preserving a strong franc. Blum had come to admire Roosevelt's pragmatism, and offered himself as a 'loyal manager' of French capitalism. The result was economic failure, satisfying neither Left nor Right, dashing the high hopes many had held of the Popular Front, and further diminishing the prestige and self-confidence of the non-communist Left in Europe. Even the much-vaunted gains of the Popular Front government – the paid holidays, forty-hour week and arbitration in industrial disputes – had already been won in many other countries.

While de Man, Mosley and others gave up on democracy, and came to believe that concerted action against unemployment was only possible through the authoritarian state, the 1930s and its lessons for democracy could also be interpreted rather differently. Some liberals came to reject state interventionism and economic nationalism entirely as the root of the problem, and saw planning itself as inherently authoritarian. This was the free-market critique of the totalitarian state. Popular in both Britain and Italy, it was espoused most forcefully by émigré Austrian economists Hayek and von Mises. The 1930s, however, were not the best time for their message to strike home, and they would have to wait another forty years to make their mark.

In the short run, liberalism's democratic critics were far more successful. Many shared the view of one analyst of the 1930s, H. W. Arndt, who wrote in 1944 that 'the Nazis developed a number of economic techniques – in the sphere of Government finance, planned State intervention, exchange control and the manipulation of foreign trade – which *mutatis mutandis* may well be applicable in a worthier cause'.[49] John Maynard Keynes, for instance, came to discern certain virtues in economic nationalism, in particular the autonomy which individual states had gained over policy as a result of the collapse of a unified international economy. 'Ideas, knowledge, science, hospitality, travel – these are the things which should of their nature be international,' he wrote in 1933. 'But let goods be homespun whenever it is reasonable and conveniently possible, and above all, let finance be primarily national.'[50]

A similar moral was drawn by Keynes's Polish contemporary, Michał Kalecki. In an article on the Blum experiment, Kalecki argued that exchange controls were necessary for governments wishing to alter the balance of industrial power to labour's advantage; otherwise capitalists could always threaten capital flight to undermine a regime's credibility. Kalecki belonged to a school of economists which argued that the state needed to 'wind the economy up' to full employment, a doctrine which underpinned the Polish 1936 Four-Year Investment Plan, one of the most important ventures in centralized planning to take place outside the Soviet Union. In Keynes, we can see the incipient rethinking of capitalism which provided guidelines for post-war policy in western Europe; in Kalecki, the doctrines which contributed to state socialism in the East. In both East and West, the memory of classical liberalism's failure in the 1930s would provoke a reassessment of the balance between public and private power in the modern economy, paving the way for the great post-war boom. That the state needed to be brought in to the life of the national economy was not, therefore, a lesson which the Europeans needed to be taught by the Russians or American New Dealers; their own experience between the wars pointed to the same conclusion.[51]

5

Hitler's New Order, 1938–45

It is my impression that Germany has certain plans . . aiming at a lasting European new order . . . along the lines of the planned economy known to Germany, which will certainly contain important advantages compared with the lack of planning hitherto reigning, which has been part of liberalist egoism. We had better calmly and willingly collaborate in the adaptation which I have here hinted at.

– Danish Prime Minister Thorvald Stauning, 8 March 1941[1]

It has become increasingly clear to us this summer, that here in the East spiritually unbridgeable conceptions are fighting each other: German sense of honour and race, and a soldierly tradition of many centuries, against an Asiatic mode of thinking and primitive instincts, whipped up by a small number of mostly Jewish intellectuals . . . More than ever we are filled with the thought of a new era, in which the strength of the German people's racial superiority and achievements entrusts it with the leadership of Europe. We clearly recognize our mission to save European culture from the advancing Asiatic barbarism. We now know that we have to fight against an incensed and tough opponent. This battle can only end with the destruction of one or the other; a compromise is out of the question.

– Colonel-General Hermann Hoth, 17 Army, 25 November 1941[2]

In the spring of 1942 a young Italian diplomat called Luciolli returned home after serving a year and half in the Berlin Embassy. His first task in Rome was to set down his thoughts on the way Italy's ally was tackling the major issues arising out of the war. The result was a penetrating critique of the foundations of the Nazi New Order in Europe; when it was brought to Mussolini's attention, the Duce's reaction was that 'he had not read anything so significant and far-reaching for a long time'. Luciolli noted:

To defend to the death the great amount that has so far been conquered, to exploit it, to organise the economic and political life of Europe so as to increase its powers of endurance and develop its offensive capacities – all this seems capable of constituting a clear and precise goal, a programme around which to collect adherents and consensus, were it not for the fact that it is precisely in this *political* mission that Germany shows herself to be decisively and obstinately inferior to her task.

The emphatic German decision to organise Europe hierarchically, like a pyramid with Germany at the top, is known to all. But this alone fails to capture the attitude of the German regime to the problems of European reconstruction. In every country, even in those which till yesterday had a rather clear anti-German attitude, there was no lack of political personalities and currents ready to admit that the international order which emerged from the French Revolution and culminated in Versailles had been definitively superseded and that the nation-states would have to give way to much larger political entities . . . Thus the concept of a hierarchical organization of Europe in itself was not unacceptable. But what strikes anyone who comes into contact with the Germans is their purely mechanical and materialistic conception of the European order. To organize Europe for them means deciding how much of this or that mineral should be produced and how many workers should be utilised. They have no idea that no economic order can rule if not based on a political order, and that to make the Belgian or Bohemian worker work, it is not enough to promise him a certain wage, but one must also give him the sense of serving a community, of which he is an intimate part, which he feels an affinity with and in which he recognises himself.[3]

As Luciolli observed, many Europeans were ready by the end of the 1930s to leave behind the liberal, democratic order created after 1918 by Britain, France and the United States for a more authoritarian future. What they did not bargain for was the brutal reality of Nazi imperialism, the reintroduction of slavery into Europe and the denial of all national aspirations apart from German ones.

Nazi governance was never more chaotic than during the war: Hitler's satraps wrestled for his attention, and a host of allies and collaborators intrigued among themselves. Yet through all the confusion, the uncertainty, the innumerable blueprints for the future which emanated from Nazi think-tanks, one may trace the broad outlines of the New Order as it was realized between 1938 and 1945. No experience was more crucial to the development of Europe in the twentieth century. As both Hitler and Stalin were well aware, the Second World War involved something far more profound than a series of military engagements and diplomatic negotiations; it was a struggle for the social and political future of the continent itself. And such was the shock of being subjected to a regime of unprecedented and unremitting violence that in the space of eight years a sea-change took place in Europeans' political and social attitudes, and they rediscovered the virtues of democracy.

European hearts and minds were not so much won by the Allies as lost by Hitler. Luciolli's assessment of German failure was echoed by many other observers. Reporting from Romania, an acute American journalist noted that on her arrival there in the summer of 1940 she had felt 'that Hitler might not only win the war, but could win the peace and organize Europe if he did'. But by the time she left 'on an icy morning at the end of January 1941, I was convinced that under no circumstances could Hitler win the peace or organize Europe'. Let us, then, begin our analysis of the New Order by dwelling on what we might call the Führer's lost opportunity.[4]

HITLER'S LOST OPPORTUNITY

Opinion in Europe at the end of the 1930s was by no means opposed to the idea of an authoritarian reconstruction of the continent under German leadership. The potential basis for a New Order which rejected the inheritance of Versailles extended well beyond pro-Nazi or Fascist extremists. Mistrust of German power was blended with admiration for their economic recovery; attachment to British notions of liberty was mixed with suspicion of the 'plutocrats' in the City of London whose defence of the gold standard and laissez-faire had doomed much of the continent to depression and failed to find an exit from it. 'These European peoples themselves had become indifferent to democracy, which was advertised to them in intellectual terms of freedom of thought and freedom of speech, but which in terms of their daily experience meant chiefly freedom to starve,' observed Countess Waldeck. 'I saw that not more than ten per cent of the people on the European continent cared for individual freedom or were vitally interested in it to fight for its preservation.'[5]

In Belgium, in the summer of 1940, public opinion greeted news of the German victory with 'palpable relief', and for a while Brussels was gripped by a genuine 'anti-parliamentary rage'. Belgians appeared well disposed towards the Germans, glad that the war was finally over and hopeful that their country would regain prosperity in a unified continent under a reformed and less divisive domestic political system. Hendrik de Man, president of the Belgian Workers' Party and a close adviser of King Leopold, declared in a famous manifesto on 28 June that the democratic era was ended. In his words: 'This collapse of a decrepit world, far from being a disaster, is a deliverance.' His vision of an authoritarian government led by the King seemed briefly – in the summer of 1940 – a more 'realistic' outcome of the war than any foreseeable revival of democracy. For politicians and diplomats who make a fetish out of realism, the summer of 1940 stands as a warning.

In the Netherlands, too, the revulsion against party politics lay behind Hendrik Colijn's attack on the 'evils of democracy'; Colijn, a former prime minister and head of the conservative Anti-Revolutionary Party, envisaged – like de Man – an authoritarian regime loyal to the royal House and willing to work with the Germans. Danish Social Democrat Thorvald Stauning, prime minister since 1924, advised collaboration in the interests of Europe's future economic well-being, and a national coalition government in Copenhagen cooperated smoothly with Berlin.[6]

In *Strange Defeat*, the historian Marc Bloch searched for the causes of France's humiliation – beyond the mistakes of the Army High Command – in the weaknesses of a parliamentary system ruled by old men, undermined by a cynical civil service and ultimately destroyed by the polarization which followed the 1936 Popular Front era. Few were capable so early in the war of following him out of the depths of 'bourgeois despair' in the search for a renewed and revived form of democracy, to 'adapt ourselves to the claims of a new age'. For many the solution to France's 'decadence' lay in a rapprochement with Nazi Germany. Accepting the inevitable, wrote André Gide, was wisdom. Teilhard de Chardin consoled himself with the thought that 'we are watching the birth, more than the death of a World'. Student enrolments for German classes at the Berlitz in Paris shot up from 939 in 1939 to 7,920 two years later; numbers taking English plummeted.[7]

The fall of France reverberated across the continent. 'This afternoon more bad news,' wrote a Polish doctor on 14 June 1940. 'Paris has fallen into German hands.' Two days later, he noted: 'The news from France is terrible. People are emotionally broken. Some have lost all hope. What will happen now?' In Bucharest, Waldeck observed a more positive, if cautious, reaction. 'The fall of France', she wrote, 'formed the climax to twenty years of failure of the promises of democracy to handle unemployment, inflation, deflation, labour unrest, party egoism and what not. Europe, tired of herself, and doubtful of the principles she had been living by, felt almost relieved to have everything settled . . . Hitler, Europe felt, was a smart guy – disagreeable but smart. He had gone far in making his country strong. Why not try it his way? That's how Europeans felt in this summer of 1940.'[8]

Such relatively favourable attitudes towards the Germans were quick to disappear. In France and Belgium, for example, the mood swung round totally within two to three months, leaving collaborationists increasingly isolated. The Netherlands Union was disbanded by the Germans in 1941 after it was declared 'untrustworthy'. This shift was to some extent the result of outrage at the behaviour of German soldiers and occupation forces, but it also stemmed from the changing international situation. Following the Battle of Britain it became clearer that the war would last longer than people had expected. And as we shall see, doubts over possible boundary shifts and annexations across Europe also undermined faith in Hitler's New Order.

LIVING IN HISTORIC TIMES

For the Germans themselves the mood was one of euphoria. The New Order had prevailed against the 'protectors of a dying epoch'. More than ever before, they felt themselves to be living in 'historic' times. After the march into Prague, Hitler declared that 'in the course of its thousand-year past the Reich has already proved . . . it alone is called to resolve the problem of restoring order in central Europe'. On the eve of the western campaign he announced that 'the struggle now beginning will decide the fate of the German nation for the next thousand years'. Goebbels hailed a 'time without precedent' in which the 'historic genius' of the Führer was helping build a 'new Europe'. As the Wehrmacht thrust eastwards towards Moscow the Führer dreamed great dreams, of 'the beauties of the Crimea, which we shall make accessible by means of an autobahn – for us Germans, that will be our Riviera. Crete is scorching and dry. Cyprus would be lovely, but we can reach the Crimea by road. Along that road lies Kiev! And Croatia, too, a tourists' paradise for us. I expect that after the war there will be a great upsurge of rejoicing . . . What progress in the direction of the New Europe!'[9]

Chatting to Ciano in October 1941 – perhaps the point of greatest excitement – the German Foreign Minister, Ribbentrop, predicted that Hitler's New Order in Europe would 'ensure peace for a thousand years'. The cynical Italian could not let that pass. As he recorded in his diary: 'I remarked that a thousand years is a long time. It is not easy to hang a couple of generations on the achievements of one man, even if he is a genius. Ribbentrop ended by making a concession: "Let's make it a century," he said.'[10] But if the former champagne salesman could not resist the chance of making a bargain, the Führer himself had no such doubts. 'When National Socialism has ruled long enough,' he declared one night after dinner, 'it will no longer be possible to conceive of a form of life different from ours.'[11]

No one in Berlin, then, doubted that a historic opportunity had been presented to the Third Reich. The question remained, however, how best to exploit it. What the soldiers had won, the politicians must now govern. Yet the land mass controlled by the Germans at the end of 1941 was staggeringly large – stretching from the Arctic Ocean to the fringes of the Sahara desert, from the Atlantic and the Pyrenees to the Ukraine. A quick succession of *Blitzkrieg* offensives had suddenly brought Hitler into possession of a vast empire much of which he had never planned to conquer.

From *Mein Kampf* onwards, the proposed site of the future Greater German Empire had been clear; it lay in the East, roughly covering the territory Germany had briefly controlled in 1918 after the Treaty of Brest-Litovsk. 'We are putting an end to the perpetual German march towards the South and West of Europe,' Hitler had written in *Mein Kampf*, 'and turning our eyes towards the land in the East.' The Ukraine was to be turned through German colonization into 'one of the loveliest gardens of the world'; it was, according to an SS leaflet, 'badly exploited, fertile soil of black earth that could be a Paradise, a California of Europe'.[12]

Poland would provide a connecting link to the East and a source of labour – an *Arbeitsreich* for the *Herrenvolk*, as Hitler put it shortly after the invasion.[13] The dismemberment of the country and brutal treatment of its population after September 1939 showed what methods would be used to this end. Yet what about Scandinavia, the Low Countries, the Balkans, even France? These areas figured less prominently in Hitler's thinking. All the signs are that at the end of 1939 he was reluctant to take on further military commitments. Why bother to invade countries which could be intimidated into alliance and acquiescence? Diplomatic pressure successfully ensured German control of vital resources in Romania, Hungary and Sweden. In early 1940 Hitler resisted as long as he could the idea of invading Norway until he became convinced of the threat British plans posed to Scandinavian ore shipments to Germany.[14] France had to be knocked out of the war, of course, but its role in the New Order remained unclear.

Greece could probably have remained neutral had not the botched Italian invasion brought in the British and demanded a German response. Plans to invade Yugoslavia had to be made on the run when news came in from Belgrade that the pro-Axis government had been toppled by a military coup.

German policy towards many of the defeated states was at first deliberately provisional: their fate was not to be decided until the war was over. Goebbels insisted in May 1940, on the eve of the attack on France, that there was to be *no* media discussion of war aims at all; during the war, these were to be formulated simply as 'a just and durable peace and *Lebensraum* for the German people'. Such a policy reflected the wishes of the Nazi leadership. Hitler insisted that declarations of war aims were beside the point: 'As far as our might extends we can do what we like, and what lies beyond our power we cannot do in any case.'[15]

Although in the summer of 1940 the Wehrmacht and the Foreign Office were both sympathetic to the French desire to conclude a peace treaty with the Third Reich, Hitler's disapproval blocked the way. The German generals in the Netherlands had assumed that the defeated country would remain independent and were taken aback by Hitler's decision to place it under civilian rule. But the Party and the SS were attracted by the racial affinity of the Dutch and swayed by dreams of annexation in order to reconstitute the Holy Roman Empire and Hitler had certainly not repudiated such ideas.[16]

West European statesmen, alarmed by the German annexation of chunks of Poland and Czechoslovakia, sought reassurance that the integrity of their states would be respected, and their sovereignty restored. They naturally did not believe the numerous German declarations to this effect in the absence of solid peace treaties with Berlin. Deluded King Leopold of Belgium had a disappointing interview with Hitler. Vidkun Quisling raised the subject at least three times but got nowhere; indeed, on the last occasion he was told that Hitler wanted no further discussion of the subject. German officials in the Foreign Office and the Wehrmacht who tried to argue for grants of autonomy – for France, for example, and after 1941, for Estonia – were no more successful.[17]

The question of peace settlements banished to the indefinite future, the Third Reich covered the New Europe with a patchwork of more or less provisional occupation regimes. At one extreme, certain countries were dismembered, their national identity entirely suppressed. Poland, Yugoslavia and Czechoslovakia endured this approach; their very names were to be erased from the map. 'In the future,' said Goebbels in the summer of 1940, 'we shall not refer any more to the "Government-General for the Occupied Polish Territories" but – without expressly drawing attention to this – simply to the "Government-General"; in this way, just as is gradually happening in the Protectorate (of Bohemia-Moravia), which is now simply called the Protectorate, the situation will clarify itself automatically. The population in those territories merely has the task of making our work easier.' Luxembourg, too, was all but annexed to the Reich and any reference to the 'Grand Duchy' or the 'country' of Luxembourg was banned. The juridical status of such countries was left unclear, even if their ultimate future was not.[18]

The customary German procedure was to appoint military or civil commanders, who ruled through the existing native civil service. In that war within a war which was the bureaucratic chaos of the Third Reich, these territories became so many fiefdoms, subject to competing claims from different ministries and ruled with varying degrees of success. The Danish government was most effective in preserving public order, perhaps because it was least disrupted by occupation. The king and parliament were allowed to function and in the beginning enjoyed – in theory at least – a considerable measure of sovereignty: as a result a total German staff of fewer than one hundred kept control of the entire country; in France, Greece, the Protectorate of Bohemia-Moravia, Serbia and Norway puppet governments interposed a fig-leaf of respectability between the conquerors and the civil service. In the Netherlands, a civilian Reich Commissioner governed through the Secretary-Generals of the civil service, while in Belgium the Secretary-Generals answered to the military authorities. Nominally independent governments in Croatia and Slovakia were, in fact, clearly subordinate to German wishes; Axis partners such as Finland, Romania, Bulgaria and Hungary had slightly more room for manoeuvre.

Hitler's imagination was captured by the example of the British in India. Their model of imperial rule, such as he conceived it, struck him as admirable. After the invasion of the Soviet Union his mind returned again and again to the problem of how the British ruled the subcontinent with a handful of men; for him the Ukraine was 'that new Indian Empire'; the Eastern Front would become Germany's North-West Frontier where generations of officers would win their spurs and preserve the martial virtues of the Aryan race. But the Führer had little understanding of British imperial techniques of governance; he was critical of the laxness of British racial attitudes and their willingness to permit some degree of local political autonomy.[19]

The India parallel cropped up on one of the very rare occasions when Nazi war aims were briefly aired in public. This was in a speech made by the prominent radio commentator, Hans Fritzsche, almost certainly following Hitler's instructions, in October 1941 when a Russian defeat seemed assured. Telling the foreign press that the war had been decided, Fritzsche went on to lay out Germany's political plans: Europe was to become economically self-sufficient under German leadership. The Germans themselves would have to be trained in the 'imperial European idea' and prepared for continual minor military operations in the East analogous to the problems the British faced in India. 'As for the nations dominated by us,' he said, 'our language to them will become very much freer and colder. There will, of course, be no question of some crummy little state obstructing European peace by some special requests or special demands – in such an event it would get a sharp reminder of its task in Europe.'[20]

Such a harsh vision reflected contemporary Nazi criticisms of liberal international law. Carl Schmitt, for instance, argued that the conquered territories now formed Germany's own *Grossraum*. Just as the Monroe Doctrine was supposed to justify the non-intervention of other powers in the western hemisphere, he wrote, so Germany had won the right to rule Europe. Above all, it had won the right to govern by new rules: the old system of international law with its universal pretensions and its basis in the relations of sovereign states had to be replaced by a genuinely National Socialist jurisprudence of '*Volk* Law'. Not all peoples, according to Schmitt, were equally capable of bearing the weight of a modern constitutional state. Departing abruptly from the liberal notion – as enshrined in the League of Nations – that all states were sovereign and juridically equal, Schmitt declared that a 'high degree of organization' and 'voluntary discipline' were required in the modern world. The Nazi rulers of the Netherlands and the General Government both indicated publicly that the era of 'absolute independence' was over.[21]

Nor indeed was neutrality any more acceptable. As one commentator stated:

What small state is there which is sufficiently independent to be neutral towards the Great Powers? The crisis of neutrality is in reality the crisis of the structure of our continent, of the collapse of old orders and empires, and of the birth of new dynasties. The small states have become the prey of an inexorable course of history, and the only question is whether they will give in without hope or full of hope.[22]

Luciolli, then, was surely right to characterize the regime's basic conception of politics as hierarchical. Europe was called to rule the world but only on the condition that it was itself ruled by the Reich. For Hitler no devolution of power to racial inferiors was permissible; it could only be a sign of weakness, not strength. German superiority had to be jealously safeguarded in every sphere, with sometimes ludicrous results. After the Czech national ice-hockey team beat the Germans 5–1 in Prague, Goebbels alluded to 'the mistaken practice of matching oneself with colonial peoples in a field in which we are inferior. Herr Gutterer is to arrange ... that a repetition of such incidents is made impossible.' Even the Italians, supposedly Germany's partners in the making of the New Order, got the same treatment; directives issued in connection with the treatment of foreign workers ordered that 'relationships with Italians are not welcomed'.[23]

At the political level, such attitudes were replicated to the detriment of Germany's would-be collaborators. As Luciolli remarked, given the pervasive sense of disaffection from the Versailles order in Europe by 1939, there was little reason to suppose that collaboration as a political project would not be successful. It is hard now to remember that the very concept had a positive ring to those who coined it in

France. Laval and Pétain saw collaboration as a partnership of two imperial powers, and thus a way of salvaging French sovereignty. Hitler stood in the way of such ideas.

He was especially wary of *soi-disant* National Socialists. If unpopular they were likely to be ineffective administrators, if popular, a threat. Quisling scrambled into power during the invasion of Norway but was kicked out after a week. Degrelle in Belgium and Mussert in Holland were put on ice. They might be allowed to recruit gullible or desperate young men to fight on the Eastern Front, but power resided in the hands of professional civil servants. The disillusioned young French collaborator, Robert Brasillach, concluded despondently in August 1943: 'There is no longer a fascist Europe.'[24]

What made the Degrelles and Musserts unsuitable partners was precisely, of course, their nationalism. 'For Norway to become germanophile it must become national,' declared Quisling. Mussert drew up a scheme for a League of Germanic Peoples in which Hitler would be head but whose members (Germany, the Scandinavian countries, the Greater Netherlands), would have independent National Socialist governments and their own military forces. It is difficult to imagine anything less likely to have appealed to Hitler. On 30 June 1941 young Ukrainian nationalists pre-empted Berlin by their 'Proclamation of the Ukrainian State' in Lviv; two weeks later, most of them had been arrested and the movement was broken. Hitler's imperialism was thus of a very different kind from that of Wilhelm II, who had supported Paul Skoropadsky during the German occupation of the Ukraine in 1918: both favoured authoritarian regimes, but Wilhelm was prepared to allow a local proxy to govern in his name. Hitler refused even that, insisting: 'I cannot set any goals which will some day produce independent . . . autonomous states.'[25]

The essential feature of the 'new European Order' is that it was a German Order. Although numerous Nazi visionaries played with the ideology of Europeanism, for Hitler himself it was only Germany, or more precisely *Deutschtum* that mattered. Following the invasion of the Soviet Union, Berlin propaganda publicized the idea that this was a 'crusade for Europe': a new 'Song for Europe' was broadcast, stamps with the slogan 'European United Front against Bolshevism' were issued and the press even claimed in late November 1941 that 'born out of discord, struggle and misery the United States of Europe has at last become a reality'. Nevertheless, such slogans clashed with the reality of occupation rule experienced by ordinary people and there was no sign that this Europeanism was taken any more seriously outside Germany than it was by the Führer.[26] After Stalingrad, when the Germans started to seek out friends and allies more seriously, it was too late. No one was convinced by the U-turn in Nazi jurisprudence which led to declarations of 'anti-imperialism', especially as these had no discernible effect upon policy. In eastern Europe, where the Red Army's advance made anti-communism a potentially fruitful form of political warfare, Nazi racialism had alienated the population beyond Goebbels's reach. In the West, beyond any plausible Soviet sphere of influence, anti-communism offered little. Only in Greece, and to a lesser extent Serbia and Northern Italy, was it possible to poison the domestic scene to the point of civil war. As the German forces withdrew, they left behind them an inheritance of bitter internecine bloodletting. By 1944, the Cold War was already casting a shadow over Europe, but not sufficiently to save Hitler's empire.

ORGANIZING EUROPE

In so far as there was a Nazi vision for Europe, it belonged to the sphere of economics not politics. Associated with the idea of a German Monroe Doctrine was the notion of a *Grossraumwirtschaft* – a regional economy with Germany at its heart. In certain forms, this bore a more than passing resemblance to the post-war Common Market. The 'New Order' beloved of the youthful technocrats at the Reich Ministry of Economics involved the economic integration of western Europe and the creation of a tariff-free zone: Minister Walther Funk went so far as to propose such a scheme in the early summer of 1940. Goering, who carried far more weight in the Nazi establishment, also discussed the need for cross-national investment in Europe under German auspices. Others looked to the Balkans, where German economic penetration had intensified during the 1930s. Trade agreements were negotiated in 1939 and 1940 with Romania and Hungary that brought vital raw materials under the control of the Third Reich.

Late in 1940, Hermann Neubacher – later Hitler's Balkan supremo – confided to an American journalist the bright future which awaited Europe after the war: 'Germany's economic organization of the Balkans is the first step in a plan to set up the entire European continent as a single *Grossraum*, which instead of individual countries would form the economic unit of the future. A common plan would regulate production across the European *Grossraum*.'[27] From this continental bloc both the United States and Great Britain were to be excluded; Europe was to become self-sufficient. The gold standard and laissez-faire of the post-Versailles order were to be replaced by barter trade and planning of production on a continental scale in an extension of German trade policy of the 1930s.

The idea of 'organizing' Europe into a vast continental economy was discussed before and after 1939 far more openly than was the continent's political future. Nevertheless, particularly during the first three years of the war, such grand schemes had little practical impact upon policy. The *Blitzkrieg* strategy for waging war dictated rather different methods of exploiting the economic resources of the conquered territories; only with the turn to 'total war' did the idea of some form of economic integration appear attractive in the context of the war effort itself.

But Nazi thinking about international economics provided no analogue to the liberal doctrine of the mutual benefits offered by the market. The regime sometimes claimed that Germany's partners would benefit from associating with her: this had after all been the case to some extent in the 1930s and was not entirely implausible, especially after the hardships associated with international capitalism in the 1920s. Nevertheless, it was increasingly clear that Europe's prime economic function was to support Germany. Only in so far as that function was best served by securing the economic prosperity of the rest of the continent did it seem at all likely that the economic benefits would be shared more widely. Countries like Greece and Romania soon suspected they had exchanged the tyranny of the City of London for the stranglehold of Berlin.

Such a narrow vision of the European economy was particularly pronounced during the war itself. To the despair of those like Goering and later Speer, who were responsible for increasing armaments production, Hitler was extremely reluctant to see living standards inside the Reich fall. He wished at all costs to avoid a repetition of the debacle of 1918, when, he believed, the collapse of the home front had led to military defeat. The regime kept food consumption as close as possible to pre-war levels and was unenthusiastic about encouraging women into the factories. Hitler knew that there was little public enthusiasm for an extended conflict and remained sensitive to Party reports of dissatisfaction. He was reluctant to test his popularity by making sharp cuts in consumer goods production. The economic resources of Europe would enable him to avoid this.[28]

With the Wehrmacht as it invaded one country after another came a variety of economic experts, private businessmen and special agents who took over existing firms, expropriated Jewish-owned businesses, and established contacts with prominent local industrialists. The Wehrmacht, and other authorities, levied 'occupation costs' and requisitioned existing stocks of strategic goods from jute to bicycles. The bulk of these were consumed by army units, or sent back to the Reich in soldiers' parcels. In the First World War, German troops in the Balkans had received food from home; this time, they sent food back.

The overall effect of these policies differed rather sharply from one area to another. In the industrial economies of the Protectorate and north-western Europe, the short-term policy of physical expropriation soon gave way to one of allowing existing installations to continue production before taking over the finished products. The Aryanization of Jewish-owned firms offered an avenue to direct control, particularly of Czech and Austrian holdings. Firms, however, owned by non-Jews or by the state were also brought under German control. In this way, much of the most important heavy industry and mining production of central Europe was incorporated into the Reichswerke AG 'Hermann Göring' by a process of what has been termed 'legalized theft'. Three quarters of France's iron-ore supply went to Germany, half of total Belgian production was for German purposes. Czech armaments production was crucial to the war effort. From these countries, there was a clear net economic gain to Germany.[29]

Ironically, Nazi economic policy worked much better there than in the territories in the East, whose economic importance had loomed so large in National Socialist thinking. Whereas Goering – the economic overlord of the Reich until 1942 – accepted the need to exploit local resources in western Europe *in situ*, in the East he pushed for straightforward 'pillage' until confronted with the resistance of local Party and military rulers in Poland and the Ukraine, who had to cope with the consequences.[30]

In the primarily agrarian economies of Russia and the Balkans, German policies of expropriation led swiftly to the most terrible conditions. The peasants' response was to stop producing for the market, the surplus vanished, and city dwellers in these regions faced starvation. Only a month after the German invasion of Greece in April 1941, observers there predicted famine. They were right: around 100,000 Greeks may have died of hunger that first winter. In the East, the Nazi regime was prepared for worse yet. 'Many tens of millions of people will be superfluous in this area and will die or have to emigrate to Siberia,' concluded one report a month before the invasion. 'Attempts to rescue the population there from famine by drawing upon surpluses from the black earth region can only be at the expense of provisioning Europe.' With the first outbreaks of guerrilla resistance to German rule, and the ruthless German response, life in the countryside became precarious, and all chances of efficiently exploiting the 'black earth' of the Ukraine vanished for the duration of the war.[31]

Whereas Goering and the Nazi Party favoured direct exploitation of the local population, Alfred Rosenberg, who was nominally in charge of policy in the East, favoured encouraging pro-German and anti-Russian nationalist groups. As political warfare this might have worked, except that it was opposed by Rosenberg's own deputies. Reichskommissar Kube promised the Belorussians 'no parliamentary nonsense and no democratic hypocrisy'. In the Ukraine there was Erich Koch, a devoted follower of Hitler. 'I will pump every last thing out of this country,' Koch had said, 'I did not come here to spread bliss but to help the Führer.' The Ukrainians were 'niggers' and their attempts at political assertion met with Koch's contempt.

The results were obvious to many of his subordinates. 'If we shoot the Jews,' protested one administrator, 'liquidate the prisoners of war, starve considerable portions of the population, and also lose part of the farmers through famine . . . who in the world is then supposed to be economically productive here?' At the start of the occupation, the farmers in the Ukraine had hailed the Germans as liberators. Had Hitler agreed to privatize the collective farms as Rosenberg and his advisers urged, agricultural output might well have risen instead of dropping. But he did not, and the great granary of Europe never fulfilled its promise. Famine spread across the Ukraine and eastern Galicia in the winter of 1941. A revival of industrial activity took place in the East following a change of heart by Goering, but too late to win back the sympathies of a by now totally disillusioned population. By 1943, many peasants were turning their thoughts back to Moscow, arguing that 'a bad mother is still better than a step-mother who makes many promises'. Rosenberg believed his underling Koch had 'ruined a great political opportunity'. Only the more moderate policy the Wehrmacht pursued with the Muslim mountaineers in the Caucasus indicated one of the great might-have-beens of the war.[32]

TOTAL WAR

'The *Blitzkrieg* is over,' wrote a military economics specialist in January 1942. 'As for the economy, it is a matter of the first priority that it should be clearly reconstructed on the basis of a long war.' In the winter of 1941, the German leadership was forced to move the economy on to a total war footing. This meant, as Milward observes, that the original scheme for the creation of a New Europe had failed and with it Goering's efforts to coordinate arms production through the Four-Year Plan; saving the National Socialist revolution would require a profound transformation of economic relationships and rationalization of the gargantuan but massively wasteful rearmament effort that had been going on since 1936.[33]

Now even more intense exploitation of the satellites was required. The young technocrat Albert Speer, a favourite of the Führer's, began to coordinate arms production. Party hack Fritz Sauckel was ordered to conscript millions more foreign workers into the service of the Reich. Having killed off nearly three million Russian POWs that winter, the regime now woke up to its desperate labour needs. As one official noted in February 1942: 'The current difficulty besetting labour deployment would not have arisen had a decision been made in proper time for a larger-scale deployment of Russian POWs. There were 3.9 million Russians available; of these now only 1.1 million are left.'[34]

The Reich was already dependent on foreign labour: some 700,000 Polish workers were employed by the summer of 1940, and one year later there were some 2.1 million civilian labourers and 1.2 million POWs. Far more, however, were now needed. From 1942 Sauckel's labour drives across the continent resulted in the forced conscription of millions of workers. The violent methods employed by his officials aroused enormous protest and spurred on the growth of resistance to German rule. One report of November 1942 gives a graphic picture of how workers were actually recruited:

Men and women, including teenagers aged 15 and above, [are being] picked up on the street, at open-air markets and village celebrations and then speeded away. The inhabitants, for that reason, are frightened, stay hidden inside and avoid going out ... The application of flogging as a punishment has been supplemented since the beginning of October by the burning down of farmsteads or entire villages as a reprisal for the failure to heed the orders given to the local townships for making manpower available.[35]

In April 1943 Sauckel's agency head in Warsaw was shot dead in his office; the following month, widespread protest caused forced conscription to be slowed down in western Europe.

Even so, foreign labour was vital to the German war effort. As early as 1942 Goering's giant Reichswerke had drawn 80–90 per cent of its 600,000 workers from foreign workers and POWs; the rest of the economy followed suit. By 1944 there were eight million, mostly civilian workers, in the Reich, and another two million working directly under German command in third countries. These workers tilled farms and provided a cheap source of domestic servants. They constituted one third of the labour force in the armaments industry by November 1944, and more than one quarter of the workforce in the machine-building and chemical industries. Their presence cushioned the German population and saved the regime from having to establish a comprehensive domestic labour policy, particularly one that would have forced German housewives into paid work. As a Nazi labour scholar wrote: 'How much more we were prepared to endure a temporary increase in the alien element in certain occupations rather than endanger the folk-biological strength of the German people by the enhanced deployment of women in the workforce.'[36]

Sauckel's continental manhunt may have aided the war effort in Germany, but it caused tremendous disruption elsewhere. Faced with the unpredictable threat of being rounded up and sent to the Reich, male workers in occupied Europe often abandoned their jobs and went into hiding. Local administrators sought ways to protect their workforce from deportation; policemen turned a blind eye. The growth of the Maquis in France and resistance in Greece was directly linked to the growing intensity of Sauckel's labour drives. Politicians and civil servants tried to persuade the Germans to change their policy. Their greatest ally was Albert Speer, the Minister for War Production.

Speer believed, unlike Sauckel, that economic cooperation with the industrialized economies of France, Belgium and Holland was essential to the Reich war effort. Bringing labourers into Germany by force made no sense if it alienated foreign governments and businessmen, disrupted production and increased resistance to German rule. In France, Sauckel's policy had pushed Laval to the point of desperation: 'It is no longer a policy of collaboration,' complained the French premier, 'but on the French side of a policy of sacrifice and on the German side of a policy of compulsion.' What Speer proposed in effect was to resuscitate the policy of collaboration – as a matter of economic rationality rather than political pride.[37]

Speer envisaged a rationalization of production which treated the whole of north-western Europe as a single economic unit. This was very different to the policies of expropriation which had characterized the early forms of German economic policy and which, in a sense, reached their culmination in Sauckel's exploitation of European labour. Speer's was a cooler, less nationalistic outlook which preferred planning to plunder and the world of business to that of National Socialist ideology. For Speer, the creation of a Europe-wide armaments industry – essential if Germany was to have a chance of winning the war – necessitated the protection of industrial economies outside the Reich, and by extension, the protection of an adequately skilled and motivated labour-force.

Speer's efforts to build up arms production in Poland and the Ukraine ran afoul of the economic havoc created there by earlier policies. But in France, where the ideological stakes were low, Speer's strategy made an impact. He managed to block Sauckel's labour drive and reached an understanding with local technocrats (like Jean Bichelonne, the Vichy Minister of Industrial Production) which allowed industrial output to be planned by committee rather than merely targeted for expropriation. 'It is imbecility if I call up one million men in France,' insisted Speer in criticism of Sauckel, 'I end up with two million workers less there and fifty to a hundred thousand more in Germany.' Not only war production but also consumer goods were going to the Reich. By the autumn of 1943, some 40–50 per cent of French industrial output was being used for German purposes. By this point Speer was thinking in terms of creating giant industrial cartels in coal, cars, aluminium and other goods which could be planned in a tariff-free European zone.[38]

Such visions made Speer look like a pioneer of the industrial arrangements that would lead to the European Coal and Steel Community and ultimately to the Common Market. There is some truth in this view, which is certainly at least as plausible as that which traces these post-war institutions back to the federalism of the anti-Nazi resistance. But the fact remains that the New Order was much more, and much less, than a proto-Common Market. In one way Speer was a realist, for he recognized the impossibility of winning a modern, highly industrialized war on the basis of Hitler's primitive economics of conquest; in another way, though, he was deluded, for without Hitler's politics the Third Reich was nothing. Speer's vision, in other words, of a world where business superseded political conflict – a world strikingly akin to that which did eventually emerge after 1945 – could not be realized in Hitler's Europe. Hitler himself limited Speer's planning and never totally withdrew his support for Sauckel: the victory of rationality over ideology was only temporary.

If Europe could not be 'organized', the fault lay largely with the 'organizers' and their concept of 'organization'. With his customary lucidity, the philologist Victor Klemperer had quietly noted its Nazi connotations of imposed discipline, of hierarchy and of order which in turn stemmed from its underlying racialism. Its mirror image turned out to be the 'organizing' (i.e. thieving, pilfering and plundering) carried out by the lowest of the low in the concentration camps. Rather than a principle of value-free, managerial efficiency, organization Nazi-style meant the economic subordination of the lesser races of Europe to the Nordic-Germanic *Volk*. Thus, economics could not be separated from ideology; ultimately, race was to be the genuine 'organizing' principle for the continent.[39]

EUROPE AS A RACIAL ENTITY

'Europe is not a geographical entity,' commented Hitler in August 1941. 'It is a racial entity.' The League of Nations had tried to keep minorities where they were, and ensure stability through international law; Hitler, in contrast, had no faith in law and aimed to ensure stability by uprooting peoples. In pursuit of racial goals, nations were rearranged and millions of people were forcibly driven from their homes, resettled hundreds of miles away in strange surroundings, abandoned, forced into labour camps, or deliberately put to death. It was in this respect, above all, that the Second World War differed from previous conflicts. A vast gulf lay between Kaiser Wilhelm's imperial aspirations of 1918 – with their old-fashioned programme of assimilation through cultural Germanization – and the biological racism of 1939.[40]

This new world of state-sponsored mass murder and cultural extermination gave birth to a new term – genocide – introduced for the first time in 1944 in a study of *Axis Rule in Occupied Europe* by a Polish-Jewish lawyer called Raphael Lemkin. After the war, the Nuremberg trials, the UN Genocide Convention, the Eichmann trial and new media interest in what became known as the Holocaust all made people familiar with the idea that the Second World War had been in some measure a race war. Often, however, this was seen exclusively in terms of 'the war against the Jews' (to cite the title of one famous study). In fact, the Final Solution of the Jewish question emerged out of a broader interlocking set of racial issues which the Nazi regime sought to 'solve' through war.

One consequence of the Nazi conquest of Europe was the extension on to a continental scale of the dialectic of the Nazi racial welfare state – a state, in other words, where police measures to repress 'racial undesirables' were the obverse of policies to safeguard the vigour of the *Volksgemeinschaft*. The New Order in Europe involved, on the one hand, measures to curb the 'threat' which Jews, gypsies, Poles, Ukrainians and other *Untermenschen* presented to the Reich, and on the other hand, grand schemes on behalf of *Deutschtum*. This meant, in particular, providing for the welfare and resettlement of the ten million so-called *Volksdeutsche* – German-speakers living outside the borders of the Reich. Expulsion and colonization, extermination and social provision were the two sides of the same imperial Nazi coin.

But the war did not merely expand the geographical reach of Nazi racial policies, it also radicalized and complicated them. War was the great catalyst. For Hitler in the late 1930s, the first resettlement of Germans from the South Tyrol was initially a matter of diplomatic necessity; in Himmler's hands after October 1939 it became the prelude to a much more ambitious vision involving the total ethnic recasting of eastern Europe. Resettlement goals changed several times as the amount of German territory increased and the outlook changed. The same might be said for Nazi policy towards 'racial undesirables'. Policy moved into uncharted waters as the war progressed.

On the 'Jewish question' new vistas, and new difficulties, opened up as first Poland, then western Europe, and finally large parts of the Soviet Union came under Nazi control. Along the 'twisted road to Auschwitz' were wrong turns like the Madagascar Plan of 1940 (by which Europe's Jewish population were to be shipped to the island)

and deathly improvisations like the gas-vans used in Serbia, the Ukraine and Chełmno before the Nazi leadership hit upon the idea of industrialized mass murder in the death camps.

The expansion and radicalization of the racial agenda was accompanied by the rapid growth of the SS. Consolidating the security services in the RSHA under Heydrich gave Himmler extensive influence in policing and intelligence throughout much of the occupied territories. Created in 1934, the concentration camp empire (excluding the death camps) expanded its population from 25,000 in 1939 to 714,000 in 1945 and was administered by another wartime SS office, the WVHA. The death camps themselves did not exist in 1939; in 1942 they killed over one million people. The creation of a new class of German colonists from the hapless *Volksdeutsche* became the responsibility of the RKFDV (see below), established in October 1939. It removed more than one million ethnic Germans from their homes, managed hundreds of resettlement camps, and settled at least 400,000 across eastern Europe. It was thus war that brought the SS close to rivalling the power of the state apparatus created in the Soviet Union for controlling the lives and fates of millions of people.[41]

The centrality of racial thinking – as well as the idea of industrializing mass murder – was what primarily differentiated Hitler's empire from Stalin's. Possessing the power to reshape the human composition of an entire continent, Himmler and the SS came face to face with the ambiguities, dilemmas and limitations of an imperial policy shaped by the premises of biological racism. What, in the first place, was to be the role of the Germans themselves? Were they to be concentrated in the Reich, which was more or less the view which prevailed until 1941, or should some form a frontier class manning the eastern marches as their medieval forebears had done? As a master race were they to lord it over Slavic helots, manning estates of thousands of serfs, or should they till the soil themselves in accordance with the Nazi view which saw *Blut und Boden* as the ultimate guarantor of Aryan vitality? How, too, was an ethnic German to be recognized – by language, looks or genealogy? Bitter doctrinal disputes on such issues took place among Nazi bureaucrats throughout the war. As for the *Untermenschen*, were they a necessary labour force or a biological threat to be exterminated? Such were the dilemmas of *apartheid* as practised on the vast and murderous scale of Hitler's New Order.

THE RACE WAR (I): POLAND, 1939–41

The Versailles approach to minorities problems in eastern Europe expired at Munich, when Ribbentrop, the German foreign minister, secretly promised the Italians that the ethnic German minority in South Tyrol would be resettled in the Reich. Together with the annexation of the Sudetenland, this pledge ended the era of the Minorities Treaties and opened up a more brutal approach to Europe's ethnic tensions. Legal guarantees were replaced by forced population transfers along the lines of the Greco-Turkish exchange of fifteen years earlier.

Initially this meant a large influx of ethnic Germans into the Reich. Just as Hitler's need for Italian support in 1938 led him to reverse earlier policy and sanction the resettlement of 80,000 Germans from the South Tyrol, so his need for Russian backing in 1939–40 led to a similar sacrificing of the German communities in the Baltic and Bessarabia. In October 1939 the SS was given the task of repatriating around 75,000 Germans from Latvia and Estonia; the following month, a further German–Soviet agreement embraced the 128,000 *Volksdeutsche* of Soviet-occupied Poland. Within weeks, these people began arriving in the Reich and occupied Poland, and questions of where and how to resettle them had to be faced.

Hitler had first intended resettlement to be a matter for the Nazi Party, but Himmler quickly persuaded him to entrust it to the SS. At the beginning of 1940, he established the Reich Commission for the Consolidation of Germandom (RKFDV) to organize evacuations, the racial screening of evacuees and reception camps. The RKFDV was trustee of the property the Baltic Germans had left behind, but it was also responsible for finding new properties for resettlement. This latter task involved organizing the expulsion of the local Polish and Jewish population from property in the conquered territories.

Between 1939 and 1941 the focus of RKFDV activities was Poland, now split into the western territories of Warthegau and Danzig which were incorporated into the Reich, and the rump General Government, ruled as a colony by Hans Frank. Himmler envisaged creating a clear line of demarcation between Germans and the 'racially inferior' population. The ethnic Germans were to be brought into the western incorporated territories, while the local Poles and Jews from those regions were to be expelled eastwards into the General Government, which he envisaged as a reservation for the *Untermenschen*.

Such a scheme, however, disturbed other Nazi bureaucrats. It involved, in the first place, a high degree of disruption of local economic life. In the annexed territories, the expulsion of the local Polish peasantry and Jewish artisan class threatened to lead to economic breakdown; at the same time, those administering the General Government were distinctly unhappy at having to receive masses of impoverished and uprooted Poles and Jews. This prospect would make it impossible for them to realize their own ambitions of turning the General Government into an important centre of economic activity. The clash between racial dogmatism and economic interest pitted Himmler, the SS and the Nazi Party ideologues against Hans Frank, the ruler of the General Government, and Goering, spokesman for major economic interests in the Reich.

This conflict was still unresolved when further German–Soviet agreements led to the 'recall to the Fatherland' of 50,000 Germans from Lithuania and 130,000 from Bessarabia and northern Bukovina. By the summer of 1941, on the eve of the invasion of the Soviet Union, the RKFDV had settled 200,000 *Volksdeutsche* in western Poland, mostly on expropriated farmsteads. Another 275,000 immigrants remained in hundreds of resettlement centres awaiting screening and transportation to a new life. As many as one million Poles and Jews had been summarily expelled to the General Government. Fifty per cent of all commercial establishments were now in the hands of German trustees from the Reich. The Jewish population there had swollen to 1,650,000, the newcomers mostly crowded into disease-ridden ghettos and work-camps. Frank had drafted 600,000–700,000 Polish workers as labourers for the Reich.

The treatment of the incoming ethnic Germans by the RKFDV, the Nazi Party and other agencies was remarkably comprehensive and indeed welcoming – a welfare programme on an imperial scale. An American journalist touring the Galatz camp in Romania, which had been set up to cater for returning Bessarabian Germans in late 1940, described how

Old people sat peacefully in the sun on benches . . . Women with the headcloth of the Germans in these parts of the world gossiped as they did their washing on troughs along the hangars. There were porches, overgrown with green, where other women did their pressing and washing. The youngsters marched and sang and heiled under the supervision of SS-men and *Volksdeutsche* . . . There were more babies and little children here than in French Canada, so it seemed, playing in the care of kindergarten teachers, chiefly young German girls from Rumania and Jugoslavia who were thus doing their voluntary labor service. Now and then a young SS-man fondly picked up a child and carried it around on his shoulders or held it on his lap . . .

It was amazing to listen to these refugees. According to all standards they had suffered a major catastrophe in being forced to leave the lands of their ancestors. Nor did they know yet where and when they would find new homes. Their immediate prospect was other camps, as their final destination had not yet been determined. Yet old and young, rich and poor, expressed a minimum of regret, and a boundless confidence in the Führer's Germany. These prolific descendants of prolific colonists, who spoke the antiquated German of the Wuerttemberg at the time of Schiller, were returning to Hitler's Germany as to the Promised Land . . . To have inspired them with such fervent belief was, one had to admit, a great triumph for Hitler. You could not help being impressed with this triumph. Here the protective state acted really protective in a grandiose manner.[42]

Although it should be noted that Stalin was at least as important an influence on these refugees as Hitler (*Volksdeutsche* outside the Soviet sphere were a lot less enthusiastic about 'repatriation'), it is certainly true that the Third Reich, remaining true to its concern with racial welfare, expended idealism, effort and money on the repatriation effort.

Not all immigrants welcomed being uprooted: significant numbers stayed behind whilst there were plenty who grumbled about wanting to return home. Hapless Lorrainers hardly wished to be settled in

Galicia to satisfy Himmler's racial experiments; Latvian Germans wanted to go home once the Baltic states were occupied by the Wehrmacht; the *Volksdeutsche* villagers from outside Athens, whose Bavarian ancestors had settled there with King Otto a century earlier, now found themselves in a camp in Passau where they muttered that 'we don't like it here in Germany, we want to return to Greece'. Nevertheless many were mollified by the eager young girls from the League of German Girls (BDM) who came east from the Reich to welcome new groups, tidying up expropriated farms for their arrival and helping with childcare. Thousands of Hitler Youth teenagers were drawn by the 'mystery of the East' and used their Land Service Year to help the newcomers settle down.[43]

Needless to say, however, the Germans' treatment of Poles and Jews was rather different. From the western territories, the hapless *Untermenschen* were deported by the SS with little advance warning. Allowed to carry a small amount of hand luggage and forbidden to take along valuables or more than a small sum of money, they were directed to the nearest railway station, or simply abandoned in open fields. No provision was made for their future welfare. In a deliberate effort to weaken or obliterate Polish resistance – what Hitler called 'political house-cleaning' – the intelligentsia and other elements of national leadership were targeted for mass murder by SS squads. The faculty members of Cracow University, for example, were deported en masse in November 1939 to the Sachsenhausen concentration camp, where most of them died. During 1940, villages were burned down and hundreds of civilians killed in a series of reprisals for assaults of German personnel, setting the pattern for a regime of brutality soon to be extended throughout eastern Europe. The 'AB Action' that summer led a further 3,000 notables to be arrested and executed: the German officials responsible were guaranteed immunity from prosecution. On 12 July, Zygmunt Klukowski, a Polish doctor, noted in his diary the 'terrible news about the executions in Lublin of more than forty people ... I have a difficult time believing this is true.' Two days later, learning that a German forestry official had shot a young Polish boy with impunity, he wrote sadly: 'It is legal for Germans to shoot Poles and Jews.'[44]

What made the Polish predicament particularly dreadful was that Soviet forces were behaving with even greater ruthlessness in the zone of Eastern Poland occupied by the Red Army between 1939 and 1941. There too forced settlement was in full swing, while the total of those killed at Soviet hands was many hundreds of thousands. This figure left even the Nazi murder tally at this time far behind. But the Germans, in their war of racial conquest, would soon overtake the Communists, and embark upon a full-scale 'war of annihilation'. Already, the inmates of Polish mental asylums had been assembled and machine-gunned to death to clear space for SS barracks. In this way, the German euthanasia programme was reaching into the occupied territories. Treatment of Polish Jews was equally alarming. The deportation programme from the western territories had not generally discriminated between Poles and Jews – both were to be cleared from the areas reserved for German settlement. But the SS, through special Death's Head regiments and SiPo/SD *Einsatzgruppen* carried out summary executions of Jewish elders, burned synagogues and looted Jewish property. Lublin was assigned as the destination for the hundreds of thousands of Jews expelled from western Poland.

Nineteenth-century Germanization in Poland had been a gradual process, with culture and language providing for a gradual transmission of German values to the population at large (often indeed via the Jews). In sharp contrast, exclusion, separation and extermination were the guiding principles of Nazi policy. The occupied territories were to be Germanized by force and as quickly as possible. Hitler told his *Gauleiters* that they had no more than ten years to complete the Germanization of their provinces. German replaced Polish in public life, and the cities, in particular, were soon transformed: Łódź was renamed Litzmannstadt; Poznań became Posen. Even in the General Government, in central and southern Poland, similar processes were at work. Klukowski noted that 'in Biłgoraj there is more and more Germanization. Everywhere there are new signs in German.'[45]

Germanization involved a fully-fledged policy of cultural denial. Polish universities were closed down (as Czech ones had been earlier) and in accordance with the policy of 'spiritual sterilization' only limited primary and vocational education was permitted. Explaining

Nazi education policy in May 1940 Himmler wrote that 'the sole goal of this school should be: simple arithmetic up to 500 at most; writing of one's name; a doctrine that it is a divine law to obey the Germans and to be honest, industrious and good. I don't think reading should be required. Apart from this school there are to be no schools at all in the East.'[46]

Having made a sharp distinction between cultures, the SS still endeavoured to sift the racially 'valuable' from the 'worthless' elements of the population. But to identify potential Germans among the Slavic population in the ethnically mixed societies of eastern Europe, the pseudo-science of biological racism offered an imperfect guide. The selection procedure was as strict as it was arbitrary. One Nazi official tasted the process at first hand when he was included by mistake in the screening of hundreds of Czechs and was declared racially valueless before he could prove his identity. But this moment of humiliation was insignificant beside the thousands of families which were split up in the effort to conserve racially valuable stock, or the hundreds of thousands of women who were shipped off to the Reich, having been declared Germanizable, in order to learn German ways in domestic service to German households. Eventually, the screening process was even extended to the concentration camps in an effort to reinforce the increasingly depleted stocks of *Deutschtum* with blue-eyed, blond-haired slave labourers.[47]

For the Jewish population, no such escape valve was offered. Jewish culture itself was to meet a 'historical death', and would exist only as a memory. Alfred Rosenberg, the regime's chief ideological theorist, sent out squads of soldiers, bibliographers and art historians to seize the cultural possessions of Jewish communities across Europe. They were destined for Frankfurt where Hitler had instructed Rosenberg to establish a research centre for Nazi ideologues. By 1943 an administrator was boasting that 'in the New Order of Europe *the* library for the Jewish question not only for Europe but for the world will arise in Frankfurt on Main'.[48]

THE RACE WAR (2):
VERNICHTUNGSKRIEG, 1941−5

The murderous dimensions of Nazi policy towards the Jews took time to emerge from out of the overall racial restructuring of eastern Europe. As Himmler's schemes for an *apartheid* state in former Poland ran foul of other Nazi bureaucrats, the aim of using the General Government as a 'reservation' for the Jews had to be abandoned. Hitler himself had come to realize by March 1940 that the idea of herding millions of Jews into the Lublin region was not feasible. In this policy vacuum, the invasion of France gave Himmler a new opening, and in May 1940 he outlined for Hitler a comprehensive new approach to Germany's racial dilemmas.

In 'Some Thoughts on the Treatment of Alien Populations in the East', Himmler suggested that the entire population of former Poland be racially screened: the 'racially valuable' could then be brought to the Reich, while the rest would be dumped in the General Government to serve as a reservoir of cheap labour for the Reich. Touching briefly on the subject of the Jews, Himmler noted: 'I hope completely to erase the concept of Jews through the possibility of a great emigration to a colony in Africa or elsewhere.' The memorandum as a whole raised the possibility of genocide, only to dismiss it: 'However cruel and tragic each individual case may be, this method is still the mildest and best, if one rejects the Bolshevik method of physical extermination of a people out of inner conviction as un-German and impossible.'[49]

The African colony which offered itself following the victory over France was Madagascar, and for some months the 'Madagascar Plan' was taken very seriously. It rested, however, upon the assumption that not only France but Britain too would be defeated, and once it became clear that the Battle of Britain had failed, Madagascar faded from Nazi minds. Hitler's short-term response was to override Hans Frank's objections to having to receive more Jews in the General Government. But as Christopher Browning has remarked, the goal of the Final Solution at this stage remained 'the expulsion of the Jews to the furthest extremity of the German sphere of influence'. What transformed Nazi policy towards the Jews was the invasion of the Soviet Union, and the consequent radicalization of the war. In 1940 the Germans killed at most approximately 100,000 Jews; the following year they killed more than one million. With Operation Barbarossa, the war changed; it became a *Vernichtungskrieg* – a war of annihilation – against the 'Judaeo-Bolshevik' foe, and plans and military orders involving mass murder on an as yet unprecedented scale were drawn up.[50]

The behaviour of the German Army and SS in the initial stages of Barbarossa demonstrated the horrific character of the *Vernichtungskrieg*. Front-line troops under new standing orders shot captured Soviet commissars in defiance of international law. The upper echelons of the Wehrmacht offered little objection. As Soviet POWs fell into German hands in extraordinary numbers, they were treated quite differently to their French or Belgian counterparts the previous year. They were starved to death or marched into the ground till they looked 'more like the skeletons of animals than humans'. Within six months, over two million Soviet POWs had starved to death in German captivity.[51]

As the front advanced eastwards, it brought violent death to millions of civilians. On the heels of the front-line troops came Heydrich's *Einsatzgruppen* – motorized SiPo/SD death squads – in search of Jews, partisans and communists. Their victims were largely Soviet Jews of all ages: more than 2.7 million lived in the former Pale of Settlement, more than five million in the 1941 borders of the Soviet Union. By mid-April 1942, the four *Einsatzgruppen* had reported the death of 518,388 victims, of whom the vast majority were Jews. A further round of killings took place in the following year, and may have led to the murder of as many as 1.5 million more: by the end of war, only some 2.3 million Soviet Jews remained alive.[52]

Mass murder on this terrifying scale marked a new stage in the German approach to the *Endlösung*, and showed that the Final Solution was no longer being considered in terms of resettlement. The execution of so many civilians, including women and children, however, was also taking its toll on the executioners themselves. In August 1941 Sonderkommando 4a killed the hundreds of adult Jewish inhabitants of the Ukrainian town of Byelaya Tserkov, but left some ninety children under guard. 'Following the execution of all the Jews in the town,' reported a Wehrmacht officer in the area, 'it became necessary to eliminate the Jewish children, particularly the infants.' This was done. Yet afterwards, the reporting officer stated bluntly – to the fury of hardline Field Marshal von Reichenau – that 'measures against women and children were undertaken which in no way differ from atrocities carried out by the enemy'. Such misgivings on the part of some perpetrators did not prevent mass murder, but they complicated it.[53]

It was partly to circumvent such unease, and partly to improve the efficiency of the killing process, that the use of gas in specially designed death camps was developed. The period when this policy was set in motion seems to have been the late summer and early autumn of 1941, at around the time that Himmler personally watched Einsatzkommando 8 carry out a mass shooting in Minsk. The SS had already tried out mobile gas vans in East Prussia and the General Government in 1939–40. And just when Himmler was searching for an alternative to shootings, public outrage forced the euthanasia campaign in the Reich to be wound down. Hitler's Chancellery had kept the T-4 programme under its own control; now it made the personnel, with their expertise in gassing techniques, available for transfer eastwards.

In September 1941, some euthanasia centres received Jewish inmates from the concentration camps, a sign that their function was already being shifted to the mass murder of Jews. At around the same time, a castle at Chełmno, near Łódź, was converted into a rudimentary death camp, and stationary gas vans operated by former euthanasia programme specialists were used to kill off the remaining Jewish population of the Warthegau from December 1941. The *Einsatzgruppen* started to use mobile vans throughout the East. SS technicians developed two types – the smaller Diamond, with a capacity of twenty-five/thirty people, and the larger Saurer which held fifty/sixty – and carefully monitored their performance, especially in bad weather. 'Since December 1941, ninety-seven thousand have been processed, using three vans, without any defects showing up in the machines,' notes one report.[54]

The key to the Final Solution, however, was the construction of special extermination centres in the General Government. The SS focused initially on the area of Lublin, which under the earlier resettlement plans had been designated as a dumping-ground for Jews from western Poland. Former euthanasia specialist Christian Wirth was put in charge of the first death camp, Belzec, and gassing by carbon monoxide began there in March 1942. Exhausted Soviet POWs built the Majdanek camp in late 1941 and the first Jews were sent there from Lublin in December. By September 1942 gas chambers were in operation there too. Other former euthanasia operatives were assigned to the death camps of Treblinka and Sobibor. Gas chambers were constructed at these and other sites, and expanded as problems with capacity emerged.[55]

Auschwitz itself had been growing from its first use as a camp for Polish political prisoners. SS town planners dreamed of turning the Polish Oświęcim into Stadt Auschwitz, a nucleus for German colonization, with orderly streets, modern cinemas and rich fields regained from the marshes which surrounded the town. In addition to the prison barracks, the camp complex housed the giant synthetic rubber factory which IG Farben executives had wanted to build out of the range of Allied bombers. A gigantic new camp at nearby Birkenau housed Soviet POWs in truly appalling conditions, and it was on these that an insecticide called Zyklon-B, patented by an IG Farben subsidiary, was tested for the first time on 3 September 1941. A little later on, new gas chambers were built purposely for mass extermination. In 1942-3 Birkenau became the main death camp for Europe's Jews.[56]

By 1942, then, the technological prerequisites for industrialized mass murder were in place. Death camps were under construction and cheap poison gases had been tested and were available. Spearheaded by the SS, backed by Hitler, the complex diplomatic, legal and logistical arrangements were now set in train for the extermination of the entire Jewish population of occupied Europe. The subject had been intensively discussed by the Nazi leadership during October and November 1941; its administrative dimensions formed the theme of the Wannsee Conference, originally scheduled for December but postponed until January 1942. By the time that Heydrich, Himmler's deputy, was assassinated in May 1942, the Jews of Poland were being killed in 'Operation Reinhard', and the first trainloads of Jews from Slovakia had arrived at Auschwitz.[57]

In early 1943, SS chief statistician Richard Korherr drafted a report on the progress of the Final Solution for Himmler, in which he noted that 1,449,692 Polish Jews had already received 'special treatment'. Himmler rebuked him for using that particular euphemism, and corrected the text to read: 'Transportation of the Jews out of the Eastern Provinces to the Russian East: [1,449,692].' But the numbers speak for themselves. By the end of 1943, when the death camps were closed down, approximately 150,000 Jews had been murdered in Kulmhof/ Chełmno, 200,000 in Sobibor, 550,000 in Belzec, and 750,000 in Treblinka – thus the Jews of Poland were mostly killed in the so-called 'Reinhard' camps. Auschwitz-Birkenau, the giant combined labour camp and extermination centre, remained in operation for another year. Between March 1942 and November 1944, well over one million people were killed there, mostly Jews from Greece, Hungary, France, Holland and Italy as well as Poland.[58]

The overall impact of the Final Solution was summarized by Korherr in the provisional report he prepared for Hitler in April 1943. 'Altogether, European Jewry must have been reduced by almost 1/2 since 1933, that is to say, during the first decade of the development of the power of National Socialism. Again half, that is a quarter of the total Jewish population of 1937, has fled to other continents.' In fact, the final death toll was considerably higher, since the killing went on, inside and outside the camps, until the end of the war.[59]

By the war's end, between five and six million European Jews had been killed, almost half of the eleven million Jews recorded at the Wannsee conference. In some countries, such as Poland and Greece, almost the entire community was murdered. Other ethnic groups were also decimated, notably between 200,000 and 500,000 gypsies (many of whom were murdered in Belzec and Birkenau), Serbs, Poles, Ukrainians and Russians; but the systematic nature of the Final Solution makes it a case apart. Compared with the primitive techniques employed by other exponents of genocide such as the Croat Ustaše (who slaughtered at least 334,000 Serbs in Croatia and Bosnia) and the Romanians (who carried out bloody pogroms in Transnistria), the *Endlösung* demonstrated the superior genocidal efficiency of an operation conducted by a modern bureaucracy with industrial equipment.[60]

We need not assume the complicity of all Germans to accept that responsibility for, and knowledge of, this crime stretched far beyond the ranks of the SS. Propaganda Minister Goebbels referred in a diary entry of 27 March 1942 to the 'liquidation' of the Jews of Poland; by May, Reich Railway Department heads were conferring with the SS over transportation aspects of 'the complete extermination' of the Jews. The Army, the Navy and the Foreign Office all played their part. In Salonika, for example, a tiny team of SS 'experts' could not have deported one fifth of the city, nearly 50,000 people, without the active support of the local military administration. As for scientists, doctors and academics, their advice and enthusiastic involvement had been integral to the Nazi racial programme from the start.[61]

When foreign governments were approached for support, their reactions depended upon the prospects for German victory, the nature of local attitudes towards the Jews and the opportunity costs of resistance. They tended to be particularly cooperative in handing over Jewish refugees and other non-nationals, but they were usually more reluctant to allow their own fellow-citizens to be deported. Some governments, notably the French, the Slovak and the Croat, were at least as enthusiastic in their anti-Semitism as the Germans and responded warmly to the chance of removing their Jewish population 'to the east'. In Romania and later Hungary where extreme anti-Semitic movements briefly held power, the bloody consequences shocked the Germans themselves. Even where the locals dragged their heels, as in Greece or the Netherlands, cooperation among the various German authorities often ensured that a high proportion of the local Jewish population was deported. Virtually none emulated the Danes in helping most Jews to escape, though the Italians – for their own reasons – did all they could to obstruct the Final Solution in the areas under their control. And as for neutral Sweden and Switzerland, recent revelations indicate their willingness to turn Nazi racial policy to their own advantage.

The British and American governments, for their part, suffered from no lack of information. Churchill was receiving Ultra decrypts of the *Einsatzgruppen* reports from the East, which summarized the killing totals. Several individuals, including Jan Karski, an astonishingly brave Polish emissary, emerged from occupied Europe to brief London and Washington with eyewitness accounts of the ghettos and even the death camps themselves. But apart from some vague public warnings to the Germans, little was done, and the chance to bomb the camps was passed over. Whether this inaction stemmed from anti-Semitism, from inability to imagine was what taking place, or from the fact simply that the Final Solution was never a central concern of the Allied war effort remains a matter of controversy.[62]

Popular opinion inside occupied Europe is also difficult to gauge. Anti-Semitism was a continent-wide phenomenon with a long history, of course, and in some areas explains an attitude of detachment and even enthusiasm for the Jews' plight. Nor should it be forgotten that genocide always offers spectacular opportunities for enrichment – abandoned factories, shops and properties, furniture and clothes – with which popular satisfaction may be purchased by the occupying power. After 1940, Eichmann extended the 'Vienna model' of 'Aryanization' of Jewish property to Amsterdam, Paris, Salonika and Europe's other major cities, while Rosenberg's agents alone plundered the equivalent of 674 trainloads of household goods in western Europe. Seventy-two trainloads of gold from the teeth of Auschwitz victims were sent to Berlin. If most of this went into German homes or Swiss bank vaults, a considerable sum lined the pockets of unscrupulous collaborators, informers and agents of every nationality. Yet it must be said that approval of the Final Solution was not a common phenomenon. In response to the horrors of occupation, most people living under Nazi control had retreated into a private world and tried to ignore everything that did not directly concern them. With traditional moral norms apparently thrown to the wind, the unusual cruelty of the Germans towards the Jews created a more general alarm among non-Jews.

What cannot escape our attention are German reactions – or the lack of them. There was no public protest inside the Reich to match the furore over the euthanasia campaign. Most Germans appear to have accepted that the Jews were no longer part of their community. Ordinary middle-aged policemen took part in mass executions; university professors, lawyers and doctors commanded the *Einsatzgruppen*. They did not do so out of fear: there is no recorded instance of a refusal to shoot innocent civilians being punished by death. Rather, the letters of concentration camp guards and death-squad killers reveal what ordinary individuals living in Europe in the middle of the twentieth century were capable of doing under the influence of a murderous ideology. Even in the midst of killing, private concerns about girlfriends, wives or children continued to worry them.

When SS-Untersturmführer Max Täubner was tried by the SS and Police Supreme Court in Munich in May 1943 for the unauthorized shooting of Jews in the Ukraine, the court offered a revealing insight into the moral values of the Third Reich. Its judgment stressed that killing Jews was not in itself a crime: 'The Jews have to be exterminated and none of the Jews that were killed is any great loss.' In the court's eyes, Taübner's offence lay rather in killing them cruelly and allowing 'his men to act with such vicious brutality that they conducted themselves under his command like a savage horde'. Even though he had acted out of 'a true hatred for the Jews' rather than 'sadism', he had revealed an 'inferior' character, and a 'high degree of mental brutalization'. 'The conduct of the accused', ran the verdict, 'is unworthy of an honourable and decent German man.'[63]

A similar acceptance of racially motivated killing was evident inside the Reich. The segregation of forced labourers and POW workers, enforced by the Gestapo, became accepted as a normal state of affairs. Denunciations of foreign workers were commonplace. The public hanging or flogging of workers who formed sexual relationships with German citizens seem to have occasioned little protest, as did the restrictions imposed by the police on their movements and activities: Polish workers were, for example, forbidden to use bicycles or to attend church. Nazi views on the inferiority of 'East workers' seem to have been commonly accepted. The inhabitants of Mauthausen grew used to seeing camp inmates shuffling through their streets and the casual brutality of their SS guards. When several hundred Russian POWs managed to escape from the camp, on 2 February 1945, only two local families are recorded as having offered a hiding-place and shelter. Most of the escapees were quickly rounded up or shot like 'rabbits' by local farmers, excited Hitler Youth teenagers and towns-people eager to participate in a terrifying bloodletting.[64]

The death camps formed part of a larger 'concentration camp universe' in which the SS ruled over hundreds of thousands of inmates in a vast network of camps stretching right across Europe. The boundaries of this 'universe' stretched as far north as Norway, as far south as Crete. By the end of the war, some 1.6 million people had been incarcerated, of whom over one million had died (in addition to those deliberately targeted for extermination). In Europe as a whole there were more than 10,000 camps, including – in addition to the eight extermination camps and the twenty-two main concentration camps with their 1,200 offshoots – over four hundred ghetto camps, some twenty-nine psychiatric homes and thirty children's homes where patients were murdered, twenty-six camps in the occupied eastern territories where mass murder was institutionalized, as well as numerous others housing POWs, civilian workers, juveniles or 'Germanizable' east Europeans.[65] Some thirty-three nationalities were to be found among the inmates at Dachau, over fourteen in Ravensbruck. The conditions of work were so oppressive that even many so-called labour camps were regarded by the inmates as centres of extermination. Describing the granite quarry at Gross-Rosen, near Breslau, a French doctor who arrived there from Auschwitz noted: 'Nowhere did I see individual murders carried out with such dexterity as at Grossrosen; murder was practised without qualms, by the kapos, by the Camp police, by the SS and their dogs. With consummate skill they could kill a man with two or three blows.'[66]

The inmates of these camps provided the basis for the main economic activity of the SS, which by 1944 extended from mining to heavy industry, from land reclamation to scientific 'research'. Four hundred and eighty thousand of the 600,000 prisoners in the camps in late 1944 were termed fit for work. Their tasks included sorting the possessions of dead prisoners for distribution to the Waffen-SS or other depart-ments, building, quarrying and mining, as well as manufacturing in the Buna works and other industrial operations. Like the Soviet Union in the 1930s, the wartime Reich became a slave labour economy.

In February 1944 armaments czar Speer enlisted Himmler's help in 'deploying concentration camp inmates in functions that I regard as especially urgent'. This request inaugurated a rapid expansion of slave labour in munitions, in aircraft construction and particularly in building the underground missile works at 'Dora' and Peenemünde. Death rates here were horrendous: 2,882 of 17,000 workers died on the 'Dora' project within a few months: Speer regarded the project as a 'sensational success'. Overall, some 140,000 prisoners were used by Speer while 230,000 were utilized as slave labour by industrial firms in the private sector. By this point the armaments crisis had reached such a point that for the first time anti-Semitic ideology was overridden and Hungarian Jews were moved from Auschwitz as additional labourers.[67]

Barbarossa also extended the range of SS responsibilities in other directions. Terror replaced the rule of law in the East, and Himmler was authorized to deal with civilians directly without reference to the courts. The Waffen-SS became Himmler's army, growing from around 75,000 men in 1939–40 to nearly 500,000 by late 1944, part-threat part-partner to the Wehrmacht and as such a key instrument for Hitler in his gradual Nazification of the Army. The SS was given responsibility for policing the occupied territories in the East, while SS-Gruppenführer Bach-Zelewski was placed in charge of coordinating anti-partisan operations.

Needless to say, such operations resulted in enormous destruction and loss of life. The basic strategy was 'to answer terror with terror'. Reprisal ratios were set for attacks on German life or property. As a result thousands of villages were burned down and hundreds of thousands of civilians killed in the course of 'cleansing operations'. Their impact upon partisan activity was almost certainly counterproductive, driving young men into clandestine activity. Efforts at a more sophisticated counter-insurgency strategy would have to wait several decades: after 1945 European colonial powers, and the Americans, studied and learned much from the failures of Nazi retaliatory anti-guerrilla policies.

While the partisans never really posed a significant military threat to German rule, they did obstruct the process of Germanization. Here, too, Barbarossa had made Nazi thinking more extreme and more ambitious. Following the conquest of the Ukraine and Belorussia, SS town planners lost no time in drawing up proposals for new small German towns dotted across the Ukraine. 'General Plan East' envisaged a massive settlement programme stretching from Lithuania to the Crimea over twenty-five years. At Auschwitz, inmates dug fish ponds and built barns for model farms where Nazi colonists could be trained before heading east.

In the real world, however, certain difficulties with the entire Germanization idea were becoming apparent. One was corruption, for among the Germans from the Old Reich was a high proportion of 'gold-diggers' (or 'golden pheasants', as they were known) and carpet-baggers, attracted by the prospects of quick riches and easy plunder. By contrast, few farmers wanted to make the move. Settlers felt exposed in rural areas where their life and property was endangered by the embittered local population.

Ironically – given the regime's obsession with 'living-space' – there did not seem to be enough settlers for the enormous amount of territory which Himmler dreamed of colonizing. 'Well, Kamerad, how are you getting on?' asked the local peasant leader in a Nazi paper of the time. 'Too much land,' is the response, as the unwilling farmer 'looks helplessly into the distance'. 'The proportions between space and people have been reversed,' commented another critic in 1942. 'The problem of how to feed a great people in a narrow space has changed into that of the best way of exploiting the conquered spaces with the limited numbers of people available.'[68]

As the regime cast around for volunteers, the screening of potential colonists threw up some knotty problems for the racial theorists: some Party hardliners were willing to take any suitable-looking candidates, even if their ties with Germany were tenuous; others insisted that knowledge of language and culture was more important than physical attributes. Some even speculated that if the SS brought home too many racially superior specimens from Russia, the inhabitants of the Reich might develop an inferiority complex and start a race war! On the other hand, of the 35,000 unwilling Slovenes who were forcibly brought to Germany, only some 16,000 were finally reckoned suitable for Germanization; as most were the relatives of Slovene partisans, it is surprising that the number was so high. The rest, together with others from Luxembourg and Alsace, had to be kept in detention camps for the duration of the war.

The limits imposed by wartime reality on Himmler's demographic engineering were sharply revealed in the case of Zamość, a town south of Lublin where a special effort was made to create a planned settlement of *Volksdeutsche*. In this, the only case where the SS brought its colonization schemes anywhere near completion, over 10,000 Poles were removed from their homes to make way for German settlers. Half the Poles fled into the forests where they joined the Underground and raided farms and villages; the rest were screened for racial purity and deported. Twenty-five thousand Germans were brought into an area still inhabited by 26,000 Ukrainians and 170,000 Poles. They were, a propagandist boasted, 'the first German cell of the modern eastern colonization, reawakened by this search to a pulsating German colonial life'. But by early 1944, the local authorities were already trying to persuade Himmler to abandon the colony and evacuate the settlers westwards: assaults on their farms were a regular occurrence and their menfolk were sleeping in fields to avoid being killed by the resistance.[69]

Yet Himmler and Hitler stuck doggedly to their vision of a German empire in the East and left the evacuation of their hardy colonists as late as possible. This lack of contingency planning for withdrawal was but one aspect of the basic unreality in their plans. Their racist colonialism was doomed to failure; it was an imitation of Habsburg frontier policy without Habsburg political flexibility. They had created such hatred among the local population that in the absence of 'an overpowering police machine' the numbers of colonists required to hold vast areas of the former Soviet Union for Germany were beyond the grasp of Berlin. Hitler's long-term policy had been to see '100 million Germans settled in these territories'. But such numbers simply did not exist. The Nazis wanted to turn Germans into peasants, but most Germans refused. Whether, as Himmler believed, the returning war heroes from the front would have welcomed a farmstead in Poland or the Ukraine as their reward must be open to doubt.[70]

As the Red Army advanced, the resettlement scheme disintegrated of its own accord. Between August 1943 and July 1944, some 350,000 Crimean Germans were evacuated to western Poland; others followed from the Ukraine and Belorussia. The German scorched-earth policy meant that it became impossible for many colonists to remain even had they wanted to. By early 1945, hundreds of thousands of German refugees were trekking westwards towards the Reich in a vast spontaneous exodus.

At the same time an even grimmer series of forced marches betrayed the dark side of the racial dream. In the last phase of the Final Solution, the extermination camps and concentration camps were closed down and, in some cases, destroyed, and the surviving inmates were driven through the snow on long marches in the general direction of the Reich. Of the 714,211 prisoners still in the camps in January 1945 around 250,000 died on these death marches.

A variety of motives lay behind the marches – including the SS's reluctance to allow prisoners to fall into Allied hands as well as the desire to exploit them as slave labourers. But in some cases, journeys on foot or by train were so aimless that it seems the intention was simply to 'continue the mass murder in the concentration camps by other means'. Marchers were starved, beaten and shot, particularly when they became too exhausted to keep up with the others. In addition to the brutality of the guards, the victims often had to contend with the active hostility of the civilian German population they passed through. Instances of help are also recorded. 'In Christianstadt German women tried to give us bread, but the women guards wouldn't permit it,' recorded one former prisoner. 'One German woman with a human heart cried: "*Ihr Elende, Ihr Unglückliche*". The brutal woman guard yelled: "What are you doing pitying Jews?"' It is worth noting that there are no known instances of German bystanders losing their life for expressing sympathy in the hearing of SS guards. Even so, disapproval and indifference outweighed pity: by early 1945, with the end in sight, many German civilians saw themselves as the prime victims of the war and remained blind to the misfortune of the marchers passing through their midst.[71]

In this terminal phase of Hitler's empire, the barriers which had previously existed between the ordered world of the *Volksgemein-schaft* and the underworld of the camps now dissolved. The inmates emerged 'like Martians' into the outside world. Their guards were no longer solely SS men, sworn to secrecy; they included retreating soldiers, civilians, Party officials and Hitler Youth members. Random shootings and massacres took place no longer within the camp perimeter, but by roadsides, in woods and on the outskirts of towns and villages in Germany and Austria.[72]

The ultimate technical problem arising from mass murder practised on this scale was how to dispose of the dead. In the extermination camps, corpses were burned on enormous pyres or in ovens. The random, ubiquitous killing of the final months could not be so easily tidied up. As the Germans retreated from the Lublin region, they made hasty and unsuccessful efforts to hide the traces of genocide. Klukowski noted with horror 'the odor of decomposing bodies from the Jewish cemetery' where mass graves had been dug. The shocked Allied troops who liberated the camps in Germany forced local citizens – at places like Nordhausen, Gusen and Woebbelin – not merely to inspect the mounds of corpses but to bury them, sometimes in the central squares and parks of their old and elegant towns.[73]

Overcome by nausea, an Austrian priest who entered Mauthausen several days after liberation noted: 'A couple of times I was on the verge of throwing up. One indeed comes from civilization. And here inside? ... What a sad achievement of our arrogant century, this hideousness, this sinking into an unprecedented lack of civilization, and on top of that in the heart of Europe!' But the dead lay outside the camps as well. In the years after the war, their graves dotted the roadsides of central Europe until local committees chose to remove these blots on the landscape by constructing collective memorials instead and disposing of the human remains. A newly sanitized rural landscape was created for the benefit of tourists and locals alike.[74]

In 1942 it had been decided to distribute the clothing and personal belongings of Auschwitz inmates as Christmas presents to *Volks-deutsche* settlers in the Ukraine. Later the scheme was expanded and trainloads of goods were sent off to the German pioneers. Genocide and resettlement were inextricably linked, for Hitler's war aimed at the complete racial reconstitution of Europe.[75]

There were no historical parallels for such a project. In Europe neither Napoleon nor the Habsburgs had aimed at such an exclusive domination, but then Hitler's upbringing as a German nationalist critic of Vienna helps explain the contrast with the methods of governance pursued by the Dual Monarchy. In its violence and racism, Nazi imperialism drew more from European precedents in Asia, Africa and – especially – the Americas. 'When we eat wheat from Canada,' remarked Hitler one evening during the war, 'we don't think about the despoiled Indians.' On another occasion he described the Ukraine as 'that new Indian Empire'. But if Europeans would have resented being ruled as the British ruled India, they were shocked at being submitted to an experience closer to that inflicted upon the native populations of the Americas.[76]

National Socialism started out claiming to be creating a New Order in Europe, but as racial ideology prevailed over economic rationality, the extreme violence implicit in this project became clearer. 'Gingerbread and whippings' was how Goebbels summed up their policy, but there was not enough of the former and too much of the latter. The 'Great Living Space [*Grosslebensraum*] of the European family of nations' promised life to the Germans, an uncertain and precarious existence to most Europeans and extermination to the Jews. 'If Europe can't exist without us,' wrote Goebbels in his pro-European phase, 'neither can we survive without Europe.' This turned out to be true. The Germans threw away their chance to dominate the continent after 1940 and their defeat led to their own catastrophe. Himmler's original vision came to pass – the Germans were henceforth concentrated inside Germany – but it is doubtful whether he would have regarded the way this came about as a triumph.[77]

6

Blueprints for the Golden Age

The foundations of twentieth-century democracy have still to
be laid.

  – E. H. Carr, *Conditions of Peace*

For a fleeting moment we have an opportunity to make an epoch
– to open a Golden Age for all mankind.

  – C. Streit, *Union Now*

The reexamination of values and the heroic effort which might
have saved the democracies from war if they had been attempted
in time, are taking place and will take place in the midst of the
ruins.

  – J. Maritain, *Christianisme et démocratie*

The Second World War and the confrontation with the reality of a
Nazi New Order in Europe acted as a catalyst inside and outside the
continent for a renewed attempt to define the place of the democratic
nation-state in the modern world. This chapter attempts to describe
the various axes along which the wartime debate took place, a debate
whose core concerned the rethinking of another New Europe to rival
the authoritarian monster created by Berlin. It goes without saying,
of course, that the Nazi New Order was not merely a spur to alternatives, but the very seedbed – in certain areas – of post-war realities;
the continuities between Hitler's Europe and Schuman's are visible in

economic – especially industrial – Franco-German cooperation, for instance; there are also the obvious continuities of personnel in state bureaucracies and administrations. But in the realm of political values and ideals these continuities were much less important.

Yet the Second World War did not start out – at least so far as London and Paris were concerned – as a war for a new order. The power of Nazi dreams contrasted from the outset with the ideological timidity of the British. 'These people,' fired off an elderly H. G. Wells, 'by a string of almost incredible blunders, have entangled what is left of their Empire in a great war to "end Hitler", and they have absolutely no suggestions to offer their antagonists and the world at large of what is to come after Hitler. Apparently they hope to paralyse Germany in some as yet unspecified fashion and then to go back to their golf links or the fishing stream and the doze by the fire after dinner.'[1]

The arrival of Churchill did not allay such criticism; indeed, following Dunkirk it intensified. At the Ministry of Information, Harold Nicolson contrasted the 'revolutionary war' waged by the Germans with the British 'conservative' war effort and urged that Whitehall respond to the need to ask people to fight for a 'new order'. Conservative Party reformers felt similarly while Attlee stressed the need not to fight 'a conservative war' with 'negative objectives'. Churchill himself disliked any talk about war aims or the post-war order; but the debate – in Addison's words – 'flowed around him'. As talk of a Nazi New Order captivated Europe in the summer of 1940, British policy-makers came under pressure to outline a New Order of their own. The debate that ensued – in Britain and abroad – gave impetus to many of the ideas and values that would form the foundations of the post-war world.[2]

REVIVING DEMOCRACY

By March 1941, one prominent British politician could write that '"everybody" is talking about the new order, the new kind of society, the new way of life, the new conception of man'. According to historian E. H. Carr, 'the point at issue is not the necessity for a new order but the manner in which it shall be built'. Hitler could not win the war, in his view, but he would have performed 'the perhaps indispensable function of sweeping away the litter of the old order'. Thus the struggle was 'an episode in a revolution of social and political order'.[3]

At the very heart of this revolution were the preservation and reassertion of democratic values in Europe. 'Democracy! Perhaps no word has ever been more devalued and ridiculed,' wrote the French resistance paper *Franc-Tireur* in March 1944. 'Only yesterday it stood for long-winded committee speeches and parliamentary impotence.' Aware of the deep disaffection with the Third Republic in France, General de Gaulle expressly avoided raising the subject in his early broadcasts. 'At the moment,' he wrote in July 1941, 'the mass of the French people confuse the word democracy with the parliamentary regime as it operated in France before the war . . . That regime has been condemned by events and by public opinion.' It was this wholesale disillusionment with democracy in inter-war Europe which had led commentators like Ambassador Joe Kennedy to predict after the fall of France that 'democracy is finished in England'. 'The necessity for re-stating the democratic idea,' asserted R. W. G. MacKay, author of the best-selling *Peace Aims and the New Order*, 'is the most fundamental question for us all just now.'[4]

Chamberlain's uncertain presentation of the case against Hitler typified for many critics the complacency, passivity and outmoded style of the prevailing 'bourgeois' democratic tradition in western Europe. What was to become the wartime consensus rested upon the belief that in order to survive in Europe, democracy would have to be reinterpreted: the old liberal focus upon the value of political rights and liberties had not been enough to win the loyalty of the masses. 'Democracy', wrote a central European émigré in the USA '. . . must set its values against new ideals; it must show that it is able to adapt its psychology and its methods to the new times.' From such a perspective, the Atlantic Charter of August 1941 seemed woefully cautious and even conservative in its promises. 'Nothing in the text suggests that we are in the middle of the greatest revolutionary war of all time . . . [This] has the drawback of suggesting that the democracies wish to preserve and maintain the methods of the past, while the totalitarian powers strive for something new and imaginative.' In Britain, even the Charter itself was downplayed, according to a scathing anonymous critic of British propaganda: 'Speakers of the Ministry [of Information] lecture about the Empire, America, France, wartime cookery, the horrors of Nazi rule and Hitler's new order, but they do not talk about *our* new order. There is, in fact, no recognition of the war of ideas or of the social revolution through which we are living.'[5]

Suspect as the notion may seem to revisionists today, social revolution hardly seems too strong a term to describe the dramatic changes wrought by the war both in Britain and in occupied Europe. Wartime dislocation and chaos – some sixty million changes of address were registered in Britain alone during the war – collapsed the social distances upon which the rigid pre-war class systems of Europe had rested. The impact of bombing, together with systematic evacuations and the mass panics and flight of millions of people (eight to twelve million, for example, covering hundreds of miles, during the mass panic in Belgium and France alone in the summer of 1940) brought classes and communities together which had formerly remained in ignorance of one another. Rationing demonstrated that government planning could be used for egalitarian ends and was as a result surprisingly popular. Hence the war itself, with the new roles assumed by government in managing the economy and society, demonstrated the truth of the reformers' argument: democracy was indeed compatible with an interventionist state. According to Mass Observation in 1944: 'Public feeling about controls is largely based on the belief that they are democratic, more democratic than the freedoms and liberties which in practice apply only to limited sections of the population.'[6]

In a *Times* editorial of July 1940 entitled 'The New Europe', E. H. Carr asserted that 'if we speak of democracy, we do not mean a democracy which maintains the right to vote but forgets the right to work and the right to live'. This was the message which socialists across Europe had been repeating for years; the war gave it a new urgency and plausibility. Imprisoned by Vichy, the former French premier Léon Blum wrote: 'A weak and perverted bourgeois democracy has collapsed and must be replaced by a true democracy, an energetic and competent democracy, popular instead of capitalist, strong instead of weak ... This popular democracy will be, indeed can only be, a Social Democracy.'[7]

The wartime reformist consensus, however, included other groups than the socialists. Liberal progressives, technocratic planners and newly assertive moderate conservatives were all keen to enlarge the social and economic responsibilities of the modern state. None was happier than Keynes, for example, to seize the chance to assert the primacy of economics over finance and the bankruptcy of laissez-faire. He too had been frustrated by the retrograde nature of the British government's initial attitude towards post-war goals. In the summer of 1940 he had turned down an invitation to broadcast a rebuttal of the economic aspects of the Nazi New Order on the grounds that he found much in them to admire. To Duff Cooper he wrote:

Your letter seems to suggest that we should do well to pose as champions of the pre-war economic *status quo* and outbid Funk by offering good old 1920–21 or 1930–33, i.e. gold standard or international exchange *laissez-faire* ... Is this particularly attractive or good propaganda? ... obviously I am not the man to preach the beauties and merits of the pre-war gold standard.

In my opinion about three-quarters of the passages quoted from the German broadcasts would be quite excellent if the name of Great Britain were substituted for Germany or the Axis ... If Funk's plan is taken at face value, it is excellent and just what we ourselves ought to be thinking of doing. If it is to be attacked, the way to do it would be to cast doubt and suspicion on its *bona fides*.[8]

At the beginning of 1941 Keynes did agree to draft a declaration of war aims in which he emphasized the need to ensure social security and to attack unemployment after the war. Never published, this memorandum marked the beginning of the British government's move towards a commitment to full-employment policies. No less important was the pioneering work he carried out with two assistants in constructing the first official national income statistics. Here were the tools which made possible the post-war Keynesian revolution in fiscal management.[9]

The wartime transformation of British social policy was far-reaching. Apart from Keynes's work in economic policy, pioneering reforms were laid down in education, health and town planning. War saw the introduction of free school meals and milk. It brought the 1944 government White Papers on Full Employment and a National Health Service. Above all, it brought William Beveridge, whose 1942 report on 'Social Insurance and Allied Services' laid the foundations of the post-war welfare state. Beveridge himself, converted by the war from a critic of welfare capitalism to a believer in planning for radical social change, even told Beatrice Webb in early 1940 that 'I would very much like to see Communism tried under democratic conditions'.[10]

This, then, was the man appointed reluctantly by the coalition government to investigate what it imagined would be the rather technical matter of social insurance reform. But Beveridge resolved – with enormous success – to see this work 'as a contribution to a better new world after the war'. His subsequent investigations forced Whitehall to travel further down the road to full-employment policies after the war than it had originally intended. Common to both Beveridge and the government's own White Paper was their insistence on the need for state planning for the social good and their denunciation of the iniquities of pre-war laissez-faire. 'If the united democracies', concluded Beveridge in 1942, 'today can show strength and courage and imagination even while waging total war, they will win together two victories which in truth are indivisible.'[11]

The reception which greeted Beveridge's reports attested not merely to his talent for self-publicity but to the very real public interest in post-war reconstruction. Like Beveridge himself, British popular opinion had shifted to the Left during the war. This could be seen in the interest aroused by a special *Picture Post* issue in January 1941 on 'The Britain we hope to build when the war is over'; it was also reflected in the sales of the Archbishop of Canterbury's best-selling 1942 Penguin Special on *Christianity and the Social Order*, and the emergence of Richard Acland's Common Wealth Party. Beveridge's proposals achieved international circulation through the BBC and underground publications, so much so that in the Third Reich his plan was regarded as 'an especially obvious proof that our enemies are taking over national-socialistic ideas'.[12]

This of course was not entirely fair. Rather, the challenge of Nazism was forcing democrats to look again at the question of social and national solidarity. The process had started already in the 1930s, notably in Sweden where the Social Democrats had pioneered an explicit alternative to the prevailing authoritarian model of coercive population policy. The Swedish welfare state which emerged in the late 1930s was a determinedly democratic programme, combining pro-natalist measures to encourage people to have more children with an affirmation that the decision whether or not to have children was an individual one which the state should respect. Sweden did maintain sterilization of the mentally ill, but it also supported birth control clinics, provided sex education in schools, liberalized abortion laws and protected the rights of working mothers at the same time that it introduced family allowances, universal free medical and dental care and school meals.

For one of the architects of these policies, Alva Myrdal, the Swedish model presented a contrast to the Nazi conception of the relationship between state and individual. It was – she argued in *Nation and Family* – a necessary amplification of the scope of modern democracy. Finishing her book in August 1940, Myrdal looked forward cautiously to a time when 'the present calamity' would be over and 'freedom and progress would again have a chance in Europe'. But, she warned, in what were fast becoming familiar terms,

Such an end of this war, even more than that of the earlier one, will present a challenge to democracy, again reasserted, to fulfill its social obligation. Political freedom and formal equality will not be enough; real democracy, social and economic democracy, will be exacted . . .

Europe will be impoverished. The fiscal structures of belligerent and nonbelligerent countries alike will seem bankrupt when measured by traditional norms of financial solvency. The rich will have seen their wealth taxed away. The masses will be hungry. When the structure of war-time economy breaks down, the dislocations of normal exchange and commerce will be left as enormous maladjustments. The demobilized millions will crave employment and security. Both courage and wisdom will be required to preserve orderly freedom and to avoid social chaos. These circumstances, however, will not prevent the undertaking of social reforms; on the contrary, they will force reforms whether we want them or not.[13]

All this formed part of the more general debate about social justice and democracy that the war had provoked. By 1942, Nazi visions of a more egalitarian New Order shielding Europe from the capitalist 'plutocracies' had lost any allure they once possessed. It was their opponents who now stood for a fairer future. In France, for example, Léon Blum's impassioned defence of the Popular Front during his trial at Riom in 1942 had won him many admirers. Another indication of disaffection with Vichy was de Gaulle's call that November for a 'New Democracy' against the reactionary regime of Pétain; by April 1943, the General was talking about the need to introduce state control of economic affairs and social security.[14]

Evidence abounds for the radicalization of ordinary people across Europe living under Nazi rule. 'The last thing we want is a return to the social conditions of 1939 with their economic chaos, social injustice, spiritual laxity and class prejudices,' wrote a young Dutch lawyer in an underground newsletter in 1942. In Greece, inflation and food shortages had led to 'a veritable social revolution' and 'the veering towards the Left of elements of the public who, before the war, were among the most conservative'.[15]

Resistance and underground movements were naturally responsive to this leftwards shift in popular attitudes, partly because many of their leading cadres were drawn from the Left and partly because resistance itself was an exercise in communal solidarity, whose values lent themselves to an egalitarian and morally elevated vision of the post-war world. After Stalingrad, people's minds turned more and more to the future; 'in the heat of the battle, amid the terror of the Gestapo and of Vichy,' proclaimed *La Revue libre* in late 1943, 'essays, political theses, draft constitutions, programmes are springing up almost everywhere, circulating, being read and discussed.' The most unlikely groups now tried to expound an 'ideology'.[16]

It would be a mistake to insist too strongly upon the similarities of resistance ideologies across the continent: after all, resistance groups were fragmented, localized and poorly informed of one another's existence; they were drawn from very diverse political and social elements of the population; above all, they were wartime phenomena, with all the flux, uncertainty and ideological confusion which the conditions of the war produced. In Italy, where twenty years of Fascism had made state intervention in socio-economic affairs less of a novelty than in Britain or France, anti-Fascists stressed the themes of justice and liberty above those of planning; in France, faith in *dirigisme* was combined with a fervent patriotism only perhaps matched in Poland. Such differences of emphasis, however, cannot obscure the remarkable convergence of resistance aspirations. Whether interpreted in terms of nationalization of major industries and banks, of state planning through price and production controls, or of vague and unspecified demands for 'social justice', the goal of a fairer and 'socialized' economy was shared by the vast majority of *résistants*. 'Finance is at the service of the Economy,' declared the plan which Émile Laffon placed before the Conseil National de la Résistance in 1943. This was the dream of Keynes and all those who had seen the prospects for economic recovery in the 1930s sacrificed before the altar of the balanced budget.[17]

Slower to respond to the new mood because of their greater distance from events, the exile governments of Europe also shaped their post-war aspirations to take account of the desire for a new domestic order. Norwegian foreign minister Trygve Lie stated that the war 'has made necessary in all countries a national planned economy under the direction of the State'. The Dutch government was rather reluctant to consider what this might mean, but the Belgians, by contrast, quickly set up a Committee for the Study of Postwar Problems committed to the extensive use of 'national planning'; an 'organized national economy' would allow the state to banish mass unemployment. Beneš's government was – rightly – proud of pre-war Czechoslovakia's enlightened social policies but still envisaged the nationalization of banks, insurance companies and heavy industry and the introduction of a 'planned economy'. What best reveals the extent of the wartime acceptance of radical social and economic engineering were the very similar pronouncements of conservative and traditionally inclined politicians like Poland's General Sikorski, de Gaulle and the Greek

Liberal prime minister Tsouderos. They, too, committed themselves to sweeping reforms when the war was over. For social democrats like Beneš or Spaak the cause of economic planning and social intervention was scarcely new; but it was the winning over to such ideas of conservative Europeans – and the consequent convergence of Left and Right – which provided one of the preconditions for post-war political stability.[18]

THE INDIVIDUAL AGAINST THE STATE

If one tendency in wartime thought was to stress the evils of pre-war economic individualism and laissez-faire and the need for greater state intervention in the interests of social harmony, another was to argue that the struggle against Hitler had revealed the importance of human and civil rights. In the legal and political sphere, in other words, the trend was to reassert the primacy of the individual vis-à-vis the state. The wartime rehabilitation and redefinition of democracy moved between these two poles.[19]

Occupation raised the question of individual choice in the most direct and inescapable form. Experiencing the terrors of Nazi rule in Poland led the science fiction writer Stanisław Lem to a theory of chance where individual autonomy and power had vanished: it was mere contingency whether venturing out for food led to a premature death, forced labour in the Reich or a loaf of bread. In Yugoslavia, diplomat turned novelist Ivo Andrić saw the onset of civil war in terms of the power of historical forces and collective traditions over the individual. In his prophetic prizewinning novel, *Bridge over the River Drina*, five centuries of Bosnian history dwarfed the individual protagonists.

Yet others reached quite different conclusions: faced with the choice between collaboration and resistance, everything boiled down not to fate but to a stark individual decision. In *Uomini e no*, the Italian novelist Elio Vittorini insisted that both resistance and Nazi brutality were the result of human choices. 'He who falls, rises also. Insulted, oppressed, a man can make arms of the very chains on his feet. This is because he wants freedom, not revenge. This is man. And the Gestapo too? Of course! . . . Today we have Hitler. And what is he? Is he not a man?'[20]

'To render myself passive in the world', wrote Sartre in *Being and Nothingness* (1943), 'is still to choose the person I am.' The experience of occupation had a powerful effect on the development of existentialist thought. Sartre denounced the fatalism of his fellow-intellectuals – men like Drieu, Brasillach or even Emmanuel Mounier – who had chosen to collaborate because – they argued – history and destiny had chosen Hitler's Germany as the way of the future. Writing one of his *Letters to a German Friend* in July 1944, Albert Camus argued similarly: 'You never believed in the meaning of this world and therefore deduced the idea that everything was equivalent and that good and evil could be defined according to one's wishes . . . I continue to believe that this world has no ultimate meaning. But I know that something in it has meaning and that is man.'[21]

To enter into resistance was often a profoundly personal act. What Alban Vistel called the 'spiritual heritage' of the resistance emerged from the sense that Nazi values were an affront to 'the individual's sense of honour'. For many insurgents this was bound up with the passionate sense of patriotism and their desire for liberty and led them naturally to stress the importance of individual freedom. 'The ideal which motivates us', declared a founder of the French MRP, 'is an ideal of liberation.' Resistance thus demonstrated that collective action could serve to defend individual liberties.[22]

Inside Hitler's Germany, too, the experience of Nazi rule encouraged a revaluation of the role of the individual on a smaller, more restricted and private scale. After the war, the German-Jewish philologist Victor Klemperer would try to explain to his students in the ruins of Dresden that the Third Reich had devalued the meaning of wartime heroism by turning it into part of the propaganda machine of the regime. The real hero, he went on, had been the lonely individual, isolated and apart from the adulation of the state. Heroes in the Nazi pantheon were borne aloft on a spurious tide of public acclaim; even activists in the anti-Nazi resistance had had the support of their comrades; for Klemperer the model of true heroism had been his non-Jewish wife, who had courageously stood by him through the Third Reich, despite the misery this had brought her, alone and with no support or recognition for her courage.

To religious thinkers, this reassertion of the individual conscience was perhaps the outstanding intellectual development of the war. At the same time as the Church rediscovered its social mission – whether Anglican in Britain, Catholic or Orthodox – so it reasserted the primacy of the human spirit over totalitarian demands for total loyalty to the state. Emmanuel Mounier's flirtation with Vichy, prompted by the desire to pass from 'bourgeois man and the bourgeois Church' led him and other religious reformers into a spiritual cul-de-sac. Pointing to a way out was Jacques Maritain, a fellow Catholic intellectual. Like Mounier, Maritain believed that social reform was urgently needed; but unlike him he argued that it was possible within a democratic context. In *Christianisme et Démocratie* (1943), Maritain insisted that the inter-war retreat from democracy could now be seen to have been a mistake: 'It is not a question of finding a new name for democracy, rather of discovering its true essence and of realizing it . . . rather, a question of passing from bourgeois democracy . . . to an integrally human democracy, from abortive democracy to real democracy.'[23]

Here in embryo was the source of post-war Christian democracy, at least in an idealized form. In his 1942 work, *Les Droits de l'homme et la loi naturelle*, Maritain developed the idea that the full spiritual development of an individual demanded contact with society. The person existed as an '*open* whole', and found fulfilment not in isolation but in the community. 'I have stressed . . . the rights of the civic person,' wrote Maritain, 'of the human individual as a citizen.' This conception of social responsibility as an individual duty, and of such behaviour as a condition of political freedom, can be encountered among other religious groups as well. Greek Orthodox Archbishop Damaskinos called for less selfishness and a greater sense of solidarity in the face of the famine in Greece. William Temple, the Archbishop of Canterbury, cited Maritain approvingly and echoed his call for a generous 'Democracy of the Person' as opposed to an egotistical 'Democracy of Individuals'.[24]

The new emphasis upon the worth of the individual reached beyond the sphere of moral philosophy and religion into that of the law. Starting with Churchill's bold declaration on 3 September 1939 that the war was being fought 'to establish, on impregnable rocks, the rights of the individual', Allied propaganda emphasized the sanctity of rights. 'In the course of World War Two,' wrote the distinguished international lawyer Hersch Lauterpacht, ' "the enthronement of the rights of man" was repeatedly declared to constitute one of the major purposes of the war. The great contest, in which the spiritual heritage of civilization found itself in mortal danger, was imposed upon the world by a power whose very essence lay in the denial of the rights of man as against the omnipotence of the State.'[25]

It was all very well, however, to proclaim a crusade in defence of rights but which rights were at issue and for whom? Quincy Wright was reflecting liberal American thought when he hazarded a definition which focused upon civil liberties, equality before the law, and freedom of trade. But others objected that this ignored the new social demands generated by the war. Nazi occupation, according to the Pole Ludwik Rajchman, 'was a process of levelling down entire populations, which creates a psychological atmosphere for compelling authorities, the powers that will be, to accept very far-reaching reforms'. He argued that hundreds of millions of people were 'thinking today in terms of the future exercise of human rights, which cannot but include the right to a minimum standard of social security'. Thus at the outset we find the debate under way between broad and narrow conceptions of human rights: starting during the war, this argument would gain in intensity during the Cold War and after, as the Soviet bloc and the Third World attacked the minimalist view of the Western powers.[26]

The new commitment to rights raised knotty problems of race and empire. In the late 1930s, lawyers had witnessed the development of a body of Nazi jurisprudence which consciously attacked liberal notions of individual autonomy in the name of the interests of the race and the state. Now they argued that anti-Semitism inside Germany had paved the way for the racist ambitions which led to the Nazi conquest of Europe, as well as to the extermination of millions of Jews discussed openly and in detail by Maritain and others by 1943.

Yet Western intellectuals – not to mention governments and public opinion – hesitated to make any connection with the ideas of racial superiority still very much current in their own societies.[27]

Noting that this was 'an ideological war fought in defense of democracy', Swedish Social Democrat Gunnar Myrdal observed that 'in this War the principle of democracy had to be applied more explicitly to race ... In fighting fascism and nazism, America had to stand before the whole world in favor of racial tolerance and cooperation and racial equality.' Some white Americans were increasingly uncomfortable at the hypocrisies involved in fighting Hitler with a segregated army. Black Americans commented upon 'this strange and curious picture, this spectacle of America at war to preserve the ideal of government by free men, yet clinging to the social vestiges of the slave system'. 'The fight now is not to save democracy,' wrote Ralph Bunche, summing up what was probably the dominant view among African-Americans, 'for that which does not exist cannot be saved. But the fight is to maintain those conditions under which people may continue to strive for realization of the democratic ideals. This is the inexorable logic of the nation's position as dictated by the world anti-democratic revolution and Hitler's projected new world order.'[28]

British attitudes were marked by similar hypocrisies. Dudley Thompson, a Jamaican volunteer arriving in England to join the RAF, was asked: 'Are you a pure-blooded European?' George Padmore, the remarkable journalist imprisoned in 1933 by the Nazis for attacking Hitler's racial policies, spearheaded the efforts of the Pan-African movement to force the British to extend their democratic crusade to the empire. Under Churchill, the archetypal romantic imperialist, this was never likely to happen. Hard though it may be now to credit it, the British government actually launched its own Empire Crusade in late 1940 to whip up support for the war. Whitehall's feeble effort to spread a 'dynamic faith' among the public contrasted Nazi efforts to build a 'slave empire' with the British version: 'The British Empire is exactly the opposite. There has been nothing like it in the world before; it is a commonwealth, a family of free nations – linked together by a loyalty to one king. It stands for progress; it is the hope of the future.'[29]

That the Empire Crusade turned out to be a complete flop may tell us something about the attitude of Europeans to their empires. During the war this seems to have been based largely on indifference, at least in Britain and France (though not perhaps in the Netherlands). In all these countries, domestic matters were of much livelier concern than questions of imperial government. The cause of empire beat weakly in British hearts. But so too did anti-imperialism. Most Europeans seemed scarcely aware that any inconsistency was involved in defending human liberties at home while acquiescing in imperial rule overseas. One examines the resistance record in vain for indications of an interest in the predicament of colonial peoples. In Italy, for example, the retention of colonies was a question of *amour propre*. In France, there was much discussion of remodelling the empire but virtually none of dismantling it; the Left more or less ignored the issue, and their silence at the Brazzaville Conference on imperial reform in early 1944 was entirely characteristic. Queen Wilhelmina simply offered to turn the Dutch Empire into a commonwealth which 'would leave no room for discrimination according to race or nationality'. To the Indian Congress Party's demands for British withdrawal, Whitehall countered by arresting Gandhi and offering Dominion status.[30]

To astute and sensitive observers of the Allied war effort, the ambiguity of European attitudes to race was one of the most striking features of the war. The American anthropologist Robert Redfield remarked on how, faced with Nazi theories, democracy had been forced to a 'self-examination' of the inconsistency between what it professed and practised: 'The ideal is now asserted as a program for an entire world – a free world,' Redfield noted. 'And yet the leaders who announce this program are citizens of the countries in which racial inequality is most strongly applied.' Redfield predicted in the future 'a moderate reaction favourable to intolerance' with a 'corresponding postponement of the resolution of the inconsistency'. This was not far from the truth: if the war, with its renewed stress on racial equality and human rights, did eventually contribute to the ending of European imperialism, it did not do so automatically: Europeans (and white Americans) remained largely unmoved by the drama of their own racial problems. So long as colonial subjects were willing to fight on their behalf, they had little incentive to alter the structure of power in a radical fashion. But here too, in ways largely invisible to British, French, Belgian and Dutch eyes, the war itself was the catalyst of change: Ho Chi Minh continued the struggle he had begun against the Japanese – against the French; Asian, African and Caribbean servicemen – Kenyatta and Nkrumah among them – returned home from fighting in Europe prepared to continue the struggle which had been started against Hitler.[31]

THE NATION-STATE AND
INTERNATIONAL ORDER

In 1944 the international lawyer Raphael Lemkin called for the United Nations, by their victory, to impel the Germans to 'replace their theory of master race by a theory of a master morality, international law and true peace'. But it was not only Lemkin who believed that the revival of international law was essential to any future world peace and moral order. The racial basis of Nazi jurisprudence and Germany's abandonment of the accepted principles of international law had been regarded since the late 1930s as among the principal causes of the breakdown of order in Europe. Nazi aggression had undermined the very existence of an 'international community'. At the same time, Nazi treatment of the Jews persuaded many people that if the individual was to be protected against the state, the traditional doctrine of state sovereignty in domestic affairs would have to be reconsidered. A revival and reinvigoration of international law thus emerged as the natural adjunct to liberal concern for world peace and, in particular, for the safeguarding of human rights.[32]

'Effective international organisation is not possible,' wrote Quincy Wright in 1943, 'unless it protects basic human rights against encroachments by national States.' Wright observed that, unlike Poland or Czechoslovakia, Germany had not been obliged to conclude a minorities treaty with the League of Nations, with the result that 'there was no formal ground on which the League of Nations could protest against the beginning of the persecutions in Germany. It was a general principle that a State was free to persecute its own nationals in its own territory as it saw fit.'[33]

But the protection of human rights required the existence of a body superior to the state to which the individual could have recourse. The Austrian jurist Hans Kelsen insisted that 'a right consists only in the legal possibility to invoke a court ... [International law] can confer rights on individuals only under the condition that individuals have direct access to an international court.' His colleague Lauterpacht warned that the international protection of human rights 'touching as it does intimately upon the relations of the State and the individual ... implies a more drastic interference with the sovereignty of the State than the renunciation of war.' But in his aptly named *Peace through Law*, Kelsen argued that only people who believed in a 'theology of the State' refused to recognize the need for all states to be bound by international law. Sovereignty was simply a red herring. 'We can derive from the concept of sovereignty', he went on, 'nothing else than what we have purposely put into its definition.'[34]

The limits of sovereignty, then, reflected political rather than jurisprudential or philosophical considerations. But who was going to make states acknowledge the supremacy of international law? Liberal thought in the inter-war period had reposed its confidence in the pressure of world public opinion to safeguard human rights. It was obvious that a more effective instrument of enforcement would be required in the post-war period. What complicated matters was the Allies' commitment, as enshrined in the Atlantic Charter, to respect traditional ideas of state sovereignty. The post-war state, in other words, was being asked in some measure to acquiesce in its own weakening. Experienced lawyers like Kelsen and Lauterpacht saw no realistic alternative to persuading individual states to make their international obligations a part of domestic law. The alternative was to push for some form of World State, but this they regarded as utopian.

An equally serious dispute centred on the question of whether the human rights to be enshrined in the new post-war order should be individual or collective. The League of Nations had chosen the latter in its system of protection for ethnic minorities in eastern Europe. Yet despite the obvious importance of safeguarding minorities, strong arguments were advanced in favour of demolishing rather than improving the collective-rights approach. President Beneš and the Czech government in exile denounced the League system on the grounds that experience had shown it had actually jeopardized their national security. 'Every protected minority will ultimately find its Henlein,' warned one observer. In addition, the states of eastern Europe resented the fact that they had been singled out for special obligations towards their minorities whereas the Great Powers, including Italy and Germany, had not had to suffer such an indignity.

'In the end,' wrote Beneš in 1942, 'things came to such an extraordinary pass that the totalitarian and dictator states – Germany, Hungary and Italy – persecuted the minorities in their own territories and at the same time posed as the protectors of minorities in states which were really democratic.' Rather than attempting to restore the League system, Beneš suggested that the post-war approach to minorities should be based upon 'the defense of human democratic rights and not of national rights'.

On top of this east European opposition, the major Allied powers – Britain, France and the United States – also showed little enthusiasm for reviving a system which had succeeded in internationalizing the most serious source of tension in Europe without finding adequate means of resolution. As the post-war settlement in Europe would show, the main interest of the major powers was in limiting their obligations to minor states, and this meant that they too were happy to bury the League's approach to collective rights. The result was that the United Nations' eventual commitment to individual human rights was as much an expression of passivity as of resolve by the Allies. It was a means of avoiding problems, not of solving them. This fact helps us understand why so few of the wartime hopes for a reinvigoration of international law were to be realized.

The wartime desire to limit national sovereignty by inducing states to surrender some of their powers to a higher authority was not confined to matters of law. One of its most striking manifestations was to be found in the vogue for federalism, which approached fever pitch around 1940. In a war which many attributed to the cancerous development of national rivalries, the idea of creating international harmony through federation seemed increasingly attractive. A Dutch resistance leader saw 'this war as the great crisis of the "sovereignty of the state"'. For one English lawyer 'the alternatives are war once in every generation, or federation'.[35]

In both Britain and France such ideas had been much in the air in the late 1930s. The Federal Union movement was founded in 1938 in London and soon proved extraordinarily popular. Its call for a union of democracies was based on the view that 'no international order based on co-operation between sovereign States will prove either effective or durable since all sovereign States in the last resort seek their own national self-interest'. In his *Federal Europe*, R. W. G. MacKay described 'a system of government for a New European Order, the establishment of which would enable the peoples of Europe to hope with some confidence that in future they might live and work in peace free from the fear of war, want and insecurity'. The spectacular proclamation in the darkest days of June 1940 of an 'indissoluble union' between Britain and France was the culmination of this vein of thought.[36]

Even though that union was never realized, the federalist idea only slowly lost its allure and remained a striking feature of official and unofficial planning for the future of Europe. A plethora of map-makers speculated upon how the continent might be carved up, and though their fantasies varied the federationist principle was common to virtually all of them. Thus an American geographer, in a 1942 article for *Collier's* called 'Maps for a New World' (heralded by the blurb: 'Here's a brave new world redesigned for lasting peace – a world from which war-breeding frictions are gone, where all nations live secure and unafraid, thanks to the new science of political geography') offered a Europe carved up into a 'British–Dutch Commonwealth' alongside the 'United States of Fennoscandia', 'Czechopolska', a German-Magyar state and a 'Balkan Union'. More serious, though scarcely more accurate, was the frontispiece of Bernard Newman's 1943 book,

The New Europe. This showed a map which divided Europe into West European, Scandinavian, Baltic, German, Central European, Balkan and Iberian federations. Only Italy escaped intact.[37]

British and American officials engaged in post-war planning also tended – as they had in 1914–18 – to see federation as an attractive solution to Europe's border problems. Austria, for example, posed British Foreign Office clerks with no less of a dilemma than the Habsburg Empire had done earlier. Few in Whitehall appear to have believed that Austria could survive as an independent state, but even fewer were happy to allow the *Anschluss* to stand: a surrogate empire in the form of Danubian 'integration' was the answer. Reviving the inter-war Balkan Union, and press-ganging Bulgaria into joining it, was an analogous pipe-dream.[38]

Churchill was drawn to the idea of a United States of Europe, envisaging an arrangement by which Britain could exert leadership on a continental scale. From May 1940, US planners for the post-war world came to believe that a new international organization, far from being incompatible with regional or continental unions, would in fact be more firmly based if they were created first. Indeed Newman's 1943 map was very similar to that envisaged by the US State Department in 1940.[39]

At the same time, though, we should keep these schemes in perspective. Federalism diminished in popularity inside and outside government as the war went on. One reason was the strong hostility of the Soviet Union to arrangements which seemed intended to create anti-Soviet blocs in eastern Europe. Another was the objection of many small countries which – despite the examples of the wartime Czech–Polish and the Greek–Yugoslav alliances – worried about disappearing into a Europe more than ever dominated by the major powers.

Inside continental resistance movements, the idea of Europe stood for an ethical heritage rather than a specific set of politico-economic arrangements. Asserting the existence of common European values was a way of denying the durability of Hitler's New Order. By talking of the struggle as a *European* civil war, the Italian Partito d'Azione set its struggle for a 'democratic revolution' firmly in a continental framework. High school pupils in Paris in 1943 demanded 'a new European order' to take the place of the Nazi order, and insisted that what they had in mind was not a Europe dominated by one hegemonic state, nor an economic and financial network like the Pan-American union, but 'a cultural and moral community which must be transformed by the war into a political and social one'. *Le Franc-Tireur* announced that 'as one regime collapses, another is being born. It arises from the fire of the struggle of liberation and from the icy cold of prisons, with the mass resistance that has sprung up from the French maquis to the Polish plains, from the factories of Milan to the German forced labour camps, from Norwegian universities to the mountains of Bosnia.'[40]

There were some more specific commitments to the ideal of federation. But in general the strength of the commitment was in inverse proportion to the size of the group concerned. The anti-Fascist 'Ventotene Manifesto' of August 1941, for example, reflecting the ideas of British federalists, had only limited circulation during the war. Resistance support for federation was rarely at the head of their programme. Hence, the efforts made by some historians to trace the origins of the Common Market back to declarations of the wartime resistance are in the last resort unconvincing, and one could with equal if not greater justice argue that its origins lay with the Nazis: by 1943 many Axis sympathizers were keener 'Europeans' than their opponents. In general, *résistants* remained motivated – as did most Europeans – by considerations of domestic social and economic policy and patriotism, their horizons bounded by the confines of the nation-state.

For at the same time as giving an impetus to federalism, the war had actually increased nationalist sentiment in Europe. Patriotism, after all, was far more important than 'Europeanism' as a motive for resistance. Intelligence reports coming out of Holland in late 1941 noted that 'the population is . . . ardently nationalistic. There is even reason to fear an intensification of Dutch nationalism. A blood-bath is imminent.' British pride at the country's stand against the Third Reich may help explain why support for federal union faded away as the war ended. France saw a resurgence of the 'idea' of the nation.

When Polish resistance groups agreed that 'the Polish Republic will be a member of the federation of free European nations', this was less an expression of federalist faith than a desire to ensure the security of an independent Poland after the war. In traditionally nationalistic countries like Greece, internationalist sentiment never took hold. There, as in Poland, Albania and Yugoslavia, a virtual civil war within the resistance led both Left and Right to insist on its nationalist credentials. In general, conservative and right-wing resisters to the Germans were more hostile to the idea of surrendering national sovereignty than were socialists or Christian Democrats; but even the latter tended to attach greater importance to the cause of reform at home. Federalism remained, in other words, a relatively weak element of the wartime consensus.[41]

THE NEW CONSENSUS: LIMITS AND CONTRADICTIONS

In 1944 the émigré Austrian economist Friedrich von Hayek published a small book entitled *The Road to Serfdom*. 'If we take the people whose views influence developments, they are now in the democracies all socialists,' bemoaned Hayek. 'Scarcely anybody doubts that we must move towards socialism.' This prospect he found deeply alarming. Why, he asked, had the West gone to war against Nazism if it was prepared to stamp out freedom at home? *The Road to Serfdom* argued incisively that freedom and what Hayek preferred to call 'collectivism' were incompatible. According to Hayek, the idea of 'democratic socialism' was simply a confusion of terms; any attempt to achieve such a synthesis would tilt society inexorably towards totalitarianism. Those, like H. G. Wells, who argued that economic planning and the protection of human rights could coexist were deluding themselves; planning required dictators and reduced parliament to impotence. Denouncing 'the totalitarians in our midst', Hayek called for people to turn away from the mirage of 'the great utopia' and to return to what he termed 'the abandoned road' of economic liberalism.[42]

Some four decades would pass before Hayek's ferocious polemic succeeded in gaining an influential audience, and then it would become the new bible of the Thatcherite laissez-faire revivalists in their assault on the post-war social order. But in 1944 Hayek was a voice in the wilderness. His insistence that Western planning was equivalent to Soviet collectivism fell on deaf ears, as did his assault upon the notion of democratic socialism. The Austrian neo-liberal tradition found a readier audience in the United States.

Far more in keeping with contemporary European opinion was the expatriate Hungarian-Jewish sociologist Karl Mannheim, who argued (in *Man and Society in an Age of Reconstruction* (1940)) the contrary view to Hayek's. For Mannheim, the age of laissez-faire was over. He argued that in a modern industrial society 'there is no longer any choice between planning and laissez-faire, but only between good planning and bad'. In a discussion which anticipated Isaiah Berlin's *Two Concepts of Freedom*, Mannheim insisted that there are different conceptions of freedom, and that the libertarian's insistence upon 'freedom from external domination' leads him to neglect the other forms of 'freedom as opportunity' which certain types of planning create in society. For Mannheim, democracy needed to come to terms with planning if it was to survive; the enemy to beware was not the planner but the bureaucrat. As he puts it: 'The problem of the democratic constitution of a planned society mainly consists in avoiding bureaucratic absolutism.'[43]

In retrospect what is striking is the lack of debate on these issues in most of Europe. The two countries where economic liberalism was most in evidence after 1945 were West Germany and Italy; there, the idea that state planning was associated with totalitarianism had a plausibility borne of bitter experience. Yet not even in those countries could there be a return to Hayek's 'abandoned road'. Elsewhere the principle of state intervention – either for a mixed economy as in western Europe, or for a planned and controlled economy, as in eastern Europe – was accepted with surprisingly little resistance. Behind this development lay the memory of capitalism's inter-war crisis, the prestige which the Soviet system won in the war against Nazism as well as the sense produced by wartime state controls and rationing that state intervention could increase social *fairness*.

It was also questionable whether economic planning was compatible with the new internationalism. It was, after all, the Left and the social reformers who tended to be in favour of *both* abandoning laissez-faire at home, and creating new international institutions with enlarged powers. E. H. Carr, for example, proposed the creation of a European Planning Authority 'whose mission will be nothing less than the reorganization of the economic life of "Europe" as a whole'. With a characteristic blend of realism and idealism, Carr did not blanch at the idea of taking advantage of the 'centralized European authority' that Hitler had established while abandoning the nationalist premises upon which it was based.[44]

But how could national planning, which Carr also advocated, coexist with planning at a continental level? What if national economic interests did not mesh with those of Europe as a whole? In general, there was little awareness on the Left of such a potential conflict. But here the critique from economic liberals was penetrating. Hayek insisted that *international* planning was a nonsense:

One has only to visualize the problems raised by the economic planning of even such an area as western Europe to see that the moral bases for such an undertaking are completely lacking. Who imagines that there exist any common ideals of distributive justice such as will make the Norwegian fisherman consent to forgo the prospect of economic improvement in order to help his Portuguese fellow, or the Dutch worker to pay more for his bicycle to help the Coventry mechanic, or the French peasant to pay more taxes to assist the industrialization of Italy?[45]

Hayek insisted that Carr was wrong; such planning could not be democratic in scope, but must always rest on 'a naked rule of force' like the Nazi *Grossraumwirtschaft*. Reviewing Carr's book, C. A. Manning enquired: 'If the Nazi way with small sovereign states is indeed to become the common form, what is the war about?' Hayek argued that the notion of European planning implied 'complete disregard of the individuality and of the rights of small nations'.[46]

Other liberals agreed with Hayek that international federation was, in principle, desirable. But in their view, it could only remain democratic in so far as it eschewed the idea of supranational planning and based itself upon the creation of free-trading areas. 'Federal government can only work under a free market economy,' stated von Mises, another Austrian neo-liberal. He suggested that, though it was unlikely to happen, the Western democracies should aim at removing barriers to trade as well as abandoning *étatisme* at home. Rather than pursuing utopian and unrealizable schemes for 'world planning', politicians should work towards the more modest goal of international economic agreements and regulations. The eminent Italian liberal economist, Luigi Einaudi, was thinking along similar lines. In *Per una federazione economica europea* (For an economic federation of Europe), issued in September 1943, the future President of the Italian Republic advocated free trade and economic federation as a realistic means of bringing harmony to Europe. States, he argued, would not surrender their political independence at a stroke to some new international federation; but they might be prepared to relinquish certain economic powers for the sake of greater security.[47]

In this debate, the liberals were ultimately more successful than they were where domestic reform was concerned. This was partly because they had logic and, for once, political realism, on their side. But it was also because their message had powerful supporters. US Secretary of State Cordell Hull was committed to the cause of free trade; the post-war planners in his department followed his lead and stressed the importance of eliminating economic nationalism in Europe through tariff reduction and the introduction of convertibility. It did not hinder matters that the US also stood to benefit from such policies. Finally, the liberal argument won the day not least because the economic planners preferred to exercise power at a national level. As a result, the post-war economic 'miracles' would be based on a delicate blend of *étatisme* at home and liberalization of trade.

UTOPIAS AND REALITIES: THE EXTENT OF
THE ACHIEVEMENT

During the war, cautious commentators had warned against utopian expectations. 'How *new* will the better world be?' asked historian Carl Becker. 'Many people are saying that what we have to do to make a new and better world is to "abate nationalism, curb the sovereign state, abandon power politics and end imperialism,"' he noted, adding, 'Maybe so. But if so, then I think we have an impossible job on our hands . . . Making a new and better world is a difficult business and will prove to be a slow one.'[48]

In England, Mass Observation reported that pessimism at the prospects of any far-reaching change after the war was growing. Following Beveridge, people hoped for full-scale reform but did not believe it would happen. They now believed that post-war unemployment was avoidable but would occur nonetheless. 'I think it will be like after the last war, dreadful unemployment,' said an older man. Increasing cynicism and uncertainty led people to dream of emigrating or living off the land. The return to civilian life provoked a sense of unease and anxiety among soldiers and their families.[49]

Inside occupied Europe, the *résistants*' expectations of a better future were tempered by the fear that just as their activities and values had emerged during the war, so too they would disappear when the war ended. This uncertainty was evident in Italy where members of the Partito d'Azione worried that the demise of Fascism might lead in turn to the end of anti-fascism. As one put it, '"Antifascist" may one day become as useless and irritating a word as "fascist".' What, then, would happen to the ideals and aspirations of the resistance? Would the world return to power politics and business as usual?[50]

From the resistance perspective, these fears were given added weight as it became clear that political power was slipping from their hands. Across Europe, former resistance leaders were being marginalized as the war came to an end. In Italy, Ferruccio Parri gave way to Alcide de Gasperi in December 1945; in Poland, the Red Army backed the Lublin Committee, who had been parachuted in from Moscow. In

France, de Gaulle ordered the demobilization of the Maquis. Across Europe exiles and refugees returned to take power and policies were imposed from above. The most striking case of all was Greece, where the British-backed royalist government actually fought with the left-wing EAM/ELAS in Athens in December 1944, crushing the main wartime resistance movement there.

We will examine in the next chapter the extent to which pro-Nazi and collaborationist elements in society and the state bureaucracy were purged after the war. In general, however, these purges left intact the same structures of power through which the Germans had ruled Europe: local civil servants, police, business organizations and the press. There may have been good reasons for this, but many former partisans and members of the underground were left with the feeling that they and their cause had been betrayed.

A later generation of historians has echoed their complaint. A recent collection of studies of the experience of women during the war describes what happened as a retreat in peacetime from the gains made during the war itself. We should compare this critique with a very different school of thought which sees the war as a forcing-house for social change. On the surface they appear incompatible; but are they really?[51]

Looking back at the way visions of the post-war world emerged during the struggle against Germany, what must surely strike us is the extent to which a genuine consensus of ideas concerning domestic reform – political, economic and social – was attained and lasted well into the post-war era. Consensus, in other words, was a reality not merely a wartime propaganda myth, as some recent scholars have argued. The Labour government's creation of a National Health Service, together with its commitment to educational reform, nationalization and full employment rested upon the studies carried out during the war and survived the changeover of power in 1951. Elsewhere in western Europe too the mixed economy and welfare state became the norm, despite stops and starts as liberals tried to halt the growth of public spending or swam briefly against the *dirigiste* current. There was, to some extent, an 'emulation effect' as, for example, France followed the British and Belgian lead in reforming social security. Under Soviet rule, eastern Europe moved towards economic planning and the development of a social security system; given the acceptance of such measures by exile governments during the war, it seems likely that not dissimilar developments would have taken place even without Soviet pressure. Across Europe, in other words, the repudiation of laissez-faire was complete. As a result, the idea of democracy was resuscitated, fitfully and abortively in eastern Europe, but with much greater success in the West.

However, in other areas of reform, advances were less durable. Women's rights had been promoted by resistance movements during the war; this was part of what many regarded as their 'dual war of liberation' – against the Germans and against the 'reactionaries' at home who opposed social reform. Moreover, the war itself had profoundly altered traditional gender roles, disrupting family ties and providing women with new tasks and challenges outside as well as inside the home. Liberation did bring some enduring changes, notably the extension of the suffrage in France, Yugoslavia, Greece and other countries where women had formerly been excluded. But just as after 1918, the ending of the war revived more traditional relations between the sexes. Governments tried to get women to withdraw from the workforce and return to the home, both in order to give employment priority to returning servicemen and to encourage the production of babies. In countries like Greece and Italy, this trend was blamed by the Left on capitalism, but as it was also occurring in such uncapitalist environments as Tito's Yugoslavia, other explanations for 'the reassertion of patriarchy' must be sought.

Part of the answer lies in the new post-war pro-natalism, based on the old concerns about the birth rate and population decline – natural enough in the aftermath of the greatest bloodletting in Europe's history. But the answer may also be found in ordinary people's reactions to the war; the feeling of sheer exhaustion after years of fighting, and the desire to retreat from the world of ideological strife contributed to an idealization of domesticity. With this nostalgia for the home, many men and many women looked forward to settling down and starting a family. 'After the war I shall get married and stay at home for ever and ever,' said a twenty-year-old, working on the day shift. 'I'll get right out of it when the war is over,' said another, older married woman. 'Straight out of it. I've been here about fifteen years now. I was married six years ago. I suppose I'll go on for a time till my hubby gets settled, and then I'll go home and increase the population.' 'For better or worse,' concluded the Mass Observation team, 'the larger number of opinionated women *want* to return to, or start on, domestic life when the war is over.'[52]

In the case of attitudes to race, one can scarcely talk of a retreat from wartime radicalism. European attitudes to race were slowly changing anyway before the war; the war itself appears hardly to have accelerated the process. Anti-Semitism did not disappear from Europe after 1945: to the contrary, it intensified across the continent immediately after the war ended as Jewish survivors returned home to find their property inhabited by others and their goods plundered.

There were also few signs in 1945 that the European powers intended to do anything other than cling on to their colonies. Being subjected to Nazi violence appears to have made them more rather than less inclined to inflict imperial violence of their own: French forces killed up to 40,000 Algerians in the aftermath of the Setif uprising in May 1945, and left perhaps as many as 100,000 dead in Madagascar in 1947. Decolonization, for all the efforts of the 1945 Pan-African Congress in Manchester, remained off the European political agenda until forced back as nationalists raised the costs of hanging on to the colonies. In so far as the European imperial powers had been humiliated by the war and were now overshadowed by the anti-imperialist superpowers, they felt more rather than less inclined to reassert their authority overseas. It was hardly a coincidence that it was the one imperial power which could have been said to have 'won' the war – Great Britain – which first accepted the need for decolonization.

The vision of a united Europe flickered on fitfully as the nation-state reasserted itself and adjusted to the exigencies of the Cold War. Early efforts to force the pace led to the creation of such bureaucratic drones as the Council of Europe, a far cry from the idealistic visions of 1943. At the start of the 1950s, the failure of the EDC (European Defence Community) marked the end of the federalist dream for three decades, making Nato rather than any purely European organization the

watchdog over the newly sovereign German Federal Republic. Thereafter, the Europeanists were a chastened but more realistic cohort,
following Einaudi's advice and adopting a gradualist programme
which, beginning with the ECSC in 1951, led in turn to the Common
Market and the European Union.

As to the revival of international law, the realization of wartime
dreams was also patchy and unsatisfying. The United Nations' commitment to human rights was as weak as its overall position in power
politics. From the doctrinal point of view, human rights were given
priority over economic and social rights in the Charter. But in terms
of the protection of minorities the UN Charter represented a step
backwards from the League. The Universal Declaration of Human
Rights of 1948 did symbolize the new status of the individual in
international law, and lasting mistrust of the Nazi doctrine of state
supremacy, but it contained no provisions for enforcement and remains
little more than a pious wish.[53]

More far-reaching in its implications was the Genocide Convention
of the same year – passed after a remarkable one-man crusade by
Raphael Lemkin, who had been disappointed at the refusal of the
International Military Tribunal at Nuremberg to judge acts committed
by the Nazis before 1939. Lemkin and others had seen the war-crimes
trials as an opportunity to secure world peace by increasing the powers
under international law to take action against individuals as well as
states. The Genocide Convention added an important new crime to
those recognized under international law, and imposed obligations
upon ratifying states to act to prevent or punish its commission. But the
Convention's potential has been entirely ignored by the international
community and there has been little evidence to back the UN's
confident assertion that 'the feeling will grow in world society that
by protecting the national, racial, religious and ethnic groups everywhere in the world we will be protecting ourselves.' For four decades,
a series of genocides went unpunished outside Europe; in 1992 that
indifference extended to Europe itself.[54]

7

A Brutal Peace, 1943–9

Now that the United Nations are beginning to reconquer Europe
from the Nazis, the 'democratic' phase of colonial policy comes
into effect ... What (the Europeans) used to refer to with a
certain disdain as 'native politics' is now being applied to them.
                        – Dwight Macdonald, 'Native Politics', 1944[1]

The Second World War – the culmination of nearly a century of
growing violence between the European powers inside and outside
the continent – was really several wars in one. It was, first and
foremost, a military conflict, fought out by armed forces, prompted
by Hitler's imperial ambitions. But it was also a war between races,
religions and ethnic groups – a bloody reopening of accounts by
extreme nationalists wishing to revise the Versailles settlement by
force. Thirdly it was, in many areas west and east, a class war in the
broadest sense, whether of landless *braccianti* against pro-Fascist
landowners in northern Italy, or poor hill farmers against the urbanites.
Finally, as resistance movements burgeoned in 1943–4 and provoked
bitter reprisals by collaborationist militias, the war became a civil war
of extraordinary ferocity stirred up by German arms and funds whose
roots stretched back to 1919, and even – in France – to 1789. This
polarized atmosphere was intensified by the approach westwards of
the Red Army and eastwards of the Allies.[2]

The death toll of approximately forty million easily outweighed
not only the thousands killed in the Franco-Prussian, the Boer or the

Balkan wars, but even the millions killed in the First World War and the Russian civil war. The proportion of civilian dead – perhaps half of the total – was far higher than ever before. They included, apart from between five and six million Jews, millions of Poles, Germans, Russians and Ukrainians. The war of annihilation in the East was the scene of the greatest slaughter; this was destruction on a different scale, and conducted according to different rules, from that experienced in western Europe. British and French military casualties, for instance, were less than one tenth of the enormous German losses. But even these were dwarfed by the Soviet Union, which lost – in addition to well over ten million civilians – three million POWs through starvation, and another 6.5 million men on the Eastern Front.[3]

The intensity of suffering and destruction which struck civilians over six years profoundly transformed European societies. Nazi extermination policies had threatened entire ethnic and national groups; much of Poland's military and intellectual elite had perished at German and Russian hands. Policies of genocide were but the most extreme forms of a war which targeted civilians, and the very structure of pre-war society. Reconstruction after 1945 was, therefore, a very different enterprise from that of the 1920s: this time, there could be no thought of going back. Wartime losses tore gaping holes in the social and physical fabric; they provoked bitter memories and angry emotions, but also new challenges and opportunities.[4]

How could conflicts of such intensity stop suddenly in 1945? The German surrender is a convenient marker for historians, but little more. Indeed it is positively misleading in so far as it suggests the ending of one epoch and the start of another. There was, in reality, no Year Zero, no clean break between hot and cold war, and the post-war regimes which emerged in the latter had their roots in the social experiences of wartime. The transition to the post-war era may be said to have begun in 1943, when the Allies invaded Italy and the problems of occupation and reconstruction began. Six years later the division of Europe was almost complete (only Austria and Scandinavia holding out against the tide) and wartime enmities had been transmuted under the pressure of the Cold War.

As Nazi occupation gave way to more enduring modes of subordination – in the East to the Soviet Union, in the West to the United States – the post-war reinvention of democracy in Europe ceased to be a project defined against the threat of fascism and became instead an arena for Cold War competition. By 1950, the winners had emerged: in the West, anti-communist Social and Christian Democrats, in the East, communist People's Democracies. Each saw the other as the successor to Hitler, themselves as his true opponents. Stalin turned out to have been right. 'This war is not as in the past,' he remarked as the war came to an end. 'Whoever occupies a territory also imposes on it his own social system. Everyone imposes his own system as far as his army can reach. It cannot be otherwise.'[5]

DISPLACEMENT AND SOCIAL CRISIS: 1944–8

Wars invariably displace populations. But this war had been waged specifically to establish a New Order through extermination, incarceration, deportation and transfer. Hitler had wanted to redraw the ethnographic map of Europe, while Stalin, for his part, also deported hundreds of thousands of class and ethnic 'enemies', including Poles, Ukrainians, Lithuanians and Chechens. Germany's defeat brought imprisonment to German POWs and liberation for millions of camp inmates, slave labourers and foreign workers. Although there had been some wartime planning to deal with refugees, the sheer scale of the humanitarian problem took the Allies aback. Those uprooted – through flight, evacuation, resettlement, use as forced labour – numbered some forty-six million in east central Europe alone between 1939 and 1948, dwarfing the refugee movements of the First World War. Some of these movements were temporary and voluntary, but the majority were not. The main reason for them, in retrospect, is clear enough: after the inter-war era's unsatisfactory experience with minorities in the new nation-states, people were being moved in order to consolidate political boundaries.[6]

Liberation revealed that there were over eleven million Displaced Persons, ten times as many as after the First World War. Some wreaked their revenge on the Germans, looting freely and threatening civilians.

On 4 May 1945, for example, Elena Skrjabina watched a group of fellow-Russians loot the German house she was staying in. They burst in and threatened the owner with a revolver, accusing him of being a Nazi and a 'Hitlerite'. 'They dispersed through the house, telling us that German property by right should go over to them . . . In about half an hour it was impossible to recognize the house. All the trunks and suitcases had been smashed, the closets were wide open, and our countrymen were disappearing down the path with huge sacks on their backs.' The DPs had borrowed a Nazi phrase for this sort of behaviour: they called it 'organizing'.[7]

Having being forcibly removed from their homes and exploited and humiliated in Germany, these *Ostarbeiter* were not inclined to show much respect for property or person. In time, they were to become a considerable headache for the occupation authorities. Yet there were surprisingly few acts of revenge. The overriding priority of most DPs was to return quickly to home and family. In the summer of 1945 the roads of Europe were packed with long lines of civilians straggling out of Germany in all directions. By the autumn most had left Germany; UNRRA alone had helped some six million. Yet 1.5 million remained in DP camps and as late as June 1947 the camps still housed around half a million who were unwilling for various reasons to go back.

Some repatriations, however, were far from voluntary. Under the terms of the Yalta agreement, the Allies were bound to hand over all Soviet citizens to Stalin. It is arguable that they had little choice in this matter, since they were anxious to secure those of their own POWs who had fallen into Russian hands during the Red Army's advance. Indeed, this was the main reason why Russian NKVD personnel were permitted to establish interrogation centres to screen Soviet repatriates. As fears of post-war communism spread, increasing numbers of east Europeans in Allied-occupied Germany resisted repatriation. One year after VE-Day these included 380,000 Poles, 125,500 Yugoslavs and 187,000 Balts, among them collaborators and former members of Waffen-SS and other German detachments. Eventually, they would profit from the anti-communist mood of the late 1940s and be allowed under special programmes to emigrate to Britain, the Commonwealth and the USA.[8]

As for Jewish survivors, they too by and large proved unwilling or unable to go back: their pre-war homes were generally occupied by others, their possessions gone. In fact the numbers of Jewish refugees swelled after the war, as around 220,000 Jews from eastern Europe moved westwards. Anti-Semitic pogroms in Poland during 1946, with dozens of dead, accelerated this movement; Zionist organizations assisted it. West European anti-Semitism barred doors to Jewish DPs that were opened to Balts and East Europeans. Thus the numbers of Jewish refugees on the continent continued to increase until 1948 when the creation of the state of Israel and the US Displaced Persons Act allowed most of them to leave Europe. Half a million Palestinian Arab refugees during the 1948 Israeli–Arab War paid the price for Europe's reluctance to absorb its diminished Jewish population. Europe itself became less central to Jewish life, and the striking intensification of anti-Semitism after 1945 suggested that while the Germans might have carried out the genocide, its socio-economic and cultural repercussions were exploited more widely across the continent.[9]

Not surprisingly, feelings of intense bitterness and 'morbid hatred' against the Germans were widespread when the war ended. As late as 1948, a traveller to Holland observed that 'the Dutch do not even want to hear the word "Germany", since the Germans had caused them so much grief during the war'. In eastern Europe, where the threat posed by sizeable German minorities to the new nation-states had just been amply demonstrated, the mood was vengeful. The two largest minorities in inter-war Europe had been the Germans and the Jews, and their fates turned out to be intertwined in more ways than one. Once the Jews had been important transmitters of German culture in eastern Europe; now their mass murder became the prelude to the destruction of German life outside Germany. For the war did not only lead to the Final Solution of the Jewish Question; it led, in a different way, to the ending – or at least the transformation – of Europe's German Question too.

This too was Hitler's legacy. His dream of consolidating *Deutschtum* was realized in a nightmarish fashion, and tolerated by the Allies in the interests of ethnic homogeneity and future security in Europe. The issue which had triggered off the Second World War was definitively, if brutally, solved through the largest single refugee movement in European history. In 1944–5, five million Germans fled from the eastern parts of the Reich in the face of the Red Army. Between 1945 and 1948, post-liberation regimes in Czechoslovakia, Poland, Romania, Yugoslavia and Hungary expelled another seven million members of their German minorities. It would not be too much to say that in western no less than in eastern Europe, the memory of this violent convulsion has, until very recently, been almost entirely repressed. Yet its effect upon Germany's place in Europe was at least as profound as that country's division, and perhaps – in the long run – more important still.[10]

The first phase of panic and flight in the face of the advancing Red Army occurred between the autumn of 1944 and the Potsdam Conference in July 1945. Hundreds of thousands of Germans fled East Prussia by land and sea; later they were followed by others from Silesia and Pomerania. Mass rapes and massacres at the hands of the Red Army created a widespread atmosphere of terror. 'The Russians entered every shelter, cellar and basement, and under menaces, demanded and took watches, rings and other valuables,' ran a report from Danzig in early 1945. 'Nearly all the women were raped – among the victims were old women of sixty and seventy-five and girls of fifteen or even twelve. Many were raped ten, twenty or thirty times.' Those who did not flee were thrown into labour or detention camps and deprived of their possessions. Many were forced to wear marks of identification – first large painted swastikas on their clothes, then badges. In these ways, the German population was collectively paid back for the racial humiliation which Nazi policies had inflicted earlier upon the *Untermenschen*.[11]

In Czechoslovakia, following liberation, hatred of the Germans was widespread, especially as many seemed unrepentant and 'sullen and dangerous'. President Beneš had already won Allied support for his plans to expel the 'disloyal' among them, but expediency rather than justice turned out to be the motive for what followed. In Brno, for instance, on 30 May 1945, young National Guards expelled the town's entire German population, roughly 25,000 people, and herded them towards the Austrian border. Discriminatory measures such as being banned from public transport, or being made to wear 'badges of defeat', added pressure on those that remained. By July 1945, several million Germans had fled or been expelled from their homes and driven into camps or herded across the border. In part, this was an act of revenge by the east Europeans for their sufferings of the previous six years; but we should not ignore the fact that running parallel with this popular anger was a more carefully thought-out official policy by the new authorities in the region. 'We must expel all the Germans,' the Polish communist Gomułka emphasized, 'because countries are built on national lines and not on multinational ones.'[12]

At Potsdam, the nature of this policy became clearer. The Allies accepted the principle of the mass expulsion of millions of Germans, including not just *Volksdeutsche* but also those who were citizens of the pre-war Reich, now living under Soviet or Polish occupation. The Allies' primary concern was to control the flow of refugees so that they could be received properly in Germany itself. Thus a temporary suspension of the transfers was agreed. In fact, the expulsions continued, especially from the former Reich territories now administered by Poland. Only during the winter of 1945–6 were more 'orderly transfers' arranged; but by then the temperature had dropped and many died in the cattle cars which brought the refugees westwards. In all, some twelve to thirteen million Germans were 'transferred', by far the largest such population movement in European history. The numbers who died en route must have been at least in the hundreds of thousands; some sources put the final tally as high as two million.

The disappearance through expulsion or killing of east Europe's Germans and Jews formed part of a still vaster process of demographic turbulence and instability in the wake of the war. More than seven million refugees from other ethnic groups (mostly Poles, Czechs and Slovaks, Ukrainians and Balts) were evicted from their homes and resettled. The result was the virtual elimination of many minorities in eastern Europe – falling from 32 per cent to 3 per cent of the population in Poland, 33 per cent to 15 per cent in Czechoslovakia, from 28 per cent to 12 per cent in Romania. The German *Volk* was now more closely aligned with the boundaries of the (divided) German state; so, too, the Ukrainians. War, violence and massive social dislocation turned Versailles's dreams of national homogeneity into realities.[13]

A total of close to ninety million people were either killed or displaced in Europe between the years 1939 and 1948. Adding together military and civilian casualties, POWs and civilians forced to move whether permanently or temporarily from their homes during and after the war, we find that these groups amounted to no less than half the total population in extreme cases such as Germany or Poland, but even to one person in five in the case of comparatively less afflicted countries like France. In Poland's Western Territories well over half the population by 1950 comprised recent settlers and migrants from other regions. Here were, in embryo, the origins of the 'new reality of an integrated national community being formed in the crucible of socialist change', which Polish sociologists analysed in the post-war period.[14]

We cannot hope to understand the subsequent course of European history without attending to this enormous upheaval and trying to ascertain its social and political consequences. The years of Nazi occupation, followed by the chaos of the immediate post-war period, had sundered human ties, destroyed homes and communities and in many cases uprooted the very foundations of society. The thousands of ruined buildings, mined roads and devastated economies were the most visible legacy of these years; but alongside the physical destruction were more intangible wounds which lasted well after the work of reconstruction had been completed. Changing moral and mental perspectives changed individual behaviour, and thence society and politics.

One of the most obvious of these changing values was the erosion of respect for property rights. Put simply, across much of central and eastern Europe a lot of people ended up living in other people's homes and enjoying their goods. Much of the Germans' property, as had that of their victims before them, passed abruptly into the hands of new owners. The expulsions – not unlike the earlier deportations of the Jews – provoked a 'lust for booty' on the part of onlookers. 'The

German peasant had scarcely left his farm and house and been taken off to the station by the police, when robbery and plunder were in full swing,' recalled an ethnic German from Hungary. 'Former have-nots were stealing by day and night. A rabble would arrive from the town in lorries and plunder everything that came to view and that they could lay their hands on. There were bandits too among the police.' Just as there had been, of course, a few years earlier among the German police battalions and Waffen-SS units stationed in eastern Europe.[15]

Places changed their identity and composition. Towns reverted from their German to their Polish, Czech or Hungarian names. Across eastern Europe, synagogues, mosques, Lutheran and Uniate churches were bulldozed, or converted to secular use, becoming barns, stables, warehouses or, later on, cinemas. Those houses which were not rendered unsafe by the wholesale looting stood vacant until new owners moved in. Owing largely to the initial plundering of unoccupied buildings, many areas of settlement remained deserted for many years. The town of Glogau, for example, met a fate shared by others in Silesia: its pre-war population of 33,500 had shrunk to some 5,000 by the early 1960s. 'To all intents and purposes Glogau no longer exists,' reported a visitor in 1960. 'Here a grotesque looking ruin, there a deep hole, then a hillock overgrown with sparse grass.' Even in 1966 the population of the city of Wrocław was only 477,000 – only three quarters the 1939 size of its former incarnation, Breslau.[16]

In Poland, because there were often too few settlers to replace the expelled Germans and Uniates, the local authorities advertised for newcomers. We read for example, from a 1953 brochure entitled 'Moving to New Farms', how an early settler was told that 'in the county of Rzeszów, in the district of Sanok, you'll find land in abundance, houses and barns; and if you think it sounds too good to be true, anyone can check it out with his own eyes and the railway will cost him nothing.' Sanok lay in a formerly Greek Catholic area, depopulated since the population transfers of 1945 and the anti-partisan sweeps of 1947.[17]

The role of officials in directing this violent exchange of property made its mark on popular attitudes towards authority. Nazi rule had already left many people with the feeling that force was all that mattered. Now they saw, and indeed participated in, the forceful expulsion and looting of fellow-villagers or townspeople under the eyes of the new political authorities. Partisans, policemen and the courts all partook of the opportunities. This experience confirmed a widespread growing cynicism about politics which fed apathy and conformity and undermined efforts to challenge the holders of power.

For the new authorities and their Soviet backers, no small part of the rationale for the expulsions was to purchase political popularity and, more pertinently, to expand the level of political dependency. By distributing Jewish possessions to their non-Jewish neighbours, the Nazis had created a web of complicity that weakened resistance; after 1945, the expulsion of the Germans allowed Communist officials to follow a similar strategy. Thus considerations of social justice and national security were often a cover for more practical concerns. The new settlers were beholden to the regime for their new station in life; uncertain of the validity of their legal claims to their new homes, anxious for protection against those families who tried to get their property back, they were from the outset a dependent class.[18]

FAMILY AND MORALITY

Derrick Sington, one of the very first British soldiers to enter Belsen, had noted how 'in the summer of 1945, after the terror of starvation and the gas chamber had been lifted, the thoughts of those thousands of survivors, healthy enough to reflect and hope, turned to the wives or sisters, parents or children, who had been snatched from them months and even years before'. They sent letters, and relatives started turning up. The British initially sent a car through the camp with a loudspeaker calling out lists of sought-for people; then they began to compile a central registry.[19]

Wartime and post-war displacement broke up innumerable families across the continent. By 1947 there were some 50,000 orphans in Czechoslovakia. In Yugoslavia the estimate was closer to 280,000 and at least 10,000 children had survived the war hiding in the woods in conditions of complete destitution. In Holland, some 60,000 children required help, including those of imprisoned collaborators; in Bucharest there were 30,000 homeless. UNRRA was caring for some 50,000 unaccompanied children in Germany alone, many of whom had forgotten who they were or where they came from.[20]

Tracing services were quickly set up by the Red Cross, national governments and UNRRA. The Central Tracing Bureau employed interviewers and researchers in twenty countries, while the US Central Location Index eventually contained more than one million entries. For years afterwards, national radio and press services carried long lists of missing persons. But the number of individuals reunited with relatives was always outweighed by the number of those still untraced. UNRRA, for example, in its first year was able to solve only about one sixth of its cases. As late as July 1948, over 4,000 children being cared for by the UN as displaced persons were still unidentified.[21]

Studies of war orphans revealed a range of traumas which many had suffered as a result of their experiences. The children were depressed, unduly serious for their age and highly nervous. They seemed cynical, despondent and distrustful of authority. To many it seemed that the war had produced a generation of anti-idealists. 'We have to realize,' one young Czech woman told an English friend, 'that the occupation produced cowards as well as heroes. During the years when young people were growing up, morals were inverted; evil was often shown to be more profitable than good and lies more profitable than truth. Those who grew used to whispering cannot speak out naturally now; they either shout or whisper . . . It is not easy to expel fear from the hearts of the people from the Continent.'[22]

Orphaned children were suspicious of signs of affection and prone to violence, often dangerous. Their 'emancipation from the rule of moral law' might manifest itself in crime, in sudden, uncontrollable rages or in brutality towards younger or weaker children. But their casual attitude towards violence also revealed itself in play. English nurses were astounded at the strange behaviour of a group of Jewish children who had survived the camps. Living in a self-contained world which excluded all outsiders, they appeared to expect no assistance or support from grown-ups. If a child went missing from the group, the others would say, quite matter-of-factly: 'Oh, he is dead.'[23]

Many such patterns of behaviour were eventually overcome by sustained attention and love. There were relatively few psychoses, as a result of wartime experiences, among either children or adults observed; the majority of problems – such as the sexual difficulties experienced by many former partisans as a result of the enforced abstinence of the war years – seem to have disappeared with time. In the longer term, it seems that the psychological impact of wartime suffering upon survivors and their children depended heavily upon the interpretation that could be placed upon that suffering – Holocaust survivors (who found it hard to heroize their experiences) and former political prisoners (for whom this was easier) thus found themselves in different situations. In the short term, such differences were less apparent and one can see how the emotional attitudes reported in wartime survivors underlay some broader social and political responses among the population at large.[24]

Cynicism towards authority and a concomitant willingness to get by were especially evident, for obvious reasons, in the ravaged lands of eastern Europe. A Polish writer summed up the mood: 'The Bolsheviks are in the country, the Communists are in power, Warsaw is burned to the ground, the legitimate London government is abandoned. Nothing worse can happen to us, we lost the war and should look after ourselves.' In 1972, another observer of the Polish scene remarked upon the 'demoralization left in the wake of the brutal occupation of World War II'; among the results were 'present-day cynicism' and 'a heightened yearning for material goods and gadgets, rather than for more idealistic values'.[25]

Even in countries less devastated than Poland, the war's end was welcomed by many people as a chance to leave behind the madness of a world torn apart by political struggle. In Germany, Franz Neumann summarized the popular mood as 'the deliberate rejection of politics and parties, ironic and sarcastic attitudes towards Nazism, denazification, democracy and anti-fascism and concentration on finishing one's education as speedily as possible, and on a position, money and consumer goods'. The greatest believers turned into disillusioned cynics. 'He who loves unduly a god, forces others to love him, ready to exterminate them if they refuse,' wrote Romanian émigré Emil Cioran in his manifesto of pessimistic indifference, *Précis de décomposition*, in exile in France in 1949 – the same Cioran who had worshipped Hitler and Codreanu in the 1930s with messianic fervour for their 'cult of the irrational'.[26]

After 1945, then, politics turned into something to be endured, while intimacy and domesticity became more important than ever as stabilizing factors in people's lives. Elio Vittorini's classic novel of reconstruction in post-war Italy – *Le donne di Messina*, first published in 1949 – describes a world in which ideology has lost its magical powers of persuasion and the search for privacy beckons. The need for human warmth extends to Uncle Agrippa, whose entire life is spent on trains passing up and down the country looking for his daughter, and to the anti-hero, Ventura, once a Fascist fanatic and an ideologue, now rooted to the land and his lover, desperately keeping his past at bay.

It was the family, above all, which became a refuge from wartime and post-war anxieties. 'As in an experiment,' noted the anthropologist Vera Erlich, 'the tendency to preserve family life became evident among the survivors of German concentration camps.' Erlich noted the speed with which these people sought not casual affairs but marriage. 'With marriage they changed completely. Only then did they begin to return to life.' Affection and intimacy were thus essential in reviving the self-described 'ghosts' after their return from captivity. Erlich observed: 'When a child was born to them, many found some mental equilibrium. Their passionate desire for married life had appeared spontaneously, as had their wish to have children. To the babies they showed extreme tenderness, and even tended to pamper and spoil them.' The more troubling psychological consequences of this sort of relationship between camp survivors and their children often only emerged ten or twenty years later.[27]

This new attachment to the family did not appear only among survivors of the camps. It was very widespread, and contributed in no small part to the remarkable and almost entirely unforeseen baby boom of the post-war period. As a result of the new upward trend, which had begun in many countries even during the war, the gloomy prognoses of population decline, so commonplace in the West before 1939 and still encountered into the 1950s, turned out to be unfounded.

The results of wartime and post-war dislocation and upheaval were therefore paradoxical. On the one hand, in many countries the new political authorities were confronted with a *tabula rasa* upon which to imprint their own social vision. To this end they could count upon the support of a radicalized population that had moved to the Left during the war and demanded reform and reconstruction. On the other hand, there is little doubt that the overwhelming feeling was one of exhaustion. 'We are tired out by History,' wrote an eminent Greek novelist, 'tired and uneasy.' In Sarajevo in 1946, the writer Ivo Andrić observed the exhausted faces and white hair of prematurely aged passers-by. Weary of conflict, suspicious of ideology and politics, people wished to remake and sometimes retreat to a secure private world of family stability and adequate living standards.[28]

The outcome was a popular mood which was both radical and conservative at the same time. People looked forward to building a new world, but they did not wish this process to be disruptive. Hence an underlying propensity, once the anger and excitement of the first moments of liberation had worn off, to opt for social calm. In eastern Europe, the extraordinary turmoil of the years from 1939 to 1948 was an important factor, therefore, in helping understand popular adaptation to the imposition of communist rule. But in western Europe, too, one sees how the social and psychological consequences of the war years laid the foundations for a social consensus based upon commitment to welfare, mass consumption and the recovery of the family.

THE POLITICS OF OCCUPATION, 1943–5

In May 1943 Anthony Eden advised the British war cabinet that the only alternative to total Russian domination of eastern Europe at the end of the war was to create an 'inter-Allied Armistice Commission', with a rotating presidency. Through this the Big Three would determine policy jointly towards the territories which fell under their control. The Russians welcomed Eden's idea. So when, a few months later, they learned that they were being shut out of Allied negotiations for an Italian surrender, they protested forcefully. In Stalin's words:

To date it has been like this: the USA and Britain reach agreement between themselves while the USSR is informed of the agreements between the two powers as a third party looking passively on. I must say that this situation cannot be tolerated any longer.[29]

Churchill, however, signed the Italian armistice terms before replying. Allied actions spoke louder than words: by the autumn of 1943, before the Red Army had pushed the Wehrmacht back into Europe, it had been made clear that there were limits to the extent of Big Three cooperation. As Italy was the first ex-combatant to drop out of the war, a precedent had been set.[30]

How conscious were the Allies of the implications of the Italian armistice for cooperation with the Russians? The Americans, in so far as they devoted much thought to post-war Europe, shied away from anything that smacked of power politics and preferred to envisage European problems being solved amicably through the new post-war United Nations Organization which they hoped to create. On the other hand, they expected to demobilize rapidly when the war ended, a prospect which necessarily undermined the persuasiveness of their arguments.

The likelihood of being left alone without American support concentrated minds in Whitehall: idealism was a luxury the overstretched British could ill afford. De Gaulle offered a potential prop for London in post-war Europe. But even if an Anglo-French understanding materialized, the fact of overwhelming Russian power remained. Hence, the British Foreign Office attached much importance to ascertaining Russian wishes, and was prepared, if necessary, to acquiesce in Soviet domination of eastern Europe. 'It is better that Russia should dominate Eastern Europe than that Germany should dominate Western Europe,' was the superbly ruthless calculation of Sir William Strang in May 1943.[31]

As for the Soviet Union, this was far from planning the swift takeover of Europe which Cold War warriors came to fear. Rather, its post-war planners envisaged a 'breathing spell' of decades in which time the borders of 1941 would be confirmed and wartime devastation made good, Germany would be nullified as a threat, and the USSR would become 'a centre of gravity for all truly democratic medium-sized and small countries, particularly in Europe'. European stability would be assured preferably by continuing the wartime Grand Alliance, and if not by at least exploiting the rivalries that were believed likely to emerge between the USA and the UK.[32]

There was thus much common ground between the Big Three and, while the war was on, the understanding between them remained intact. When Stalin broke off relations with the Polish government in exile, the weak Allied response can only have encouraged him to assume that he had their support for his efforts to ensure a pro-Soviet regime in Poland after the war. Was there not then, at the highest levels, a tacit quid pro quo here regarding Poland and Italy? At the Teheran conference at the end of 1943, the Allies agreed to shifting Poland's borders westwards, a move which astute observers realized must inevitably turn Poland into a client state of the Soviet Union since it meant taking territory from Germany. By 1944, Strang's precept seemed to be underlying Western policy towards Poland, at least.

Once the British and Americans decided not to invade the Balkans from the Mediterranean, it became clear that nothing could stop the Red Army's march into eastern Europe. During the Romanian armistice negotiations in September 1944, the British and American ambassadors to Moscow watched silently as Molotov agreed terms with the Romanian delegation which gave the Soviet High Command sweeping political powers in the occupied country. The following month Anglo-Soviet talks in Moscow allowed Churchill and Stalin openly to discuss spheres of influence. The two men's so-called Percentages Agreement, followed by some surreal bargaining between Eden and Molotov, clarified the balance of power in the region: Stalin's demand for a free hand in Romania was balanced by British control in post-war Greece. Soviet predominance was also conceded in Hungary and Bulgaria.[33]

We should not, however, make the mistake of assuming that the Great Power carve-up of the continent was necessarily intended at this stage to be comprehensive. There could be little doubt by the end of 1944 about Soviet intentions in Poland, Romania and Bulgaria, just as it was obvious that Stalin was conceding Italy to the Allies and allowing Churchill a free hand in Greece, where British fighter planes were strafing suburbs of Athens in order to defeat a communist-led uprising. Yet in Hungary, Stalin's tactics were very different and intended to form a reassuring contrast with Soviet policy towards Poland. In both France and Italy, the Communist Parties – which had accumulated considerable military power as a result of their leading role in the resistance – were under strict instructions to pursue a legalist policy. In Italy, the result was that the PCI agreed to support the largely discredited monarchy ahead of most other parties. By December, Communist Party secretary Togliatti was one of two vice-presidents in the government and more insistent than ever – in view of the rift which had opened up in Greece between the Left and the British – upon abstaining from revolutionary temptation.

The Yalta Declaration on Liberated Europe – with its promise of a dawning era of liberty and democracy – must be evaluated in the light of this emerging Great Power understanding. Just prior to Yalta Roosevelt had indicated that: 'The Russians had the power in Eastern Europe, that it was obviously impossible to break with them and that, therefore, the only practicable course was to use what influence we had to ameliorate the situation.'[34] Yalta's lofty commitment to free elections across the continent could hardly be squared with the real-politik of the Percentages Agreement of three months earlier, when Stalin and Churchill secretly carved up eastern Europe into spheres of influence. None of the Big Three could have believed that Yalta would have much effect upon Soviet attitudes towards Poland, Romania and Bulgaria, countries which Stalin regarded as keys to Russian security. Strikingly, both the Polish communists and their opponents interpreted Yalta as a victory for Stalin. By the spring of 1945, the Red Army was rounding up and deporting thousands of Home Army guerrillas, forcing others into the forests to take up arms. At the same time, the Polish Workers' Party launched an immense and highly successful recruitment drive to build up a mass base. Thus in Poland, as in Romania and Bulgaria, the twin bases of Soviet domination – massive repression of the opposition combined with membership drives into local Communist Parties – were in evidence even before the German surrender.

Yet in 1945 we are still some way from the polarization of three years later. In Poland itself communist tactics shocked Western public opinion and provoked forceful if largely ineffectual protests from Churchill and Roosevelt. Moreover, the spheres of influence tacitly confirmed at Yalta left much of Europe untouched. Austria, Finland, Czechoslovakia, Hungary, Yugoslavia, Albania and eastern Germany formed what Geir Lundestad has called Moscow's 'middle sphere'. In this area Stalin could not count upon Western toleration, nor indeed was he convinced that countries like Yugoslavia or Hungary were ready for revolution. So keen were the Russians to play the parliamentary game according to the rules in 1945 in the areas outside their own sphere of influence that in at least two cases – Austria and Finland – Communist Parties entered elections, did poorly and were effectively marginalized from politics.

The future of Germany remained the key issue. It would be quite inaccurate to assume that partition was a foregone conclusion as early as 1945. On the contrary, the Big Three were all genuinely committed to preserving the unity of the country. Thus when the war finally ended and Europeans began to tackle the problems of social and political reconstruction, they found themselves in a situation of growing tension but not deadlock between the Powers. Nor, in 1945, was polarization common in domestic affairs. Across Europe coalition governments were the norm, pledged to embark upon the sweeping socio-economic reforms required for a renovation of parliamentary democracy. For later generations, the years 1945–6 came to represent a moment of promise, before the Iron Curtain dropped.

A NEW START?

On 18 September 1944 the first High Court trial of a collaborator in Rome was disrupted when a key witness, Donato Carretta, former director of the city's main prison, was attacked in the courtroom.

Spectators, led by a woman whose son had been shot by the Germans a few months earlier, seized Carretta and amid shouts of 'Paris, let's imitate Paris!', dragged him out of the building and eventually killed him. His battered body was left hanging, by the feet, outside his former prison.[35]

All over Europe, the withdrawal of the Germans left large numbers of people vulnerable to the charge of collaboration or treachery. Their existence was a shameful reminder of the Nazi New Order; their removal from public life – sometimes from life itself – seemed vital to establish a break with the past. Occupation had revealed disturbingly deep fault-lines in the unity of the European nation. It was hard to imagine a genuine democracy flourishing anew without the punishment of its enemies, hard too to see a revival of independent nation-states without their purification of those who had betrayed them to a foreign power. However, the legal anarchy and diffusion of power which characterized the first days of liberation allowed a number of very different conceptions of punishment to emerge.

The first was that evident in the death of Carretta – a spontaneous, popular demand for revenge which manifested itself in instant executions, lynchings and public humiliations. Emerging out of the internecine war of 1943–4, this vengeful mood was most evident in countries like Italy, France and Belgium, which had seen high levels of repression by collaborationist squads under German rule. In Italy, above all, liberation offered a chance to turn the tables on two decades of Fascist domination. One partisan recalled an episode where 'a guy who'd been made to drink castor oil seized a Fascist and told him: "Now you go home and don't appear in the village for a week." And he did. They did to the Fascists what they had done to them for twenty years.' But often the mood was more violent and attacks upon snipers soon turned into a wider wave of killings. In Bologna 'the people . . . roamed the streets on their hunt' and 'justice was meted out with a certain freedom to anyone in trouble with the partisans . . . Some people certainly paid for personal animosities or for quarrels over women.'[36]

The random and brutal nature of such killings served in the long run to help discredit the whole idea of punishing collaborators at all;

but in the short run they raised the spectre of outright civil war and prompted resistance movements to intervene and assert their own authority.

The second response, then, was that of the organized resistance, which steered a difficult course between the passions of its rank and file and the restraint and legalism of its leadership. During the fighting, resistance movements had singled out collaborators for 'liquidation'; their commitment to punish traitors after the war was one of their main weapons in demoralizing their opponents. In France, for example, the Conseil National de la Résistance instructed its local leaders to prepare 'immediate measures to purge and neutralize traitors'. Of course, defining involvement in Vichy as treason also helped to assert the legitimacy of the de Gaulle government in the eyes of the Allies. But the resistance was well aware of the need to control the 'people's desire for revenge'. The ad hoc field courts martial which partisans throughout Europe had employed during the war persisted into the first weeks of liberation; in addition, they set up rudimentary internment camps to secure and sometimes protect suspected collaborators from mob justice. Inside the resistance itself there were bitter disputes about what sort of justice to mete out. Thus, from northern Italy: 'Some partisans said it would be better to chuck a pair of grenades into the room where the prisoners were kept and exterminate them there and then, but the commander and others decided to send the prisoners to the prisons at Rovigo for a regular investigation.'[37]

Within a decade of the end of the war, anti-communist accounts of this phase would talk darkly of the excesses of *résistentialisme*, and the horrors of 'class justice'. This was sheer exaggeration. 'It was astonishing that the Liberation happened as it did,' the wartime SOE (Special Operations Executive) agent Francis Cammaerts reminds us. 'All you hear about is shaving women's heads, personal vendettas and so on. But I had a lieutenant who came up to me and said: "I've got 300 German prisoners. What do the international conventions say about how much food and exercise they are entitled to every day?" And those were Germans who had strung up resisters and their families. There was something extraordinarily civilized about the Liberation.' However, it is true that an aura of shame surrounded the whole subject (which resistance organizations mostly preferred to forget), and the number of dead in the first wave of purges was certainly high in comparison with the slower pace of official justice that followed – perhaps 10,000–15,000 victims in Italy during 1943–6, 9,000–10,000 in France (with another 40,000 or so held in detention).[38]

The third source of power, which eventually asserted itself over these 'improvisations of authority' (in de Gaulle's phrase), was that of the new political authorities returning from exile, backed up by some degree of foreign recognition. Here the desire for revenge was milder, the concern with public order and due process of law stronger. In many countries tensions quickly emerged between the slow pace of official justice and popular expectations. This was true, especially while the war was still going on, for both the Allied-backed Italian government, whose relationship with Fascism remained equivocal, and even for the Free French, whose modest initial efforts to try Vichy officials in Algiers in late 1943 led to harsh criticism inside France.[39]

But by 1945–6 a pattern was beginning to emerge. Coalition governments responded to the call for a new start by embarking upon sweeping judicial investigations of collaborators with show trials of senior politicians, writers and actresses. (Businessmen usually got off lightly.) Multi-tiered systems of courts were established and new crimes were defined where necessary. Yet few trials ended with severe punishment, and by 1946 disillusionment with the whole process was growing in certain sectors of society. The first amnesty laws were introduced, to be followed by others. By the early 1950s, most judicial investigations had been wound down.

In Norway, for example, the entire membership of the pro-Nazi Nasjonal Samling – some 55,000 people – was brought for trial. But few of these were sentenced to more than five years in jail. Only twenty-five death sentences were carried out and by 1957 the last life prisoner had been released. In the Netherlands, over 200,000 cases were investigated, resulting in some forty death sentences actually carried out. Again, most prisoners were released by the early 1950s. Although French courts tried over 300,000 cases, and sentenced over 6,700 to death, the actual numbers executed or jailed were relatively low. A series of amnesties reduced the numbers in prison from 29,000 in

1946 to fewer than 1,000 in 1954. Much more important in France and elsewhere was the loss of full citizenship rights: the charge of 'dégradation nationale' or 'incivisme' was important in symbolically distancing post-war regimes from the memory of collaboration and reaffirming the democratic essence of the nation.

Even more fraught with ambiguity were the purges of state administrations, police forces and armies. On the one hand, new political elites desired to govern on the basis of post-Fascist principles; on the other, they needed to ensure effective and orderly government as rapidly as possible to cope with the horrendous socio-economic problems which the Nazis left in their wake. In Italy, or for that matter Austria, the impracticability of a clean sweep was obvious. By July 1946, Chancellor Figl was telling the Allies that the Austrian administration was now 'free of the National Socialist spirit'; some 70,818 out of 299,000 civil servants had been dismissed – not enough for anti-Nazis, too many for the bulk of the population.[40] In Italy, the violence of the initial 'wild purges' led to an even swifter backlash: the administrative purges were wound down as early as the autumn of 1945. Only 6,500 out of 850,000 civil servants were dismissed in France, mostly in the Interior Ministry, but outside the police and the army officer corps, little was done, and de Gaulle insisted there could be no question of 'sweeping aside the vast majority of the State's servants'. In the Netherlands, perhaps because there had been much less violence at liberation itself, the purge went deeper, with 17,500 civil servants dismissed and another 6,000 disciplined.[41]

Overall, west European governments opted for continuity rather than prosecution. Some civil servants were disciplined. But the bastions of state power, notably the police, remained mostly immune to investigation. De Gaulle's creation of a new republican police force, the CRS, was unusual; more typical in western Europe were the cases of the Italian *carabinieri* or the Greek National Guard, whose personnel simply changed uniforms between 1943 and 1946. Other key areas of society – the judiciary, education and business – escaped with little more than perfunctory investigation. If the Nation was to be reborn, the state machine remained largely the same.

Within the post-war coalition governments, Christian Democrats and conservatives preached the benefits of amnesia and charity. 'We have the strength to forget! Forget as quickly as possible!' urged *Il popolo* in April 1945. Fears of 'Jacobin improvisations', intensified by the Greek civil war, contributed to this position as much as any electoral calculation. Conservative anti-communism helps explain the emergence of determined resistance to the idea of any wholesale purge. But so does a more basic popular desire in 1945-6 to see governments focus their energies upon rebuilding the economy and raising living standards, assuaging political passions instead of arousing them.[42]

Inside the resistance such attitudes appeared scarcely comprehensible. Often the very policemen who had persecuted resisters in 1943 were still telling them what to do five years later. In late 1944 fighting broke out in Athens and Belgium, in part because of resistance fears that there would be no substantial turnover of personnel by incoming exile governments. Elsewhere, partisan forces were demobilized with extraordinary difficulty only on the basis of pledges of genuine reform. Now it appeared that resistance fears of betrayal had been justified all along. They had been outflanked and found themselves helpless before 'the continuity of the State'. Such resentments were highly dangerous and occasionally spilled over into acts of violence. Greece was the extreme case where the temporary truce of 1945 turned into a civil war lasting three years. But the threat was always beneath the surface in Italy too and emerged for one brief, frightening moment in the insurrection which followed the shooting of the communist leader Palmiro Togliatti in July 1948. But by this date, the Cold War had changed people's perceptions: now the radicalization of the war years had vanished, and with it, the public support for revolutionary violence.

In eastern Europe, too, there were extensive purges after the war, but they served a very different purpose and followed a different course to those in the West. They were not based upon the judicial investigation of individual misdeeds but upon a more sweeping attribution of collective guilt derived from social position or ethnic attribution. This reflected the key difference behind the two social projects, West and East. The philosophy underlying the purges in western Europe separated the punishment of guilty individuals from questions of socio-economic reform, and regarded the latter as matters for democratic debate. In eastern Europe, on the other hand, purges against 'Fascists' and 'war criminals' became a central part of the construction of society on something approaching the Soviet model.

'Anti-Fascist' campaigns targeted entire social categories for dismissal, deportation, expropriation or worse. In Hungary, for instance, Moscow insisted upon the need to purge 'Fascist elements' during the negotiations which preceded the formation of a provisional government in December 1944. It quickly emerged that this was meant to encompass not merely the pro-German Arrow Cross extremists who had seized power in October, but also the 'full liquidation of feudal structures' and measures against 'reactionaries' in the state and society.[43] During 1945 over 3,000 local committees were set up to imprison and try suspected collaborators. They also formed special police units drawn from workers and farm labourers. At the same time, 'People's Courts' were set up to try high-profile political cases: public executions of war criminals drew large crowds. Though at first these trials focused upon the Arrow Cross, over time the definition of 'enemy of the people' broadened. By April 1945, communist papers were criticizing the courts for their moderation, asserting that 'the Democracy is behaving too humanly towards these fascist beasts'. Interestingly, there is evidence to suggest that the judicial process ran into the same difficulties in Hungary as it did in western Europe, and produced the same low rate of guilty verdicts.[44]

In Yugoslavia, Tito ordered the massacre of thousands of members of Serbian, Croatian and Slovenian collaborationist formations who were handed over by the British in April–May 1945. He saw this, according to Djilas, as a 'pragmatic solution' since he feared the courts could not cope with so many individual investigations. Overall estimates of the numbers of quislings and collaborators killed in post-war Yugoslavia are highly controversial, but as many as 60,000 may have lost their lives in this way. In Greece, the December 1944 fighting saw the communists conduct mass shootings of 'people's enemies', often identifying them solely on the basis of their status as 'bourgeois'. Meanwhile, on the Greek Right, nationalist guerrillas killed hundreds of Chams (Albanian-speaking Muslims) and drove the remaining 15,000 into Albania on the grounds that they had aided the Axis.[45]

Russian-backed regimes in eastern Europe developed this kind of ethnic cleansing more systematically. Anti-communist underground armies, stay-behind teams and sabotage units, in many cases equipped by the Germans in 1944-5, constituted a thorn in the side of these new regimes and prompted them to respond with both repression and expropriation. In Romania, for example, where the Waffen-SS was parachuting paramilitaries into Transylvania late in 1944, the Soviet authorities acted swiftly and harshly to stamp out any potential resistance. On 7 January 1945, nearly 100,000 *Volksdeutsche* were deported for forced labour to the Soviet Union. The reform decree of March 1945 – yoking together wartime, class and ethnic enemies – expropriated the farms of those who had collaborated with the Germans, of war criminals and of anyone who held more than ten hectares but had not farmed it themselves.[46]

In Hungary, the land reform decree of the same month singled out the 'enemies of the Hungarian people', thus again targeting both the class enemy – the large landowners – and the ethnic foe – the German minority. Such measures, introduced under a communist Minister of Agriculture, were enormously popular among the peasantry. In the words of an impartial source: 'It was a social revolutionary measure of supreme importance that ruined the powerful landowners and released a pent-up energy which enlivened the countryside some time after.'[47]

Confiscation of German property took place on an even vaster scale in Czechoslovakia and Poland. Large estates and thousands of urban properties were abandoned and became available for resettlement, a means for incumbent governments to purchase popular backing by appealing to nationalist sentiment as well as economic interest. Sometimes, the expulsion of the Germans formed part of a more concerted scheme for eradicating minorities from the country. Following bitter internecine struggles during the inter-war years and under the German occupation, the Poles also took their revenge on the large Ukrainian minority, forcing 480,000 to leave for the Soviet Union; in 1947, some

150,000, who had escaped the earlier deportations, were forcibly resettled in the west of the country.[48]

Such examples indicate the contrasting nature of the purges in western and eastern Europe. In the former, they were limited in scope, rapidly brought under the control of the courts, and quickly scaled down as the Cold War developed. In the latter, judicial activity formed only part of a variety of measures against 'war criminals' and 'enemies of the people'. Post-war purges became an instrument for a total economic and ethnic reshaping of society. As such they were a means for post-war regimes to mobilize genuine popular support (just as bourgeois governments had used land reform after 1918 in much of eastern Europe), and allowed left-wing figures to claim leadership of the nation. As before in the Soviet Union so now in eastern Europe, social revolution went hand in hand with national assertion.

THE DIVISION OF GERMANY

'Already it is clear,' wrote Basil Davidson in 1950, 'that the drawing of a frontier line down the middle of Germany has meant as well the dividing of Europe.' In retrospect there can be little doubt that even in defeat Germany held the key to Europe's fate, and that it was partition which finally divided the continent. What, however, is far from obvious is at what point partition became inevitable and as a result of whose actions. After all, the Big Three were all agreed in 1945 on the need to keep Germany together. How, then, did partition happen? Was it the result of Soviet intransigence? Was it rather, as Davidson argued, the result of Western policy? Or did it flow from the basic incompatibility of the ideologies of the occupying powers, an incompatibility which some observers believed had revealed itself even before May 1945 in the very first steps taken by the military governments that the Allies and the Red Army set up in the territory they had conquered?[49]

The Allied policy of 'unconditional surrender', first announced in 1943, finally prevailed. Hitler's successor, Admiral Dönitz, authorized the signature of surrender on 7 May 1945 and his government led an increasingly controversial half-life until he and the remainder of the German High Command were arrested two weeks later. His efforts to win Allied support for a rejuvenated Third Reich standing against the Bolshevization of Europe were belatedly rejected, and central political control in Germany passed into the hands of the conquerors.[50]

The victors shared many basic goals at the start. All were agreed upon the need to eliminate Nazism for the sake of European security; all were pledged to punish German war criminals. The Yalta Declaration alluded to the possible 'dismemberment' of the country, but also made reference to central German institutions. Both the Russians and the Americans accepted the desirability of sweeping economic reform through decartelization and land reform in order to break the power of those interests which were believed to have backed Hitler. Finally, all were agreed upon the need to 'democratize' Germany. Such goals amounted to nothing less than a social and political revolution.

This common ground formed the basis for the declarations which followed the Potsdam Conference in July 1945. Drawing a distinction between National Socialism and the German people, the agreement talked of preparing the latter 'for the eventual reconstruction of their life on a democratic and peaceful basis'. At the same time Potsdam skated over the widening areas of Big Three disagreement. Yet none of these was of such immediate significance in the summer of 1945 as the position taken by the French, who were not invited to Potsdam at all, but who had been given their own occupation zone. De Gaulle was the prime opponent of a united Germany. He doggedly opposed the idea of a central German administration operating under the control of the Control Commission, and wanted to annex German territory and break up the old central state. Ultimately the French would fail in their territorial ambitions. But by then their veto had obstructed the chances of German unity, and in the meantime, the policies being pursued in the different Occupation zones created increasingly divergent social and political regimes.

In small but far from meaningless ways, the repudiation of the Nazi regime took similar forms across the country. Street names were changed (once more), Nazi literature was cleared out of public libraries and in general visible signs of the old regime were erased. But beyond such measures, the differences of approach became more obvious. In the Soviet zone, de-Nazification was regarded as a means of destroying the economic and social bases of reaction. There was no systematic search for Nazis or war criminals and their life was often easier there than in the Allied zones. Lumping together Nazis with other 'enemies of democracy' the authorities focused upon a swift and far-reaching administrative purge, extending into the judiciary and the teaching profession, and set up short training courses to create new cadres.[51] As in eastern Europe, anti-Nazi slogans became the justification for sweeping economic reforms. Large landed estates were confiscated in 1945, bringing into being a new class of smallholders tied to the new regime. Banks and heavy industry were expropriated. The dismantling of industrial plant proceeded rapidly, despite the fact that it caused tremendous wastage and threw thousands out of work.

Soviet policy reflected two key considerations. One was the prevailing communist analysis of Nazism itself. Walter Ulbricht argued in 1945 that 'Hitler fascism' had emerged from the reactionary nature of German capitalism; hence it was necessary to destroy capitalism and socialize the economy if German authoritarianism was to be eradicated. But even more important than this was the overwhelming Soviet concern to exploit German resources to the hilt to rebuild their own shattered economy and to take full advantage of the reparations provisions agreed with the Allies. In the long run these two goals – the creation of a pro-Soviet Germany and high levels of reparations – were incompatible, but this was not clear in 1945.[52]

De-Nazification in the Western zones took the form of judicial investigation on a case-by-case basis. This satisfied Western conceptions of fairness but proved increasingly impracticable, especially as the scope of the purges *increased* in 1945 following publicity over a number of de-Nazification failures. The infamous *Fragebogen* (questionnaires), a basic element in the investigations, accumulated in enormous numbers – over 1.6 millions in the US zone alone by June 1946 – and as a result the whole de-Nazification process turned into a bureaucratic nightmare. By late 1946, with more than two million cases still to be dealt with, it was already being wound down. A case study of the town of Marburg under US occupation concludes unambiguously that de-Nazification was a failure: it neither excluded former Nazis from office, nor made for a more democratic life. The more pragmatic British and French reached a similar conclusion early on. Several million Germans were affected by the purges but German public opinion believed that they had targeted the lesser fry while allowing big fish to swim free. In short, Allied procedures were not obviously superior to those adopted in the Eastern zone.[53]

Just as in the Soviet case, so in the Western zones de-Nazification practices reflected more general theories of the nature of the Third Reich. Rather than seeing Nazism as a socio-economic phenomenon (requiring drastic intervention in the economy for its eradication), the Allies were more inclined to see it as a dictatorial regime imposed from above. This suggested that the conscientious removal of former Nazis would simply release the natural democratic urges of the German people. Social reform was therefore less important than juridical surgery.

Unfortunately, German attitudes to defeat did not bear out this rosy view. As they monitored public opinion, the Allies were increasingly concerned at what they found. On the one hand, the resistance to occupation which many had feared failed to materialize: the Werewolves proved toothless and the Alpine redoubt a fantasy. Total defeat, following the SS violence of the final apocalyptic months of the war, seemed to have discredited Nazism. Unlike 1918, no one had been left in doubt about the scale of the catastrophe. Yet the Allies expected more than this: they hoped to see signs of repentance for the events of the past six years, and some kind of desire for democracy's return.

The initial reports from Germany were disheartening. People seemed dazed by the total and sudden collapse of the Reich. They were apathetic and individualistic, concerned about food rather than democracy. 'Without me' was the stock response to thoughts of grass-roots political activism. Having once feared the prospect of class revolution, the Allies now worried more about political passivity. When they circulated a film about the death camps, most Germans who watched it regarded it as propaganda.[54]

Nazi patterns of thought outlived the fall of the regime, often manifesting themselves in the most incongruous ways. Saul Padover, one of the first US intelligence officers to assess the popular mood in Germany, describes meeting the Social Democrat who advocated stern measures against the Nazis, stating that: 'Nazi blood is something unclean, biologically unhealthy and incurable . . . Those with Nazi blood cannot be redeemed. They must be made permanently sterile.' And there was the Bürgermeister of Hamborn, who greeted Padover with an instinctive Hitler salute before stammering: 'It's an old habit. One has to stop oneself.' Few Allied officers realized that the ugly term *Entnazifizierung* (de-Nazification) itself replicated the pattern of Nazi jargon.[55]

Slowly seeing that de-Nazification alone would not change mentalities, the Allies embarked upon an ambitious peacetime extension of psychological warfare targeted at the German public. 'Re-education' – a propaganda campaign to democratize an entire society – turned into one of the most extensive such ventures of the twentieth century. School books were rewritten, schools and universities restructured and exposed to new theories and interpretations. And whereas de-Nazification was painful because it looked back to the past, 're-education' offered the promise of a brighter future.

The British remained the least optimistic about its chances of success; as late as 1952 a senior civil servant observed gloomily that 'it is unlikely democracy will develop in Germany in the near future'. The French, by contrast, attached far more importance to it and focused with some success on German youth. De-Nazification, after all, was not really the issue for the French; they were concerned about Germans not Nazis, and felt that transforming German culture was the key to peace. Their travelling exhibition 'Message from French Youth' was visited by 120,000 Germans, and their teacher-training reforms and exchange-visit programmes were highly successful. The American effort was more wholehearted than the British, and resulted in a purge of German universities in 1946. Yet like the British, the Americans found their efforts to reform the school system ran into vocal German opposition. They too were forced to retreat, though it took them longer.[56]

Thus in both de-Nazification and re-education the Allies reaped meagre returns for massive outlay. In the Soviet zone, by contrast, substantial educational reforms took place – notably the establishment of a comprehensive school system – largely because the sources of opposition which were so important in the Western zones were silenced. But this reflects the basic divergence in the occupation regimes: in the West, de-Nazification took place without radical social reform, while in the East, it provided the opportunity for this. Backpedalling from their earlier policy commitments, the Allies were reluctant to countenance sweeping social and economic change. They vetoed land reforms, for example, and allowed Ruhr industrialists to escape the vigorous decartelization which was envisaged in 1944. The main reason for this social conservatism during 1945–6 was not so much anti-communism as the Allies' reliance upon existing interest groups in their zones and their fear of adding to the food shortages and economic difficulties which were currently the chief political concern throughout the country.

This was also why they reacted with growing hostility to the Russian insistence on dismantling German industry, as had been agreed at Potsdam. There is no doubt about the wastefulness of much of the Soviet dismantling effort. (A good example was provided by the dismantling of the Meissen china works: the benches and kilns were smashed, while the iron fragments were sent to a Russian china factory near Leningrad where they rusted away for several years.) Intensified by bureaucratic competitition, the plundering of German resources – not just in the Soviet zone – created enormous confusion and unemployment. Yet it is striking that economic conditions in the Eastern zone in 1945 were no worse than in the West and quite possibly better, thanks to the rapid implementation of economic planning. Despite the high level of reparations shipments, industrial growth started relatively early. Perhaps because of the land reform, the population in the Eastern zone was relatively well fed, at least until 1947.[57]

Reparations, however, became the issue which led most directly to the collapse of Four-Power government. The Potsdam agreement had provided for the Soviet Union to receive 15 per cent of usable capital equipment from the Western zones 'as is unnecessary for the German peace economy'. During the winter of 1945–6, however, food shortages forced rations down dangerously low and the prospect of mass starvation loomed. Relief problems were exacerbated by the millions of refugees entering Western zones from the East. As the Western military governments coped with this manifold social crisis, they began to insist upon the need for a new approach to German reconstruction. On 27 May 1946 they halted reparations deliveries to the Soviet Union from the American zone until such time as a general agreement was reached on the German economy as a whole. With the Soviet authorities refusing to scale down their reparations demands, economic traffic across zonal boundaries quickly dwindled. Just as after 1918, reparations threatened to tear apart the understanding among Germany's conquerors.

The dispute over reparations was stimulated in the first place by the appalling food shortages and economic dislocation of the immediate post-war period. But behind the American–Soviet rift lay the great gulf in their wartime experiences. The Soviet Union had borne the brunt of the German war effort and had suffered enormous damage as a result. By 1945 over twenty million of its citizens were dead and much of its territory was devastated. It was natural for Moscow's policy to be guided above all by the desire to exploit German economic resources for its benefit. The United States, in contrast, had seen its economy boom as a result of the war. It had suffered few casualties at German hands and there was in its relations with the Germans none of the racial antagonism with which the Nazis had invested their *Vernichtungskrieg* in the East. In Washington, policy towards Germany had been split between those who argued for a punitive peace and those who wanted – as they saw it – to avoid the mistakes of 1918 and favoured a more supportive and less radical approach. Up to Potsdam, the first group exerted the upper hand; by late 1945, however, they were losing ground as the scale of the economic crisis became more widely known.

The reparations quarrel should also be seen in the context of political developments in Germany. Just a fortnight after the formation of the Soviet Military Administration, the Communist Party was officially registered in the Eastern zone. Shortly afterwards, the Soviet authorities registered several other political parties. The Western authorities were far more cautious, only permitting parties to act on a local basis until much later. They thereby rebuffed many groups keenest to cooperate in reforming existing structures, preferring to rely on more conservative, ostensibly apolitical administrators. The strict control of Communist Party activities in particular suggested much uncertainty about the loyalties of the electorate.[58]

The Soviet political strategy for Germany became evident as early as 15 July 1945, with the formation of a four-party anti-Fascist bloc. By pressing at Potsdam for a common Allied approach towards party activity – a policy resisted by all the others, most notably by the French – the Russians were permitted to present themselves as sponsors of those forces in Germany that wished Germans to be granted a greater measure of political responsibility. The Communist Party underlined its commitment to a parliamentary democracy for Germany through a 'bloc of antifascist democratic forces'. Nationalism and parliamentary democracy was a persuasive combination in the aftermath of defeat: at this time it must have seemed to many Germans that the Soviet Union was no less likely than the Western allies to provide it.[59]

With the emergence of SPD activity in the Western zones during the summer and autumn of 1945, Soviet policy switched from urging the creation of several separate parties to insisting upon the unification of the SPD and the KPD (the Communists). The poor performance of Communist Parties in elections in Austria and Hungary may have prompted this shift. So undoubtedly did the increasingly independent and assertive line taken by the SPD leadership. At the end of February 1946, the fusion of the two parties was announced. Social Democrats in Berlin protested, and when the new Socialist Unity Party (SED) held its first rallies in April in the Eastern zone, it failed to carry the entire SPD with it. As a result relations in the Western zone between the SPD and the SED were frosty, while the Allies became increasingly suspicious of Soviet tactics.

In the following eighteen months relations between the Soviets and the Allies worsened. A public dispute between Molotov and his

American counterpart Byrnes over the Polish–German frontier was followed in October 1946 by elections in the Eastern zone and Berlin, which revealed the strength of feeling against joining the SED by SPD members. Just over a month later, the US and British zones were fused, and pressure was applied to the French to join. The Four-Power Control Commission had more or less stopped working, unable to agree on much more than the abolition of the state of Prussia. Against this background, it is not surprising that the Conference of Foreign Ministers in Moscow in March–April 1947 failed to agree upon a basis for a German peace treaty. That failure, which coincided with the proclamation of the Truman Doctrine, marked the start of a more decisive and openly anti-communist policy by Washington towards Europe. It also marked the beginning of the Cold War.[60]

Suspicion of *Germany* was with surprising speed ceasing to become the defining factor in post-war international relations. The 1947 Treaty of Dunkirk, signed by the Benelux countries, France and the United Kingdom, had been directed against Germany, which was still regarded as the main threat to peace in Europe. But the Treaty of Brussels signed the following year was less specific about the potential aggressor. East–West relations followed a dialectic of suspicion. Russia regarded the Marshall Plan as an attempt to subvert its rule in eastern Europe. The British and Americans were alarmed by the establishment of the Cominform in September. But probably the key event which turned Russia in Western eyes into the main threat to European security was the Communist *coup d'état* in Prague in February 1948.

Events in Prague pushed the French and the Americans together. In return for pledges of US military and economic support, the French gave up their dreams of obtaining part of the Rhineland. The French zone was merged with Bizonia and the Allies began to plan for currency reform and economic reconstruction within the framework of the European Recovery Plan. The Russians walked out of the Control Commission, which never met again, and blockaded the Western sectors in Berlin. At the height of the Berlin crisis, a separate municipality was created in the Soviet zone. The division of the city anticipated the division of the country. On 23 May 1949, the West German constitution was signed in Bonn; one week later, a rival constitution was adopted by the People's Congress in Berlin. The German Democratic Republic was officially declared in October.

THE COLD WAR IN EUROPE

The Cold War brought a brutal stability to an exhausted continent and ensured that the revival of political life would take place on the terms permitted by the international balance of power. Contrary to Nazi expectations the Second World War was not succeeded by war between the members of the Grand Alliance. Stalin would scarcely have demanded the Allies invade Europe to form a Second Front if he had aimed then to get them out. Soviet losses – after suffering the greatest wartime destruction in history – and the American nuclear monopoly both made Stalin shy away from belligerence. For their part, both the British and the Americans reluctantly and privately accepted the reality of their partnership with the Russians. They could not help recognizing Soviet military predominance in eastern Europe, and its genuine security interests there. The dissolution of the Comintern in 1943 had been Stalin's way of signalling the abandonment of world revolution. If the establishment of its successor, the Cominform, in 1947, marked the deterioration in Moscow's relations with the Allies since the war, it just as importantly – though it was little noticed at the time – signalled a Soviet policy of conservative consolidation behind the Iron Curtain. For the Americans, too, containment was an essentially defensive doctrine. Dulles's talk of a 'roll-back' of communism in the 1950s was not meant seriously: the Western reaction to the 1953 riots in East Germany or 1956 in Hungary demonstrated how uninterested the West was in challenging the prevailing balance of power. Fear of actual hostilities proved unfounded; despite the tension in relations, especially in 1948, neither side seriously considered using military force to intervene in the other's sphere of influence. The most dangerous flashpoints were where the Iron Curtain frayed – Trieste, for example, in 1945 (and that largely because of Tito's belligerence), Hungary and Greece.

One consequence of this division of the continent was that remaining border disputes and minority issues within each Power's sphere of influence no longer threatened international stability, as they had done earlier in the century. In the West, the Americans sorted out French claims to the Val d'Aosta and to western Germany. It had been decided at the post-war Peace Conferences that quarrels between, say, Czechoslovakia and Hungary, were to be left to the two countries concerned to hammer out. There was to be no repeat of the League of Nations' attempt to solve minorities problems by internationalizing them. Neither the Peace Treaties with the defeated Axis partners, nor the United Nations, devoted much attention to minority rights. In a divided Europe, such problems appeared to be of secondary importance. Security from the sorts of border disputes which had plagued the continent in the past was obtained by its subordination to the Superpowers.

There were, of course, high costs to be paid for such stability. The struggle between the Superpowers was henceforth conducted not on the battlefield, but through forms of warfare more compatible with the overwhelming perils of the nuclear era. The covert, psychological and underground warfare which both sides had developed in the struggle against Hitler were now turned upon each other. The spy became the characteristic Cold War warrior. The 'gospel of national security' led to the expansion of vast state organizations for surveillance and espionage. Intelligence activities were no longer regarded as appendages to military operations; they developed their own bureaucratic interests. In western Europe vetting was introduced on the American model, offering a new arena for spymasters to prove their indispensability. The 'stay-behind' networks, set up in the late 1940s by American intelligence, determined not to be caught napping by a Soviet invasion, formed malignant anti-communist nuclei in the body politic. Only in the 1980s with revelations about the Gladio ring in Italy would the extent of their activities become appreciated.

The predominance of Cold War anti-communism, combined with the signs of growing popular political disillusionment, gave the democratization of the West a highly conservative cast which troubled liberals and those on the Left in the late 1940s. 'The burning question for one concerned with the future of democracy in Europe,' wrote the historian Carl Schorske in 1948, 'is the extent to which the loyalty of the middle class to democracy will continue.' In Italy, France and western Germany he noted the rightward thrust of politics since the war and the 'signs of a return to anti-democratic authoritarianism' under the pressures of the Cold War. Writing about Germany a year later, another observer was equally gloomy, noting that 'the promised democratisation has not yet been effected'.[61]

Anti-communism in western Europe threatened to make deep inroads into civil liberties and to prevent the social reforms which many had looked forward to. In 1946-7, Communist Parties were pushed out of government. By 1948-9 the state was drawing upon paramilitary units to stamp out resistance on the Left. The struggle for democracy was now couched in Cold War terms: thus from the Left came accusations that conservative administrations were making anti-Fascism suspect and succouring Fascists, while Christian Democrats responded by arguing that the real threat to democracy came from the communist attack on freedom. In 1951 Unesco mounted an inquiry into the meaning of democracy in the post-war world. It concluded that although everyone professed to want it, a vast gulf in understanding separated the two halves of Europe.

By 1949 the forces of the Free World had triumphed in the West. In Italy and Greece, where violent resistance to the post-war regimes lasted longest, suspected Leftists entered the prisons as collaborators were released. Following the critical Christian Democrat victory in Italy's 1948 elections Mario Scelba's paramilitary assault units, armed with grenade launchers and flame-throwers, threw hundreds of partisans and workers into jail. A decade after the end of the Spanish civil war, Franco's police were still mopping up left-wing resisters in the hills. In Greece, the American-trained royalist army, backed by napalm, overcame the communist Democratic Army and interned thousands of suspected sympathizers in makeshift camps.

In eastern Europe, of course, the resistance to the Cold War order was met by an even harsher repression. In Yugoslavia, Mihailović's Chetniks had been rounded up by the time of their leader's arrest in early 1946. But in Poland and the Ukraine, NKVD and native pro-communist troops conducted ferocious anti-partisan sweeps of the forests late into the 1940s. Perhaps the most tenacious resistance struggle took place in the Baltic states. There Soviet policy – deportations and collectivization – drove many men into the forests from early 1945. The Forest Brothers, as they were known, attacked Russian troops, disrupted elections and killed collaborators. They were encouraged by their belief that there would soon be war between the West and the Soviet Union. In Latvia and Estonia their numbers were dwindling by the end of 1946, but in Lithuania the movement was more organized. By 1948 the authorities needed 70,000 troops as well as special death squads, infiltrators and regular Red Army divisions.

There are some striking cases of individuals who rejected the postwar structure of power for several decades. Tadeusz Konwicki's nightmarish novel of Poland in the 1960s, *A Dreambook for Our Time*, shows what ghosts from the war still lurked in the forests. An Estonian Forest Brother, August Sabe, was discovered by KGB agents as late as 1978 and drowned himself rather than surrender. Similarly, after the fall of the Colonels' Junta in 1974, a Greek partisan was reportedly discovered hiding in the White Mountains in Crete, reluctant to return to normal life. A French woman was discovered living as a recluse in 1983 in a town in the Auvergne: at liberation she had been accused of collaboration and her hair had been shorn; she had not been seen for thirty years and had gone mad.[62]

People like this who had refused to make their re-entry into post-war society were very much the exceptions. Most Europeans accepted the division of the continent and the post-war balance of power, and therefore participated in the social projects which developed on either side of the Iron Curtain. The wartime alliance preserved its basic understanding, and the brutal peace of the Cold War brought the continent the most precious commodity of all – time – which allowed an extraordinary and largely unexpected regeneration of its economic life and a sweeping transformation of its political habits.

8

Building People's Democracy

> We have chosen our own Polish path of development which we
> call the path of people's democracy. Under the present conditions
> no dictatorship of the working class, and even less the dictatorship
> of one party, is necessary or intended. We believe that the govern-
> ment in our country can be carried out through all democratic
> parties cooperating one with another.
>
> – Władysław Gomułka, 1947[1]

> Every change in the social order is an historical process accom-
> panied by difficulties, unsolved problems, shortcomings and,
> inevitably, mistakes.
>
> – from the Report of the Dubček Government Commission
> of Inquiry into the Czechoslovak Political Trials, 1968[2]

Eastern Europe has been the unfortunate laboratory for all three of
the century's ideological experiments. The first, that of the liberal
democratic victors of 1918, lasted little more than a decade, before
collapsing in the aftermath of the world depression. Hitler's New
Order lasted only half as long. Nazi defeat opened the way for Stalin
to make a third attempt, and his creations – the People's Democracies
– were to prove more durable than any of their predecessors.

   In the early 1950s, as Stalinist terror reached its apogee in a series
of bizarre and terrifying show trials, Western political scientists
developed the theory of totalitarianism, which emphasized the similarities between communism and fascism. In both cases, they argued,

political power resided essentially in coercion. At a time when the labour camps were filled with hundreds of thousands of prisoners and the secret police were in the ascendant such views were highly plausible. Today, however, the limitations of the theory of totalitarianism are more obvious. If we wish to explain why Russian rule lasted so much longer than German in eastern Europe, the differences between Nazism and communism are no less important than their similarities. Both relied upon military and police to subdue a basically hostile population but in varying degrees and at different times. More important, in their ultimate goals and political strategies, the Russians and the Germans diverged sharply.[3]

For the Nazis, as we have seen, the goal of occupation was defined entirely in terms of *German* interests. This was the principal reason why the dissatisfaction many Europeans felt with pre-war liberal (or 'bourgeois') democracy could not be satisfied by a Nazi New Order. It also explains Berlin's reluctance to give any power to non-German political groups, its basic vision of eastern Europe as a source of land and foodstuffs worked by Slavic helots for the benefit of their racial superiors, and the miserable failure of German *political* warfare among the Slavs.

Soviet Russia, like Germany, sought imperial security through control of eastern Europe; like Nazi Germany, it regarded the system of independent states set up at Versailles as hostile to its interests. However, its policy was shaped not by racial nationalism but by the philosophy of socio-economic transformation known as communism. This ideology was inclusive rather than exclusive, and all the more powerful for it. The Russian empire, unlike the Nazi one, depended upon local elites, and accommodated – if not without difficulty – east European nationalism: this explains both the limits and the durability of Soviet control. Hitler's vision of a feudal, ethnically purified farming belt was succeeded by that of an urbanized, industrial utopia: unlike Hitler, Stalin and his successors aimed at a total modernization of the region. In its own way, this happened: the rapid growth of cities and industry after 1945 dwarfed any previous changes. Communism profited from these extraordinary developments; later they helped cause its demise. Industrialization changed society in ways the

Party had not anticipated: society raced ahead while the Party stagnated.[4]

ESTABLISHING POLITICAL CONTROL

Soviet takeover, or social revolution? Today most people would unhesitatingly plump for the former to describe communism's emergence in post-war eastern Europe. In the 1940s, however, well-informed and impartial observers saw things rather differently. They remembered the inter-war legacy of failed democracy, economic depression and ethnic strife – grim memories which weakened opposition to communism inside and outside the region. The British scholar Hugh Seton-Watson underlined the harsh, chauvinistic and corrupt rule of earlier regimes, and spoke of a widespread 'desire for violent change, and distrust of everything said by the ruling class'. The Masaryk Professor of Central European History at London University, R. R. Betts, referred to 'the revolution in central and eastern Europe' which was taking place, and stressed that 'much of [the achievement, for good and evil] is native and due to the efforts of the peoples and their own leaders'. 'It is clear', he went on, 'that even if the Soviet Union had not been so near and so powerful, revolutionary changes would have come at the end of so destructive and subversive a war as that which ended in 1945.'

Such commentators may have felt later that their views were coloured by wishful thinking. Seton-Watson confessed in 1961 that 'the years after 1945 brought not a New Deal of liberty and social justice but a totalitarian tyranny and colonial subjection to the Soviet Empire'. But the illusions, beliefs and hopes which he later castigated were to prove no less important an instrument of imperial rule than force of arms itself; as for the social revolution, that was a reality.[5]

Soviet prestige may have been boosted by the military achievement of defeating the Germans, but the wartime Red Army was never envisaged as a permanent force of occupation, except perhaps in Germany itself: demobilization diminished its military strength from twelve million in 1945 to around three million three years later; in

Germany itself, Soviet troop strengths dropped from some 1.5 million at the end of the war to 350,000 by July 1947. This was slower than the astonishingly rapid American demobilization but striking nonetheless. In fact, troop strengths fell quickly in all countries and the Red Army pulled out of Czechoslovakia in keeping with its international agreements. Stalin reminded the Hungarian Communists: 'Soviet power cannot do everything for you. You must do the fighting, you must do the work.' For the Kremlin it was clear that Germany must never again be allowed to threaten the Soviet Union, and that eastern Europe must form part of its own sphere of influence; both objectives, however, were conceived in primarily political rather than military terms.[6]

For action against the Germans in the final stages of the war, as also against the opposition that emerged to communist control in the forests of the Baltic states and Poland, the Carpathians, and along the Albanian–Yugoslav frontier, reliable local armed forces needed building up. Reconstructed armies loyal to the new regime were quickly pulled together around a core of pre-war officers, resistance fighters and POWs 're-educated' in Soviet captivity. Some of these armies were purged of many former career officers as early as 1945 – a necessity in the case of an army like the Romanian which had been fighting the Russians a year before – but others kept much of their pre-war character. The Polish Army was a special case, as thousands of its pre-war officers had been seized by the Russians when the war began, and shot en masse in the Katyn forest and elsewhere. More reliable instruments for the new masters were the various security, police and paramilitary formations that emerged very rapidly under Soviet guidance, and played a vital role in policing elections, and targeting opponents of the new order. They were recruited not from reliable Party cadres, since these did not exist in any numbers, but from a strange mix of former partisans, collaborators, criminals and others. In Romania, for instance, the paramilitary Patriotic Combat Formations, directly under the orders of the Party, grew to 60,000 strong by March 1945. Overall, within a year of Russian 'liberation', hundreds of thousands of East Europeans were serving in military, policing and paramilitary formations under Soviet control.[7]

There was little domestic military resistance. Anti-Soviet armed bands and resistance units continued their doomed struggle into the late 1940s, but they were systematically repressed – shot, imprisoned in camps (often taken over from the Germans, as at Majdanek) or deported – and never seriously threatened communist plans. Of the estimated 100,000 anti-communist partisans fighting in Poland between 1944 and 1947, the vast majority laid down their arms in two government amnesties. The Serb Chetnik leader Mihailović was captured in 1946. Apart from the Baltic states, opposition was scattered and ineffectual.[8]

The really serious challenges to Soviet predominance were not military; they came, instead, from the various parties that re-emerged after the Occupation. If the chief arena in which the struggle for power took place in post-war eastern Europe was political, the main question facing communist activists was how to obtain the ascendancy from a position of domestic weakness. In most countries, the Party membership at liberation was tiny. State repression and public indifference in the inter-war era had kept the communist movement small; Stalin's purges in the 1930s had made it even smaller. Now the survivors were hurled into the spotlight. How should they act?

The obvious revolutionary option was to seize power as soon as possible. The paradox is that this only happened where the Red Army was *not* in control – in Yugoslavia where Tito, backed by his partisans, installed a one-party state within a year of liberation, and in his satellite, Albania. The idea appealed to many communists outside Yugoslavia, but Tito was the one communist leader in a position to ignore Stalin's wishes, and Stalin clearly had other tactics in mind which would be more compatible with his evident desire not to alienate his wartime Allies. For as Molotov later recalled: 'It was to our benefit to stay allied with America.'[9]

During the war, the Department of International Information of the Soviet Communist Central Committee had publicized the path ahead: cooperation with other democratic forces, not communist revolution. Eastern Europe, it decreed, was not ready for socialism. Rather the residues of feudalism must be swept aside, and the abortive bourgeois revolution of 1848 completed. There would be elections, in which workers and peasants would have a new voice. Not surprisingly, many communist cadres apart from Tito found it hard to take such advice seriously.[10]

Thus in defeated Germany, Stalin and his henchmen were furious with the old-time sectarian communist cadres who went around shouting 'Heil Moskau!', hanging red flags or painting the hammer and sickle on requisitioned cars. From Moscow's point of view, bloodthirsty declarations of imminent revolution, preaching dictatorship of the proletariat, tearing down statues of Luther and erecting monuments to Lenin – all implied a complete misreading of the situation. It showed that pre-war communists had learned nothing, and would only disturb the administration of the country. As early as 10 June, and with bewildering speed, the Soviet Military Administration issued an order permitting the creation of other parties and trade unions; the German Communist Party's own manifesto explicitly ruled out the idea of 'forcing the Soviet system on Germany' and called for the establishment of a parliamentary democracy.[11]

All this indicated that from Stalin's perspective in 1945, other parties would be tolerated and parliamentary elections would be held. The model for eastern Europe was to be the Popular Front of the mid-1930s not the Leninist revolutionary elite of 1917. Fascism's triumph between the wars, according to Moscow's theorists, had showed the necessity for unifying progressive forces under the banner of a broad anti-Fascist coalition, winning over the masses by a gradualist programme of land reform (not collectivization), expropriation of the elites and state-led economic controls. But even the theory itself was not so important as it would later become. The situation was, in fact, highly fluid. It is a striking reflection of the improvised character of east European politics at this time, and of the pragmatic character of Soviet attitudes, that not until early 1947 did there appear any official interpretations of the meaning in Marxist theory of People's Democracy, and only in December 1948 was it identified unambiguously with the dictatorship of the proletariat. The fact was that until this point Soviet policy was focused upon the question of creating a friendly Germany and there was no overall strategy for eastern Europe.[12]

Time was required, meanwhile, to build up what were in effect

new parties, since communism had been effectively crushed throughout most of the region in the preceding three decades. Just as in Russia
earlier, so now in eastern Europe, it was necessary to make the transition
from the small conspiratorial organization which had struggled in
opposition to a party capable of wielding power. Only in Czechoslovakia had the party remained legal and popular. Membership of the
Polish Communist Party, renamed a more palatable Polish Workers'
Party, grew from 20,000 in July 1944 to 300,000 in under a year; in
Hungary it grew from 2,000 in late 1944 to 864,000 by the end of 1947;
the Romanian party grew similarly. When we examine the ballooning
party membership figures for the early post-war years, it would be easy
to write off most of those who joined as opportunists or time-servers.
It was not difficult to recognize the new realities, and many 'realists'
adjusted their expectations, swallowed hard and compromised with the
new masters and their Soviet backers. Others were simply too worn
out by the years of war to struggle further. But there was also genuine
enthusiasm underlying the rise of the party after 1945.

In part, this was enthusiasm for the Soviet Union and respect for
its achievements. The enormous prestige which had accrued to the
Red Army in defeating the Third Reich was not immediately dispelled
by its soldiers' ill-disciplined behaviour. Moreover, the defeat of the
Third Reich did not allay traditional fears of German power: on the
contrary, the experience of half a century, and especially the previous
six years, persuaded many that Russian protection was more than
ever a necessary insurance against future German expansion.

At home, memories of the war generated a widespread suspicion
of collaborators and underlined the ambiguous status and doubtful
performance of most pre-war political parties. Zdeněk Mlynar, for
instance, who was later to play a leading part in the Czech Spring,
recollected the vehemence with which, as a teenage recruit into the
party in 1946, he had criticized the 'pusillanimous prudence of our
parents' generation that had made collaboration with the enemy so
excusable'. Growing up through the war had given the young a
'Manichean view of the world' and a 'primitive radicalism'. 'We were
children of the war who, having not actually fought against anyone,
brought our wartime mentality with us into those first post-war years,

when the opportunity to fight for something presented itself at last.'[13]

But this struggle was not merely, in Mlynar's words, 'a holy struggle against the infidel'. Sweeping away the past was necessary in order to construct a better future. The general radicalization which occupation had stimulated across Europe manifested itself after liberation in a widespread desire for socio-economic change. The Hungarian elections of 1945 – the first in the country's history under universal suffrage – demonstrated that this desire extended far beyond communist voters. Many looked eastwards for inspiration. 'In 1945,' writes Mlynar, 'deification of the Soviet Union and Stalin did not necessarily exclude one from the general excitement felt . . . concerning the prospects of establishing freedom and justice as the cornerstones of the new state. On the contrary, it was part of that excitement . . . The Soviet Union was, in that sense, a land of hope for all who desired a radical departure from the past after the war and who also, of course, knew nothing of the real conditions in the Soviet Union.'[14]

Even among non-communists, who were much less inclined to idolize Stalin, Party policy in the first two or three years after liberation encouraged their hopes by its relative flexibility and gradualism. 'Though the nation did not want to accept the alien system of rule imposed by Stalin,' Jacek Kurczewski has argued in the case of Poland, 'civil war in the first post-1945 years was rejected by the majority in favour of reconstruction of homes for the people and of the country as the home for all.' In central–eastern Europe, communist energy and dedication in the work of reconstruction could win people over. A striking illustration is provided by the anti-communist Hungarian refugees who gave credit for the reconstruction drive to 'the communists, who handled economic reconstruction with enthusiasm and even a touch of genius'. Gerö 'the Bridge-Builder' was the leading Party official who as Minister of Transport was hailed for the swift rebuilding of the Danube bridges.[15]

The basic point is that social justice and economic efficiency were for many higher priorities than a return to – or creation of – party or 'bourgeois' democracy. Communism, which had swept away the remnants of feudalism and held out the promise of Soviet industrialization to contrast with the capitalist stagnation of the inter-war years, offered a way forward, especially through the palatable compromise of People's Democracy. If no less a figure than Czech President Beneš could publicly reject a 'purely political conception of democracy in a liberalistic sense' in favour of a system 'in the social and economic sense also', is it surprising that many less sophisticated thinkers should be ready for effective rather than necessarily representative government? This was the legacy of the inter-war crisis of liberal democracy in eastern Europe.[16]

But the sharing of power in the People's Democracies through coalitions and bloc-building was more easily reconciled with Soviet security concerns in some countries than in others. In Romania and Poland – countries where both communism and Russia were historically unpopular, and whose anti-Russianism, incidentally, was heartily reciprocated in Moscow – the strains became apparent early on. Foreign Minister Vyshinsky had to come to Bucharest in February 1945 to order King Michael to appoint the prime minister the Russians wanted. Moscow's man, Petru Groza, was not a communist, though his secretary-general, Emil Bodnaras, was not merely a communist but an NKVD officer. It is significant that there was no Western response to the King's appeals for help, perhaps because Churchill was not behaving very differently in Greece at about the same time. When Michael ordered Groza to resign, the prime minister simply ignored him and then went to Moscow to meet Stalin. 'We talked', Groza recollected, 'as a small pupil to an old teacher.'

The Poles put up greater resistance than anyone else to Russian domination; unfortunately for them, Poland was the most important country in eastern Europe to the Russians, especially while the fate of Germany remained undecided, and Polish public opinion of little consequence to Moscow. As the West acknowledged this fact, Stalin could use a greater degree of force there than elsewhere. Yet even there the politics of the initial phase of communist rule also aimed to garner support. The pro-Soviet 'Provisional Government' was a coalition, led by a socialist prime minister, and the West put pressure on genuinely independent political figures to cooperate with the Russians. Added pressure came in the form of show trials of anti-Soviet public figures in the summer of 1945.

And as in Romania, so in Poland, the Soviet Union gained enormous leverage over domestic politicians by its ability to readjust international borders at the peace table. Regaining Transylvania from Hungary was the carrot for the Romanians; taking over the vast and prosperous formerly German 'New Territories' along the Oder–Neisse line the incentive for the Poles. The result in both cases was that nationalists had every incentive to placate Moscow as the guarantor of their new lands.

Although the rhythms differed across eastern Europe, the subsequent pattern looked similar in retrospect: government by coalition, in which the Communist Party played an influential and dominant part; then, marginalization and outright repression of those parties and splinter groups which remained outside the coalition. Finally elections, which gave the Government Front 89 per cent in Poland, 98 per cent in Romania (up in 1948 from 91 per cent in 1946!) and 79 per cent in Bulgaria. By 1947–8, this process had succeeded in crushing the agrarian and socialist parties which were the most serious threat in a democratic setting to communist hegemony; some of their leaders had been executed or forced to flee, while others had led splinter groups into government.

Was this a Machiavellian strategy carefully planned in advance? Some contemporary observers had no doubts. Hugh Seton-Watson discerned a pattern of three stages: genuine coalition; bogus coalition; the 'monolithic' regime. Yet in a curious way, this series of stages mirrored the emerging Soviet view which also saw the region moving by stages to communism. Both perhaps were trying to see a logic and a tidiness to events which did not exist. The actual course of events suggested – at least before 1947 – a far more hesitant and uncertain Soviet Union than Seton-Watson implied. The 1945 elections in Hungary, for example, resulted in a humiliating defeat for the communists and a 57 per cent triumph for the Smallholders. Some coalitions (Poland, Yugoslavia in early 1945) *were* mere showpieces from the start, disguising communist control; others were genuine coalitions for several years (Hungary, Czechoslovakia); Romania and Bulgaria fell somewhere between the two. Nor should one forget the vital case of Finland in this context: Finno-Soviet diplomacy resulted in an agreement which satisfied Soviet concerns while preserving Finnish autonomy of action.[17]

It is also important to remember that an impatience with pre-war party politics and a desire to solve the immediate problems of the post-war era in a spirit of national unity made coalition government popular right across the continent: democracy – it was widely felt – must be made to work the second time around, by sinking party differences if necessary, especially on the Left. As this spirit frayed under the pressure of the Cold War, coalitions West and East fell apart. Thus the emergence and disappearance of coalition governments was not solely an east European development, nor only explicable as a Soviet conspiracy.[18]

The communists also profited from several factors in addition to Soviet backing. One was the weakness and lack of cohesion of many of their rival parties: although some could only be crushed through police terror, others – like the Hungarian Smallholders – were friable and splintered easily, especially in the absence of Western support. Marxist Social Democrats were often as drawn to the Soviet example as repelled by it. And anyway, outside Czechoslovakia and East Germany social democracy had weak roots in the region. The historical memory of the Left's fatal split in the 1920s added weight to the communists' demands for unity.

More fundamentally still, the rival parties' commitment to the principles of democracy had to be understood in the light of their own pre-war political traditions and experience. For many this included both the lack of a legacy of successful parliamentarism, and a familiarity with the idea of large governing coalitions operating – as in inter-war Hungary and Romania, for instance – in an authoritarian context. Outside Czechoslovakia, the memory of inter-war parliamentary government conjured up ambiguous associations. Pre-war 'bourgeois democracy' found few supporters; sociologically and ideologically its old constituencies had shrunk, fled or been killed. In Poland, the war – thanks to both Germans and Russians – had more or less wiped out the liberal intelligentsia; in Romania it was largely tainted with collaboration.

Liberal, Catholic and peasant politicians were uncertain about whether to move to total opposition or some kind of compromise with the new order. Advocates of intransigence placed their hopes in the outbreak of a Third World War, and this led many to wait indefinitely for salvation from the West. In the Balkans, noted Elisabeth Barker, 'There were many in the Opposition who had little interest in the peasants or in constructive programmes. The one question which obsessed them, and which they often put only to foreigners, was: "When do you think the war against Russia will start?" . . . They let the expectation of war become the assumption on which most of their thinking was based. So they tended just to wait passively with a strange mixture of hopelessness and hopefulness, for the outbreak of the war.' They were understandably misled by the warlike tone of Cold War rhetoric on both sides. 'The final stage of preparation for war is under way,' insisted a Lithuanian partisan bulletin at the time of the Truman Doctrine. The Korean War gave a further boost to the surviving believers. Only Western passivity over Hungary in 1956 killed off their dreams for good.[19]

At the same time, the ambiguity of communist policy towards nationalism further confused matters, and disorientated opponents. By expelling the ethnic Germans, communist regimes claimed to be turning countries like Poland into nation-states at last. By forcibly resettling members of one ethnic group in another part of the country – Ukrainians in western Poland, Banat Serbs and Macedonians in eastern Romania, Bosnian peasants in the Yugoslav Vojvodina – the regime weakened old local and regional ties and asserted the authority of the centralized state. The contrast is striking with the Soviet policy pursued in the Baltic states, where it was precisely the dominant national group which was targeted for deportation. But then the Baltic states faced a far worse fate than the rest of eastern Europe: they were to be absorbed within the Soviet Union itself, and subjected to a conscious policy of Russification.

Building up a ruling Party was one thing; controlling the administration was another, for that required an obedient state machine. In western Europe, occupation gave British and American policy-makers enormous influence over the internal affairs of both former enemies like

Italy and Germany, and of former allies like Belgium and Greece. Soviet advisers intervened as much if not more, and took steps to consolidate their influence over the bureaucratic apparatus of the various east European states. Both West and East, most civil servants had wartime pasts to live down, and willingly conformed to the wishes of their new masters. In many cases, too, political control of the civil service was nothing new, and the communists simply inherited wartime and pre-war instruments of domination.

The independence of the judiciary, where this still existed after years of authoritarianism and wartime occupation, was almost immediately undermined by decrees making judges subordinate to the Ministry of Justice. It was not necessary after this sort of measure to force pre-war appointees to resign: in Poland, for instance, some 60 per cent of judges as late as 1950 had begun their careers on the bench before the war. It was a similar story in the military, where pre-war generals took their orders from the new Higher Political Administration, which ensured a pro-Soviet line.[20]

Culture, education and the media, formerly censored by domestic right-wing regimes or by the Germans, now came under Moscow's influence: some conservative papers were closed (on the grounds that they had served the 'Fascists'); others were controlled through a licensing system and the distribution of paper and newsprint. Censorship gradually extended from 'anti-Soviet' material to more sweeping definitions of what was harmful to the state: by 1949 some 8,000 previously published works were banned in Romania, and similar lists grew elsewhere. By 1949 at the very latest, formal censorship systems had been established which effectively placed all literary and journalistic output under Party control. It took longer to bring the universities into line, and the rhythm and rate of success varied enormously from east Germany, on the one hand, where the old order was swept away almost at once, to Poland, where it remained tolerated by an uncertain Party for years.[21]

Most important of all, there were the security forces. Military intelligence was subordinated to GRU, the Soviet military intelligence agency. Virtually from the moment of liberation, the KGB made control of internal security a priority. Prompted by the Russian security services, Party apparatchiks both infiltrated the regular police forces and outflanked them by creating new special security units – like the Bulgarian People's Militia – under Party control. In Czechoslovakia – the last country to fall under communist control – the reorganization of the police became *the* critical political question, prompting a struggle between the communist-controlled Interior and the non-communist Justice Ministry.

The police – like civil servants generally – were in a weak position to resist communist pressure. Many of them had worked through the war for the Germans and were vulnerable to being purged; they found it awkward to act against politicians backed by the forces of liberation. They also had to watch for their jobs as politically reliable youngsters were being drafted en masse. Sándor Kopacsi, a future police chief of Budapest, recollected that 'all underground fighters of the Mokan group [a Leftist wartime partisan outfit] were rearmed and became part of the law-enforcement apparatus of the new Republic of Hungary that was just being born. That's how I became a cop.' Yet such inexperienced novices could hardly be relied upon from the start. In the police, as elsewhere, high percentages of officers remained in post from the old force, and simply bowed their head to the new realities, trading their professional expertise for job security.[22]

TOWARDS STALINISM

The turning point in what Mastny calls the *Pax Sovietica* came in 1947: in the face of increasingly decisive Western anti-communism, the foundation of the Cominform that September revealed a shift in Soviet policy from gradualism to embattled militancy, from an acceptance of divergent national paths to socialism to an insistence upon bloc uniformity. Stalin used the Yugoslavs to attack other Communist Parties for their 'fetish of coalitionism'. Humiliated just the previous month in national elections, Hungarian cadres were criticized for admitting that their government was a 'mixture made up of elements of the people's democracy and bourgeois democracy'. A year earlier Gomułka in Poland and Gottwald in Czechoslovakia had stressed the need for each country to find its own path to socialism. Henceforth, this line was abandoned. In economic planning, politics, architecture – across the board came an increased subservience to Moscow.

In 1948 it was the Yugoslavs' turn to be the whipping boy: the Tito–Stalin split, unforeseen and undesired by Tito, essentially came about because the Yugoslavs would not accept the kind of Soviet domination of their internal affairs which was becoming routine throughout the region. Meeting Soviet officers in Romania, Milovan Djilas was shocked by 'this attitude of a "superior race" and the conceit of a great power'. Djilas and his colleagues, proud of their wartime record, resented the need to publish Soviet books on demand, or to subordinate their own economic development to the needs of the Soviet Union; in foreign policy, Tito's intervention in the Greek civil war and his evident ambitions in the Balkans angered Stalin, just as the Yugoslav attempt to take Trieste had done two years earlier. The breach opened up rapidly, and became the means for Stalin to impose his authority even more powerfully upon the rest of the bloc. For the next five years, until his death, the region experienced a wave of show trials, police terror and forced industrialization – in a word, Stalinism.[23]

'We study and take as an example the Soviet system,' Tito had stressed to Stalin, 'but we are developing socialism in our country in somewhat different forms.' After Yugoslavia was expelled from the Cominform, cadres in other countries hastened to distance themselves from accusations of 'national communism'. The gap which had opened up in the Soviet bloc was attributed to 'despicable traitors and imperialist hirelings', 'traitors to proletarian internationalism', 'gangs of spies, provocateurs and murderers', and 'dogs tied to American leashes, gnawing imperialist bones, and barking for American capital'. The need to reconfirm the infallibility of Soviet authority led not merely to purges and mass expulsions, which cut deep into the Party and state apparatus but also – notably in Hungary and Czechoslovakia – to a series of show trials.[24]

The effort to demonstrate loyalty to Moscow by unmasking 'enemy agents' spread the terror like a virus into the heart of the Party. In August 1948 Romanian minister Lucretiu Patrascanu was arrested;

another 'nationalist deviationist', Władysław Gomułka, was removed as secretary-general of the Polish party the following month. Senior figures in the Albanian and Bulgarian leadership were arrested and tried. The Hungarian Interior Minister, László Rajk, was transferred to Foreign Affairs in August 1948, and arrested the following May.

Reflecting the paranoid atmosphere in the Kremlin in Stalin's last years as well as real fears over the extent of Soviet control in eastern Europe, the show trials turned into a visible demonstration of Party loyalty which extended even to the victims themselves. According to bugged tapes of a private dialogue between Interior Minister Kádár and Rajk, the chief defendant in the first Hungarian trial, Kádár told Rajk: 'We *know* you're not guilty; we'll admire you even more for this sacrifice. Not even your life – we won't kill you; just moral sacrifice and then we'll spirit you away.' Rajk initially resisted this line, but worn out at the trial, complied. He was then executed.[25]

When the Hungarians started the Rajk trial they warned the Czechs that some Czech names would come up. Why hadn't they arrested them? Accusations of 'Titoism' led to an acceleration in the Czech investigations. Moscow sent security advisers to Prague to uncover the 'Czechoslovak Rajk' and his links with Western imperialism. Hastening to prove his own loyalty, former Secretary-General Rudolf Slánsky warned: 'Nor will our Party escape having the enemy place his people among us and recruiting his agents among our members . . . We must be all the more vigilant, so that we can unmask the enemies in our own ranks, for they are the most dangerous enemies.' In 1950 Slánsky himself was among those senior Party figures arrested on the grounds that they were 'Trotskyist-Zionist-Titoist-bourgeois-nationalist traitors, spies and saboteurs, enemies of the Czech nation, of its People's Democratic order and of Socialism'.

Cold War spy fever was an epidemic which afflicted the East even more than the West. In Czechoslovakia alone, there were monster trials of former Socialists, Catholics and Social Democrats – 'the leaders of a terrorist conspiracy' – as well as the notorious 'Trial of Vatican Agents' which took place in early 1950. Among the victims were wartime opponents of the Party, soldiers, intellectuals and religious leaders. But they also included suspect Party members like the 'Spaniards' (activists who had fought in the Spanish civil war and were often thought to be dangerously independent), ethnic minorities deported to work camps, and, of course, 'class enemies'.

The victims of these few years numbered tens if not hundreds of thousands. More communists were killed in Hungary as a result of the purges than Horthy had managed in twenty-five years. The secret police rose to power (as their backers were doing under Beria's leadership in the Soviet Union), but were themselves riven by suspicion, informers and feuds. Nevertheless, they managed to superintend the elaboration of a sprawling network of work camps – at least seventy in Bulgaria, holding perhaps 100,000 inmates (mostly in the infamous 'Little Siberia'). Those arrested numbered some 200,000 in Hungary, 136,000 in Czechoslovakia, 180,000 in Romania, an incredible 80,000 in Albania. Only Poland, nearing the end of its own civil war, escaped repression on this scale.[26]

The Stalinist terror cannot, in the final analysis, be separated from the ultimate justification for the Party's existence – its role in the transformation of society. Despite the large numbers killed, the majority of those arrested were sent to labour camps. As in the Soviet Union earlier, work became both punishment and means of redemption, both a right and a duty, through which enemies of the 'working classes' could rejoin society in the great task of Socialist Construction. In other words, the Stalinist terror of 1948–53 was bound up not only with Soviet efforts to stamp out heresy or independence within the Party but also with the grand project of state-driven industrialization. Terror accompanied the Party's march towards modernity.[27]

The model for eastern Europe's development was to be the forced industrialization of the Soviet Union in the 1930s through five-year plans. Although the region was more advanced economically than the Soviet Union had been, the effort to create a modern industrial sector still presupposed a profound social upheaval. The communists aimed to transform society completely through an industrial revolution, and the only way to finance growth domestically on the scale required was by squeezing both the agricultural sector and consumption: but this was impossible without coercion by the state. Hence, as one émigré put it: 'The essence of the situation in the countries of eastern

Europe is the communist police state and the industrial revolution.'

Eastern Europe's basic economic problem had been evident for over a century. As western Europe industrialized, the region fell further and further behind. For the newly independent states created after 1918, the challenge had been how to respond. Peasant parties had traditionally argued that the answer lay not in imitation of the West but rather in support for the independent smallholder and agricultural development. This message carried tremendous emotional appeal but cooler heads realized that it offered no lasting solution to overpopulation and low agricultural productivity.

The chief alternative in the inter-war period was that urged by east European urban elites: gradual industrialization financed by capital inflows from the West. For roughly a decade this policy had actually been tried, and produced rapid but patchy industrial growth. The trouble was that it handed over investment decisions and ultimately ownership of key industries to foreign capitalists without ensuring growth high enough to solve the problem of rural underemployment. Economic nationalists hated the results and felt vindicated when the world slump terminated the experiment. After the failures of inter-war liberalism and the peasantist movement, the socialist strategy of forced industrialization organized by the state and financed out of domestic savings looked increasingly appealing.

The world depression of the 1930s had already popularized the idea of state-led industrial growth. In the wake of the catastrophic failure of market capitalism, *étatisme* became fashionable: in eastern Europe technocratic planners and army officers (in Poland and Bulgaria) agreed that the state should expand not merely into labour relations and social services but into planning and directing investment. The crisis of 1929–32 had led to new public-sector control of banking, allowing the state greater control over monetary policy and industrial investment. The state's economic reach extended further after 1939 as the Germans expropriated key businesses and introduced wartime controls on production and pricing. Often – in economics as in politics – the Germans' successors simply took over the new tools of control.

After liberation, the new vogue for planning and the repudiation of liberalism spread right across the continent. Enlarging the welfare state, greater intervention in the economy, control of heavy industry and banking all formed part of the accepted wisdom of the day. The key issue in the years 1944–7 was not whether or not to plan, but whether to follow the social democratic or the communist variant of planning.

In Poland and Czechoslovakia, there were powerful pre-war traditions of state planning, and in 1945–6, socialist planners seemed to be winning the ear of local communists in arguing for a mixed economy, private trade and non-collectivized farms. But after the formation of the Cominform and Stalin's refusal to allow East European countries to participate in the Marshall Plan, Stalinist orthodoxy took over. Communists criticized the 'so-called primacy of consumption'. Poland's Central Board of Planning, which had called for a mid-course between the 'heroic road' of forced savings and 'middle-class' demands for an immediate gratification of consumer desire, was wound up. It was replaced in early 1949 by the Party-controlled State Commission of Economic Planning for whom 'the struggle for the planned economy is a class struggle waged on the political, economic and ideological fronts'.[28]

Between 1948 and 1951 every country behind the Iron Curtain introduced a Five- or Six-Year Plan. These were very different from the shorter reconstruction plans which had been introduced after liberation. By this point pre-war levels of output had been regained in most countries, while nationalization had delivered industry into the hands of the state. These new Plans set out highly ambitious targets for heavy industry and power generation. Far less attention was paid to consumer goods, and Party experts – ignoring the signs of social exhaustion – warned that in this 'heroic' phase of development, living standards would remain depressed as resources were ploughed back into investment. Czech premier Zápotocký attacked 'any fond illusions that a rise in the standard of living may be regarded as a necessary corollary, or even ought to precede the successful implementation of the Plan. The exact opposite is the truth: in order to make it possible that our material and cultural level might be raised, it will first be necessary to fulfil the Plan . . . so that we might henceforth live better, more contentedly and more joyfully!' Eastern Europe, observed the UN, was aiming at 'an industrial revolution far more radical than anything seriously attempted in western European countries'.[29]

A vigorous propaganda drive hyped the results. The J. W. Stalin steelworks in East Germany, the Klement Gottwald steelworks in Ostrava, the V. I. Lenin iron and steelworks in Bulgaria were the cathedrals of the new era – their monumental entranceways, their very creation, a testimony to the power of man and science to conquer nature. Petru Dumitriu's painting *The Light of Lenin in the Mountains of Romania* celebrated the building of the hydroelectric plant at Bicaz. The 'light of Stalin shines on Albanian soil', was Hoxha's slogan in 1952.

But it was certainly not all propaganda. Growth rates in certain sectors, starting from a low base, were spectacular. Industrial production and employment both grew at least as quickly as in western Europe – perhaps faster – in the 1950s and early 1960s, despite the fact that there was no east European Marshall Plan; indeed the Soviet Union was actually *extracting* resources from the region, not putting them in. 'A revolutionary transformation of the industrial structure has been carried out,' noted the Economic Commission for Europe from Geneva. 'East European governments have on the whole planned successfully.' Very high investment ratios – twice as high as in western Europe – delivered fast rates of growth in favoured sectors such as mining and iron and steel production.[30]

Yet this pattern of development was storing up innumerable problems for the future. The use of a labour-intensive Soviet model was not illogical in an area where capital was scarce and labour relatively abundant; but it did lead east European countries to favour industries reliant on outmoded technologies. While in the world economy the number of miners was falling during the 1950s, in Hungary, for example, it doubled. Large numbers of workers were being funnelled into problem areas of industry, making for economic and political turmoil in the future once the region became more exposed to international competition.

Perhaps politically most serious of all was the problem of agriculture. After nearly two decades in which farmers had enjoyed an advantage over urban dwellers, the late 1940s ushered in a period in which the city took its revenge. In the Baltic states, where collectivization was introduced several years ahead of the rest of eastern Europe, hundreds of thousands of 'kulaks' were deported, just as they had been in the Ukraine in the 1930s: a staggering 3 per cent of the total population went in a mere ten days in March 1949. Because communism had little support among the peasantry, the Party elsewhere had initially denied any interest in collectivization and tried to win favour through land reform. Now, this policy was thrown into reverse throughout the region. Stalinism placed the burdens of development on to the agrarian sector by introducing collectivization drives, raising taxes, and cutting back loans and credits for farmers. Like a sort of internal colony, the countryside was to provide both food and labour for the growing cities. But state control of the land turned out to be a disaster, just as it had earlier in the Soviet Union. While industrial output soared, agricultural production barely attained pre-war levels. Indeed as late as the early 1960s, per capita output remained depressed and 'meatless days' testified to the depletion of livestock herds.[31]

As the authorities tried to secure the harvest by force, farmers resisted with every means – arson, deliveries of damaged grain, sabotaging machinery – at their disposal. In Romanian Transylvania, peasants burned the new cooperative farms; after one incident in July 1949, security forces only restored order by shooting twelve peasants on the spot and making mass arrests. Party efforts to terrorize the peasantry into submission led to widespread unrest and the inevitable accusations of 'sabotage' by 'well-off peasants'. These 'bitter enemies of the new order' were 'capable of any crime to ruin Socialist construction'. The typical 'kulak' 'fails to deliver his quotas, sabotages agricultural production and even resorts to murder'. In fact, the resistance was on an enormous scale, as was even indirectly admitted occasionally by the official press. 'How can one talk about the proper ideological attitude of such members as Mikula from Mosina in Człuchów?' demanded the *Green Banner*, the official journal of the Polish United Peasant Party in November 1951. 'He has said that he will not sell grain or potatoes to the State, and that if the surplus is taken from him by force, he will hang himself and let the Western radio know about it.'[32]

Peasant rebellions were a traditional part of the political landscape in eastern Europe and the new state authorities suppressed them much as their predecessors had done, through the militia and army. At least 80,000 peasants were deported or tried in Romania alone, 30,000 in humiliating public show trials. Others had their homes ransacked by the militia, their produce and livestock requisitioned, their families beaten up or threatened. In Hungary, thousands of farmers languished in internment camps, further disrupting the rural economy.[33]

Although these rebellions – even when, as in Transylvania, they obtained the support of anti-communist partisans in the mountains – did not threaten the grip of the Party directly, they did reveal the extent of peasant dissatisfaction. Moreover, as one of the causes of food shortages, they constituted an indirect threat to communist power. Hardliners might try to blame the shortages on the surviving private smallholders, but Party critics increasingly realized that collectivization was a folly which threatened the entire industrialization effort. From as early as 1951 (in Romania) the policy was modified, to reduce the elements of coercion and compulsion. 'The ideal collective farm is a socialistic form too far ahead of present conditions,' ran the new rationale, 'A lower form should be used in this intermediate period.' Hardly a message likely to quieten peasant fears![34]

Other 'class enemies' were also being created by the industrialization drive. As millions of young peasants flocked into the cities, the regimes tried solving a looming housing shortage by clearing out 'bourgeois' property-owners. These 'unproductive people' were now to pay the price for the slow rate of housing construction (four times slower in East than in West Germany, for example). Operation 'B' in Czech cities in the early 1950s led to mass evictions of 'class enemies'. 'As far back as last November,' ran a report from 1952, 'rumours started circulating in Romania that a mass deportation of "unnecessary city dwellers" was slated for the near future.' Thousands of residents were deported from Bucharest, Budapest and elsewhere. Bulgarian police took advantage of the 1948 'Measures against Socially Dangerous

Persons'. Official permission was now required to reside in an increasing number of 'workers' cities'.[35]

The victims went to swell the armies of slave labourers used on such high-profile construction projects as the Danube–Black Sea canal (involving 40,000 prisoners). Kept behind barbed wire fences, they lived in the open until they succeeded in building reed shacks and digging wells for water. Food shortages and poor sanitary conditions led to high rates of suicide. This forced labour – sometimes institutionalized as in the Romanian Directorate of Labour Reserves, or the Bulgarian Labour Army – played an important part in helping the bureaucracy aim for the fantastic targets set under the Plan. In Bulgaria there were 100,000 slave labourers compared with an industrial workforce of 361,000.

Even ordinary workers – supposedly the favoured class of the new order – found themselves hemmed in, and urged on, by restrictions and pressures which they had not anticipated. 'To fight mercilessly against the enemies of the working people' – as, say, the Romanian Party was committed to doing – meant attacking the workforce itself. The authorities not only banned strikes and work stoppages; they restricted labour mobility and tried to clamp down on 'absenteeism'. In Bulgaria the 'arbitrary quitting' of one's job was punishable by 'corrective labour'. Workers needed to register with the local police to obtain ID and work cards, and faced prosecution for 'violations of labour discipline'. In the absence of wage rises or convincing incentives, the low living standards, shortages of food and other consumer goods, increasingly strict labour discipline and unmasking of 'saboteurs' and 'agents' alienated the workforce. Yet outright resistance was difficult as the unions were extensions of the state, while workers were encouraged to police themselves. 'The tightening of labour discipline', insisted a Hungarian paper, 'must be achieved by pillorying [loafers and idlers] at production conferences, by reporting their nefarious activities ... by visiting them in their homes, and if all else fails, by expelling them from the ranks of honest workers.'[36]

In the midst of this extraordinary turmoil came Stalin's seventieth birthday. The end of 1949 saw roads, monuments, buildings and entire towns dedicated to the Soviet leader. New cities emerged – like

Stalinstadt in East Germany, Sztalinvaros in Hungary – as symbols of 'the great construction projects of Communism'. In Prague, the State Commission for Coordinating the Celebration of General Stalin's Seventieth Birthday commissioned a monument thirteen metres high overlooking the city. These edifices were intended to mark 'Man's triumph over nature and the social forces that have fettered him'. Instead, they were soon to reveal the fragility of the Stalinist system itself.

In December 1949 Frankfurter Allee in the Soviet sector of Berlin was renamed 'Stalinallee'. 'The first socialist street in Germany' – as it was hailed – was to be flanked by ambitious building projects. Just as the street was supposed to symbolize the achievements of the communist regime, the workers building it symbolized the 'new men' who were making it possible. Otto Nagel's painting of the *Young Bricklayer of Stalinallee* depicted one of these heroes against a back-drop of scaffolding and flags. Yet shortly after the completion of this picture, these very same building workers downed tools in the first serious internal challenge to communist rule.

The workers' uprising in East Berlin in the spring of 1953, coming soon after Stalin's death, marked the end of the initial industrialization drive across the Soviet bloc. Similar discontent – which quickly took on an anti-Russian character – was manifest in Czechoslovakia and elsewhere. Angered at wage cuts (masquerading as 'higher work norms') the 'Heroes of socialist construction' were, in reality, alienated from the regime that glorified them. Eventually, the street placards on Stalinallee were quietly removed: part of the street reverted to its old name, while part was renamed 'Karl-Marx-Allee'.

REFORMING COMMUNISM?

Stalin's successors followed a rather hesitant 'New Course' in the mid-1950s that was supposed to allay this discontent by slowing the pace of industrialization. Collectivization came under attack and where it was reversed – as in Poland and Yugoslavia – the 'socialist sector' shrank with extraordinary speed. Taxes were lowered as were the compulsory crop deliveries demanded by the authorities. At the same time, it was announced that more consumer goods would be made available, and that the housing shortage would be tackled. The harsh labour discipline of the 'heroic' phase of Stalinism was replaced by a more conciliatory approach.

Politically, too, there was a change of course. Just as Stalin's death led to an emphasis on 'collective leadership' in Moscow, so too in eastern Europe the 'little Stalins' were challenged. In East Germany, from where nearly one million (mostly young people) had fled in the years after 1945, Ulbricht came under fire, and there was a row provoked by such pseudo-Stalinist follies as the creation of a Commission for the Preparation of Comrade W. Ulbricht's Sixtieth Birthday. One by one, the 'little Stalins' were toppled; few foresaw that they would be succeeded by others.

More crucially, the departure of the Stalinist leadership was accompanied – as in the Soviet Union – by the discrediting of their chief instrument of power, the secret police. Once the security forces had been above the party; now they were disorientated and uncertain. 'The sad ones', as they were known, were thrown on to the defensive. Never again would they be so sure of themselves, or so reliable an instrument of repression. It was the end of what one victim called 'the dictatorship of the party within the party'. When Hungarian Party Secretary Mátyás Rákosi tried addressing a meeting of secret-police officers in June 1956 he was roundly booed.[37] The victims of the purges were thus rehabilitated, their persecutors purged. The party managed to pin the blame for Stalinism's excesses on agencies which had escaped its control: rehabilitating former party leaders like Rajk, Gomułka and Pauker became paradoxically a way of reasserting communist control of the state.

In this way, de-Stalinization made any future clampdown far more awkward for the authorities to contemplate and facilitated a new openness and debate. Police powers were restrained by new laws (or by a greater willingness to observe old ones), as the party emphasized the need to 'return to socialist legality'. Labour camps were shut down and tens of thousands of prisoners returned home. In Poland, for instance, some 30,000 prisoners benefited from an amnesty in April

1956 which coincided with a purge of the upper echelons of the security services.[38]

But what did liberalization within a communist system mean? To some it meant independence from Moscow; but as the examples of Romania (and to a lesser extent Yugoslavia) showed, 'national communism' was compatible with one-man rule of the harshest sort. To others, among them many shocked and guilty party cadres, it meant recapturing the 'original purity' of the movement. Thus as the People's Democracies emerged from the 'heroic' phase of the immediate post-war years, uncertain party cadres had to confront the question of how the Party itself should react to de-Stalinization. This debate was fought out between Stalinists and liberalizers in an atmosphere punctuated and to some extent shaped by explosions of popular protest in East Germany (1953), Poland and Hungary (1956). The liberalizers argued that such events demonstrated the need for a change of course; the Stalinists retorted that they were triggered off by rising expectations which had been stimulated by the signs of panic and division in the highest echelons of the Party after Stalin's death. But powerful forces were behind the liberalizers: Khrushchev, in Moscow, for one, who publicly accepted the idea in 1955 of 'several roads to socialism', and tried to mend his fences with Tito. Even the occasional returns to a hard line – after 1956, for example, and again after 1968 – never approached the paranoiac excesses of Stalinism, except perhaps in the Zhivkov, Hoxha and Ceauşescu dynasties in the Balkans.

De-Stalinization raised in particular the question of the rule of law under communism, and the relationship between law and ideology (as expressed by its watchdog, the Party). On the one hand, none other than Stalin himself had reasserted the significance of the law; and yet his most important theoretician, Andrei Vyshinsky, had insisted that 'if the law lags behind life it needs to be changed'. According to the 1950 Polish Judiciary Act (a typical expression of the Stalin era) judges were instructed to behave as 'revolutionary constructors of a socialist society'. Throughout the empire, in fact, post-war constitutions had followed Vyshinsky in explicitly rejecting the 'bourgeois principle of a separation of powers'. Instead, all authority converged in the hands of the Party, even in those cases where the Party was not mentioned in so many words.[39]

So was the Party above the law? If it was, what was to prevent the re-emergence of a police state especially in a case where – as in Bulgaria for instance – Party theorists insisted that 'to speak about vested rights in socialism is the same as to favour counter-revolution'? The aftermath of the show trials saw party bosses trying to square the circle. To the throng gathered before the grave of László Rajk – in a setting of multiple and tragic ironies – a senior Hungarian party official proclaimed: 'Many are asking themselves: what guarantee do we have that illegalities, offences against the law such as these, will never again take place in the future? – It is a justified question. It is a question to which we are obliged to give our people an answer. The guarantee is the party. We communists are the guarantee.' An unsettling reassurance! Trying to distance himself from the old days, János Kádár insisted: 'A whole nation cannot be suspect.' Or, in another pithy reversal of Stalinism: 'He who is not against us is for us.' Yet even under Kádár, there was no real move towards judicial independence. The Party retained its control over the security apparatus; it was just that the Party became more moderate.[40]

At the heart of these debates was the question of the character of the Party itself. In his controversial 'Anatomy of a Morality', Tito's fiery colleague Milovan Djilas charged that the ideological purists of the revolution had been replaced by a 'new class' of self-aggrandizing time-servers. The 'heroes' of the partisan war had turned into corrupt 'practical men' married to grasping wives. But, if this was true – and even Tito's spreading waistline gave support to Djilas's criticism – what was to be done? Djilas himself talked about building a genuine multi-party democracy and doing away with the Party's monopoly on power. Later, but in like vein, Czech reformers argued for a separation of the Party and state.

Such a revival of the postulates of 'pure bourgeois democracy' was anathema to most cadres. Perhaps there was another way. Tito's favourite theorist, Edvard Kardelj, argued that between 'classical bourgeois democracy' and Soviet 'socialism of the apparatus' lay the 'direct democracy' of workers' self-government and the realization of Marx's dream of the 'withering away of the state'. Workers' self-management sounded wonderful in theory, and attracted the attention of curious foreign economists (who showed less interest in the millions of Yugoslav workers who preferred employment as migrant workers in the capitalist West). But though brilliant as propaganda for foreign consumption, Kardelj's theories – as modified by reality – turned out to involve little more than a very pragmatic response to calls for reform. Tito, after all, was hardly going to preside over the dismantling of the Party apparatus he had fought a war to bring to power. Nor, of course, would the Soviet Union acquiesce more generally in the Party's demotion: liberalization would have to take place under its gaze.

If a certain decline in the Party's ideological influence did take place it was due to pressures less easily evaded than Djilas's broadsides. A new technical intelligentsia was indeed coming to dominate the Party machinery, ousting the pre-war 'heroes'. These cadres were economic pragmatists not ideologues, and they recognized the need for scientists, managers and specialists to spearhead the reforms without which the Party must eventually be doomed. Their ideology was that of technocrats everywhere in the late fifties and sixties – a belief that science, technological progress and a state run by experts held the answers to modern life. They sought a depoliticization of the system on the grounds that the modernization of the economy now required not ideologues but administrators.

What made such arguments plausible was the Soviet insistence in the 1950s that capitalism and communism were competitors in a race towards a material utopia. Khrushchev, in particular, liked to boast that communism would soon demonstrate its superiority to the West by overtaking it in the production of consumer goods: 'Within a period of, say, five years following 1965, the level of US production per capita should be equalled and overtaken. Thus by that time, perhaps even sooner, the USSR will have captured first place in the world both in absolute volume of production and per capita production, which will ensure the world's highest standard of living.' His Master's Voice, Ulbricht, talked of 'overtaking and surpassing' West Germany. Strange and implausible as such boasts may sound today, they were not dismissed by the West. This was, after all, the Sputnik era. 'Can Moscow match us industrially?' asked one leading American commentator in 1955. His conclusion: the possibility could not be ruled out.[41]

THE NEW SOCIETY

If such boasts were taken seriously, it was because people were struck by the dramatic social changes which communism had brought to eastern Europe. In less than two decades the region became a predominantly urban society. More than twenty million people moved into the war-ravaged towns and their abandoned apartments. New cities emerged; old ones were ringed by estates of high-rise apartment blocks; even villages acquired industrial workforces. In the late 1940s the urban population of the region stood at 37.5 million – some 36 per cent of the total workforce – figures which had remained unchanged for a decade. Twenty years later, the urban population had grown to some 58 millions and nearly half the labour force now lived in the towns. In the recession-bound 1980s, places like Hoyeswerda, Nowa Huta and Dimitrovgrad were shabby, decaying reminders of communism's failure; in the 1950s they evoked its glorious future.[42]

Of course, even in the 1950s, the careful observer could discern the priorities of the new order in the ideological elephantiasis which seemed to be afflicting the region. The centre of Warsaw was dwarfed by a new Palace of Culture, described by one analyst as 'an architectural three-stage rocket' – a Stalinist skyscraper 'donated' by the Soviet Union; central Sofia was dominated by the neo-Byzantine Ministry for Heavy Industry. In Bucharest the mammoth Casa Scînteii housed a printing and publishing complex which produced newspapers, school books, brochures and symbolized 'man's triumph over nature and the social forces that have fettered him'. These 'great construction projects of communism' took precedence over private housing. Even after the 'New Course' increased the emphasis on housing, the shortage of living space remained acute.[43]

Yet while homes remained scarce, there were dramatic improvements in the provision of other social goods. The creation, for instance, of a nationalized health service offered vast improvements in care. In Bulgaria, where the government had passed the 'Free and Universal Medical Care' Bill in 1951, the number of beds per 1,000 inhabitants was soon more than double the pre-war level. In Czechoslovakia, where the entire health sector was nationalized, child mortality dropped dramatically from a pre-war rate of nearly 50 per 1,000 to under 15 by the 1960s. Life expectancy converged equally rapidly on west European norms.

Family allowances (often linked progressively to income), the provision of childcare and the liberalization of abortion were all presented as 'part of the emancipation of women' and were not unrelated to the needs of an economy desperate for female labour. It should of course be remembered that although large numbers of married and unmarried women did enter the workforce, they were still paid less than men. And what allowed them to do this were not only official childcare facilities but also the plentiful and indispensable supply of grandmothers, often cooped up in tiny flats with their grandchildren.[44]

This example should alert us to the particular character of the east European welfare state; if (to simplify matters) the Nazi equivalent had been geared to the needs of the race, and the post-war west European model to the rights of the individual citizen, the Communist model was designed to respond, above all, to the needs of economic production. Hence not only the incentives to female labour, but also the relative lack of concern with the elderly or with the rural as opposed to the urban population. Lenin had warned that 'he who does not work shall not eat'. In accordance with this precept social insurance was used as a weapon; not only 'persons with fascist activities' (as in Bulgaria) but also peasants and others outside the socialist sector were often excluded from proper coverage.

Yet under the 'enlightened despotism' of communism some truly dramatic changes were afoot. Education became available to a much wider range of social groups than it had been before the war: the number of primary schools built in Yugoslavia nearly doubled; so did the universities, and the student population leapt from a pre-war

17,000 to 97,000. Schooling was vital to create the cadres for the new order: in Poland there were 250,000 students in higher education compared with 50,000 before the war; in Hungary some 67,000 by the early 1960s compared with a pre-war 11,000. Technical studies in particular enjoyed rapid increases in enrolments, partly because they offered the best job prospects and partly because they were often preferred to the more ideologically charged humanities.[45]

All these changes formed part of a social philosophy which aimed to break down the traditional hierarchies of the past. Communism may have created its own governing class, but there can be little doubt that it was a lot less elitist than any previous kind of ruling system eastern Europe had known. In purely economic terms, there was a striking flattening of income differentials across the board: differentials between manual and non-manual were greatly reduced, despite the persistence of traditional respect for 'the trousered ones'. Upward mobility from the working class into the new administrative elite was deliberately encouraged by quotas for jobs and university admissions. 'Poverty as a social phenomenon had disappeared,' wrote Mlynar. 'People going about in rags, beggars in the streets, slums in the urban periphery ... had disappeared for good and were known to the younger generation only from movies.' By the 1960s Czechoslovakia was – in terms of income distribution – the most egalitarian country in Europe; Poland and East Germany were not far behind.[46]

All in all, this constituted a social revolution. Living standards were slowly rising. From Yugoslavia was reported 'the increased use of bicycles and motorcycles, and many people had even cause to hope that one day they would own an automobile'. Radio, TV and telephone ownership spread rapidly, posing all sorts of new challenges to Party control as village loudspeakers gave way to personal sets. Families shrank: torn between 'baby or car', an increasing number of couples were plumping for the car, or at least the hope of one.[47]

The changing pattern of daily life was mirrored in school textbooks: by the 1960s, these displayed an attention to consumption and leisure which had been unthinkable even a decade earlier. One illustration of the image of a little boy reading to his grandparents (parents presumably out at work), marked the change. A 1952 Serbian primer had shown them all sitting on low stools in a sparsely furnished simple home. The 1963 version showed them in comfortable chairs, in a room with a smart modern cabinet with a shelf of books and a carpet on the floor.[48]

Despite these achievements, however, there was real dissatisfaction within society. In particular, the constant shortages and scarcity of consumer goods undermined the Party's proud boasts. At one level, scarcity, far from being a threat to the rule of the Party, was in fact basic to its power: one of the main reasons for joining or cooperating with the Party was to enjoy privileged access to scarce resources. Were goods suddenly to become plentiful, the Party would have lost one of its main sources of support. At another level, though, the shortages of consumer goods in particular did undermine the main justification the Party under Khrushchev offered for its leadership, namely its ability to outstrip the West in material terms.

Shortages focused popular discontent on corruption and favouritism among Party cadres themselves, as well as on national subservience to Soviet economic interests. Whereas western Europe received capital from its superpower, eastern Europe saw money and goods flow out instead through requisitions, rigged barter deals and Soviet-controlled joint companies. One estimate puts the total cost to eastern Europe up to Stalin's death at roughly $14 billion, which is the equivalent of the US investment in western Europe through the Marshall Plan. The formation of Comecon as a rival to the Marshall Plan did not ease the discontent of countries like Romania and Bulgaria, which saw themselves destined to serve as agricultural producers in the new communist division of labour.[49]

By the 1960s the gap between East and West was widening. Czechs and Austrians had had roughly the same rate of car ownership before the war; by 1960 the Austrians had three times as many per capita. Most other east Europeans only reached the Czech level of 1960 in the 1970s and traffic congestion – that symbol of modern consumerism – came very late to the great cities of the region. The economic 'miracle' in Japan overshadowed everything Moscow had to offer and as Moscow's share of world GNP fell so that of Japan rose. Growth in eastern Europe, despite the reforms, dropped in the 1960s. Unlike western Europe, agricultural production barely exceeded the pre-war level. More worrying in the long term, that growth which had taken place since the war was based not – as in the capitalist world – on improvements in productivity, but rather on huge injections of labour. What would happen as the reserves of labour dried up? Communist cadres in eastern Europe were like a runner who makes a huge effort to catch up with a rival, only to see the latter disappearing over the horizon.[50]

Looking to the future, the authorities could not fail to be alarmed by the disaffected attitudes to be found particularly among the offspring of this social revolution. The 'Hero's children' (as Hungarian émigré Paul Neuburg called them) had been in many ways the beneficiaries of the dramatic changes of the first decade of communism. Yet they did not appear to be grateful. A communist education, far from brainwashing them, had left them with a deep mistrust of ideology and critical of a political system which treated them 'like babies' and deprived them of information. Unlike their elders, they did not compare their lives with the pre-war or war years but rather with their contemporaries in the West.[51]

They developed lifestyles which alarmed their parents and the Party – based around a private world of transistor radios, cassette players and the dream of Western affluence and autonomy. While some young idealists were attracted to the reform communism of the New Left or aimed a Maoist critique at the tired cadres around them, far more had 'embraced materialism with a vengeance'. They tended to be both nationalistic (i.e. anti-Russian) and 'cosmopolitan'. The Romanian politburo were not alone in criticizing their youth for their 'servitude to the cultural and scientific achievements of the capitalist countries'. Parties across the region sponsored endless teams of sociologists to research the 'youth problem'.[52]

Yet not even social science could save communists from the truth. It was the Party itself which had brought the West to these young people – through its insistent materialism, through urbanization, and more directly and concretely through the tourists who were flocking to eastern Europe in the 1960s. Earlier generations had needed to migrate westwards to experience Western culture. Now the West came to them. One million seven hundred thousand tourists hit the Yugoslav beaches in 1963 (compared with a meagre 150,000 in 1926); two years later there were 2.6 million, by 1973 an incredible 6.2 million visitors formed a mainstay of the Yugoslav economy. Other Communist states quickly entered the field. At the same time it became easier for people from central Europe to travel westwards. 'The craze for foreign travel has swept our country like a summer storm,' observed a Czech journalist.[53]

They might have been bored of communist ideology; but in their worship (not too strong a word) of modernity and material progress, these young people showed that they were the Party's children still: it was striking how completely the image of peasant life, which had captivated a previous generation of east Europeans before communism, had been relegated to the dustbin of history. (But then the cities had become the homes of the peasants and their children, less prone to romanticizing the rural life than the old urban bourgeoisie, which had been decimated by the war.)

This was the paradox of the Party: its great achievement was precisely what now cast doubt upon its own existence. 'In proposing itself as the Ultimate Hero of History, Rationality Incarnate and the Sole Champion of Progress,' wrote Neuburg, 'the Party created the situation by which it was now ensnared.' This would have been the moment for the Party to retire. But of course it could not: it was committed to the eastern centralism which had once worked so dramatically but was now leading to failure.[54]

THE END OF EMPIRE?

'Bulgaria will not be a Soviet republic, it will be a people's republic,' Georgy Dimitrov had insisted in December 1947. Yet Dimitrov would not have made this pronouncement without Moscow's permission. With the exception of the Baltic states, Stalin had decided not to incorporate eastern Europe into the Soviet Union, preferring a form of indirect rule through national communist elites. In their external as well as their domestic relations, the People's Democracies were an experiment under constant review. The tensions generated by such a form of imperialism remained a challenge to Moscow throughout the post-war era. But was Soviet hegemony ever really in jeopardy?[55]

If the years from 1945 to 1953 were a phase of increasing Soviet control over their European empire, the decades after 1953 saw a gradual decentralization whose rhythms and extent were the subject of continual trial and error. In 1955 the Red Army actually withdrew from the Soviet occupation zone in Austria in exchange for a pledge of Austrian neutrality, a move which caught the West by surprise and was almost certainly inspired by the desire to settle the German question in the same way.

Only rarely did the widespread anti-Soviet feelings which existed across the region manifest themselves publicly (as in the flowers placed on T. G. Masaryk's grave each year, which led it to be guarded in 1953 by more than one hundred policemen), but Party officials were always aware of their existence. So, too, of course was Moscow, which was prepared to allow, indeed to an extent even encourage, the drift towards 'national communism' as the price to be paid for maintaining power. This was Khrushchev's line, which prevailed over that of the more hardline Molotov and which led directly to the dissolution of the Cominform in 1956.

Occasionally popular anti-Soviet sentiment spilled out into the streets. When it did, as in Hungary in 1956, it tended to be in periods of relaxation, by those groups – workers, students – who far from being the chief victims of communism, were (in theory at least) among the elect. 'No more compulsory Russian' was one of the slogans chanted in Budapest during the uprising, 'Russians go back to Russia' another. Workers' uprisings tended to alarm the authorities much more than students' – but neither group could resist for long when armed force was deployed against them. Moreover, astute and flexible handling by the political elite – as in Poland in 1956, or Yugoslavia in 1971–2 – usually served to drive unrest underground again. Moscow disliked having to intervene directly, but was prepared to do so where it felt it was necessary.

Djilas talked about a state of virtual civil war existing between the Party and the rest of the population. But Djilas was as given to exaggeration in opposition as he had been when in power. Popular dislike, even contempt, for 'democratic socialism' was always mixed with fear. Communism was highly successful in breaking up possible centres of resistance. Secret police, with the help of vast networks of hundreds of thousands of informers, penetrated the workplace and the home. If the queue could be turned (by Konwicki in his *The Polish Complex*) into a symbol of social relations under communist rule it was because it was organized around the principles of scarcity, rumour and the satisfaction of individual desires. Sullen acquiescence and withdrawal from politics were increasingly in evidence except among a small minority. Indeed a sullen populace was to be preferred to one that took communism seriously, for that only produced idealists and critics of socialist reality. Popular dissatisfaction, in other words, was not the most serious of threats to Soviet rule.

Far more serious for Moscow was the threat posed by communist cadres themselves. The key to Soviet control lay in the obedience of the satraps. After Stalin's death this was never assured. In 1956, for example, Soviet will prevailed in Hungary against the crowds on the streets but was powerless against the Polish Party's defiant insistence on bringing Gomułka back into power. Battles in Moscow itself between hardliners and reformists confused the East European leadership, who increasingly kept their distance from both the verbose but unpredictable Khrushchev and the more laconic and cautious Brezhnev. Moscow tried to reimpose discipline through the Warsaw Pact but although it gave Nato planners nightmares (and work) the Pact was basically little more than an instrument for legalizing the presence of Soviet troops in Hungary and Romania after the Austria Peace Treaty was signed in 1955. Neither it nor Comecon could bring back the discipline of the late 1940s.

The Sino-Soviet split harmed Moscow's prestige still further. Not only did it open up another front to worry Soviet policy-makers, but Chinese influence among east European hardliners was a threat from the late 1950s, and as Albania showed, could open up the opportunity for disobedient satellites to play Moscow off against Peking. From the early 1960s onwards, the 'Mother of realized socialism' was fighting a rearguard action in eastern Europe. What made the Prague Spring so much *more* threatening to Moscow in some ways than Hungary in 1956 was the fact that this time the impetus for revolt was coming from within the Party itself. Of course, neo-Stalinist nationalists like Ceauşescu caused Brezhnev as many headaches as idealistic reformers like Dubček; wily long-term players like János Kádár in Hungary perhaps caused even more.

And yet in retrospect it must be confessed that this rearguard action from Moscow was on the whole strikingly successful. Observers, after all, spent decades predicting the break-up of the Soviet empire in eastern Europe. Ionescu, in 1965, argued that 'the internal history of the Soviet bloc since the death of Stalin is the story of its progressive disintegration and the unchecked decline of Russian authority within it'. According to Pierre Hassner, 'the Balkanization of Communism has prevailed over the Communization of the Balkans'.[56]

More percipient observers, however, were cautious. The machinery of Soviet control had proved its durability; despite the increasing senility of the Party leadership and its loss of ideological appeal, there were few signs of where a political challenge might come from. Gyorgy argued that the failure of the rebellions of 1956 'cannot augur well for future revolutionary success from below'. Paul Kecskemeti concluded his masterly analysis of the Hungarian uprising with the caveat that eastern Europe was unlikely to be the main centre of political upheaval in the Soviet bloc; instability was more likely to occur in the Soviet Union itself – the heart of the empire – than in its satellites. Most remarkably of all, François Fejtö saw in the Prague Spring not only the revival of Soviet obscurantism, but at the same time, the revelation that communism contained the seeds of reform within itself. 'One may hope', he wrote presciently in 1969, 'that the next Dubček will appear in the nerve centre of the system: Moscow.'[57]

9

Democracy Transformed:
Western Europe, 1950–75

The number of communist voters in European countries stands
in inverse proportion to the number of housing units per thousand
inhabitants.

> – Eberhard Wildermuth (West German Federal
> Housing Minister)[1]

High employment, fast economic growth and stability are now
considered normal in western capitalism.

> – Michael Kidron, 1968[2]

The vastness of their desires paralysed them.

> – Georges Perec[3]

REVIVING DEMOCRACY

After 1945 western Europe rediscovered democracy. The remnants of
the inter-war authoritarian Right – Franco's Spain and Salazar's
Portugal – were shunned as hangovers from an unwelcome past,
excluded from the new international organizations – the United
Nations, the European Economic Community, even the Marshall Plan
– at least until the Cold War turned them once more into ambiguous
allies of the Free World. In the UK, Eire, Sweden and Switzerland
wartime restrictions were lifted and the normal functioning of parliament resumed. The anti-democratic strongholds of the New Order –
France, Germany and Italy – put the past behind them and built new

constitutional systems. In Greece, the authoritarian legacy of the 1930s was abandoned, despite a civil war, and parliamentary rule shakily re-established.

But this rebirth of democracy was no simple return to 1919; on the contrary, what emerged after 1945 was profoundly altered as a result of the region's memories both of war and of the pre-war democratic crisis. The role of parliament, the nature of political parties and of politics itself all emerged transformed from the struggle with fascism. Democracy now encompassed both a fuller suffrage – as women acquired voting rights where they had previously lacked them (except in socially backward Switzerland and Liechtenstein) – and a greater degree of commitment across the political spectrum to real social and economic rights as well.[4]

As after 1918, the change in attitudes could be charted through constitutional reforms. These displayed a concern for human rights born of bitter wartime experience, and an awareness of the need to defend the individual against the power of the state. According to article 2 of the 1948 Italian constitution: 'The Republic recognizes and guarantees the inviolable rights of man.' 'The German people . . . acknowledge inviolable and inalienable human rights to be the basis of every human community,' ran article 1 of the new German Basic Law, which provided a tighter safeguard on arbitrary state power, and especially the police, than had been delivered by the Weimar Constitution.[5]

Given the strong feeling that in the inter-war years democracy had been undermined by over-powerful or disputatious assemblies, it is hardly surprising that many people also wanted a stronger executive. West Germany created what some came to call a 'Chancellor democracy', and others – more pointedly – 'Demokratur' (a combination of democracy and dictatorship). But France illustrated the difficulties involved in asking parliamentarians to divest themselves voluntarily of power. The Fourth Republic looked little different from this point of view to its predecessor: if anything it handed over *more* power into the hands of parliament, and it was not until 1958 that a disgusted de Gaulle, backed by an exasperated public, managed to create a more presidential regime. In Italy, too, the new 1946 referendum ousted the monarchy but otherwise altered little of the forms of pre-Fascist parliamentary procedure.

Moderation was the new virtue: explicitly in the Italian and German cases (where the Allies anticipated serious right-wing opposition after the war), implicitly elsewhere, governments committed themselves to the suppression of anti-democratic political movements. West Germany's Basic Law, for example, laid down conditions governing the role of a political party, its democratic structure and the need for it to comply with the constitution. In some cases this led to neo-Nazi parties being banned by the Federal Constitutional Court. But such measures were probably not the main reason for the relatively poor performance of the extreme Right in post-war elections. More significant, apart from public disaffection, was the success of the mainstream Right in diverting the extremists' natural constituency into their own ranks. The leniency shown by Adenauer and Italian Christian Democrats helped keep the extreme Right at bay.

In the long run, for all the disgust such tactics now excite, it is not obvious that a total marginalization of the Right would have offered the very fragile new democracies greater security. We should recall how far the anti-democratic Right had predominated in Europe in the 1930s. There seemed a real prospect of its popularity reviving immediately after the end of the war: Allied opinion polls indicated no great commitment to democracy in the German public. Nationalistically minded refugees from East Prussia, Silesia and the Sudetenland in particular were reluctant to give up their dreams of *Heimat*. 'To a demagogue', warned *The Times* in December 1950 – with an eye to the past – 'refugees are what blood in the water is to a shark and the refugee problem is large enough to create a revolutionary situation.' Adenauer may have given jobs and protection to a scandalously large number of former Nazis (some 34 per cent of Foreign Ministry officials in 1952 had been Party members); but his defusing of the potentially explosive refugee vote in the fifties and early sixties was masterly. Had he not brought about the decline of the nationalist Refugee Party, by breaking it up and bringing one faction into his CDU, the millions of German refugees from eastern Europe might have jeopardized the very foundations of the new Federal Republic.[6]

Fewer compromises, of course, were made with the extreme Left: conservatively inclined governments in the first decade of the Cold War felt a lot more comfortable excluding the Left than the Right. The Communist Party was outlawed in West Germany and Greece, tolerated but harassed elsewhere. Across western Europe, domestic custodians of anti-communism – especially in the police and security services – worked together with American Cold War warriors, whose centre, the CIA's Office of Policy Coordination, saw its budget mushroom from $4.7 million in early 1949 to $200 million by 1953. Anti-communism was a growth industry.[7]

European governments helped the youthful CIA try out its latest theories of psychological warfare against the Left, attacking communism through advertising, cultural publishing, travelling exhibitions and film. Socialist and Labour parties were supported in their struggle with communists over control of trades unions. At the height of the Cold War, the Americans anticipated a possible Russian invasion of the West, and provided a few reliable anti-communists with weapons to organize armed resistance, just as had been done during Nazi occupation. Only in the late 1980s and early 1990s did the afterlife of these bizarre cells, their links with the secret services in Italy and Belgium, and their involvement in right-wing terrorism, become public knowledge.[8]

Although such paranoia evaporated with the ending of the Korean War, many of the institutions of the new 'national security' state became permanent: West European spy services expanded enormously, and vetting public-sector jobs became standard practice. In the UK, for example, the Attlee government rejected proposals from a Tory MP to form a parliamentary Committee on Un-British Activities, but did set up a secret cabinet committee on subversive activities and began regular 'negative vetting' of civil servants. The much more intrusive 'positive vetting' into applicants' views and past activities began in 1950 at the urging of the Americans: a process originally forecast to apply to some 1,000 posts encompassed 68,000 by 1982.[9]

The public showed only limited concern at the consequent infringements of civil liberties. Partly there was a general suspicion of Soviet intentions towards western Europe. More fundamentally, though, there was a widespread feeling that 'all -isms are now wasms'. The war had left people with a deep antipathy to ideological politics. And the reflection of this could be seen in the changed attitudes of mainstream political parties, which moved away from the polarized attitudes of the past in favour of compromise. Both Left and Right were coming to terms with parliamentary democracy, and losing their earlier reservations.[10]

On the Left, the ending of the war had originally been seen – in the words of Léon Blum – as ushering in socialism's 'triumphant period'. 'After Hitler, us!' proclaimed the German Social Democrat Rudolf Breitscheid. It was not to be. The new era of social reconstruction would not take place based on socialist principles, as Blum had thought. Fascism might have been defeated, but the menace of communism posed socialists serious problems in its turn; outside the UK, Marxism was the umbilical cord which bound them together, and even anti-communist socialists – an increasingly common breed – found it hard to cut it. Moreover, both capitalism and conservatism proved more tenacious and indeed more popular in western Europe than had seemed possible in the dark days of Nazi occupation, and socialists were forced to come to terms with these realities. Thus, the Left's initial euphoria gave way to a protracted rethinking of the relationship between socialism, capitalism, and class.[11]

The retreat from Marxism began in some countries almost immediately after the war. In the Netherlands, for example, the Social Democratic Workers Party changed its name to the Dutch Labour Party in an effort to broaden its appeal and downplay its class character. In West Germany, Sweden and Austria, the process took social democrats into the late 1950s or even 1960s. Opposition to reform was even more prolonged in France and Italy, with their strong Marxist traditions, and above all in that bastion of non-Marxism, the British Labour Party. Nevertheless, even in these countries socialists were forced one way or another to recognize electoral and economic truth: the only way to avoid gradual extinction was to escape the ghetto of class politics and undergo the transformation into a broader-based type of party. Gaitskell, for instance, warned that Labour was doomed to defeat unless it took account of 'the changing character of labour, full employment, new housing, the new way of life based on the television, the fridge, the car and the glossy magazines'. Opposing him, Richard Crossman tried arguing that managed capitalism would not be able to match the achievements of Soviet-style planning in eastern Europe; but in fact neither the British Labour Party nor any other mainstream socialist movement made any radical attempt on the virtues of post-war capitalism.[12]

The Right exploited the Cold War far more effectively. Less encumbered than the Left by theory and dogma, able to embrace anti-communism with greater ease, and more attuned to the widespread desire in the 1950s for political quiescence, family stability and domesticity, pragmatic right-wing politicians rethought their earlier authoritarian impulses and built up new, powerful movements committed to democracy and sharing many of the social concerns of the Left. A former bastion of fiscal caution like the inter-war British Conservative Party succumbed to 'One Nation' Toryism: Tory governments in the 1950s were as committed as Labour to a national housing policy, for example. Where economic liberalism survived, as it did in West Germany and Italy, it competed and compromised with very different traditions: Catholic paternalism, social concern and anti-materialism. The rise of Catholic democratic parties was a key here. Germany's CDU, for example, offered a 'socially committed market economy' as a third way between laissez-faire and state planning.[13]

In this way the old polarization and class antagonism between Left and Right slowly yielded to a new emphasis on consensus. In the extreme case, as in Austria, the outcome was a grand coalition of Left and Right (1945–66) whose durability reflected the two partners' determined avoidance of ideological conflict after their civil war in the 1930s: Vienna's two-party state, in fact, turned out to be far more impregnable than the older one-party version. Coalition became the norm in Western parliaments, a source of instability in France but not in countries like Italy or Denmark where frequent changes of government hid the continued hold on power of at least one of the major parties. Though on average west European governments were not particularly durable for much of the post-war period, this does not seem to have bred dissatisfaction with democratic politics, and there was relatively little civil protest or public violence. The chief reason for this public tolerance – so striking a contrast with the unsupportive stance of the inter-war years – was surely that the revival of democracy coincided with the most remarkable period of sustained economic growth in history. As people's lives became more comfortable and prosperous, the political system reaped the rewards.[14]

THE MIRACLE OF GROWTH

It was not easy, at first, to foresee the extended economic upswing that would transform the West in the two decades after 1950. Mindful of the experience of the years immediately after the First World War, most experts anticipated a post-war boom followed by some kind of slump. The slowdown in industrial production in western Europe from 12 per cent per annum in 1947–8 to 5 per cent in 1949–50 apparently confirmed their caution. In 1951 the *Economist* observed gloomily: 'In the third year of the Marshall Plan, which has succeeded beyond expectation, in conditions of prosperity and restored standards of living – in short in what ought to be a good year – a quarter of both the French and Italian electorates voted communist . . . There is almost nowhere a positive faith in the possibilities of progress, such as the Russians and the Americans both have.'

Gloom at the long-term outlook was evident. The Dutch government encouraged emigration on the grounds that the country was unlikely to be able to solve its unemployment problem by internal growth; in less than a decade, the country would be a net importer of labour. In West Germany, many economists predicted that the loss of the agrarian lands of East Prussia and Silesia would lead to permanent food shortage, and unemployed men wandered the streets as they had done before the war carrying placards or signs indicating their desire to find work. The stifling impact of the Cold War on business confidence was reflected in the caution of a French farmer, Lucien Bourdin, who told an American scholar: 'Plant an apricot orchard so the Russians and Americans can use it as a battlefield? Thanks. Not so dumb.'[15]

As late as 1953, the overall verdict of the UN's Economic Commission for Europe was distinctly lukewarm: the 'general progress of the western European economy has not been entirely encouraging'. Balance-of-payments pressures were acting as a brake on expansion. The ECE was pessimistic about the chances of employment growth without inflation getting out of control in what it called a 'private enterprise economy'. Growth had so far been patchy and based on internal factors, with little sign of international cooperation so that 'the historical trend towards national autarky has not been clearly reversed'.[16]

As it happens, the experience of a few countries in western Europe did bear out just such a gloomy forecast. 'National autarky' was exactly the economic strategy followed by the authoritarian fossils of the Iberian peninsula, and by the conservative Catholic government in Eire. The outcome was in every case an unambiguous failure, with sluggish growth and high unemployment or underemployment which looked less and less impressive as the 1950s progressed and the rest of western Europe prospered. Exporting tens of thousands of workers annually – as all three did – to take advantage of the boom was really admitting defeat. In the late 1950s, Eire and Spain changed course dramatically and embraced modernization: Portugal – under its pre-Keynesian economics professor Salazar – remained the odd man out.[17]

By this point there could be no doubt about the quite exceptional character of the economic upswing across the rest of western Europe. Growth was faster and smoother than ever before. Between 1913 and 1950 per capita growth in the region had averaged 1 per cent a year; between 1950 and 1970 this rose to an incredible 4 per cent. For the most part, the swings in the business cycle which had so disrupted businessmen before 1939 gave way to much milder fluctuations. Pre-war mass unemployment seemed to have been banished for good: unemployment rates in western Europe fell from an average of 7.5 per cent in the 1930s to just under 3 per cent in 1950–60 and 1.5 per cent in the succeeding decade. 'Today having a million unemployed and more is thought of as a disastrous possibility,' wrote a British commentator in 1967. 'We should greet it as a decisive mark of national failure.' With astonishing speed, full employment came to be seen, not as a precarious and hard-won achievement, but as a natural part of a modern, scientifically managed capitalist economy.[18]

There were substantial differences in performance between countries. Austria, West Germany, France, Italy and the Netherlands notched up relatively rapid growth rates; Britain and Belgium somewhat slower. Some economies did better in the 1950s than in the 1960s; for others, it was the other way round. Yet the really important point is that in all cases growth was well above any levels previously recorded. Even in sluggish Britain, whose poor performance alarmed domestic analysts, growth after 1950 was – at 3.0 per cent per annum – higher than the 1.3 per cent averaged between 1913 and 1950, or even the 1.9 per cent recorded between 1870 and 1913.[19]

The causes of this unprecedented achievement – the so-called 'economic miracle' – remain fiercely disputed. Abundant labour – in the shape of refugees and underemployed peasants – may have kept wages low and encouraged investment. Yet labour was abundant in the Iberian peninsula, but did not by itself lead to growth there, just as it had not by itself brought prosperity in the 1930s. The abundance of labour was basically a permissive factor, contributing to growth where other circumstances were also favourable.

Much the same applied to capital. Wartime destruction of industrial plant was far less than originally believed. In fact, given the tremendous expansion of capacity during the war, there can be little doubt that western Europe's capital stock after 1945 was greater than in 1939, and growing fast. Tight government control of credit and investment, as well as rationing and other forms of forced saving, kept consumption low and investment ratios high – 16.8 per cent of GNP in 1950–70 compared with 9.6 per cent in 1928–38. But this pattern reflected not only the availability of capital but also the willingness of the public authorities to direct its use, as well as the willingness of populations to forgo consumption in the present for the sake of a better future.[20]

In the mythology of the time, the European recovery is often attributed to the Marshall Plan, the massive American financial contribution which the USA committed itself to providing western Europe following the initiative of Secretary of State George Marshall in the summer of 1947. It is certainly true that the solid economic, political and military commitment which the USA made to western Europe after 1945 was instrumental in making the recovery from the Second World War so much more successful than that from the First. Nevertheless, in purely quantitative terms it is now clear that, except in Greece and perhaps Italy, the Marshall Plan was less important economically than its propagandists – or their opponents – made out. Most European investment was domestically generated, while growth rates in the West were no higher than in eastern Europe where, far from enjoying Marshall Plan aid, countries were financing their superpower rather than being supported by it. What Marshall Plan funds did do was ease foreign-exchange bottlenecks, providing scarce dollars, and allowing growth to continue.[21]

Americans helped change European capitalism – just as they had begun to do before the war – transforming industrial relations, preaching the gospel of scientific management and modernizing working practices and equipment. Productivity growth, averaging around 4 per cent per annum, undoubtedly underpinned the boom. The Marshall Planners and other propagandists for the 'American way' launched an array of Productivity Councils, exchange programmes for union leaders and managers, publications and exhibitions. In the late 1940s, a time of considerable labour unrest, 'productivity' was hymned as an ideological alternative to class war, a means of boosting *both* wages *and* company profits.[22]

The debate over the Marshall Plan has highlighted the significance of other aspects of American economic influence. These include not merely the new gospel of productivity, but also attitudes to fiscal policy, investment strategy and class harmony. In general, Marshall Planners tried to encourage European policy-makers to boost consumer spending (in order to reduce social discontent and the likely spread of the communist virus), and to break free of the rigid social hierarchies of the past in a kind of European New Deal.

Perhaps most important of all, in the long run, was the broader political impact of the American presence in western Europe. The Cold War – at its height in the early 1950s – induced not only fear and alarm but also a greater degree of cooperation among the nation-states of western Europe than had ever been seen in the past.

Washington's ambitious visions of closely coordinated European planning may have been quickly thwarted by devious Europeans like Bevin and Schuman. But American money and security could not be gained without strings attached, and these – by tying the recipients to some form of inter-state dialogue – changed the international economic environment in western Europe. In particular, they laid the foundations of the astonishing revival of trade which lay at the heart of the boom in the mid-1950s. France and especially Britain, locked into expensive imperial commitments, were less inclined to take advantage of such opportunities than the Benelux states, West Germany or Italy. But through the European Payments Union and later the European Economic Community – all encouraged by American policy-makers – intra-European trade boomed. Noting how quickly Germans had abandoned the old inter-war obsessions with land and autarky, Elizabeth Wiskemann commented in 1956 that 'in a Europe which has plans to prevent sharp recessions in trade and their consequences, in a Europe which is striving after peaceful integration, and whose communications have seemed to melt distances to nothing, the aim of national self-sufficiency seems to have become irrelevant'.[23]

European governments, though, were not simply the passive recipients of American generosity. They had effectively thwarted a return to isolationism by dragging Washington back into Europe with their scare stories of the menace of communism. If the Americans were now the imperialists, they were there (in Lundestad's words) 'by invitation'. The Europeans too had their priorities and strategies and the post-war boom needs to be assessed in the light of their domestic policy choices. To be sure, the old concerns about inflation (especially during the Korean War), the balance of payments and the balanced budget had not disappeared: they survived particularly in countries like Italy and Germany which came out of the recent past with a deep mistrust of *étatisme*. But by the 1960s, governments across western Europe were placing demand management, the pursuit of full employment and economic growth above price stability. In other words, they were more willing than ever before to accept a degree of inflation in return for prosperity. 'In all European countries', Postan wrote, 'economic growth became a universal creed and a common expectation to which governments were expected to conform. To this extent economic growth was the product of economic growthmanship.'[24]

We can chart the development of the new creed fairly precisely. In the early 1950s, the annual reports of the new OEEC (the Organization for European Economic Cooperation) spotlighted the need to improve productivity as the key to expansion. In 1956 it used the phrase 'economic growth' for the first time. When the organization was refounded in 1960 as the OECD, article 1 of its founding charter stated that the organization aimed 'to achieve the highest sustainable economic growth and employment and a rising standard of living in Member countries'. In Walt Rostow's *The Stages of Economic Growth* (subtitled 'a Non-Communist Manifesto') – which explained 'take-off' into prosperity as a universal, historical process – the growth creed acquired its gospel.[25]

'Growthmanship' was not only to be found in official circles. In the private sector, too, confidence grew out of the uncertainty of the early 1950s, and private investment soared alongside public. Indeed, the striking feature of the post-war boom was the way public and private sectors seemed to have achieved a mutually acceptable and beneficial symbiosis. As the egalitarian mood of liberation faded, the socialist assault on capitalism failed to materialize; planning gave way to nationalization, and then to 'direction' and 'guidance'. The planned economy which the CDU had committed itself to in Germany in early 1947 melted before the triumph of Ludwig Erhard's 'social market economy'. In Britain, where Labour seemed initially so hostile to the private sector, employers were treated with a respect which would have startled, say, the more directive Dutch authorities; even in France, 'planification' turned out to be a largely hands-off affair, though apparently none the less successful for that. 'What was it', asked Andrew Shonfield, perhaps the most acute analyst of the new European economy, 'that converted capitalism from the cataclysmic failure which it appeared to be in the 1930s into the great engine of prosperity of the post-war world?' The answer, according to him, lay in the 'changing balance of public and private power'.[26]

Contrary to the UN Economic Commission for Europe's 1953 fears, private-enterprise economies achieved high rates of investment and growth rivalling those in eastern Europe. Entrepreneurs benefited from official demand management and full-employment policies, and could invest more confidently in the knowledge that counter-cyclical economic management by the state was smoothing out the trade fluctuations which had bedevilled inter-war economic life. As this management was widely regarded as resting on scientific foundations, it is not surprising that Shonfield should have concluded confidently that there was 'no reason to suppose that the patterns of the past . . . will reassert themselves in the future'. Wise policy, social solidarity and adaptable institutional cooperation guaranteed for western Europe one of the most remarkable achievements of its history.[27]

THE WELFARE STATES

This 'unexpectedly dazzling' revival of capitalism took place, of course, in a world where the extension of state power was accepted not only in the economic sphere itself, but also in the area of social welfare. For many commentators at the time, the two – a booming economy and an extended welfare state – seemed closely connected. 'Without the underpinning of welfare-state policies,' argued the SPD reformist Karl Schiller, 'the free market economic system might well have collapsed . . . Welfare state and dynamic market economy are mutually indispensable.'[28]

In the Thatcher years, of course, such ideas came under attack. Spending on the welfare state, it was argued, had actually held back economic growth, not helped it forward. Less an argument about the economics of the 1950s than about the politics of the 1980s, it must be said that the historical record fails to bear out such a critical assessment. In Britain spending on welfare was actually a lower proportion of GDP than it was in West Germany, for example. In western Europe as a whole, low growth was accompanied by low spending on social services.[29]

Because the state's post-war involvement in social welfare coincided with the consolidation of European democracy, some have argued that it was an essentially democratic phenomenon. The phrase 'welfare state' had, after all, been coined in opposition to Hitler. In 1950 Attlee talked of his government having laid 'the foundations of the Welfare State', and within a few years the term had passed into common usage. It seemed to mark a watershed in the relationship between state and individual, and perhaps also as the sociologist T. H. Marshall argued, to inaugurate a new understanding of the notion of citizenship in a democracy, with social and economic rights now added to political ones.[30]

But Marshall's linkage of democracy and welfare reflected the specific experiences of Britain and Sweden. Elsewhere, post-war welfare arrangements reflected strong continuities with pre-war conservative and fascist regimes, while in eastern Europe they emerged under communism. It is salutory to remember that the term 'the life-ensuring state', introduced into West German discussions of social policy by the constitutional lawyer Ernst Forsthoff, had in fact been first employed by him – approvingly – in 1938 in the context of the Third Reich. Post-war Italian social services, too, basically worked through the network of semi-autonomous agencies set up under Mussolini.[31]

Yet despite these continuities of tradition, the Second World War did separate two very different policy environments. The world of the post-war welfare state was one of full employment, fast population growth and relative internal and external peace inside Europe. Inter-war social policy, by contrast, had been made against a backdrop of mass unemployment, fears of population decline, revolution, political extremism and war. In both eras, the state took the lead, but whereas before 1940 it aimed to secure the health of the collectivity, the family, and above all, the nation, after the war it acted chiefly in order to expand opportunity and choices for the individual citizen. Each epoch reacted against its predecessor: post-1918 against the individualism of mid-nineteenth-century liberalism, post-1945 against inter-war collectivism. To that extent Marshall's stress on citizenship hits the mark.

The post-war welfare state reflected some real differences of philosophy and institution across western Europe. West Germany, for instance, like the UK, had an ambitious housing policy and was building hundreds of thousands of council homes each year, while the post-war 'sack of Rome' and the sprawling concrete jungle surrounding Athens testified to the indifference of the state in southern Europe where housing was concerned. The British welfare system was financed through national taxation, free at the point of delivery and designed to provide a basic minimum to all citizens. In France, Belgium and Germany on the other hand, the government supported voluntary insurance schemes where contributions were linked to earnings. In these systems, welfare arrangements perpetuated existing income and status differences and were thus basically conservative in their social impact, whereas in Sweden the state was at the other extreme, intervening actively to reduce income inequality. Thus there were, according to one scholar, at least 'three worlds' or models of welfare capitalism in western Europe: conservative Catholic; liberal; and social democratic.

Everywhere, though, state spending on social services was rising. In the UK, spending on social services as a percentage of GNP rose from 11.3 per cent in 1938 to 16.3 in 1955 and 23.2 per cent in 1970. Over the same period total public expenditure was rising from 30.0 per cent of GNP to 47.1 per cent by 1970, by which point social services accounted for nearly half of all public spending. Across most of western Europe, public spending rose after the war proportionate to national income; simultaneously the composition of that spending changed, as the proportion spent on defence fell and welfare rose. Because national income itself was rising fast, as a result of the boom, the result was that per capita welfare spending by the state everywhere rose dramatically, accelerating in the 1960s before slowing down once more at the start of the following decade. During the two decades of the economic boom, moreover, the divergences between different countries became less apparent. In 1950, for example, it was only in Denmark, Britain, Norway and Sweden that the proportion of the labour force covered by accident, health, old-age and unemployment insurance topped 70 per cent; by 1970, this figure had been reached everywhere except in the southern fringe of Greece, Portugal and Spain.[32]

To generalize, it seems as though the war had created – or intensified – a demand for social solidarity, while the economic upswing created the resources to support this change. Nor, of course, should it be forgotten that the change in attitudes applied to government revenues as well as spending: in other words, after 1945 people enjoying the security of full employment accepted rates of taxation which would have seemed unthinkable ten or twenty years earlier. Why they did so remains a question entirely ignored by historians – the history of taxation is not the most glamorous of subjects – yet it is a fundamental feature of the post-war evolution of west European society which marks off its own experience of capitalism from that of the USA or Asia.[33]

Strangely, perhaps, the expansion of the state's responsibilities in the 1950s and 1960s was accompanied by a growing sense of disillusionment. 'All the impulses and ideals of the 1940s to recreate, rebuild and replan have now collapsed,' lamented the British social theorist Richard Titmuss. Rising expectations had certainly raised hopes and demands, and pushed poverty thresholds upwards. But neither the 'rediscovery of poverty' of the early 1960s, nor the more general concern at the nature of welfare provision, could be wholly attributed to rising expectations. The limits of the new welfare democracy were becoming clear.[34]

As the egalitarian hopes of the 1940s faded, people slowly realized that the coming of the welfare state had made little difference to inequalities of wealth. Income distribution was not significantly altered (outside Scandinavia) since there was little attempt to use either the tax or the benefits system for broader redistributive purposes. For whom, then, had the welfare state come into existence? It looked increasingly as though the answer was not for the poor but rather for the better-off, the middle classes and that element of the old working class which was sharing in the fruits of full employment. This suspicion underpins a new view of the origins of the welfare state, which now tends to be seen as the outcome not so much of heroic working-class pressure as of middle-class interest groups, do-gooding paternalistic intellectuals and the risk-averse of all social strata.[35]

What was so surprising about this? It was just a further instance of the way post-war west European democracy had been stabilized by the middle classes turning radical agendas to their own ends. 'It may look at first sight as if the *bourgeoisie* had, as usual, filched what should have gone to the workers,' Marshall wrote. 'But in the circumstances, that was bound to happen in a free democracy and is bound to go on happening in the Welfare State. For the Welfare State is not the dictatorship of the proletariat and is not pledged to liquidate the *bourgeoisie*.'[36]

What some saw as the product of 1950s individualism, irresponsibility and selfishness, others regarded more neutrally as the growth of acquisitiveness and affluence. But the coming of the Affluent Society did pose new challenges to the Welfare State, which was linked in people's minds with the years of austerity, and based on a principle of universality that the rise in living standards made seem less urgent and even 'rather silly'. 'The acquisitive society', Marshall concluded, 'has succeeded in expanding its frontiers and converting its natural antagonists to its own creed.'

THE INDIVIDUALISTIC MOBILIZATION OF EUROPE

'Many people of my generation,' wrote Shonfield in 1965, 'who in the 1930s had come to take for granted the ineradicable destructiveness of capitalism, have lived through a major personal experience in witnessing the metamorphosis of the system since the war.' This metamorphosis could be interpreted negatively – by disappointed socialists – in terms of waning social responsibility and the decline of wartime egalitarian goals; it could also, however, be cast in a more positive light as part of a profound social transformation – what Alessandro Pizzorno termed the 'individualistic mobilization' of Europe. Capitalism's success eroded class rivalries and replaced the activist and utopian mass politics of the inter-war era with a more bloodless politics of consumption and management. Goods not gods were what people wanted.[37]

The origins of Europe's consumer society of course could be traced back well before the Second World War. If Henry Ford's USA was the prototype, it is true that even in inter-war Europe first signs could be found of the change in attitudes and aspirations that would become so evident in the 1950s and 1960s. Opening the 1934 Berlin Automobile Show, Hitler had stated that:

As long as the automobile remains a means of transport for especially privileged circles, it is with a bitter feeling that millions of obedient, diligent, and able fellows, who in many cases live lives of limited opportunities, know themselves to be denied a mode of transportation that would open for them, especially on Sundays and holidays, a source of unknown, joyous happiness ... The class-emphasizing and therefore socially divisive character that has been attached to the automobile must be removed; the car must not remain an object of luxury but must become an object of use![38]

Such bold proclamations, however, ran up against the realities of the 1930s. Hitler's words were belied by the fact that economic stringency and war mobilization prevented a single Volkswagen being sold to the public in the Third Reich. But once the war ended, the popular tolerance of rationing and austerity quickly vanished. Even when people recognized the fairness of rationing, they increasingly demanded its ending and the reinstatement of the market. From the early 1950s onwards, as wartime controls were cast aside, the outlines of the new shopping culture became clearer.

The production of desires preceded the purchase of goods. Well before more than a small minority were able to afford the new consumer durables and other wonders, advertising agencies and retailers had revolutionized their practices. In the words of the Burton's Manager's Guide for 1953: 'Create desire to possess strong enough to overcome a natural antipathy to parting with money and you will make sale after sale.' Traditional salesmanship was transformed. Women, far from being ignored, were spotlighted as the 'motor' of 'modern life': advertisers saw them in the 1950s chiefly in domestic terms and concentrated on 'hitting the housewife'. 'You can't do any longer without electricity, espresso and Cola,' ran one German ad. 'But you can do without cooking! All these wonders are now yours, dear housewife! What your grandmother and mother had to suffer through by hand, a tiny miracle machine will handle in seconds ... Tell your husband to dig a little deeper into his pocket!' 'I put the woman in first place,' commented an Italian businessman, 'then the dog, the horse and finally the man.' By the early sixties, advertisers were starting to distinguish the 'little Mums' from the 'timid mouseburger' and the sexy, single 'Cosmo girl' whom models popularized with the new 'leaping about' style.[39]

Old-fashioned snob appeal, which in a way acknowledged the permanence of status and class differences, was now being challenged by advertising which made a purchaser believe it was possible to move a few steps up the social ladder. 'American' advertising methods targeted the 'new status hunters ... the C2 commuters who drink lager instead of beer, smoke tipped instead of plain, eat plain chocolate instead of milk, and the young AB executives who've just acquired an open-plan and garden in the suburbs'. In 1937 only four American agencies had branches outside the USA; by 1960 there were thirty-six, with over 280 offices.[40]

Their techniques of classifying potential buyers rested on a foundation of new disciplines – market research, testing and applied psychology – dissected in Georges Perec's novel of sixties consumerism, Les Choses (Things). 'Psychology, the science which we thought was to be the handmaiden of education,' wrote one alarmed observer, 'has been prostituted to serve the ends of salesmanship, the panjandrum of the inflated economy.' Such voices were crying in the wilderness: advertising as a profession lost the disreputable associations it had had before the war and became an exciting and even glamorous occupation.[41]

The advertising revolution spread through the new mass media: commercial advertising appeared on television from the mid-1950s, while the growth of telephone ownership stimulated the emergence of Yellow Pages retail directories at the start of the 1960s. In that same period, the Sunday papers began to introduce colour supplements which carried articles as well as adverts extolling the new 'lifestyles' on offer. And there was even help for the anxious purchaser negotiating this proliferation of goods. In 1957 the new Association for Consumer Research, supported by the American Consumers' Union, began publishing Which?, and in a few years acquired a readership of nearly half a million.

The new desires thus created and diffused were satisfied faster than before. Attitudes to credit and debt were changing. The French peasant's view that 'credit is a festering sore on the body of commerce' was challenged, not only by the spread of hire-purchase schemes, but even by the commercial banks themselves through 'the active merchandizing of a range of banking services that are increasingly being adapted to cater for customers who have never before held bank accounts'. Thanks to these financial innovations, the consumer revolution got under way. Mild inflation acted as an incentive. As one cautious French villager put it in 1961: 'The way prices keep going up, it's stupid not to get what you want when you want it – within reason, of course.'[42]

'Well-being' started in the home: all the evidence points to people purchasing refrigerators, washing machines, televisions and other domestic appliances as a priority. Although sales of such goods boomed, it must be emphasized that it was only gradually that the poorer social strata shared in their enjoyment. In this respect, contemporary adverts from the 1950s and early 1960s were not so much depicting reality as proposing the future. In 1959, for example, roughly three quarters of all French executives owned a car, compared with a fifth of workers and an eighth of agricultural workers; TV ownership lagged even more slowly, becoming widespread only late in the 1960s.

The car was perhaps the single most important consumption good of them all. Car production in western Europe grew from half a million per annum in 1947 to over nine million annually by 1967. Ownership soared from 51,314 in 1950 to 404,042 in 1960, and 876,913 in 1966 in Austria; from 342,000 to 4.7 million in Italy between 1950 and 1964; from 1.4 million in 1949 to 9.5 million in 1962 in West Germany. As rail usage declined, the network of motorways spread across the continent. Work on the Paris Périphérique started as early as 1956; the expressway along the right bank of the Seine in 1967; in October 1964, at the completion of the Autostrada del Sole which united Milan and Naples, the Archbishop of Florence held a thanksgiving service in the Florence North service station.[43]

Congestion created a need for specialist traffic planners – competing with wartime bombers to level Europe's historic city centres – for traffic wardens, parking meters (first spotted around 1959) and yellow no-parking lines. From the late 1960s, cars also stimulated the development of out-of-town shopping, hitting small retailers in town centres and reinforcing the spread of the new supermarkets. In France, for instance, there were just forty supermarkets in 1960; by 1970 there were over 1,000: the age of Prisunic and Monoprix had arrived.[44]

Rising living standards also encouraged spending on leisure. Not by chance did Coca-Cola stick for two decades to its winning slogan for the German market: 'Mach mal Pause' (Give yourself a Break). In 1948 some 3.1 million manual workers in Britain enjoyed two weeks' paid holiday; by the mid-1950s that figure had risen to 12.3 million – virtually the entire manual workforce. More people were taking holidays than ever before, and spending more on them. From the late 1960s, package deals to foreign destinations became increasingly popular: in 1971 only one third of British adults had ever been abroad on holiday; by 1984 only one third had not. As the United Nations recognized in making 1967 'International Tourist Year', tourism was now a major industry and Europe was at its heart, both supplying and receiving the bulk of the world's tourists. For the OECD, tourism was 'one of the most spectacular features of the "leisure civilization" which is gradually developing in the western world'. Tourism was also redistributive, channelling money – at some environmental cost – back into those areas which had been left behind by the boom, places like the continent's southern fringes, now lined with new tourist developments, or its unspoilt rural landscapes, now as often visited as worked.[45]

These tourists were easy meat for cultural critics, who rarely admitted that tourism might have any merit in, say, breaking down the insularities of the past. American Paul Fussell contrasted the gentlemanly and perceptive 'traveller' of pre-war vintage with the modern package barbarians. Hans Magnus Enzensberger's *Theorie des Tourismus* saw tourists as engaged in a hopeless, fundamentally bourgeois quest for freedom from the travails of industrial society. Alternatively, they were just part of that 'flight from freedom' which according to Erich Fromm betrayed the bourgeoisie's susceptibility to fascism.[46]

But such intemperate attacks formed part of a much broader assault on the new consumerism that brought together everyone from Catholic clerics, alarmed at the threat to the 'family and moral order', to high-minded Marxists like Pasolini who despised the fetishism of goods. In Franco's Spain, conservatives saw the boom of the 1960s corroding their 'Organic Democracy', driving the new 'tele-addict consumers' away from the old Catholic values. But even in genuine democracies, the dramatic social repercussions of the 'economic miracle' were encouraging alarm as well as satisfaction. Giorgio Bocca in his *Discovery of Italy* (*La scoperta dell'Italia* (1963)) described 'Italia boom! . . . transformed, hypnotized by *benessere* [prosperity]'.

The consumer – a passive, conformist object of commercial pressures – seemed to have replaced the active citizen imagined by social theorists during the 1940s. Now – in this brave new world of market research and TV advertising – perhaps not even people's desires were truly their own. For the influential early theorists of consumerism, centred around the Marxist Frankfurt school, the new 'mass society' allowed the forces of modern capitalism to play on the 'false consciousness' of ordinary people. As these left-wing elitists saw it, the same masses who before the war had abdicated their own judgement to follow Hitler, were now flocking mindlessly in droves into the stores.

Such interpretations were propped up by snobbery and exaggerated the homogenizing and conformist tendencies of the new consumerism; in fact – as a later generation of cultural critics pointed out – by the 1960s, 'lifestyle' merchandising was actually breaking down the standardization of 1950s fashion. For some optimists, like Baudrillard and Bourdieu, consumer cultures actually offered people a new freedom to define themselves and shape their own identity.

Against this, the rise of the new individualism *had* apparently eroded older, collectivist solidarities. The strike wave of the late 1940s – especially visible in France and Belgium – tapered off in the 1950s. 'There is little point in talking about the "proletariat" . . . because it simply no longer exists,' observes a source in 1958. As a former miner explained to an American journalist: 'I look around me here in Doncaster. It's not so long ago since I saw people ill-nourished, ill-clad, their homes sparsely furnished. Now you see them well-dressed, well-fed. You go into their homes and they have decorations, pianos, carpets, radios, some of them are getting TV sets. It's all changed.'[47]

Working and middle classes alike split between those able to enjoy the new wealth and those left out in the cold. The white-collar and managerial sectors expanded, while the peasantry rapidly contracted. Ferdynand Zweig, in his study of the British worker, found the connotation of class changing. The term was 'invariably linked with snobbishness but rarely, if at all, with class struggle'. Its range of associations had shrunk, and was increasingly regarded as belonging only to the workplace itself. As one worker told him: 'I am working-class only in the works, but outside I am like anyone else.' Classes in the old-fashioned sense – offering collective action, identities and activities inside and outside the factory – were vanishing. Converging patterns of consumption (and reproduction) were blurring the old social boundaries.[48]

German commentators seemed especially conscious of the dangers in a society which had swung from one extreme – of political fanaticism and violence – into passivity and apathy. A society once torn apart by class struggle seemed now to have fallen asleep. Karl Bracher warned of 'the frightful image of a mere technocracy' leading to an 'authoritative remodeling of parliamentary democracy'. Without an active citizenry, Europe would degenerate into a 'self-satisfied expertocracy' which placed all its faith in managerial solutions. Jürgen Habermas insisted that technology and science had themselves become a sort of ideology 'that penetrates into the consciousness of the depoliticised mass of the population'. American political scientists who hailed the 'end of ideology' were talking about the same process, but more positively.[49]

If the Americans had indeed intended to defuse class tensions in western Europe through their 'politics of productivity', it looked – during the fifties – as if they had succeeded. One is reminded of the American official in Italy who had opined back in 1947 that 'there is little hope that the Italians will achieve a state of prosperity and internal calm until they start to be more interested in the respective merits of cornflakes and cigarettes than in the relative abilities of their political leaders'. Had his desires now been realized? Had western Europe in its turn abandoned politics and been transformed into the society of 'happy slaves' which French anti-Americans saw across the Atlantic?[50]

THE AMERICANIZATION OF EUROPE?

'Ten years ago we could still look down on the snack bars, the supermarkets, the strip-tease houses and the entire acquisitive society,' wrote a French critic in 1960. 'Now all that has more or less taken hold in Europe. This society is not yet ours, but it – or one resembling it – could be our children's. The United States is a laboratory exhibiting life forms into which we have entered whether we like it or not.'[51]

In the 1950s, the homogenization of patterns of living across national and social boundaries seemed to many people to mark a loss of identity, and the evolution of a typically American model of society. If mass consumption was an American invention, then did not the spread of the car, Coca-Cola and the TV presage the end of Europe's distinctiveness? 'Is what we have here the tendency of a new age through which it is possible to make out the pattern of future societies,' asked Pizzorno, 'or only a momentary flash after which we can expect the return of the same old problems and impasses, the same old contradictions and conflicts?'[52]

So far as most American policy-makers were concerned, Americanization was indeed the goal. In other words, they regarded the USA as providing a model for the resolution of social and economic conflicts which should if possible be applied faithfully to western Europe: this was the conviction underlying the productivity drive, the promotion of European federalism and free trade, and the advocacy of new types of technology (such as TV) and marketing (scientific management, aggressive advertising).

But how far had Europeans entered this new world? Their protests were certainly loud enough; American hegemony elicited a growing anti-Americanism, particularly in France. Keeping out Coca-Cola, struggling hard to gain a foothold in France, was seen by *Le Monde* in a revealingly hopeless metaphor as fighting for the 'Danzig of European culture'. Across the Channel, playing Greece to Washington's

Rome, the British too found themselves torn between humiliation and pride at their subordination in 'the special relationship'.[53]

Yet anti-Americanism was markedly less pronounced lower down the social scale among those enjoying the new popular cultures than among the intellectuals and defenders of the old high culture. It was also weaker in the countries that had lost the war (Germany, Austria and Italy) than in those which believed they had won it. This was surely because anti-Americanism (and by extension fears of 'Americanization') was closely connected first with the goal of neutralism ('neither Coca-Cola nor vodka') and second with a sense of post-imperial humiliation. It was not enough that the former imperial powers should be forced to lose their colonial possessions; they – or their elites – now saw themselves turned into a colony in their turn. By contrast, in Germany and Austria, the *Amis* were seen as more of a positive force, offering a new modern identity to mask the awkward national memories of the recent past.

Moreover, the shaping of a less deferential, more egalitarian and forward-looking society was not indeed solely nor even primarily the product of American influence. Images of American life certainly helped, as seen in films from the 1920s onwards. But mass democracy, fascism, the war and Nazi occupation had all effectively swept away much of the old order in Europe before the Americans arrived. The process continued under their hegemonic gaze, it is true, but reflected forces rooted deep in European politics as well. The cinema – often regarded as the spearhead of Americanization – in fact betrayed a more complex relationship: Hollywood films were, of course, immensely popular in Europe. But indigenous film-making traditions – British 'Carry-On' farces, the German *Heimatfilm*, and the French *nouvelle vague* – survived and flourished, even if they did not export well.

In general, American influences were modified once they came into contact with European traditions and wishes. Coca-Cola might have tasted the same on either side of the Atlantic, but other goods were altered. Cars, for example, looked smaller and more modest: Europeans embraced the VW, the Fiat 500, the Morris Minor and the Mini, not to mention the Vespa and Lambretta, which had no obvious parallel in the USA. Even large cars looked different: an expensive, crafted 'European' look – as on the Jaguar XK 140, the Gordon Keeble and the Bristol – was deliberately retained; the Sunbeam Rapiers, Vauxhall Victors and Ford Zephyrs – plebeian 'dream cars' with their rocket fins – hardly swept the board. Flashy Crestas and Zodiacs were easily outsold in the UK, for instance, by the resolutely traditional Austin Westminster.

It was the same story in architecture. Modernism came back eastwards out of exile and brought skyscrapers and apartment blocks, American embassy buildings, and corporate HQs. Yet the resultant skyline was not quite American; the buildings tended to be lower, and blended more deliberately with the existing street frontage. Suburbs never destroyed the life of urban centres as they did in the USA, perhaps because the flight to the suburbs lacked the disturbing racial impetus it had there.[54]

America was anyway not a homogeneous set of influences; it was an amalgam of different, often contradictory, strands, some real, others mythical. It was as much an idea as a reality, capable of turning into the vehicle for the creative fantasies of Europeans, whether young fashion victims, rock 'n' roll stars like 'Freddy Quinn' (real name Manfred Nidl-Petz) and Ray Miller (Rainer Müller) or film director Sergio Leone, reinventing the Western as Homeric epic in Spain or Ciné-Città.[55]

America offered a variety of models for Europeans to draw on in their own social and political struggles. There was, for example, the 'national security' state (which of course also built upon respectably indigenous traditions of anti-communism everywhere in western Europe); there was the new consumerism. But then there was also the anti-advertising movement, which benefited from American critics like Vance Packard, whose best-selling *The Hidden Persuaders* appeared just as commercial TV advertising started in the UK. The struggle for civil rights, above all, helped to shape both local protest and national legislation in Europe in the mid-1960s and 1970s.

In retrospect what is striking about the 'Americanization' debate is the way it fizzles out some time in the 1960s. It is as though by then most Europeans had lost their feelings of inferiority to their transatlantic protector. Loss of empire had not, it was becoming clearer, led to economic decline; on the contrary, Europe was becoming more and more powerful a force in the international economy, while American power was showing signs of faltering. The old fears of being taken over by American multinationals (expressed most vociferously by Servan-Schreiber in *Le Défi américain*), were allayed by the knowledge that western Europe was now a net investor in the USA. The old nation-state had not disappeared, as many had feared when confronted with the federalist enthusiasm of the Marshall Planners in the late forties. Instead it had survived and grown even stronger. Even TV, originally heralded as the ultimate dissolver of national cultures, had turned out in fact to have created a *stronger* feeling of nationhood, destroying the sense of allegiance to locality and region. Western Europe had accepted the new consumerism as its own.[56]

PROTEST IN THE GROWTH SOCIETY

In 1955 the jurist Piero Calamandrei, one of the architects of the post-war Italian constitution, attacked the extent of his country's recent democratic achievement. The hopes of the resistance had been dashed by conservative obstruction, he argued, the constitution itself remained 'unrealized', and behind the façade of a 'formal democracy' lay the reality of continuities and compromises with Fascism and the 'police state'. The continued use of the 1931 Law on Public Security was but the most blatant example of democracy's imperfections in Italy; there was no real freedom of movement or assembly or genuine equality between the sexes.[57]

In the 1960s, a younger, more urban Europe became conscious of the vast social changes which had taken place since the war, and demanded that politics and the law catch up. The old world of peasants and aristocrats was disappearing through economic growth, where it had not been destroyed by the war, and a more mobile, less deferential society emerged. This wanted real liberty in the Free World, and was no longer prepared to accept that calls for social reform be written off as communist subversion. It was bolstered by changes in Washington, where the elderly Eisenhower was replaced by Kennedy and the Democrats.

As Cold War fears receded in Europe, conservatives in office looked increasingly tainted by the past. There was near civil war in Italy in 1960 when the Tambroni government took office with the support of neo-Fascists. In France, the war in Algeria spilled over on to the mainland. When police in Paris broke up a demonstration and killed dozens of protesters, hurling them into the Seine in one of the least-publicized and most atrocious acts of mass violence in post-war western Europe, the man in charge was Maurice Papon, who had been a prominent Vichy official. In Greece, the Karamanlis government was rocked by revelations of the wartime collaboration of senior ministers, and clung to power through rigged elections. In West Germany, the 1962 Spiegel affair reawoke memories of the Gestapo, while both Chancellor Kiesinger and President Lübke were haunted by their Nazi past. Adolf Eichmann's trial in 1961 brought the whole issue into the spotlight. It seemed increasingly that Cold War normalcy and prosperity had allowed only a partial or even nominal democracy behind which lurked older authoritarian forces.

The political beneficiaries of this new mood were the parties of the centre–left – Harold Wilson in the UK, the SPD in West Germany, the 'opening to the Left' in Italy, and George Papandreou with his 'unending struggle' in Greece. Labour and social democratic parties returned to power, as managers of a more modern society. Like the conservative Right before them, they were slowly emancipating themselves from class affiliation, and turning themselves into broader catch-all parties which could respond to deep, gradual shifts in popular opinion. These governments were keener than their predecessors to use the state to improve educational and health services, and to legislate for reform in areas of social and civil rights. The real prospect of change, in turn, fed the appetite of movements and lobby groups calling for reform and modernization. Thus the 1960s marked the beginning of a new deepening of democracy in western Europe, the real break with traditional social values and institutions, and – for many – the onset of modernity.

In December 1965, the case of a young Sicilian peasant woman called Franca Viola hit the Italian headlines after she was abducted and raped by a young man whose offer of marriage she had refused.

Normally in such situations – by no means uncommon – the woman was expected to yield, so that what the Italian Penal Code defined as *matrimonio riparatore* could cancel out the man's offence. For the first time anyone could remember, however, the raped woman refused to get married. As a result, her suitor was arrested and eventually sentenced to jail. It was Viola's obstinacy which local opinion in her home town regarded as dishonourable. But in the rest of Italy the case caused a sensation, and underlined women's lack of equal status and dignity in the eyes of the law.[58]

In the 1960s, the demand for greater democracy was spearheaded by a growing awareness of women's continuing social and economic subordination. Constitutions might promise equality to all citizens irrespective of gender, but under existing penal codes, men and women were often treated quite differently. Men could commit adultery with impunity while women laid themselves open to punishment. Husbands could prohibit their wives seeking work outside the home, and fathers retained absolute power over the children. In Switzerland women did not even gain the vote until the 1970s; in France many could not open their own bank accounts. Large numbers of women continued to enter the labour market, yet once there they faced discriminatory pay and working prospects.

In many ways, the move for female emancipation had been on the retreat in Europe since the early 1920s; certainly the inter-war years, beset by fears of national decline through falling birth rates and by mass unemployment, had seen women's rights eroded. Even Soviet Russia, which had given women unprecedented legal equality after 1918, reverted to the ideology of motherhood in the mid-1930s. Now reforms to benefit women, and to increase their autonomy, independence and equality before the law, threatened the basis of the traditional European family as it had been sanctified in the inter-war years and reaffirmed in the conservative 1950s. Demands for sexual liberty were even more frightening. An Italian Catholic sociologist castigated 'the exasperated individualism which is carrying the American and North European family to the edge of total disintegration' and warned against 'a conception of matrimony as a mere sexual benefit for the individual'.[59]

Yet the tide was turning in favour of reform, as an army of social commentators and psychiatrists discovered the costs of home-bound isolation, and what the French called the 'Madame Bovary syndrome'. In *The Captive Wife*, sociologist Hannah Gavron stood the 1950s ideal of domesticity on its head, to reveal the depressions and frustrations it bred, as extended family and communal bonds withered, and television and traffic pushed the nuclear family indoors.

Changing sexual practices (chiefly through the pill, which entered western Europe in the early 1960s), and the emergence of a newly independent generation that aimed at higher education and professional autonomy, prefigured the legal reforms which came at the end of the decade. Birth control liberated itself from its pre-war eugenic implications and family-planning clinics spread across Europe. Most Scandinavian countries had legalized abortion very early; Britain followed in 1967. But in Catholic Europe, the battle took longer, mobilized hundreds of thousands of women and led to major political conflicts before decriminalization occurred, chiefly – and very hesitantly – during the 1970s. Even today, abortion is only available in Germany and Portugal on very limited grounds, and illegal abortions continue to be widespread.

Legal changes were more rapid where contraceptives were concerned, no doubt because the baby boom had made the old fears of population decline seem irrational. In 1961 Nazi police ordinances against the sale of contraceptives were finally taken off the books in West Germany, and France relaxed its prohibitions in 1967; Italy repealed Fascist legislation four years later. As for realizing the equal status of women in marriage and the family, the reform of divorce procedures and of family law generally took place in the 1970s, and – in post-dictatorship southern Europe – in the 1980s, more than sixty years after civil divorce by mutual consent was introduced in Sweden and Bolshevik Russia.[60]

Slowest of all was effective action to secure equal rights in the workplace. Constitutional guarantees and Common Market directives mostly remained empty promises, and although a few countries such as the UK, the Netherlands, France and the Scandinavian north did bring in legislation on equal pay and treatment, too often provisions were unenforced, or realized only through lengthy court battles. In West Germany and Austria, entrenched conservatism made the outlook even bleaker.[61]

Overall, the battles for female emancipation and equality bore out Calamandrei's critique of post-war democracy: formal guarantees of constitutional rights had meant little without effective political action for their realization. This applied as much to the post-dictatorial constitutions of southern Europe (Spain, Portugal and Greece) as to the earlier post-1945 models. Constitutions might offer women full *political* rights; but without equality in private law and commercial practice as well, women remained subordinate to men. In the 1960s and 1970s, the struggle to achieve such equality formed one of the most remarkable and sustained examples of social protest in western Europe. Full equality was not gained, and neither were many of the rights which women claimed were necessary for their protection and well-being; but the paternalist basis of social institutions was exposed and gradually reformed. As so often, the starting point for reform in liberal democracies was exposing the gap between what they promised and what they really provided.

Nothing so revealed the continued authoritarianism in post-war conservative European politics as the generational warfare which broke out during the boom. In 1957 a law was passed in Austria to protect young people from immoral influences, including 'dangers in the streets, the indiscriminate visits to restaurants and events, the consumption of alcohol and nicotine, and from all harmful influences from outside'. Such measures, it seemed to those in authority, were urgently needed. When Elvis Presley came to Europe, he turned teenagers into 'wild barbarians in ecstasy' or even 'haunted medicine men of a jungle tribe governed only by music', threatened western civilization with African primitivism, and drove young girls into 'intoxicating' sexual delinquency.[62]

Behind the rock 'n' roll hysteria of the 1950s and the equally hysterical reaction of the mainstream press and politicians was a very real challenge to post-war conservatism. A new front opened up between the adults who had gone through the war and their children.

Post-war economic growth helped fuel this. Generational authority was threatened by the emergence of a separate youth culture, based on the fourfold rise in teenage earnings between 1938 and 1960. Young people – more of them than ever before thanks to the post-war baby boom – were being sought after by employers and retailers. What puzzled and concerned commentators in the late 1950s was the way this growing affluence appeared to be accompanied by a new violence and lawlessness. This was what the Germans, faced with the rock 'n' roll cinema riots, called 'prosperity criminality' (*Wohlstandskriminalität*). In 1956 Bavaria's Interior Minister declared that, as 'humanitarian molly-coddling' had failed to make the *Halbstarken* behave, the authorities would now act 'with brutality'. In Italy the activities of the *teppisti*, gangs of teenage joyriders, pushed an anxious government into passing 'regulations for the repression of hooliganism'. (Conservatives in Greece followed suit.) Observers were quick to point out the link between the new vandals' love of cars and the consumer boom with its spreading auto culture.[63] In England – whose Victorian mores had probably been less shaken up by the war than anywhere else – the problem seemed equally serious. 'Get rid of that suit and try to become a decent member of society,' an outraged magistrate told one Teddy boy. 'Dance halls, cinemas, police and public join forces to wage WAR ON THE TEDDY BOYS,' reported the *Sunday Dispatch* on 27 June 1955. 'Menace in the streets of Britain being cleared up at last.'[64]

Some put the problem down to the effects of the war on family stability. Yet it was around 1954 – coinciding with the ending of austerity – that juvenile crime and disorder had suddenly taken an upward turn, with large gangs brawling in cafés and clubs. A sympathetic observer of 'rebellious youth' connected these trends with the disintegration of older social norms: on the one hand, the working class was splintering; on the other, the 'bourgeois age' of a dominant middle class was being replaced by a broader, mass culture. Some working-class youths could rise socially in this setting; but others were marginalized more than before.

In fact, retrospect suggests that the whole problem was blown up out of all proportion; there was rather *little* youth violence, considering the extent of social disruption during and after the war. Conservatives demonized the *teppisti*, the Teddy boys and the *Halbstarken*, and exaggerated their significance. Most countries had long traditions of urban youth riots. But in the stolidly conformist climate of the 1950s and early 1960s even small disturbances and signs of independence threatened the authority of a ruling generation which – just as in eastern Europe – felt increasingly unable to understand its own children. They were disobedient, wore scandalous clothes and hairstyles, and took for granted – when not actually attacking – the achievements that their parents had made through self-sacrifice and hard work since the war.

'My parents, relatives and their friends live like mice in a closed cage . . . and want us to live the same way,' wrote a girl to the Italian teenage magazine *Mondo Beat* in 1965. 'They want more money and spend it on stupid things: a bigger television, covers for their cars . . . But they don't know how to really enjoy themselves.' German student leader Rudi Dutschke fulminated against 'aggressive and fascist consumerism'. The children of the consumer revolution were thus turning against it and coming back to politics and protest. What was so enigmatic was the way they combined an anti-consumerist stress on spiritual enjoyment, on love, Flower Power and individual self-fulfilment with older kinds of political visions – of social revolution, class war, strikes and barricades.[65]

First in West Berlin, later in France and Italy, youthful dissatisfaction with the mainstream Left was expressed in a radical critique of post-war social development. In December 1966, for instance, students demonstrated down the Ku'damm, symbol of Berlin's new shopping culture, just before Christmas. They attacked the 'myth of Western democracy' and drew on Marxist critiques of consumerism to decry the emptiness and authoritarianism they saw around them. The Vietnam War had shattered the American dream even – perhaps particularly – in countries like West Germany and Italy, where it had been so strong before.[66]

The signs of a revival of mass protest were already visible – in the marches of CND in the early 1960s, in the violent demonstrations against American involvement in Vietnam, against the Greek colonels' coup in 1967, and the Shah's tyranny in Iran. TV images of the civil-rights marches in the USA, together with a reawakening interest in the legacy of resistance from the Second World War, fed a growing anti-authoritarianism. In 1968 came the explosion: campus sit-ins, riots, strikes and demonstrations rocked Europe, threatening at one point to topple the de Gaulle government; street fighting returned to the streets of Paris, Berlin and Milan. The scale of the turmoil shocked and delighted those who had observed the apathy and conformism of middle-class youth in the previous decade. For subsequent generations, '68' came to assume the proportions of a myth, a myth fed subsequently by the large number of its participants who as writers, broadcasters, teachers or film-makers found themselves able to provide a public interpretation of what it had all meant. 'It would not be unjust', writes Sunil Khilnani in his study of the intellectual Left in France, 'to see 1968 as an interpretation in search of an event.'[67]

To a later and perhaps more cynical generation, the turmoil of 1968 looks less impressive than it did to its protagonists, more noise than lasting achievement, a product in many ways of the very prosperity the students were attacking, and an unrepresentative product at that. Despite the rapid expansion of student numbers – itself, of course, an achievement of post-war democracy – only a small proportion of the youthful population was actually involved in the upheavals: in the mid-sixties only 5.5 per cent of twenty-year-olds in the UK were in higher education (8.6 per cent in Italy, 7.7 per cent in West Germany, 16 per cent in France). Their demands too were unclear: stressing the present rather than the future, absolute liberty and freedom of expression, hindered the expression of unified, concrete demands. Indeed when these finally emerged in an organized shape, they took the form of an extreme Marxist sectarianism – 'Stalin, Mao and the "great Popular Republic of Albania"' – which left many of the original participants cold.

The events of 1968 thus created a fragmented and bitterly dogmatic Leftist fringe, tempted by violence and unable or unwilling to comprehend the scale of capitalism's triumph. It had its own way of life, with endless proclamations, critiques and public theses, and a fondness for intellectual gurus whose pronouncements did not save their followers from a complete misreading of the political situation. This detachment from the realities of power reached its culminating expression in the terrorist Red Army Faction in West Germany, which saw itself as a 'city guerrilla force' carrying out an armed 'anti-imperial struggle' under the slogan 'Victory in the People's War!' These terrorist groups and the police repression and right-wing counter-terrorism they provoked mostly disappeared by the end of the 1970s. But for a time they raised the spectre of that inter-war political extremism and ideological polarization which most of western Europe hoped had been left behind for good.[68]

And yet the student radicals did have some real achievements to their credit. First, they drew attention to a vacuum of belief at the heart of post-war politics. Their passionate idealism reminded people of the need for political and ideological debate; not all problems are reducible to questions of scientific management or interest-group bargaining. Second, their often satirical attack on post-war authoritarianism, if exaggerated, was well aimed, and encouraged a more critical look at the centres of corporate, military and political power. Finally, they acted as a typical interest group, securing resources for the university system and opening it up to more democratic influences.

Effective if less glamorous interest-group action was also being mounted by the organized working class, as student dissatisfaction coincided with an upsurge in labour unrest and inflationary pressures. The protests of 1968 showed that class activism had been written off too quickly: in fact, post-war state-led corporatism was coming under strain as never before. With full employment, the unions pressed for long-delayed wage rises, and used the opportunity provided by the students' actions to attack the prevailing distribution of wealth. In Italy and France, the result was that the protests of thousands of students were quickly supplemented by a wave of strikes as millions of unionists demanded a fairer share in the growth society.

Yet if the students wanted to do away with capitalism, the workers aimed instead to enjoy more of its profits. Their aims were thus divergent, and it is not surprising that once the unions had achieved most of their demands, hopes of a continued student–worker alliance quickly faded. The working class was no longer revolutionary: its bargaining power was at its height in these last years of the boom, and its most advanced sectors were able to use this to their advantage. As a result, in the early 1970s, union bosses and frightened conservative opponents both fell into the trap of exaggerating labour's political strength. In fact, the fortunes of western Europe's workers rose and fell with capitalism itself. This was to prove the last victory for the old working class in a century of organized struggle, before recession, mass unemployment and global restructuring wiped it out in little more than a decade.

MIGRATIONS

In 1964 the German magazine *Der Spiegel* devoted its cover to a Portuguese worker called Armando Rodríguez, hailed as the one millionth 'migrant worker' to enter the country, and greeted at Cologne with an official welcome and the present of a motorbike. This was an era when immigrants were welcomed and regarded as indispensable for continued prosperity.[69]

Post-war capitalism thirsted for labour, and demanded human mobility. Europe's nation-states, on the other hand, aimed to patrol their borders and to distinguish between their own citizens, to whom they offered an increasing array of rights and benefits, and foreigners. Thus there was – and remains – an inherent tension between the demands of capitalism and the nation-state where immigration is concerned. After 1950, mass immigration started out as an economic necessity but soon turned into a cultural and political issue which brought to the surface the racism still entrenched in European society. Fascism and communism had between them more or less eliminated many of eastern Europe's ethnic minorities; now capitalism introduced quite different minorities into the West. The evolution of multiracial societies became as great a challenge to post-war democracy in Europe as the struggle for gender equality.[70]

Of course western Europe, like the continent as a whole, had long supplied and received vast flows of human beings. The immigration wave after the war – somewhere around ten to fifteen million people in total – was dwarfed by the fifty-five to sixty million who had emigrated from the continent to the Americas before 1921. So far as labour mobility was concerned, German industry and agriculture in the nineteenth and early twentieth centuries had relied heavily upon Polish labour, while the French working class which evolved over the same period included many Belgians, Italians, Poles and Swiss. The use of migrant labour, much of which would become permanent, was nothing new in Europe's history.[71]

Yet the great post-war immigration was so completely unforeseen that after 1945 a wave of emigration took place from the continent, as governments viewed pessimistically the chances of avoiding long-term mass unemployment: this was why the Dutch, British, Italians and others encouraged overseas settlement. But at the same time, refugees were pouring into West Germany, while other countries accepted some of the millions of DPs who refused to return to eastern Europe. 'People were afraid for their jobs,' recalls a Polish man who settled in the UK after the war. 'They still remembered the slack before the war and that was understandable.'

Even at this stage, a link between immigration policy and racism was evident: Whitehall, for example, operated its European Volunteer Workers scheme in the late 1940s on the basis of a racial classification, granting priority to Balts and keeping out Jews. Still haunted by the old fears of population decline, Britain's post-war Royal Commission on Population – worried about national weakness in the face of Soviet expansionism – recommended that 'immigration on a large scale into a fully established society like ours could only be welcomed without reserve if the immigrants were of good human stock and were not prevented by their religion or race from inter-marrying with the local population and becoming merged with it'. Immigration and racial issues remained intertwined thereafter.[72]

Yet the dynamics of capitalism pushed in quite another direction. From the mid-1950s, sustained economic growth fed an apparently insatiable demand for labour. At first, this was satisfied domestically – either by refugees, as in Germany, or by the rural economy, which supplied hundreds of thousands of workers annually to the urban centres of western Europe. In Italy alone over nine million people moved from one part of the country to another. Between 1950 and 1972 the numbers working in the agricultural sector overall in the West fell from thirty million to 8.4 million, or from one third to one tenth of the total workforce of the original Six. The curtain fell on the centuries-old history of the European peasantry, and only the EEC's Common Agricultural Policy acted as a form of historic preservation of this vanishing species. In the cities, villagers found work, anonymity (from the repressive surveillance of relatives, the gendarme and the state) and new, more modern ways of living.[73]

As these sources were exhausted, employers started to look further afield. Switzerland and Sweden had been recruiting Italian labourers from as early as 1945, but the main effort started in the late 1950s. By the 1960s, France, Germany and Switzerland were competing for labour in southern Europe. The state tried, not very successfully, to control this trade: the West German Bundesanstalt für Arbeit set up recruiting offices in six countries round the Mediterreanean; the French, through the Office National d'Immigration, had no fewer than sixteen, mostly in Africa, operating on the basis of bilateral agreements between host and supplier country. In Britain, the state was less involved, partly because labour requirements could be satisfied by British citizens, and partly because of a traditional reluctance to intervene in, still less encourage, recruitment of workers from the empire. It was thus left to employers, like the National Health Service and London Transport, to arrange their own schemes. Even so, immigrants from Cyprus, the Indian subcontinent and the West Indies soon responded to the needs of the British labour market.

In fact, even in France and West Germany, the state actually had little control over the immigration process, and channelled only a small proportion of incoming workers through its offices. But in the 1960s this seemed scarcely to matter. In 1958 55,000 foreign workers entered Germany; by 1960 the number had risen to 250,000. In France numbers rose from around 150,000 annually in the late 1950s to 300,000 by 1970. What makes the trend even more remarkable is that both countries had, by British standards, enormous refugee influxes at the same time – three million young men fleeing East Germany by 1961, and one million *pieds noirs* from Algeria. Mass unemployment seemed a figment of the past; modern capitalism's insatiable demand for labour coped simultaneously with several millions of refugees, the twenty million or so west Europeans who moved from agricultural work to industry or services, *and* with the approximately ten million workers from southern Europe, the Mediterranean fringes or more far-flung colonies. European labour markets were internationalized, as the number of foreigners living in western Europe trebled in three decades.

The initial newcomers were young men, without families, lodged in inadequate accommodation and poorly treated by locals. Entrances to public parks in Switzerland carried signs saying 'No entry for dogs and Italians'. In English lodging houses the placards read: 'No Blacks, Irish or dogs.' Greek 'guest workers' in Germany were following in the steps of the forced labourers taken to the Reich during the war, barely a decade earlier: living conditions sometimes seemed little better. In Germany and Switzerland, those who came on the basis of the bilateral labour agreements were placed on short-term contracts and housed in hostels, segregated from the rest of the population. They enjoyed minimal rights and could be deported. Although legally the situation of workers in Britain and France was better than this, socially they suffered a similar degree of segregation and discrimination. Across western Europe, immigrant workers tended to cluster in urban centres, forming 12 per cent of the Paris population, 16 per cent in Brussels, 11 per cent in Stuttgart and 34 per cent in Geneva by the early 1970s.

One reason why governments had failed to plan any kind of long-term strategy for immigration on this scale was that they assumed it was a temporary phenomenon. For at least a century, migrants had provided a useful cushion, taking up the slack in the boom and shielding the indigenous workforce from unemployment during a downturn. In France, Germany and elsewhere, short-term and even seasonal contracts were the traditional instrument for regulating labour flows. Within a short time, however, it became apparent that not all immigrants intended to return home quickly: many Italians, Yugoslavs, Greeks and Spaniards did, but not so many from Turkey, the West Indies and India.

In a pattern identical to that observed among those European migrants to the USA in the nineteenth century, these incomers now brought over wives and started families. In the early 1970s, they were in fact pushed to do so by the threat of forthcoming immigration controls. Although they moved out of unpleasant hostels into flats of their own, their segregation did not cease, for as in the USA – though on a lesser scale – many whites moved house rather than live in a racially mixed neighbourhood, and enclaves began to appear in the cities. Soon a second generation emerged. Of the approximately 924,000 members of the 'coloured' population in the UK in 1966, 213,000 had been born there: what had started out as a question of immigration policy inescapably raised issues of race, citizenship and national culture.[74]

In his 1973 film, *Fear Eats the Soul*, Rainer Werner Fassbinder depicted a love affair between a Moroccan 'guest worker' and an older German woman, Emmi. They are 'just a rabble', her friends tell her, 'mean, filthy swine'. Surrounded by prejudice, the two get married, however, and have their wedding meal in a Munich restaurant once frequented by Hitler. As Fassbinder implied, pre-war and post-war racism were closely linked, and the influx of foreign workers brought out the enduring sense of superiority, the cultural anxiety and prejudice that were never far beneath the surface in west European society. In 1955 it had been London's Cypriots whom Teddy boys had attacked in the name of the 'white man'; three years later it was the West Indians living in Notting Hill. Although racist violence and overtly xenophobic politics were relatively uncommon, and indeed criticized by mainstream opinion, a milder form of racism was widespread and growing. In the early 1970s, the economic climate changed and became more hostile to continued immigration on a large scale.[75]

The late 1960s and early 1970s saw a series of restrictions placed upon immigration, with an increasingly evident racial bias. Both Britain and France retreated from their earlier relatively liberal imperial citizenship policies; the empire had collapsed more quickly than anyone could have predicted, and citizenship rights were swiftly confined to the *métropole*. In Britain legislation between 1962 and

1971 closed the door on new arrivals, except for the Irish, who remained the largest ethnic minority in the country. From 1968 British citizenship was, for the first time, made dependent on having a British parent. Similar developments followed in France, which tightened up its immigration procedures in the early 1970s. Further immigration was halted into France in 1974, and recruitment into Germany stopped at about the same time.

But stopping immigration was easier than taking action to improve race relations. West Germany, unlike the former imperial powers, always differentiated between ethnic Germans and 'guest workers'. The 1965 'Foreigners' Act' (*Ausländergesetz*) was an even more stringent measure than the National Socialist legislation it replaced; expulsion no longer depended on the behaviour of the individual worker but simply on the needs of the state. Keeping its head in the sand, the Bonn government steadfastly refused to acknowledge the new social realities. In the resolute words of the Federal Commission of 1977: 'The Federal Republic is not an immigrant country. Germany is a place of residence for foreigners who will eventually return home voluntarily.' Yet there were 1.3 million foreign workers there in 1966 and 2.6 million by 1973; foreigners were responsible for 4.3 per cent of all births in the country in 1966, and 17.3 per cent in 1974.[76]

Most countries took a long time to grapple seriously with racial prejudice. 'We were foreigners and treated as such,' recalled an east European who settled in Yorkshire. 'You – every time you had to prove yourself – that you were, well perhaps not equal, but almost.' The existence of prejudice was generally regarded as an unfortunate fact of political life, to be found on both Left and Right. There was no anti-discrimination machinery, and in most countries the state clearly believed that encouraging migrants to return home was the best answer to racial tensions (as in Bonn's 1983 Act to Promote the Preparedness of Foreign Workers to Return). Only a few people argued that such policies actually made the problem worse.[77]

Even in Britain, where limited race-relations legislation *was* enacted, the stimulus was effective lobbying by small groups rather than wide-scale public protest. The 1971 Immigration Act too contained provisions for 'repatriation', though these were never publicized or promoted, to avoid jeopardizing 'good race relations'. In fact, to judge from opinion polls, although west Europeans recognized that the expression of racial prejudice was no longer as acceptable as before the war, much of their underlying hostility towards foreigners, especially those from outside Europe, remained. Labour unions suspected immigrants of undercutting wages, conservatives feared them corrupting the national culture. Few seemed aware that Britain, for example, remained a net *exporter* of migrants for most of this period, that immigrants brought net economic gains to their host societies, or that immigrant populations formed a mere 2.3 per cent of the total population of western Europe (1970–71). Few would have agreed with one immigrant that 'as (your) culture enriches ours, ours enriches yours as well'. As economic optimism evaporated in the early 1970s, immigrants were transformed almost overnight from valued factors of production into a threat to jobs, a drain on the welfare state and unwanted aliens.[78]

IO

The Social Contract in Crisis

There is no such thing as society.
                                   – Margaret Thatcher, 1987

In those days no one knew what [time] was moving towards.
Nor could anyone quite distinguish between what was above and
below, between what was moving forwards and what backwards.
                        – Robert Musil, *The Man without Qualities*[1]

In the rethinking of democracy that took place during the Second
World War, the political forms of liberal parliamentarism were supplemented by a new commitment to social provision. The Golden Age
that followed was less collectivist than most wartime thinkers had
imagined, and owed much to something they had not expected – the
flowering in the 1950s of conservative individualism and economic
growth through regulated capitalism. The social contract which grew
out of this dual reform of capitalism and democracy evolved over
twenty-five years. It was influenced rather less by the Cold War and
superpower interventions than seemed apparent at the time, and rather
more by popular aspirations, historical memories of inter-war failure,
and economic performance. It rested, above all, upon the twin achievements of full employment and growth. Full employment brought in
the tax revenues to finance the burgeoning welfare state; growth
allowed gains in living standards to be shared out across the board.
Upon these bases, the democratic nation-state was built anew.

But in the early 1970s, this remarkable period in European history

– a time of extraordinary political stability compared with preceding decades – suddenly came to an end. A sense of crisis and malaise gripped the West, and tensions between labour and capital resurfaced with a new intensity. The oil shocks revealed European capitalism's vulnerability to the outside world. Growth was no longer seen as an unmitigated good, and its environmental dangers were spotlighted. Full employment became a memory, and neo-liberal economics came back into vogue.

Some intellectuals were quick to find evidence of a crisis of 'post-modernity', and certainly the contrast with the buoyant prosperity of the 1950s and 1960s was striking. Yet how deep a break was there with previous decades? Despite rising unemployment, and economic instability, there was no return to the 1930s. The rebuilt democratic order managed to adapt and weather the storm, far better in fact than its communist rival. Welfare regimes cushioned societies against the worst effects of impoverishment and insecurity. Conservatives momentarily feared the collapse of Western democracy; but it was actually the last remnants of the old dictatorial Right which fell – in Greece, Spain and Portugal – and then communism itself. The post-war social contract was thrown into crisis, but not destroyed, as west European nation-states came to realize the limits of their power and the need for concerted action to defend their way of life against global competition.

THE CRISIS OF INFLATION

Through the 1950s and 1960s, growth in western Europe was accompanied by a persistent gentle rise in prices. This was tolerated as necessary for social and industrial harmony, since it offered an apparently painless and unobtrusive means of buying off the working class, and avoiding the bitter social conflicts which had bedevilled Europe in the past. But as historian Charles Maier has pointed out, something began to go wrong in the late 1960s, and instead of acting as a 'social lubricant', inflation started to 'aggravate not smooth over distributional conflicts'. In the 1970s inflation developed from a technical issue in economics, to a fact of everyday life and, eventually, to a determinant of politics itself. Inflation introduced a new instability into the economic order and made people vote as consumers.[2]

The rise in price levels in the years before 1973 was certainly connected with the labour militancy of the late 1960s. The struggle between labour and capital coincided with the ending of the rapid productivity growth that had bought industrial peace for two decades, and the villains – according to taste – were either the workers and their exorbitant demands, or the employers and their reluctance to countenance a drop in profits. Either way, the upshot was the pessimistic view that full employment could not be sustained by west European capitalism without endangering price stability.

It should be remembered, though, that wage pressure was certainly not the sole cause of accelerating inflation. In the international economy, too, inflation was being stoked, both by the war in Vietnam (as the USA printed dollars to finance this) and by the rise in commodity prices on world markets. The two factors were connected – with the depreciation of the dollar brought about by the strain of financing the war in Vietnam forcing the end of the gold standard, introducing a new era of currency instability and encouraging primary producers to compensate by raising commodity prices. It was when the oil producers followed this course and announced a major price hike in 1973 that the world suddenly took note.[3]

The inflationary disease afflicted all western Europe. For the whole of OECD Europe, on aggregate, the rate shot up from an average of 3.7 per cent in 1961–9 and 6.4 per cent in 1969–73, to a remarkable 10.9 per cent for 1973–9. At the same time national experiences were diverging more and more widely. Thus while the UK, Italy, Spain and Eire all averaged around 16 per cent per annum in the 1970s, West Germany, Austria, the Netherlands and Switzerland were closer to 5 per cent. Such disparities discouraged a unified response. Floating exchange rates allowed countries to move in different directions, and for perhaps the last time, each state was in a position to pursue a separate monetary policy.[4]

In the past, inflationary pressures had been countered by tightening fiscal policy; the striking feature of the 1970s was that this no longer seemed to work. Demand management appeared impotent, and economic slowdown was no longer an alternative to inflation but accompanied it. A new term was coined for this bizarre phenomenon – 'stagflation'. Reflation simply made matters worse. One response was to supplement demand management with increasing state involvement in incomes and price bargaining. If inflation was generated by unregulated corporatism, perhaps it might be contained by government getting involved in encouraging or even enforcing restraint on employers and unions. This was the road taken by both Labour and Conservative governments in the UK, but it turned out to be a cul-de-sac. When Edward Heath lost his battle with the powerful British miners' union, the very authority of the government was thrown into question and raised the basic issue of the country's political governability. Labour governments were more successful in imposing wage restraint after 1976, but they eventually failed too. This meant that in the UK, neo-corporatist incomes policy was discredited, and even blamed for making matters worse.

It was easy for the British to forget that not dissimilar policies continued to be followed elsewhere – for example, in Sweden and Austria – with much success right through the 1970s and into the 1980s: both kept unemployment well below British levels, and the Austrians kept inflation lower too. The explanation for the difference with Britain surely lay in the combative tradition in the latter's industrial relations, compared with the conciliation, joint action and compromise found in the former. Where trade-union movements owned banks, for instance, as they did in Austria, they had an interest in the overall health of the economy which moderated their demands.[5]

There was, of course, another way to rein in prices: deliberate deflation through a tight monetary policy. The West Germans had pioneered this approach, very effectively, in 1973–4; the Callaghan government followed at the behest of the IMF in 1976. In neither case was this seen as an alternative to state involvement in wage bargaining. But with Margaret Thatcher's victory in 1979, monetary policy was elevated into dogma and became a new creed: monetarism. The state's ambitions were to be curtailed, its role confined to balancing the books and monitoring the supply of money. Both supporters and opponents of the new government recognized that this was a historic moment – the revival of economic liberalism after fifty years in the wilderness. 'It is the second time this century', wrote Nicholas Kaldor, one of Thatcher's bitterest critics, 'that monetarist dogma has become the official creed of the Government of Britain.' For his fellow economist, John Vaizey, who left the Labour Party for the Conservatives in 1979, 'there is no longer a set of social democratic ideas that will work. Keynesianism is intellectually dead.'[6]

THE THATCHERITE EXPERIMENT

The attractions of monetarism were many. Intellectually, there was the excitement of participating in a counter-revolution against the Keynesian orthodoxies which had held sway since the war. Individual energies would be liberated from the nanny-state; collectivism would give way to freedom; the state would be rolled back, and the attention of government and policy-makers focused upon the one indicator which held the key to economic success – the quantity of money. This was a seductively simple formula for success, and many were seduced.

Did 'Thatcherism' – as the new creed was termed in 1980 – actually set out to increase unemployment? This was taken for granted by many critics, particularly as jobless totals soared. Many years earlier, the Polish economist Michał Kalecki had warned that capitalists disliked full employment since it weakened labour discipline, and that therefore they would always look to create a certain level of unemployment in order to control the workforce. In the early 1980s, Kaldor and others saw this happening; in his words, '[the "new monetarism"] offered the prospect of reversing the growing imbalance between the power of labour in relation to the power of capital which was the result of the full-employment situation maintained during the previous decades'.[7]

It may seem hard to refute this, especially in view of the notorious anti-union attitude in the Thatcher government. A determination not to be 'held to ransom' by the unions – who had humiliated her predecessor – slid easily into a desire to break them. Even so, it must be stressed that this did not mean that the new government aimed at the deliberate creation of mass unemployment on a scale unseen for fifty years. Consequence should not be conflated with cause. All the evidence indicates that what happened took Whitehall by surprise. As Ian Gilmour – Minister turned critic – notes: 'In February 1980 [Mrs Thatcher] would hardly have criticized the Callaghan government for having doubled unemployment if she had thought that her government on top of that doubling would go on to triple it.' But, equally, since her government saw the control of inflation as a higher priority than full employment, it did not regard the re-emergence of mass unemployment as a sign of fundamental policy failure.[8]

Monetarism – like Marxism – far from offering policy-makers essential truths about the economy, drove them further and further away from what was really happening. It made government policy dependent upon a metaphysical concept – the money supply – that it had difficulty defining and even greater difficulty controlling. A variety of indicators – M1, M2, the PSBR (Public Sector Borrowing Requirement) – came and went. Traditional policy instruments – interest rates, the exchange rate, fiscal policy – remained. In the mid-1980s, monetarism was quietly abandoned. Reality had triumphed even over Mrs Thatcher, who henceforth sought electoral success by the time-honoured means of a government-engineered consumer boom. Intellectually, then, monetarism seems to have offered little advance on Keynesianism. Quite the contrary, in fact: its stark simplicity and dogmatic quality represented an intellectual regression; it was, in Gilmour's words, 'the Thatcherite equivalent of the Marxist materialist conception of history', less a new start than the final gasp of that long and multifarious search for a pure ideology to explain and therefore to rule society.

It would, however, be a mistake to limit the effects of the 'Thatcherite Revolution' to economics when its historical significance lay instead in its reappraisal of what the modern state could and could not do. The Iron Lady herself, after all, when asked what her government had changed replied: 'Everything' – pointing if nothing else to the scale of her ambitions. 'We offered a complete change in direction,' she stated. 'I think we have altered the balance between the person and the state in a favourable way.'[9]

In fact, claims of a neo-liberal sea change were misleading for two reasons. In the first place, this was a peculiarly authoritarian form of neo-liberalism: cutbacks in some areas of state involvement went hand in hand with increased state powers in others. Local authorities lost much power to Whitehall in a striking process of centralization, so that central government became more rather than less powerful in housing and education and whittled away the residual tax-raising competences of local councils. Police forces, universities and schools all lost autonomy. In addition, a new Official Secrets Act gave unprecedented powers to Britain's political police. The new Right – in Levitas's words – sought the twin utopias of competition and compliance. The UK's economic 'privatization', in other words, turned out to be perfectly compatible with its administrative 'nationalization'.[10]

Perhaps more unexpected is the clear evidence of the *failure* of Thatcherism to effect any far-reaching roll-back of state economic activity. Public expenditure as a percentage of GDP was 42.5 per cent in 1977/8, and 41.7 per cent ten years later; this hardly looked like roll-back on a revolutionary scale. Over the same period welfare spending remained virtually stationary as a proportion of general government spending (55.7 per cent in 1977/8 and 55.6 per cent in 1987/8), and as a proportion of GDP (23.7 per cent and 23.2 per cent respectively). Tax, too, despite the government's promises, remained more or less unchanged in proportion to national income. One of the most careful studies of retrenchment is clear: there was *no* conservative revolution where the British welfare state was concerned. A major LSE investigation concluded that there was 'no evidence here to support a story of serious decline'.[11]

Of course, closer analysis reveals that a number of important changes were taking place. Mass unemployment pushed up spending on social security, despite the tightening of eligibility rules for benefits. Spending on housing plummeted, and combined with the freezing of council-house building helped to generate a visible rise in the homeless population. City-dwellers grew accustomed to the sight of people sleeping rough in doorways or on park benches. On the other hand, spending on education and health care did not, contrary to popular perceptions, fall substantially.

It is not surprising that this state of affairs went largely unnoticed: Thatcherite governments were not keen to boast of their achievement in keeping state spending high; neither were their opponents. One saw cutbacks as desirable, the other as wicked, but both liked to exaggerate their impact. So why was the Thatcherite revolution such a failure? Leaving aside mere inertia, or the difficulty of forcing through change on a reluctant Whitehall, the main reason was simply the high level of public support for state provision of basic services. This, combined with the centralization produced by Thatcher's more authoritarian tendencies, meant that the state sector overall was strengthened rather than weakened by her years in power. But if this was true in Britain, scene of the most radical experiment in neo-liberalism anywhere in Europe, then what impact did the neo-liberals have on the mainland?

THE ENDURING STATE

The Thatcherite experiment represented the most concerted and ideologically charged attempt to break with the post-war status quo in western Europe. Coinciding with Reagan's presidency in the USA, it was regarded as ushering in a new period of conservative ascendancy. If Thatcher ultimately fell short of these expectations, it is not perhaps surprising that her influence on the rest of Europe's domestic policies was also rather limited. Fellow conservatives like Helmut Kohl showed little inclination to follow her lead. In three key areas – industrial relations, privatization, and the welfare state – the British example remained at the extreme end of the conservative spectrum.

There were two fundamental differences between the UK and continental Europe which help explain why the former ended up – in Gilmour's words – 'the most right-wing state in West Europe'. The first was a question of historical memory: it was surely no coincidence that the kind of deliberately confrontational politics espoused by Mrs Thatcher unfolded in the country with the least experience of ideological turmoil and political violence on the entire continent. Elsewhere, the memory of polarization in the past constrained policy-makers; social cohesion and political unity meant most where they had been bloodily and recently fractured. Gambling with class conflict surely worried Mitterrand and Kohl rather more than the British prime minister.

The second factor was connected with the first – the gulf in values and outlook which divided British Conservatism under Thatcher from European Christian Democracy, which has perhaps been the single most important political force in post-war Europe. It is hard to think of a Christian Democrat politician who would have endorsed Mrs Thatcher's famous dictum that there was no such thing as society. Christian Democrats may have varied in the closeness of their attach-ment to the Church; often, it seems hard to find what was distinctively religious about their policies. Even so, their core beliefs clearly revolved around notions of mediation and reconciliation – whether for indi-viduals or social groups. They aimed, in the words of one scholar, to 'restore the natural and organic harmony of society' – a goal which had made many hostile to both democracy and capitalism before the war. Reconciled after 1945 to both, Christian Democracy remained conscious of the importance of social policy, and suspicious of neo-liberal individualism; in countries such as Italy and West Germany, real differences of view separated them from Liberals and Free Democrats. Emphasizing the family and the role of charitable institutions, they emerged as the key architects of 'social capitalism'. Put simply, but not entirely misleadingly, the main differences between them and British conservatives were firstly Catholicism, and secondly, the memory of occupation.[12]

What was more, their support for the welfare state was not simply the result of their beliefs and values. In the 1950s, the expansion of the state had offered a means of expanding their power and patronage and acquiring new bases of electoral support. In countries such as Italy, Belgium, Austria and the Netherlands, clientelism fed off public-sector growth. Roll-back thus implied weakening the party itself. When national memory, political expediency and morality all dictated against a radical assault on the state sector, it was hardly surprising that the Thatcherite experiment should look about as attractive as collective suicide, especially in view of the strong and continued popular attachment across western Europe to social solidarity. The lack of any 'tax protest' along American lines deterred politicians seeking votes in a radical diminution of the role of the state. From this point of view, the 1980s exposed once again the limited Americanization of western Europe.[13]

In industrial relations, too, European conservatives stuck to a more consensual approach than in the UK, and continuities with the 1970s were greater. Even where tighter monetarist policies were adopted in the fight against inflation, as in West Germany, they were pragmatically accompanied by more traditional modes of wage negotiation and pay bargaining. Structures of neo-corporatist mediation remained in place. Despite substantial changes in shop-floor patterns of unionization, collective bargaining was seriously eroded only in Belgium and the Netherlands. Unions and their workers adjusted their expectations after 1973 so that everywhere converged upon the pattern of West German industrial relations, with wages decoupling from prices and following productivity.[14]

It was the same story with privatization. Neo-liberalism was stimulated by financial deregulation (London's 'Big Bang' of 1986 triggered off minor explosions in Paris, Stockholm, Vienna, Rome and elsewhere), by EC trade liberalization (culminating in 1992's single market), by the need to combat high government debt and by the weakening of state monopolies as a result of technological change or intensified international competition. Even so, countries were slow to follow Britain's lead in selling off major nationalized industries; they doubted whether this would necessarily lead to greater competitiveness and feared the damage to national interests. Across the Channel, national sovereignty usually trumped British chancellor Geoffrey Howe's 'consumer sovereignty'. Outside France, denationalization was not carried far and popular capitalism remained limited by the small size of domestic equity markets.[15]

Many sympathized with the need to cut back bureaucracy – Portugal, for instance, declared a 'National Day for Debureaucratization' in 1990, while in Italy the 'Movement for the Defence of the Citizen' formed in 1987 to protest against 'bureaucratic micro-persecution'. But none of this led very far and no one equalled the British cuts in civil-service employment. The British mania for exposing the public sector to a 'management revolution', which rapidly produced a plethora of monitoring and auditing bodies, contrasted with continental caution; so too did the impact of 'contracting out', the rise of the quango (*qu*asi *a*utonomous *n*on-governmental *o*rganization) and the consequent blurring of public- and private-sector values.[16]

If, then, the so-called 'conservative revolution' starts looking like a rather self-deluded Anglocentric view of events after 1973, perhaps the collapse of the Left which so worried British commentators needs to be viewed in the same light too. Labour's defeat in the UK was followed by that of Germany's SPD in 1983. The two oil crises ushered in a stream of gloomy predictions: Eric Hobsbawm warned that 'the forward march of Labour' had been halted. Dahrendorf heralded the 'end of the social democrat century'. Marxists, liberals and conservatives all agreed that social democracy had had its day. Commentators warned that the entire political spectrum had shifted to the Right during the 1970s and 1980s. But even if this was true, did it necessarily imply the decline of the Left?

THE LEFT IN DECLINE?

As ever, it was largely a matter of perspective. Left-wing parties suffered in north-west Europe, but held their ground in Scandinavia and prospered in southern Europe: Mitterrand, Craxi, Gonzáles and Papandreou, for instance, all held power during the 1980s. At the beginning of the 1990s, eleven of sixteen west European social democratic parties were in power – more than at any time since 1945. Overall, there was no decline in social democracy electorally; if anything, concluded the author of a searching examination of the subject, what required explanation was 'the striking stability of the social democratic vote'.[17]

In retrospect, the 'crisis' of social democracy in the 1980s reflected other factors. Electorates tended to punish whoever had been in government in the late 1970s: Kohl and Thatcher profited on the Right, but equally so did Mitterrand and Papandreou. The second was that the policy environment *had* changed, and become far less favourable to traditional Keynesian state-led national recovery plans: Mitterrand and Papandreou both tried this and were forced back into 'austerity' and *rigueur*. Hence socialists and social democrats had to find new approaches to their traditional goals of social equity and workers' rights; for many, these would lead to Brussels. As a result, some would argue that Leftists in government in the 1980s were not really pursuing socialism. It is certainly true that Mitterrand was indeed implementing a state-led 'socialism without workers', while in Spain and Greece, the socialists won because they offered the prospect of full-scale social renewal and national reconciliation after authoritarian rule and civil war. In all three countries, the Left adopted a national mission and avoided being labelled as a labourist movement. But this was not only a reflection of the specific political pasts they faced: it was also because the workers were disappearing as a class. Across western Europe the old, organized working class was following the peasantry into history. This was where the real crisis was taking place.

Whereas the evidence for a political 'revolution' in western Europe after 1973 is at best patchy, there can be no disputing the scale of the changes which were taking place in society and the economy. Pre-eminent among these were the related phenomena of de-industrialization and the declining power of organized labour. De-industrialization hit the headlines in the UK with the decimation of British manufacturing in the first three years of Mrs Thatcher's government, when no fewer than one million manufacturing jobs were lost. To a large extent this drop was the product of astonishing economic mismanagement, and in particular of an overvalued exchange rate. Nevertheless, a longer-term secular decline in the relative importance of the industrial sector was taking place more widely.

From the late 1960s the absolute size of the industrial workforce started to decline in western Europe. Between 1960 and 1985 it fell as a proportion of the total labour force from 47.7 per cent to 32.3 per cent in the UK, from 47 per cent to 41 per cent in the FDR, from 40 per cent to 26.5 per cent in the Netherlands. Southern Europe followed suit about a decade later: from 36.1 per cent to 31.8 per cent between 1980 and 1985 in Spain, for instance. Industrial output fell as a proportion of GDP. European output was also falling over this period as a proportion of world industrial output, indicating the difficulty countries faced in keeping up with international levels of competitiveness, especially against Asian newcomers.

Many of the great centres of European industrialization fell into decline: coal and textiles were among the first industries to be hit, followed by shipbuilding, steel and car production. Not surprisingly, social theorists – in an ironic echo of Mrs Thatcher herself – were quick to spot the onset of 'post-industrial' society, sometimes overlooking the vital role industry and manufacturing in particular continued to play in the economy. For while some traditional heavy industries suffered 'restructuring', others such as electronics and pharmaceuticals prospered. The drop in industrial value added was far less than in *employment*. Long-term economic well-being continued to depend on such factors as the level of investment in training, research and development. Nevertheless, the overall decline of industry sent shock-waves through society.[18]

In the first place, it radically altered the nature of union power, shifting the balance away from the old centres of working-class activism – the mines, docks and railways – towards white-collar, technical and especially public-sector unions. Unionization rates fell in some countries – France and Spain (where they had traditionally been low, anyway), the Netherlands and the UK – but not everywhere: they remained high, for example, in Sweden, Denmark, Norway and Belgium where corporatist pay bargaining continued.

Mass unemployment reduced the effectiveness of strike action. In the 1980s there were only sporadic strikes on a large scale, and their outcomes tended to be at best ambiguous (the I. G. Metall strike in West Germany), at worst clear defeats (the NUM in the UK in 1984). When the great Fiat strike unfolded in Turin in 1980 shortly after the Solidarity movement emerged in Poland, the limits of industrial action in the West became obvious: unlike Solidarity, the Fiat workers found that their popularity was constrained by internal division and the sense that they were fighting for their own interests, not those of the nation. Fiat managers mounted a successful counter-demonstration, and the disillusioned strikers were forced back to work. 'Have you seen what they've managed to do in Poland since they've got the backing of all the workers?' exclaimed one. 'We know that in Italy, in a country like Italy, we can never have the backing, and above all the physical and moral participation of all the workers; within the working class today there are conflicting interests.'[19] Thus labour's share of income fell from the mid-1970s onwards, and most union leaders realized that this could not be reversed. Their continued influence depended not merely upon their own actions, but also upon the willingness of employers and government to accept them as partners.

These trends were connected with broader shifts in labour patterns and the very meaning of work. Large corporations promising long-term employment to a largely male workforce were gradually replaced by smaller companies with short-term contracts, employing an increasingly female staff. 'Flexibilization' and the rise of part-time work, the growth of unregulated 'black economies', together with the destruction of the old blue-collar labour aristocracy, led some commentators to mourn the passing of the working class. 'Did the working class ever exist at all?' asked Blackwell and Seabrook in their 1996 study of changing work practices. Certainly it was no longer the heroic protagonist at the heart of European politics that it had been for a century, much less the vanguard of revolution. Collective working-class rituals such as the May Day festival were petering out; a study of the sales figures for May Day badges in Sweden showed figures rising from the 1960s until the early 1980s and then declining precipitously. Elsewhere the decline set in even earlier.[20]

Work itself was assuming a different significance in people's lives. As we have seen, for both communism and fascism work had occupied a central place, both as right and as duty, in their claim to have superseded liberal democracy: work was redemption from uselessness and an entry-ticket into the community, an idea parodied even on the gate into Auschwitz with its mocking slogan 'Arbeit macht frei'.

Post-war liberal democracy had responded to the challenge by itself guaranteeing the right to work, a commitment enshrined in the UN Declaration of Human Rights and realized in the full-employment policies of the post-war years.

Suddenly there were no longer jobs for all. It began to look as though full employment had been nothing but what Göran Therborn called 'a strange experience in the history of capitalism'.[21] Mass unemployment and the rise of social-security spending meant that work and income were less directly connected than ever before in modern history. In the UK, for example, income from work as a proportion of gross household income fell from more than 80 per cent of the total in the mid-1970s to 73 per cent by 1982.[22]

The spread of higher education and the pressure to take early retirement, combined with increasing longevity and longer paid holidays, meant that an ever-larger portion of people's lives was spent outside paid work (unpaid housework remained inescapable for many women). Sociologists observed a waning work ethic as people sought satisfaction and fulfilment outside work rather than inside it, and tried to husband their energies for their free time. Polls indicated that in 1962 only 33 per cent of Germans preferred leisure over work; by 1979 the figure had risen to 48 per cent. German newspapers became alarmed: 'We are *not* idle,' ran a headline in *Bild Zeitung*. Such attitudes reflected the fact that on average even those in work spent as much time in a year outside the workplace as at it. But they also showed the great contrast between the rapidity of economic change and the persistence of deeply rooted ethical traditions which associated idleness and leisure with moral deficiency.[23]

Mass unemployment emerged in the mid-1970s and remained a major social problem in the following decade, despite economic recovery and the creation of jobs in the service sector. By the early 1990s, unemployment averaged 11–12 per cent in the EU, and totalled some eighteen million people. Yet this figure, unimaginable to most people twenty years earlier, was accompanied by very little serious unrest. Certainly there was no parallel to events in the early 1930s, and no fundamental challenge to the political order. That this was so must surely be attributed to the continued resilience of the welfare state in cushioning society, even – or perhaps especially – after the ending of the post-war boom.

LOSING OUT

Compared with two decades earlier, however, people had come to accept high levels of poverty and inequality. Over forty-five million people – some 14 per cent of the population – were living in poverty in the EU by the late 1980s, 17 per cent by 1993 – a figure comparable with the situation in the USA, and a striking contrast with the egalitarian 'tiger economies' of East Asia. In the UK, thanks to monetarism and tax breaks for the rich, the rise was particularly glaring – Mrs Thatcher had urged people to 'glory in inequality' – reversing nearly half a century's trend the other way. As Gilmour put it acidly, 'trickle down' policies had actually produced 'an upward trickle'. The leading British scholar of income distribution stated bluntly that 'the 1980s have seen a departure from the historical trend, with a definite rise in inequality'. By the 1990s the UK was the most unequal society in the Western world, with around fourteen million living in poverty, including over four million children, but other west European countries were heading in the same direction.[24]

It was not long before the poor were – as in the past – being blamed for their misfortune: declining faith in social engineering naturally encouraged more moralistic and individualistic explanations of poverty. During the inter-war slump, conservative eugenicists had talked of the 'social problem group'. Now the idea reappeared in a new guise: the 'underclass'. According to the American Charles Murray, the leading propagandist for the term, this identified not the degree but a type of poverty. Single mothers – an increasingly impoverished group – were attacked for scrounging off the welfare state, and the unemployed were accused – despite scholarly evidence refuting the idea – of preferring generous handouts to proper work at low wages. Such accusations helped justify cuts in child allowances and supplementary benefit, as well as schemes which tied welfare entitlements to workfare. Another growing section of the 'new poor' – the elderly

– were suffering, first in Britain, later elsewhere, from the fall in the real value of state pensions. For those who most needed it, the welfare safety net was looking threadbare, inadequate and unfocused in the benefits it offered.

Impoverishment had its own geography. As the old industrial heartlands – the Clyde and the north-east of England, the Ruhr – fell into decline, jobs and people tilted towards the suburbs or other regions. In 1980s Germany, for instance, there was the 'Nord–Sud Gefälle' – the Great Trek to the South. The destitution of the Italian Mezzogiorno contrasted more strikingly than ever with the wealth of the Veneto and Emilia, whose inhabitants' protectionism expressed itself in large votes for the autonomist *Lega*. Those left behind found themselves stranded in pockets of high unemployment. People started to talk of 'inner cities' as zones of social tension and poverty. Within cities, housing patterns also changed as those in work abandoned public housing estates: by the 1990s, council houses were inhabited overwhelmingly by the poor, something which had not been true a decade or so earlier. Homelessness was on the increase too, and by the early 1990s had reached the staggering figure of three million across the European Union.

As poverty increased, and the gulf widened between those in and out of work, prison populations also rose – unevenly but persistently – across western Europe. We need not follow Marxist penologists who argue capitalism uses prison as a means of labour discipline and a way of keeping public order, to see possible connections between social distress and a return to hardline law-and-order policies. As ever, the poor were most at risk of imprisonment; white-collar theft, corruption and fraud were rarely regarded as 'real' crimes, despite the enormous sums of money involved – £6 billion from EU subsidies alone. Effectively, the crimes of the economically powerful were left to the margins of policing work.

So far as crime was concerned there were two possibilities: either the figures were unreliable; or there actually was more crime. The unreliability of crime figures was acknowledged on all sides, but few believed that statistics alone explained the increase. Were people behaving worse than in the past, or had definitions of what constituted criminal behaviour changed so that more kinds of act were now being defined as criminal? Conservatives preferred the first kind of explanation; radicals the second.

In fact, of course, the two are not incompatible, and while it was difficult to prove moral deterioration (except through markers such as the rise in violent crime), there was some evidence of a tendency to criminalize new kinds of behaviour, such as homelessness, trespass, peaceful protest and vagrancy. Social policy was hopelessly confused where drugs were concerned – criminalizing possession of cannabis, for example, but not alcohol or tobacco. The radical critique was justified in targeting economic factors, even if they worked less mechanistically than was often suggested. It was true that unemployment played a part in pushing prison rates up, but mostly because it increased re-conviction rates (i.e. it made it harder for prisoners to find work when they were released from prison), and because the unemployed found it difficult to pay fines.

At the same time, the consumer society – with its car radios and mobile phones – generated new temptations and attitudes to crime. So did the welfare state itself: government publicity campaigns targeted benefit fraud – trying to reassure taxpayers that their money was not being squandered – and called on the public to inform on cheats. At the most general level, some argued that the alienation of modern life led people to treat one another with suspicion and to rely on the law to settle disputes which might once have been settled privately. But though this may be true, it remains difficult to see how such a long-term explanation could help explain a relatively recent surge in crime.

Comparison among European countries also shows no clear relationship between crime and incarceration rates. The latter varied enormously, and some countries were far keener to send people to jail than others. European prison populations were proportionately far lower than in the Soviet Union (let alone the USA), and west European rates lower than east European, though rising fast. But in general there was a startling upward trend in prison populations: between 1979 and 1993 the number of prisoners per 100,000 inhabitants rose, for example, in the Netherlands, from 23 to 52, from 44 to 62 in

Norway and from 37 to 117 in Spain. The UK had the highest rate in western Europe, and this too rose under the increasingly draconian policies of successive Conservative governments. The Norwegian Nils Christie saw Europe moving 'towards GULAGS, Western style' and warned of the dangers of ending up with a crime-control industry on an American scale. Yet some of the symptoms are here already – a buoyant private security industry, the emergence of electronic tagging and other means of surveillance as prisons became overcrowded.[25]

The new conservative mood of the 1980s could be seen particularly clearly in the Netherlands, traditionally a country reluctant to imprison criminals. This reluctance had been led by a wartime generation of judges whose own experiences during the occupation had given them a deep aversion to incarceration. Now they were passing into retirement just when social engineering and social reformism more generally were being called into question. In March 1994 an official announcement from the Ministry of Justice noted that 'punishing is again "allowed", and the legitimation of penal sanctions is no longer sought in its resocializing effect, but again in incapacitation and retribution as well'. The conservative trend even reached Sweden in the early 1990s, where the centre-right fought the 1991 election with the slogan: 'Keep them locked in, so we can go out!'[26]

And there was also an inescapable racial dimension: the proportion of foreign and ethnic minority prisoners shot up alarmingly in the 1980s. By 1987 they amounted to nearly a third of the prison population in Belgium and France, and above a third in Switzerland. Rates of increase were staggeringly high in countries like Spain and Portugal. Many people were in prison for breaches of immigration law, and in Belgium one third of foreigners detained were in jail 'for administrative reasons as a measure of social defence'.[27]

In some cases this increase reflected the social situation of certain ethnic groups – with higher levels of drug use, or higher rates of unemployment – as well as pervasive racism in the ranks of the police. Although there was much dispute about the reasons, there was no doubt that ethnic minorities were disproportionately afflicted both by unemployment and by imprisonment. In the UK, for instance, the unemployment rate among young black men in London reached a staggering 51 per cent in the early 1990s, and was 37 per cent across all ethnic minorities. It was hard to believe that these statistics did not reflect – among other factors – the persistence of racial prejudice, and a reluctance to admit the members of minorities (as indeed was still the case for women, too) as full citizens in west European society.

With the rise of unemployment, European states threw their previously welcoming immigration policies into reverse. In most countries, the 1970s marked the end of mass immigration and the beginning of restriction. The French Office of National Immigration (founded in 1946) was renamed the International Migration Office, and sought to encourage return. Yet ethnic-minority populations of course did not decline and policies to encourage repatriation made little impact. In West Germany, for instance, neither Helmut Schmidt's 'consolidation policy' nor Kohl's 'return policy' were effective in reducing numbers: 17,000 migrants took up Kohl's offer, while the number of foreigners in the country increased by nearly two million in his first decade in office.[28]

After 1989, new fears emerged of a flood of migrants from the East. Amid predictions that millions of impoverished former Communist-bloc workers would head for the Golden Land of the West, the European Union states tightened immigration controls and asylum laws still further. Immigration and refugee issues were often conflated, casting doubt on the bona fides of refugee applicants, who were increasingly portrayed in the press as scroungers on Western generosity.

Such anxieties were not entirely groundless: asylum seekers in western Europe rose from 65,400 in 1983 to 544,000 in 1991, and rose further with the war in Bosnia; Germany alone took some 80 per cent of the total. Once granted asylum, they generally received benefits and entitlements. Yet wealthy western Europe hosted a rather small share of the world's total refugee population, most of whom were settled in much poorer parts of the globe – some six and a half million in Asia, for example, and four million in Africa. Countries like Iran and Pakistan hosted far greater numbers of refugees both absolutely and proportionately to their total population than relatively generous European states like Sweden and West Germany, let alone misers like the UK.

As a rather ineffective deterrent, conditions for hosting refugees were made deliberately unattractive. They were housed in camps, detention centres, old barracks and elderly offshore rustbuckets. In some cases, rights to welfare assistance and benefits were whittled away. At the same time they were often prevented from working. Not surprisingly, they were pushed into the black economy and various forms of illegality. The numbers of those refused asylum rose, yet most remained nonetheless. By the early 1990s it was estimated that there were some three million undocumented foreigners in western Europe. Occasional amnesties were one way of regularizing their plight; another was the mass deportations of tens of thousands of illegal workers and residents carried out in Italy, Greece and France. Particularly hard hit were those affected by retrospective changes in citizenship laws who faced deportation and separation from their own children.

The persistent and indeed increased attention paid to refugees and immigrants was linked to the racial hostility which the members of minority communities settled in western Europe continued to endure on a daily basis. The situation of different minorities varied considerably, while despite (or because of) the high unemployment rates they faced, many of the second and third generation were staying on into higher education and becoming at least as well educated (and in the British case generally better) than the white population as a whole. Yet these and other favourable social trends do not obscure the persistence of racism.

Even in the UK, with the most substantial race-relations legislation in the EU, racial harassment – especially outside the major cities – was a serious and growing problem. 'Harlow is a very racist town,' said a young black man who grew up there. 'It's a minority of white people who give us the trouble, but the others don't stop them . . . I've not been into the town centre since 1991. We're actually prisoners.' Embattled minorities had to choose – as ever – between relying on the protection of a police force that was itself riddled with racism, bowing to street violence, or self-defence, Suicide rates were high. 'I've been bullied about it for ten years,' said one sixteen-year-old. 'I feel like killing myself sometimes.'[29]

Outside the UK, levels of racism were higher and much less inhibited. British publishers of children's books found illustrations showing non-white children reduced sales abroad and routinely changed the pictures as a result. 'What bothers me with English books', said one French publisher, 'is that there are lots of children from different cultures. We do have our different races here, but the public don't want to buy books which represent them.' France's republican ideal of assimilation meant that ethnic diversity was seen in negative terms as something which should disappear; few gloried openly in their immigrant past, or appreciated that without immigration France's population in the 1990s would have been one fifth smaller than it was.[30]

In central Europe old attitudes still ran close to the surface. In West Germany, sixteen university professors in 1982 signed a manifesto calling for the deportation of all migrant workers in order to preserve 'the Christian Occidental values of Europe'. The lack of effective laws in many countries outlawing racial discrimination allowed flats to be advertised 'Only for Europeans'. In xenophobic Switzerland there were grass-roots attacks on the 'over-foreignization' (*Überfremdung*) of the country. Overall in western Europe, between 1984 and 1990 the European Parliament registered an alarming increase in racist attacks.[31]

These trends were, of course, linked to the new salience of race and immigration issues in national politics. The 1980s saw avowedly right-wing parties achieve national prominence for the first time in fifty years. In France the National Front linked the issues of immigration, unemployment and crime to become a national force in the mid-1980s; Le Pen, its leader, himself polled 14 per cent in the first round of the 1988 presidential elections. In West Germany, the Republican Party was formed in 1983 with a similar platform and polled around 11 per cent in 1992. A more violent neo-Nazi fringe seized the headlines both East and West after unification, and there was a spate of attacks on asylum seekers' hostels. In Austria, the Freedom Party under Jörg

Haider's leadership rose on the back of the immigration issue. Its 1992 anti-immigration petition failed, but won the signatures of 417,000 voters. 'Vienna must not become Chicago' was the FPÖ's slogan in the Austrian capital – a curiously 1930s view of America, which bore out how little attitudes on race had changed across much of Europe in half a century.

In all this were echoes – visual and rhetorical – of inter-war fascism, and journalists flocked around young goose-stepping neo-Nazis like bees round honey. But history rarely repeats itself, and these groups had to struggle with the memory of their antecedents. No longer was it obvious that they had the key to the future; they could just as easily seem locked in the past. Anti-immigrant rhetoric boosted support for these parties, but also limited it, and the emergence of the Right prompted fierce opposition through organizations such as SOS-Racisme and the church sanctuary movement. Racism may have remained a powerful current in European attitudes, but anti-racism was also growing, and migrants' rights were defensible in domestic courts. International human rights law could also be used to curb domestic restrictions, as in Austria where in 1985 the Foreigners Police Law was declared unconstitutional because it conflicted with the European Convention on Human Rights.

The real problem lay less with the new Right than with the crisis of post-war conservatism. The weakness of the Gaullist Right in France, cleverly exploited by Mitterrand, was what allowed the National Front its opportunity. Where conservative parties were stronger, radical anti-immigrant parties found it more difficult to make headway. Where weak, the conservatives themselves often flirted with the same rhetoric: in Vienna, for instance, the ÖVP slogan of 'Vienna for the Viennese' was hardly less inflammatory than the FPÖ version. In the UK, the Major government toyed briefly with the anti-immigrant card: 'We must not be wide open to all comers just because Rome, Paris and London are more attractive than Bombay or Algiers,' Major told the 1991 Conservative Party conference. The Gaullist Chirac conjured up 'an overcrowded family with the father, three or four wives and twenty or so kids, who receives 50,000 francs in social security payments, obviously without working . . . not to

mention the noise and the smell'. From this point of view, the significance of Le Pen and Haider lay in the extent to which they were able
to take the mainstream Right hostage.[32]

Citizenship itself was clearly at the heart of the immigration debate.
At the same time as entry was becoming harder, some countries were
loosening their citizenship procedures in order to ease social tensions.
The rise of the welfare state and the decline of the militarized state
meant that citizenship was now understood in terms of costs and
benefits rather than political rights (voting) and duties (defending the
nation-state). This was why the immigration issue was so often used
by the Right as a peg for other concerns – unemployment, the equity
of tax burdens and job insecurity. It was also why some commentators
argued the need for a new 'post-national model of membership' in
Western society. After all, foreigners already partook of some of the
traditional attributes of citizenship such as paying tax and national
insurance, or claiming certain benefits. In that sense they were already
citizens, even if they lacked the right to vote or to enter the civil
service.[33]

Overall, the character of European attitudes towards ethnic minorities is becoming clearer. Europe is not an American 'melting-pot' (but
then neither is the USA any longer), and assimilation as a goal has
had its day; post-war immigrant communities have become permanent,
but often remain culturally distinct and in some cases 'foreign'. In
many countries they remain excluded from full citizenship rights, and
even in the UK, where this is less true, they are pushed to the margins
in more informal ways. They are not necessarily better off in a country
like France whose secular republican assimilationism allows little
space for cultural and religious diversity than they are in Germany or
Greece, where nationalism is more exclusive but also more inclined
to accept difference. For many reasons – historical, ethical, economic
– deportation is no longer acceptable to mainstream opinion, yet the
development of a new kind of civic identity which can encompass
cultural diversity seems unlikely to emerge in much of Europe, where
national insecurities prevail, religion remains a powerful marker of
belonging and where multiracial coexistence is a very recent phenomenon. The experience of British society – for all its hesitancies in this

area – does suggest that such an evolution is possible even in the context of the nation-state. But then British nationalism is itself a hybrid and is not inclined to fetishize purity.

What is certain is that the effort to stabilize the current situation through a twin policy of 'assimilation' and barriers to further immigration is doomed to fail. Societies will not cease to be multicultural just because politicians – or even their voters – declare that they are against it. European capitalism still requires cheap workers, especially as its ageing wealthy societies draw on more youthful, poorer pools of labour to work for them and generate the taxes to pay their pensions. Geography makes Fortress Europe impossible to police, particularly on its porous southern and eastern borders, and as smuggling people in becomes big business, numbers may grow from the currently estimated 300,000–500,000 illegal entrants annually. In recent years, would-be illegal immigrants have drowned in the Aegean, frozen to death in the holds of international airliners and been thrown overboard by Ukrainian sailors in the Atlantic. Such cases rarely make the headlines, but they indicate the scale of this traffic. International disparities in wealth and political stability will continue to propel people into Europe whatever the wishes of the state authorities.

INDIVIDUALISM TRIUMPHANT?

In the mid-1980s the Italian Socialist Gianni De Michelis looked back on 1968 as 'the "twilight of the Gods", the last great collective moment in Italian history, the end of all dreams of a new era'. The decline of class struggle coincided with the crisis of Keynesianism and, more generally, of optimism in social planning. The 'Requiem for large-scale planning models', which appeared in the *Journal of the American Institute of Planners* in 1973, seemed to refer to a far broader phenomenon than urban management. *Small is Beautiful* was the new gospel. From the mid-1970s, the era of collective political mobilization was superseded by more fragmented forms of politics. *Adieu au prolétariat* was one French intellectual's summing up; more ambitious colleagues turned their disappointment into something grander. For the former

Leftist Jean-François Lyotard, the 1970s ushered in no less than the end of 'modernity'.[34]

The idea of social progress as a collective project based on the accumulation of goods had lost its charm. Economic growth and material prosperity were no longer unchallenged blessings. *The Limits to Growth* – the 1972 manifesto of the Club of Rome – sold ten million copies, marking a new environmental and conservationist consciousness. Therborn notes the striking changes in mood between the forward-looking scientific confidence of Expo 1958 in Brussels – with its focus on the atom – and the retrograde nostalgia of Expo 92 in Seville. It seemed fitting that the theme in that year of supposed Euro-optimism should be the discovery of a New World five hundred years earlier. The only New Worlds still to be discovered in the 1990s lay in the past.[35]

Science and technology were also losing their allure; they were seen less as means of liberation from drudgery than as sources of pollution, discomfort and even death. Sociologists talked about the new 'risk society' which overwhelmed individuals with threats over which they had no control and limited information. While politicians berated the 'whining cultural pessimism' that resulted from 'the fear of life, fear of technology, and fear of the future', the proportion of West Germans who saw technology as a blessing dropped from 72 per cent in 1966 to 30 per cent in 1981.[36]

Behind their disaffection lay the realities of daily life. The Great Car Economy of Mrs Thatcher's dreams seemed less and less attractive as traffic jams lengthened and respiratory illnesses multiplied. In 1974 the president of the German Automotive Industry Association had talked of 'the automobile as another bit of freedom'; less than a decade later advertisers were featuring 'the man who travels slowly because he gets where he's going faster, who has enough personality to do without horsepower, who saves energy and gains strength'. In fact between 1975 and 1994 people walked and cycled on average 20–30 per cent less and spent 50 per cent more time in cars, increasing anonymity and insecurity, and turning communal spaces into parking lots and race tracks.[37]

Ecological movements were the natural expression of this disaffection. Galvanized by the oil crises, they were boosted in the 1980s by the debate over cruise missiles and nuclear power. In West Germany, the new Green Party drew on a longer tradition of anti-materialism, as well as new concern at the 'death of the forests', and became a small but important presence in the Bundestag, able to force through environmental measures out of all proportion to its strength. Elsewhere, environmental mobilization occurred less through political parties than via campaigning movements such as Greenpeace and Survival International. Single-issue organizations of this kind, dependent upon a large membership for their existence, became more and more important instruments for bringing issues to the public.

In general, political activism increasingly revolved not around class but around issues of 'identity'. At some point in the 1970s this term was borrowed from social psychology and applied with abandon to societies, nations and groups. By the 1980s, a debate on 'national', 'cultural', 'gender' identity had begun which shows no signs of abating. The prominent social theorist Anthony Giddens talked about the emergence of what he called 'life politics', which dealt with a range of biological, emotional and existential concerns 'repressed' by more traditional conceptions of politics, in which 'self and body become the sites of a variety of new life-style options'.[38]

While the advance of the working class was checked, new groups progressed. First and foremost, the women's movement won real gains. It is true that mass unemployment, the feminization of poverty and growing job segregation in a time of economic crisis all undermined women's position in European labour markets. 'Glass ceilings' were hard to break through and professional, industrial and administrative elites remained overwhelmingly male. Attitudes were slow to change: as late as 1983 Kohl tried to attract women voters by remarking that 'our pretty women are one of Germany's natural resources'.[39]

Nevertheless, the rethinking of gender roles which had begun in the 1960s achieved its greatest legislative impact in the 1970s and 1980s, especially in Catholic and Orthodox Europe. Divorce laws were liberalized, and the legal equality of husbands and wives was reaffirmed. The 1977 West German Marriage Law did away with the clause which permitted a wife to work only with her husband's permission. In the 1980s civil marriage was legalized in Greece, and women gained new rights as Spain and Portugal emerged from dictatorship. The movement for gay and lesbian rights also gathered momentum during the 1970s, and despite the persistence of entrenched homophobia, which surfaced especially during the start of the AIDS crisis in the 1980s, public attitudes and state policies were changing. The criminalization and medicalization of 'deviant' sexual behaviour were increasingly regarded as anachronisms: yet the age of consent for gays was still higher in most countries than for heterosexuals.

These dramatic changes led some commentators to herald the decline of the family. But it was rather a question of the way the goals, meaning and attractiveness of this fundamental social institution were being transformed. Marriage itself was turning into a choice rather than a duty. Sexual pleasure, love and affection between partners were demanded, scrutinized and the subject of expert advice, with helplines for those unable to cope. While marriage itself only slowly lost popularity, divorce (and remarriage) rates shot up. 'Living in sin' turned into cohabitation, and by 1981 even Debrett's *Etiquette and Modern Manners* felt it necessary to advise upper-class hostesses how to deal with 'live-in lovers'. By the early 1990s, it was no longer safe to assume that children in north-western Europe would live with two married natural parents. Southern and Catholic Europe was slower to change, but even there cohabitation and divorce were becoming more common. Extramarital birth rates doubled between 1970 and 1990 in West Germany, Portugal, Greece and Austria; they more than trebled in the UK, Sweden, Norway, the Netherlands and France.[40]

Medical technology introduced further challenges to traditional morality. Reproductive medicine now allowed single women and infertile couples the chance to become parents. Contraceptive technologies were more and more accessible; so too was abortion, now widely legalized and available on demand through the welfare state in much of Europe. Sperm banks and frozen embryos posed new moral dilemmas for doctors and society at large. Bearing children was still widely regarded as the main goal of marriage, but it could be made on an increasingly individualistic basis with timing and to some extent quantity (though not yet quality) arranged to suit the would-be parent(s).

From one point of view, the responsibility for sexual order was shifting from the public to the private domain, and becoming almost another aspect of consumption. Yet at the same time, the state's role was expanding – through its interpretation of legal rights, and its provision of health, educational and welfare services. Hence there was no diminution in the public debate over issues of sexuality and reproduction. The difference with earlier periods, and particularly with the inter-war era, was that these issues were debated in terms of the ethics of individual choice and not of the collective politico-military needs of the ethnically pure nation-state. But the lack of any common basis upon which to reach agreement – apart from the shaky one of cost – has rendered most of these debates inconclusive. What was striking was that there was no replay of the pre-war scares of population decline, despite the resumption of similarly falling birth rates.

'Identity politics' was also being offered on a very different basis by an increasingly rampant consumer culture. 'New Colonial or Savile Row?' the *Guardian* clothes column asked its male readers in 1987. Neither pop nor fashion was offering (if they ever had) anything as simple as *one* alternative to the dominant cultural norm. The 'teenager' of the 1950s and 1960s was dead, a fashion journalist gleefully announced in 1986: youth culture had dissolved into a fizz of alternative styles. So, too, had culture generally. Rock and pop might occasionally claim to offer an anti-politics, but even punk's anarchism was suspect, the creation of art-school fashion entrepreneurs like Malcolm McLaren: for punk politics you went to *A Clockwork Orange* not the Sex Pistols. The very distinction between 'high' and 'low' culture was itself looking increasingly shaky, a product of an earlier era of elite intellectual self-confidence and benevolent moral superiority.[41]

Late-twentieth-century capitalism saw in images, services and events a far more lucrative source of instantly obsolescent desires than goods had ever been. Hence the marked commercialization of both leisure and culture in the last three decades: corporate sponsorship of sports in the UK, for instance, rose from £2.5 million sterling in 1970 to

£128 million in 1986, and in the arts, from £0.5 million in 1976 to £25 million a decade later.[42] Space and time were being ransacked, compressed and encompassed. 'World music' and 'ethnic fashions' revealed the global reach of an industry which was busy plundering the past, and – more and more often – the future. Was it by chance that the Henley Centre for Forecasting should have been founded in 1974 to offer businesses a guide to a future into which social and economic grand theory could no longer claim access? The expertise of the market analyst filled the vacuum left by the collapse of confidence in social science.

According to some commentators the whole pattern of Western consumer capitalism, forcing people to live daily life at a dizzying pace, was leading to a sort of existential crisis. With people harangued by 'experts' and thus encouraged to mistrust their own intuitions, presented with 'identities' to select and discard at random, was it not natural that there should be an increasing sense of anomie, which manifested itself in growing fear, on the one hand, and a sporadic search for 'genuineness' on the other? 'Post-modernity' had spawned an obsession with 'roots' and 'heritages' among a politically immobilized electorate, too sophisticated any longer to trust the media, and deprived of any dependable sources of knowledge. Television opened up a world of images, but robbed personal experience of its authenticity. The spread of astrology, New Age philosophies and other forms of irrationalism reflected this growing anxiety in the face of an uninterpretable world. Journalists talked of the 'fretful 1990s, when fear is the new badge of citizenship'.[43]

It was tempting to accept this line of argument – how else to reconcile increasing wealth with a decreasing sense of personal security – but there were good reasons not to exaggerate the post-modern fin-de-siècle malaise. After all, the complaint was not a new one, owing much to older theories of capitalist alienation and individual anomie. To be sure, modernity was now being defined differently, but the basic analysis had been around for a while. 'The times were on the move. People who were not born then will find it difficult to believe, but the fact is that time was moving as fast as a cavalry-camel; it is not only nowadays that it does so': Robert Musil had ironically opened his novel *The Man without Qualities* by describing 1914 Vienna in terms which sounded very familiar to theorists of post-modernity. Heidegger greeted National Socialism as an escape into Being from the Becoming of the 'dreary technological frenzy' of American/Russian mass culture. Contemporary theorists do not date the beginning of post-modernity back to the 1930s, still less to 1914. But it is not easy to see what is fundamentally different about the post-modern existential crisis from earlier versions.[44]

Where the late twentieth century did differ from earlier periods was that politics was no longer regarded as the prime arena for personal fulfilment or action. Voter apathy and abstention were on the increase, and party memberships dropped. The ranks of what the Spaniards called *pasotas* ('pass-men') increased. In Belgium, Italy, France and Britain, corruption scandals rocked public confidence in political elites. They bred disillusionment but nothing like a 'crisis of democracy' along inter-war lines, since that too had been the product of an era when people still believed in ideological and redemptive politics and looked forward to collectivist solutions. Polls consistently demonstrated that the vast majority of western Europeans – 93 per cent in 1989, for instance – firmly believed in the idea of democracy as a principle of government.[45]

The sense of uncertainty was in fact chiefly social and economic rather than political. Class was bound up less with work than with lifestyles and fashion choices. Patterns of employment and personal relations were more varied and less settled than ever before, while the memory of two severe recessions had undermined the confidence of the 1950s and 1960s. Greater choice also meant greater uncertainty; increased individualism reduced the opportunity for collective mobiliz-ation. The great demonstrations and marches of the past became more and more sporadic: mass groupings of people were more likely to be generated by sports events and pop festivals. Individualism opened up a world of vulnerability to risks which had formerly been met with familial, local or national solidarity – crime and pensions were two instances where the state tried to throw back responsibility on to the individual. One reaction was a 'communitarianism' which tried to revive a civic morality based upon neighbourhoods and localities – a backward and rosy-tinted glance at earlier social harmonies. But another was surely the revival of a politics of resentment against 'scroungers', 'benefit cheats' and immigrants – reminders of the processes of global change which mocked both individual and national destinies. Conservatives – and increasingly social democrats too – sought a return to the language of duties to counterbalance what they saw as an excessive emphasis on rights. Yet the language of rights had become entrenched in individualistic post-war Europe. Despite social crisis and economic readjustment, there was no return to the authoritarianism of the 1930s, and the new moralizing stress on duties made only very limited headway.

GLOBALIZATION AND THE CRISIS OF THE NATION-STATE

Despite the sense of economic vulnerability, western Europe remained one of the powerhouses of the global economy even after the crises of the 1970s. Although European economies were under pressure to remain globally competitive, they managed restructuring in the 1970s and 1980s fairly successfully while preserving high standards of living. What was changing was the power of government to pursue national economic policies, and thus capitalism's impact upon the European nation-state. During the *Pax Americana*, national elites had been aided by the imperfect currency convertibility which existed for much of that era, by the need for domestic reconstruction in areas such as housing, and by the small size of non-governmental financial markets. Constraints increased sharply with the emergence of floating rates – which encouraged currency speculation – and in particular the rise of the Eurodollar market in the 1970s. With global capital markets awash in petrodollars, and then with the release of Eurodollar issues, an enormous new market emerged, outside the control of any single central bank. Flows of 'hot money' – sensitive to interest rates or budget deficits – directed into or out of given currencies could entirely disrupt national economic policy.

UK governments came face to face with this phenomenon in the mid-1970s. In 1981 France's Socialists tried Keynesian-style demand stimulus, weakening the franc and increasing the trade deficit. By early 1983 they had had to give up what was known as the 'Albanian' option and opted instead for an anti-inflationary policy of *rigueur*. This narrowed substantially the policy distance between the Socialists and Chirac's Gaullists when they returned to power with a neo-liberal programme in the mid-1980s. The whole scenario was repeated on a smaller scale in Greece with Papandreou's Pasok U-turn in the same period. Thus the 1980s demonstrated that even governments aiming for a social democratic national economic recovery package could no longer go it alone.

It was at this point that the European option started to look increasingly attractive, and it was no coincidence that after a period in the doldrums, the 'European project' should gather speed again in the 1980s. Of course, there were several variants of this 'project' with very different backers. Some – perhaps one might call them the descendants of Albert Speer – saw the Community building up world-class industries on a European scale, rationalizing excessive national competitition, and providing protection from global competition; others, the free marketers (descendants of the British bankers of the 1920s?), saw trade liberalization as the key to Europe's post-war growth and wanted this to continue through the Single European Market. Finally, European social democrats like Mitterrand's Finance Minister Jacques Delors and others on the centre-left, saw the Community replacing or supporting the nation-state as the guarantor of welfare and social solidarity. These three options perhaps only seemed incompatible to the neo-liberal British; to most other west Europeans, free trade was perfectly compatible with support for industrial research and restructuring, and for 'social capitalism'. There was an unsubtle British effort to undercut its European partners by opting out of the Social Chapter, and offering Japanese and American investors a cheap-labour alternative; few other EU members – despite periodic groans about labour costs – seriously considered following the British lead.

What did make the three visions of 'Europe' more difficult to reconcile was the decision to push ahead for full monetary union on terms that would compel budgetary retrenchment in the member states. EMU was one response to the currency speculators who made international exchange rate coordination so difficult, but it was not the only response – the earlier 'snake' with its system of shadowing and banding currencies had been more flexible – and it was not necessary to have agreed on such stringent terms for achieving it.

Even leaving the substantial symbolic issues of national independence on one side, monetary union posed some serious difficulties. National government's economic function would be sharply curtailed, posing an unprecedented challenge to national independence. Moreover, the harshness of the convergence criteria chosen for full monetary union caused increasing levels of unemployment and fiscal retrenchment, making social stability more rather than less difficult to achieve. Some argue that this harshness was a deliberate choice by national governments as a way they could push through unpopular fiscal policies while fixing the blame on Brussels. But a wave of strikes and protests across western Europe in 1994–8 indicated the depth of popular resentment. In France, the pursuit of the *franc fort* by successive governments – desperate to join the mark – prompted occasional bursts of speculation and record levels of unemployment. Chirac was forced to abandon neo-Keynesian policies of reflation almost as soon as he entered government. In Spain, Greece and the Netherlands, governments battled with austerity programmes against popular protest. Nation-states were becoming mere shells with no real hold over policy, while social problems and alienation from government increased. In effect, cautious and unelected German central bankers were being handed control over economic policy across most of western Europe.

There were two possible responses to this pessimistic outlook. One was to point out that EMU involved little that was not already happening, as, in practice, the German Bundesbank was already setting interest rates which other currencies were forced to respond to. Thus economic sovereignty had largely been eroded by the overwhelming strength of the mark. Was it not better in that case to share responsibility for policy throughout the Union more formally? The second consideration was that ultimately there was no particular reason why monetary policy made at the Union level should be more deflationary than when made by national governments. The chief problem was convergence not union – the journey not the destination. EMU itself was not incompatible with expansionist fiscal and monetary policies. Everything depended on how far the authorities allowed control of inflation to override other economic and social concerns.

Interestingly, while the Germans – facing the enormous task of reconstructing the former East Germany – remained anxious about inflation, there were signs in the mid-1990s that the old obsession with inflation elsewhere was starting to wane. The lessons to be drawn from the experience of East Asia's 'tiger' economies turned out to be unexpected, and contrary to the principles followed by European capitalism in its neo-liberal phase in the 1980s. High growth depended upon high levels of government and private investment in research; this would have reassured countries like Germany which preserved high R&D ratios, but undermined the Conservative achievement in the UK where spending on civil research remained very low, overshadowed by the presence of an excessively large arms-export industry. East Asian growth also depended upon high levels of government spending on education, and more generally on egalitarian social policies that equalized income and wealth.

The World Bank drew some startling conclusions: inequality was not beneficial to growth, equality was. 'Reducing inequality not only benefits the poor immediately but will benefit all through higher growth,' stated the chief economist of the World Bank in 1996. Skills and training, not 'flexibilization' and cheap labour, were the way to reduce unemployment. 'Future prosperity', noted the OECD in 1996, 'depends on reducing high unemployment . . . and in some instances, inequalities in earnings and income.' Though it would require redefinition and retargeting, welfare spending was not therefore the great obstacle to economic success. On the contrary, social cohesion was a greater virtue than individualism. By the late 1990s, it looked as though the conservative 'revolution' had had its day. The sweeping Labour victory in the 1997 British elections suggested that neo-liberalism was dead even in its homeland: the capitalist social contract might have to be reworked, but it had proved its popularity and would survive.[46]

Sharks and Dolphins: The Collapse
of Communism

Patiently endured so long as it seemed beyond redress, a grievance
comes to appear intolerable once the possibility of removing it
crosses men's minds.

— De Tocqueville[1]

. . . small fish will turn into dolphins
so will the sharks so will the sharks because
it has to be so.

— Rudolf Rimmel, 1968[2]

'Despite [the] problems, liabilities and handicaps that the Soviet
Union incurs from its continuing imposition of Communism on East
Central Europe,' an authoritative textbook on the region concluded
in 1988, 'there is no signal that Stalin's heirs are prepared to retreat
from it, nor any flagging of their political will to dominate the
area.'[3]

The almost universal failure to predict the collapse of communism
drove a large nail into the coffin of Western political science. But it
was not just the academics who were taken by surprise; so were
policy-makers and intellectuals. In 1984 the Hungarian writer György
Konrad proposed — not entirely seriously — in response to the failed
uprisings of 1956 (Hungary), 1968 (Czechoslovakia) and 1980–81
(Poland): 'Now let the Russians do it.' His preposterous suggestion
was shot down by Vaclav Havel: 'To me personally', wrote Havel,
'that seems just lovely, though it is not entirely clear to me who or

what could induce the Soviet Union to dissolve the entire phalanx of its European satellites – especially since it is clear that, with its armies gone from their territory, it would sooner or later have to give up its political domination over them as well.'[4]

To recall such prognoses is not to mock their authors, who were after all entirely in sympathy with the outlook of their times, but rather to recapture some essential elements of what happened in 1989 itself. The collapse of Soviet control was fast, unexpected and peaceful, and it swept across the region as a whole. None of these features should be forgotten or taken for granted: they are clues as to the real nature of what happened.

The mistaken forecasts of continued Soviet domination should also make us wary of some of the more naive or triumphalist explanations of its demise. In what sense did the West 'win' the Cold War? A victory for democracy there was, to be sure, but hardly of the kind or in the manner anticipated, since no such victory had really been foreseen. Was this a glorious triumph for 'the people' and for the cause of European freedom over tyranny? But popular protest had – as Konrad observed – been tried and found wanting in the past, and came late in the day this time round. Freedom was the outcome; desire for it was not necessarily the cause. The subject of the fall of communism has scarcely begun to attract the interest of historians; this chapter serves simply to map out some ways of understanding this final act in Europe's ideological drama.

THE WORLD ECONOMIC CRISIS AND EASTERN EUROPE

Although Stalinism as an ideology was in decline after 1956, the political *economy* of Stalinism was little altered in the following decades: a centralizing party and state apparatus promoted economic growth through the expansion of heavy industry and the tight control of trade, agriculture and consumer goods. Political discontent was periodically assuaged by adjusting the balance of investment in favour of light industry and improved living standards, but such adjustments were temporary and reversible. The economy was run according to the Plan not the market, in conditions of information scarcity and total political responsibility for economic performance. State socialism was, as one Polish economist put it, not a good idea badly implemented, but a bad idea which was implemented surprisingly well. A development strategy which enjoyed considerable success in the early post-war era outlived any usefulness it might once have had, and ended up causing the collapse of communism as a whole.[5]

In the 1950s and 1960s, growth was spectacular across Europe. The real challenge came with the great crisis of the post-war world economy which began around the end of the 1960s and the early 1970s. In capitalist western Europe, surging inflation and mass unemployment bankrupted the post-war Keynesian consensus. The same economic forces buffeted eastern Europe, and post-war growth slowed down there too: from an average of 4.9 per cent p.a. in 1970–75 to 2.0 per cent in 1975–80 to 1.4 per cent in 1980–85. This drop was relatively slow at first: in the 1970s, east European growth rates (3.4 per cent) fell more slowly and were higher than in the OECD West (3.2 per cent), which may have even increased a sense that centrally planned economies were less vulnerable to the crisis than capitalist ones; but by the mid-1980s, they were lagging far behind.[6]

East as well as West, economic slowdown strained the welfare systems which had been created in the previous decades. Life expectancy actually fell, largely because of hazards at work – the deterioration of the capital stock was killing workers. From the 1970s, the gap with western Europe, which had been narrowing since the war, widened again. Only in terms of alcohol consumption was the East outstripping the West.[7]

Not only was the communist welfare model less and less attractive compared with its western counterpart; it was also failing to live up to its promises in the eyes of societies which took its egalitarian pledges seriously. Income equality was threatened by reforms to increase efficiency, and social mobility was blocked, provoking a growing anger within the working class at the privileges and perks of a relatively wealthy administrative, professional and technical elite. Welfare benefits were failing to equalize real incomes as they turned into Party privileges rather than universal social rights. Living conditions were dire: the average female Polish factory worker got up before 5 a.m., spent over an hour getting to work, fifty-three minutes a day queuing for food, nine hours working and less than six and a half hours asleep. The shortage of housing, above all, preyed on people's minds. 'There's no future here,' complained a Polish shipyard worker in 1972. 'To receive an apartment you have to wait ten years. A man grows old, he wants to marry.' 'The housing situation is worse than before, indeed it is hopeless,' wrote a senior Hungarian housing official in 1985. 'Nothing has essentially changed, nothing has improved.' The communist 'social contract' which western commentators discerned as the basis for regime legitimacy was, if it had ever existed, now coming apart.[8]

Politically, communists found it impossible to make the kinds of adjustments taking place in the West. In other words, the illness was (more or less) the same – declining productivity, the collapse of the old heavy industries which had formed the bedrock of the working class – but the symptoms were different. Inflation was marked by growing shortages, deteriorating quality and lengthening queues, not rising prices, which were controlled tightly by the authorities; black and informal private markets were another expression of the same trend. The result was empty shelves, increasing time wasted in queues and, at the extreme, food riots which threatened the rule of the Party itself when it did try pushing price increases through.

The crisis of heavy industry, too, had more serious implications in the East than in the West. The great iron- and steelworks – spearheads of post-war economic growth, following the Soviet model of the 1930s (which was itself modelled upon German growth patterns from the early part of the century) – were increasingly economically irrational but still possessed tremendous symbolic power. Stalinization as pursued in Romania, for example, led in the 1970s to the creation of monsters like the oil refineries which operated at 10 per cent of capacity, or the aluminium complex which used up as much energy as the whole of Bucharest.

The costs were visible on people's skins and in their lungs. Pollution, by the 1980s, had become a frightening reminder of Communism's failed attempt to master nature. Eastern Europe had become an eco-logical disaster zone of dying rivers and barren forests, grimy cities, crumbling monuments and disease-ridden humans. It pumped out roughly double the amount of sulphur dioxide emitted by the European Community – East Germany's alone was four times that of the Federal Republic.[9] Yet this kind of outmoded industrialization – expensive, unproductive and destructive of the natural environment – far from being disowned, received as much investment as ever. Party bosses had formed power bases around the old industries which fought off challenges from would-be modernizers, and even, as in the case of Poland's Gierek, took them to national leadership.

The obsession with heavy industry had also brought into being a vast working class which the regime claimed to speak for: how could this be sacrificed on the altar of economic rationality? Hence commu-nist regimes could not for political reasons adjust the economy through deflation or through mass unemployment after the fashion of their Western counterparts. They therefore chose the opposite strategy to that followed in the West, and kept consumers suffering through scarcity and shoddy goods in preference to throwing workers out of their jobs. But workers were consumers too, and did not always reciprocate the regime's sentiments. In 1980 the rise of Solidarity showed the threat posed by workers turning against the Party which claimed power in their name.

In retrospect, the central communist dilemma of the 1980s was that economic transformation was necessary but impossible. At the time, however, it did not seem out of the question that communism might reform itself in the same sort of way that capitalism had done in the 1940s. Many in the West saw capitalism and communism as two converging ways of managing a modern industrial economy. Political scientists emphasized the striking formal similarities of the two rival systems – their enormous bureaucracies and reliance on experts, their encouragement of higher education, science and technology, their pursuit of the common goals of material prosperity. Such theorists argued that Western and Eastern economies existed at different points on a continuum with varying combinations of state intervention and market. The implication was that communist reformers could succeed in peacefully transforming east European economies into something closer to the mixed economies of the West.

This belief in the reformability of communism was shared in the East as well and underpinned a series of debates and experiments in eastern Europe and the Soviet Union, curtailed but not ended by the Soviet invasion of Czechoslovakia in 1968. In general, Brezhnev's long reign was a period of conservative reaction to Khrushchev's efforts at improvising reform. But even under Brezhnev, some east European leaders initiated reform movements as a means to modernization and greater efficiency. In East Germany and Bulgaria, this took the form of administrative decentralization, which left the basic central-planning mechanisms untouched. More radical in its implications was the economic decentralization pursued in Czechoslovakia (until the invasion) and Hungary, which tried tentatively to introduce real prices and costs into the economy.

Hungary's was the most enduring and intriguing case. Through the so-called New Economic Mechanism (NEM) which was introduced in 1968, János Kádár cautiously encouraged a process of gradual marketization. Trading with the outside world was decentralized and measures to encourage greater efficiency and productivity were introduced. Firms were encouraged to make profits rather than solely to meet production targets. In the West there was a good deal of interest in the NEM, and much talk of the reformability of communism. But there was just one problem: it was not very successful economically. Hungary ended up with the highest per capita hard-currency debt behind the Iron Curtain, and growth rates which lagged well behind those of such resolute Stalinists as the Czechs, the East Germans and the Romanians. Honecker's own acerbic view was that capitalism and communism were 'as different and incompatible as fire and water' and he insisted as late as 1986 that the GDR was 'no field of experimentation'.[10]

His thinking could not be faulted on economic grounds, as East Germany's record was far superior to that of the Hungarians. Hungarian reform was a soft variant of adjustment which shied away from allowing bankruptcies or unemployment. In retrospect, its main significance was not economic but political, enabling Kádár cautiously to detach Hungary from the Soviet embrace, and to tiptoe through trade policy towards more autonomy. There is an illuminating parallel with another Hungarian leader trying to manoeuvre alongside a great power – Admiral Horthy and his astute handling of Hitler in the decade after 1933.[11]

Borrowing capital from the West was – as it had been in the 1920s, too – another inviting means of avoiding painful decisions and cushioning the shock of modernization. The path beaten to the City and Wall Street by Yugoslavia and Romania was followed by the rest. The transnational and volatile financial markets which emerged in the 1970s, awash with petrodollars, saw eastern Europe, with its highly stable regimes and well-trained workforce, as a neglected area for investment. Bankers with short memories (which certainly did not stretch back the requisite fifty years) convinced themselves that the Soviet 'guarantee' over the Eastern bloc ruled out any chance of default. Communist elites saw Western capital as a means of buying off public opinion and delaying the harsh impact of structural change in the economy. Communists and bankers fell into each other's arms.

As a result, hard-currency debt grew fast everywhere in East Europe. From $6.1 billion in 1971 it rose to $66.1 billion in 1980 and $95.6 billion in 1988. Perhaps the country most affected was Poland, whose borrowing rose from $1.1 billion in 1971 to $25.0 billion in 1980. In the last phase of unquestioned Party rule – during the early 1970s – first secretary Gierek borrowed heavily to engineer a consumer boom. When this began to falter, in the second half of the decade, and living standards fell again, two things emerged: first, that the use of foreign capital had been unsuccessful in modernizing the Polish economy and improving its technological base; and second, that levering up living standards temporarily and artificially had not purchased social peace.

Poland's problems were more generally shared. The rigid structure of command economies made it easier to use foreign credits for food and consumer goods than in acquiring foreign technology and making good use of it. Eastern-bloc exports did shift slowly away from the Soviet Union towards hard-currency partners, but not sufficiently: EC barriers to trade helped keep goods out, increasing the strain on foreign-exchange reserves. Hence these vast debts did not help to modernize the economic base; they simply bought unpopular regimes a breathing space. For a tyrant like Ceauşescu this was not such a problem: thanks to his security system, he could depress living standards still further in order to clear his accounts with Romania's creditors. But for less repressive regimes – and few were as harsh as his – the costs of debt repayment, often now accompanied by supervision from the IMF and World Bank, had to be borne by an increasingly alienated workforce. Thus foreign capital did not ease the plight of communism; it made it worse.

By the early 1980s the overall picture was grim. The once backward economies of southern Europe – Portugal, Spain and Greece – had escaped the shackles of dictatorship, gained access to EC markets and, as a result, were pulling ahead of the communist bloc. Inside eastern Europe, there was considerable variation in economic performance, with hardline East Germany and Czechoslovakia outperforming Hungary and Poland. Everywhere, though, living standards were falling, goods were scarce and the inadequacies of the system were evident. But did this necessarily point to its imminent demise? The GDR's chief statistician has claimed that it was around 1982–3 that he realized 'we were heading for economic collapse'. But in almost the next breath he goes on to admit that Western credits did help stabilize the short-run situation. The mere fact of economic slowdown did not threaten regimes which had perfected reliable ways of defending themselves. What it did was to undermine their claims to rule.[12]

THE ATROPHIED PARTY

By virtue of the care for a good supply of the people with all the necessary goods, for the improvement of trade, of public services, price stability, the population often meet Nicolae Ceauşescu in the town's shopping centres, when opening new shops, when examining the supply of the market with goods. On these occasions, President Ceauşescu listens to what they say and what else should be done, and when possible, takes measures on the spot to improve things. These signs speak by themselves to the honest-minded man that the final scope of building a new society in Romania according to President Ceauşescu's view is Man and his interests, the satisfaction of his spiritual and material demands, the realization of his ideals of progress and civilization.[13]

This Stalinist propaganda puff from 1983 coincided with a period of austerity harsh even by Romanian standards: consumption was being squeezed to pay off the foreign debt, and daily life was ravaged by the insanely destructive programme of 'systemization' through which the regime demolished thousands of villages, scores of towns and eventually a large part of Bucharest itself. There and elsewhere, a growing gulf was opening up between an increasingly harsh reality and official ideology. Or rather, since that gulf had always been present in communism, what was fundamentally happening in the 1980s was the growing recognition by society generally – elite and base – that reality and ideology were parting company.[14]

In Ceauşescu's Romania such recognition counted for little, since it did not extend to the 'Giant of the Carpathians' himself. Elsewhere, however, it permeated the echelons of power. The sense that reality had mastered socialist theory rather than been mastered by it fatally undermined the Party's sense of its own governing mission. Here lay the chief political trend through much of the last two decades of communism – not the emergence of outright opposition, but rather this slow decline of a Party which believed in itself, and its replacement by other organs of government – civil servants in the state apparatus, the military, and the elderly 'little Stalins'. The collapse of belief in socialist ideology, and the abandonment by the early 1980s of any convincing hope of surpassing the West economically, left the Party with little general purpose. It was degenerating into a privileged *nomenklatura*, and a decreasingly effective instrument of crisis management.

The Party's decline was most visible in Poland. In the official Kubiak Report, which it commissioned in September 1981 to reflect upon the causes and origins of the Solidarity crisis, its author – on the liberal wing of the Party – noted that the origins of social conflict lay not only in the political opposition but more basically, 'when the gap between the declared aims of socialism and the results achieved widened'. Solidarity proved that the workers of Gdańsk took socialism seriously – they criticized the perks of Party bosses and showed no signs of interest in capitalism or the market; it was precisely because the Party was no longer a convincing guide to socialism that the assault it faced was so devastating.[15]

Poland had offered a paradigm of the continuation of Stalinist economic priorities through the 1970s: growth of producer goods outstripped consumer goods for much of the period, and there was little structural change or modernization. The priority given to investment in heavy industry continued even into the 1980s. Hence the shock generated by the shipyard workers' strike movement, not to mention the astonishing expansion of the associated Free Trade Unions to some eight million members – more than double the PUWP's own membership – in just a few months.

Solidarity's legacy was a ruling Party stripped of purpose and legitimacy. The 1970s had already seen state officials and industrial managers assuming power at its expense. In a striking departure from all socialist political experience – a move which summoned up echoes of the inter-war years – the government was now handed over to a military man, General Jaruzelski. Jaruzelski claimed that his rule, and the imposition of martial law, were necessary in order to avoid Soviet invasion. This claim now appears to be false, though that was not widely known at the time. What was important was the common perception that the PUWP lacked the authority to continue.

'The principal reason for the December 13 coup [introduction of martial law],' wrote Adam Michnik, 'was not the radicalism of Solidarity but the weakness of the base of the PUWP.' Party numbers fell from 3.1 million in 1980 to 2.1 million in 1984: worryingly, it was primarily the young who were leaving; more than half the Party membership by 1987 were over fifty years old. The true state of relations between populace and governing class was expressed in the martial law which Jaruzelski proclaimed, and which lasted for nearly two years. 'For the first time,' writes the philosopher Leszek Kołakowski, 'the apparatus of communist power was compelled to wage war . . . against its own society.'[16]

Nowhere else in the communist bloc was the Party's situation or outlook as obviously desperate as in Poland; nevertheless, outside East Germany and Czechoslovakia, it could hardly be said to function as a cohesive administrative force. Mostly it had been displaced by the 'little Stalins' at its head, and their coteries. Yet these elderly figures who clung to power across the region seemed by their very age to point to the dangers of predicting what might follow their demise: by 1985 the oldest in the bloc, Gustáv Husák of Czechoslovakia, was seventy-six, the youngest (apart from Jaruzelski), Ceauşescu, was sixty-seven; the seventy-four-year-old Bulgarian Todor Zhivkov had come to power in 1954; Honecker, the newcomer, had succeeded to the East German leadership in 1971. This was an elite of arthritic geriatrics, bitterly resisting change. The succession crisis which followed the octogenarian Tito's death in Yugoslavia in 1980 was a worrying portent.

The danger of personal rule was that, especially in the Balkans, it encouraged the creation of family dynasties. Romania was the most egregious instance – wags called it 'Ceauschwitz' – turned virtually into a personal fiefdom. Even the most senior echelons of the *nomenklatura* were sidelined, as all decisions were taken, without prior discussion, by the Conducator and his powerful, sinister wife, Elena. Party officials were treated much like their Ottoman predecessors, moved from posting to posting, to prevent their building power bases which might threaten their master. After their daughter Zoia, a mathematics student, tried to flee her parents, an angry Ceauşescu closed down the Bucharest Mathematical Institute, provoking a massive brain drain of some two hundred of the country's leading mathematicians. Even in less flagrant abuses of power, accusations and rumours of nepotism were common, indicating the deep popular mistrust of an elite regarded as having betrayed its own principles.[17]

Romania also exemplified another way in which communist elites tried to regain some popularity – through the cultivation of national aspirations. Ceauşescu pushed the use of nationalism further than any other leader, and achieved an apparent detachment from Moscow which brought rich rewards from the West. But national communism became part of a common strategy for clinging on to power. Older gods from the nationalist pantheon were introduced into the Marxist-Leninist liturgy: Marshal Piłsudski started to appear on Polish postage stamps; Luther and Frederick the Great were commemorated in East Germany. Compliant professors produced works like the Bulgarian Academy of Sciences' fourteen-volume history of the country, or the infamous nationalist memorandum of the Serbian Academy of Arts and Sciences. Archaeology, history and ethnography all helpfully uncovered socialism's deep roots in the nation. 'Folk art has been a powerful active factor in the history of the people,' wrote an Albanian professor, 'because for centuries on end it has transmitted the demo-cratic, patriotic and revolutionary ideals of the working masses.'[18]

But national communism also involved a tenser and more antagon-istic relationship towards the surviving remnants of the region's ethnic minorities: anti-Semitism, for instance, surfaced briefly in Poland in 1968, despite the almost total disappearance of what had once been the largest Jewish community in Europe. Tito's legacy was abandoned in Yugoslavia as Milošević used the issue of Kosovo to play to reawakening Serb nationalism. In Bulgaria, decades of a central-izing assimilationist policy towards the minorities culminated in the 1984–5 drive to rename the Turkish population, or rather, to 'restore' their original Bulgarian names. When Romania similarly sanctioned the official persecution of its Hungarian minority, it enflamed a grievance with Hungary which, as we shall see, would play an important part in the events of 1989.

Nationalism was anyway an unpredictable card for the elite to play, since the communists' subservience to Moscow was always in the back of people's minds. Other groups, more independent of Moscow, could pose as more convincing voices for national aspirations. But did such groups exist in the 1980s? This raises the question of the state of the political opposition, its goals and limits. A quick survey reveals two things: first, that the opposition was no longer primarily interested in national independence – the lessons of 1956 and 1968 had been well learned; and second, that apart from Poland its ability to force change was very limited indeed. The revival of nationalism, in other words, was far more a consequence than a cause of 1989.

There were, however, various ways in which opposition manifested itself beyond outright, public confrontation, a very rare event indeed. There was widespread withdrawal from the system – most directly expressed by the millions who fled to the West (a net flow of some 3.5 million East Germans, hundreds of thousands of Poles and others). A Polish opinion poll taken in 1987 showed that 70 per cent of young people wanted to leave the country either temporarily or for good. Their motivation could certainly not be reduced to consumer envy, or to a desire to have the freedom to travel, strong though both these elements were; the Stasi noted that it also implied 'a rejection of the social system'. In 1989 this form of opposition would be crucial in triggering off change across the region.[19]

Leaving the country, though, was not merely discouraged by the rulers of eastern Europe; it was also frowned upon by many of their opponents, by the Church, by reformers inside the Party and outside who had elected to stay and fight for change at home. This was the path followed by Church leaders and many intellectuals, but it did not – outside Poland – seriously threaten the regimes themselves. Intellectuals as an opposition varied from complete irrelevance – as in Romania and Bulgaria – to outspoken sources of irritation and hope in Czechoslovakia and Poland. Political opposition outside Marxism had been crushed in the Stalin years; within it, it remained hesitant and sectarian. Where the Marxist tradition remained strong, as among the most prominent dissidents in East Germany, one heard voices calling for improvements to socialism, not its abandonment. The greater emphasis on ethics, human and civil rights which came across with Charter 77 in Prague, or the KOR group in Poland, made opposition a broader and less sectarian issue; yet it also meant sidestepping the question of a political alternative to communism.

A further problem for the intellectual opposition – especially that situated outside the Party – was that by itself it was powerless. The desire to retain some ability to shape events was precisely what made many opponents of the existing order hang on to their Party membership. For the rest, their influence depended crucially upon whether they could build alliances with other powerful social forces such as the Church or the workers. Yet a gulf divided the three groups for most of this period. The shadow of anti-Semitism, for instance, separated Church leaders and key intellectuals in Poland through the 1970s; even where this was not a factor, anti-clerical intellectuals often found it hard to reach an understanding with Church leaders. The divide between intellectuals and workers was exploited by the Party in Czechoslovakia, which made sure after 1968 to keep the workers loyal; in Poland, it weakened the opposition in 1970. Bridging it was part of the secret of Solidarity's strength in the 1980s.

Also weakening opposition was the fact that all these groups were permeated by the system and to some extent compromised by it. This was true in the most obvious sense that they were often effectively penetrated by security services and their informers; the scale and terrifying intimacy of such operations – with husband spying on wife, for example – has only emerged with revelations from official archives after 1989. But compromise and collusion occurred more indirectly as well. The religious authorities, for example, rarely encouraged outright protest and preferred a more indirect and cautious attitude towards power; their primary goal, after all, was the protection and defence of their own institutions and privileges. The Catholic Church in Poland under Cardinal Głemp, a British observer noted in 1983, was 'alarmed at its own strength' in the aftermath of Solidarity. If this was the case with the most vigorous potential opponent to communism behind the Iron Curtain, it is easy to see how limited a role the more subservient Catholic, Lutheran or Orthodox authorities elsewhere chose to play.[20]

Such an attitude rested on an assessment of the basic durability of East European communism which was broadly shared by another potentially powerful source of opposition – the West. Western governments – and in general, Western public opinion, too – never seriously challenged the communist hold over the region. In fact, given the West's basic acquiescence – right through the 1980s – in the Cold War division of Europe, it is hard to criticize East Europeans for their lack of more vigorous opposition. Few people anywhere, after all, believed in the possibility – or even perhaps the desirability – of a rapid introduction of multi-party democracy.

On the contrary, the 1970s saw a new acceptance of communist rule by the capitalist West. Financially, as we have seen, this took the form of extensive credits. Politically, it was expressed in West German *Ostpolitik*, and superpower détente. By the early 1980s, too much was at stake to let Reaganite neo-conservatism, the onset of the so-called 'second Cold War' and the row about nuclear-missile deployments in western Europe, erode this basic understanding. Western policy aimed to wear the Soviet Union down in the long run through an expensive arms race. But the other side of this 'dual track' strategy was the continued provision of trade credits to eastern Europe, the decision not to declare Poland in default, and to prop up the Hungarian and East German banking system. West Germany's Chancellor Kohl was as committed to *Ostpolitik* as his Social Democrat predecessors had been, buying out East German dissidents and massively subsidizing the communist economy, backing Jaruzelski's imposition of martial law, and eventually even allowing Honecker to make an official visit to the FRG in 1987.

In sum, the opposition which existed in the East was fragmented, inchoate and without determined foreign backing. Western individuals and NGOs offered their support to dissidents, but Western governments were chiefly interested in stability. In the 1980s, opposition to communism coalesced not around political reform but around more general issues of moral renewal, human rights, freedom and peace. In a one-party state these could not but be political in their implications, but they tended – and this was, of course, a condition of their existence – not to produce mass organizations or to offer political alternatives.

One key focus for protest was environmental pollution, especially after the Chernobyl disaster: the Stasi got very irritated by posters in an East German churchyard which read: 'Ride a bike, don't drive a car.' The Hungarian Danube Circle was an unofficial movement with thousands of signatories and strong links in Austria. In Czechoslovakia, Charter 77 circulated a document in 1987 entitled 'Let the People Breathe', which disclosed grim official estimates of the republic's pollution levels. Yet arguably, even here, the level of activism was rather less than in the Soviet Union itself, and especially in the Baltic states.

The vast security services which monitored popular opinion do not appear to have been unduly alarmed by levels of opposition. 'Conformity and grumbling' was the pattern discerned by the Stasi, and the former had probably grown rather than diminished over time. Soviet-sponsored Stalinism had come to be seen as the region's fate, against which only the headstrong or saintly rebelled. Compared with the Nazi Gestapo, the Stasi and the Romanian Securitate were enormous, technically advanced apparatuses of terror, easily able to coerce and intimidate the mass of the population into compliance. Only one source of destabilization eluded their control – Moscow itself. In 1987 Poland's deputy prime minister Mieczysław Rakowski, musing on the ever-present threat that 'somebody' might intervene in the country's internal affairs, was struck by a sudden thought: 'What if that *somebody*, bearing in mind his own interests, does not *want* to intervene?' And what, indeed, if he did intervene – to challenge the old order? It is to this possibility that we must now turn.[21]

THE EVOLUTION OF SOVIET POLICY

Murder or suicide? Revolution or retreat? The same questions which are often asked of the ending of British rule in India, or of the Dutch in Indonesia, can be posed in the case of 1989 too. This is not by chance: communism's demise formed part of the broader canvas of European decolonization.

The long age of empire, begun by Portugal and Spain in the fifteenth century, came to an end in the middle of our own. After the Second World War, itself a defeat for German imperial ambitions, the remaining European powers reluctantly divested themselves of their colonies too. The speed varied, but overall the process of decolonization was incredibly fast – a matter of decades – set against the lengthier rhythms of imperial conquest and consolidation. Whatever Marxist theorists of neo-imperialism may have felt – and it is true that Western economic influence did *not* in general decline after decolonization – the political act of dismantling empires was an act of tremendous significance.

Explaining the causes of decolonization – and especially its speed

– has occupied historians ever since. Several points have become clearer. First, empire did not, on the whole, pay; to be more specific, while it offered huge profits to some individuals and companies, it burdened the treasuries of most imperial powers. Thus the exploitation of colonial peoples was not incompatible with net losses to taxpayers at home. Second, imperial powers were rarely forced to retreat as a direct result of military insurrection – Algeria was the exception not the rule. Insurgencies could usually be squashed; the problem was at what cost in lives and money. Nationalist historians like to argue that brave resistance fighters threw off the shackles of imperial rule; in practice, the warders in Whitehall and Paris usually decided when to close down (or unlock) the prison and retire.

Their decision was a compound of considerations – financial, military and politico-ideological. Imperial powers always had a choice whether or not to resort to force to uphold their rule. When they did – like the French in Algeria and Vietnam or the Portuguese in southern Africa – they often ended up jeopardizing political stability at home. Increasingly, in the post-war era, they chose not to do so. One reason, of course, was that they came to realize that military domination was an expensive and clumsy way of getting what they wanted. Another for the Western powers was that their continued grip on empire suited neither their patron, the United States, nor their own domestic publics, who were chiefly concerned about prosperity inside a new Europe. The glamour of empire looked increasingly tarnished, its morality and rationality thrown into question in a continent which operated not according to global imperial rivalries and the possession of territory, but through transnational economic cooperation.

Thus, in the modern era, military defeat was not necessary to bring empires to their knees. It brought the collapse of the Ottoman, Spanish and Habsburg empires of course, but hardly that of the mightiest empire of them all, the British. As for Russia, the Tsarist empire had collapsed in 1917 under the pressure of war, yet Stalin's empire survived and prospered after an even more vicious and destructive war only to collapse with such speed in a period of peace. One way to look at Soviet rule in eastern Europe is simply as an anachronism, a relic of past modes of rule no longer suited to the modern world.

With a swiftness and political sophistication comparable to the British pull-out from India in 1947 or from West Africa a little later, the Kremlin chose to pull out from eastern Europe and the empire disintegrated almost overnight. Suicide, then, not murder. The reasoning underlying the Kremlin's choice – the priority attached to domestic economic reform, the disillusion which followed the Afghanistan quagmire – becomes the key to the events of 1989.[22]

Although the Brezhnev years were ones of stagnation and ideological conservatism – the high priest of Soviet doctrinal purity, Mikhail Suslov, only died in 1982 – beneath the surface there were indications of new ways of thinking about Soviet relations with eastern Europe. Brezhnev's eventual successor, Yuri Andropov, had been Soviet ambassador to Hungary in 1956, before heading the Kremlin's main liaison department with east European communist parties. There he gathered around him a group of reformers who would rise to senior positions in the 1980s. Andropov himself, who headed the KGB for most of the Brezhnev era, had a better idea than most in the Kremlin of the ruinous state of the communist empire, and after the Polish crisis of 1980–81 he spoke bluntly of the need for fresh thinking and urgent economic reform.

From the Soviet perspective, several factors encouraged new approaches towards eastern Europe. In the first place, the region, after acting as a net asset to Moscow in Stalin's time, had now become an enormous economic burden, equivalent on one reckoning to 2 per cent of GNP per year: in the 1970s, massive subsidies, chiefly through cheap Soviet exports of fuels, meant that poorly-off Russians were subsidizing better-off Poles and Czechs. Eastern Europe's CMEA, unlike the Common Market, was failing to generate a virtuous circle of greater productivity and wealth; rather it ossified bilateral trading arrangements (95 per cent of all CMEA activity) and encouraged mutual accusations of exploitation. Brezhnev's 1971 plan for 'socialist integration' was a damp squib compared with its capitalist counterpart. By the 1980s CMEA looked to the east Europeans like an instrument of Soviet nationalism; it was, in the words of one commentator, 'a framework without much substance'. In the second half of the 1980s, the overall volume of Soviet–east European trade failed to grow at all.[23]

To make matters worse, the cost of supporting hundreds of thousands of troops in eastern Europe was also draining the economy. Moscow's security policy had made the region entirely dependent upon Soviet arms, but the consequence was that the Soviet Union footed the bill for generating new weapons systems. On average, the Soviet Union spent 12–15 per cent of GNP on defence compared with 6 per cent by its satellites. Ironically, it faced exactly the same issue of unequal burden-sharing which preoccupied Nato states too; the difference was that the USA was far better equipped to handle the burden of being a superpower. To rub salt into the wound, the east Europeans were actually cutting back defence spending in the 1980s.[24]

From the strategic point of view, too, the importance of eastern Europe to Soviet security needs had changed vastly since 1945. The Cold War was now being fought out in Asia as well as Europe. Détente diminished the threat from Germany and allowed Moscow to focus on its rival China, an infinitely more powerful and less predictable foe. Then came the war in Afghanistan and a Soviet military performance which increased doubts about its usefulness in eastern Europe. At the same time, east European elites responded to the breakdown of détente by insisting, against Soviet wishes, on the need to preserve links to Western economies. Bloc unity was less and less assured.

All this helps explain why the Soviet elite seemed to be coming round to the view, through the 1980s, that force had had its day. Unlike the Nazis, communists had never formally renounced the idea of the juridical equality of sovereign states. They had traditionally, however, justified granting a 'leading role' to Moscow by appealing to the notion of 'socialist internationalism' and 'joint defence for the achievements of socialism', phrases whose real meaning emerged in 1968. By 1983, stimulated by Brezhnev's death and the rise of the reformist Andropov, a vigorous debate was under way among Russian scholars about whether or not a socialist community really existed. Reformers talked instead of 'common-democratic principles of non-interference in internal affairs'.[25]

In 1985 Gorbachev was elected general secretary, the youngest ever to hold the post. His priority was domestic – to meet the economic challenge facing the USSR by replacing the Stalinist growth model of extensive development based around heavy industry with a more modern pattern using up-to-date technology and high productivity. The Lenin of the NEP – experimental, pragmatic yet committed to the cause of socialism – became his model. In the mind of this adroit product of the communist system, *perestroika* was thus intended to regenerate the Soviet economy, not to destroy it.

In many ways, the Gorbachev reform programme was similar to that pursued earlier in parts of eastern Europe. But there was a key doctrinal difference. Gorbachev was far freer than, say, Kádár to speculate about the political aspects of reform. Soon it became clear that for the Soviet leader, a successful restructuring of the economy – and revitalization of socialism – depended upon greater freedom of information, and even – in an arresting phrase – upon 'the democratization of all parts of our society'.[26]

The foreign-policy implications took time to emerge. It was obvious that Gorbachev did not envisage the break-up of the Soviet empire, still less the Union itself. Yet he did stress that future cooperation between states and republics would need to occur on a non-coercive basis. 'The time is ripe', he wrote in 1987, 'for abandoning views on foreign policy which are influenced by an imperial standpoint . . . It is possible to suppress, compel, bribe, break or blast, but only for a certain period.'[27]

Running to some extent counter to the new emphasis on cooperation was an insistence that east European regimes emulate the Soviet Union in its reform effort. Elites were told openly that 'the administrative-state model of socialism, established in the majority of East European countries during the 1950s under the influence of the Soviet Union, has not withstood the test of time'. Now Moscow was ordering them to reform, while expecting its influence to remain undiminished. Gorbachev himself won astounding popularity in the region, except among the hardline leaders, like Honecker, Husák and Ceaușescu. But then perhaps they saw more clearly than he did that his policies spelled the end of communism.[28]

THE CRISIS OF 1989

The fall of the empire began inside the USSR itself. In 1987 powerful environmental protest movements gave way in the Baltic states to large unofficial demonstrations commemorating the anniversary of the 1939 Molotov–Ribbentrop pact, which had effectively sealed the fate of the inter-war independent republics. Further anniversaries also gathered large crowds, plunging the authorities into disarray and paving the way for the more intense political struggle of the following year. At the end of 1988 Estonia proclaimed its sovereignty as an autonomous republic – the first to do so in the USSR – and declared the primacy of republic over federal law. 'National' emblems of the pre-war republics were increasingly visible in demonstrations organized by massively popular pro-autonomy groups which wrested unofficial recognition from the local authorities.

What weakened the latter and made them hesitate to crack down on the demonstrators were the signs from the Kremlin that it was opposed to a hard line. By early 1989 the popular fronts had scored a resounding success, trouncing the Party in elections to the new USSR Congress of People's Deputies, and they started moving cautiously from demands for 'autonomy' to full independence.[29]

But in eastern Europe, there was – outside Poland – little indication at the start of 1989 of the momentous events that were shortly to unfold there. In Poland itself, the post-Solidarity balancing act was clearly over, and a new wave of strikes threatened to escape the control, not only of the government, but more worryingly of the old Solidarity leadership as well. This time the threat was not of Soviet intervention, but of civil war – forcing the government first to invite Solidarity for round-table talks, and then to grant elections, in July 1989, at which the Party suffered a resounding defeat. Amidst these extraordinary events, Gorbachev reasserted his doctrine of non-intervention, and a meeting of Warsaw Pact member states proclaimed that 'there does not exist any kind of universal socialist model, (and) no one possesses a monopoly on truth'. The government formed by

Tadeusz Mazowiecki in August 1989 was the first in eastern Europe to be headed by a non-communist since the 1940s.[30]

In retrospect, communism had already ended that April, when the Polish communists implicitly recognized Solidarity's legitimacy by inviting them to the round-table talks. Still, few at this stage predicted the changes that would so swiftly be triggered off across the region. After all, Gorbachev's reform programme was really only safe after the defeat of his main conservative rival Ligachev in October 1988. Chance and error continued to reign as the empire fell apart. If change had occurred in Poland because of the Party's weakness, it occurred next in Hungary because the Party was strong, overbearing and overconfident in the face of a fragmented opposition which it mistakenly thought it could control. What it did not realize until too late was that behind the political opposition was a massive public desire for change – manifested in the enormous crowds that gathered to celebrate the anniversary of the 1848 uprising (far larger than the previous year), the reburial of Nagy, or the alternative 1 May rally which dwarfed the official one.

Because change had come about in Poland where the economy was desperately weak, the regimes in East Germany and Czechoslovakia felt confident that they were protected by economic strength. Yet economic turmoil was not the only trigger for collapse. There was a kind of domino effect, too. When the Hungarians liberalized their border requirements with Austria in order to draw international attention to the plight of the Hungarian minority locked inside Romania, the unforeseen result was an exodus of East Germans through Hungary that summer which underlined the unpopularity of Honecker's rule. The crisis of the *ancien régime* took months in Poland, but only weeks in the DDR and Czechoslovakia. As in 1848 one uprising triggered off another, but this time there was no imperial reconquest because no one believed any longer in empire.

In general, the changeover was astonishingly peaceful, marred only by police brutality in Czechoslovakia and the DDR; serious street fighting took place only in Romania, where the Ceauşescu tyranny was deaf to other forms of dialogue. Tiananmen Square was a model to be avoided for all but the most hardline apparatchiks, though

Honecker came close. The smoothness of this transition – in contrast to the bloodshed in China – was in part a reflection of the ruling Party's sense of its own weakness, its abandonment by Moscow and its own historic failure. But it also reflected the opposition's weakness as well, insecure in its claim to power. What confronted all would-be participants in the political reformation of 1989 was the danger posed by the power vacuum created by communism's failure. Public opposition to communism was unmistakable, and immediately reflected in the elections which followed over the next two years.

It is therefore understandable why many observers seemed transfixed by the enormous crowds which emerged to demonstrate against the old order in its dying moments. These crowds – making perhaps their last appearance in European history – were both an affirmation of communism's bankruptcy, and a portent of the instability that might follow if a new and more legitimate political order was not constructed.

Working out the new rules was the immediate task of post-communist politics. There was a striking parallel here with 1919: seventy years later, a new generation was again attempting to remake democracy in the region. Once again, but for different reasons, West European political and constitutional norms were imported into eastern Europe, and clashed with divergent socio-political realities and historical memories. Political parties had to be founded in an environment where the very notion of a political party had been tainted by communism. Hence the Salvation Fronts, Solidarity, the Democratic and Civic Forums, and Union of Democratic Forces – anything to avoid the dreaded appellation. The suspicion of parties actually increased as the heterogeneous opposition coalitions which had been formed and held together to combat communism, fell apart in 1990–91. Solidarity's split between liberal intellectuals around Mazowiecki and populist nationalists around Wałęsa prefigured the key fault line, as political and intellectual elites struggled to reforge links to the masses.

As in 1919 the constitutional order had to be remade, but this time the trend was distinctly gradualist and unrevolutionary. In Hungary and Poland, amended communist constitutions served for several years in place of completely new versions, underlining the desire for a smooth transition rather than an abrupt dismissal of the past. Remaking constitutions was hampered initially by the uncertain legal situation created by the communist abdication of power – who had the legitimacy to make a new constitution in 1990? – and later by the collapse of the initial anti-communist consensus. Only in Romania and Bulgaria were entirely new constitutions brought in swiftly.

And as in 1919, these looked better on paper than in reality. The desperate economic crisis made new promises of social and economic rights sound hollow, even (perhaps especially) in comparison with the communist past, while civil, human and political rights were often checked and limited by arbitrary state power and nationalist authoritarian impulses. Free speech could be curbed, for example, when adjudged to conflict with 'public morality' or the 'constitutional order', while in Romania, the law prohibited the 'defamation of the country and the nation' as well as 'obscene acts contrary to good morals'. The fact that similarly illiberal statutes remain on the books in countries like Greece and Italy is a reminder that it is not just in eastern Europe that residues of past authoritarian attitudes survive.[31]

Just as in 1919, moreover, the new constitutions failed to address what remained of minority rights. Democracy once again involved the re-creation of a *national* community, and there was less international concern about minorities, or protest on their behalf, than in the days of the League of Nations. The Baltic republics introduced citizenship laws which turned ethnic Russians and Belorussians into 'foreigners' – some 50 per cent of Latvia's population, and 40 per cent of Estonia's: protests from the Council of Europe brought only minor improvements in their situation. In the Balkans, the constitutional commitment to national languages allowed local authorities to block the teaching of minority languages in schools and universities. The citizenship laws of the new Czech republic excluded gypsies and Slovaks. Hungary stood out for the liberal way it treated its own minorities, even if its constitution talked unsettlingly of a 'responsibility for what happens to Hungarians living abroad'.[32]

But the parallels were with 1945 as well as with 1919. As after the Nazi occupation, the question of the continuity of the state – of law and administration – with the old order had to be faced. As the communist apparatus of terror was dismantled, East Europeans had to decide who should be punished, who compensated. 'Lustration' of the communist *nomenklatura* recalled the 1940s purges of elites tainted by wartime collaboration. Similar debates about the focus and range of such purges took place, as it became clear that there was simply no way to remake society afresh. In Czechoslovakia and the former DDR – perhaps the two most enthusiastic purgers – it soon became clear that secret police files were an unreliable instrument of vengeance. In general, there were surprisingly few witch-hunts, probably because everyone was aware of how deep complicity in the old system had gone. As in the 1940s, there were strong practical arguments in favour of burying the ghosts of the past. Transition rather than revolution meant keeping the administrative and economic expertise that lay in the hands of the old elite, even if this allowed it the chance to expropriate state property and retain some degree of power. In fact the transition after 1989 was smoother than either of those after the First and Second World Wars, a sign perhaps of the growing political sophistication and experience of the region.[33]

Perhaps the best proof of the new system's resilience were the victories won by former communists in parliamentary elections in 1994. 'Do people forget so quickly?' complained a conservative Hungarian politician facing defeat at the hands of former communists. 'Yes, the bad things, at any rate. Voters associate the Left less with the horrors of the 1950s and more with the easygoing "goulash communism" that made Hungary the "jolliest barracks in the socialist camp".' The problem for Hungarian conservatives was that before 1989 Hungarians had compared themselves to Romania, now it was Austria which provided the benchmark.[34]

In general, the newly liberated east Europeans had one dream: nervous of being left alone, they could hardly wait to 'rejoin Europe'. But what Europe were they rejoining? A Europe of freedom, to be sure, but beyond that lay a Europe they had thought little about and that thought little about them, preoccupied by its own welfare crisis, fiercely protective of its industries, and largely uninterested in the practical difficulties of helping smooth their transition to democracy and capitalism. Western neo-liberalism, and political introversion at the highest levels, ruled out any attempt to emulate the kind of comprehensive aid provided by the Marshall Plan after 1945. On the contrary, in the first few years at least, Western advisers implied that the mere dismantling of the institutions of state socialism, and the creation of a legal framework for functioning markets, would allow capitalism to take root and flourish.

Thatcherite policies which had been sensibly shunned by most of western Europe were implemented on a breathtaking scale in the East. Directed by an army of Western economists, consultants, accountants and lawyers, privatization swept across the region. Nearly 80 per cent of the Czech economy, 40–60 per cent elsewhere, was in private hands in five years. It was a transfer of resources – within countries, and from states to foreign investors – on an unprecedented scale.[35] The result was the destruction of the old communist welfare system without anything being put in its place. At most, Western banks provided the kind of short-term financial aid for monetary stabilization which had been forthcoming to communist regimes throughout the 1980s. As once before – in the 1920s – Western governments tended to keep out of the region, leaving the provision of investment capital to the private sector. It was simply not enough. Between 1990 and 1993, foreign investment in the entire former Soviet bloc came to $12.5 billion, yet Singapore alone attracted almost half that amount in one year. Faced with legal uncertainty over property claims – the German federal restitution office alone had more than one million claims outstanding in 1993 – foreign investors remained cautious. Meanwhile the European Bank of Reconstruction and Development – a worthy heir to Lloyd George's abortive scheme after the First World War – spent most of its initial funds on marbling sumptuous headquarters in London rather than on eastern Europe.

The outcome was a massive 20–40 per cent drop in industrial output and sharply rising unemployment, offset only by increased flows of workers migrating elsewhere. The new democracies thus faced the reckoning with global competition which their predecessors had postponed. Whole towns and industries collapsed, decontrolled rents soared and income differentials suddenly widened as a new class of capitalists flaunted their wealth in societies which had taken the egalitarian rhetoric of communism very seriously. 'Now there is no social safety net,' complained one Hungarian worker. 'At least then there was. There are terrible lay-offs. They turn off the electricity if people can't pay.' The old system had, after all, had benefits as well as drawbacks, and people had been accustomed to both. The new capitalism was more unstable, creating new *mafiosi*, breeding crime and destroying the savings of honest people through pyramid scams which they mistook out of inexperience for regular banks. The moral economy of communism was bankrupt, but nothing has yet replaced it except perhaps a new individualism and sense of suspicion.[36]

GERMANY REUNIFIED

The most fundamental alteration in the European balance of power created by the collapse of the Soviet empire was the reunification of Germany. Yet this was as unforeseen as partition had been forty years before. The original division of Germany might not have figured in the plans of any of the major powers (except France), but once it had happened, none of them hurried to reverse it. In both West and East Germany, the issue of reunification declined in importance as time passed and appeared forgotten by the time of Honecker's state visit to Bonn in 1987. *Ostpolitik* was a substitute for unification more than a strategy for achieving it. Of course, this reflected the perception inside and outside the country that calling for unification would reawaken dormant fears of German power. As it was, opinion polls confirmed that fear of Germany was declining sharply in eastern Europe as the memory of the Second World War receded: it was this very decline which undercut the old justification for the Soviet Army's continued presence in Europe, and which therefore – by a paradox more apparent than real – permitted the retreat of communism that ultimately made German reunification not merely advisable but unavoidable. For as Kohl's chief foreign-policy adviser had realized, should the ideological divergence between the two Germanys disappear, then there would no longer be any reason for the country's partition.

Gorbachev talked about overcoming the division of Europe, but did not apparently contemplate overcoming the division of Germany. Like a Stalin in reverse, Gorbachev came to unification only gradually. Many in the West too envisaged the ending of the Cold War while keeping two Germanys; Mrs Thatcher, for instance, declared in November 1988 that 'we're not in a Cold War now' but remained suspicious of German power and opposed to reunification. Only George Bush saw matters differently. Unlike Gorbachev he wanted the unity of Europe based unambiguously on 'Western values'; unlike Kohl he was not ready to hold eastern Europe hostage to good relations with Moscow.[37]

Yet would reunification have ever happened without the opening of the Berlin Wall in November? In the chaotic and unpredictable summer of 1989, many commentators suddenly discovered the virtues of the Cold War and the stability it had created. Writing in June, the historian Hugh Trevor-Roper speculated: 'Perhaps if controls were removed, communism in East Germany would shrivel like a scroll. But would that not be a revolution, a de-stabilisation of Europe, which for 44 years has lived in a balanced peace? . . . The only questions are, do the Germans really want it, and if so, how can it be achieved without destroying the delicate balance of Europe which has been based on division?'[38]

Certainly, neither the refugee exodus of August, nor the demonstrations of October, seemed at the time necessarily to spell the end of the East German state. The demonstrators in Leipzig, who in December would be shouting 'Wir sind ein Volk!' (We are one people), were two months earlier shouting the very different 'Wir sind das Volk!' (We are the people). Behind the Wall, the first calls for unification came barely a month before the Wall itself fell.

Perhaps the Cold War ended therefore as a result of a simple administrative error. More than one Western journalist claims the credit for having posed the vital question at the 9 November press conference in East Berlin: from when did the newly liberalized travel regulations for East Germans – just announced by Günter Schwabowski, the government's exhausted press spokesman – come into effect? Without instructions on this point, Schwabowski replied off the cuff:

'From this moment.' Later he admitted the authorities had not anticipated 'the rush, the emotional drive' that drove thousands within
hours to Checkpoint Charlie. Bewildered border guards had no idea
what to do with them; by the time the politicians ordered them to let
people through, they had started to do so anyway.

In a final act of the revolution which had begun in 1917, a popular
uprising swept away the last vestiges of communism in Germany, and
swept the political elite along with it. Yet even after 9 November,
many politicians and intellectuals – from Gorbachev to Günter Grass
– still sought to preserve a separate East German state, linked to its
Western partner in confederation. At the end of November, Kohl
himself suggested a long-term, phased approach to reunification. But
the popular mood inside Germany was impatient, and Kohl too
astute a politician to hold out against it. Within a year of the Wall's
demolition, currency union and then full constitutional unification
were achieved.

'A final line is being drawn under post-war German history,'
declared General Matvei Burlakov, the last commander of Russian
troops in eastern Germany on the eve of withdrawal in 1994. Western
forces had already left; Soviet war memorials were beginning to
crumble. With a swift resurgence of neo-Nazism, and the spread of
mass unemployment among the Ossis, it was natural to feel a certain
apprehension at Europe's newly dominant power. This apprehension
was, of course, a reflection of those historical fears – held with especial
tenacity in Britain and France, the two countries most desperate to
cling to their illusions of great-power status – which often obscure a
more balanced view of the present. But it was also based on simple
bewilderment at the speed and unpredictability of reunification, which
had underlined the difficulty of foreseeing, still less controlling, events
in the new Europe. Interestingly, ordinary people – to judge from
opinion polls taken in 1990 – were less perturbed by German unification
than intellectuals and politicians.

To the historian, it seems obvious that Kohl's Germany is not the
threat to Europe which Hitler's was. It is buoyed up by the resilience
of its post-war democratic experience and the historical failure of
communism and fascism. Its lack of militarism reflects the memory

of five million German war dead from the last war; its lack of expansionism, the disappearance of German minorities in the East as a primary concern of foreign policy, and the collapse of the Darwinist views of international relations which held sway for nearly a century between the eras of romantic nationalism and the Third Reich.

The most powerful country in Europe is now forced to devote itself to the reconstruction of its eastern half. Should it be criticized for introspection, or attacked for seeking to dominate eastern Europe through economic aid and investment there, more than half the West's total? Should it be praised for halving the Bundeswehr's troop strength, or attacked for lack of assertion in projecting its strength abroad? It was expected to take the lion's share of refugees from the former Yugoslavia, while any tightening of its asylum laws provokes cries of Fascism. It sometimes seems as though other Europeans find it as hard to come to terms with German democracy as Germans do with their former dictatorship. But that may be less because of the past than because Germany today – with its loose federalism and its faltering social-market economy – seems likely to be their future.

THE WAR IN THE FORMER YUGOSLAVIA

After 1989, Western commentators became transfixed by nationalism. As national memories and old hatreds resurfaced, it was easy to see the revival of nationalism as the return of history and the root of Europe's future troubles. The study of ethnic minorities has now become a growth industry for academics, security experts and international lawyers. Communist elites may have made an easy switch to new roles as nationalist figureheads, but their Western observers were not far behind them, expertly retooling their own Cold War analytic skills.

The fall of communism underlined nationalism's disruptive potential for several reasons. First, liberation from communism was often seen in the context of demands for national independence – this was most obviously true in the Baltic states, but also for most of Eastern

Europe too. Second, the old mechanisms for smoothing minorities disputes inside the Warsaw Pact, already badly worn out, no longer operated after 1989. Third, the greater ease of access to eastern Europe for Westerners meant a harsher light now shone on xenophobia and racism in the region. 'The flame-thrower is the only weapon I need to win/All Gypsy adults and children we'll exterminate,' sang a Hungarian skinhead band. 'But we can kill all of them at once/When it's done we can advertise: Gypsy-free zone.' Anti-gypsy prejudice united such foes as Slovak premier Meciar and the Hungarian politician István Csurka, as did the new passion for commemorating wartime nationalists with nasty collaborationist and anti-Semitic records like Tiso, Pavelić and Marshal Antonescu.[39]

On the other hand, a lot of the talk about a return to past hatreds was beside the point, part of a fashionable *fin de siècle* gloom that was not based on any serious appraisal of the overall political outlook. In fact, the international context differed dramatically from the first half of the century, when nationalism had threatened the stability of Europe. Wartime genocide, mass expulsions and population engineering had led the proportion of east Europeans who made up minorities to drop dramatically from the high levels of the inter-war years. Jews, Germans and Ukrainians had been wiped out, deported or expelled and their return was neither biologically nor politically possible. The German Question in consequence was now a matter of unification not irredentism, and no one in the 1990s seriously anticipated a German *Anschluss* with Austria. Compared with the Basques and Catalans in Spain, the ethnic Germans in northern Italy and the increasingly restless subject peoples of Great Britain, eastern Europe on the whole looked fairly peaceful. The only minority there capable of triggering off a wider conflict were the ethnic Russians in the Baltic states, who faced discrimination and pressure to leave. Elsewhere, minorities remained a focus for prejudice and assault, an Other (to use a fashionable French term) against which the Nation might define itself, but hardly at the centre of daily political concerns. In this respect, at least, east and west Europe were coming to resemble one another.

It was, of course, the bloody disintegration of Yugoslavia which set nationalism centre stage – the one case where the failure of communism had devastating consequences (and showed what Russia had escaped). Slovenia's defection in 1991, after a few days' desultory fighting with the rump Yugoslav Army, showed that break-up was possible in a relatively peaceful fashion. But then Slovenia had no Serb minority. Croatia and Bosnia did, and when they sought to secede from the federation, the Serbs refused to let them.

Serbia's communist boss – Slobodan Milošević – guaranteed his own hold on power for years longer than his former comrades elsewhere in eastern Europe by going to war as a Serbian nationalist and Yugoslav socialist at one and the same time. When Ceauşescu had tried to play the nationalist card, he found the crowds and the army against him. Milošević purged the army of his opponents and tanks drove demonstrators off the streets of Belgrade. Thereafter there was little overt opposition – though much desertion, emigration and withdrawal – inside Serbia until the war reached its inglorious conclusion in 1995. Nationalism, self-obsession and the regime's lock on the media minimized Serbian opposition to the war itself.

In Bosnia, the Serbs were clearly fighting for ethnic purity and land – in a reversion to the kinds of methods and values last employed by the Germans, in Hitler's bid for *Lebensraum*. Ethnic cleansing was the first stage in this process, a strategy of terror designed to force non-Serbs out of their homes and push local Serbs into line. It worked brilliantly, creating hundreds of thousands of refugees within months, and eventually more than two million in all. The West tried to contain the refugee crisis without addressing its fundamental cause, and waited for a Serb victory. If this failed to come it was because ethnic cleansing itself could not guarantee military success. So long as the cities – above all Sarajevo – held out against bombardment, the Serbs' massive superiority in artillery was not decisive, and they needed to go in for street fighting, with the heavy losses that could entail, in order to win. They shied away from this, and settled for stalemate. But time shifted the balance of forces in favour of their enemies: with American support, the Bosnians and Croats became more powerful, while Serb morale fell. In 1995 they suddenly learned a truth which had eluded the Nazis half a century earlier: it is not enough to win land, it must also be held. Ethnic cleansing had brought them too much land, and driven away the hands to make it productive.

Thus the Serb defeat in 1995 was a defeat for the idea of *apartheid* in Europe. But it was also a defeat for the West, which failed to meet the first serious challenge to liberal values after the Cold War. It was bad enough that it chose realpolitik over the protection of rights and the prevention of genocide; worse that even its realpolitik was a failure. Having declared for three years that military intervention was bound not to work, it suddenly found in the summer of 1995 that it worked all too well. Bosnian government forces had to be prevented by Western diplomatic pressure from taking the vital Serb stronghold of Banja Luka, a prize which would have guaranteed a viable Bosnian state. The outcome of the war was therefore that there were no outright victors – a recipe for continued uncertainty in the region, and a triumph for Western indecision.

To speak of the West is to disguise the fact that all the major initiatives to break the deadlock in Bosnia came from the Americans. It might have seemed to the neutral observer that Bosnia was a European problem, but this could not have been deduced from the behaviour of the Europeans themselves. EU policy-making was completely marginalized, and the West European Union seemed little better. The British and the French preferred to operate through the UN and Nato, bodies in which they shared power with the Americans, and – in the former case – with the Russians too. London and Paris vaunted their commitment by sending troops, but were confused for long periods as to what they wanted them to do. Both liked complaining about American arrogance and hypocrisy, but neither was able to summon sufficient resolve to act alone. Thus Bosnia showed how hard it was for Europeans to handle their own conflicts without Washington, even after the end of the Cold War.

One of the arguments of the pro-interventionists in the Bosnian war was that left to run unchecked it might destabilize the rest of eastern Europe. In the short run, at least, this fear was not borne out. Scenarios of a domino effect across the Balkans – with fighting spreading through Kosovo, Macedonia and Albania – ignored the war's deterrent impact. Television footage of burning villages and shelled cities brought home the real costs of nationalist hysteria, and thus may have helped inhibit inflammatory rhetoric, and contain expansionist or irredentist plans, encouraging compromise and mediation.

At the same time, the West's inability to bring the fighting to an end, and its seeming reluctance to enforce norms of international behaviour, increased nervousness throughout the region. A serious arms race between Greece and Turkey escalated in the early 1990s, and brought the two countries closer to war than they had been for decades. In Kosovo it was starting to look as if the Serbs could not repress the Albanian majority for very much longer, while in Macedonia, ethnic tensions and violence spilling over from Albania itself threatened to destabilize a precariously balanced regime. The deterrent effect of the Bosnian war will not last indefinitely and is no substitute for a coherent European security policy towards the Balkans.

The war in Yugoslavia can perhaps best be seen as a product of the collapse of federalism after 1989. This was the only case in Europe where the outcome was settled by fighting. In Czechoslovakia – the only other surviving federal creation of Versailles – a Velvet Divorce ensured a peaceful and civilized separation between Czechs and Slovaks. The real difficulties lay mostly in the sphere of the former Soviet Union, with its large Russian minorities on the western and southern periphery of the old empire. In fact, in the European zone, the conflict – with the partial, brief exception of Moldova, and the Baltic republics in 1991 – remained confined to the political level and did not escalate.

In general eastern Europe, and therefore Europe as a whole, was a far more stable place than at any time earlier in the century. Inter-war revisionism had sought to change the borders laid down at Versailles. But in the end people moved – or were moved, or killed – and with the exception of Poland, the USSR and Germany, there was little alteration of borders by the end of the 1940s. After 1989 it was generally accepted that borders should stay where they were. This was what had been agreed at Helsinki in 1975, and it remained an article of faith even when this meant accepting the injustices of the post-1945 settlement. Germany finally recognized Poland's western border and gave up all claims to the old eastern territories. The Baltic states too accepted independence within the post-war boundaries and did not seek a return to the pre-1939 status quo ante. Stability was too precious to be jeopardized, and much of the West's seemingly amoral and contradictory policy towards the former Yugoslavia is best understood as a desperate attempt to uphold this principle.

This general acceptance is all to the good, since there is little sign of any greater willingness on the part of east European states to cooperate with one another. On the contrary, the old suspicions remain: the West is still expected to act as saviour, the Russians still regarded as the enemy. Western indifference is matched by Eastern irresponsibility. The Western excess of realpolitik is counterbalanced by excessive east European nationalist myopia. How to fit perennial geopolitical truths – that Russia, for instance, will always be more important to the West than Poland or Romania – with the new post-1989 realities is a task that so far neither half of the continent seems willing to contemplate.

Epilogue: Making Europe

In these last years there has been and still is much talk of Europe and European civilization, of anti-Europe and forces opposed to European civilization and so on. Appeals, articles in newspapers and magazines, discussions and polemics: in all, the word 'Europe' has been tossed around with unusual frequency, for good reasons and bad. But if we stop to analyse a little more closely what is meant by 'Europe' we immediately become conscious of the enormous confusion which reigns in the minds of those who talk about it . . .

– F. Chabod (1943–4)[1]

'Democracy has won,' wrote Zbigniew Brzezinski in 1990. 'The free market has won. But what in the wake of this great ideological victory is today the substance of our beliefs?' As the euphoria which greeted the end of the Cold War gave way to gloomy misgivings, Francis Fukuyama saw communism's collapse ushering in the end of history and the dawning of a more prosaic and less heroic era. Others foresaw instead the rebirth of history's demons – nationalism, fascism and racial and religious struggle. They talked about 'the return of history' and drew grim parallels – as Sarajevo hit the headlines – between 1992 and the eve of the First World War.

In fact, history had neither left Europe nor returned to it. But with the end of the Cold War, Europe's place in history changed. Europe is once again undivided, but it no longer occupies the central role in world affairs which it held before the Cold War began. Understanding where we stand today thus requires not only seeing how the present resembles the past, but how it differs from it as well. Sometimes it is easier to dream the old dreams – even when they are nightmares – than to wake up to unfamiliar realities.

'With the passing of the centuries', two French historians concluded in 1992, 'Europe discovers that beyond the differences of its tongues and customs, its people partake of a common culture . . . Europe is becoming conscious of the existence of a European identity.'[2] Made with unfortunate timing in the year civil war broke out in Yugoslavia, this bold claim has a respectable pedigree. In 1936, another year of civil war, the British historian H. A. L. Fisher asserted that Europe was unified by a civilization which was 'distinct . . . all pervading and preponderant', resting upon 'an inheritance of thought and achievement and religious aspiration'. And a few years later, in *The Limits and Divisions of European History*, the émigré Polish scholar Oskar Halecki pleaded for the fundamental unity of the continent at the very moment his country formed part of the Communist bloc.[3]

It is as though one response to the bloody struggles of this century has been to deny their internecine character: one side is made to stand for the true Europe – *l'Europe européenne* in the striking phrase of Gonzague de Reynold – while the others are written off as usurpers or barbarians. The intellectual tradition which identifies Europe with the cause of liberty and freedom goes back many centuries. But if we face the fact that liberal democracy failed between the wars, and if we admit that communism and fascism also formed part of the continent's political heritage, then it is hard to deny that what has shaped Europe in this century is not a gradual convergence of thought and feeling, but on the contrary a series of violent clashes between antagonistic New Orders. If we search for Europe not as a geographical expression, but as what Frederico Chabod called 'an historic and moral individuality', we find that for much of the century it did not exist.[4]

What was new in Europe's history was not the existence of conflict, but rather its scale. Compared with the great dynastic empires of the past – the long centuries of Byzantine, Habsburg and Ottoman rule – the utopian experiments of twentieth-century ideologies came and went with striking speed: yet their struggle brought new levels of violence into European life, militarizing society, strengthening the state and killing millions of people with the help of modern bureaucracies and technologies. In the 1870–71 Franco-Prussian War the death-toll was 184,000; in the First World War it was above eight million, and more than forty million Europeans – half of them civilians – died in the Second World War. The depth of these wounds was directly proportionate to the grandeur of the ambitions held by the various protagonists, each of whom aspired to remake Europe – inside and out – more thoroughly than ever before. It is not surprising if today Europe is suffering from ideological exhaustion, and if politics has become a distinctly unvisionary activity. As Austria's former chancellor Franz Vranitsky once supposedly remarked: 'Anyone with visions needs to see a doctor.'

This disillusionment colours the strange post-1989 triumph of democracy in Europe. Seventy years earlier, the consolidation of democracy across the continent after the First World War fitted liberal dreams of a new world order: Europe seemed destined to become the model for mankind. Through the League of Nations the new states of eastern Europe would learn the habits of democracy from the more advanced and mature states of the West, while through colonies and mandates, the great imperial powers would spread democracy more widely. The defeat of communism in Europe in 1989 carried no such global implications, and no such evangelical dreams. Democracy suits Europeans today partly because it is associated with the triumph of capitalism and partly because it involves less commitment or intrusion into their lives than any of the alternatives. Europeans accept democracy because they no longer believe in politics. It is for this reason that we find both high levels of support for democracy in cross-national opinion polls and high rates of political apathy. In contemporary Europe democracy allows racist parties of the Right to coexist with more active protection of human rights than ever before. It encompasses both the grass-roots politics of Switzerland and near-dictatorship in post-communist Croatia.

The real victor in 1989 was not democracy but capitalism, and Europe as a whole now faces the task which western Europe has confronted since the 1930s, of establishing a workable relationship between the two. The inter-war depression revealed that democracy might not survive a major crisis of capitalism, and in fact democracy's eventual triumph over communism would have been unimaginable without the reworked social contract which followed the Second World War. The ending of full employment and the onset of welfare retrenchment make this achievement harder than ever to sustain, especially in societies characterized by ageing populations. The globalization of financial markets makes it increasingly difficult for nation-states to preserve autonomy of action, yet markets – as a series of panics and crashes demonstrates – generate their own irrationalities and social tensions. The globalization of labour, too, challenges prevailing definitions of national citizenship, culture and tradition. Whether Europe can chart a course between the individualism of American capitalism and the authoritarianism of East Asia, preserving its own blend of social solidarity and political freedom, remains to be seen. But the end of the Cold War means that there is no longer an opponent against whom democrats can define what they stand for in pursuit of this goal. The old political signposts have been uprooted, leaving most people without a clear sense of direction.

This sense of *fin de siècle* disorientation is largely a European problem which reflects the specific historical experience of Europe this century, and the carnage that followed its once-fervent faith in utopias. A self-belief rooted in Christianity, capitalism, the Enlightenment and massive technological superiority encouraged Europeans to see themselves over a long period as a civilizational model for the globe. Their trust in Europe's world mission was already evident in the seventeenth and eighteenth centuries and reached its apogee in the era of imperialism. Hitler was in many ways its culminating figure and through the Nazi New Order came closer to its realization than anyone else. Now that the Cold War has ended, Europe is once more undivided, and this makes its loss of belief in the pre-eminence of its civilization and values all the more obvious. Many of the newly freed states of the former Soviet empire cannot wait to join 'Europe'. Yet what that 'Europe' is, and where it stands in the world, seem less and less clear.

The only visionaries meeting the challenge are the Europeanists clustered in Brussels, and the only vision offered that of an ever-closer European union. Its acolytes still talk in the old way – as if history moves in one direction, leading inexorably from free trade to monetary union and eventually to political union too. The alternative they offer to this utopia is the chaos of a continent plunged back into the national rivalries of the past, dominated by Germany and threatened by war.

Dreams of perpetual peace have a long history in European thought, and emerged naturally once more out of the bloodletting of the mid twentieth century. The desire in particular to staunch the Franco-German conflict which generated three wars in under a century played an important part in the formation of the Common Market. In earlier formulations, perpetual peace was to be secured in Europe through its very multiplicity of states. But the rise of the nation-state and the bloodshed it has provoked led, during and after the Second World War, to the view that the nation-state was itself a cause of wars. The ghosts of the past, however, offer a poor guide to the future: the fear of another continental war, and the associated pessimism in relation to the nation-state, need to be matched against the facts of the present situation and not merely taken as resting on self-evident truth. Stanley Hoffmann's comment of some thirty years ago remains to the point: 'An examination of the international implications of "nation-statehood" today and yesterday is at least as important as the ritual attack on the nation-state.'[5]

It is now clear that Europe's twentieth century divides sharply into two halves. Before 1950, more than sixty million people died in wars or through state-sponsored violence; by contrast, the number of those who died in such a fashion after 1950 is well under one million, even taking the war in Yugoslavia into account. Thus if the nation-state is blamed for the bloodshed of the first half of the century, it should also be given some credit for the peaceful character of the second. After all, it is now clear that the nation-state has flourished in Europe right through the century, surviving the Nazis, and the Cold War too.

Both the USA and the Soviet Union, in different ways, were forced to come to terms with the continuing resilience of their European allies. The Common Market itself started out as a series of negotiations among nation-states and remained a forum for such negotiations for most of its life: only in the mid-1980s did the federalist impulse grow, largely because of French unease at growing German strength.

Yet the fear of Germany is a classic example of what happens when the past is projected into the future. Germany and Russia between them provided, it is true, liberal democracy's two greatest threats this century, but they also suffered the highest death tolls of any European countries. The predominance of Germany remains the fundamental feature of the European power structure as it has done for a century, but Germany's dreams of empire are gone – surviving only in nostalgic photo albums of pre-war Silesia or East Prussia. Its military caste has been destroyed, its minorities in eastern Europe are reduced to a remnant of the millions who constituted Hitler's *casus belli*. Five million war dead weigh more heavily on German minds than all of Hitler's triumphs. If German companies invest today in eastern Europe it is not because they represent the vanguard of a Fourth Reich, but because they are capitalists, whose capital is as vital as ever to Europe's economic health.

History seems even less likely to repeat itself with Russia. The country is smaller than at any time in the last two centuries, shorn of its Baltic states and the old western and southern Soviet republics. Internally, the collapse of communism has given rise to a kind of jungle capitalism, where massive fortunes are made alongside poverty unparalleled elsewhere in Europe. The desperate need for social reconstruction and the sad state of the Russian Army produce nationalism and a nostalgia for communism, but they also make irredentism and empire-building unlikely and risky eventualities. The Russian minorities who remain in the Baltic states are less of a threat to European stability than the decaying nuclear warheads and unsecured military installations left behind by the end of the Cold War.

The danger is that the West will not take this weakened Russia as seriously as it should. The EU, in particular, has given it paltry financial assistance – the contrast with American aid to western Europe after the Second World War is a depressing reminder of Europe's inability to plan its own affairs with long-term vision. 'Once we were great and now we are small,' runs a Danish school song, but it is not easy for a great power to adjust to imperial disengagement, especially when there are no attractive alternatives such as the European colonial powers found in the Common Market.

Here, after all, has been the great change in the nation-state since the Second World War: cooperation has replaced competition. Imperial nation-states shed their colonies and found that they were unnecessary for their prosperity. Nuclear weapons rendered much older strategic thinking obsolete and made it harder to envisage war as part of national policy. Armies are getting smaller rather than larger, as conscripts are replaced by specialist professional forces. Borders are chiefly now a matter for police rather than the military: illegal immigrants are a greater concern than neighbouring armies. Minorities still exist but in far smaller numbers than before 1950: thanks to genocide, expulsion and assimilation, the chief cause of the Second World War has effectively disappeared. In all, Europe has entered a new era in which war, empire and land have all come to seem far less important for national well-being than they once did. As a result, population decline in Europe today evokes none of the frenzied panic about national virility, racial purity and military performance that it did in the 1930s, and is more likely to be discussed in terms of pension schemes and welfare reform. Most of Europe is either in or wishes to join the EU and Nato, a situation with no historical precedent. From today's perspective, therefore, the 'Europeanist' project seems to be based on unreal fears and expectations. Nation-states are as strong as ever and cannot be willed away. Nor need they be, since they pose no threat to continental peace.

Perhaps the European Union can most fruitfully be seen as the West European nation-state's concession to capitalism. In other words, its existence is based on the fact that member states recognize national economic policies can no longer guarantee success, and see their prosperity lying in the kinds of cooperation and joint action made possible through the EU. This is why the EU remains most important as an economic entity; it is part of the attempt to adapt European capitalism to the needs of an increasingly global era.

But economics is not everything and the globalization of capital does not mean that the nation-state is finished in Europe, as many argue today. The Italian Luciolli criticized the Nazi New Order for assuming that material goods were enough to create a feeling of belonging among diverse European nationals, but his accusation could more fairly be levelled at the European Union with its disquieting 'democratic deficit'. The fact is that capitalism does not create feelings of belonging capable of rivalling the sense of allegiance felt by most people to the state in which they live. If anything, contemporary capitalism is destroying older class solidarities and making individuals feel more insecure, thus rendering other forms of collective identity more and more important. So capitalism requires the nation-state for non-economic as well as economic reasons, and will not further reduce its power. 'Consciousness of the nation remains infinitely stronger than a sense of Europe,' wrote Raymond Aron in 1964. The same is true today, and the European Union is therefore likely to remain – in the words of a Belgian diplomat – 'an economic giant, a political dwarf and a military worm'.[6]

All this means that the current state of affairs in Europe is untidy and complicated and likely to remain so: there are more nation-states in Europe than ever before, cooperating in a variety of international organizations which include – in addition to the EU and Nato – the Council of Europe, the OSCE, the WEU and many others. The great era of nation-state autonomy is past, and the globalization of capital (and labour) forces countries to give up exclusive control of some areas of policy; but this Europe of overlapping sovereignties should not be confused for one in which nation-states are vanishing and disappearing into larger and larger entities. Europe's great variety of cultures and traditions which was so prized by thinkers from Machiavelli onwards remains fundamental to understanding the continent today.

This panoply of national cultures, histories and values does make it hard for Europeans to act cohesively and swiftly in moments of crisis, though this hardly mattered in the Cold War as Europeans on both sides of the Iron Curtain surrendered the initiative over their affairs to the superpowers. For decades, they got into the habit of blaming the Americans and Russians while expecting them to sort out their affairs. But the war in Bosnia showed that even after the end of the Cold War, this habit has not died. None of the European organizations played anything other than a marginal role in the Yugoslav conflict. The year 1992 was supposed to herald the making of a new, confident and unified Europe: the ethnic cleansing of the Drina valley that spring and summer showed this up for the windy rhetoric it was. Lack of a unified will, not objective circumstance, held back Europe from a decisive response in Bosnia, and its nation-states could not agree among themselves on a policy until they were forced into one by Washington.

But although Europe's refusal to take responsibility for its own affairs is not an edifying sight, perhaps it matters less than it once did. Were Bosnia the prelude to a new era of bloodshed in Europe, such indecision in the face of crisis might be alarming. The war in the former Yugoslavia, however, was not the start of a new era of ethnic conflict – at least in Europe – so much as the final stage in the working out of the First World War peace settlement, and the definitive collapse of federal solutions – in this case through communism – to minorities problems. Conflict is still imaginable in the Balkans and the Aegean, but can scarcely threaten continental peace. There is a good reason why the Yugoslav war of 1991–5 did not lead to a more general war while the Balkan Wars of 1912–13 did: today Europe's major powers are partners with one another rather than military rivals.

Globally, Europe has lost its primacy, and perhaps that is what most Europeans find hardest to accept. Yet compared with other historical epochs and other parts of the world today, the inhabitants of the continent enjoy a remarkable combination of individual liberty, social solidarity and peace. As the century ends, the international outlook is more peaceful than at any time previously. If Europeans can give up their desperate desire to find a single workable definition of themselves and if they can accept a more modest place in the world, they may come to terms more easily with the diversity and dissension which will be as much their future as their past.

Maps and Tables

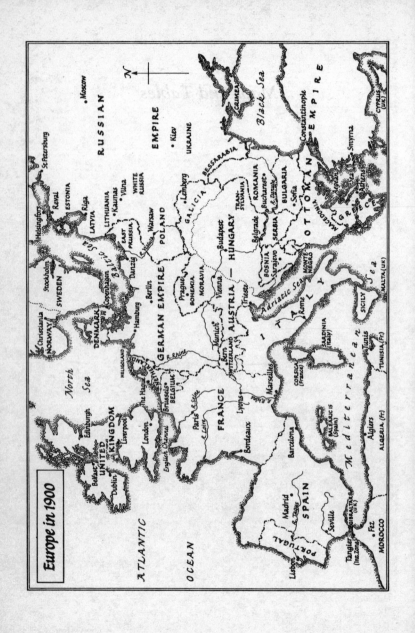

Europe in 1900

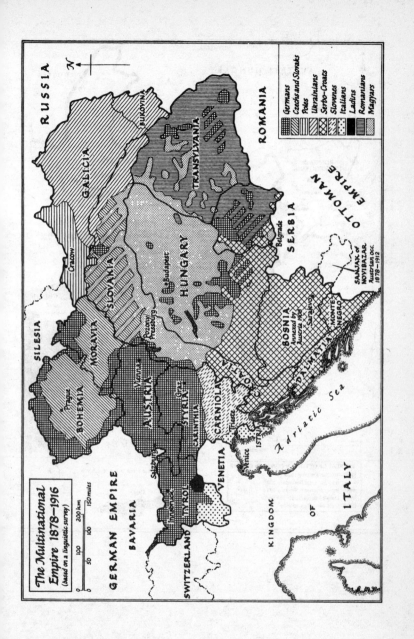

The Multinational Empire 1878–1916
(based on a linguistic survey)

GERMAN EMPIRE

BAVARIA

SWITZERLAND

RUSSIA

ROMANIA

OTTOMAN EMPIRE

SERBIA

Belgrade

SILESIA

BOHEMIA

Prague

MORAVIA

SLOVAKIA

GALICIA

Cracow

BUKOVINA

TRANSYLVANIA

HUNGARY

Budapest

AUSTRIA

Vienna

STYRIA

Graz

CARINTHIA

CARNIOLA

Trieste

TYROL

Innsbruck

Salzburg

VENETIA

Venice

ISTRIA

CROATIA

BOSNIA
Annexed by
Austria 1908

Sarajevo

DALMATIA

MONTE-
NEGRO

SANJAK of
NOVIBAZAR.
Austrian occ.
1878–1912

Adriatic Sea

KINGDOM

OF

ITALY

Germans
Czechs and Slovaks
Poles
Ukrainians
Serbo-Croats
Slovenes
Italians
Ladins
Romanians
Magyars

0   50   100   150 miles
0   100   200 km

N

RUTHENIA

AUSTRIA-HUNGARY

RUSSIA

Drava

Danube

TRANSYLVANIA

BOSNIA &
HERZEGOVINA
1908

Belgrade

RUMANIA
1878

Bucarest

Danube

DOBRUDJA

Sarajevo

S
E
R

Nish
1878

1878

BESSARABIA
1913

SANJAK
NOVIBAZAR

MONTE-
NEGRO

Sofia

BULGARIA

Black
Sea

Dubrovnik

Adriatic
Sea

Durazzo

Sea of
Marmara

Corfu

G
R
E
E

Cephalonia

Athens

1830

Mediterranean Sea

| 0 | | 200 km |
| 0 | 100 miles | |

Crete

To Greece 1908–13

RETREAT OF OTTOMAN POWER IN EUROPE
- Turkish Empire 1880
- – – – International boundary 1880
- ▬▬ International boundary 1914
- *1885* Date of aquisition from Turks
- **1913** Date of independence

RUSSIA IN THE GREAT WAR

Russian Empire in 1914

Central Powers and their allies 1914

Allies of the Entente 1914

Neutral 1914

Cease-fire line in 1917

Occupied by the Central Powers 1918

NORWAY

SWEDEN

GERMANY

AUSTRO-HUNGARIAN EMPIRE

MONTENEGRO

ALBANIA

BULGARIA

ESTONIA

LITHUANIA

POLAND

Arctic Ocean

Murmansk

Petrograd

Baltic Sea

Moscow

Rostov-on-Don

Black Sea

OTTOMAN EMPIRE

Mediterranean Sea

N

0   400 km

0   250 miles

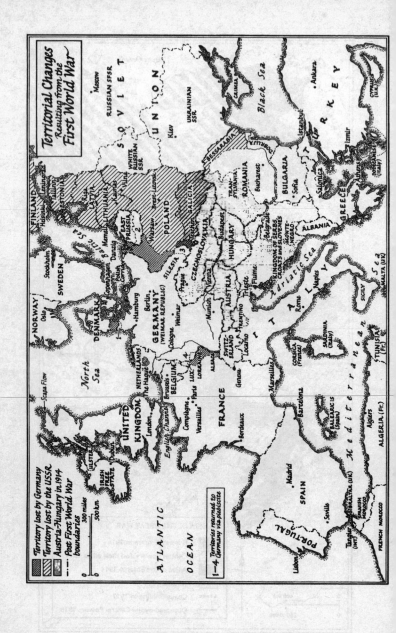

Territorial Changes
Resulting from the
First World War

Territory lost by Germany
Territory lost by the USSR
Austria-Hungary in 1914
Post First World War
boundaries

1—4 Territories returned to
Germany via plebiscite

0   300 miles
0   500 km.

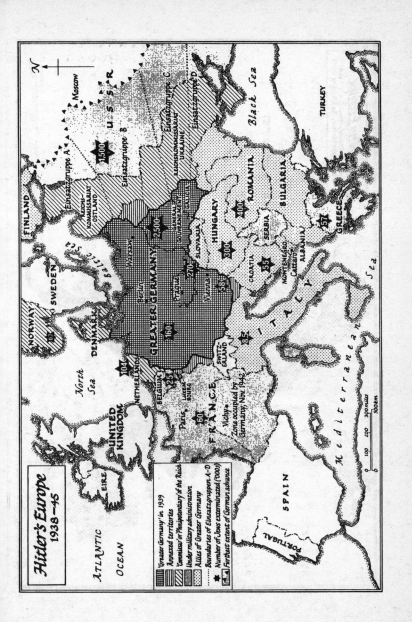

Hitler's Europe
1938–45

The New Europe?

A wartime vision of post-war Europe drawn from Bernard Newman, *The New Europe* (1943)

Territorial Adjustments after
the Second World War, 1945
--- International boundaries in 1938
[dotted] Territory which changed hands
after the Second World War

0   100   200   300 miles
0   100 200 300 400 500 km

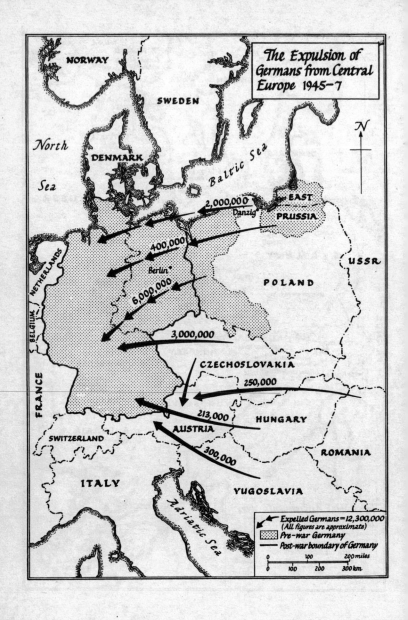

The Expulsion of Germans from Central Europe 1945–7

NORWAY

SWEDEN

North Sea

DENMARK

Baltic Sea

2,000,000

Danzig

EAST PRUSSIA

USSR

400,000

Berlin

POLAND

6,000,000

BELGIUM

NETHERLANDS

3,000,000

CZECHOSLOVAKIA

250,000

FRANCE

213,000

AUSTRIA

HUNGARY

SWITZERLAND

300,000

ROMANIA

ITALY

YUGOSLAVIA

Adriatic Sea

Expelled Germans = 12,300,000
(All figures are approximate)
Pre-war Germany
Post-war boundary of Germany

100   200 miles
0   100   200   300 km

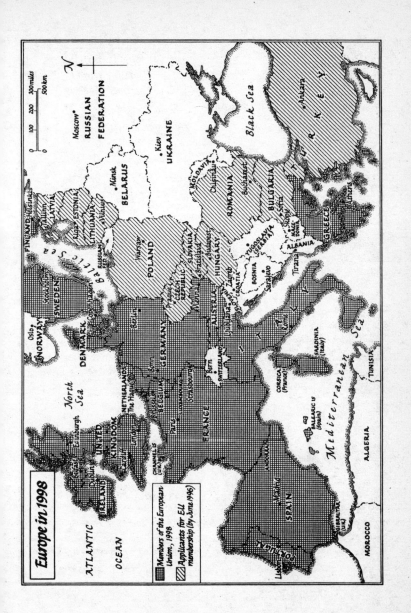

Europe in 1998

Members of the European Union, 1998

Applicants for EU membership (by June 1996)

Table 1 The Disappearing Minorities of Eastern Europe, 1931–91

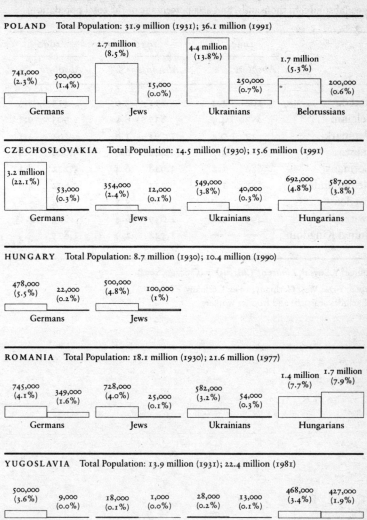

POLAND   Total Population: 31.9 million (1931); 36.1 million (1991)

741,000 (2.3%) · 500,000 (1.4%) — **Germans**
2.7 million (8.5%) · 15,000 (0.0%) — **Jews**
4.4 million (13.8%) · 250,000 (0.7%) — **Ukrainians**
1.7 million (5.3%) · 200,000 (0.6%) — **Belorussians**

CZECHOSLOVAKIA   Total Population: 14.5 million (1930); 15.6 million (1991)

3.2 million (22.1%) · 53,000 (0.3%) — **Germans**
354,000 (2.4%) · 12,000 (0.1%) — **Jews**
549,000 (3.8%) · 40,000 (0.3%) — **Ukrainians**
692,000 (4.8%) · 587,000 (3.8%) — **Hungarians**

HUNGARY   Total Population: 8.7 million (1930); 10.4 million (1990)

478,000 (5.5%) · 22,000 (0.2%) — **Germans**
500,000 (4.8%) · 100,000 (1%) — **Jews**

ROMANIA   Total Population: 18.1 million (1930); 21.6 million (1977)

745,000 (4.1%) · 349,000 (1.6%) — **Germans**
728,000 (4.0%) · 25,000 (0.1%) — **Jews**
582,000 (3.2%) · 54,000 (0.3%) — **Ukrainians**
1.4 million (7.7%) · 1.7 million (7.9%) — **Hungarians**

YUGOSLAVIA   Total Population: 13.9 million (1931); 22.4 million (1981)

500,000 (3.6%) · 9,000 (0.0%) — **Germans**
18,000 (0.1%) · 1,000 (0.0%) — **Jews**
28,000 (0.2%) · 13,000 (0.1%) — **Ukrainians**
468,000 (3.4%) · 427,000 (1.9%) — **Hungarians**

Source: After P. R. Magocsi, *Historical Atlas of East Central Europe* (Washington, 1993)

Table 2 Foreign Population in Selected European Countries, 1960, 1976, 1990 (absolute, in thousands, and as a percentage of the total population)

	1960 Absolute	%	1976 Absolute	%	1990 Absolute	%
Austria	102	1.4	271	3.6	413	5.3
Belgium	453	4.9	835	8.5	905	9.1
Denmark	17	0.4	91	1.8	161	3.1
France	—	4.7	3,442	6.6	3,608	6.4
Germany*	686	1.2	3,948	6.4	5,242	8.2
Netherlands	118	1.0	351	2.6	692	4.6
Sweden	191	—	418	5.1	484	5.6
Switzerland	495	9.2	1,039	16.4	1,100†	16.3†
United Kingdom	—	—	1,542	2.9	1,875	3.3

Source: Y. Soysal, *Limits of Citizenship* (Chicago, 1994).

*1960, 1976: West Germany; 1990: Germany, FRG.
†Excludes seasonal and frontier workers.

Table 3 The Flight from the Land, 1930, 1980 (percentage of working population in agriculture)

Country	1930	1980
Denmark	30	7
Finland	71	11
Norway	36	7
Sweden	39	5
Austria	32	9
Belgium	17	3
France	36	8
Germany	29	—
FRG	—	4
GDR	—	10
Ireland	34	18
Netherlands	21	6
Switzerland	21	5
UK	6	3
Bulgaria	80	37
Czechoslovakia	37	11
Hungary	55	20
Poland	66	31
Romania	77	29
Yugoslavia	78	29
Greece	54	37
Italy	47	11
Portugal	55	28
Spain	50	14

Adapted from G. Ambrosius and W. Hubbard, *A Social and Economic History of Twentieth Century Europe* (Cambridge, Mass., 1989), pp. 58–9

Notes

Preface

1 J. Roth, *Juden auf Wanderschaft* (Cologne, 1985 edn), p. 84

2 Figures for the First World War from *Encyclopaedia Britannica*, vol. 23 (Chicago, 1949), p. 775; Masaryk cited in E. Goldstein, *Winning the Peace: British Diplomatic Strategy, Peace Planning, and the Paris Peace Conference, 1916–1920* (Oxford, 1991), p. 4; El Lissitsky in M. Rowell and A. Z. Rudenstine (eds.), *Russische Avantgarde aus der Sammlung Costakis* (Hannover, 1984), p. 52

3 Ignazio Silone (1955) from 'The choice of comrades' in N. Mills (ed.), *Legacy of Dissent: Forty Years of Writing from Dissent Magazine* (New York, 1994), p. 58

4 H. Arendt, *The Origins of Totalitarianism* (New York, 1958), p. ix

5 J. Keegan, 'A primitive tribal conflict only anthropologists can understand', *Daily Telegraph*, 15 April 1993. See also the same author's *A History of Warfare* (London, 1993), pp. 6, 55–6

6 R. Aron, *The Century of Total War* (London, 1954), p. 325

1: The Deserted Temple: Democracy's Rise and Fall

1 H. Kelsen, *La Démocratie: sa nature, sa valeur* (Paris, 1932), p. viii

2 F. Nitti, *Bolshevism, Fascism and Democracy* (New York, 1927), p. 15

3 'Kings in exile', in A. Wat, *Lucifer Unemployed* (Evanston, Ill., 1990), pp. 17–35

4 B. de Jouvenel, *Après la défaite* (Paris, 1941), p. 7

5 James Bryce, *Modern Democracies*, i (New York, 1921), p. 4

6 F. Cambo, *Les Dictatures* (Paris, 1929), p. 98

7 V. M. Dean, 'The attack on democracy', in Dean *et al.*, *New Governments in Europe: The Trend towards Dictatorship* (New York, 1934), p. 15; M. J. Bonn, *The Crisis of European Democracy* (New Haven, Conn., 1925); Eustace Percy, *Democracy on Trial* (London, 1931); H. G. Wells, *After Democracy: Addresses and Papers on the Present World Situation* (London, 1932); S. de Madariaga, *Anarchy or Hierarchy* (New York, 1937), p. 14; W. E. Rappard, *The Crisis of Democracy* (Chicago, 1938), pp. 2–3.

8 De Jouvenel, op. cit., pp. 7–8, 229

9 M. W. Graham, *New Governments of Central Europe* (London, 1924), pp. 604ff

10 B. Mirkine-Guetzevitch, *Les Constitutions de l'Europe nouvelle* (Paris, 1929), 25

11 A. J. Zurcher, *The Experiment with Democracy* (New York, 1933), p. viii

12 Mirkine-Guetzevitch, op. cit., pp. 16–21

13 ibid., pp. 9, 34–5; B. W. Diffie, 'Spain under the Republic', in V. M. Dean *et al.*, *New Governments in Europe*, op. cit., pp. 404–5

14 Hugo Preuss cited by E. Kennedy, 'Introduction', p. xxi, in her translation of C. Schmitt, *The Crisis of Parliamentary Democracy* (Cambridge, Mass., 1987)

15 Lvov cited in O. Figes, *A People's Tragedy: The Russian Revolution, 1891–1924* (London, 1996), p. 355

16 J. Burbank, 'Lenin and the Law', *Slavic Review* (1995), pp. 23–44

17 On voting, see O. Radkey, *Russia Goes to the Polls* (Ithaca, NY, 1990 edn), ch. 2; E. H. Carr, *The Bolshevik Revolution, 1917–1923*, vol. 1 (London, 1986 edn), pp. 116, 191f; I. Getzler, 'Lenin's conception of revolution as civil war', *Slavonic and East European Review*, 74: 3 (July 1996), pp. 469–72; Z. Zik (ed.), *Ideas and Forces in Soviet Legal History* (New York, 1992), no. 78

18 H. Shukman (ed.), *The Blackwell Encyclopaedia of the Russian Revolution* (Oxford, 1988), pp. 192–3; Carr, op. cit., p. 182

19 G. Serventi, *Ascesa della democrazia europea e prime reazioni storiche* (Rome, 1925), 358; F. Cambo, *Autour du fascisme italien* (Paris, 1925), p. 196; see also F. Lyttelton, 'Fascism in Italy: the second wave', in G. Mosse and W. Laqueur (eds.), *International Fascism, 1920–1945* (New York, 1966), pp. 75–101

20 B. Mussolini, *Le Fascisme* (Paris, 1933), pp. 19f

21 G. Gentile, *Che cos'è il fascismo* (Florence, 1925), p. 38

22 H. Rogger and E. Weber (eds.), *The European Right: A Historical Profile* (Berkeley, Calif., 1966), p. 8

23 Cambo, *Les Dictatures*, op. cit., p. 51; cf. Bonn, op. cit., p. 80

24 Kelsen, op. cit., p. 22

25 S. Neumann, *Die deutschen Parteien: Wesen und Wandel nach dem Kriege* (Berlin, 1932), pp. 110–12; Bonn, op. cit., p. 82; Kelsen, 'Die Krise des parlamentarischen Systems', cited in J. Bendersky, *Carl Schmitt: Theorist for the Reich* (Princeton, NJ, 1983), p. 110 n. 8

26 E. Giraud, *La Crise de la démocratie et le renforcement du pouvoir exécutif* (Paris, 1938), pp. 73–4, 166

27 J. Stengers, 'Belgium', in Rogger and Weber, op. cit., pp. 136–7; Giraud, op. cit., p. 35; E. Beneš, *Democracy: Today and Tomorrow*: (London, 1940), p. 215

28 Cited by Giraud, op. cit., p. 150; on Poland, see J. Holzer, 'The political right in Poland, 1918–1939', *Journal of Contemporary History*, 12 (1977), pp. 395–412

29 Bendersky, op. cit., pp. 130–31

30 M. S. Wertheimer, 'The Nazi revolution in Germany', in Dean *et al.*, op. cit., pp. 206–7; Bendersky, op. cit., pp. 132–5, 169

31 Bonn, op. cit., p. 84

32 R. Wohl, *The Generation of 1914* (Cambridge, Mass., 1979); Drieu cited by Weber, 'The right: an introduction', in Rogger and Weber, op. cit., p. 18

33 Montherlant cited in de Jouvenel, op. cit., pp. 36–7; Eliade and Cioran in L. Volovici, *Nationalist Ideology and Antisemitism: The Case of Romanian Intellectuals in the 1930s* (Oxford, 1991)

34 Musil in D. Luft, *Robert Musil and the Crisis of European Culture* (Berkeley/Los Angeles, Calif., 1980), p. 279; H. G. Wells, 'Liberalism', in his *After Democracy* op cit., p. 24

35 E. di Nuoscio, 'La democrazia dei partiti nel pensiero politico di Guglielmo Ferrero', in L. Cedroni (ed.), *Guglielmo Ferrero: itinerari del pensiero* (Milan, 1994), p. 670; see also A. Lyttelton, 'The "crisis of bourgeois society" and the origins of Fascism', in R. Bessel (ed.), *Fascist Italy and Nazi Germany: Comparisons and Contrasts* (Cambridge, 1996), pp. 12–23; Keynes, 'Am I a Liberal?', cited in P. Mandler and S. Pedersen (eds.), *After the Victorians: Private Conscience and Public Duty in Modern Britain* (London, 1994), p. 10

36 D. Sassoon, *One Hundred Years of Socialism: The West European Left in the Twentieth Century* (London, 1996), pp. 36–41; Cited by Kennedy, op. cit., p. xxxviii

37 de Madariaga, op. cit., R. Paxton, 'France: the Church, the Republic and the Fascist temptation', in R. J. Wolff and J. K. Hoensch (eds.), *Catholics, the State and the European Radical Right, 1919–1945* (New York, 1987), p. 83

38 F. Morstein Marx, *Government in the Third Reich* (New York, 1937), p. 33; Graham, op. cit., p. 292; Hitler cited in A. Bullock, *Hitler and Stalin: Parallel Lives* (London, 1991), p. 271

39 *The Times*, 10 August 1936

40 K. Loewenstein, 'Autocracy versus democracy in contemporary Europe', *American Political Science Review*, 29: 4 (August 1935), pp. 571–93, ibid., 29: 5 (October 1935), pp. 755–84

41 M. Oakeshott, *The Social and Political Doctrines of Contemporary Europe* (London, 1940), pp. xvii, 4

42 Oakeshott, op. cit., p. xiii; H. Arthur Steiner, *Government in Fascist Italy* (London, 1938), p. 141; Kennan in M. Weil, *A Pretty Good Club: The Founding Fathers of the US Foreign Service* (New York, 1978), p. 171

43 F. C. Egerton, *Salazar, Rebuilder of Portugal* (London, 1943), pp. 224–7

44 For the idea that the NSDAP realized the 'basic lessons of democracy', see the review article of P. Fritzsche, 'Did Weimar fail?', *Journal of Modern History*, 68 (September 1996), pp. 629–56; also Bullock, op. cit., p. 271

45 J. P. Diggins, *Mussolini and Fascism: The View from America* (Princeton, NJ, 1972), pp. 164–5

46 T. Gallagher, *Portugal: A Twentieth Century Interpretation* (Manchester, 1983), pp. 64–74

47 U. Kluge, *Der österreichische Ständestaat, 1934–1938* (Vienna, 1984), chs. 1–3; F. Stadler and P. Weibel (eds.), *Vertreibung der Vernunft: The Cultural Exodus from Austria* (Vienna/New York, 1995)

48 Cited in ibid., p. 15

49 ibid., p. 86

50 See P. Diehl-Thiele, *Partei und Staat im Dritten Reich* (Munich, 1971)

51 K. Loewenstein, 'Law in the Third Reich', *Yale Law Journal*, 45 (1936), p. 811; H. W. Koch, *In the Name of the Volk: Political Justice in Hitler's Germany* (London, 1989), chs. 3–4

52 I. Müller, *Hitler's Justice: the Courts of the Third Reich* (tr. D. Schneider) (Cambridge, Mass., 1991), pp. 6–27

53 E. Fraenkel, *The Dual State A Contribution to the Theory of Dictatorship* (New York, 1941), p. 13; Loewenstein, 'Law in the Third Reich', op. cit., p. 803; cited by M. Burleigh and W. Wippermann, *The Racial State* (Cambridge, 1991), p. 177; cf. Dickinson, *Politics of Child Welfare*, p. 218

54 Fraenkel, op. cit.

55 Müller, op. cit., pp. 91–2

56 Fraenkel, op. cit., pp. 52, 94

57 R. C. van Caenegem, *An Historical Introduction to Western Constitutional Law* (Cambridge, 1995), p. 284

58 C. Beradt, *The Third Reich of Dreams: The Nightmares of a Nation, 1933–1939* (Wellingborough, Northants, 1985), p. 21

59 Fraenkel, op. cit., pp. 43–4, 54, 56, 58

60 ibid., pp. 40, 48–9

61 E. Gentile, *The Sacralization of Politics in Fascist Italy* (Cambridge, Mass., 1996)

62 Müller, op. cit., p. 197; M. Broszat, 'The concentration camps, 1933–1945', in H. Krausnick and M. Broszat, *Anatomy of the SS State* (London, 1970)

63 See Bullock, op. cit., ch. 10

64 D. Bankier, *The Germans and the Final Solution: Public Opinion under Nazism* (Oxford, 1992), ch. 3

65 G. L. Weinberg, 'Germany's war for world conquest and the extermination of the Jews', *Holocaust and Genocide Studies*, 10: 2 (fall 1996), pp. 119–33; M. Knox, 'Conquest, foreign and domestic, in Fascist Italy and Nazi Germany', *Journal of Modern History*, 56 (1984), pp. 1–57; Bankier, op. cit., p. 55

2: Empires, Nations, Minorities

1 Acton cited by C. A. Macartney, *National States and National Minorities* (New York, 1968), p. 17

2 D. G. Kambouroglou, *Toponymika Paradoxa* (Athens, 1920), p. 5

3 Von Horvath cited in J. Rupnik, *The Other Europe* (London, 1988), p. 41

4 Cited in R. R. Wisse, *I. L. Peretz and the Making of Modern Jewish Culture* (Seattle, 1991), p. 96

5 On the borderlands, see now A. Applebaum, *Between East and West: Across the Borderlands of Europe* (London, 1995); O. Jaszi, *The Dissolution of the Habsburg Monarchy* (Chicago, 1929), p. 3; on Renner, T. Bottomore and P. Goode (eds.), *Austro-Marxism* (Oxford, 1978), p. 31 (by an irony of history, this staunch advocate of a supranational state was to become the first chancellor of the Austrian Republic)

6 V. H. Rothwell, *British War Aims and Peace Diplomacy, 1914–1918* (Oxford, 1971), p. 159

7 ibid., pp. 193f; R. L. Koehl, 'A prelude to Hitler's Greater Germany', *American Historical Review*, 59: 1 (October 1953), pp. 43–65

8 P. Stirk (ed.), *Mitteleuropa: History and Prospects* (Edinburgh, 1994), pp. 14–15; Rosenberg cited in G. Stoakes, *Hitler and the Quest for World*

Dominion: Nazi Ideology and Foreign Policy in the 1920s (New York, 1986), p. 125

9 The question is asked by Henryk Szlaiffer in R. L. Rudolph and D. F. Good (eds.), *Nationalism and Empire: The Habsburg Empire and the Soviet Union* (New York, 1992), p. 152

10 E. Traverso, *The Marxists and the Jewish Question: The History of a Debate (1843–1943)* (New Jersey, 1994), chs. 4–5; J. Frankel, *Prophecy and Politics: Socialism, Nationalism and the Russian Jews, 1862–1917* (Cambridge, 1981), p. 235

11 Traverso, op. cit., p. 132; J. Jacobs, *On Socialists and 'the Jewish Question' after Marx* (New York, 1992), ch. 5; H. Carrère d'Encausse, *The Great Challenge: Nationalities and the Bolshevik State, 1917–1930* (New York, 1992), ch. 4

12 R. Pipes, *The Formation of the Soviet Union: Communism and Nationalism, 1917–1923* (Cambridge, Mass., rev. edn, 1964), pp. 43–50, 108

13 A. J. Motyl, *Sovietology, Rationality, Nationality* (New York, 1990), p. 88

14 ibid., p. 85; O. Subtelny, *Ukraine: A History* (Toronto, 1988), p. 389; A. J. Motyl, 'Ukrainian nationalist political violence in inter-war Poland, 1921–1939', *East European Quarterly*, 19: 1 (March 1985), pp. 45–56

15 J. A. Armstrong, *Ukrainian Nationalism* (New York, 1990 edn), pp. 10–12; J. T. Gross, *Revolution from Abroad: The Soviet Conquest of Poland's Western Ukraine and Western Belorussia* (Princeton, NJ, 1988), pp. 31–2. Needless to say, such celebrations were short-lived

16 R. Conquest, *Soviet Nationalities Policy in Practice* (London, 1967), pp. 26–9; R. Szporluk, *Communism and Nationalism: Karl Marx versus Friedrich List* (New York, 1985), p. 218

17 L. E. Gelfand, *The Inquiry: American Preparations for Peace, 1917–1919* (New Haven, Conn., 1963), p. 148; Rothwell, op. cit., p. 221

18 Dmowski in P. Latawski, 'Roman Dmowski, the Polish question and Western opinion, 1915–1918: the case of Britain', in P. Latawski (ed.), *The Reconstruction of Poland, 1914–1923* (London, 1992), p. 9; two visions of Poland, O. Halecki, *The Limits and Divisions of European History* (London, 1950), p. 136

19 P. Wandycz, 'Dmowski's policy at the Paris Peace Conference: success or failure?', in Latawski, op. cit., p. 120

20 M. Levene, *Wars, Jews and the New Europe: The Diplomacy of Lucien Wolf, 1914–1919* (Oxford, 1992)

21 ibid., p. 266; Wandycz in Latawski, op. cit.; see also A. Polonsky and M. Riff, 'Poles, Czechs and the "Jewish Question", 1914–1921: A Comparative

Study', in V. Berghahn and M. Kitchen (eds.), *Germany in the Age of Total War* (London, 1981), pp. 63–101; F. M. Leventhal, *The Last Dissenter: H. N. Brailsford and His World* (Oxford, 1985), p. 159

22 Goldstein, op. cit., p. 139

23 J. Headlam-Morley, *A Memoir of the Paris Peace Conference, 1919* (London, 1972), pp. 112f; Macartney, (London, 1968 edn), pp. 282–3

24 Cited by P. B. Finney, '"An evil for all concerned": Great Britain and minority protection after 1919', *Journal of Contemporary History*, 30 (1995), pp. 536–7

25 C. Fink, '"Defender of Minorities": Germany in the League of Nations, 1926–1933', *Central European History*, 5: 4 (1972), pp. 330–57; R. Brubaker, *Nationalism Reframed: Nationhood and the National Question in the New Europe* (Cambridge, 1996), ch. 5

26 Figures from O. Junghann, *National Minorities in Europe* (New York, 1932), pp. 116, 119

27 Headlam-Morley, op. cit., pp. 112–13

28 Mill cited in A. Ryan, *J. S. Mill* (London, 1974), p. 207; S. Sierpowski, 'Minorities in the system of the League of Nations', in P. Smith (ed.), *Ethnic Groups in International Relations* (New York, 1991), p. 27; Schmitt, op. cit., pp. 9–10

29 Schmitt, op. cit., pp. 9–10; A. Sarraut, *Grandeur et servitude coloniale* (Paris, 1931), p. 102

30 H. Solus, *Traité de la condition des indigènes en droit privé* (Paris, 1927), pp. 117, 126; Algerians deported in A. Bockel, *L'Immigration au pays des Droits de l'homme* (Paris, 1991), p. 27

31 I. Livezeanu, *Cultural Politics in Greater Romania: Regionalism, Nation Building and Ethnic Struggle, 1918–1930* (Ithaca, NY, 1995), p. 47

32 E. Mendelsohn, *The Jews of East Central Europe between the World Wars* (Bloomington, Ind., 1983), p. 105; R. Weisberg, *Vichy Law and the Holocaust in France* (New York, 1996), p. 13

33 Cited by I. Claude, *National Minorities: An International Problem* (Cambridge, Mass., 1955), p. 30; numbers of petitions in Macartney, op. cit., p. 504 and J. Robinson *et al.*, *Were the Minorities Treaties a Failure?* (New York, 1943), p. 252

34 M. J. Somakian, *Empires in Conflict: Armenia and the Great Powers, 1895–1920* (London, 1995), pp. 86, 137; A. J. Toynbee, *The Western Question in Greece and Turkey* (London, 1923, 2nd edn), pp. 16–17

35 The whole idea of transfers is powerfully criticized by O. Janowsky, *Nationalities and National Minorities* (New York, 1945), pp. 136–45

36 F. Carsten, *The First Austrian Republic, 1918–1938* (London, 1986), p. 30; C. Skran, *Refugees in Inter-War Europe: The Emergence of a Regime* (Oxford, 1995), p. 104

37 See M. Matsushita, *Japan in the League of Nations* (New York, 1929)

38 Headlam-Morley, op. cit., p. 132

39 S. A. Schuker, *The End of French Predominance in Europe: The Financial Crisis of 1924 and the Adoption of the Dawes Plan* (Chapel Hill, NC, 1976)

40 A. Ramm, *Europe in the Twentieth Century, 1905–1970* (London, 1984), p. 186; G. Riou, 'A French view of the League of Nations', *The League and the Future of the Collective System* (London, 1937), pp. 28–40; E. H. Carr, 'Public opinion as a safeguard of peace', *International Affairs* (November 1936), pp. 846–62

41 F. Berber, 'The Third Reich and the future of the collective system', *The League and the Future of the Collective System* (London, 1937), pp. 64–83

42 Stoakes, op. cit., p. 186; E. Jäckel, *Hitler's World View: A Blueprint for Power* (Cambridge, Mass., 1981)

43 Stoakes, op. cit., p. 160

44 Quoted in US Department of State, *National Socialism: Basic Principles, Their Application by the Nazi Party's Foreign Organization, and the Use of Germans abroad for Nazi Aims* (Washington, DC, 1943), p. 70

45 P. Stirk, 'Authoritarian and national socialist conceptions of nation, state and Europe', in Stirk (ed.), *European Unity in Context: The Inter-War Period* (London, 1989), pp. 125–48

46 J. Herz, 'The National Socialist doctrine of international law and the problems of international organization', *Political Science Quarterly*, 44: 4 (December 1939), pp. 536–54; also D. Diner, 'Rassistisches Völkerrecht. Elemente einer nationalsozialistischen Weltordnung' in his *Weltordnungen: Über Geschichte und Wirkung von Recht und Macht* (Frankfurt, 1993), pp. 77–124

47 Macartney, op. cit., foreword to 2nd (1934) edn; W. Friedmann, 'The disintegration of European civilisation and the future of international law', *Modern Law Review* (December 1938), pp. 194–214

48 Adenauer in H. Stoecker (ed.), *German Imperialism in Africa* (London, 1986), p. 323; D. Glass, *Population Policies and Movements* (London, 1940), p. 220

49 G. Rochat, *Guerre italiane in Libia e in Ethiopia: Studi militari, 1921–1939* (Padua, 1991)

50 G. W. Baer, *Test Case: Italy, Ethiopia and the League of Nations* (Stanford, Calif., 1967), pp. 296–7

51 G. Bernardini, 'The origins and development of racial anti-semitism in Fascist Italy', *Journal of Modern History*, 49 (September 1977), pp. 431–53

52 Baer, op. cit., p. 56; J. Delarue, 'La guerra d'Abissinia vista dalla Francia: le sue ripercussioni nella politica interna', in A. del Boca (ed.), *Le guerre coloniali del fascismo* (Bari, 1991), pp. 317–39; E. Weber, 'France', in Rogger and Weber, op. cit., p. 97

53 Cited in R. Schlesinger, *Federalism in Central and Eastern Europe* (New York, 1945), pp. 457–8

54 'Politics and right', tr. from *Europäische Revue*, January 1941, in US Department of State, *National Socialism*, op. cit., pp. 471–7

55 A. J. P. Taylor, *The Origins of the Second World War* (London, 1961), *passim*

56 W. Schmokel, *Dreams of Empire: German Colonialism, 1919–1945* (New Haven, Conn., 1964); Stoecker, op. cit.; G. L. Weinberg, 'German colonial plans and policies, 1938–42', in his *World in the Balance* (London, 1981), pp. 96–136

57 J. S. Huxley and A. C. Haddon, *We Europeans: A Survey of 'Racial' Problems* (London/New York, 1936), pp. 13, 132, 236; more generally, E. Barkan, *The Retreat from Scientific Racism: Changing Concepts of Race in Britain and the United States between the World Wars* (Cambridge, 1992)

58 Cited by P. Kluke, 'Nationalsozialistische Europaideologie', *Vierteljahreshefte für Zeitgeschichte*, 3: 3 (1955), pp. 240–69

3: Healthy Bodies, Sick Bodies

1 P. Corsi, *The Protection of Mothers and Children in Italy* (Rome, 1938), p. 3; M. Hirschfeld, *Sittengeschichte des Weltkrieges*, ii (Leipzig, 1930), p. 437

2 A. Pfoser, 'Verstörte Männer und emanzipierte Frauen', in F. Kadrnoska (ed.), *Aufbruch und Untergang: Österreichische Kultur zwischen 1918 und 1938* (Vienna, 1981); R. J. Sieder, 'Behind the lines: working-class family life in wartime Vienna', in R. Wall and J. Winter (eds.), *The Upheaval of War: Family, Work and Welfare in Europe, 1914–1918* (Cambridge, 1988), pp. 109–38

3 S. Pedersen, *Family, Dependence and the Origins of the Welfare State: Britain and France, 1914–1945* (Cambridge, 1993), p. 129

4 M. L. Roberts, *Civilization without Sexes: Reconstructing Gender in Postwar France* (Chicago, 1994), pp. 70, 125

5 W. Z. Goldman, *Women, the State and Revolution: Soviet Family Policy and Social Life, 1917–1936* (Cambridge, 1993), chs. 1, 3

6 Cited in T. Verveniotis, 'I thesmothetisi tou dikaiomatos tis psifou ton gynaikon apo ton elliniko antistasiako kinima (1941–1944)', *Dini: Feministiko periodiko*, 6 (1993), pp. 180–95 (p. 181)

7 The Irish constitution cited by D. Keogh and F. O'Driscoll, 'Ireland', in T. Buchanan and M. Conway (eds.), *Political Catholicism in Europe, 1918–1965* (Oxford, 1996), p. 292

8 Hanna Hacker, 'Staatsbürgerinnen' in Kadrnoska, op. cit., pp. 225–66; V. de Grazia, *How Fascism Ruled women: Italy, 1922 1945* (Berkeley/Los Angeles, Calif., 1992), p. 25; Goldman, op. cit., chs. 5–6

9 J. M. Winter, 'The fear of population decline in western Europe, 1870–1940', in R. W. Hiorns (ed.), *Demographic Patterns in Developed Societies* (London, 1980), 178–81; P. Ogden and M.-M. Huss, 'Demography and pro-natalism in France in the nineteenth and twentieth centuries', *Journal of Historical Geography*, 8:3 (1982), pp. 283–98; S. Weiss, 'Wilhelm Schallmeyer and the logic of German eugenics', *Isis*, 77 (March 1986), p. 45; C. Pagliano, 'Scienza e stirpe: eugenica in Italia (1912–1939)', *Passato e presente* (1984), pp. 61–97

10 M.-M. Huss, 'Pronatalism and the popular ideology of the child in wartime France: the evidence of the picture postcard', in Wall and Winter, op. cit., pp. 329–69; C. Usborne, 'Pregnancy is the woman's active service', in ibid., pp. 389–416

11 D. Glass, *Population Policies and Movements in Europe* (Oxford, 1940), pp. 84, 152, 274; Corsi, op. cit., p. 4

12 Mussolini cited in de Grazia, op. cit., p. 41; W. Schneider, *Quantity and Quality: The Quest for Biological Regeneration in 20th Century France* (Cambridge, 1990), p. 139; Pedersen, op. cit.

13 R. Bridenthal, ' "Professional housewives": stepsisters of the women's movement', in R. Bridenthal, A. Grossmann and M. Kaplan (eds.), *When Biology Became Destiny: Women in Weimar and Nazi Germany* (New York, 1984), pp. 153–74

14 Goldman, op. cit., pp. 288–9

15 de Grazia, op. cit., p. 55; Schneider, op. cit., p. 120; G. McCleary, 'Prewar European population policies', *The Millbank Memorial Fund Quarterly*, pp. 104–20; Glass, op. cit., pp. 282–4

16 M. Nash, 'Pronatalism and motherhood in Franco's Spain', in G. Bock and P. Thane (eds.) *Maternity and Gender Policies: Women and the Rise of*

European Welfare States, 1880s–1950s (London/New York, 1991), p. 169

17 Glass, op. cit., pp. 45–50

18 A. Hackett, 'Helene Stocker: leftwing intellectual and sex reformer', in Bridenthal, Grossmann and Kaplan op. cit., pp. 153–74

19 Glass, op. cit., conclusion; L. Thompson, '*Lebensborn* and the eugenics policy of the *Reichsfuhrer-SS*', *Central European History*, 4 (1971), pp. 54–77

20 A. Gramsci, *Selections from the Prison Notebooks* (London, 1971), p. 242

21 J. Lewis, *The Politics of Motherhood: Child and Maternal Welfare in England, 1900–1939* (London, 1980), pp. 30–33; de Grazia, op. cit., pp. 63–5

22 J. Lewis, 'Red Vienna, socialism in one city, 1918–1927', *European Studies Review*, 13: 3 (July 1983), pp. 335–54; B. Schwan, *Städtebau und Wohnungswesen der Welt: Town Planning and Housing throughout the World* (Berlin, 1935), pp. 303–4; A. Lees, *Cities Perceived: Urban Society in European and American Thought, 1820–1940* (Manchester, 1985), p. 272

23 F. Smejkal *et al.*, *Devetsil: the Czech Avant-Garde of the 1920s and 1930s* (Oxford, 1990), p. 46

24 Lees, op. cit., 272; Schwan, op. cit.

25 G. Jones, *Social Hygiene in Twentieth Century Britain* (London/Sydney, 1986)

26 *Eugenics, Genetics and the Family*, i (Scientific Papers of the Second International Congress of Eugenics) (Baltimore, Md, 1923), p. 1

27 D. Kirk, *Europe's Population in the Interwar Years* (Princeton, NJ, 1946), pp. 10–33; A. Keith, *An Autobiography* (London, 1950), pp. 552–3; T. Kalikow, 'Konrad Lorenz's ethological theory: explanation and ideology, 1938–1943', *Journal of the History of Biology*, 16 (1983), pp. 39–73; A. Funk, *Film und Jugend: Eine Untersuchung über die Psychischen Wirkungen des Films im Leben der Jugendlichen* (Munich, 1934)

28 Lees, op. cit., p. 275

29 D. Horn, *Social Bodies: Science, Reproduction and Italian Modernity* (Princeton, NJ, 1994), p. 103

30 Churchill cited in D. Kevles, *In the Name of Eugenics: Genetics and the Uses of Human Heredity* (New York, 1985), p. 99

31 H. Laughlin, 'The present status of eugenical sterilization in the United States', in *Eugenics in Race and State* (Baltimore, Md, 1923), p. 290; J. Noakes, 'Nazism and eugenics: the background to the Nazi sterilization law of 14 July 1933', in R. J. Bullen *et al.* (eds.), *Ideas into Politics: Aspects of European History, 1880–1950* (London, 1983), p. 80

32 M. E. Kopp, 'Eugenic sterilization laws in Europe', *American Journal of*

Obstetrics and Gynaecology, 34 (September 1937), pp. 499–504; Jones, op. cit., pp. 88–97; B. Mallet, 'The reduction of the fecundity of the socially inadequate', in *A Decade of Progress in Eugenics* (Baltimore, Md, 1934), pp. 364–8

33 See esp. Burleigh and Wippermann, op. cit.

34 Cited by Burleigh and Wippermann, op. cit., p. 177

35 Sir Harry Johnston, 'Empire and anthropology', *The Nineteenth Century and After* (August 1908); B. Müller-Hill, *Murderous Science: Elimination by Scientific Selection of Jews, Gypsies and Others: Germany, 1933–1945* (Oxford, 1988)

36 Schneider, op. cit., pp. 228, 242–54

37 Barkan, op. cit.

38 J. S. Huxley and A. C. Haddon, *We Europeans: A Survey of 'Racial' Problems* (London/New York, 1936), p. 13

39 ibid., pp. 132, 136; see also G. M. Morant, *The Races of Central Europe* (London, 1939), pp. 9, 15

40 M. Kohn, *The Race Gallery: The Revival of Scientific Racism* (London, 1995)

4: The Crisis of Capitalism

1 Cited in D. Peukert, 'The lost generation: youth unemployment at the end of the Weimar Republic', in R. J. Evans and D. Geary (eds.), *The German Unemployed* (London, 1987), p. 180

2. S. Asch, *The Calf of Paper* (London, 1936), p. 24

3 Cited in A. Orde, *British Policy and European Reconstruction after the First World War* (Cambridge, 1990), p. 178

4 ibid., p. 310

5 ibid., p. 143

6 Priestley cited in C. Waters, 'J. B. Priestley' in Mandler and Pedersen (eds.), op. cit., p. 211

7 Cited in R. Boyce, *British Capitalism at the Crossroads, 1919–1932: A Study in Politics, Economics and International Relations* (Cambridge, 1987), pp. 115–16

8 Cited by Orde, op. cit., p. 317; Boyce, op. cit., p. 108; also Boyce, 'British capitalism and the idea of European unity between the wars', in Stirk, *European Unity in Context. . .* , op. cit., pp. 65–84

9 O. Spengler, *Man and Technics* (New York, 1932), pp. 101–2

10 Cited in R. Skidelsky, *Politicians and the Slump: The Labour Government of 1929–31* (London, 1967), p. 244

11 Cited in Boyce, *British Capitalism. . .* , op. cit., pp. 172–3

12 D. Kazamias, *Sta ftocha chronia tis dekaetias tou '30* (Athens, 1997), p. 71; M. Jahoda, P. Lazarsfeld and H. Zeisel, *Marienthal: The Sociography of an Unemployed Community*, cited by R. Overy, *The Interwar Crisis, 1919–1939* (London, 1994), p. 113

13 C. Webster, 'Hungry or Healthy Thirties?', *History Workshop Journal*, 13 (spring 1982), pp. 110–29; M. Mitchell, 'The effects of unemployment on the social condition of women and children in the 1930s', *History Workshop Journal*, 19 (spring 1985), pp. 105–23

14 The most reliable figures are in S. G. Wheatcroft and R. W. Davies, 'Population', in R. W. Davies, M. Harrison and S. G. Wheatcroft (eds.), *The Economic Transformation of the Soviet Union, 1913–1945* (Cambridge, 1994), pp. 57–80; see also F. M. Wilson, *In the Margins of Chaos: Recollections of Relief Work in and between Three Wars* (London, 1944), p. 145

15 Cited in R. Pethybridge, *One Step Backwards, Two Steps Forwards: Soviet Society and Politics in the New Economic Policy* (Oxford, 1990), p. 143

16 ibid., op. cit., p. 415

17 See M. Lewin, 'The immediate background of Soviet collectivisation' in his *The Making of the Soviet System* (London, 1985), pp. 91–121; on numbers shot, see R. W. Davies, 'Forced labour under Stalin: the archive revelations', *New Left Review*, 214 (November/December 1995), pp. 62–80; see generally, R. Conquest, *Harvest of Sorrow: Soviet Collectivization and the Terror-Famine* (New York, 1986), esp. pp. 120–28

18 Cited in M. Fainsod, *Smolensk under Soviet Rule* (London, 1989 edn), p. 240

19 Cited by M. Lewin, ' "Taking grain": Soviet policies of agricultural procurements before the war', in his *Making of the Soviet System*, op. cit., p. 166

20 ibid., pp. 142–77; V. Kravchenko, *I Chose Freedom: The Personal and Political Life of a Soviet Official* (London, 1947), pp. 111, 130

21 Fainsod, op. cit., p. 248

22 Cited by G. Hosking, *A History of the Soviet Union* (London, 1985), p. 150

23 Cited by Bullock, op. cit., p. 311

24 L. Siegelbaum, 'Masters of the shop floor: foremen and Soviet industrialisation', N. Lampert and G. T. Rittersporn (eds.), *Stalinism: Its Nature and Aftermath* (London, 1992), pp. 127–56

25 L. R. Graham, *The Ghost of the Executed Engineer: Technology and the Fall of the Soviet Union* (Cambridge, Mass., 1993), pp. 54–8

26 Davies, op. cit., p. 67

27 ibid.; J.-P. Depretto, 'Construction workers in the 1930s', in Lampert and Rittersporn, op. cit., p. 197

28 H.-H. Schröder, 'Upward social mobility and mass repression: the Communist Party and Soviet society in the Thirties', in Lampert and Rittersporn, op. cit., pp. 157–84

29 F. Furet, *Le Passé d'une illusion* (Paris, 1995), p. 474

30 See T. von Laue, *Why Lenin? Why Stalin?* (New York, 1971), p. 181; Leventhal, op. cit., p. 248

31 Cited in Boyce, *British Capitalism*, op. cit., p. 314

32 ibid., p. 307

33 M. Mazower, *Greece and the Inter-War Economic Crisis* (Oxford, 1991), p. 315

34 But see S. Reich, *The Fruits of Fascism: Postwar Prosperity in Historical Perspective* (Ithaca, NY, 1990)

35 W. Murray, *The Change in the European Balance of Power, 1938–39* (Princeton, NJ, 1984)

36 Cited in Steiner, op. cit., p. 91

37 M. Kele, *Nazis and Workers: National Socialist Appeals to German Labor, 1919–1933* (Chapel Hill, NC, 1972), p. 178; D. Schoenbaum, *Hitler's Social Revolution: Class and Status in Nazi Germany, 1933–1939* (New York, 1966), p. 53

38 Kele, op. cit., p. 205; B. F. Reilly, 'Emblems of production: workers in German, Italian and American art during the 1930s', in W. Kaplan (ed.), *Designing Modernity: The Arts of Reform and Persuasion, 1885–1945* (London, 1995), pp. 287–315

39 A. Lyttelton, *The Seizure of Power: Fascism in Italy, 1919–1929* (Princeton, NJ, 1987), pp. 348–9

40 Cited in J. Noakes and G. Pridham (eds.), *Nazism, 1919–1945*, vol. 2: *State, Economy and Society, 1933–1939* (Exeter, 1988 edn), pp. 373–4; see also: A. Lüdtke, 'The "Honor of Labor": industrial workers and the power of symbols under National Socialism', in D. Crew (ed.), *Nazism and German Society* (London, 1994), pp. 67–110; F. L. Carsten, *The German Workers and the Nazis* (Aldershot, 1995); on Italian workers see T. Abse, 'Italian workers and Italian Fascism', in R. Bessel (ed.), *Fascist Italy and Nazi Germany: Comparisons and Contrasts* (Cambridge, 1996), pp. 40–61; comparative unemployment figures in B. Eichengreen and T. J. Hatton

(eds.), *Unemployment in International Perspective* (Dordrecht, 1988), p. 7

41 P. Hayes, *Industry and Ideology: IG Farben in the Nazi Era* (Cambridge, 1987), p. 172; G. Toniolo, *L'economia dell'Italia fascista* (Rome, 1980), 266; Bullock, op. cit., pp. 181–2

42 R. Overy, *Why the Allies Won* (London, 1995), ch. 6

43 D. S. White, *Socialists of the Front Generation, 1918–1945* (Cambridge, Mass., 1992), p. 81

44 ibid., p. 128

45 ibid., p. 109

46 N. Mosley, *Rules of the Game* (London, 1982), p. 150

47 H. W. Arndt, *The Economic Lessons of the 1930s* (London, 1963 edn), p. 210

48 E. Hansen, 'Hendrik de Man and the theoretical foundations of economic planning: the Belgian experience, 1933–1940', *European Studies Review*, 8 (1978), pp. 235–57

49 Arndt, op. cit. (London, 1944 edn), p. 152

50 Cited by C. Kindleberger, *The World in Depression, 1929–1939* (London, 1973), p. 261

51 Kalecki cited in J. Jackson, *The Popular Front in France: Defending Democracy, 1934–38* (Cambridge, 1990), p. 174; see also, G. Ranki and J. Tomaszewski, 'The role of the state in industry, banking and trade', in M. C. Kaser and E. A. Radice (eds.), *The Economic History of Eastern Europe, 1919–1975*, vol. 2: *Interwar Policy, the War and Reconstruction* (Oxford, 1986), pp. 44–6

5: Hitler's New Order, 1938–45

1 Cited by G. Therborn, 'The autobiography of the twentieth century', *New Left Review*, 214 (November/December 1995), p. 87

2 Cited by O. Bartov, *Hitler's Army: Soldiers, Nazis and War in the Third Reich* (Oxford, 1992), pp. 130–31

3 Ministero degli Affari Esteri, *I documenti diplomatici italiani*, 9th series (1939–43), vol. 8 (Rome, 1986), p. 410: Luciolli to D'Ajeta, 14 March 1942; Mussolini's reaction is noted in M. Muggeridge (ed.), *Ciano's Diary: 1939–1943* (London, 1947), pp. 448–9

4 R. G. Waldeck, *Athene Palace* (New York, 1942), p. 13

5 ibid., p. 14

6 P. Struye, *L'Évolution du sentiment public en Belgique sous l'occupation*

allemande (Brussels, 1945), pp. 20, 30; M. Conway, *Collaboration in Belgium: Léon Degrelle and the Rexist Movement, 1940–1944* (New Haven, Conn./ London, 1993), p. 30; W. Warmbrunn, *The Dutch under German Occupation, 1940–1945* (Stanford, Calif., 1963), pp. 130–35

7 M. Bloch, *Strange Defeat* (New York, 1968), pp. 149, 156–68; F. Bédarida, 'Vichy et la crise de la conscience française', in J.-P. Azéma and F. Bédarida, *Vichy et les Français* (Paris, 1992), pp. 77–96; de Chardin cited in J. Lukacs, *The Last European War* (New York, 1976), p. 515; Berlitz enrolments in R. Cobb, *French and Germans, Germans and French* (Hanover/London, 1983), p. 125

8 Z. Klukowski, *Diary from the Years of Occupation, 1939–1944* (Urbana, Ill./Chicago, 1993), p. 90; Waldeck, op. cit., p. 124

9 R. E. Herzstein, *When Nazi Dreams Come True* (London, 1982), p. 38; C. Moret, *L'Allemagne et la réorganisation de l'Europe (1940–1943)* (Neuchâtel, 1944), p. 43; H. Trevor-Roper (ed.), *Hitler's Table Talk: 1941–1944* (London, 1973), pp. 4–5

10 R. G. Reuth, *Goebbels* (New York, 1993), pp. 268–70

11 Muggeridge, op. cit., p. 390; Trevor-Roper, op. cit., p. 6 (entry for 11–12 July 1941)

12 Noakes and Pridham, op. cit. (New York, 1990 edn), p. 615; N. Rich, *Hitler's War Aims*, vol. 2: *The Establishment of the New Order* (New York, 1974), p. 330; I. Kamenetsky, *Secret Nazi Plans for Eastern Europe* (New Haven, Conn., 1961), p. 38

13 E. L. Homze, *Foreign Labor in Nazi Germany* (Princeton, NJ, 1967), pp. 26–30

14 N. Rich, *Hitler's War Aims*, vol. 1: *Ideology, the Nazi State and the Course of Expansion* (New York, 1973), pp. 134–42; K. Hildebrand, *The Foreign Policy of the Third Reich* (London, 1973), p. 114

15 C. Child, 'The concept of the New Order', in A. and V. Toynbee (eds.), *Survey of International Affairs, 1939–1946: Hitler's Europe* (London, 1954), p. 61

16 W. A. Boelcke (ed.) *The Secret Conferences of Dr. Goebbels* (New York, 1970), pp. 38, 65; Warmbrunn, op. cit., pp. 24–7; Child, op. cit., p. 57

17 P. M. Hayes, *The Career and Political Ideas of Vidkun Quisling, 1887–1945* (Bloomington, Ind./London, 1972), pp. 247, 283–6

18 Boelcke, op. cit., p. 66; Toynbee and Toynbee, op. cit., p. 511

19 Trevor-Roper, op. cit., pp. 92, 621

20 Boelcke, op. cit., pp. 185–6

21 See Schmitt's *Völkerrechtliche Grossraumordnung mit Interventionsver-*

bot für raumfremde Mächte: Ein Beitrag zum Reichsbegriff im Völkerrecht (Berlin, 1939), and 'Reich und Raum: Elemente eines neuen Völkerrechts', *Zeitschrift der Akademie für Deutsches Recht*, 7: 13 (1 July 1940), cited in Bendersky, op. cit., pp. 253–5; Seyss-Inquart and Frank cited in Moret, op. cit., pp. 55–7

22 Cited in Child, op. cit., p. 53

23 Boelcke, op. cit., pp. 17–18; Homze, op. cit., p. 62; Hitler described the Italians as 'the only people on earth with whom we can see eye to eye'. Rich, *Hitler's War Aims*, vol. 2, p. 317; cf. also F. Taylor (ed.), *The Goebbels Diaries: 1939–1941* (London, 1982), p. 328

24 W. Tucker, *The Fascist Ego: A Political Biography of Robert Brasillach* (Berkeley/Los Angeles, Calif., 1975), p. 253

25 Y. Durand, *Le Nouvel Ordre européen nazi* (Paris, 1990), p. 34; J. A. Armstrong, *Ukrainian Nationalism* (New York/London, 1963), p. 79; A. Dallin, *German Rule in Russia, 1941–1945: A Study of Occupation Policies* (Boulder, Colo., 1981, 2nd edn), p. 164

26 Child, op. cit., pp. 50–51

27 A. S. Milward, *War, Economy and Society, 1939–1945* (London, 1977), pp. 162–3; Waldeck, op. cit., pp. 65–72

28 League of Nations, *Food Rationing and Supply 1943/44* (Geneva, 1944), pp. 34–5; on the debate about Hitler's *Blitzkrieg* strategy and its economic implications see R. J. Overy, *Goering: the 'Iron Man'* (London, 1984), ch. 4

29 Milward, op. cit., pp. 132–69; Overy, *Goering: the 'Iron Man'*, op. cit., p. 136

30 Overy, ibid., pp. 120–21

31 Cited in C. Browning, 'The decision concerning the Final Solution', in his *Fateful Months: Essays on the Emergence of the Final Solution* (New York/London, 1985), p. 28; Homze, op. cit., p. 71

32 ibid., 376; Rich, op. cit., vol. 2, p. 381; Dallin, op. cit., pp. 159, 204, 244

33 A. S. Milward, *The New Order and the French Economy* (Oxford, 1970), p. 110; cf. Overy, *Goering: the 'Iron Man'*, op. cit., chs. 6, 8, and Overy, *Why the Allies Won*, op. cit., pp. 198–205

34 Cf. the memo of Otto Brautigam (Head of the Main Political Department, OMi), 25 October 1941, in J. Noakes and G. Pridham (eds.), *Documents on Nazism: 1919–1945* (London, 1974), pp. 626–30; cf. Overy, *Goering: the 'Iron Man'*, op. cit., ch. 8; U. Herbert, *A History of Foreign Labor in Germany, 1880–1980* (Ann Arbor, 1990), p. 145

35 Cited in Herbert, op. cit., p. 149

36 Overy, *Goering: the 'Iron Man'*, op. cit., p. 128; E. M. Kulischer, *Europe on the Move: War and Population Changes, 1917–1947* (New York, 1948), pp. 263–4; Herbert, op. cit., p. 133
37 Cited by Milward, *The New Order and the French Economy*, op. cit., p. 119
38 ibid., pp. 142–51, 165
39 V. Klemperer, *'LTI': Die unbewältigte Sprache* (Munich, 1969), pp. 105–6
40 Trevor-Roper, op. cit., p. 24
41 J. Billig, *Les Camps de concentration dans l'économie du Reich hitlérien* (Paris, 1973), p. 72; R. Koehl, *RKFDV: German Resettlement and Population Policy, 1939–1945* (Cambridge, Mass., 1957), pp. 210–11
42 Waldeck, op. cit., pp. 306–8
43 T-81/307/2435373, 'Abschlussbericht über die Durchschleusung von 95 Griechenlanddeutschen in Passau/Gau Bayr. Ostmark durch die Einwanderzentralstelle des Chefs der Sicherheitspolizei und des SD' (Washington DC, US National Archives)
44 On 'political house-cleaning' see R. Breitman, *The Architect of Genocide: Himmler and the Final Solution* (London, 1991), pp. 70–71; Klukowski, op. cit., pp. 100–101; T. Cyprian and J. Sawicki, *Nazi Rule in Poland, 1939–1945* (Warsaw, 1961), pp. 116–24
45 Gross, op. cit., pp. 226–30; Klukowski, op. cit., pp. 117, 124–5
46 I. Kamenetsky, *Secret Nazi Plans for Eastern Europe* (New Haven, Conn., 1961), p. 106
47 ibid., pp. 93f
48 American Jewish Conference, *Nazi Germany's War against the Jews* (New York, 1947), I-24–5
49 C. Browning, 'Nazi resettlement policy and the search for a solution to the Jewish Question, 1939–1941', in his *The Path to Genocide: Essays on Launching the Final Solution* (Cambridge, 1992), pp. 16–17
50 ibid., p. 24; M. Marrus, *The Holocaust in History* (London, 1988), p. 55
51 Klukowski, op. cit., p. 173
52 G. Robel, 'Sowjetunion', in W. Benz (ed.), *Dimension des Völkermords: Die Zahl der jüdischen Opfer des Nationalsozialismus* (Munich, 1991), pp. 499–560; see also, H. Krausnick, *Hitlers Einsatzgruppen: Die Truppen des Weltanschauungskrieges, 1938–1942* (Frankfurt am Main, 1985)
53 Cited in E. Klee, W. Dressen and V. Riess (eds.), *'Those were the Days': The Holocaust through the Eyes of the Perpetrators and Bystanders* (tr. D. Burnstone) (London, 1991), pp. 138–53
54 E. Kogon, H. Langbein and A. Rückerl (eds.), *Nazi Mass Murder: A*

Documentary History of the Use of Poison Gas (New Haven, Conn., 1993), ch. 4

55 Y. Arad, *Belzec, Sobibor, Treblinka: The Operation Reinhard Death Camps* (Bloomington, Ind., 1987)

56 R. van der Pelt and D. Dwork, *Auschwitz: 1270 to the Present* (New Haven, Conn., 1996)

57 Browning, 'The decision concerning the Final Solution', in *Fateful Months: Essays on the Emergence of the Final Solution*, op. cit., p. 33

58 van der Pelt and Dwork, op. cit., pp. 326, 336, 343

59 ibid., p. 327

60 S. Della Pergola, 'Between science and fiction: notes on the demography of the Holocaust', *Holocaust and Genocide Studies*, 10: 1 (spring 1996), pp. 354–51; on the Ustaše genocide, see A. Djilas, *The Contested Country: Yugoslav Unity and Communist Revolution, 1919–1953* (Cambridge, Mass., 1991), pp. 125–7

61 Goebbels and Kohl of the Railway Dept. cited in Kogon, Langbein and Rückerl, op. cit., pp. 10–11

62 W. Laqueur, *The Terrible Secret: An Investigation into the Suppression of Information about Hitler's Final Solution* (London, 1980); T. Kushner, *The Holocaust and the Liberal Imagination* (Oxford, 1994)

63 Klee, Dressen and Riess, op. cit., pp. 196–207

64 G. J. Horwitz, *In the Shadow of Death: Living outside the Gates of Mauthausen* (New York, 1990), ch. 6

65 G. Schwarz, *Die nationalsozialistischen Lager* (Frankfurt, 1990), pp. 221–2

66 J. Billig, op. cit., pp. 57, 99, 241

67 Herbert, op. cit., p. 174; for an earlier criticism of the economic harm caused by the murder of 150,000–200,000 Jews in the Ukraine, see 3257-PS, cited in *Nazi Germany's War against the Jews*, op. cit., I-50–51

68 Kamenetsky, op. cit., p. 74; Kulischer, op. cit., p. 261

69 See SS/Police chief O. Globocnik in the *Krakauer Zeitung*, 15 June 1941, tr. in US Department of State, *National Socialism*: op. cit., pp. 485–6

70 On reports that mismanagement had led to the need for 'an overpowering police machine' see Dallin, op. cit., p. 219; Trevor-Roper, op. cit., pp. 468–76

71 Y. Bauer, 'The death-marches, January–May, 1945', *Modern Judaism*, 3 (1983), pp. 1–21, esp. 11

72 See Horwitz, op. cit., chs. 7–8

73 Klukowski, op. cit., p. 345; see also R. H. Abzug, *Inside the Vicious Heart: Americans and the Liberation of Nazi Concentration Camps* (New York/Oxford, 1985)

74 Horwitz, op. cit., p. 165

75 V. Lumans, *Himmler's Auxiliaries: The Volksdeutsche Mittelstelle and the German National Minorities of Europe, 1933–1945* (Chapel Hill, NC, 1993), p. 203

76 Trevor-Roper, op. cit., pp. 33, 69, 92, 316, 354–5

77 C. Child, 'Administration', in Toynbee and Toynbee, op. cit., p. 125; E. K. Bramsted, *Goebbels and National Socialist Propaganda, 1925–1945* (Ann Arbor, Mich., 1965), p. 303

6: Blueprints for the Golden Age

1 H. G. Wells, *The New World Order* (New York, 1940), p. 45

2. I. McLaine, *Ministry of Morale: Home Front Morale and the Ministry of Information in World War II* (London, 1979), pp. 30–31, 101; P. Addison, *The Road to 1945: British Politics and the War* (London, 1975), p. 121

3 R. Acland, *The Forward March* (London, 1941), p. 9; E. H. Carr, *Conditions of Peace* (New York, 1942), p. 9

4 W. Lipgens (ed.), *Documents on the History of European Integration*, vol. 1: *Continental Plans for European Union, 1939–1945* (Berlin/New York, 1985), p. 39; Kennedy in *The Times*, 18 November 1940; on de Gaulle, A. Shennan, *Rethinking France: Plans for Renewal, 1940–1946* (Oxford, 1989), pp. 53–6; R. W. G. MacKay, *Peace Aims and the New Order* (London, 1941 edn), p. 7

5 E. Ranshofen-Wertheimer, *Victory is not Enough: The Strategy for a Lasting Peace* (New York, 1942), pp. 122–3; 'Metropoliticus', 'The Ministry of Information', *Political Quarterly*, 13 (1942), p. 300

6 cf. R. M. Titmuss, 'War and social policy', in his *Essays on the 'Welfare' State* (Boston, Mass., 1969), esp. pp. 84–6; and the comments of J. Harris, 'Some aspects of social policy in Britain during the Second World War', in W. J. Mommsen (ed.), *The Emergence of the Welfare State in Britain and Germany, 1850–1950* (London, 1981), pp. 247–63; *The Journey Home* (a report prepared by Mass Observation for the Advertising Service Guild) (London, 1944), p. 104; on the exodus, see J. Vidalenc, *L'Exode de Mai–Juin 1940* (Paris, 1957) and N. Ollier, *L'Exode: sur les routes de l'an 40* (Paris, 1970)

7 Cited by Addison, op. cit., p. 118; Blum cited by Lipgens, op. cit., pp. 278–9

8 Cited by McLaine, op. cit., p. 149

9 Addison, op. cit., pp. 170–71

10 J. Harris, *William Beveridge: A Biography* (Oxford, 1977), p. 366

11 Harris, op. cit., p. 387; W. Beveridge, *Social Insurances and Allied Services* (London, 1942), p. 172

12 Harris, op. cit., p. 420; for parallel thinking in the Nazi labour organization, see R. Smelser, 'Die Sozialplanung der deutschen Arbeitsfront', in M. Prinz and R. Zitelmann (eds.), *Nationalsozialismus und Modernisierung* (Darmstadt, 1991), pp. 71–92

13 A. Myrdal, *Nation and Family: The Swedish Experiment in Democratic Family and Population Policy* (London, 1940), p. vi

14 M. Sadoun, *Les Socialistes sous l'occupation: résistance et collaboration* (Paris, 1982), p. 136; C. Andrieu, *Le Program commun de la Résistance: des idées dans la guerre* (Paris, 1984), pp. 114f

15 Lipgens, op. cit., p. 569; M. Mazower, *Inside Hitler's Greece: The Experience of Occupation, 1941–1944* (New Haven, Conn., 1993), p. 267

16 Shennan, op. cit., p. 36

17 Andrieu, op. cit., p. 38

18 L. W. Lorwin, *Postwar Plans of the United Nations* (New York, 1943), pp. 128, 135–40, 144–5

19 *New World Order*, Wells, See, e.g., op. cit., p. 58

20 E. Vittorini, *Men and not Men* (tr. Sarah Henry) (Marlboro, Vt, 1985), p. 157

21 J. D. Wilkinson, *The Intellectual Resistance in Europe* (Cambridge, Mass., 1981), p. 47; Camus in G. Brée and G. Bernauer (eds.), *Defeat and Beyond: An Anthology of French Wartime Writing (1940–1945)* (New York, 1970), pp. 347–9

22 A. Vistel, *Héritage spirituel de la Résistance*, in Lipgens, op. cit., p. 268; Shennan, op. cit., p. 82

23 J. Hellman, *Emmanuel Mounier and the New Catholic Left, 1930–1950* (Toronto, 1981), p. 180; J. Maritain, *Christianity and Democracy* (San Francisco, Calif., 1986), p. 22

24 J. Maritain, *The Rights of Man and Natural Law* (San Francisco, Calif., 1986), pp. 91, 165; W. Temple, *Christianity and Social Order* (Harmondsworth, Middx, 1942), p. 80

25 L. Holborn (ed.), *War and Peace Aims of the United Nations* (Boston, Mass., 1943), p. 158; H. Lauterpacht, *An International Bill of the Rights of Man* (New York, 1945), pp. v–vi; E. Hamburger *et al.*, *Le Droit raciste à l'assaut de la civilisation* (New York, 1943)

26 *The World's Destiny and the United States* (A Conference of Experts in International Relations) (Chicago, 1943), pp. 101–37

27 J. Maritain, 'Le droit raciste et la vraie signification du racisme', in Hamburger, op. cit., pp. 97–137

28 G. Myrdal, *An American Dilemma: The Negro Problem and Modern Democracy*, vol. 2 (New York, 1944), pp. 1004, 1007–9

29 D. Thompson, *From Kingston to Kenya: The Making of a Pan-Africanist Lawyer* (Dover, Mass., 1993), pp. 23–33, 45–7 (thanks to Rupert Lewis for drawing my attention to this remarkable book); McLaine, op. cit., pp. 223–4

30 C. Pavone, *Una guerra civile: saggio storico sulla moralità nella Resistenza* (Turin, 1991), pp. 202–3; Shennan, op. cit., pp. 142–3; E. Rice-Maximin, *Accommodation and Resistance: The French Left, Indochina and the Cold War, 1944–1954* (New York, 1986), pp. 14–15; Holborn, op. cit., pp. 522–3

31 R. Redfield, 'The ethnological problem', in G. de Huszar (ed.), *New Perspectives on Peace* (Chicago, 1944), pp. 80–82

32 R. Lemkin, *Axis Rule in Occupied Europe* (Washington, DC, 1944), p. xiv; W. Friedman, 'The disintegration of European civilisation and the future of international law', *Modern Law Review* (December 1938), pp. 194–214; J. Herz, 'The National Socialist doctrine of international law', *Political Science Quarterly* (December 1939), pp. 536–54

33 *The World's Destiny and the United States*, op. cit., pp. 102–5

34 ibid., p. 113; Lauterpacht, op. cit., p. vi; H. Kelsen, *Peace through Law* (Chapel Hill, NC, 1944), esp. pp. 41–2

35 W. Lipgens, 'European federation in the political thought of resistance movements', *Central European History*, 1 (1968), p. 10; W. I. Jennings, *A Federation for Western Europe* (New York/Cambridge, 1940), p. 10

36 'Statement of Aims' cited in W. Lipgens, *A History of European Integration*, vol. 1: *1945–1947* (Oxford, 1982), p. 143; MacKay, op. cit., p. 23; see the special issue, 'Anglo-French Union?' in *The New Commonwealth Quarterly*, v: 4 (April 1940)

37 G. T. Renner, 'Maps for a new world', *Collier's* (6 June 1942), pp. 14–15; B. Newman, *The New Europe* (New York, 1943), frontispiece; for an important survey of earlier moves towards federalism, see R. Schlesinger, *Federalism in Central and Eastern Europe* (New York, 1945)

38 Representative of the time is A. Kolnai, 'Danubia: a survey of plans of solution', *Journal of Central European Affairs* (January 1944), pp. 441–62

39 H. Notter, *Postwar Foreign Policy Preparation, 1939–1945* (Westport, Conn., 1975), pp. 458–60

40 Pavone, op. cit., pp. 305–6; Lipgens, *Documents*, op. ct., pp. 319, 339

41 ibid., p. 563; Lipgens, 'European federation . . .', op. cit., p. 12

42 F. A. von Hayek, *The Road to Serfdom* (Chicago, 1944), pp. 4, 67, 84

43 K. Mannheim, *Man and Society in an Age of Reconstruction* (London, 1950 edn), pp. 6, 380

44 Carr, *Conditions of Peace*, op. cit., pp. 256–61

45 Hayek, op. cit., p. 203

46 ibid., p. 231; see also, F. A. von Hayek, 'Economic conditions of inter-state federalism', *The New Commonwealth Quarterly*, v: 2 (September 1939), pp. 131–50

47 L. von Mises, *Omnipotent Government: The Rise of the Total State and Total War* (New Haven, Conn., 1944), p. 286

48 C. Becker, *How New Will the Better World be?* (New York, 1944), pp. v, 243

49 *The Journey Home*, op. cit., pp. 43–52

50 Pavone, op. cit., p. 570

51 M. Higonnet (ed.), *Behind the Lines: Gender and the Two World Wars* (New Haven, Conn., 1987)

52 Cf. B. Jancar-Webster, *Women and Revolution in Yugoslavia, 1941–1945* (Denver, Colo., 1990), p. 163; *The Journey Home*, op. cit., pp. 55–6

53 I. Szabo, 'Historical foundations of human rights and subsequent developments', in K. Vasak (ed.) *The International Dimensions of Human Rights*, i (Paris, 1982), pp. 11–42; H. Lauterpacht, *International Law and Human Rights* (New York, 1950), p. 353; H. Lauterpacht, *Report: Human Rights, the Charter of the United Nations and the International Bill of the Rights of Man* (Brussels, 1948), p. 22

54 N. Robinson, *The Genocide Convention: A Commentary* (New York, 1960), p. 52; see also H. Kelsen, 'Collective and individual responsibility in international law with particular regard to the punishment of war criminals', *California Law Review*, XXXI (December 1943), pp. 530–71; H. Lauterpacht, 'The subjects of the Law of Nations', *Law Quarterly Review*, LXIII (October 1947), pp. 438–60; LXIV (January 1948), pp. 97–116

7: A Brutal Peace, 1943–9

1 In his *Memoirs of a Revolutionist: Essays in Political Criticism* (New York, 1957), p. 119

2 On the war as a civil war, see Pavone, op. cit., and A. J. Mayer, *Why Did the Heavens Not Darken?* (London, 1990)

3 Kulischer, op. cit., pp. 274–81; P. R. Magosci, *Historical Atlas of East*

Central Europe (Seattle, 1993), p. 164; R. Overy (ed.), *The Times Atlas of the Twentieth Century* (London, 1996)

4 See J. T. Gross, 'Social consequences of war: preliminaries to the study of imposition of communist regimes in east central Europe', *East European Politics and Society*, 3: 2 (spring 1989), pp. 198–214

5 M. Djilas, *Conversations with Stalin* (New York, 1962), p. 114; on 'Red Fascism', see L. Adler and T. Paterson, 'Red Fascism: the merger of Nazi Germany and Soviet Russia in the American image of totalitarianism, 1930s to 1950s', *American Historical Review*, 75 (1970), pp. 1046–64

6 Magosci, op. cit., cf. J. Vernant, *The Refugee in the Post-War World* (London, 1953), p. 30; M. J. Proudfoot, *European Refugees, 1939–1952: A Study in Forced Population Movement* (London, 1957), p. 34

7 On German POWs, see G. Bischof and S. E. Ambrose (eds.), *Eisenhower and the German POWs: Facts against Falsehood* (Baton Rouge, La/London, 1992); E. Skrjabina, *The Allies on the Rhine, 1945–1950* (Carbondale, Ill., 1980), p. 29

8 Vernant, op. cit.

9 ibid., op. cit., pp. 60–63; Proudfoot, op. cit., p. 361; A. Königseder and J. Wetzel, *Lebensmut im Wartesaal: Die jüdischen DPs im Nachkriegsdeutschland* (Frankfurt am Main, 1994)

10 Skrjabina, op. cit., p. 109; W. Benz (ed.), *Die Vertriebung der Deutschen aus dem Osten* (Frankfurt am Main, 1995)

11 Danzig report cited in C. Tighe, *Gdansk: National Identity in the Polish–German Borderlands* (London, 1990), p. 197; T. Schieder (ed.), *The Expulsion of the German Population from the Territories East of the Oder–Neisse Line* (Bonn, n.d.), p. 269

12 A. M. de Zayas, *Nemesis at Potsdam: The Expulsion of the Germans from the East* (Lincoln, Nebr./London, 1988 edn), pp. 104–6; J. B. Schechtman, *Postwar Population Transfers in Europe, 1945–1955* (Philadelphia, Pa, 1962), pp. 56–67; Gomułka cited in N. Naimark, *The Russians in Germany: A History of the Soviet Zone of Occupation, 1945–1949* (Cambridge, Mass., 1995), p. 147

13 Schechtman, op. cit., p. 363

14 Kirk, op. cit., p. 69, n. 24 for civil and military casualties; Proudfoot, op. cit., p. 34 for forced movements of civilians during the war. Total population estimates from B. R. Mitchell, *European Historical Statistics, 1750–1975* (New York, 1980 edn); on western Poland, J. Ziolkowski, 'The sociological aspects of demographic changes in Polish Western Territories', *Polish Western Affairs*, 3: 1 (1962), pp. 3–37; quote from J. Wiatr, 'Polish

society', cited in C. M. Hann, *A Village without Solidarity: Polish Peasants in Years of Crisis* (New Haven, Conn./London, 1985), p. 157

15 T. Schieder (ed.), *Documents on the Expulsion of the Germans from Eastern-Central Europe* (Bonn, 1961), pp. 146–7, 152

16 A. Scholz, *Silesia: Yesterday and Today* (The Hague, 1964), p. 69

17 Hann, op. cit., p. 179; Scholz, op. cit., p. 50

18 See Gross, 'Social consequences of war', op cit., *passim*

19 D. Sington, *Belsen Uncovered* (London, 1946), p. 187

20 D. Macardle, *Children of Europe* (Boston, Mass., 1951), pp. 58, 107, 154, 200, 231

21 ibid., pp. 231–5, 294–6

22 ibid., p. 64

23 ibid., p. 242

24 A. Mando Dalianis-Karambatzakis, *Children in Turmoil during the Greek Civil War 1946–49: Today's Adults* (Stockholm, 1994); cf. A. Karpf, *The War After* (London, 1996), and A. Hass, *Aftermath: Living with the Holocaust* (New York, 1995)

25 Z. Zaluski, *Final 1945* (Warsaw, 1968), p. 17, cited in P. Wandycz, *The Price of Freedom: A History of East Central Europe from the Middle Ages to the Present* (London, 1992), p. 240; J. R. Fiszman, *Revolution and Tradition in People's Poland: Education and Socialization* (Princeton, NJ, 1972), p. 25

26 F. Neumann, 'Re-educating the Germans: the dilemma of reconstruction', *Commentary* (June 1947), pp. 517–25; post-war Cioran cited in S. Guilbaut, 'Postwar painting games: the rough and the slick', in Guilbaut (ed.), *Reconstructing Modernism: Art in New York, Paris and Montreal, 1945–1964* (Cambridge, Mass., 1990), p. 53; pre-war Cioran in L. Volovici, *Nationalist Ideology and Antisemitism: The Case of Romanian Intellectuals in the 1930s* (Oxford, 1991), pp. 78–9

27 V. St Erlich, *Family in Transition: A Study of 300 Yugoslav Villages* (Princeton, NJ, 1966), pp. 452–3; D. Pines, 'Working with women survivors of the Holocaust', *Journal of Psychoanalysis* (1986), pp. 67, 295–307

28 G. Theotokas, *Tetradia imerologiou* (Athens, n.d.), p. 486

29 G. Warner, 'Italy and the Powers, 1943–49' in S. J. Woolf (ed.), *The Rebirth of Italy, 1943–50* (New York, 1972), p. 30

30 D. Ellwood, *Italy, 1943–1945* (New York, 1985), pp. 22–30

31 L. Kettenacker, 'The Anglo-Soviet alliance and the problem of Germany, 1941–1945', *Journal of Contemporary History*, 17 (1982), pp. 435–58 (cited on p. 449)

32 V. Zubok and C. Pleshakov, *Inside the Kremlin's Cold War: From Stalin to Khrushchev* (Cambridge, Mass., 1996), pp. 28–30

33 See the excellent discussion in C. Gati, *Hungary and the Soviet Bloc* (Durham, NC, 1986), pp. 28–33; on Romania, G. Ionescu, *Communism in Rumania, 1944–1962* (London, 1964), p. 90

34 K. Kersten, *The Establishment of Communist Rule in Poland, 1943–1948* (Berkeley/Los Angeles, Calif., 1991), p. 122

35 R. Palmer Domenico, *Italian Fascists on Trial, 1943–1948* (Chapel Hill, NC, 1991), pp. 92–4

36 Cited in M. Dondi, 'Azioni di guerra e potere partigiano nel dopoliberazione', *Italia contemporanea*, 188 (September 1992), pp. 457–77 (citations pp. 465–6)

37 ibid., p. 467

38 H. R. Kedward, *In Search of the Maquis: Rural Resistance in Southern France, 1942–1944* (Oxford, 1993), p. 279

39 H. Lottman, *The People's Anger: Justice and Revenge in Post-Liberation France* (London, 1986), pp. 50–56

40 K.-D. Henke and H. Woller (eds.), *Politische Säuberung in Europa: Die Abrechnung mit Faschismus und Kollaboration nach dem Zweiten Weltkrieg* (Munich, 1991), pp. 184, 215–39, 272, 292–9

41 ibid., p. 128; J.-P. Rioux, *The Fourth Republic, 1944–1958* (Cambridge, 1987) p. 36

42 Domenico, op. cit., p. 157; Rioux, op. cit., p. 40

43 M. Szöllösi-Janze, '"Pfeilkreuzler, Landesverräter und andere Volksfeinde": Generalabrechnung in Ungarn', in Henke, op. cit., pp. 317–18

44 P. Zinner, *Revolution in Hungary* (New York/London, 1962), p. 25

45 E. Völkl, 'Abrechnungfuror in Kroatien', in Henke and Woller, op. cit., pp. 366–74

46 On German measures behind Soviet lines, see P. Biddiscombe, 'Prodding the Russian Bear: pro-German resistance in Romania, 1944–5', *European History Quarterly*, 23 (April 1993), pp. 193–232; J. Schechtman, 'Elimination of German minorities in southeastern Europe', *Journal of Central European Affairs* (July 1946), pp. 151–66; Ionescu, pp. 110–11

47 Hungary, in Henke, op. cit.; Zinner, op. cit., pp. 51–2

48 Kersten, op. cit., pp. 390–92; see also Hann, op. cit., pp. 33–5

49 B. Davidson, *Germany: What Now? Potsdam–Partition, 1945–1949* (London, 1950), p. 2; L. Krieger, 'The inter-regnum in Germany: March August 1945', *Political Science Quarterly*, 64: 4 (December 1949), pp. 507–32

50 D. Botting, *From the Ruins of the Reich: Germany 1945–49* (New York, 1985), pp. 109–11; A. Grosser, *Germany in Our Time: A Political History of the Postwar Years* (New York, 1971), pp. 26–7

51 J. P. Nettl, *The Eastern Zone and Soviet Policy in Germany, 1945–1950* (London, 1951), ch. 3

52 W. Ulbricht, *Der faschistische deutsche Imperialismus (1933–1945)* (Berlin, 1945)

53 H. Zink, *American Military Government in Germany* (New York, 1947), p. 143; J. Gimbel, *A German Community under American Occupation: Marburg, 1945–1952* (Stanford, Calif., 1961), pp. 109, 140–42, 163;. A. J. Merritt and R. L. Merritt (eds.), *Public Opinion in Occupied Germany: The OMGUS Surveys, 1945–1949* (Urbana, Ill., 1970), pp. 79–80, 304–5

54 D. Culbert, 'American film policy in the re-education of Germany after 1945', in N. Pronay and K. Wilson (eds.) *The Political Re-Education of Germany and Her Allies after World War Two* (Totowa, NJ, 1985), p. 179; also B. S. Chamberlain, 'Todesmühlen: ein früher Versuch zur Massen-"Umerziehung" im besetzten Deutschland 1945–1946', *Vierteljahreshefte für Zeitgeschichte*, 29 (July 1981), pp. 420–36

55 S. Padover, *Experiment in Germany: The Story of an American Intelligence Officer* (New York, 1946), pp. 135, 339

56 K. Jürgensen, 'The concept and practice of "re-education" in Germany, 1945–50', in Pronay and Wilson, op. cit., p. 93; F. Roy Willis, *The French in Germany, 1945–1949* (Stanford, Calif., 1962), pp. 163–77; J. F. Tent, *Mission on the Rhine: Re-education and De-Nazification in American-Occupied Germany* (Chicago/London, 1982), pp. 313–14

57 V. Rudolph, 'The execution of policy, 1945–47', in R. Slusser (ed.), *Soviet Economic Policy in Postwar Germany* (New York, 1953), p. 40; Nettl, op. cit., pp. 167–81

58 Zink, op. cit., pp. 180–83

59 H. Krisch, *German Politics under Soviet Occupation* (New York/London, 1974), p. 40

60 Grosser, op. cit., p. 66

61 C. Schorske, 'The dilemma in Germany', *Virginia Quarterly Review*, 24: 1 (winter 1948), pp. 29–42; Krieger, op. cit., pp. 507–32

62 Lottman, op. cit., p. 68

8: Building People's Democracy

1 Cited in F. J. Kase, *People's Democracy: A Contribution to the Study of the Communist Theory of State and Revolution* (Leyden, 1968), p. 21

2 J. Pelikan (ed.), *The Czechoslovak Political Trials, 1950–1954: The Suppressed Report of the Dubček Government's Commission of Inquiry, 1968* (London, 1971), p. 38

3 See now, A. Gleason, *Totalitarianism: The Inner History of the Cold War* (Oxford, 1995)

4 See D. J. Dallin, *The New Soviet Empire* (London, 1951)

5 H. Seton-Watson, *Eastern Europe between the Wars, 1918–1941* 1962 edn, first pub. 1945), pp. 262–3; R. R. Betts (ed.), *Central and South East Europe, 1945–1948* (London, 1949), p. 212

6 Soviet military strengths are cited from W. Park, *Defending the West: A History of NATO* (Brighton, 1986), pp. 23–5; Naimark, op. cit., p. 17; see also M. Evangelista, 'Stalin's postwar army reappraised', *International Security*, 7: 3 (winter 1982–3), pp. 110–38; op. cit., Gati, p. 37; Myant, *Socialism and Democracy in Czechoslovakia, 1945–1948* (Cambridge, 1981), p. 58.

7 See J. Adelman, *Communist Armies in Politics* (Boulder, Colo., 1982); D. Deletant, *Ceauşescu and the Securitate: Coercion and Dissent in Romania, 1965–1989* (London, 1995)

8 A. Korbonski, 'The Polish Army', in Adelman, op. cit., p. 111

9 Zubok and Pleshakov, op. cit., p. 32

10 See N. Naimark, 'Nationalism and the East European Revolution, 1944–1947', paper prepared for Conference on 'Remembering, Adapting, Overcoming: The Legacy of World War Two in Europe' (New York University, 24–27 April 1997)

11 Naimark, *Russians in Germany*, op. cit., pp. 260–75; G. Sandford, *From Hitler to Ulbricht: The Communist Reconstruction of East Germany, 1945–1946* (Princeton, NJ, 1983), pp. 49–51

12 F. J. Kase, *People's Democracy: A Contribution to the Study of the Communist Theory of State and Revolution* (Leyden, 1968), p. 103; Zubok and Pleshakov, op. cit., p. 106

13 Z. Mlynar, *Night Frost in Prague: The End of Humane Socialism* (London, 1980), pp. 1–2

14 ibid., p. 2

15 J. Kurczewski, *The Resurrection of Rights in Poland* (Oxford, 1993), p. 10; Zinner, op. cit., pp. 52, 62

16 Gati, op. cit., p. 89

17 Zubok and Pleshakov, op. cit., pp. 116–19

18 Gati, op. cit., pp. 86–8

19 Barker, *Truce in the Balkans*, p. 148; T. Remeikis, *Opposition to Soviet Rule in Lithuania, 1945–1980* (Chicago, 1980), pp. 210–11

20 On judges, op. cit., Kurczewski, p. 70

21 J. Connelly, 'Foundations for reconstructing elites: Communist higher educational policies in the Czech lands, East Germany and Poland, 1945–48', *East European Politics and Societies*, 10: 3 (fall 1996), pp. 367–92

22 S. Kopacsi, *In the Name of Working Class* (London, 1989), p. 42; Myant, op. cit., p. 59, states that *after* the purge of the Czech police, there were still 25,000 from the old force as against 12,000 new ones.

23 See the excellent analysis in Gati, op. cit.; A. Mastny, 'Pax Sovietica', in R. Ahmann, A. M. Birke and M. Howard (eds.), *The Quest for Stability: Problems of European Security, 1918–1957* (Oxford, 1993), 379–89; Djilas, op. cit., p. 140

24 Cited in B. Jelavich, *History of the Balkans*, vol. 2: *Twentieth Century* (Cambridge, 1983), pp. 326–7

25 Cf. B. Szasz, *Volunteers for the Gallows: Anatomy of a Show-Trial* (London, 1971), pp. 146–7

26 Estimates from Dallin, op. cit., p. 157; Zinner, op. cit., p. 115; F. Fejtö, *A History of the People's Democracies* (Harmondsworth, Middx, 1974 edn), p. 18; Ionescu, op. cit., pp. 131, 199; *News from Behind the Iron Curtain*, 1: 5 (May 1952)

27 See S. Kotkin, *Magnetic Mountain: Stalinism as a Civilisation* (Berkeley/ Los Angeles, Calif., 1995), pp. 198–203

28 T. P. Alton, *Polish Postwar Economy* (New York, 1955), pp. 108–14

29 UN Economic Commission for Europe, *Economic Survey of Europe since the War* (Geneva, 1953), pp. 21, 31 n. 1

30 ibid., pp. 33, 35; G. Ambrosius and W. Hubbard, *A Social and Ecnomic History of 20th Century Europe* (London, 1989) p. 200

31 On the Baltic states, see R. Misiunas and R. Taagepera, *The Baltic States: Years of Dependence, 1940–1990* (Berkeley, Calif., 1993), pp. 94–107; it was the communist theorist Evgenii Preobrazhenskii who once termed the peasantry an 'internal colony'.

32 Deletant, op. cit., p. 26; *News from Behind the Iron Curtain* 1: 1 (January 1952), p. 10; ibid., 1: 9 (September 1952)

33 Ionescu, op. cit., p. 200; Kopacsi, op. cit., pp. 58–9

34 *News from Behind the Iron Curtain*, 1: 1, p. 16

35 Mlynar, op. cit., p. 37; Zinner, op. cit.; *News from Behind the Iron Curtain*, 1: 4 (April 1952), p. 13; A. Aman, *Architecture and Ideology in Eastern Europe during the Stalin Era* (New York, 1922), p. 82, for rates of housing construction

36 *News from Behind the Iron Curtain*, 1:4 p. 18

37 Szasz, op. cit., p. 231; P. Kecskemeti, *The Unexpected Revolution: Social Forces in the Hungarian Uprising* (Stanford, Calif., 1961), p. 71

38 Kecskemeti, op. cit., p. 31; Fejtö, op. cit., p. 81

39 See Kurczewski, op. cit., chs. 2–3

40 Szasz, op. cit., p. 237

41 Z. Brzezinski, *The Grand Failure: The Birth and Death of Communism in the 20th Century* (London, 1990), p. 53; P. Mosely, 'Can Moscow match us industrially?' reprinted in his *The Kremlin and World Politics: Studies in Soviet Policy and Action* (New York, 1960)

42 Ambrosius and Hubbard, op. cit., p. 40; J. Kosinski, 'Urbanization in East-Central Europe after World War 2', *East European Quarterly*, 8: 2 (June 1974), p. 135

43 See Aman, op. cit., p. 141

44 L. A. Dellin (ed.), *Bulgaria* (New York, 1957), p. 253; V. Srb, 'Population development and population policy in Czechoslovakia', *Population Studies*, 16 (November 1962), pp. 147–60; M. Fulbrook, 'On Germany's double transformation', *European History Quarterly*, 20: 3 (1990), pp. 402–15, on G. Helwig, *Frau und Familie: Bundesrepublik Deutschland–DDR* (Cologne, 1987)

45 G. W. Hoffman and F. W. Neal, *Yugoslavia and the New Communism* (New York, 1962), p. 373; Fejtö, op. cit., pp. 424–5

46 Mlynar, op. cit., p. 49; Ambrosius and Hubbard, op. cit., p. 70

47 Hoffman and Neal, op. cit., p. 361

48 W. Vucinich (ed.), *Contemporary Yugoslavia: Twenty Years of Socialist Experiment* (Berkeley/Los Angeles, Calif., 1969), p. 341

49 Jelavich, op. cit., pp. ii, 344

50 A. S. Deaton, 'The structure of demand, 1920–1970', in C. Cipolla (ed.), *The Fontana Economic History of Europe*, vol. 5: *The Twentieth Century*: 1 (London, 1982), pp. 124–5

51 M. Pundeff, 'Education for communism', in S. Fischer-Galati (ed.), *Eastern Europe in the Sixties* (New York, 1963)

52 Ionescu, op. cit., p. 267; P. Neuburg, *The Hero's Children: The Postwar Generation in Eastern Europe* (London, 1972), p. 273

53 Fejtö, op. cit., p. 306

54 Neuburg, op. cit., p. 265

55 G. Ionescu, *The Break-Up of the Soviet Empire in Eastern Europe* (Harmondsworth, Middx, 1965), p. 26

56 ibid., p. 41; Fejtö, op. cit., p. 158

57 A. Gyorgy, 'The internal political order', in Fischer-Galati, op. cit., p. 190; Fejtö, op. cit., p. 463

9: Democracy Transformed: Western Europe, 1950–75

1 Cited in J. Diefendorf, *In the Wake of War: The Reconstruction of German Cities after World War II* (Oxford, 1993), p. 132

2 M. Kidron, *Western Capitalism since the War* (London, 1968), p. ix

3 G. Perec (tr. D. Bellos), *Things: A Story of the Sixties* (London, 1991), p. 31

4 W. F. Murphy, 'Constitutions, constitutionalism and democracy', in D. Greenberg (ed.), *Constitutionalism and Democracy* (New York, 1993), pp. 3–25

5 See the discussion in J. F. Golay, *The Founding of the Federal Republic of Germany* (Chicago, 1958), pp. 175–81

6 E. Wiskemann, *Germany's Eastern Neighbours* (Oxford, 1956), p. 191; I. D. Connor, 'The Bavarian government and the refugee problem, 1945–1950', *European History Quarterly*, 16: 2 (1986), pp. 131–53; D. Childs, 'The far Right in Germany since 1945', in L. Cheles *et al.* (eds.), *Neo-Fascism in Europe* (London, 1991), p. 70

7 T. Barnes, 'The secret cold war: the CIA and American foreign policy in Europe, 1946–1956', *Historical Journal*, 24: 2 (1981), pp. 399–415, and 25: 3 (1982), pp. 649–70

8 P. Coleman, *The Liberal Conspiracy: The Congress for Cultural Freedom and the Struggle for the Mind of Postwar Europe* (New York, 1989); I. Wall, *The United States and the Making of Postwar France, 1945–1954* (Cambridge, 1991), pp. 213–16

9 P. Hennessy and G. Brownfield, 'Britain's cold war security purge: the origins of positive vetting', *Historical Journal*, 25: 4 (1982), pp. 965–73

10 C. Friedrich, 'The political theory of the new constitutions', in A. Zurcher (ed.), *Constitutions and Constitutional Trends since World War II* (New York, 1955)

11 S. Padgett and W. Paterson, *A History of Social Democracy in Postwar Europe* (London, 1991), pp. 13, 110

12 Gaitskell in B. Moore-Gilbert and J. Seed (eds.), *Cultural Revolution? The Challenge of the Arts in the 1960s* (London, 1992), p. 22; Crossman cited in M. Pinto-Duschinsky, 'Bread and circuses? The Conservatives in office, 1951–1964', in V. Bogdanor and R. Skidelsky (eds.), *The Age of Affluence, 1951–1964* (London, 1970), p. 93

13 A. J. Nicholls, *Freedom with Responsibility: The Social Market Economy in Germany, 1918–1963* (Oxford 1994), p. 11; also M. Mitchell, 'Materialism and secularism: CDU politicians and National Socialism, 1945–1949', *Journal of Modern History*, 67 (June 1995), pp. 278–308

14 Lane and Ersson, *Politics and Society in Western Europe*, pp. 304–6

15 P. Armstrong, A. Glyn and J. Harrison, *Capitalism since World War II: The Making and Breakup of the Great Boom* (London, 1984), pp. 156, 161–2; Dutch emigration policy, L. Kosinski, *The Population of Europe* (London, 1970), p. 71; L. Wylie, *Village in the Vaucluse* (Cambridge, Mass., 1974 edn), p. 33

16 UN, *Economic Survey of Europe since the War: A Reappraisal of Problems and Prospects* (Geneva, 1953), pp. 81–3, 234

17 R. Carr, *Modern Spain, 1875–1980* (Oxford, 1980), pp. 156–8; Gallagher, op. cit., p. 138; A. Cochrane and J. Clarke (eds.), *Comparing Welfare States: Britain in International Context* (London, 1993), pp. 211–14

18 Figures from A. Maddison, 'Economic policy and performance in Europe, 1913–1970', in Cipolla, op. cit., vol. 5: *The Twentieth Century: 2* (London, 1981), pp. 442–509; J. Holloway, 'The Dickensian environment', *The Listener*, 12 January 1967

19 J. Tomlinson, *Public Policy and the Economy since 1900* (Oxford, 1990), p. 238

20 A. Boltho (ed.) *The European Economy: Growth and Crisis* (Oxford, 1982), pp. 11–16; E. Denison, *Why Growth Rates Differ* (Washington, DC, 1967)

21 The debate is chiefly between A. Milward, *The Reconstruction of Western Europe, 1945–1951* (London, 1984) and M. Hogan, *The Marshall Plan: America, Britain and the Reconstruction of Western Europe, 1947–1952* (Cambridge, 1987). For US aid, M. Postan, *An Economic History of Western Europe, 1945–1964* (London, 1967), p. 106

22 A. Maddison, *Phases of Capitalist Development* (Oxford, 1982), pp. 96–9; C. Maier, 'Politics of productivity', in P. J. Katzenstein (ed.), *Between Power and Plenty: Foreign Economic Policies of Advanced Industrial States* (Madison, Wis., 1978); from a growing literature on productivity, D. W. Ellwood, *Rebuilding Europe: Western Europe, America and Postwar Reconstruction* (London, 1992); R. Kuisel, *Seducing the French: The Dilemma of*

Americanization (Berkeley, Calif., 1993); for TU suspicions, see A. Carew, 'The Anglo-American Council on Productivity (1948–1952): the ideological roots of the post-war debate on productivity in Britain', *Journal of Contemporary History*, 26 (1991), pp. 49–69

23 Wiskemann, op. cit., p. 176

24 G. Lundestad, *The American 'Empire' and Other Studies of US Foreign Policy in a Comparative Perspective* (Oslo, 1990); Postan, op. cit., p. 25

25 Ellwood, op. cit., pp. 218–19

26 A. Shonfield, *Modern Capitalism: The Changing Balance of Public and Private Power* (Oxford, 1965), p. 3

27 ibid., p. 62; N. F. R. Crafts, 'The golden age of economic growth in Western Europe, 1950–1973', *Economic History Review*, 48: 3 (1995), pp. 429–47

28 Nicholls, op. cit., p. 321

29 The argument is made for Britain by C. Barnett, *The Audit of War* (London, 1986), and refuted by J. Harris, 'Enterprise and welfare states: a comparative perspective', *Transactions of the Royal Historical Society* (1990), pp. 175–95

30 Attlee in R. Lowe, *The Welfare State in Britain since 1945* (London, 1993), p. 10; T. H. Marshall, *Class, Citizenship, and Social Development* (New York, 1965)

31 G. Esping-Andersen, *The Three Worlds of Welfare Capitalism* (Cambridge, 1990); Titmuss in Lowe, op. cit., p. 12

32 Cited in K. D. Bracher, *The Age of Ideologies: A History of Political Thought in the 20th Century* (London, 1985), p. 200

33 Cochrane and Clarke, op. cit., p. 32

34 T. H. Marshall, 'The welfare state – a comparative study', in his *Class, Citizenship and Social Development*, op. cit., p. 313; Ambrosius and Hubbard, op. cit., p. 128; Titmuss, *Essays on the Welfare State*, op. cit., p. 241

35 Baldwin denies any necessary link between specific classes and redistributive social policy: P. Baldwin, *The Politics of Social Solidarity: Class Bases of the European Welfare State, 1875–1975* (Cambridge, 1990), p. 290

36 Marshall, *Class, Citizenship and Social Development*, op. cit., pp. 297–300, 330

37 Shonfield, op. cit., p. xv; on the resilience of French conservatism, see R. Vinen, *Bourgeois Politics in France, 1945–1951* (Cambridge, 1995); A. Pizzorno, 'The individualistic mobilisation of Europe', *Daedalus*, 93: 1 (winter 1964)

38 Cited in W. Sachs, *For Love of the Automobile: Looking Back into the History of Our Desires* (Berkeley/Los Angeles, Calif., 1992), pp. 55–6

39 On women, see S. Weiner, 'The *consommatrice* of the 1950s in Elsa Triolet's *Roses à crédit*', *French Cultural Studies*, vi (1995), pp. 123–44; C. Duchen, *Women's Rights and Women's Lives in France, 1944–1968* (London, 1994); *Bikini: Die Fünfziger Jahre* (Berlin, 1983), p. 200; M. Boneschi, *La grande illusione: i nostri anni sessanta* (Milan, 1996), p. 93

40 F. Mort and P. Thompson, 'Retailing, commercial culture and masculinity in 1950s Britain: the case of Montague Burton, the "Tailor of Taste"', *History Workshop Journal*, 38 (1994), pp. 106–29; J. Pearson and G. Turner, *The Persuasion Industry* (London, 1965), pp. 30–31

41 T. R. Nevitt, *Advertising in Britain: A History* (London, 1982)

42 Wylie, op. cit., pp. 181, 347; R. Harris and A. Seldon, *Advertising in Action* (London, 1962), pp. 23–4

43 A. Sampson, *Anatomy of Europe* (New York, 1968), p. 116; R. Wagnleiter, *Coca-Colonization and the Cold War: The Cultural Mission of the United States in Austria after the Second World War* (Chapel Hill, NC/London, 1994), p. 294; S. Gundle, 'L'americanizzazione del quotidiano: televisione e consumismo nell'Italia degli anni cinquanta', *Quaderni storici*, 62 (August 1986), pp. 561–94; Hiscocks, *Germany Revived*, p. 55; K. Ross, *Fast Cars, Clean Bodies: Decolonization and the Reordering of French Culture* (Cambridge, Mass./London, 1995), p. 53; Gundle, op. cit., p. 588

44 C. Dyer, *Population and Society in 20th Century France* (London, 1978), p. 222

45 N. Stacey and A. Wilson, *The Changing Pattern of Distribution* (Oxford, 1965 edn), p. 390; J. Benson, *The Rise of Consumer Society in Britain, 1880–1980* (London, 1994), p. 88; Sampson, op. cit., p. 232

46 P. Fussell, *Abroad*, Hans Magnus Enzensberger, *Eine Theorie des Tourismus* (Frankfurt, 1963)

47 Stacey and Wilson, op. cit., p. 334; Joe Curry cited in Ellwood, op. cit., p. 208

48 Cited in Marshall, 'The affluent society in perspective', in *Class*, p. 341; on the convergence in reproduction patterns, D. V. Glass, 'Fertility trends in Europe since the Second World War', *Population Studies*, 22:1 (March 1968), pp. 103–47

49 K. D. Bracher, 'Problems of parliamentary democracy in Europe', *Daedalus*, 93:1 (winter 1964), p. 185f; Habermas cited in R. Kearney, *Modern Movements in European Philosophy*, p. 230

50 Cited in P. Ginsborg, *A History of Contemporary Italy: Society and Politics, 1943–1988* (London, 1990), p. 248; Duhamel in Kuisel, op. cit., p. 11

51 Jean-Marie Domenach, 'Le modèle américain', *Esprit* (July–August 1960), p. 1221 cited in Kuisel, op. cit., p. 109

52 Pizzorno, op. cit., p. 199

53 Cited in Kuisel, op. cit., p. 65

54 Pizzorno, op. cit.; R. Willett, *The Americanisation of Germany, 1945–1949* (London, 1989), pp. 49–51

55 See D. Strinati, 'The taste of America: Americanisation and popular culture in Britain', in Strinati and S. Wagg (eds.), *Come on Down? Popular Music and Culture in Postwar Britain* (London, 1992), pp. 46f

56 On European role in the world economy, see D. Aldcroft, *The European Economy, 1914–1990* (London, 1993 edn), ch. 5

57 P. Calamandrei, *Questa nostra costituzione* (Milan, 1995 edn), p. v

58 Boneschi, op. cit., pp. 119–21

59 Gundle, op. cit., p. 589

60 G. Kaplan, *Contemporary Western European Feminism* (New York, 1992)

61 F. Thebaud (ed.), *A History of Women: Toward a Cultural Identity in the 20th Century* (Cambridge, Mass., 1994)

62 Austrian law in K. Schmidlechner, 'Youth culture in the 1950s', in G. Bischof, A. Pelinka and R. Steininger (eds.), *Austria in the 1950s: Contemporary Austrian Studies*, vol. 3 (New Brunswick, 1995), pp. 116–37; Elvis quotes from U. Poiger, 'Rock 'n' roll, female sexuality and the Cold War battle over German identities', *Journal of Modern History*, 68: 3 (September 1996), pp. 577–617

63 R. Dorner, 'Halbstark', in *Bikini: Die Fünfziger Jahre*, op. cit., p. 164; S. Piccone Stella, '"Rebels without a cause": Male youth in Italy around 1960', *History Workshop Journal*, 38 (1994), pp. 157–74

64 Bogdanor and Skidelsky, op. cit., pp. 300–314

65 Boneschi, op. cit., p. 319

66 G. Statera, *Death of a Utopia: The Development and Decline of Student Movements in Europe* (New York, 1975), pp. 78–89

67 S. Khilnani, *Arguing Revolution: The Intellectual Left in Postwar France* (New Haven, Conn., 1993), p. 122

68 Figures from G. Therborn, *European Modernity and Beyond: The Trajectory of European Societies, 1945–2000* (London, 1995), p. 259; Red Army Faction in Linke Liste (eds.), *Die Mythen knacken: Materialen wider ein Tabu* (Frankfurt, 1987), *passim*

69 Cited in H. Fassmann and R. Münz (eds.), *European Migration in the Late 20th Century: Historical Patterns, Actual Trends and Social Implications* (Aldershot, Hants., 1994), p. 3

70 J. F. Hollifield, *Immigrants, Markets and States: The Political Economy of Postwar Europe* (Cambridge, Mass., 1992)

71 R. King (ed.), *Mass Migrations in Europe: The Legacy and the Future* (London, 1993)

72 Cesarani, *Justice Delayed*, p. 70

73 J. Salt and H. Clout (eds.), *Migration in Postwar Europe: Geographical Essays* (Oxford, 1976), 34; Ginsborg, op. cit., p. 219

74 D. Hiro, *Black British, White British: A History of Race Relations in Britain* (London, 1991 edn), p. 51

75 See generally, P. Rich, *Race and Empire in British Politics* (Cambridge, 1990 edn)

76 King, op. cit., p. 96; Rogers Brubaker, *Citizenship and Nationhood in France and Germany* (Cambridge, Mass., 1992), pp. 171–4

77 S. Collinson, *Beyond Borders: West European Migration Policy and the Twenty First Century* (London, 1993), pp. 92–6; A. Nocon, 'A reluctant welcome? Poles in Britain in the 1940s', *Oral History* (spring 1996), p. 81

78 Figures from Fassmann and Münz, op. cit., p. 7; Minority Rights Group, *Race and Law in Britain and the United States* (London, 1983 edn), pp. 11–13; Nocon, op. cit., p. 85

10: The Social Contract in Crisis

1 R. Musil (tr. E. Wilkins and E. Kaiser), *The Man without Qualities*, vol. 1 (London, 1982), p. 8

2 C. Maier, 'The politics of inflation in the 20th century', in his *In Search of Stability: Explorations in Historical Political Economy* (Cambridge, 1987), p. 223

3 On the factors behind the crisis of the early 1970s, see N. Kaldor, *The Scourge of Monetarism* (Oxford, 1985, 2nd edn), pp. xi–xii; Maddison, op. cit., pp. 133–42; C. Allsopp, 'Inflation', in Boltho op. cit., pp. 72–104

4 Allsopp, op. cit., p. 79

5 R. Mishra, *The Welfare State in Capitalist Society* (Toronto, 1990), ch. 3

6 Kaldor, op. cit., p. xx; Vaizey cited in R. Cockett, *Thinking the Unthinkable: Think-Tanks and the Economic Counter-Revolution, 1931–1983* (London, 1995), p. 229

7 Kalecki, 'Political consequences of full employment', op. cit.; Kaldor, op. cit., p. xii

8 I. Gilmour, *Dancing with Dogma: Britain under Thatcherism* (London, 1992), p. 60

9 ibid., p. 131

10 R. Levitas, 'Competition and compliance: the utopias of the New Right', in Levitas (ed.), *The Ideology of the New Right* (Oxford, 1986); S. Jenkins, *Accountable to None: The Tory Nationalization of Britain* (London, 1995)

11 P. Pierson, *Dismantling the Welfare State? Reagan, Thatcher and the Politics of Retrenchment* (Cambridge, 1994), pp. 147–9; N. Barr *et al.*, *The State of Welfare: The Welfare State in Britain since 1974* (Oxford, 1991), pp. 339–40

12 K. van Kersbergen, *Social Capitalism: A Study of Christian Democracy and the Welfare State* (London, 1995)

13 H. Döring, 'Public perceptions of the proper role of the state', *West European Politics*, 17: 1 (January 1994), pp. 1–11

14 G. Baglioni and C. Crouch (eds.), *European Industrial Relations: The Challenge of Flexibility* (London, 1990)

15 J. Vickers and V. Wright, 'The politics of industrial privatisation in Western Europe: an overview', *West European Politics*, 11 (1988), pp. 1–30

16 V. Wright, 'Reshaping the state: implications for public administration', *West European Politics*, 17: 1 (January 1994), pp. 102–33

17 W. Merkel, 'After the golden age: is social democracy doomed to decline?' in C. Lemke and G. Marks (eds.), *The Crisis of Socialism in Europe* (Durham, NC, 1992), pp. 136–70

18 M. Sharp, 'Changing industrial structures in Western Europe', in D. Dyker (ed.), *The European Economy* (London, 1992), pp. 233–55

19 Ginsborg, op. cit., p. 405

20 T. Blackwell and J. Seabrook, *Talking Work: An Oral History* (London, 1996), p. 201; May Day badges in Therborn, *European Modernity*, op. cit., p. 237

21 Therborn, *European Modernity*, op. cit., p. 57

22 A. B. Atkinson, *Incomes and the Welfare State: Essays on Britain and Europe* (Cambridge, 1995), p. 28

23 J. Ardagh, *Germany and the Germans* (London, 1995), pp. 114–15

24 Gilmour, op. cit., p. 134; Thatcher cited in the *Guardian*, 21 July 1996; Atkinson, op. cit., p. 39

25 N. Christie, *Crime Control as Industry: Towards GULAGS, Western Style* (London, 1994 edn)

26 Cited in V. Ruggiero. M. Ryan and J. Sim (eds.), *West European Penal Systems: A Critical Anatomy* (London, 1995), pp. 40, 169

27 B. A. Hudson, *Penal Policy and Social Justice* (London, 1993), p. 68

28 P. O'Brien, 'Migration and its risks', *International Migration Review*, 30: 4 (1996), pp. 1067–77

29 Blackwell and Seabrook, op. cit., p. 123; 'Ethnic minority children "still suffer racism daily" ', *Guardian*, 23 July 1996

30 'Publishers bow to colour bar on children's books', *Observer*, 27 October 1996

31 M. Kohn, *The Race Gallery: The Return of Racial Science* (London, 1995); N. Abadan-Unat, 'Turkish migration to Europe', in R. Cohen (ed.), *The Cambridge Survey of World Migration* (Cambridge, 1995), p. 281

32 Cited in Joly, *Refugees: Asylum in Europe*, pp. 118–19

33 Y. Soysal, *Limits of Citizenship: Migrants and Postnational Membership in Europe* (Chicago, 1994)

34 Cited in Ginsborg, op. cit., p. 424; D. Harvey, *The Condition of Postmodernity* (Oxford, 1989), p. 40

35 Therborn, *European Modernity*, op. cit., p. 268

36 Ardagh, op. cit., pp. 95–6

37 Cited in Sachs, op. cit., pp. 97, 200–202, *Guardian*, 21 August 1996, citing the National Travel Survey

38 A. Giddens, *Modernity and Self-Identity: Self and Society in the Late Modern Age* (Cambridge, 1991), ch. 7: 'The emergence of life politics', quote from p. 225

39 Ardagh, op. cit., p. 165

40 C. Haste, *Rules of Desire: Sex in Britain, World War 1 to the Present* (London, 1994), p. 235

41 F. Mort, *Cultures of Consumption: Masculinities and Social Space in Late 20th Century Britain* (London, 1996), pp. 16, 25

42 Cited in Strinati and Wagg, op. cit.

43 The *Guardian*, 19 August 1996

44 Musil, op. cit., p. 8

45 Council of Europe, *Disillusionment with Democracy: Political Parties, Participation and Non-Participation in Democratic Institutions in Europe* (Colchester, 1993)

46 Cited in the *Independent on Sunday*, 21 July 1996

11: Sharks and Dolphins: The Collapse of Communism

1 Cited by B. Geremek, 'Between hope and despair', in S. Graubard (ed.), *Eastern Europe ... Central Europe ... Europe* (Boulder, Colo., 1991), pp. 95–113, cited on p. 103

2 Cited by Misiunas and Taagepera, op. cit., p. 202

3 J. Rothschild, *Return to Diversity: A Political History of East Central Europe since World War 2* (Oxford, 1989), p. 221

4 Cited by T. Garton Ash, *The Uses of Adversity* (Cambridge, 1989), pp. 180–81

5 B. Kaminski, *The Collapse of State Socialism: The Case of Poland* (Princeton, NJ, 1991), p. 3

6 Growth rates from K. Dawisha, *Eastern Europe, Gorbachev and Reform: The Great Challenge* (Cambridge, 1990 edn), p. 169

7 M. Bernstam, 'Trends in the Soviet population', pp. 185–214, and N. Eberstadt, 'Health of an empire: poverty and social progress in the CMEA bloc', pp. 221–55 in H. Rowen and C. Wolf (eds.), *The Future of the Soviet Empire* (New York, 1987)

8 A. Shub, *An Empire Loses Hope* (London, 1971), p. 109; D. N. Nelson (ed.), *Communism and the Politics of Inequality* (Toronto, 1983); R. Laba, *The Roots of Solidarity: A Political Sociology of Poland's Working-Class Democratization* (Princeton, NJ, 1991), pp. 118–19; P. Hauslohner, 'Gorbachev's social contract', *Soviet Economy*, 3 (1987), pp. 54–89, and J. McAdams, 'Crisis in the Soviet empire: three ambiguities in search of a prediction', *Comparative Politics*, 20: 1 (October 1987), pp. 107–18; S. Miskiewicz, 'Social and economic rights in Eastern Europe', in G. R. Urban (ed.), *Social and Economic Rights in the Soviet Bloc* (New Brunswick, NJ, 1988), p. 98

9 J. Rupnik, 'Central Europe or Mitteleuropa?' in Graubard op. cit., pp. 247–8

10 Cited in Dawisha, op. cit., p. 192

11 Gati, op. cit.

12 Fulbrook, op. cit., pp. 38–9

13 Cited by E. Behr, *'Kiss the Hand You Cannot Bite': The Rise and Fall of the Ceauşescus* (London, 1991), pp. 180–81

14 On systemization, see D. Giurescu, *The Razing of Romania's Past* (New York, 1989)

15 L. Labedz (ed.), *Poland under Jaruzelski* (New York, 1984), p. 102

16 Kaminski, op. cit., p. 193; Labedz, op. cit., p. 3

17 Behr, op. cit., pp. 165–6

18 A. Uci, 'The place of folk art in Socialist artistic culture', in anon., *Questions of the Albanian Folklore* (Tirana, 1984), p. 6

19 See N. Naimark, ' "Ich will hierraus": emigration and the collapse of the German Democratic Republic', in I. Banac (ed.), *Eastern Europe in Revolution* (Ithaca, NY, 1992), pp. 72–95

20 Garton Ash, op. cit., p. 48

21 Cited by ibid., p. 264

22 For some interesting reflections, see A. Nove, 'The fall of empires – Russia and the Soviet Union', in G. Lundestad (ed.), *The Fall of Great Powers: Peace, Stability and Legitimacy* (Oxford, 1994), pp. 125–46

23 Cited by C. Gati, *The Bloc that Failed: Soviet–East European Relations in Transition* (London, 1990), p. 127

24 Dawisha, op. cit., pp. 104–5

25 J. Valdez, *Internationalism and the Ideology of Soviet Influence in Eastern Europe* (Cambridge, 1993), p. 98

26 M. Gorbachev, *Perestroika: New Thinking for Our Country and the World* (London, 1988), p. 107

27 ibid., p. 138

28 From 'The place and role of Eastern Europe in the relaxation of tensions between the USA and the USSR' (1988), cited in Gati, *The Bloc that Failed*, op. cit., p. 206

29 Misiunas and Taagepera, op. cit., pp. 303–12

30 ibid., p. 120

31 See A. E. Dick Howard (ed.), *Constitution Making in Eastern Europe* (Washington, 1993)

32 'Getting better, getting worse: minorities in East Central Europe', *Dissent* (summer 1996)

33 On purges, see T. Rosenbaum, *The Haunted Land* (London, 1993)

34 *Financial Times*, 4 May 1994

35 A. Robinson, 'Painful rebirth from the ashes', *Financial Times*, 11 November 1994

36 *Financial Times*, 4 May 1994

37 P. Zelikow and C. Rice, *Germany Reunified and Europe Transformed: A Study in Statecraft* (Cambridge, Mass., 1995)

38 'On the unification of Germany', *Independent*, 17 June 1989 cited by G.-J. Glaessner, 'German unification and the West', in Glaessner and I. Wallace (eds.), *The German Revolution of 1989: Causes and Consequences* (Oxford, 1992), pp. 208–9

39 L. Kürti, 'Rocking the state: youth and rock music culture in Hungary, 1976–1990', *EEPS*, 5: 3 (fall 1991), pp. 483–513

Epilogue: Making Europe

1 F. Chabod, *Storia dell'idea d'Europa* (Bari, 1961), p. 8

2 S. Berstein and P. Milza, *Histoire de l'Europe*, vol. 3 (Paris, 1992), conclusion

3 A. Fisher, *A History of Europe*, vol. 1 (London, 1960 edn), pp. 13–18; Halecki, (Notre Dame, Ind., 1962 edn)

4 Chabod, op. cit., p. 20

5 S. Hoffmann, 'Obstinate or obsolete: the fate of the nation-state and the case of western Europe', *Daedalus* (summer 1966), pp. 862–915

6 R. Aron, 'Old nations, new Europe', *Daedalus* (winter 1964), pp. 43–67. See too M. Mann, 'Nation-states in Europe and other continents: diversifying, developing, not dying', in G. Balakrishnan (ed.), *Mapping the Nation* (London, 1996), pp. 295–317

Guide to Further Reading*

For general approaches to twentieth-century European history, George Lichtheim, *Europe in the Twentieth Century* (1972), is the most thought-provoking, James Joll, *Europe Since 1870* (1990), the clearest. Robert Paxton, *Twentieth Century Europe* (New York, 1985), is an excellent textbook. Eric Hobsbawm, *Age of Extremes: The Short Twentieth Century* (1994), is more ambitious than this book in aiming to cover the entire globe. About the only serious overview of twentieth-century value-systems is K. D. Bracher, *The Age of Ideologies: A History of Political Thought in the 20th Century* (1985). For the Left, there is now Donald Sassoon's monumental *One Hundred Years of Socialism: The West European Left in the Twentieth Century*. Michael Oakeshott, *The Social and Political Doctrines of Contemporary Europe* (1940), remains well worth reading.

On the idea of Europe, there is F. Chabod, *Storia dell'idea d'Europa* (Bari, 1961), O. Halecki, *The Limits and Divisions of European History* (1950), and D. Hay, *Europe: The Emergence of an Idea* (Edinburgh, 1968). K. Wilson and J. van der Dussen (eds.), *The History of the Idea of Europe* (1993), is a good recent survey. I have found Norman Cohn, *Cosmos, Chaos and the World to Come* (1995) and A. Pagden, *Lords of All the World: Ideologies of Empire in Spain, Britain and France, c. 1500–c. 1800* (1995) valuable in offering perspectives on the utopian and universalistic traditions in European thought which underpinned the emergence of twentieth-century political ideologies.

General surveys of social and economic history include G. Ambrosius and W. Hubbard's brilliant *A Social and Economic History of 20th Century Europe* (1989) and the excellent Fontana *Economic History of Europe* series edited by Carlo Cipolla. G. Therborn, *European Modernity and Beyond*

*Place of publication is London unless otherwise stated.

467

(1995), contains much fascinating information, especially on the post-war period. Statistics are easily consulted in the publications of the League of Nations, the UN's Economic Commission for Europe, Eurostat and B. R. Mitchell, *European Historical Statistics, 1750–1975* (1980 edn). L. Kosinski, *The Population of Europe*(1970), is a concise introduction. E. M. Kulischer, *Europe on the Move: War and Population Changes, 1917–1947* (New York, 1948), is a classic, to be supplemented with Joseph Schechtman's two volumes on population transfers between 1939 and 1955, by M. Marrus, *The Unwanted: European Refugees in the 20th Century* (1985), and also by R. Cohen (ed.), *Cambridge Survey of World Migration* (Cambridge, 1995). Excellent historical atlases include *The Penguin Atlas of World History*, vol. 2 (1974), P. R. Magocsi, *Historical Atlas of East Central Europe* (1993), and R. Overy (ed.), *The Times Atlas of the Twentieth Century* (1996).

Post-war historians usually discuss inter-war politics in terms of the rise of fascism. There is a vast literature on this, to which good guides are W. Laqueur (ed.), *Fascism: A Reader's Guide* (1976), H. Rogger and E. Weber (eds.), *The European Right: A Historical Profile* (Berkeley, Calif., 1965), and R. Bessel (ed.), *Fascist Italy and Nazi Germany: Comparisons and Contrasts* (Cambridge, 1996). Much of this literature tries to define fascism and then works out which regimes were and were not fascist. This approach forms the basis for Stanley Payne's wonderfully comprehensive *A History of Fascism, 1914–1945* (1995). The approach adopted here is rather different, taking as its starting point not fascism's rise but the crisis and weakness of inter-war democracy. One of the few post-war interpretations to formulate the problem in this way is K. Newman's unjustly neglected *European Democracy between the Wars* (1970). Inter-war scholars confronted democracy's failings more directly. See A. J. Zurcher, *The Experiment with Democracy in Central Europe* (New York, 1933), and V. Dean *et al.*, *New Governments of Europe* (New York, 1934), as well as W. E. Rappard, *The Crisis of Democracy* (Chicago, 1938). C. Schmitt (ed. E. Kennedy), *The Crisis of Parliamentary Democracy* (Cambridge, Mass., 1985) is a seminal critique by one of Weimar's foremost opponents.

On the Russian Revolution, H. Shukman (ed.), *The Blackwell Encyclopaedia of the Russian Revolution* (Oxford, 1988), is handy. O. Figes, *A People's Tragedy: The Russian Revolution, 1891–1924* (1996), is a vivid and panoramic account whose pessimism contrasts strikingly with both E. H. Carr, *The Bolshevik Revolution, 1917–1923* (1950), and with S. Fitzpatrick, *The Russian Revolution, 1917–1932* (Oxford, 1982). O. Radkey, *The Election to the Russian Constituent Assembly of 1917* (Cambridge, Mass., 1950), is an incisive study of Russian popular political opinion at the start of the revolution. V. Shklovsky, *A Sentimental Journey: Memoirs, 1917–1922* (Ithaca, NY, 1984), is a brilliant memoir. For polemical interpretations of the long-run significance of the Russian Revolution, see Z. Brzezinski, *The Grand Failure: The Birth and Death of Communism in the 20th Century* (New York, 1990), M. Malia, *The Soviet Tragedy: A History of Socialism in Russia, 1917–1991* (1994), and F. Furet, *Le Passé d'une illusion: essai sur l'idée communiste* (Paris, 1995). G. Hosking, *A History of the Soviet Union* (1992 edn), is no less useful for being less polemical.

For Weimar Germany, see P. Gay, *Weimar Culture* (1968), F. L. Carsten, *The Reichswehr and Politics* (1966), K. Sontheimer, *Antidemokratisches Denken in der Weimarer Republik* (Munich, 1974), C. Maier, 'The vulnerabilities of interwar Germany', *Journal of Modern History*, 56 (March 1984), pp. 89–99, and P. Fritzsche's thought-provoking, 'Did Weimar fail?', *Journal of Modern History*, 68 (September 1996), pp. 629–66. I. Kershaw, *The Nazi Dictatorship: Problems and Perspectives* (1985), and P. Aycoberry, *The Nazi Question: An Essay on the Interpretation of National Socialism (1922–1975)* (New York, 1981), survey the historical debates surrounding the Third Reich. See also K. D. Bracher, *The German Dictatorship* (1969), and D. Crew (ed.), *Nazism and German Society* (1994). W. S. Allen, *The Nazi Seizure of Power* (1965), remains unsurpassed as a vivid portrayal of the collapse of German democracy in a small town. The best collection of documents is the three volumes edited by J. Noakes and G. Pridham.

Law and legal theory – largely neglected by historians – are discussed by J. Bendersky, *Carl Schmitt: Theorist for the Third Reich* (Princeton, NJ, 1983), and by Ellen Kennedy in her introduction to Schmitt's *Crisis of Parliamentary Democracy*. See also Karl Loewenstein, 'Law in the Third Reich', *Yale Law Journal*, 45 (1936), I. Muller, *Hitler's Justice: The Courts of the Third Reich* (Cambridge, Mass., 1991), and E. Fraenkel's classic *The Dual State* (New York, 1941). F. Morstein Marx, *Government in the Third Reich* (New York, 1937), and H. Arthur Steiner, *Government in Fascist Italy* (1938), both have the advantage of taking their subjects seriously as functioning forms of modern administration, avoiding some silly post-war scholarly debates about whether inter-war dictators controlled what was going on inside their administrations or not. C. Beradt, *The Third Reich of Dreams: The Nightmares of a Nation, 1933–1939* (Wellingborough, Northants, 1985), shows how totalitarianism pervaded the unconscious. H. Krausnick and M. Broszat, *Anatomy of the SS State* (1970), and R. Gellately, *The Gestapo and German Society* (Oxford, 1990), lay bare the mechanics of the Nazi terror system, while A. Bullock, *Hitler and Stalin: Parallel Lives* (1991), and I. Kershaw and M. Lewin (eds.), *Stalinism and Nazism: Dictatorships in Comparison* (Cambridge, 1997), compare the repressiveness of the two major totalitarian regimes. Despite all the discussion of totalitarianism, however, we still lack searching comparative analysis of Nazism and communism.

Fascist Italy is best approached through A. Lyttelton, *The Seizure of Power* (1972), and P. Corner, *Fascism in Ferrara, 1915–1925* (Oxford, 1975). E. Gentile, *The Sacralization of Politics in Fascist Italy* (Cambridge, Mass., 1996) may be compared with I. Kershaw, *The Hitler Myth* (Oxford, 1987). E. R. Tannenbaum, *The Fascist Experiment* (1972), is comprehensive but dated. A lot of the most interesting recent work focuses on relations between regime and society: see V. de Grazia, *The Culture of Consent: Leisure in Fascist Italy* (1981), T. H. Koon, *Believe, Obey, Fight* (1985), D. Thompson, *State Control in Fascist Italy* (1991), and A. de Grand, 'Cracks in the facade: the failure of Fascist totalitarianism', *European History Quarterly*, 21: 4 (October 1991), pp. 515–37. C. Delzell (ed.), *Mediterranean Fascism* (1971), and A. Lyttelton (ed.), *Italian Fascisms from Pareto to Gentile* (1973), are useful collections. A. Stille, *Benevolence and Betrayal: Five Italian Jewish Families under Fascism* (1992), is a brilliantly readable study of the complex relationship between Fascism and Italy's Jews. Fascist anti-Semitism is covered by G. Bernardini, 'The origins and development of racial anti-semitism in Fascist Italy', *Journal of Modern History*, 49 (September 1977), pp. 431–53, and by F. Levi, *L'ebreo in oggetto* (Turin, 1991). Italian imperialism has been largely neglected by historians, but see G. W. Baer, *Test Case: Italy, Ethiopia and the League of Nations* (Stanford, Calif., 1967), and E. M. Robertson, 'Race as a factor in Mussolini's policy in Africa and Europe', *Journal of Contemporary History*, 23 (January 1988), pp. 37–59. Luisa Passerini, *Fascism in Popular Memory: The Cultural Experience of the Turin Working Class* (Cambridge, 1987), reconstructs popular attitudes through memories and oral testimonies.

The rise of the nationalist Right in eastern Europe and much more is covered by H. Seton-Watson, *Eastern Europe between the Wars, 1918–1941* (1962 edn), A. Polonsky, *The Little Dictators* (1975), P. Sugar (ed.), *Native Fascism in the Successor States, 1918–1945* (Oxford, 1971), and J. Rothschild, *East Central Europe between the Two World Wars* (1984). More detailed analysis is provided by N. Nagy-Talavera, *The Green Shirts and Others: A History of Fascism in Hungary and Rumania* (1970), and by B. Vago, *The Shadow of the Swastika: The Rise of Fascism and Anti-Semitism in the*

Danube Basin, 1936–1939 (1975). C. Codreanu's collected speeches in *For My Legionaries* (Madrid, n.d.) convey the crazed flavour of Romanian fascism. A self-serving intellectual reminiscence is offered by M. Eliade, *Autobiography*, vol. 1 (Chicago, 1981) which is best read alongside L. Volovici, *Nationalist Ideology and Antisemitism: The Case of Romanian Intellectuals in the 1930s* (Oxford, 1991). For Poland see A. Polonsky, 'Roman Dmowski and Italian Fascism', in R. J. Bullen (ed.), *Ideas into Politics* (1984), pp. 130–47, and J. Holzer, 'The political right in Poland, 1918–1939', *Journal of Contemporary History*, 12: 3 (1977).

C. A. Macartney, *National States and National Minorities* (1968) is a good introduction to the national aspects of the Versailles settlement. T. Bottomore and P. Goode (eds.), *Austro-Marxism* (1978), and E. Traverso, *The Marxists and the Jewish Question* (New Jersey, 1994), discuss Marxist approaches to nationalism. G. Liber, *Soviet Nationality Policy, Urban Growth and Identity Change in the Ukrainian SSR, 1923–1934* (Cambridge, 1992), can be read alongside R. Pipes, *The Formation of the Soviet Union: Communism and Nationalism, 1917–1923* (Cambridge, Mass., 1964), or H. Carrère d'Encausse, *The Great Challenge: Nationalities and the Bolshevik State, 1917–1930* (New York, 1992). League of Nations policies are examined in I. Claude, *National Minorities: An International Problem* (Cambridge, Mass., 1955), and J. Robinson *et al.*, *Were the Minorities Treaties a Failure?* (New York, 1943). Recent studies include C. Fink, 'Defender of Minorities': Germany in the League of Nations, 1926–1933', *Central European History* (1972), pp. 330–57; P. B. Finney, ' "An evil for all concerned": Great Britain and minority protection after 1919', *Journal of Contemporary History* (1995), pp. 533–51, A. J. Motyl, 'Ukrainian nationalist violence in interwar Poland, 1921–1939', *East European Quarterly* (1985), and I. Livezeanu, *Cultural Politics in Greater Romania* (Ithaca, NY, 1995). As yet we have no study comparing the nationalities policies adopted by Geneva and Moscow between the wars. For Asia Minor, the classic contemporary account is A. J. Toynbee, *The Western Question in Greece and Turkey* (1923). Y. Ternon, *Les Arméniens: Histoire d'un génocide* (Paris, 1996 edn), is better than anything in English, though M. J. Somakian, *Empires in Conflict: Armenia and the Great Powers, 1895–1920* (1995), is a balanced, recent account. L. Stavrianos, *The Balkans since 1453* (1958), is a classic textbook; R. J. Wolff, *The Balkans in Our Time* (1956), is as good for the modern period. P. Kitromilides, 'Imagined communities and the origins of the national question in the Balkans', *European History Quarterly*, 19: 2 (1989), pp. 149–92, discusses the rise of nationalism in the Ottoman empire. On refugees, see J. Hope Simpson, *The*

Refugee Problem (1939), and C. Skran, *Refugees in Interwar Europe* (Oxford, 1995). Nazi attitudes towards international law are discussed in J. Herz, 'The National Socialist doctrine of international law and the problems of international organisation', *Political Science Quarterly* (December 1939), pp. 536–54. See too P. Stirk, 'Authoritarian and national socialist conceptions of nation, state and Europe', in Stirk (ed.), *European Unity in Context: the Interwar Period* (1989).

Capitalism's crisis is reviewed in R. Overy, *The Interwar Crisis, 1919–1939* (1994), P. Fearon, *The Origin and Nature of the Great Slump* (1979), H. W. Arndt, *The Economic Lessons of the 1930s* (1963 edn), and C. Kindleberger, *The World in Depression, 1929–1939* (1973). B. Eichengreen, *Golden Fetters: The Gold Standard and the Great Depression, 1919–1939* (1992), and S. Pollard, *The Gold Standard and Employment Policies between the Wars* (1970), show what was wrong with the gold standard. Capitalism's chief sponsors are discussed by D. Silverman, *Reconstructing Europe after the Great War* (Cambridge, Mass., 1982), C. Maier, *Recasting Bourgeois Europe* (Princeton, NJ, 1975), R. Boyce, *British Capitalism at the Crossroads, 1919–1932* (Cambridge, 1987), R. Skidelsky, *Politicians and the Slump: The Labour Government of 1929–31* (1967), S. Schuker, *The End of French Predominance in Europe* (Chapel Hill, NC, 1988), and J. Jackson, *The Politics of Depression in France* (Cambridge, 1985) and *The Popular Front in France: Defending Democracy, 1934–38* (Cambridge, 1988). D. S. White, *Socialists of the Front Generation, 1918–1945* (Cambridge, Mass., 1992), shows why capitalism's crisis pushed several brilliant young socialists to the Right. R. Kuisel, *Capitalism and the State in Modern France* (Cambridge, 1981), charts capitalism's adaption before, during and after the depression.

On communism as an economic system, see R. W. Davies, M. Harrison and S. G. Wheatcroft (eds.), *The Economic Transformation of the Soviet Union, 1913–1945* (Cambridge, 1994). For communism as modernization see M. Lewin, *The Making of the Soviet System* (1985). R. W. Davies, 'Forced labour under Stalin: the archive revelations', *New Left Review*, 214 (November/December 1995), pp. 62–80, judiciously reviews new evidence. M. Fainsod's classic, *Smolensk under Soviet Rule* (1989 edn), brings the world of Stalin's Russia to life. Forced industrialization as lived experience is the subject of S. Kotkin, *Magnetic Mountain: Stalinism as Civilization* (Berkeley, Calif., 1995). V. Kravchenko, *I Chose Freedom: The Personal and Political Life of a Soviet Official* (1947), is a gripping memoir. L. Lih *et al.* (eds.), *Stalin's Letters to Molotov, 1925–1936* (New Haven, Yale, 1995), though offering few revelations, do give an insight into the tone and rhythm of high-level policy-making.

For the relationship between fascism and capitalism, the best place to start is H. James, *The German Slump: Politics and Economics, 1924–1936* (Oxford, 1988), and G. Toniolo, *L'economia dell'Italia fascista* (Rome, 1980). For the big corporations see P. Hayes, *Industry and Ideology: IG Farben in the Nazi Era* (Cambridge, 1987) and the collected essays in R. Overy, *War and Economy in the Third Reich* (1994). M. Kele, *Nazis and Workers: National Socialist Appeals to German Labor, 1918–1933* (Chapel Hill, NC, 1972), covers the period before Hitler came to power. Tim Mason, *Social Policy in the Third Reich* (Oxford, 1993), covers the period after. For capitalism's evolution in eastern Europe, see M. C. Kaser and E. Radice (eds.) *The Economic History of Eastern Europe, 1919–1975*, vol. 2 (Oxford, 1986), and G. Berend and I. Ranki, 'L'évolution économique de l'Europe orientale entre les deux guerres mondiales', *Annales*, 33 (1978). M. Jackson and J. Lampe, *Balkan Economic History, 1550–1950* (Bloomington, Ind., 1982), has much good data. L. Neal, 'The economics and financing of bilateral clearing agreements: Germany, 1934–38', *Economic History Review* (1979), demystifies Nazi trade policy. M. Mazower, *Greece and the Interwar Economic Crisis* (Oxford, 1991), tries to show there were advantages as well as disadvantages to backwardness.

The spectre of population decline hung over inter-war Europe: see M. S. Quine, *Population Policies in Twentieth Century Europe* (1996), J. M. Winter, 'The fear of population decline in western Europe, 1870–1940', in R. W. Hiorns (ed.), *Demographic Patterns in Developed Societies* (1980), D. V. Glass, *Population Policies and Movements in Europe* (1940), D. Kirk, *Europe's Population in the Interwar Years* (1940), and P. Weindling, 'Fascism and population in comparative European perspective', in M. S. Teitelbaum and J. Winter (eds.), *Population and Resources in Western Intellectual Traditions* (1988). G. Mosse, *Nationalism and Sexuality* (1984), is a pioneering study. M. E. Kopp, 'Eugenic sterilization laws in Europe', *American Journal of Obstetrics and Gynaecology*, 34 (September 1937), casts an approving eye over what now seem rather sinister practices.

On racism in Germany, see M. Burleigh and W. Wippermann, *The Racial State: Germany, 1933–1945* (Cambridge, 1991), D. Peukert, *Inside Nazi Germany: Conformity, Opposition and Racism in Everyday Life* (1987) and P. Weindling, *Health, Race and German Politics between National Unification and Nazism, 1870–1945* (1989). B. Müller-Hill, *Murderous Science: Elimination by Scientific Selection of Jews, Gypsies and Others, 1933–1945* (1988), and R. R. Proctor, *Racial Hygiene: Medicine under the Nazis* (1988), focus on the race professionals. G. Mosse, *Towards the Final Solution* (1978), sets German anti-Semitism in a European context. For France, see W. Schneider, *Quality and Quantity: The Quest for Biological Regeneration in 20th Century France* (1990); for Britain, see the debate between M. Freeden, 'Eugenics and progressive thought', *Historical Journal*, 22 (1979), pp. 645–71 and G. Jones, 'Eugenics and social policy between the wars', *Historical Journal*, 25 (1982), pp. 717–28. The impact of Nazism on Western thinking about race is described by E. Barkan, *The Retreat of Scientific Racism* (1992), and manifested in J. S. Huxley and A. C. Haddon, *We Europeans: A Survey of 'Racial' Problems* (1935). The link between racial fears, eugenics and social policy generally is explored in a fine survey, G. Bock and P. Thane (eds.), *Maternity and Gender Policies: Women and the Rise of the European Welfare States, 1880s–1950s* (1991), and for the UK in J. Lewis, *The Politics of Motherhood* (1980). On gender policies under Fascism, see R. Bridenthal *et al.*, *When Biology Became Destiny* (1984), and J. Stephenson, *Women in Nazi Society* (1975). For Italy we have V. de Grazia, *How Fascism Ruled Women: Italy, 1922–1945* (California, 1992), and A de Grand, 'Women under Fascism', *Historical Journal*, 19: 4 (1976).

Hitler discusses his dreams for Europe in H. Trevor-Roper (ed.), *Hitler's Table-Talk* (Oxford, 1988). The best survey remains A. and V. Toynbee (eds.), *Hitler's Europe* (1954), which also prompted the meditation of a great historian, P. Geyl, 'Hitler's Europe', reprinted in his *Encounters in History* (1963). A. S. Milward, *War, Economy and Society, 1939–1945* (1977), is essential on the economics, while J. Noakes and G. Pridham (eds.), *Nazism*, vol. 3 (New York, 1990), is a superb collection of documents. N. Rich, *Hitler's War Aims*, vol. 2 (1974), is reliable; G. Wright, *The Ordeal of Total War, 1939–1945* (1968), excellent, though more general. U. Herbert, *A History of Foreign Labor in Germany, 1880–1980* (Ann Arbor, Mich., 1990) and J. Schechtman, *European Population Transfers, 1939–1945* (Philadelphia, Pa, 1946), cover population movements. Recent research into the Wehrmacht is encapsulated in O. Bartov, *Hitler's Army* (Oxford, 1991).

Out of a vast literature on the Final Solution, E. Klee, W. Dressen and V. Riess (eds.) (translated by D. Burnstone), *'Those were the Days': The Holocaust through the Eyes of the Perpetrators and Bystanders* (1993), is the best collection of documents. M. Marrus, *The Holocaust in History* (1988), is a good survey of the debates, to be supplemented by his excellent extended reviews in *Journal of Modern History*. *Fateful Months* (1985) and *The Path to Genocide* (1992) contain important essays by the most measured and scrupulous of Holocaust historians, Christopher Browning, whose *Ordinary Men* (1993) is a contrast in argument, tone and style with D. Goldhagen, *Hitler's Willing Executioners* (1996). On Nazi demographic engineering, see R. Koehl, *RKFDV: German Resettlement and Population Policy, 1939–1945* (1957), and I. Kamenetsky, *Secret Nazi Plans for Eastern Europe* (1961). On occupation policies in specific countries, see A. Dallin, *German Rule in Russia, 1941–1945* (1981 edn), and A. S. Milward, *The New Order and the French Economy* (1970). Charles Cruikshank's *The German Occupation of the Channel Islands* (Oxford, 1979) is a comprehensive, if mandarin account of an occupation experience of special interest for the British. It may now be contrasted with M. Bunting, *The Model Occupation: The Channel Islands under German Rule, 1940–1945* (1995). M. Mazower, *Inside Hitler's Greece* (1993), tries to show what occupation felt like for those involved, but this is more forcefully conveyed in diaries such as Z. Klukowski, *Diary from the Years of Occupation, 1939–1944* (Chicago, 1994), or in memoirs such as the nightmarish O. Pinkus, *The House of Ashes* (1991). J. Gross, *Polish Society under German Occupation* (Princeton, 1979), is a searching sociological analysis of the impact of occupation upon Polish society. It may be read alongside the same author's *Revolution from Abroad: The Soviet Conquest of Poland's Western Ukraine and Western Belorussia* (Princeton, NJ, 1988) to compare the experience under Stalin's occupation forces.

The failure of collaboration is the subject of M. Conway, *Collaboration in Belgium: Leon Degrelle and the Rexist Movement, 1940–1944* (1993). R. Paxton, *Vichy France, Old Guard, New Order* (1972), broke a taboo which forms the subject of H. Rousso's *Le Syndrome de Vichy* (Paris, 1987). P. M. Hayes, *The Career and Political Ideas of Vidkun Quisling, 1887–1945* (1972), probably contains everything most people will want to know on the subject, while J. Armstrong, 'Collaborationism in World War II: the integral nationalist variant in eastern Europe', *Journal of Modern History*, 40 (1968), pp. 396–410, surveys eastern Europe. Two vivid journalistic accounts of the moral ambiguities of occupation are R. G. Waldeck, *Athene Palace* (New York, 1942), and C. Malaparte, *Kaputt!* (1948).

On resistance, see J. D. Wilkinson, *The Intellectual Resistance in Europe* (1981), for ideas, S. Hawes and R. White (eds.), *Resistance in Europe, 1939–1945* (1975), M. R. D. Foot, *Resistance* (1976), and T. Judt (ed.), *Resistance and Revolution in Mediterranean Europe, 1939–1948* (1989), for achievements. C. Delzell, *Mussolini's Enemies* (1961), discusses the anti-Fascists, a subject which also forms the focus of C. Pavone, *Una guerra civile: saggio sulla moralità nella resistenza* (Turin, 1991), which ignited a debate across

Italy about the meaning of the resistance. On France, there are two fine studies by H. R. Kedward, *Resistance in Vichy France* (Oxford, 1978), and *In Search of the Maquis* (Oxford, 1993). On Yugoslavia, there is M. Milazzo, *The Chetnik Movement and the Yugoslav Resistance* (1975), and W. Roberts, *Tito, Mihailovic and the Allies, 1941/45* (New Brunswick, NJ, 1973), as well as two classic memoirs, F. W. Deakin, *The Embattled Mountain* (Oxford, 1971), and M. Djilas, *Wartime: With Tito and the Partisans* (1977). On Poland, see R. Lukas, *Forgotten Holocaust: The Poles under German Occupation, 1939–1944* (New York, 1986); for Albania, J. Amery, *Sons of the Eagle: A Study in Guerilla War* (1948).

Working out why Britain was at war is the subject of I. McLaine, *Ministry of Morale: Home Front Morale and the Ministry of Information in World War Two* (1979), in the general political context discussed by P. Addison, *The Road to 1945: British Politics and the War* (1975). A. Shennan, *Rethinking France* (Oxford, 1989), discusses French visions of the post-war order, as does C. Andrieu, *Le Program commun de la Résistance: des idées dans la guerre* (Paris, 1984). W. Lipgens (ed.), *Documents on the History of European Integration*, vol. 1 (New York, 1985), and his 'European federation in the political thought of resistance movements', *Central European History*, 1 (1968), tries valiantly to turn the wartime resistance to Hitler into the seedbed of the post-war drive to European cooperation; this view may be corrected by reading R. E. Herzstein, *When Nazi Dreams Come True* (1982), and in a drier vein, J. R. Gillingham, *Coal, Steel and the Rebirth of Europe, 1945–1955* (Cambridge, 1991), which trace other kinds of continuities back into the war. L. W. Lorwin, *Postwar Plans of the United Nations* (New York, 1943), and L. Holborn, *War and Peace Aims of the United Nations* (Boston, Mass., 1943) are useful.

The chaos and human misery in the aftermath of the war emerge from J. B. Schechtman, *Postwar Population Transfers in Europe, 1945–1955* (Philadelphia, Pa, 1962), D. Macardle, *Children of Europe* (1951), J. Vernant, *The Refugee in the Postwar World* (Geneva, 1953), and M. J. Proudfoot, *European Refugees, 1939–1952* (1957). A. de Zayas, *Nemesis at Potsdam* (1977) covers the expulsion of the Germans, as do the official volumes of documents, T. Scheider *et al.* (eds.), *Documents on the Expulsion of the Germans from East-Central Europe*, 4 vols. (Bonn, n.d.). E. Wiskemann, *Germany's Eastern Neighbours* (Oxford, 1956), is a masterly survey. Revenge, purges and trials are surveyed in K.-D. Henke and H. Woller (eds.), *Politische Sauberung in Europa* (Munich, 1991), and for individual countries, in R. Palmer Domenico, *Italian Fascists on Trial, 1943–48* (Chapel Hill, NC, 1991), and H. Lottman, *The People's Anger: Justice and Revenge in Post-Liberation France* (1986). The de-Nazification and redemocratization of Germany are covered by J. Gimbel, *A German Community under American Occupation: Marburg, 1945–1952* (Stanford, 1961), N. Pronay and K. Wilson (eds.), *The Political Re-education of Germany and Her Allies after World War Two* (Totowa, NJ, 1985), and J. Tent, *Mission on the Rhine* (1982). S. Padover, *Experiment in Germany: The Story of an American Intelligence Officer* (New York, 1946) gives the flavour of the times, as does E. Wilson, *Europe Without Baedeker* (1967). J. F. Golay, *The Founding of the Federal Republic of Germany* (Chicago, 1958), describes the establishment of new political institutions; I. D. Connor, 'The Bavarian government and the refugee problem, 1945–1950', *European History Quarterly*, 16: 2 (1986), pp. 131–53 gives insights into a dog that failed to bark.

A pioneering historical treatment of the Soviet occupation of Germany is N. Naimark, *The Russians in Germany: A History of the Soviet Zone of Occupation* (Cambridge, Mass., 1995). J. T. Gross, 'Social consequences of war: preliminaries to the study of imposition of communist regimes in east central Europe', *East European Politics and Society*, 3: 2 (spring 1989), pp. 198–214 argues that wartime social change influenced the imposition of Soviet rule in the region. See too, K. Kersten, *The Establishment of Communist Rule in Poland, 1943–1948* (Berkeley, Calif., 1991). H. Seton-Watson, *The East European Revolution* (1951), R. R. Betts (ed.), *Central and South-East Europe, 1945–1948* (1950), and R. J. Wolff, *The Balkans in Our Time* all remain useful, as does R. V. Burks, *The Dynamics of Communism in Eastern Europe* (Princeton, NJ, 1961). M. McCauley (ed.), *Communist Power in Europe, 1944–1949* (1977), remains a useful survey. V. Mastny, *Russia's Road to the Cold War* (1979), is a fine example of Western scholarship on Soviet foreign policy before the Russian archives were opened up; V. Zubok, *Inside the Kremlin's Cold War* (1995), gives a taste of the rethinking to come. Case studies include C. Gati, *Hungary and the Soviet Bloc* (Durham, 1986), and P. Zinner, *Revolution in Hungary* (1962); J. Korbel, *The Communist Subversion of Czechoslovakia, 1938–1948* (Princeton, NJ, 1959), and M. Myant, *Socialism and Democracy in Czechoslovakia, 1945–1948* (Cambridge, 1981).

C. Milosz, *The Captive Mind* (1953), is unsurpassed as an analysis of the ethical dilemmas posed by communism. F. Fejtö, *A History of the People's Democracies* (1974), is the best introduction. Among the many insider accounts which blend personal experience and political reflection one should mention Z. Mlynar, *Night Frost in Prague* (1980), on the difficulties of reform, A. Oras, *Baltic Eclipse* (1948), on the plight of the Baltic states, B. Szasz, *Volunteers for the Gallows* (1971), on the frenzy of the purges, and M. Djilas, *The New Class: An Analysis of the Communist System* (1958), for the corruption of the new regime. F. J. Kase, *People's Democracy* (Leyden, 1968), shows how the ambiguities of communist constitutional theory shed light on the uncertainties of Stalin's foreign policy for the region. For social change, there is S. Fischer-Galati (ed.), *Eastern Europe in the Sixties* (New York, 1963), W. Vucinich (ed.), *Contemporary Yugoslavia* (Berkeley, Calif., 1969), and P. Neuburg, *The Hero's Children: the Postwar Generation in Eastern Europe* (1972). A. Aman, *Architecture and Ideology in Eastern Europe during the Stalin Era* (New York, 1992), is a well-illustrated study. D. Deletant, *Ceauşescu and the Securitate: Coercion and Dissent in Romania, 1965–1989* (1995), demonstrates how much more comprehensive post-war communist surveillance systems were than pre-war fascist and authoritarian ones. The Baltic states under communism are surveyed in R. Misiunas and R. Taagepera, *The Baltic States: Years of Dependence, 1940–1990* (Berkeley, Calif., 1993); opposition there is covered in T. Remeikis, *Opposition to Soviet Rule in Lithuania, 1945–1980* (Chicago, 1980). P. Kecskemeti, *The Unexpected Revolution: Social Forces in the Hungarian Uprising* (Stanford, Calif., 1961), is a masterly study of the most serious revolt against Soviet rule.

Until very recently historians have mostly left the subject of post-war western Europe to social scientists. It is still hard to see this as a period of history rather than as a series of contemporary social, political and economic issues. The readings cited below necessarily reflect this problem. General treatments include W. Laqueur, *Europe in Our Time, 1945–1992* (New York, 1992), and M. Crouzet's still excellent *The European Renaissance since 1945* (1970). P. Ginsborg, *A History of Contemporary Italy: Society and Politics, 1943–1988* (1990), is a model country study. It is difficult to think of anything quite as comprehensive for another west European country, though Stanley Hoffmann's writings on France and Ralf Dahrendorf's on West Germany are indispensable. G. Therborn, *European Modernity and Beyond: The Trajectory of European Societies, 1945–2000* (1995), is a sweeping survey and interpretation of social trends. P. Flora, *State, Economy and Society in Western Europe, 1815–1975*, 2 vols. (Frankfurt, 1983–7), is also valuable.

Historians *have* started to write on post-war reconstruction and the USA's contribution to it: see D. Ellwood, *Rebuilding Europe: Western Europe, America and Postwar Reconstruction* (1992), a vigorous survey which spans the debate between A. Milward, *The Reconstruction of Western Europe,*

1945–1951 (1984), and M. J. Hogan, *The Marshall Plan: America, Britain and the Reconstruction of Western Europe, 1947–1952* (Cambridge, 1987). C. Maier, 'The two postwar eras and conditions for stability in twentieth century western Europe', *American Historical Review*, 86: 2 (April 1981), makes an important comparison. R. Kuisel, *Seducing the French: the Dilemma of Americanization* (Berkeley, Calif., 1993) and I. Wall, *The United States and the Making of Postwar France, 1945–1954* (Cambridge, 1991), cover the USA's impact on the country which tried hardest to resist it. R. Wagnleiter, *Coca-colonisation and the Cold War: The Cultural Mission of the United States in Austria* (1994), is a rollicking account of the country which arguably resisted it least. For Italy, we have J. Harper, *America and the Reconstruction of Italy, 1945–1948* (Cambridge, 1986); on Greece, there is L. Wittner, *American Intervention in Greece, 1943–1949* (New York, 1982), and H. Jones, *'A New Kind of War': America's Global Strategy and the Truman Doctrine in Greece* (New York, 1989). T. Barnes, '"The secret Cold War": the CIA and American foreign policy in Europe', *Historical Journal*, 24/25 (1981/2), covers a different kind of influence. Essays in M. Mazower (ed.), *The Policing of Politics in the Twentieth Century* (1997), suggest that Europeans did not need the CIA to teach them about anti-communism. P. Hennessy and G. Brownfield, 'Britain's Cold War security purge: the origins of positive vetting', *Historical Journal*, 25 (1982), pp. 965–73, makes fascinating reading.

On the boom, the classic account is M. Postan, *An Economic History of Western Europe, 1945–1964* (1967). To this should be added P. Armstrong, A. Glyn and J. Harrison, *Capitalism since World War II* (1984), A. Boltho (ed.), *The European Economy: Growth and Crisis* (Oxford, 1982), A. Maddison, *Phases of Capitalist Development* (Oxford, 1982), and A. Shonfield, *Modern Capitalism* (Oxford, 1965). The winter 1964 issue of *Daedalus* ('A New Europe?'), contains brilliant analyses of the post-war socio-economic changes in western Europe. A. Sampson, *Anatomy of Europe* (1968), is a misnamed but highly readable view of the same region. J.-E. Lane, *Politics and Society in Western Europe* (1994 edn) has a lot of useful information conveyed very accessibly. The origins of European union are covered by E. Haas, *The Uniting of Europe* (Stanford, Calif., 1958), and more historically – and controversially – by A. Milward *et al.*, *The European Rescue of the Nation State* (1992).

For consumerism, no historical study beats the novel by G. Perec (tr. by D. Bellos), *Things: A Story of the Sixties* (1991), though V. Bogdanor and R. Skidelsky (eds.), *The Age of Affluence, 1951–1964* (1970), has some very readable essays. A. Pizzorno, 'The individualistic mobilization of Europe', in *Daedalus*, 93: 1 (winter 1964) is a remarkable analysis. S. Gundle, 'L'americanizzazione del quotidiano: televisione e consumismo nell'Italia degli anni cinquanta', *Quaderni storici*, 62 (August 1986), pp. 561–94 opens up the Italian case. S. Weiner, 'The *consommatrice* in Elsa Triolet's *Roses à crédit*', *French Cultural Studies*, 6 (1995), pp. 123–44, does something similar for France. F. Mort and P. Thompson, 'Retailing, commercial culture and masculinity in 1950s Britain', *History Workshop Journal*, 38 (1994), is good fun. Post-war advertising has still not found its historian. T. R. Nevitt, *Advertising in Britain: A History* (1982), is a good basic guide. Historians have also left the rise of tourism to anthropologists and social theorists, though P. Mandler, *The Fall and Rise of the Stately Home* (1997), shows what can be done.

T. Marshall, *Class, Citizenship and Social Development* (Chicago, 1963), and R. Titmuss, *Essays on the 'Welfare' State* (1963 edn) show the thinking of two major British social theorists. A French view is F. Ewald, *L'État de providence* (Paris, 1986). The best treatment of the German social market is A. J. Nicholls, *Freedom with Responsibility: The Social Market Economy in Germany, 1918–1963* (Oxford, 1994). More comparative treatments are to be found in P. Flora and A. Heidenheimer (eds.), *The Development of Welfare States in Europe and America* (1987), G. Esping-Andersen, *The Three Worlds of Welfare Capitalism* (Cambridge, 1990), P. Baldwin, *The Politics of Social Solidarity* (Cambridge, 1990), A. de Swaan, *In Care of the State: Health Care, Education and Welfare in Europe in the Modern Era* (Oxford, 1988), A. Cochrane and J. Clarke (eds.), *Comparing Welfare States: Britain in International Context* (1993), and P. Thane, *The Foundations of the Welfare State* (1982). J. Harris, 'Enterprise and welfare states: a comparative perspective', *Transactions of the Royal Historical Society* (1990), pp. 175–95, scrutinizes the Thatcherite critique of welfare spending. On politics, the Left is covered in S. Padgett and W. Patterson, *A History of Social Democracy in Postwar Europe* (1991); there is nothing comparable for the Right. C. Lemke and G. Marks (eds.), *The Crisis of Socialism in Europe* (Durham, NC, 1992), is very useful: we must await a similar account of the crisis of contemporary conservatism. Christian Democracy is well treated in several excellent works, M. P. Fogarty, *Christian Democracy in Western Europe, 1820–1953* (1957), D. L. Hanley (ed.), *Christian Democracy in Europe* (1996), and the excellent K. van Kersbergen, *Social Capitalism: A Study of Christian Democracy and the Welfare State* (1995). There is a good essay by M. Mitchell, 'Materialism and secularism: CDU politicians and National Socialism, 1945–1949', *Journal of Modern History*, 67 (June 1995), pp. 278–308, and the whole question of post-war political Catholicism is put in historical perspective in T. Buchanan and M. Conway (eds.), *Political Catholicism in Europe, 1918–1965* (Oxford, 1996). The extreme Right is the subject of L. Cheles *et al.* (eds.), *Neo-Fascism in Europe* (1991).

Demographic trends are surveyed in D. V. Glass, 'Population trends in Europe since the Second World War', *Population Studies*, 22: 1 (March 1968), pp. 103–47, M. Kirk, *Demographic and Social Change in Europe, 1975–2000* (Liverpool, 1981), and D. Noin and R. Woods (eds.), *The Changing Population of Europe* (Oxford, 1993). C. Dyer, *Population and Society in 20th Century France* (1978), covers the post-war period. On women, and official policies towards them, see D. Dahlerup (ed.), *The New Women's Movement* (1986), C. Duchen, *Women's Rights and Women's Lives in France, 1944–1968* (1994). C. Haste, *Rules of Desire: Sex in Britain, World War 1 to the Present* (1992), is good on British sexual politics. On the rise of the teenager, see J. G. Gillis, *Youth and History* (New York, 1974), T. R. Fyvel, *The Insecure Offenders* (1961), and S. Piccone Stella, '"Rebels without a cause": Male youth in Italy around 1960', *History Workshop Journal*, 38 (1994), pp. 157–74. On the revolting student, G. Statera, *Death of a Utopia: The Development and Decline of Student Movements in Europe* (New York, 1975), is admirably clear-sighted. There are also fine essays in *Daedalus* in the 1968–9 issues. On crime, we have N. Christie's polemic, *Crime Control as Industry* (1993), and on penal policy, V. Ruggiero, M. Ryan and J. Sim (eds.), *West European Penal Systems* (1995). Still, there is little comparative research in this area, and virtually none with any kind of historical perspective.

Immigration is discussed in R. King (ed.), *Mass Migrations in Europe* (1993), and J. Salt and H. Clout (eds.), *Migration in Postwar Europe: Geographical Essays* (Oxford, 1976). S. Collinson, *Beyond Borders: West European Migration Policy and the 21st Century* (1993), is clear. Rogers Brubaker, *Citizenship and Nationhood in France and Germany* (Cambridge, Mass., 1992), is an important treatment of forms of citizenship. Racial attitudes and their influence on policy are dealt with by P. Rich, *Race and Empire in British Politics* (Cambridge, 1990), Z. Layton-Henry, *The Politics of Immigration* (1992), G. Freeman, *Immigrant Labor and Racial Conflict: The French and British Experiences, 1945–1975* (1979), and T. Hammar (ed.), *European Immigration Policy* (1985). M. Wie? (ed.), *Racisme et xénophobie en Europe* (1994), is a good survey.

Inflation as a political phenomenon is analysed by C. Maier, 'The politics of inflation in the 20th century', in his *In Search of Stability* (Cambridge, 1987). N. Kaldor, *The Scourge of Monetarism* (Oxford, 1985) is a vigorous polemic against the kind of neo-liberalism whose revival is wittily recounted in R. Cockett, *Thinking the Unthinkable: Think-Tanks and the Economic Counter-Revolution, 1931–1983* (1995). S. Graubard (ed.), 'The European predicament', *Daedalus* (spring 1979) gives the gloomy flavour of the time. D. Dyker (ed.), *The European Economy* (1992) is comprehensive and clear. G. Baglioni and C. Crouch (eds.), *European Industrial Relations: The Challenge of Flexibility* (1990) covers the reality of 'flexibilization'. On the rise of mass unemployment, changing attitudes to work and the crisis of the post-war consensus, see B. Showler and A. Sinfield (eds.), *The Workless State* (Oxford, 1981). The politics of the welfare state in the 1980s is dissected in P. Pierson, *Dismantling the Welfare State? Reagan, Thatcher and the Politics of Retrenchment* (Cambridge, 1994); see also N. Barr *et al.*, *The State of Welfare: The Welfare State in Britain since 1974* (Oxford, 1991), and, for poverty, A. B. Atkinson, *Incomes and the Welfare State: Essays on Britain and Europe* (Cambridge, 1995). J. Vickers and V. Wright, 'The politics of privatisation in Western Europe: an overview', *West European Politics*, 11 (1988), pp. 1–30, is excellent, as too V. Wright, 'Reshaping the state: implications for public administration', *West European Politics*, 17 (1994), pp. 102–33. Some of the more thoughtful and historically nuanced accounts of 'modernity' and its aftermath include D. Harvey, *The Condition of Postmodernity* (1989), A. Giddens, *Modernity and Self-Identity* (1991).

J. Rothschild, *Return to Diversity: A Political History of East Central Europe since World War Two* (1989 edn), is good on the final phase of Soviet rule. The rumblings of discontent with communism are best described by T. Garton Ash, *The Uses of Adversity* (Cambridge, 1989): brilliant political reportage. On Solidarity there is B. Kaminski, *The Collapse of State Socialism: the Case of Poland* (Princeton, NJ, 1991), R. Laba, *The Roots of Solidarity* (Princeton, NJ, 1991), a good collection of documents and testimonies in L. Labedz (ed.), *Poland under Jaruzelski* (New York, 1984) and T. Garton Ash, *The Polish Revolution* (1991). D. N. Nelson (ed.), *Communism and the Politics of Inequality* (Toronto, 1983) analyses communism's social crisis. Gorbachev's reforms are discussed by K. Dawisha, *Eastern Europe, Gorbachev and Reform* (Cambridge, 1990 edn) and by M. Gorbachev, *Perestroika* (1988). J. Valdez, *Internationalism and the Ideology of Soviet influence in Eastern Europe* (Cambridge, 1993), is a thoughtful study. S. Graubard (ed.), *Eastern Europe . . . Central Europe . . . Europe* (1991) is an incisive collection of essays on communism's collapse. A. J. McAdams, 'Crisis in the Soviet empire: three ambiguities in search of a prediction', *Comparative Politics*, 20: 1 (October 1987), pp. 107–18 asks what kind of crisis there really was.

G. Hosking and J. Aves (eds.), *The Road to Post-Communism* (1992), looks at the rise of opposition inside the Soviet Union. The revolutions are analysed in I. Banac (ed.), *Eastern Europe in Revolution* (Ithaca, NY, 1992); a vivid eyewitness account is T. Garton Ash, *The Magic Lantern* (1990). G. Lundestad (ed.), *The Fall of Great Powers: Peace, Stability and Legitimacy* (Oxford, 1994), sets the Soviet withdrawal in historical context. On eastern Europe after communism, I found A. E. Dick Howard (ed.), *Constitution Making in Eastern Europe* (Washington, 1993), full of echoes of the past. *Dissent* (summer 1996) has some good articles on minorities. T. Rosenbaum, *The Haunted Land* (1993) is one of the most evocative of many accounts of the region's efforts to settle past scores. A. Applebaum, *Between East and West: Across the Borderlands of Europe* (1995) is a highly readable travelogue informed by a fine historical sensibility.

Index